# Global Perspectives on the Strategic Role of Marketing Information Systems

Jose Melchor Medina-Quintero
*Tamaulipas Autonomous University, Mexico*

Miguel A Sahagun
*High Point University, USA*

Jorge Alfaro
*Universidad Catolica del Norte, Chile*

Fernando Ortiz-Rodriguez
*Tamaulipas Autonomous University, Mexico*

A volume in the Advances in Marketing, Customer Relationship Management, and E-Services (AMCRMES) Book Series

IGI Global
PUBLISHER of TIMELY KNOWLEDGE

Published in the United States of America by
IGI Global
Business Science Reference (an imprint of IGI Global)
701 E. Chocolate Avenue
Hershey PA, USA 17033
Tel: 717-533-8845
Fax: 717-533-8661
E-mail: cust@igi-global.com
Web site: http://www.igi-global.com

Library of Congress Cataloging-in-Publication Data

Names: Medina Quintero, José Melchor, editor. | Sahagun, Miguel Angel, 1972- editor. | Alfaro, Jorge, 1963- editor.
Title: Global perspectives on the strategic role of marketing information systems / edited by Jose Melchor Medina, Miguel Angel Sahagun, Jorge Alfaro, and Fernando Ortiz-Rodriguez.
Description: Hershey, PA : Business Science Reference, [2023] | Includes bibliographical references and index. | Summary: "Global Perspectives on the Strategic Role of Marketing Information Systems communicates the recent advances in marketing information systems. Covering topics such as digital entrepreneurship, international business, and micro and small enterprises, this premier reference source is a cuttingedge resource for marketers, entrepreneurs, business leaders and managers, IT managers, students and educators of higher education, librarians, researchers, and academicians"-- Provided by publisher.
Identifiers: LCCN 2022061134 (print) | LCCN 2022061135 (ebook) | ISBN 9781668465912 (hardcover) | ISBN 9781668465929 (paperback) | ISBN 9781668465936 (ebook)
Subjects: LCSH: Marketing--Management. | Management information systems.
Classification: LCC HF5415.13 .G546 2023 (print) | LCC HF5415.13 (ebook) | DDC 658.8--dc23/eng/20221222
LC record available at https://lccn.loc.gov/2022061134
LC ebook record available at https://lccn.loc.gov/2022061135

This book is published in the IGI Global book series Advances in Marketing, Customer Relationship Management, and E-Services (AMCRMES) (ISSN: 2327-5502; eISSN: 2327-5529)

British Cataloguing in Publication Data
A Cataloguing in Publication record for this book is available from the British Library.
All work contributed to this book is new, previously-unpublished material.
The views expressed in this book are those of the authors, but not necessarily of the publisher.
For electronic access to this publication, please contact: eresources@igi-global.com.

# Advances in Marketing, Customer Relationship Management, and E-Services (AMCRMES) Book Series

ISSN:2327-5502
EISSN:2327-5529

Editor-in-Chief: Eldon Y. Li, National Chengchi University, Taiwan & California Polytechnic State University, USA

**MISSION**

Business processes, services, and communications are important factors in the management of good customer relationship, which is the foundation of any well organized business. Technology continues to play a vital role in the organization and automation of business processes for marketing, sales, and customer service. These features aid in the attraction of new clients and maintaining existing relationships.

**The Advances in Marketing, Customer Relationship Management, and E-Services (AMCRMES) Book Series** addresses success factors for customer relationship management, marketing, and electronic services and its performance outcomes. This collection of reference source covers aspects of consumer behavior and marketing business strategies aiming towards researchers, scholars, and practitioners in the fields of marketing management.

**COVERAGE**

- Ethical Considerations in E-Marketing
- Relationship Marketing
- Mobile Services
- Customer Retention
- Data mining and marketing
- Text Mining and Marketing
- Electronic Services
- Cases on CRM Implementation
- Online Community Management and Behavior
- E-Service Innovation

IGI Global is currently accepting manuscripts for publication within this series. To submit a proposal for a volume in this series, please contact our Acquisition Editors at Acquisitions@igi-global.com or visit: http://www.igi-global.com/publish/.

The Advances in Marketing, Customer Relationship Management, and E-Services (AMCRMES) Book Series (ISSN 2327-5502) is published by IGI Global, 701 E. Chocolate Avenue, Hershey, PA 17033-1240, USA, www.igi-global.com. This series is composed of titles available for purchase individually; each title is edited to be contextually exclusive from any other title within the series. For pricing and ordering information please visit http://www.igi-global.com/book-series/advances-marketing-customer-relationship-management/37150. Postmaster: Send all address changes to above address. 

# Titles in this Series

*For a list of additional titles in this series, please visit:*
*http://www.igi-global.com/book-series/advances-marketing-customer-relationship-management/37150*

***Big Data Marketing Strategies for Superior Customer Experience***
Jose Ramon Saura (Rey Juan Carlos University, Spain)
Business Science Reference • © 2023 • 346pp • H/C (ISBN: 9781668464540) • US $240.00

***Managing Festivals for Destination Marketing and Branding***
Sharad Kumar Kulshreshtha (Department of Tourism and Hotel Management, North-Eastern Hill University, Shillong, India)
Business Science Reference • © 2023 • 366pp • H/C (ISBN: 9781668463567) • US $250.00

***Cultural Marketing and Metaverse for Consumer Engagement***
Amandeep Singh (Chitkara Business School, Chitkara University, India) Sandhir Sharma (Chitkara Business School, Chitkara University, India) Amrinder Singh (Jain University, India) Murat Unanoglu (İstanbul Aydin University, Turkey) and Sanjay Taneja (Uşak University, Turkey)
Business Science Reference • © 2023 • 335pp • H/C (ISBN: 9781668483121) • US $250.00

***Handbook of Research on Consumer Behavioral Analytics in Metaverse and the Adoption of a Virtual World***
Pantea Keikhosrokiani (School of Computer Sciences, Universiti Sains Malaysia, Malaysia)
Engineering Science Reference • © 2023 • 404pp • H/C (ISBN: 9781668470299) • US $325.00

***Global Developments in Nation Branding and Promotion Theoretical and Practical Approaches***
Andreas Masouras (Neapolis University, Cyprus) Sofia Daskou (Neapolis University, Cyprus) Victoria Pistikou (Democritus University of Thrace, Greece) Dimitrios Dimitriou (Democritus University of Thrace, Greece) and Tim Friesner (University of Winchester, UK)
Information Science Reference • © 2023 • 320pp • H/C (ISBN: 9781668459027) • US $240.00

*For an entire list of titles in this series, please visit:*
*http://www.igi-global.com/book-series/advances-marketing-customer-relationship-management/37150*

IGI Global
PUBLISHER of TIMELY KNOWLEDGE

701 East Chocolate Avenue, Hershey, PA 17033, USA
Tel: 717-533-8845 x100 • Fax: 717-533-8661
E-Mail: cust@igi-global.com • www.igi-global.com

# Table of Contents

# Detailed Table of Contents

# Preface

This book constitutes one of a kind, exploring the intersection between Marketing and Information Systems. It may lead to future research in the area. The level of decision-making is concerned with deciding on the organization's objectives, resources, and policies. A significant problem at this decision-making level is predicting the organization's future and its environment and matching the organization's characteristics to the environment. This process generally involves technology and knowledge from the market and clients, which usually deal with very complex, non-routine problems.

The book is organized as follows:

Chapter 1 deals with Cause-Related Marketing (CRM) is a corporate strategy that assertively communicates the degree of commitment made due to social or philanthropic action, and in some cases, it actively involves consumers in this practice through the marketing of products or services for a cause. These activities are represented as a "shared value", to the extent that both companies and social causes mutually benefit. This research aims to examine the link between CRM and the construction of shared value, so a theoretical discussion on the subject is conducted regarding the post-pandemic environment, due to the significant influx of the use of information and communication technologies (ICT). According to the literature review, cause-related marketing as a strategic tool has the potential to create shared value through effective communication management of corporate philanthropy and corporate social responsibility activities.

In Chapter 2, library and information centers have begun to realize that by using marketing principles and techniques, they can understand better their user's needs, justify finding, communicate more effectively with a variety of internal and external audiences, and achieve greater efficiency and result in delivering product and services that meet the identified needs of their client. In contemporary society, people can now easily access information and information-bearing resources on the go if they relate to their laptops, smartphones, iPad, etc. Even though users can have access to information via the internet and other technology, the fact remains that the place of the library in society cannot be put aside. As such, librarians are now dwelling in a highly competitive world of marketing.

In Chapter 3, technology and interconnectivity make it possible to buy worldwide, more competition is in the market, and the client must find other ways to choose a product besides their utility, and that is where the experience takes place. Therefore, this study aims to explore the role of the five human senses in consumer shopping intention by their satisfaction. Grounded on the Consumer Culture Theory (CCT) and the Stimulus Organism Response (SOR) model, we propose a model to explain the relationship between the human senses and shopping intention. The study used a sample of 313 store clients in northeastern Mexico. A questionnaire was utilized for the recollection of the data, and the testing of the hypotheses, structural equation modeling (SEM). Research supports four of the five hypotheses, suggesting that taste, sight, hearing, and touch, through satisfaction, conduct a shopping intention. On the other hand, the smell did not correlate with consumer satisfaction.

The objective of Chapter 4 is to analyze some work areas of interest as a result of the COVID-19 pandemic such as Content Marketing and Social Networks, Artificial Intelligence, 3D Printing, Virtual Reality, Big Data, Devices through the Voice, Robotization, automation, and digital transformation of companies, Electronic Commerce and Digital Leisure for the development of digital entrepreneurship with the aim of promoting self-employment of young people, mainly from generation Z. A qualitative methodology with a cross-sectional and descriptive scope was used with secondary sources. The results show that technological tools are the new source for business development. Although Mexico is prepared for the implementation of businesses via the Internet, it should be noted that there are still barriers such as bureaucracy, training, greater investment, ignorance, and resistance to change. It is urgent to develop collaborative public-private-academy strategies to strengthen institutions, infrastructure, and human skills focused on new technologies to guarantee decent employment.

In Chapter 5, target tourists' behavior at global events could be one of the interesting topics for business houses. Business Intelligence System (LBA-BIntelligent) framework to predict target tourists' behavior at global events. The organizing countries create new businesses and gain a competitive advantage from tourists. This framework streamlines marketing to the right people at right time. This study focuses on implementing Bagging and Boosting ensemble approaches. These classifiers have been evaluated on various parameters such as accuracy, precision, recall, F-score, Kappa score, and ROC-AUC score. The classification results show that the Bagging approach gives better results through all the evaluation metrics.

In Chapter 6, mobile technologies play a transcendental role in the development of organizations. The banking industry has become the world's economic engine, and when combined, they seek to generate a competitive advantage and attract more users. For this reason, this research aims to determine the influence of users' trust in their satisfaction when they use e-Banking through mobile phones. A survey was applied to 98 users in northeastern Mexico who use a commercial banking computer application and inferential analysis with SmartPLS. The main results indicate that trust is essential in using this computer technology to perceive its usefulness and ease of use. However, the most relevant contribution is the use of e-Banking by providing greater satisfaction to users.

In Chapter 7, in a globalized world, companies must be effective and efficient with all resources (tangible and intangible, and personal). The information and communication technologies (ICTs) were built quickly due to the large and different social problems, in addition to trying to exclude all the barriers of MiPymes that have arisen over time through the implemented information systems. On the other hand, the high demand of companies has marked certain precedents that have determined competitive excellence and increased any size productivity that technologies such as the internet, social media, connectivity, and the internet of things (IoT) necessary to the daily technological activities that help to make decisions in the different types of MiPymes (homes, offices, workshops, banks, pharmacies, convenience stores, etc.).

Chapter 8 addressed what smartphones, mobile applications, programming languages, mobile operating systems are. The development, implementation and results obtained from mobile applications in the following areas are discussed in detail: educational platforms, citizen participation with the government, teaching the pronunciation of the English language and citizen participation in public security. Android, being the main operating system for smartphones is the most suitable for the development of mobile applications since it guarantees that it will have the greatest possible visibility and reach, not only for its popularity but for its presence in many devices other than cell phones and its "open system" feature so that everyone who wants it can develop compatible software.

In Chapter 9, the city of Reynosa, Tamaulipas is full of maquiladoras that come from abroad to settle here, in turn, these export mostly to the United States, because Reynosa is a border with the aforementioned country, businesses and agreements have been created that until now have prospered successfully. Speaking English has long ceased to be an added value and its importance is increasingly evident to professionals and companies, who see this language as the door to better job opportunities, expansion into the world, and new businesses. In Reynosa, there are about 125,945 students pursuing a university degree, among which are to mention a few: bachelor's degree in economics, bachelor's degree in international trade, computer systems engineering, architecture, production systems engineering, industrial engineering, and mechatronics engineering, among others. In the present research it is expected to know the main factor why students from 18 to 23 years old in Reynosa, Tamaulipas between 2022 and 2023 are interested in learning English.

The objective of Chapter 10 is to determine the critical success factors of a tax collector website in a country with an emerging economy. In the method, a questionnaire is applied to 488 taxpayers in northeastern Mexico and factor analysis as a statistical tool. The results show that the top five success factors are citizen satisfaction, service quality, information quality, ease of use, and confidence. The results show the need to adapt the technologies to the citizens for their better performance and usefulness, so the originality of the research is because there are few empirical studies in the country.

The marketing and the information system playing together, ensures efficient communication within an organization. It provides reliable and valuable information to keep all informed and focused on specific tasks and goals. This can also help prevent miscommunication by providing everyone with the same access to shared information.

This book also aims to foster the overall success of your organization. By using well-organized data and analyzing and interpreting it, you may make better, more strategic decisions. You may also identify new ways to upgrade or expand your systems to further collect and analyze data to build a more efficient business.

We want to thank all authors and reviewers to make this book and support this edition.

*Jose Melchor Medina*
*Tamaulipas Autonomous University, Mexico*

*Miguel Sahagun*
*High Point University, USA*

*Jorge Alfaro*
*Universidad Catolica del Norte, Chile*

*Fernando Ortiz-Rodriguez*
*Tamaulipas Autonomous University, Mexico*

# Chapter 1
# Relationship Between Cause-Related Marketing and Shared Value in Pandemic Times:
## A Theoretical Discussion

**Lidia Rangel Blanco**
https://orcid.org/0000-0003-3574-6462
*Autonomous University of Tamaulipas, Mexico*

**Madelyn Avila Vera**
*Autonomous University of Tamaulipas, Mexico*

**Ramiro Esqueda Walle**
*Autonomous University of Tamaulipas, Mexico*

## ABSTRACT

*Cause-related marketing (CRM) is a corporate strategy that assertively communicates the degree of commitment made due to social or philanthropic action, and in some cases, it actively involves consumers in this practice through the marketing of products or services for a cause. These activities are represented as a "shared value" to the extent that both companies and social causes mutually benefit. This research aims to examine the link between CRM and the construction of shared value, so a theoretical discussion on the subject is conducted regarding the post-pandemic environment due to the significant influx of the use of information and communication technologies (ICT). According to the literature review, cause-related marketing as a strategic tool has the potential to create shared value through effective communication management of corporate philanthropy and corporate social responsibility activities.*

DOI: 10.4018/978-1-6684-6591-2.ch001

## INTRODUCTION

The COVID-19 pandemic caused irreversible economic damage for companies of different sizes, industries, and regions, undermining their ability to survive in an increasingly complex landscape. Due to mandatory confinement many of these companies will implement new strategies to obtain sales, mainly through the use of digital platforms and marketing.

The use of information technology (ICT) experienced significant growth in developing countries due to the use of mobile devices such as mobiles, tablets, and computers, the digital economy boosted due to the electronic commerce, consumers, companies, and suppliers increased their activity in this type of market. Nevertheless, uncertainty and animosity caused by the pandemic affected consumers' perspective and their behavior of consumption, what forced them to rethink more efficient selling strategies through digital marketing with different approaches. Some of these are social marketing and cause-related marketing (CRM).

According to Álvarez et al., (2021), during pandemic companies look at social marketing strategies development, supporting them with campaigns to educate and raise consumer awareness to follow sanitary measures and prevent the spread of COVID-19. On the other hand, cause-related marketing (CMR) proved to be an important strategy to develop stronger links and build consumer brand loyalty, it is therefore considered by Adkins (1999) as a commercial activity based on a collaborative relationship between the company and a non-profit organization or the cause, with the aim to promote an image, product or service, for mutual benefit.

The benefits are numerous when a good CRM strategy is implemented, both for companies and causes. A successful CRM campaign can increase sales, create a positive brand image, enhance corporate reputation, strengthen brand equity, increase visibility, differentiate the organization from competitors, build consumer loyalty and access new customers, among other advantages (Buil et al., 2012). And from the point of view of non-profit organizations, they can obtain a larger network of donors and volunteers, other sources of funding due to the dissemination of the cause, increased efficiency of social programmers, etc.

In addition, Galan et al., (2021) point out that CRM used to be considered exclusively a commercial activity, i.e., namely a marketing tool related to sales promotion or public relations. Today, CRM is seen as a corporate social responsibility (CSR) initiative belonging to the holistic approach to marketing, where sustainability is also considered; Woodroof et al., (2019) recognizes CRM to communicate their commitment while achieving their strategic objectives. These characteristics relate to 'shared value'.

Value creation has long been a recognized idea in business, appearing repeatedly in academic and professional management texts in relation to decision-making, for example, on the commercial side of creating value for customers, or on the financial side of creating value for shareholders.

Traditionally, "creating value" in a company refers to increasing profit and profitability, but a few decades ago, also creating value means contributing to CSR, business ethics and social progress. Thus, the approach of Porter & Kramer (2006) about the importance of create "shared value" relapses to the degree that the social aspect is equally important as the economic-financial aspect (Díaz & Castaño, 2013; Manríquez et al., 2005).

The idea of creating value is not new in the marketing literature, however, no evidence positions CRM as a tool for creating shared value. This research aims to examine the link between CRM and the construction of shared value, so a theoretical discussion on the topic is conducted regarding the post-pandemic environment, due to the significant influx of the use of information and communication technologies (ICT).

However, this research does not directly address the impact of COVID-19 on CRM and ICT strategies, but it is necessary to contextualize its effects in the face of the "new normality".

## LITERATURE REVIEW

Cause-related marketing (CRM), also known as cause marketing, appeared in the 1980s in the United States through the American Express campaign to restore the Statue of Liberty in the early 1980s and is considered by virtually all authors to be the first time it was referred to in this way (Galan et al, 2005).

CRM is a strategy through which a company collaborates with a social cause in exchange for consumers buying its products and services (Buil et al., 2012). Moreover, it was defined by Kotler and Andreasen (1996) as "any effort made by a company to increase its own sales, contributing to the objectives of one or more non-profit organizations".

CRM is also a new and innovative instrument for the promotion of companies, allowing them to make themselves known according to a new facet of action, thus providing a vision of these companies that is much more committed to society (Penelas et al., 2004).

Porter & Kramer (2006) denounce that the social (or philanthropic) actions of many companies were distant from the real activity of the company and had become, in the best of cases, a pure advertising tool trying to improve their reputation.

In fact, these activities were more focused on purely advertising arguments than on trying to ensure that they had a real social impact, the serious proposal then was to try to carry out an authentic "strategic philanthropy" that would be based on two main lines: the first would be to use philanthropy and social action activities to improve the company's competitive context; and the second would consist of accepting that this type of company action generates both social and economic benefits (Muñoz, 2013).

The marketing concept traditionally recognizes that organizations thrive on a day-to-day basis by identifying customers' current needs and wants and satisfying those needs and wants more effectively and efficiently than competitors (Armstrong & Kotler, 2017). However, this definition neglects other aspects also pursued by consumers and a wider group of stakeholders involving the issue of sustainability that calls for socially and environmentally responsible actions that meet both the immediate and future needs of customers and the company.

Contreras (2013) explains that organizations should always think about applying the principle of continuity or ongoing concern, and that means that objectives should always be set in the long term so that they can be structured in a way that is congruent with what the market demands.

According to Cavazos & Puente (2014), many companies have the resources and willingness to make significant contributions to different social, cultural or environmental causes. Such companies can take advantage of different mechanisms and means to generate credibility and a positive response from different audiences, while at the same time obtaining benefits for the firm.

Certainly, the nature of organizations demands that companies produce positive economic, environmental, and social results, even though companies are inserted in a competitive market, subject to changing customer tastes and in a globalized economy, where society is increasingly aware of its influences, supported by information technologies (ICT) (Ramos & Cañadillas, 2013).

Legitimacy theory argues that a company can legitimize its business operations by disclosing to its stakeholders its contribution to the welfare of society to shape its stakeholders' opinions about the company (Sindhu, 2020). From this perspective, scholars view CRM-led CSR as a type of disclosure strategy that enables a firm to communicate its efforts and establish a philanthropic reputation to gain legitimacy.

Corporate reputation and corporate social legitimacy remain important intangible values for organizations. Corporate reputation is the overall stakeholder assessment of a company over time, i.e., the extent to which consumers, investors and/or suppliers hold it in high regard (Lee et al., 2017).

Some companies use CRM campaigns where they pledge to donate or contribute to a cause for every unit of product they sell. Although some authors consider CRM to be just another type of sales promotion, these actions should be understood as a type of corporate philanthropy planned according to much broader objectives (Buil et al., 2012).

However, according to Cavazos & Puente (2014), there is a clear distinction between CRM and corporate philanthropy that is worth mentioning (See table 1).

*Table 1. Differentiation of cause-related marketing, philanthropy, and social marketing*

| Concept | Aspects of its application in practice |
|---|---|
| Cause-related marketing | • Donation conditional on/after sales.<br>• Transaction-based.<br>• Relationship between the observed value of the for-profit company's output and the value of the non-profit organisation's cause.<br>• It is usually included in advertising and promotion budgets. |
| Social Marketing | • Application of commercial tools in programmes or campaigns that influence voluntary behavioural change of target audiences.<br>• Its purpose is to improve the well-being of people and society.<br>• It is not dependent on the sales of the commercial organisation. |
| Philanthropy | • Selflessly procuring the good of people.<br>• It expects nothing in return.<br>• It is granted on pre-tax income. |

Source: based on Cavazos & Puente (2014).

At first, according to Keim (1978) the issue of corporate philanthropy is a set of altruistic corporate activities, which are not necessarily communicated by corporations as part of an advertising campaign.

Nevertheless, if these actions are disseminated they can exert effects that work in both directions; positive effects are generated when customers identify with philanthropic donations by the company and a greater corporate reputation is generated; on the other hand, negative effects are generated when consumers do not legitimize these actions because they assume that there is a greater interest than the social cause.

Regarding CRM, Armstrong & Kotler (2017) explain that critics worry that it is more of a sales strategy than a strategy for giving, i.e., that "CRM" is actually "cause-exploitative" marketing. Thus, companies that use cause marketing may find themselves walking a fine line between increased sales and enhanced image whilst facing exploitation charges.

Indistinctly, either if it is a philanthropic action or CRM action, institutionalist theorists assure companies should achieve isomorphism, i.e., namely become members of the society they are part of and adapt to local social norms, thus, they would be reassuring legitimacy. Consequently, CRM actions communicated through CRM represent to be an adequate tool to create value.

Finally, regarding social marketing refers to the use of commercial marketing concepts and tools within programmes designed to influence the behavior of individuals to improve their well-being and that of society (Armstrong & Kotler, 2017; Cavazos & Puente 2014). Thus, the promotion of the culture of recycling among their customers promoted through multinational campaigns such as Coca-Cola and H&M, are a clear example of social marketing.

The rise of social media and ICT, in general, has managed to amplify aspects or problems of companies on a global scale, regardless of whether they are large or small. Poor management of advertising or marketing campaigns has an immediate effect on their market share, share price, etc.

The following is a typology of criteria by which CRM programmes are carried out. The aim is to clarify how a CRM programme is executed and how it differs from other areas of marketing. This is followed by a review of the relationship of marketing to the value creation process and its possibilities in creating shared value. Finally, the ICT perspective is added as an important component that brings the effectiveness of marketing as a tool for creating shared value closer.

## Types of Cause Marketing

According to Galan et al., (2013) and Galan et al., (2021) there are nine ways to carry out a CRM programme:

I. By type of product, this is done through the donation of producer units or services such as groceries, toys, food, clothes, electrical appliances, etc., in favour of a particular cause or problem.
II. For cash or monetary donations, in favour of a social cause, such as a scholarship programme, infrastructure investment, etc.
III. Campaign-related products, where a percentage of sales is allocated to certain branded products or services.
IV. Through a non-profit organization, and this is when a company participates voluntarily with this type of organization.
V. For a specific period, in the sense of promoting fundraising or collection goals in favour of a particular social cause.
VI. For a specific region, involving a country, state, or community.
VII. By the cause supported, where a wide variety of possible causes are distinguished, such as children in need, research on a certain disease, the fight against hunger and poverty, etc.
VIII. In terms of the media used, some campaigns use traditional media, such as television, radio, or the press, but many of them also use social media.

IX. Who pays the donation, which can involve the company alone, other companies or the consumer who donates to the cause.

## Marketing in the Process of Shared Value Creation

The relationship between "value" and "marketing" has been the subject of study for some decades, as Virvilaitė & Dovalienė (2021) explain, the first definitions emerged in the 1980s with the neoclassical economic theory that related the consumer's benefits from the product or service to the cost experienced.

However, the role of marketing in value creation has been approached from three established approaches, Reichheld (1996) and Payne et al., (2010) conceive of three key stakeholders in value creation: employee, customer, and shareholder value.

*Table 2. Domains of employee, shareholder, and customer value*

| Employee Value | Customer Value | Shareholder Value |
|---|---|---|
| • Employee satisfaction<br>• Employee retention and loyalty<br>• Employee commitment<br>• Employee productivity<br>• Leadership<br>• Internal Service Quality | • Customer attraction<br>• Customer satisfaction<br>• Customer loyalty<br>• Customer retention<br>• Customer profitability | • Shareholder engagement<br>• Shareholder satisfaction<br>• Shared retention<br>• Lifetime profit flows<br>• Company growth<br>• Shareholder profitability |

Source: adapted from Payne, Holt & Frow (2010).

According to Payne et al. (2010) employee value is the least examined in the academic literature, however, concerning customer value, it is acknowledged that it drives shareholder value, evidence was also found of a significant positive relationship between customer satisfaction and customer loyalty, while others believe that shareholder value drives customer value; by focusing on maximizing shareholder value, it almost automatically needs to please customers.

However, for Gallarza et al. (2011) three barriers have made it impossible to clarify the links between marketing and value creation. First, conceptual obstacles, due to the multiple definitions surrounding the topic; second, methodological problems related to the dispute over the "best" methodological approach to the construction of "value"; and third, the shortcomings of value measurement that further lead to problems in conceptualizing it.

While each of these three barriers deserves further clarification to bring marketing's involvement in value creation closer, it is pertinent to answer the following question: What is shared value?

Forero (2012) explains that the concept of shared value was first introduced by Porter & Kramer in 2006 and is defined as "practices and policies that refine competitive strategies, where the company and the community interrelate to obtain a common benefit, improving the social conditions of the community in which it operates".

As mentioned by Porter and Kramer (2006), the fulfilment of corporate social and economic responsibilities can be a strategic device for building corporate reputation and other vital intangibles for companies. Thus, shared value is carried out to the extent that the creation of social value and business value are equated (see figure 1).

*Figure 1. Spheres of shared value in relation to business and social value*
*Source: Own elaboration.*

In addition, companies create shared value when they meet their economic objectives, and in parallel, when they realize their social and environmental objectives. However, stakeholders have focused their attention on the social orientation of companies, consumers exert greater pressure in the purchasing decision process and are more often inclined to choose brands that make a social contribution.

In this way, the strategies used in marketing contribute to a favorable result for the creation of shared value.

Namely, Virvilaitė & Dovalienė (2021) spoke about how marketing or a business strategy emphasizes reciprocal company and consumer value generation and realization. In this respect, markets are treated as forums where companies and active consumers share, negotiate, and renew each other's resources and possibilities in creating shared value through new forms of interactions, services and learning mechanisms. According to the researchers, the created shared value emerges out of personalized, unique experience on the consumer's part and revenue, knowledge, and better marketing results on the company's part.

The concept has clear origins and associations with the concept of corporate social responsibility. Porter and Kramer (2011) further develop the idea of shared value and argue that CSR programmes are mainly oriented towards reputation management and do not have clear associations with business performance, which aggravates the long-term sustainability of this initiative.

However, the creation of shared value is embedded in the profitability and competitive position of the firm and allows for the creation of economic value along with social value (Porter and Kramer, 2011). This view is also held by Pinho et al. (2014), who argue that in the context of a new business environment it is essential to move from single customer to supplier, i.e., where consumer networks interact with supplier networks in favour of social causes.

The central idea in creating shared value lies in the interdependence between the competitiveness of the company and the well-being of the surrounding community. Evaluating decisions and possibilities in terms of shared value can lead to a new approach that generates innovations and revenue growth for a company along with greater benefit for society (Virvilaitė & Dovalienė, 2021).

Payne et al. (2001) had already addressed this issue when they talked about the "co-creation of value". Authors of publications on the topic of value co-creation agree on the need to involve the consumer in the value-creation process. Only if the consumer is involved, reciprocal, unique and experience-based value can be created.

However, co-creation of value is a term that makes sense when examining this consumer-value-firm relationship. According to Prahalad & Ramaswamy (2004), co-creation is about the joint creation of value by the firm and the customer. High-quality interactions that enable an individual customer to co-create unique experiences with the firm are the key to unlocking new sources of competitive advantage.

In this sense, Payne et al. (2008) define value co-creation as "the totality of three interdependent processes where both the firm and consumers learn from each other during their interaction". These value co-creation processes concern customer co-creation, firm co-creation, and interaction co-creation.

Particularly "co-creation interaction" refers to company-customer transactions. The customer is no longer just a part of the exchange of products or services, but an actor involved in the marketing process of the company, which allows for shaping value creation capabilities.

Virvilaitė & Dovalienė (2021) conclude that when analysing behavioural value, the perspective of consumer perceived value and firm value should be analysed. Both constructs should be studied multidimensionally and context dependent. Their expression depends on the effectiveness of the value co-creation process, which in turn determines the level of consumer engagement.

In a context of global uncertainty, CRM strategies must be approached from the consumer's perspective, and this involves both an economic and a psychological dimension. As part of this task, each dimension should be assessed according to the characteristics that arise in the study environment.

In the aftermath of the COVID-19 pandemic, SCR assessments have become relevant as companies look after the interests of their employees, customers, suppliers, shareholders, and the community in which they operate. In this way, CRM contributes to the process of building value, particularly shared value by communicating with the company's stakeholders about its contributions to social causes.

## ICT Growth and Its Relationship With CRM

With the increasing advancement of information and communications technologies (ICT), the creation of value through this medium is becoming particularly important. As Gatautis (2021) explains, the development of ICT has led to major changes in consumer behaviours, the consumers have become easily accessible and active.

The change experienced in the COVID-19 global pandemic accelerated the growth of ICT in regions where ICT use lagged significantly behind.

CRM has gained increased visibility due to the public opinion that can be raised through social media. Social media has been a phenomenon discussed in scientific research on the subject.

Social networks are transforming the participation and engagement of consumers, some authors consider the use of social networks as one of the elements of change in the way companies compete in the globalized world, and their analysis can be a valuable tool for obtaining relevant information. The possibilities offered by the internet are of significant importance to all companies in the world, and little by little they have positioned themselves in social networks and marketing (Esqueda et al., 2021).

The most used social networks in the world, such as Facebook, Twitter, YouTube, Instagram, and WeChat can contribute to consumers engaging and talking to the brand, which is why Armstrong & Kotler (2017) suggest that successful marketing can be obtained to the extent that contributions are relevant and genuine to consumer conversations.

In this way, appropriate dissemination of a cause marketing campaign can bring customers into solidarity with a social cause, and even involve other actors and companies in the cause.

## CONCLUSION

Creating shared value is not a single solution to end most of the problems afflicting society, involving not only social conditions but also those related to sustainability and the environment. However, it offers extraordinary opportunities for companies to change the paradigm through which they approach strategy, help mitigate social problems and build long-term competitive advantage.

According to the literature review, cause-related marketing as a strategic tool has the potential to create shared value through effective communication management of corporate philanthropy and corporate social responsibility activities.

This work has attempted to theoretically verify the determinants of the success of cause-related marketing actions through the review of various perspectives that allude to an area of study with a growing presence in marketing research.

The rise of ICT has increased the opportunities for disseminating social causes, so their development remains an essential condition that determines the popularity and applicability of CRM strategies. To the extent that CRM actions are legitimized, they will be able to contribute to the construction of value, and in particular, the shared value theoretically proposed by Porter and Kramer.

## REFERENCES

Adkins, S. (1999). Cause related marketing: who cares wins. Butterworth-Heinemann.

Álvarez, M., Guerrero, C., & Larios, M. (2021). Mercadotecnia con causa en tiempos de Coronavirus. *Revista de Investigaciones Universidad Del Quindío*, *33*(S1), 96–112. doi:10.33975/riuq.vol33nS1.486

Armstrong, G., & Kotler, P. (2017). *Fundamentos de Marketing* (P. Educación, Ed.).

Buil, I., Melero, I., & Montaner, T. (2012). La estrategia de marketing con causa: Factores determinantes de su éxito. *Universia Business Review*, *36*, 90–107.

Cavazos, J. A., & Puente, R. D. (2014). Conceptualización y características de la mercadotecnia relacionada con causas. In Facultad de Contaduría y Administración (Ed.), Mercadotecnia Sustentable y su aplicación en México y Latinoamérica (pp. 1–43). Academic Press.

Contreras, E. R. (2013). El concepto de estrategia como fundamento de la planeación estratégica. *Pensamiento y Gestión*, *35*(8), 152–181.

Díaz, N. C., & Castaño, C. A. (2013). El Valor Compartido como Nueva Estrategia de Desarrollo Empresarial. *International Journal of Good Conscience*, *8*(2), 82–100.

Esqueda, R. W., Mendoza, L., & Quiroga, F. (2021). Marketing, network marketing y marketing digital: antecedentes, tendencias y principales características. Teoría y Estudios Regionales de la toma de decisiones de marketing, 15-66.

Forero, Y. M. (2012). *Creación de valor compartido*. Ploutos.

Galán, M., Clementina, L., Casquet, G., & Amaro, V. (2005). *El marketing con causa como estrategia publicitaria*. Academic Press.

Galan, M. L., Galera, C. C., & Alves, H. M. (2021). Cause-Related Marketing Case Studies from a Global Perspective Classroom Companion: Business. In M. L. Galan, C. C. Galera, & H. Alves (Eds.), Cause-Related Marketing: case studies from a Global Perspective (pp. 1–18). Springer. doi:10.1007/978-3-030-54205-4_333

Kotler, P., & Andreasen, R. (1996). Strategic Marketing for Nonprofit Organization. *Journal of Marketing*, (43), 37–44.

Lee, C.-Y., Chang, W.-C., & Lee, H.-C. (2017). An investigation of the effects of corporate social responsibility on corporate reputation and customer loyalty – evidence from the Taiwan non-life insurance industry. *Social Responsibility Journal, 13*(2), 355–369. doi:10.1108/SRJ-01-2016-0006

Manríquez, S., Gallegos, J., & Valenzuela, I. (2005). Análisis y aplicación de la medición y gestión del valor económico agregado (EVA) a una empresa que cotiza en la bolsa. *Capic Review, 3*, 4.

Payne, A., Holt, S., & Frow, P. (2001). Relationship Value Management: Exploring the Integration of Employee, Customer and Shareholder Value and Enterprise Performance Models. *Journal of Marketing Management, 17*(7–8), 785–817. doi:10.1362/026725701323366827

Payne, A. F., Storbacka, K., & Frow, P. (2008). Managing the co-creation of value. *Journal of the Academy of Marketing Science, 36*(1), 83–96. doi:10.100711747-007-0070-0

Penelas, A. L., Cuesta, P. V., & Sarro, M. del M. A., & Guriérrez, P. R. (2004). El Marketing y las organizaciones no lucrativas: El marketing con causa (MCC). *Revista Internacional de Marketing Público y No Lucrativo, 1*(1), 125–137.

Porter, E., & Kramer, M. R. (2006). Estrategia y sociedad: El vínculo entre ventaja competitiva y responsabilidad social corporativa. *Harvard Business Review América Latina, 12*(84), 42–56.

Porter, M. E., & Kramer, M. R. (2011). La creación de valor compartido. *Harvard Business Review*, 32–49.

Prahalad, C. K., & Ramaswamy, V. (2004). Co-creation experiences: The next practice in value creation. *Journal of Interactive Marketing, 18*(3), 5–14. doi:10.1002/dir.20015

Ramos, J. A., & Cañadillas, I. P. (2003). Delimitación del Marketing con Causa o Marketing Social Corporativo mediante el análisis de empresas que realizan acciones de responsabilidad social. *Cuadernos de Gestión*, *3*(1–2), 65–82.

Reichheld, F. F. (1996). Learning from customer defections. *Harvard Business Review*, *74*(2), 56–67.

Sindhu, S. (2020). Cause-related marketing— An interpretive structural model approach. *Journal of Nonprofit & Public Sector Marketing*, *00*(00), 1–27. doi:10.1080/10495142.2020.1798851

Virvilaitė, R., & Dovalienė, A. (2021). The Concept of Shared Value in the Contexto of Newest Marketing Theories. In *Gamification and Consumer Engagement* (pp. 7–32). https://www.springer.com/series/10440

Woodroof, P. J., Deitz, G. D., Howie, K. M., & Evans, R. D. Jr. (2019). The effect of cause-related marketing on firm value: A look at Fortune's most admired all-stars. *Journal of the Academy of Marketing Science*, *47*(5), 899–918. doi:10.100711747-019-00660-y

Zhou, L. J., Qiu, H., & Zhang, X. (2021). How Does the Market React to Corporate Philanthropic Behavior? Evidence from the COVID-19 Pandemic Shock. *Emerging Markets Finance & Trade*, *57*(6), 1613–1627. doi:10.1080/1540496X.2021.1898367

# Chapter 2
# Marketing Information Products and Services in the Digital Age in the Academic Library Environment

**Peter Olubunmi Olubiyo**
*Adeyemi Federal University of Education, Ondo, Nigeria*

## ABSTRACT

*Library and information centers have begun to realize that by using marketing principles and techniques, they can understand better their users' needs, justify finding, communicate more effectively with a variety of internal and external audiences, and achieve greater efficiency and result in delivering product and services that meet the identified needs of their client. In contemporary society, people can now easily access information and information-bearing resources on the go if they relate to their laptops, smartphones, iPad, etc. Even though users can have access to information via the internet and other technology, the fact remains that the place of the library in society cannot be put aside. As such, librarians are now dwelling in a highly competitive world of marketing.*

## INTRODUCTION

Information is an indispensable factor for promoting the development of society (Elavazhagan, n.d.). According to Ramadevi (2018) in Baquee and Sevukan (2019), marketing is an essential aspect of organizations irrespective of profit-making and non-profit making and the library is not an exception to it. However, Marketing of

DOI: 10.4018/978-1-6684-6591-2.ch002

library and information services is a nascent development in developing countries (Kendadamath, n.d.). Dike (2009) in Horsfall (2020) observed that marketing involves advocating for libraries, publicizing resources and services, convincing people of the value and relevance of the library. It means not waiting passively for users but actively going out to seek them. A number of librarians around the world have gone to the streets, playgrounds, shopping centres, markets, etc. in search of users. Marketing can also involve envisioning the library as a business (from where the concept of marketing came) selling commodities to customers.

Adekumisi (2013) in Benson, Udo-Anyanwu, and Onuoha (2016) described the rapid growth of internet that it has drastically changed and transformed the way and manner which library and information product and services are offered and as well put the libraries and librarian at the center of hyper-competition. Adekumisi (2013) in Benson, Udo-Anyanwu, and Onuoha (2016) expressed that if librarians and libraries must survive, then marketing must be seen as a necessity. Library and information centers have began to realize that by using marketing principles and techniques, they can understand better their users needs, justify finding, communicate more effectively with a variety of external audiences and achieved greater efficiency and optional result in delivering product and services that meet the identified needs of their client. In contemporary society, people now easily access information and information- bearing resources on the go as long as they are connected with their laptop, smart phones, ipad e.t.c. Even though users can have access to information via the internet and other technology, the fact remains that the place of the library in the society cannot be put aside. Librarians are now dwelling in a highly competitive world of marketing (Benson, Udo-Anyanwu, & Onuoha, 2016). Three main factors, namely the information explosion, the technology revolution, and escalating library costs are responsible for encouraging the library profession to develop a marketing approach in its operations and services (Joseph & Parameswari, 2002).

Renborg (1997) in Kumar and Diksha (2014) traced the history of marketing library activities long before the concept was born. Samuel Swett Green in his often quoted speech at the ALA Conference in 1876 advocated "improved personal relations between librarians and readers". It could be said that today's marketing of library services has its roots in parts of those words in USA and Northern Europe, in countries with few illiterates and more money, libraries, and library schools than the rest of the world. This certainly does not mean that the idea of libraries reaching out to "the common man" has not occupied librarians in other parts of the world. For instance, there is the example of the "library movement" in Nigeria at the beginning of the 20th century. Marketing of library and information products and services is a new concept in Nigeria. It is not too old as a compared to the developed countries also. The above said concept has emerged during the early 1970s. Since then, it has gained much attention in the USA and is considered as most important profession.

Information institutions have grown into information industries which are providing free web based information services (Patange, 2013).

Marketing of library and information products and services is an area which is now beginning to attract the attention of research scholars, market researchers, and the business people. Marketing in the broadest sense ranks as one of the most popular topics of the day. Marketing basically starts with the market research, identifying the consumer needs and demands, their pricing and promoting them to the appropriate consumers. The main purpose in marketing is attracting and retaining a growing base of satisfied customers. These information industries have employed more than 50% of human resources. Marketing approach is useful to academic libraries to improve their image and to attract more and more users. It helps the library staff to upgrade their innovative knowledge both within their organizations and as a profession within the society. It is the need of the hour to adopt this concept (Patange, 2013).

Acquisition of knowledge in learning resources, processing, storage, retrieval and utilization are activities which like any other human endeavor engender cost. The problems of information acquisition are certainly not without their economic ramifications. It has been established that information is an economic resource. It has been recognized as a powerful saleable commodity. The present day society is rapidly changing. Information plays an effective role in the transformation of the society. This is an information era. It is almost identified as the fifth need of man ranking after air, water, food and shelter (Patange, 2013). Most of the librarians view that marketing of products and services is not possible in the profession of librarianship. But, authors such as Kotler (n.d.) in Patange (2013) is of the view that marketing is not limited to large corporations seeking profits only. It is equally applicable to non-profit organizations as well as colleges, universities, charitable institutions, libraries, information centers and services organizations also.

Marketing of library and information services require the applications of ICT. Furthermore, to effectively handle and manage information, librarians need to market library and information services to their clientele. The question now is, "how can librarians effectively market library and information services in the digital age to their users so that the information needs of their users can be met?" One of the primary functions of the library is to make available to the reader the information materials needed without waste of time. The library's basic need for survival is through information as information is a source for development. As mentioned earlier, marketing of library and information services in the digital age require the application of ICT through web 2.0 tools; these include WhatsApp, email, Face book, You-tube, Twitter, LinkedIn, etc, to reach out to their clientele (Horsfall, 2020).

With ICT facilities in the library, an e-newsletter can be produced. Marketing of library and information services can be achieved by libraries and librarians through; creating awareness, fliers, checkout for sponsorships, selective dissemination of information (SDI), talk shows promotions, exhibition, posters etc. Posters offer good visual communication. They can draw attention when displayed at prominent locations and provide brief information about an event, service, etc. Old and defaced posters should be replaced on a regular basis. These are information marketing (Horsfall, 2020).

## Information Products

The products of information refers to sources of information and knowledge contents that are available in electronic and non electronic formats such as CD- ROMs, interactive video, films, audio digital products, online publishing, public domain and commercial online databases available through internet and other databases available through various private network providers; textbooks, encyclopedia, almanac, handbooks, dictionaries, thesauruses, patent information, journals, etc. (Kumar, 2014). Similarly, the products that can be marketed in order to satisfy the needs of library users according to Vig (2012) in Benson, Udo-Anyanwu, and Onuoha (2016) ranges from books, periodicals, reports to electronic documents. Abdulsalami, and Salami (2013) as cited in Benson, Udo-Anyanwu, and Onuoha (2016) in their study of marketing information products and services in polytechnic libraries in Nigeria using a survey method revealed that information products that are available in most polytechnic library are books, journals, pamphlets as well as information communication technology with library orientation and current awareness services as mostly used strategy in marketing of information resources.

## Information Services

Information Services (IS) in library, according to Kumar and Diksha (2014), are current awareness services, newspaper clippings, indexing/abstracting services, translation services, literature search, photocopying of periodical articles, selective dissemination of information, circulation of periodical content, reference services, inter library loan, information repacking and condensation services.

Marketing of Library and Information Services (LIS) by librarians is an attempt to influence library users on how library resources and services can be effectively utilized to advance the position of information services in the digital age. For effective marketing of LIS, librarians/libraries can either learn to adapt and seek out creative solutions to change in society or find themselves going the way of the dinosaurs. Librarians should embrace change; they are to be honest with themselves about how comfortable they are with change because change is constant. Librarians should advocate for excellent library services, appropriate staffing and facilities in the context of marketing themselves and the services they provide (Horsfall, 2020).

Advocacy such as promotion, public relations, and marketing to indicate what is currently being done within the library and its environment will be greatly enhanced by what the librarians can offer. With increased alternatives for information, librarians must learn to gain a competitive edge and promote the added value in the services they provide. For effective information handling and management, effective marketing should be used to promote access to library, and information services as a panacea towards sustainable libraries in the digital age (Horsfall, 2020).

## Marketing Mix for Academic Libraries

Komolafe-Opadeji and Haliso (2012) in Benson, Udo-Anyanwu, and Onuoha (2016) pointed out that marketing is an important weapon for handling competition and that for academic libraries in Nigeria to remain relevant to the academic community, marketing concept must be embraced. Shapiro (1981) in Patange (2013) opined that there are four key marketing concepts that provide the basis for marketing thought and action in the nonprofit environment which are considered. The core concepts of marketing are considered to be the marketing mix.

Borden's concept of marketing mix has given due recognition to marketing theory and the concept of marketing mix which was accepted as the set of marketing tools. Singh and Shukla (2009) as cited in Horsfall (2020), opined that marketing is the process of planning, pricing, promoting, and distributing goods and services to create "exchanges" that satisfy the library and the customers. Also, Patange (2013) expressed that Borden's marketing mix was summed up into 4Ps – Product, Price, Place and Promotion.

1. **Product:** It is anything which is offered to the market for exchange of consumption. It is tangible (which can be seen and touched). Product is the most important thing in the marketing system. Thus, information product such as books, theses, email, google, etc. are the products.
2. **Price:** Pricing is another variable of the marketing mix. It is the most difficult issue. Lot of things are to be kept in mind while fixing the price. Two types of pricing are suggested (1) cost recovery, by which the libraries cover only budgeted cost of acquiring information materials and (2) commercial pricing, where the libraries make a profit through fine placed on defaulters.
3. **Place:** Place is the process of getting the goods or services from the producer to the destination where consumer can have access. In this business it is a matter of access. It is the channel that links product and consumer.
4. **Promotion:** It is yet another important factor in marketing. It can only be successful if the other factors of the mix have been considered. It was pointed

out that promotion, in general, involves one or more, or all, of the following methods to reach the client:

- Public relations.
- Advertising a library can advertise its products and services in newspapers, scholarly journals, magazines, newsletters, radio, television, Web, etc. Advertisements help in image-building. They can be in a short message, or staff can write longer articles on new and existing library services. Librarians can appear on local radio and TV, highlighting the new role the libraries play in the present era. There are a variety of ways of advertising online. Traditional print advertisements include brochures, pamphlets, newspaper advertisements, etc.
- Personal selling.

## Marketing of Information Products in Academic Libraries

Okogwu (2006) in Benson, Udo-Anyanwu, and Onuoha (2016) pointed out that marketing has become important in library environment because it sets the librarians toward organizational strategic thinking and planning, thereby offering the opportunity to develop more effective library services which could lead to over all improved organizational decisions. Marketing of information product, according to Ibrahim (2010) in Horsfall (2020) is defined as any activity that is undertaken in order to provide information goods and/or services that can satisfy the needs of customers. The library is a marketplace of ideas and information. Hence, when customers/users realize they are getting more from their libraries, they become advocates and passionate supporters for what the library do. Librarians are therefore to convince users to accept their help/assistance.

In this digital age, librarians are introduced to the concept of branding and rebranding its products, marketing strategies and different online platforms are open to design and market products and services to remain relevance in their role. Marketing of library and information services is absolutely a necessary agenda to librarians, situation, or activity for all kinds of libraries all over the world. It is a very important area for library and information science professionals. It shows that librarians are not book worms, they maintain a competitive air over other professional. They adopt social management principles, stand and face the individual with facts and figures [making self-services]. They possess the knowledge of identifying the information needs of clients (client-oriented), and have effective communication, interviewing, and presentation skills, as well as managerial skills and good sense of humour. It must be emphasized that marketing and communication become as important as delivering the services.

Thus, Fisher and Pride (2006), Mathews (2009), and Webreck Alman (2007) in Otobrise and Omagbon (2019) opined that promotional tools that can be used to market information products by academic libraries to promote their services and resources are digital media, such as the library's website, e-mail lists, blogs and podcasts; print materials, such as posters, handouts and giveaways; events such as orientation tours and workshops; and other tools such as library publications, contests, brochures, direct mail, Web 2.0 applications and displays.

## Marketing of Information Services in Academic Libraries

Patange (2013) expressed that successful marketing of information services includes the act of deciding the strategies/ techniques used in different situation for upkeep, management, and growth of the library. As non-profit-making organization, library and information center cannot avoid marketing practices. Although libraries/ information centers as non-profit organizations, yet they have two assignments –they are responsible to clients to whom they provide services and the parent institution/ donor agencies from whom they receive funds. The library should be a growing organism and this is why they should market their services for the following reasons:

1. Marketing enables librarian or information manager to understand the real needs of users for taking good management decisions, which will in turn help in providing maximum information services to users more efficiently and effectively.
2. Librarian or information manager is not only interested for the people who do use the services regularly. He is also interested in non-user groups. Marketing play a vital role to identify the information needs of non-users and helps to draw them with necessary information.
3. Librarians and information managers need to present their services as an indispensable part of the organization and try to justify the claim that their clients/users cannot do their job efficiently or effectively without a library service. In this way, marketing techniques will help libraries and information services receive more funding from their patrons.
4. Marketing will help to improve the image of the library and information profession through collection of revenue through library users' registration to performing different services to users.

According to Bhatt (2011) as cited in Horsfall (2020), marketing library and information services can be effectively managed to advance the position of information literacy in sustaining library services in the digital age. It helps to achieve organizational goals by determining the needs and wants of target audience, in other to make them satisfied. Effective marketing of library and information services is a way of making sure libraries and librarians market their services and themselves to meet their users' information need. Activities such as book displays, lectures, quiz, debates, seminars, competitions, exhibitions, etc., can have a positive impact on the image of the library, motivate people to come to the library and promote the use of its products and services. This will help solve the problems of the users' and their needs and also enable them to visit and use the library often.

## Challenges to Marketing Information Product and Services in Academic Libraries

A literature review conducted revealed that marketing of information was a relatively new issue in developing countries and that most of the case-study literature on the subject were scanty. The review concluded that marketing potential is underestimated by librarians and information service professional and that they were generally reluctant to embrace the marketing concept (Lafond, 1999). Librarians and information managers seem to be reluctant to become fully involved in marketing their information products and services and when they attempt to market their information services they neglect or fail to understand the behavior of the user. The librarians should understand the nature of information, needs of users, the transfer process between people and information. Understanding of this new dimension of library and information services will help concerned policy makers in formulating appropriate plans and programs to make the library and information services most effective, and long sustainable. But this is not the case. (Patange, 2013).

There are some challenges associated with marketing of Library and Information Services. These according to Horsfall (2020) include the following:

- **Ignorance Among Librarians:** Some of the librarians are ignorant about the marketing services of the library in the digital age.
- **Lack of ICT Infrastructure:** A lot of libraries do not have up to date ICT infrastructure for information marketing.
- **Lack of Awareness of the Public on Their Access to Information:** It is a common problem for some individual to have access to the right information and at the right time and place.
- **Lack of Funds:** For any organization to stand firm and aid development in any angle, fund is needed. For instance, in Nigeria, libraries are not well funded to help them procure their needed materials and improve on current marketing services needed by the library in this age to promote their image.
- **Lack of Training and Retraining of Library Staff:** Training and retraining of staff has posed problems in most libraries in Nigeria. This denies them of

the current marketing strategies of the 21st century obtainable in the western world.

- **Lack of Marketing Strategies and Skills:** This has posed challenges to librarians/libraries who do not have the strategies to market library and information services in the digital age.

## Way Forward

Abdulsalami and Salami (2013) in Benson, Udo-Anyanwu, and Onuoha (2016) opined that librarians must begin to change their orientation about traditional approach to library services in order to experience the modern dividends of marketing library and information services. Information professionals need a better understanding of marketing concepts and approaches to be able to introduce them into their services and to recover the costs of the information services and products that they provide (Lafond, 1999). Bamigbola (2013) as stated in Horsfall (2020) that marketing strategy is a well-structured plan that highlights the organization's goals and quest and the specific process of achieving those set of goals. Below are some strategies for marketing library and information services:

- **Be a Productivity Expert:** Think of those who have connections to make things work and be creative by bringing new ideas that can attract customer.
- Maintaining a good relationships with colleagues in libraries will create a peaceful atmosphere for skill exploration.
- **Keep Daily Statistics of Users:** It speaks for you as a librarian. Use statistics meaningfully to show the value of what has been achieved and the extent of the usage of the library facilities and infrastructure.
- **Being ICT Literate:** Apply ICT in library-know how to use web 2.0 tools like Facebook, twitter, LinkedIn, WhatsApp, e-mail, etc. to reach out to users.
    - Better provision for the library staff to attend in-service training and career advancement courses should be made by government (Kumar & Diksha, 2014).
- **Library Advocacy:** Librarians/information experts should advertise libraries; make use of advocacy for resources. Librarians can advocate through the services they provide. If librarians are not their own advocates through involvement in issues, professional organizations and our Institutions, to a great extent would not.
- Library tour for new and existing members of users can be used to promote the library services. While on a library tour, users can be prompted to ask questions and find out more about new activities, products, and services.

- Talk about library issues with other interest groups. For librarians to maintain a competitive air over other professionals, they need to market themselves and library and information services in the following ways.
- As part of developing Nigerian library's access to information, librarians have to continue to learn about resources and users' needs outside their area of specialization, always learning for learning is a lifelong thing.
- Create awareness in the library environment, thereby learning how to market themselves; by knowing how to sell themselves and their skills not just to their future employer but to the constituency they are hired to serve. They need to get out of the library environment and introduce themselves to faculties, staff and students, through fliers, magazines, placing their library home page prominently on a departmental web page with their names on it especially the faculty librarians.
- There should be the urge to share information, any organization benefits from the free flow of information. Closed-mouthed librarians foster inefficiency, rumours and resentments. Make them aware of what you can offer them and be proactive in getting them what they need; send them alert or articles that may help them with either teaching, research, or learning needs.
- They must focus on self-promotion and review resource allocation in an increasingly competitive field. Librarians must keep basic principles of librarianship and merge them with the changing face of knowledge, information, and society. Life is about change; technology has not changed what librarians do; it merely changed the way in which librarians do things.
- The librarian needs to continuously update his/her professional knowledge and skills through relevant staff training and development programmes by going to conferences, workshops, seminars, educational centres and in-house training, always learning for learning is a lifelong thing. Although there is inability to have needed funding which is a problem that militates against taking advantage of staff training and development programmes.
- Library web 24/7(24 hours 7 days in a week) access, initiating information desk with liaison librarians, information literacy programmers, establishment of virtual reference-telephone, e-mail and chat reference service were the major ways to increase the marketing orientation in the library (Kumar, 2014).

## CONCLUSION AND RECOMMENDATIONS

Abdulsalami and Salami (2013) in Benson, Udo-Anyanwu, and Onuoha (2016) expressed that librarians must begin to change their orientation about traditional approach to library services in order to experience the dividends of marketing library and information services. Presently, the need for marketing of information services is being felt by all types of libraries. Libraries are facing competition from other information service providers. They need to make daily decisions on the form and formats for acquiring and archiving information. Librarians are striving to provide free access to information. They are struggling with space constraints, shrinking budgets and rising cost of materials. At the same time, users' expectations are going high with the emergence of online access to information. In response to these factors, management philosophies and administrative operations of libraries have changed. Librarians are embracing marketing techniques to be more efficient managers and effective information service providers.

## REFERENCES

Baquee, A., & Sevukan, R. (2019). Marketing of Information Products and Services through Library Websites: An Analytical Study of Indian Central University Library. *Library Philosophy and Practice*. Available at: https://digitalcommons.unl.edu/libphilprac/2652

Benson, O. V., Udo-Anyanwu, A. J., & Onuoha, C. O. (2016). *Strategies Used in Marketing Library and Information Services in Tertiary Institutions in Imo State. Journal of Applied Information Science and Technology, 9(1).*

*Elavazhagan, K. (n.d.). Marketing of information products and Services. Being a Course Material for Library and Information Science*. Bharathidasan University.

Horsfall, M. N. (2020). Marketing of Library and Information Services in the Digital Age: Challenges, Strategies and Implications. *Journal of Information and Knowledge Management*, *11*(2), 13–20. doi:10.4314/iijikm.v11i2.2

Joseph, J., & Parameswari, B. (2002). Marketing of Information Products and Services for Libraries in India. *Library Philosophy and Practice.* Available at: https://digitalcommons.unl.edu/libphilprac/32

Kendadamath, G. C. (n.d). Marketing of Library and Information Services. In D. De & B. Jirli (Eds.), *Communication Support for Sustainable Development* (p. 221001). GangaKaveri Publishing House.

Kumar, A. (2014), Marketing of Information Products & Services in Kurukshetra University Library in the Disciplines of Social Science: A study. *IOSR Journal of Humanities and Social Science, 19*(2), 72-85. Available at: www.iosrjournals.org

Kumar, A., & Diksha, J. S. (2014). Marketing of Information Products & Services by the Research Scholars & Scientists in Central Soil Salinity Research Institute, Karnal: A study. *IOSR Journal of Humanities and Social Science, 19*(11), 58-78. Available at: www.iosrjournals.org

Otobrise, H. C., & Omagbon, A. B. (2019). Digital marketing of library, information and knowledge products and services among librarians in selected university libraries in South-South, Nigeria. Journal of ICT Development. *Applications and Research, 1*, 47–60.

Patange, J. T. (2013). Marketing of Library and Information Products and Services. *Global Journal of Human, Social Science, Linguistics, and Education, 13*(1).

# Chapter 3
# Do You Feel It?
## Sensory Marketing in Stores in Northeast Mexico During COVID-19

**Anabel-Sofía Villegas-Garza**
*Autonomous University of Tamaulipas, Mexico*

**José Melchor Medina-Quintero**
*Autonomous University of Tamaulipas, Mexico*

**Jorge Alfaro-Pérez**
*Universidad Católica del Norte, Chile*

**Demian Abrego**
*Autonomous University of Tamaulipas, Mexico*

## ABSTRACT

*Technology and interconnectivity make it possible to buy worldwide. More competition is in the market, and the client must find other ways to choose a product besides their utility, and that is where the experience takes place. Therefore, this study aims to explore the role of the five human senses in consumer shopping intention by their satisfaction. Grounded in the consumer culture theory (CCT) and the stimulus organism response (SOR) model, the authors propose a model to explain the relationship between the human senses and shopping intention. The study used a sample of 313 store clients in Northeastern Mexico. A questionnaire was utilized for the recollection of the data, and the testing of the hypotheses, structural equation modeling (SEM). Research supports four of the five hypotheses, suggesting that taste, sight, hearing, and touch, through satisfaction, conduct a shopping intention. On the other hand, the smell did not correlate with consumer satisfaction.*

DOI: 10.4018/978-1-6684-6591-2.ch003

## INTRODUCTION

Years ago, stores used to implement techniques related to the product, place, and service to increase sales, all of them applied to marketing strategies (Fernández, Arribas & Martín, 2020). Nowadays, information technology and interconnectivity give consumers new ways of shopping worldwide. In the same way, that provides more products, brands, and stores to compare before buying (Sachdeva & Goel, 2015). As a result, the competition and the commodities increase giving people to choose not only a product necessity, but they also need to connect with the product itself (Mostafa & Kasamani, 2020), they need to feel something more, and there is where sensory marketing goes. People are feeling more than any decade, that is a crucial line to cross-talking about emotions and feelings because they appeal to stimulate the five senses through an experience.

Pine and Gilmore (2011) talked about the experience as a new wave, they named a new economy: The experience economy. They said the product is not enough, all the product alternatives to shop make the consumer oversaturate, giving a chance to increase and create value through their experiences. Feel is more than tactile, it involves the five senses to have a perception, which also incites imagery processing (Haase et al., 2020, p. 4), and that is why they are involved together. In consequence, new tools in sensory marketing terms have been increasing online (Reina & Jiménez, 2020) and in-store. That is why nowadays is impressible to connect with customers' experiences by their senses (Gómez-Suárez et al., 2019). Now, small and medium-sized enterprises (SMEs) need to pay attention to actions to innovate on that way (Nencheva, 2018).

There have been some studies related in northeast Mexico, for example, the one made by González et al. (2019), the article concludes that sight, smell, and touch impact the decision-making of the people in the state of Tamaulipas; but it has its limitations, and this investigation could decrease the gap left behind. In the same way, we haven't noticed more papers talking about sensory marketing in the region, so this kind of studies must increase the information. Also, this research study aims to provide an extended understanding of the consumers' behavior, focusing on the influence of the sensory marketing used by the stores at the point of sale and how they influence their shopping intention.

Consequently, the objective of this paper is to analyze if the stimulus perceived by the five senses evoke satisfaction and if they end with a shopping intention. According to the main purpose of the study, the structure of the document has the next structure: in the first place we present the literature review about sensory marketing, satisfaction, and shopping intention; in the second place, a description of the methodological elements used; in third place, the results are presented, and finally, we abord the findings and the discussions of this piece of work.

## Literature Review

In the last years, the consumer has been involved in new ways of shopping, increased by information technology and interconnectivity, this has been elevating the research interest to create a store experience and brand value because it brings differentiation between brands and stores (Barrios, 2012; Wibisono & Syah, 2019). For instance, sensory marketing involves people's senses through perceptions (Krishna, 2012), perceived thru their bodies (Yakhlef, 2015), and this has positive effects on clients (Moreira et al., 2017).

Lindstrom (2015) describes the five human senses (sight, taste, hearing, touch, and smell) correlated to engagement and perceived value, arguing that if a brand evokes more senses, the customer relates it to a higher perceived value. The same author creates a *5-Dimensional brand sensogram* shown in Figure 1. He suggests every store communicate, consequently, every store can apply for the sensogram evaluation, proposing five areas to consider.

*Figure 1. Lindstrom's sensogram*
*Source: Lindstrom (2015)*

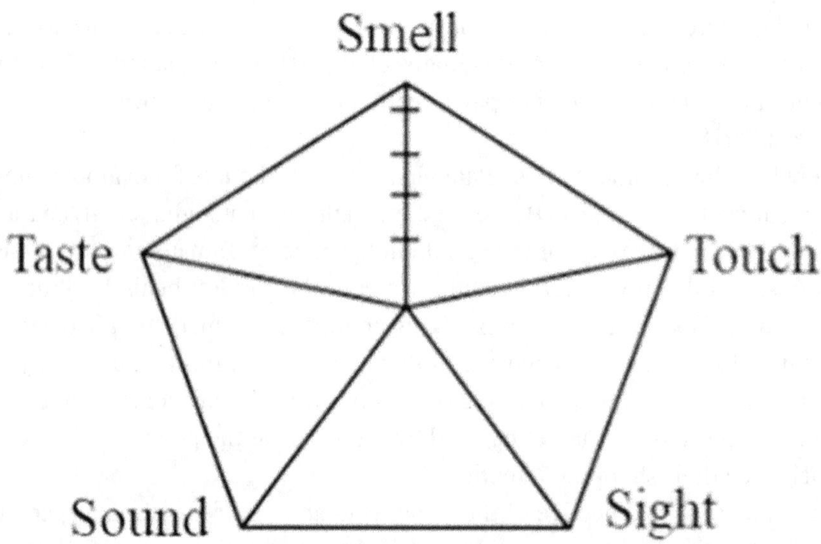


Following the research, all the stores could be sized into a sensogram, because they used stimulus, but not at the same level; that is why Lindstrom (2015) suggests the use of the sensory experience in a major way. It has been measured by cities, hospitals, stores, etc., and anything that includes a name on it. Correspondingly to Lindstrom, Brakus et al. (2009) said customers interact with brands thus, the stimulus is perceived as brand identity, brand design, marketing communications, and the environment where the brand is promoted, for example, in stores. In sum, stores should engage customers' cognition and emotions to make them a memorable experience (Raposo, 2022).

## Sensory Marketing (SM) and Its Relationship With the Experience

SM has a strong relationship with the senses because is thru our senses that people perceive and have sensations, this has been synthesized in the work of Safeer et al. (2021). In sum, they integrate into the proposed model the sensory aspects as part of the store's experience. That is why the researchers consider the consumer behavior theory basis for the study and the SOR model by Mehrabian y Russel (1974). The S refers to the stimulus perceived by the five human senses, de Organism is an internal process thru the external stimulus perceived and the R is the response to the stimulus by the organism (in this case consumer). Clearly, that theory is from 1974, but it is still in vogue, for one thing, because the Consumer Culture Theory (CCT) came from the same derivation, the Consumer Behavior Theory, but at the same time, it tries to explain cognitive and affective states, in other words, it refers to "the dynamic relationships between consumer actions, the marketplace and cultural meanings" (Arnould & Thompson, 2005), which are included in the SOR model. Now, there are some conceptualizations of the variables.

The smell is defined as a dynamic sense that identifies and decodes meanings thru the nose, it can influence taste, identity, and spatial levels (Canniford et al., 2018). Similarly occurred with Biswas and Szocs (2019), mentioned that smell influence taste, and it can increase the smell by the vision only with the color perception. Sound emerges from the sense of hearing, has a particular effect on memory, and a lot of information is perceived by this (Jang & Lee, 2019), it includes the music and the noise in store (Biswas et al., 2018). The sense of sight includes everything that the human can see in the store and its atmosphere, such as the product, the arrangement of it, the windows, the colors, etc. (Lund, 2015). This is the most effective and important sense, it can register color, light, intensity, graphics, design, and look (Koszembar, 2019). Touch is the sense that helps to feel the products thru the body, it occurs when the consumer gets in touch with the product or something, bringing an emotion, and in some cases, can affect the communication or their moves in store (Jang & Lee, 2019). Taste is usually studied in the food industry field, leaving the stores with their own decision on how to evoke that sense. It makes the customer differentiate between sweet, spicy, and salty, for example.

On the other hand, satisfaction is the result of the perceived function and utility with a previous expectation before the use and if the experience exceeds expectations (Carrizo et al., 2017). Meanwhile, the present paper used a result of an emotional state between a positive association of the product and their expectations aligned with an experience of ideal consumption. In the same way, shopping intention is a shopping intention in the future (Villiers et al., 2018). This research, it's taken because the stimulus increases the interest for a shopping intention in the present or the future as a result of an extraordinary experience in the store.

## Sensory Marketing in Stores

Sensory marketing (SM) is in constant evolution as consumers do. Some studies mention a huge increment in shopping intention when SM is implemented in stores, first of all, because it evokes experiences, and those can't be easily removed (Sachdeva & Goel, 2015; Perumal et al., 2021). Indeed, there is evidence that a positive experience influences customer´s loyalty (Mostafa & Kasamani, 2020). In the same way, it could be remembered, thus the senses (Moreira et al., 2017), plus that is the way a relationship lasts until time, between the client and the shop or even the stores (Zha et al., 2022).

In brief, to connect and communicate between the stores and the customer in a memorable way, there is SM because of the experience brought by their interaction with the product in the atmosphere built in the store, which causes a stronger and long-term emotion (Randhir et al., 2016). In addition, Wörfel et al. (2022) found that music and scent need to be congruent with the atmosphere, Garaus (2017) mentions the need of congruence between the atmosphere elements, specifically visuals, and both conclude in the increase of the factors such as satisfaction and shopping.

SM needs different strategies for each sense, and the previous experiences must be considered by looking at the consumer and their needs (Biswas et al., 2019b; Carrizo et al., 2017; Hepola et al., 2017). Next, there is a summary of the constructs and at the end the hypotheses.

Furthermore, smell has been used mostly in the food field, chiefly, because people can smell before they eat, which give a reason to have a reaction or even a shopping intention (Moore, 2014). Also, it wakes the memories, which is a reason why it influences consumer behavior (Helmefalk, 2019; Sandell, 2019; Lund, 2015). On the other hand, SM uses smell to create and form stimulus to bring satisfaction because of an experience (Roggeveen, 2020). Also, Lund (2015) found that it could help to stay longer or shorter in stores; for example, if the smell experience was positive, the customer stays longer than if the smell experience was negative, the customer stays shorter. It includes everything that produce an aroma in the atmosphere. But, also, some papers only include the intensity of the aroma in general (Marin & Gomez, 2022).

Thanks to the ear, people can hear the sounds in stores, and the researchers incorporate the sound as music and noise. Biswas et al. (2019b) include the volume of the music in the consumer's choice, the conclusion was a moderating effect of the volume of the music. However, the effect changes with the retail setting as presented; for instance, is not the same as the ambient strategy used for a salad bar or a sports bar, the first one needs to be low, and the second high volume. Equally important, sensory aspects of the own product affect the consumer experience, the name of the product, the branding in general, and the design of the package (Spence, 2012). By the sounds of the words, consumers can imagine shapes and more (Krey, 2016); that is why people, in some cases, feel related to products at first sight. Reynolds-Mcllnay and Morin (2019) confirm in their research the importance of a confirmatory sound at the register, in other words, at the moment of payment, besides, it increases satisfaction and shopping intention.

The sight includes everything seen with the eyes inside the store atmosphere, and the result in an experience. Is the most effective sense (Jang & Lee, 2019), and the most used as a stimulus receptor that registers light, color, brightness, intensity, design, graphics, and look and feel (Koszembar, 2019). All of them help to form a perception of the atmosphere and influence consumer behavior (Elder y Krishna, 2022). By the way, sight gives visual clues to our body without touch or taste, showed by Hamacher and Buchkremer (2022). Correspondingly, Kotler (1973), Stillman et al. (2020), and Baek et al. (2018) found direct relation, so it can evoke other senses.

Touch in common language is to feel something with our hands or a closer feeling (Tu & Yang, 2019), but it is also a bodily perception (Yakhlef, 2015). In other words, "bodily response to a stimulus" (Krishna & Schwarz, 2014, p. 3). At the time, is correlated to other senses to form a perception. Talking about the action of touching something, Madzharov (2019) found an increased value if the clients touch the product. Beyond, Gómez and Mejía (2012) discover a relationship between satisfaction and touch, they argue that when the client has the chance to touch and feel a product, they could have a better perception of the product in itself, and that could bring satisfaction without buying before, just by the way its feeling. Otherwise, Decré and Cloonan (2019) detect as, in other senses, people don't need to touch the product to have a sensation, as Hamacher and Buckremer (2022) found.

On the other hand, the taste is derived from the mouth and food in a simple way, which is why is more common to find information about taste related to restaurants, except the ones that manage food. For instance, Perumal et al. (2021) analyzed the brand image of an airline applying the SOR model to the tactile stimulus and taste, resulting in a positive and significate relationship. The SOR model explains the client process to take an action: S is for stimulus, O is for the organism that perceives the stimulus and R is for Response, which indicates how is going to action the organism (Mehrabian & Russel, 1974)._

By the way, this sense commonly has been studied before as a factor of satisfaction related to food, but in this paper, the researchers try to look at this variable as optional, now, if the store has something to buy or give something to eat, it could increase the satisfaction on them, not necessarily because of the taste, just because they were given a gift. To answer the current aim, and the literature review we present the next hypotheses:

**$H_1$.** Taste will be associated in a positive and significate way that could affect satisfaction.
**$H_2$.** Sight will be associated in a positive and significate way that could affect satisfaction.
**$H_3$.** Sound will be associated in a positive and significate way that could affect satisfaction.
**$H_4$.** Touch will be associated in a positive and significate way that could affect satisfaction.
**$H_5$.** Smell will be associated in a positive and significate way that could affect satisfaction.
**$H_6$.** Shopping intention is influenced by satisfaction.

## Method

The instrument has two parts: the demographic characteristics, and the measures of the constructs. In total, every questionnaire has 39 items, and the foundations have their roots in works from Fernandez et al. (2009), Alan et al. (2015), Carrizo et al. (2017), Hepola et al. (2017), Ringler et al. (2019), Biswas et al. (2019), and Haase and Wiedmann (2020), all of them were in English, except Fernández et al. (2009) that was in Spanish. Additionally, the researchers translate to Spanish and contextualize those questions for the Mexican consumers, specifically those who live in Tamaulipas. All the items were measured in a 5-point Likert scale, from 1 (strongly disagree) to 5 (strongly agree). The questionnaire was conducted in two pre-tests, involving the validity and pilot testing to get the final version before the data collection. Subsequently, at the calculation of the demographic factors, the reliability and validity of the results were calculated for the measurement of the model. Likewise, Table 1 is shown the operational definitions of the seven constructs listed before.

*Table 1. Construct definitions*

| | |
|---|---|
| Taste | Eating products inside the store that relax and satisfice the client in the store. |
| Sight | It consists on the look, the arrangement, and the order of the atmosphere of the stores that the client can see. |
| Sound | Music, sounds, and volume inside the stores that the client can hear. |
| Touch | It is integrated from the atmosphere temperature for the stores to the product feel that the client can touch. |
| Smell | It's how the atmosphere smell. |
| Satisfaction | Feeling results of a well-chosen selection, in other words, it's an emotional response of a good experience. |
| Shopping intention | The intention to buy in the future as a response of a good experience. |

Source: own elaboration

Data was collected from consumers of SMEs in northeast Mexico with an online survey (individual questionaries). There wasn't any reward if they answer because it was completely voluntary. It was executed in two months, thru October and November 2021. Table 2 shows the demographic characteristics of the consumers, which has the frequency and the percentage of age, gender, marital status, level of education, and income. About the income, there are Mexican pesos.

The sample was limited to SMEs shoppers, and they were asked to answer the items based on their own experiences inside those kinds of stores in Tamaulipas.

*Table 2. Consumers demographics*

| Demographics | Items | Frequency | Percentage |
|---|---|---|---|
| **Gender** | **Male** | **110** | **35.14** |
| | Female | 203 | 64.86 |
| Age | 14 to 19 years | 92 | 29.39 |
| | 20 to 29 years | 86 | 27.48 |
| | 31 to 29 years | 73 | 23.32 |
| | 40 to 49 years | 23 | 7.35 |
| | More than 50 years | 39 | 12.46 |
| Marital status | Single | 201 | 64.22 |
| | Married | 79 | 25.24 |
| | Widowed | 4 | 1.28 |
| | Divorce | 12 | 3.83 |
| | Consensual union | 12 | 3.83 |
| | Separated | 5 | 1.6 |
| Education | Middle school | 1 | 0.32 |
| | High school | 132 | 42.17 |
| | University/Postgraduate | 180 | 57.51 |
| Income | $0 to $2400 | 126 | 40.26 |
| | $2401 to $5400 | 44 | 14.06 |
| | $5401 to $9000 | 42 | 13.42 |
| | $9001 to $15000 | 35 | 11.18 |
| | $15001 or more | 66 | 21.09 |

Source: own elaboration

An inferential analysis with a second-generation statistical tool with the help of the SmartPLS software was used (Ringle et al., 2015). It has been recommended if the normality of the data cannot be guaranteed (Molinillo et al., 2017, p.7), it shows two biases, the first one: identify the effects between the constructs and the dependent variable; and the second, it shows the significance of factor loadings, and the path coefficients (Chin, 1998).

After the demographic analysis, the VIF was calculated, and it could show multicollinearity on the formative indicators. If the VIF is above 5 indicates collinearity, it must be “close to 3 and lower” (Hair et al. 2019, p.10). Table 3 demonstrates that the results were in those accepted values.

*Table 3. Variance inflation factor (VIF)*

| | Shopping Intention | Satisfaction |
|---|---|---|
| Taste | | 1.183 |
| Shopping intention | | |
| Smell | | 2.222 |
| Sound | | 1.543 |
| Satisfaction | 1.000 | |
| Touch | | 2.372 |
| Sight | | 2.558 |

The item reliability is assessed by examining loads (λ) that must have a load equal to or greater than 0.707 (Chin, 1998). The 29 reflective items present acceptable values (Table 4, Column 2), and the loads oscillate between 0.790 and 0.954, exceeding the recommended minimums. As for the composite reliability, it is measured by Cronbach's alpha (0.700). Table 4 (Column 4) shows that this validation is adequate for the investigation.

The convergent validation: is carried out through Average Variance Extracted (AVE), its values must be greater than 0.50 (Fornell and Larcker, 1981). It can only be applied to reflective items, as in this research. The values in Table 1 (Column 7) exceed the accepted minimum, ranging between 0.704 and 0.890.

*Table 4. Factor loading and internal consistency*

| Construct | Items | Loadings | Cronbach's Alpha | rho_A | Composite Reliability | AVE |
|---|---|---|---|---|---|---|
| Taste | Gus1 | .933 | 0.939 | 0.942 | 0.961 | 0.890 |
| | Gus2 | .954 | | | | |
| | Gus3 | .944 | | | | |
| Shopping intention | Int1 | .917 | 0.946 | 0.947 | 0.959 | 0.822 |
| | Int2 | .925 | | | | |
| | Int3 | .909 | | | | |
| | Int4 | .888 | | | | |
| | Int5 | .894 | | | | |
| Smell | Olf1 | .854 | 0.862 | 0.865 | 0.907 | 0.709 |
| | Olf2 | .837 | | | | |
| | Olf3 | .883 | | | | |
| | Olf4 | .790 | | | | |
| Sound | Oido1 | .849 | 0.861 | 0.871 | 0.905 | 0.704 |
| | Oído3 | .824 | | | | |
| | Oído4 | .807 | | | | |
| | Oído5 | .875 | | | | |
| Satisfaction | Sati1 | .888 | 0.949 | 0.949 | 0.961 | 0.830 |
| | Sati2 | .925 | | | | |
| | Sati3 | .935 | | | | |
| | Sati4 | .913 | | | | |
| | Sati5 | .893 | | | | |
| Touch | Tac1 | .888 | 0.825 | 0.825 | 0.896 | 0.743 |
| | Tac2 | .890 | | | | |
| | Tac3 | .805 | | | | |
| Sight | Vis1 | .869 | 0.931 | 0.932 | 0.947 | 0.783 |
| | Vis2 | .906 | | | | |
| | Vis3 | .903 | | | | |
| | Vis4 | .855 | | | | |
| | Vis5 | .889 | | | | |

After, for the discriminant validity, the researchers utilized the Heterotrait-Monotrait ratio of correlations (HTMT) criteria. Hair et al. (2019) mention a value less than 0.90 for similar constructs and less than 0.85 for different constructs. The results in Table 5 show less than 0.85, so, all the constructs meet the discriminant validity, except shopping intention with satisfaction, showing 0.878, but it is still in the margins of an acceptable correlation. In the same way, the rho_A indicator from Dijkstra and Henseler (2015) is used, which must be greater than 0.700, Table 1, Column 5, contains values that exceed the recommended minimums.

*Table 5. Heterotrait-Monotrait ratio of correlations (HTMT)*

| | Taste | Shopping Intention | Smell | Sound | Satisfaction | Touch | Sight |
|---|---|---|---|---|---|---|---|
| Taste | | | | | | | |
| Shopping intention | 0.425 | | | | | | |
| Smell | 0.338 | 0.722 | | | | | |
| Sound | 0.297 | 0.622 | 0.556 | | | | |
| Satisfaction | 0.460 | 0.878 | 0.621 | 0.540 | | | |
| Touch | 0.419 | 0.831 | 0.750 | 0.657 | 0.726 | | |
| Sight | 0.369 | 0.813 | 0.785 | 0.541 | 0.728 | 0.795 | |

Table 6 shows the evaluation of the model and the hypotheses, based on the previous theory. Regarding the results of the hypothesis and the model, bootstrapping and PLS algorithms were used. $F^2$ demonstrates if there is an impact on the dependent variable, if it is less than <0.02 has a small effect, =0.15 a moderate effect, and 0.35 a big one, according to the parameters marked by Cohen (1998). The path coefficients connect the PLS model, it indicates a direct effect as a reason of the dependent (Briones, 1996). Chin (1998) recommends the path coefficients have at least a value more than 0.2, but it could be better a higher one, such as 0.3. For the t-statistic must be <.05 for 5000 bootstrap sample size (Hair et al., 2019).

*Table 6. Results of hypothesis testing*

| | $f^2$ | Path Coefficients | t-Statistic | p-Values | Remarks |
|---|---|---|---|---|---|
| Taste → satisfaction | 0.061 | 0.178 | 3.899 | 0.000 | Significant |
| Sight → satisfaction | 0.134 | 0.387 | 4.6 | 0.000 | Significant |
| Sound → satisfaction | 0.020 | 0.117 | 2.233 | 0.026 | Significant |
| Touch → satisfaction | 0.045 | 0.217 | 3.097 | 0.002 | Significant |
| Smell → satisfaction | 0.002 | 0.041 | 0.641 | 0.521 | Not significant |
| Satisfaction → shopping intention | 2.254 | 0.832 | 36.825 | 0.000 | Significant |

Note: N=113. Bootstrap sample size = 5000.

H1 is accepted with a $\beta=0.178$ and t-statistic of 3.899 ($p<0.001$), the consumer prefers to eat inside the store, fomenting a satisfactory experience. H2 is accepted with a $\beta=0.387$ and t-statistic of 4.6 ($p<0.001$), there is a significant relationship between how the store is visually organized and arranged, fomenting order, and looking pretty, concluding in a satisfactory experience for the client. H3 is accepted by $\beta=0.117$ and a t-statistic of 2.233 ($p<0.001$), resulting in a satisfactory experience of what they heard in the store (the volume, the noise, and the music).

H4 is accepted with $\beta=0.217$ and a t-statistic of 3.097 ($p<0.001$), there is a significant relationship between the air conditioner temperature and how the product feels in the client's hands, giving them a chance to try the product before buying, in sum in a satisfactory experience. H5 is not supported; in other terms, there is not a significant matter of how the store smells for the clients related with their satisfaction. $H_6$ is accepted with a $\beta=0.832$ and a t-statistic of 36.825 ($p<0.001$), so there is a significant relationship between satisfaction and shopping intention. If the client experiment satisfaction with their senses (taste, sight, sound, and touch) inside the store, a shopping intention will have.

R square ($R^2$) calculates the impact between the independent variables on the dependent. The $R^2$ can be converted to a percent that will shows how well the model fits with the data to explain the problem, the establishment parameters as 0 to 100 percent. Now, Table 7, named R square, demonstrates that the model fits in the Sensory marketing elements such as taste, sight, sound, and touch, they demonstrate to have a positive and significate association with satisfaction with 55.6% positive and statistical percent, which also impacts shopping intention in 69.2% percent, which is a considerable impact.

*Table 7. R square*

| | $R^2$ |
|---|---|
| Shopping intention | 0.692 |
| Satisfaction | 0.556 |

Figure 2 (PLS nomogram) shows the results described above. Taken together, these results, suggest an association between sensory marketing, satisfaction, and shopping intention, which, were found before by other authors. The relationship between satisfaction and sensory marketing has similar results by Satti et al. (2019), Carrizo et al. (2017), Sina and Kim (2019), Garaus (2017), Mostafa and Kasamani (2020). Between satisfaction and shopping intention, there are more studies, such as Reynolds and Morrin (2019), Tu and Yang (2019), Carrizo et al. (2017), Padilla (2017), Sina and Kim (2019), and Tandon et al. (2017).

*Figure 2. Structural model*

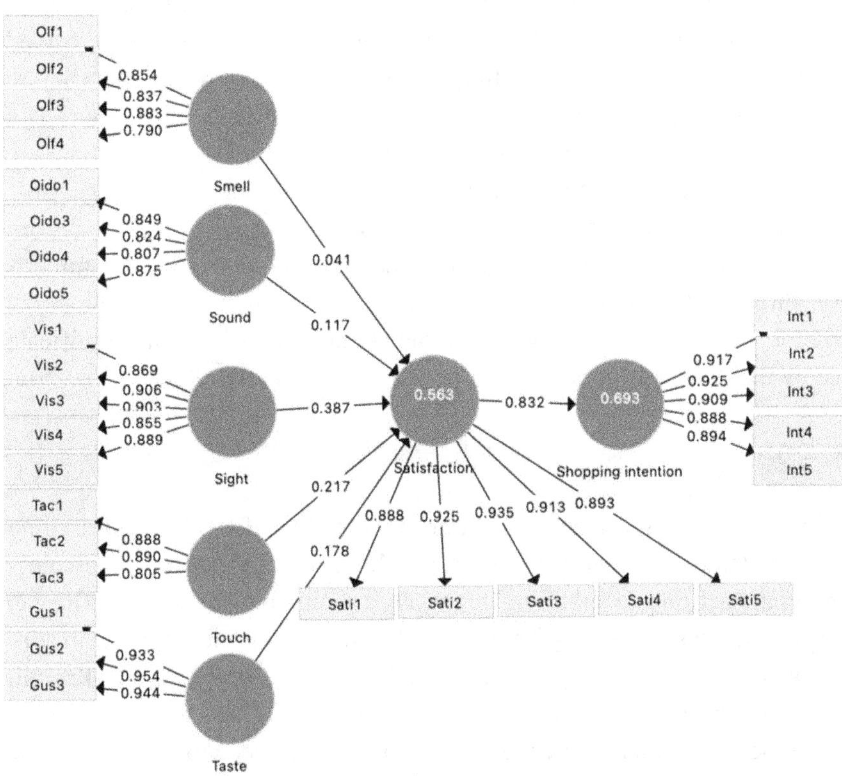

## CONCLUSION

Technology has brought new ways of communication between consumers and stores. They give the client the tools to compare any products or stores worldwide. Those interconnectivities bring an important duty to physical stores, connect with their clients thru unique experiences, giving them a chance to be at the top of mind of the client. That can be formed by associations perceived by a diverse stimulus. Focusing on taste, sight, sound, and touch.

Findings of the study revealed that Tamaulipas's (México) consumers consider taste, sight, sound, and touch as providers of satisfaction. If the SMEs manage the store in an atmosphere that includes the right elements, the client will have a shopping intention. Now, when a store manages sight, it means the arrangement of the products, the distribution of the products, the colors presented, the order inside the store, and anything that the eye could see and influence the look of it. Talking about taste means letting the client eat inside the store, and giving them food to try during their shopping. Sound influences their shopping intention too, that includes the music provided by stores to hear as ambient music, the volume, the kind of music, and the sounds produced inside the stores. Touch is formed by the temperature inside the store, in other words, the air conditioner has to be at the right temperature to incite shopping, how the products feel in the client's hands, it could be perceived as cheap or expensive, and in that way, they important touching the products before a buying intention. In conclusion, consistent with other investigations, there is a strong and direct association with the human senses.

However, the smell does not play the same role as the other senses. A possible explanation for these results may be the lack of stimulation in stores in northeastern Mexico or memory. Findings also reveal how the stores can stimulate costumer's satisfaction through their senses, improving the atmosphere in which the client interact to buy products. Also, if it gets it to the client in a positive and significate experience by their senses, the result will be a shopping intention.

### Implications

These findings point to a significant contribution for the SMEs, first of all contributing to the knowledge of the consumers in northeastern Mexico and about sensory marketing in relation to satisfaction and shopping intention. It should help to decrease the gap between big enterprises and SMEs. They can utilize the findings to improve sensory marketing, satisfaction, and shopping intention. In northeastern Mexico SMEs still using old marketing techniques, nowadays globalization pushes stores to a global market of competition with all kinds of stores. Small stores need to find their niche using the client experience thru sensory marketing to satisfy clients.

## REFERENCES


Alan, A., Kabadayi E. & Yilmaz, C. (2015). Cognitive and affective constituents of the consumption experience in retail service settings: effects on store loyalty. *Service Business, 10*(4), 715-735. doi:10.1007/s11628-015-0288-8

Arnould, E., & Thompson, C. (2005). Consumer Culture Theory (CCT): Twenty years of research. *The Journal of Consumer Research, 31*(4), 868–882. doi:10.1086/426626

Baek, E., Choo, H., & Lee, S. (2018). Using warmth as the visual design of a store: Intimacy, relational needs, and approach intentions. *Journal of Business Research, 88*, 91–101. doi:10.1016/j.jbusres.2018.03.013

Barrios, M. (2012). Marketing de la experiencia: Principales conceptos y características. *Palermo Business Review, 7*, 67–89.

Biswas, D., Lund, K., & Szocs, C. (2018). Sounds like a healthy retail atmospheric strategy: Effects of ambient music and background noise on food sales. *Journal of the Academy of Marketing Science, 47*(1), 37–55. doi:10.100711747-018-0583-8

Biswas, D., & Szocs, C. (2019). The Smell of Healthy Choices: Cross-Modal Sensory Compensation Effects of Ambient Scent on Food Purchases. *JMR, Journal of Marketing Research, 56*(1), 123–141. doi:10.1177/0022243718820585

Biswas, D., Szocs, C., & Abell, A. (2019b). Extending the Boundaries of Sensory Marketing and Examining the Sixth Sensory System: Effects of Vestibular Sensations for Sitting versus Standing Postures on Food Taste Perception. *The Journal of Consumer Research, 46*(5), 1–17. doi:10.1093/jcr/ucz018

Brakus, J., Schmitt, B., & Zhang, S. (2009). Experiential product attributes and preferences for new products: The role of processing fluency. *Journal of Business Research, 67*(11), 2291–2298. doi:10.1016/j.jbusres.2014.06.017

Canniford, R., Riach, K., & Hill, T. (2018). Nosenography: How smell constitutes meaning, identity and temporal experience in spatial assemblages. *Marketing Theory, 18*(2), 234–248. doi:10.1177/1470593117732462

Carrizo, A., Freitas, P., & Ferreira, V. (2017). Les effets des expériences de marque sur la qualité, la satisfaction et la fidélité: Une étude empirique dans le domaine des services multiples de télécommunications. *Innovar (Universidad Nacional de Colombia), 27*(64), 23–38. doi:10.15446/innovar.v27n64.62366

Chin, W. W. (1998). *The partial least squares approach for structural equation modeling. Modern Methods for Business Research, 2, 295–336.*

Cohen, J. (1988). *Statistical Power Analysis for the Behavioral Sciences* (2nd ed.). Lawrence Erlbaum Associates, Publishers.

Decré, B., & Cloonan, C. (2019). A touch of gloss: Haptic perception of packaging and consumers' reactions. *Journal of Product and Brand Management*, *28*(1), 117–132. doi:10.1108/JPBM-05-2017-1472

Dijkstra, T. K., & Henseler, J. (2015). Consistent Partial Least Squares Path Modeling. *Management Information Systems Quarterly*, *39*(2), 297–316. doi:10.25300/MISQ/2015/39.2.02

Elder, R., & Krishna, A. (2022). A Review of Sensory Imagery for Consumer Psychology. *Journal of Consumer Psychology*, *32*(2), 293–315. doi:10.1002/jcpy.1242

Fernández, C., Arribas, F., & Martín, C. (2020). Marketing sensorial en el sector de la moda femenina: El olor de las tiendas en Madrid. *Revista Academia & Negocios*, *7*(1), 31–40. doi:10.29393/RAN6-1SMCF20001

Fernández, R., Ángeles, M., & Bonillo, I. (2009). La estética y la diversión como factores generadores de valor en la experiencia de consumo en servicios. *Innovar (Universidad Nacional de Colombia)*, *19*(34), 7–24. http://www.scielo.org.co/scielo.php?script=sci_arttext&pid=S0121-50512009000200002

Fornell, C., & Larcker, D. F. (1981). Evaluating structural equation models with unobservable variables and measurement error. *JMR, Journal of Marketing Research*, *18*(1), 39–5. doi:10.1177/002224378101800104

Garaus, M. (2017). Atmospheric harmony in the retail environment: Its influence on store satisfaction and re-patronage intention. *Journal of Consumer Behaviour*, *16*(3), 265–278. doi:10.1002/cb.1626

Gómez, R., & Mejía, J. E. (2012). La gestión del Marketing que conecta con los sentidos. *Revista Escuela de Administración de Negocios*, *73*(2), 168–183. doi:10.21158/01208160.n73.2012.592

Gómez-Suárez, M., Yagüe, M. J., Schmitz, A., & García-Gumiel, C. (2020). Sensorial and Experiential Marketing in Shopping Centers: Effects on Retailer Performance. In F. Musso & E. Druica (Eds.), *Handbook of Research on Retailing Techniques for Optimal Consumer Engagement and Experiences* (pp. 162–182). IGI Global. doi:10.4018/978-1-7998-1412-2.ch008

González, N. H., Guzmán, J. C., Olguin, J. A., & Gamboa, F. (2019). La mercadotecnia sensorial en la zona comercial del sur de Tamaulipas, México. *Revista Observatorio de la Economía Latinoamericana*. Recuperado de: https://www.eumed.net/rev/oel/2019/10/mercadotecnia-sensorial-mexico.html

Haase, J., Wiedmann, J., & Bettels, J. (2020). Sensory imagery in advertising: How the senses affect perceived product design and consumer attitude. *Journal of Marketing Communications*, *26*(5), 475–487. doi:10.1080/13527266.2018.1518257

Haase, J., & Wiedmann, K. (2020). The implicit sensory association test (ISAT): A measurement approach for sensory perception. *Journal of Business Research*, *109*, 236–245. doi:10.1016/j.jbusres.2019.12.005

Hair, J., Risher, J., Sarstedt, M., & Ringle, C. (2019). When and how to report the results of PLS-SEM. *European Business Review*, *31*(1), 2–24. doi:10.1108/EBR-11-2018-0203

Hamacher, K., & Buckremer, R. (2022). Measuring Online Sensory Consumer Experience: Introducing the Online Sensory Marketing Index (OSMI) as a Structural Modeling Approach. *Journal of Theoretical and Applied Electronic Commerce Research*, *17*(2), 751–772. doi:10.3390/jtaer17020039

Helmefalk, M. (2019). Browsing behaviour as a mediator: The impact of multi-sensory cues on purchasing. *Journal of Consumer Marketing*, *36*(2), 253–263. doi:10.1108/JCM-10-2017-2392

Hepola, J., Karjaluoto, H., & Hintikka, A. (2017). The effect of sensory brand experience and involvement on brand equity directly and indirectly through consumer brand engagement. *Journal of Product and Brand Management*, *26*(3), 282–293. doi:10.1108/JPBM-10-2016-1348

Jang, H., & Lee, S. (2019). Applying Effective Sensory Marketing to Sustainable Coffee Shop Business Management. *Sustainability*, *11*(22), 6430. doi:10.3390u11226430

Koszembar, M. (2019). Sensory Marketing - Sensory Communication and its Social Perception. *Communication Today*, *10*(2), 146–156.

Kotler, P. (1973). Atmospherics as a marketing tool. *Journal of Retailing*, *49*(4), 48–64.

Krey, N. L. T. E. (2016). *Enough is enough! Understanding environmentally driven multisensory experiences* [Doctoral dissertation]. https://digitalcommons.latech.edu/dissertations/141

Krishna, A. (2012). Sensory marketing: research on the sensuality of products. Routledge, Taylor & Francis Group, USA

Krishna, A., & Schwarz, N. (2014). Sensory marketing, embodiment, and grounded cognition: A review and introduction. *Journal of Consumer Psychology, 24*(2), 159–168. doi:10.1016/j.jcps.2013.12.006

Lindstrom, M. (2015). *Brand Sense: Convierta su marca en una experiencia de cinco sentidos*. Patria.

Lund, C. (2015). Selling through the Senses: Sensory Appeals in the Fashion Retail Environment. Fashion Practice. *Journal of Design Creative Process & The Fashion Industry, 7*(1), 9–30. doi:0.2752/175693815X14182200335619

Madzharov, A. (2019). Self-Control and Touch: When Does Direct Versus Indirect Touch Increase Hedonic Evaluations and Consumption of Food. *Journal of Retailing, 95*(4), 170–185. doi:10.1016/j.jretai.2019.10.009

Marin, P., & Gomez, D. (2022). Application of sensory marketing techniques in fashion shops: The case of Zara and Stradivarius. *Vivat Academia, 155*, 17–32.

Mehrabian, A., & Russell, J. (1974). *An approach to environmental psychology. An approach to environmental psychology*. The MIT Press.

Moore, D. (2014). Is anticipation delicious? Visceral factors as mediators of the effect of olfactory cues on purchase intentions. *Journal of Business Research, 67*(9), 2045–2051. doi:10.1016/j.jbusres.2013.10.005

Moreira, A., Fortes, N., & Santiago, R. (2017). Influence of sensory stimuli on brand experience, brand equity and purchase intention. *Journal of Business Economics and Management, 18*(1), 68–83. doi:10.3846/16111699.2016.1252793

Mostafa, R., & Kasamani, T. (2020). Brand experience and brand loyalty: Is it a matter of emotions? *Asia Pacific Journal of Marketing and Logistics, 33*(4), 1033–1051. doi:10.1108/APJML-11-2019-0669

Padilla, R., Milton, S., Johnson, L., & Nyadzayo, M. (2017). Impact of service value on satisfaction and repurchase intentions in business-to-business cloud computing. *Service Science, 9*(1), 5–13. doi:10.1287erv.2016.0163

Perumal, S., Ali, J., & Shaarih, H. (2021). Exploring nexus among sensory marketing and repurchase intention: Application of S-O-R Model. *Management Science Letters, 11*, 1527–1536. doi:10.5267/j.msl.2020.12.020

Pine, J., & Gilmore, J. (2011). *The Experience Economy*. Harvard Business Review Press.

Randhir, R., Latasha, K., Tooraiven, P., & Monishan, B. (2016). Analyzing the impact of sensory marketing on consumers: A case study of KFC. *Journal of US-China Public Administration*, *13*(4), 278–292. doi:10.17265/1548-6591/2016.04.007

Raposo, D. (2022). *Design, visual communication and branding*. Cambridge Scholars Publishing.

Reina, M., & Jimenez, D. (2020). Consumer Experience and Omnichannel Behavior in Various Sales Atmospheres. *Frontiers in Psychology*, *11*, 1972. doi:10.3389/fpsyg.2020.01972 PMID:32849155

Reynolds-Mcllnay, R., & Morin, M. (2019). Increasing Shopper Trust in Retailer Technological Interfaces via Auditory Confirmation. *Journal of Retailing*, *95*(4), 128–142. doi:10.1016/j.jretai.2019.10.006

Ringle, C. M., Wende, S., & Becker, J. M. (2015). *SmartPLS 3.2.8*. Boenningstedt: SmartPLS GmbH. http://www.smartpls.com

Ringler, C., Sirianni, N., Gustafsson, A., & Peck, J. (2019). Look but Don't Touch! The Impact of Active Interpersonal Haptic Blocking on Compensatory Touch and Purchase Behavior. *Journal of Retailing*, *95*(4), 186–203. doi:10.1016/j.jretai.2019.10.007

Roggeveen, A., Grewal, D., & Schweiger, E. (2020). The DAST Framework for Retail Atmospherics: The Impact of In- and Out-of-Store Retail Journey Touchpoints on the Customer Experience. *Journal of Retailing*, *96*(1), 128–137. doi:10.1016/j.jretai.2019.11.002

Sachdeva, I., & Goel, S. (2015). Retail store environment and customer experience: A paradigm. *Journal of Fashion Marketing and Management*, *19*(3), 290–298. doi:10.1108/JFMM-03-2015-0021

Safeer, A., He, Y., & Abrar, M. (2020). The influence of brand experience on brand authenticity and brand love: An empirical study from Asian consumers' perspective. *Asia Pacific Journal of Marketing and Logistics*, *33*(5), 1123–1138. doi:10.1108/APJML-02-2020-0123

Sandell, K. (2019). Olfactory cues and purchase behavior: Consumer characteristics as moderators. *European Journal of Marketing*, *53*(7), 1378–1399. doi:10.1108/EJM-12-2017-0918

Satti, Z., Babar, S., & Ahmad, H. (2019). Exploring mediating role of service quality in the association between sensory marketing and customer satisfaction. *Total Quality Management & Business Excellence*, *32*(7-8), 719–736. doi:10.1080/14783363.2019.1632185

Sina, A., & Kim, H. (2019). Enhancing consumer satisfaction and retail patronage through brand experience, cognitive pleasure, and shopping enjoyment: A comparison between lifestyle and product-centric displays. *Journal of Global Fashion Marketing*, *10*(2), 129–144. doi:10.1080/20932685.2019.1573698

Spence, C. (2012). Managing sensory expectations concerning products and brands: Capitalizing on the potential of sound and shape symbolism. *Journal of Consumer Psychology*, *22*(1), 37–54. doi:10.1016/j.jcps.2011.09.004

Stillman, P., Lee, H., Deng, X., Unnava, H., & Fujita, K. (2020). Examining consumers' sensory experiences with color: A consumer neuroscience approach. *Psychology and Marketing*, *37*(7), 995–1007. doi:10.1002/mar.21360

Tandon, U., Kiran, R., & Sah, A. (2017). Customer Satisfaction as mediator between website service quality and repurchase intention: An emerging economy case. *Service Science*, *9*(2), 106–120. doi:10.1287erv.2016.0159

Tu, J., & Yang, C. (2019). Consumer Needs for Hand-Touch Product Designs Based on the Experience Economy. *Sustainability*, *11*(7), 2064. doi:10.3390u11072064

Wibisono, N., & Syah, E. (2019). The rol of experiential marketing towards satisfaction and re-intention to visit a tourist destination. *Journal of Tourism & Sports Management*, *1*(1), 1–14.

Wörfel, P., Frentz, F., & Tautu, C. (2022). Marketing comes to its senses: A bibliometric review and integrated framework of sensory experience in marketing. *European Journal of Marketing*, *56*(3), 704–737. doi:10.1108/EJM-07-2020-0510

Yakhlef, A. (2015). Customer experience within retail environments. *Marketing Theory*, *15*(4), 545–564. doi:10.1177/1470593115569016

Zha, D., Foroudi, P., Jin, Z., & Melewar, T. (2021). Making sense of sensory brand experience: Constructing an integrative framework for future research. *International Journal of Management Reviews*, 1–38, 130–167.

# Chapter 4
# Digital Entrepreneurship and Micro and Small Enterprises in the Time of the COVID-19 Pandemic in Mexico

**Cesaire Chiatchoua**
*Escuela Superior de Economía, Instituto Politécnico Nacional, Mexico*

## ABSTRACT

*The objective of this research is to analyze some work areas of interest as a result of the COVID-19 pandemic such as content marketing and social networks, artificial intelligence, 3D printing, virtual reality, big data, devices through the voice, robotization, automation, and digital transformation of companies, electronic commerce, and digital leisure for the development of digital entrepreneurship with the aim of promoting self-employment of young people, mainly from Generation Z. A qualitative methodology with a cross-sectional and descriptive scope was used with secondary sources. The results show that technological tools are the new source for business development. Although Mexico is prepared for the implementation of businesses via the internet, it should be noted that there are still barriers such as bureaucracy, training, greater investment, ignorance, and resistance to change. It is urgent to develop collaborative public-private-academy strategies to strengthen institutions, infrastructure, and human skills focused on new technologies to guarantee decent employment.*

DOI: 10.4018/978-1-6684-6591-2.ch004

## INTRODUCTION

The pandemic crisis that appeared in 2020 left endless consequences in the human, economic and environmental fields. For Fierro Moreno, Cuauhtémoc Gaxiola and Linares (2021) the world economy will lose 9 trillion dollars in the course of 2020 and 2021 and those developing countries will lose 220,000 million dollars of GDP in 2020 alone. there were several from the loss of more than 1 million jobs in the first 6 months of confinement according to data from the National Institute of Statistics and Geography (INEGI, 2022a) to the closure of millions of companies. For Velázquez and Rivero (2020), more than 70% of the established Micro, Small and Medium-sized Enterprises (MSMEs) had to temporarily close their doors due to the imposition of confinement that significantly reduced mobility with the intention of curbing the rate of contagion. among the population.

MSMEs represent a very important segment for the world economy and for the Mexican economy. In fact, according to INEGI (2022b) there are more than 5,528,698 million companies, and of these 5,514,815 million are within the classification of MSMEs, which in turn represent 52% of the Product National Gross Domestic and provide approximately 72% of the jobs in the country. Also, within the classification of Micro and Small Enterprises (MaSEs) that is the interest of this research, there are 5,459,659 million companies, which represents 98.75% of all companies. It means in the first instance that almost all companies are in this segment and secondly, the MYPES are important for the economy and development of the country.

From the above, Bejarano, Hancevic and Núñez (2021) speculate that this class of micro and small businesses are the first affected by any temporary closure policy or restrictions that limit the operation of establishments. The lack of operation of the MYPES entails multiple economic effects that translate into a decrease in production, loss of jobs with a high uncertainty for the reopening, an increase in the number of families in a situation of poverty and extreme poverty (Cueva-Rivera and Erazo-Álvarez (2021), decrease in income, demand and cancellation of orders, abide by health and hygiene measures (Santiago Hernández., Martínez Sandoval., Alcaraz Miranda and Córdova Yánez, 2021), as well as the strategies that businessmen of the sector have implemented according to Rodríguez González; Tagle Zamora and Granados Márquez (2020).

Therefore, Durán (2017) concludes that, in Mexico, MYPES play an important role in developing countries in terms of job creation and economic growth in their regions, contributing up to 45% to formal employment and at 33% in terms of GDP in emerging economies, they provide work to vulnerable strata such as women and youth.

Faced with the aforementioned social difficulties, entrepreneurial activity appears as a possible solution for self-employment and the need to generate income, which is why entrepreneurship has aroused great interest in recent years. This responds to the need to boost employment, especially in underdeveloped economies according to Ortiz García (2016). By the way, entrepreneurship is considered an essential part of the economic and social development of any community, region and country since it generates innovative alternatives for products, processes or inputs in the production of goods and services (Hernández-Ramírez., Mora-Esquivel, and Leiva, 2022) that with the profits generated support the entrepreneur and his family.

The confinement forced companies to opt for work at home with the intention of maintaining activities, this form of work called Telecommuting or Home Office (in English) completely changed the labor sector. The introduction of technology is here to stay and is adapted to various sectors of activity, even to entrepreneurship. Digital entrepreneurship, which is the ability to generate companies or businesses on the Internet, distribute their products and services online without the need to invest in physical spaces or offices, has been required during the closure of companies to survive.

Traditional entrepreneurs, those who use physical spaces for their activities, could not survive the confinement because they were not prepared to face the pandemic crisis, they were not trained in the use of new technology and also, according to Baltazar Vilchis and Velázquez Ramírez (2022) during this period, the low level of support from the authorities towards microenterprises (entrepreneurs) in the retail trade sector was observed in the municipalities of Region II Atlacomulco, of the State of Mexico during the first quarter of 2021, as well as the ability they have had to continue their economic work through the use of ICT and the different communication platforms with their clients.

From the above, the objective of this research is to analyze some work areas of interest as a result of the COVID-19 pandemic such as Content Marketing and Social Networks, Artificial Intelligence, 3D Printing, Virtual Reality, Big Data, Devices through the Voice, Robotization, automation and digital transformation of companies, Electronic Commerce and Digital Leisure for the development of digital entrepreneurship with the aim of promoting self-employment of young people, mainly from generation Z.

The work is distributed as follows. After the introduction, section 1 presents the theoretical framework of this document that is articulated on digital entrepreneurship and the classification of companies in Mexico. Part 2 shows the methodology used, which is descriptive and analytical with a qualitative approach using secondary data from various databases such as INEGI as well as previous research. Part 3 details the results of the research, in this case the areas indicated and their importance in generating employment using technology will be addressed. Finally, conclusions and recommendations are presented.

## THEORETICAL FRAMEWORK: DIGITAL ENTREPRENEURSHIP AND COMPANIES IN MEXICO

### Digital Entrepreneurship

The different crises around the world and mainly in Latin America, such as the 2008 financial crisis in the United States and currently the crisis derived from the COVID-19 pandemic, have increased unemployment in the countries, as well as inequality. Entrepreneurial activity appears as a possible solution due to the uncertainty about employment and the need to generate income. By the way, entrepreneurship is considered an essential part of the economic and social development of any community, region and country since it generates innovative alternatives for products, processes or inputs in the production of goods and services, which with the profits generated support the entrepreneur and his family, but it also generates jobs and attracts other investments to form an innovative entrepreneurial ecosystem (Shapero, 1981).

In this regard, Gálvez Albarracín, Guauña Aguila and Ravina Ripoll (2020) argue that entrepreneurship and its manifestation in the creation of companies are considered catalysts for the development of nations and regions, for which the public, private and academic sectors They show growing interest in understanding these phenomena and the elements that stimulate or discourage them.

In another study, Mora Pabón (2011) shows:

*A deep link between entrepreneurs and their beliefs that leads them to act and feel in a way that they take measured risks, have control over what they do, feel satisfied with themselves, are in a permanent search for innovation and have a high achievement motivation. Additionally, they indicate that not only social norms intervene in the attitude of creating a company, but that this can also influence people to achieve a favorable acceptance of the behavior of undertaking, generating a bidirectional or two-way feedback. (pp. 70-83)*

This shows that social norms, beliefs and the ability to take risks are personal factors that are related to the entrepreneurial attitude. There are also elements such as the public, private and academic sectors that are relevant in the business creation process. During the COVD-19 period Chaturvedi and Karri (2022) found prime barriers which affected the firms: organizational readiness, infrastructural support by government, technological inadequacy and financial crises. The main strategies emphasized by founders to overcome the barriers of organizational readiness and financial crunch were marketing, strategic networking and product and services, and for technological ineptness was digitization. The COVID-19 crisis forced us to permanently consider the use of technology in organizational processes, whether in sales, recruitment, production, marketing, and other business areas. Hence the interest in digital entrepreneurship in this study.

Although technological progress has led companies to digitize, the COVID-19 pandemic accelerated this process due to the restriction of mobility due to confinement. The way organizations work changed completely, teleworking was implemented, online sales increased and home deliveries were also adopted. According to Wim & Werner (2020) In a digital economy, digital entrepreneurs pursue opportunities to produce and trade in digital artifacts on digital artifact stores or platforms, and/or to create these digital artifact stores or platforms themselves.

In this context, digital entrepreneurship becomes a tool for greater competitiveness for organizations in developed and emerging countries that want to compete both nationally and internationally. Recent results of the Digital Economy and Society Index (52, 45%) and the European Index of Digital Entrepreneurship Systems (EIDES) (48%) illustrate an improved level of the digital performance in European Union countries and a significant progress towards unlocking the productivity of digital value co-creation and collaborative networks. It is also agreed that the rapid digitalization of the economy and the digital entrepreneurship approach fosters a transition of traditional business models to networked and integrated digital platform business models following Baranauskas and Raišiene (2022).

By the way, Jawad, Naz, and Maroof, (2020) in a research paper reconnoiters the digital entrepreneurship and its influence on the business setting in developing economies. The outcomes highlighted that entrepreneur's knowledge act as a sensitive social expectation and enhances support, even the non-contributively factor of institutional trust. Findings demonstrated that administrative initiatives toward digitalization are pledged to consume invigorated entrepreneurship in all emerging economies consequently providing better chances for advancement and prevailing institutions requirements for further development in order to confirm the economic growth and supportable entrepreneurial situation.

According to Kraus, Palmer., Kailer, Kallinger, and Spitzer (2018) digital entrepreneurship is of high topicality as technological developments and advances in infrastructure create various opportunities for entrepreneurs. Society's great attention to new digital business models is opposed to very little research regarding opportunities, challenges and success factors of digital entrepreneurship. These authors mention that digital entrepreneurship is an opportunity to generate independent jobs and respond satisfactorily to the needs of consumers, which continue to be more complex. Technological development plays a key role in promoting products and/or services. Companies must adapt to technological tools to boost sales.

The above presented shows that Most of these studies have reported a positive influence of digital transformation on entrepreneurial activities globally in accordance with Haitham and Mehroz (2020). Therefore, entrepreneurs must reorient or readapt their training needs towards new technologies to achieve a better insertion of their business in the markets.

For Recker and von Briel (2019) the intersection of digital technologies and entrepreneurship—is gaining increasing importance in the global economy and scholarly community. Although digital entrepreneurship is important for the transformation of entrepreneurial activities, what are the challenges faced by entrepreneurs for its implementation?

Answering the question above, Anim-Yeboah, Boateng, Awuni Kolog, Owusu, and Bedi (2020) comment that the capabilities and capacities of enterprises, as well as the strategies in implementing digital technologies and harnessing the opportunities of digitalization, are key issues that have not hitherto received much attention. Also, Baranauskas and Raišiene (2022) point out that the well-recognized benefits of the digital entrepreneurship and the digital business ecosystem, application of emerging technologies and modern business models also brings inevitable sustainable management challenges. The main negative outcomes are in the disruption or exposure of vulnerabilities within collaborative organizational and social networks, the additional socio-technical pressure for both network supervisors and incumbents, and the asymmetry of digital information and resources, etc.

## Micro, Small, and Medium Enterprises Facing the Digital in Mexico

According to Economist Impact (2021a), of Mexico's 4.9 million MSMEs operating in 2019, over a million have not survived the pandemic driven recession. Mexico's microenterprises—ten staf or less—employ almost half of the workforce. The country's SMEs need a productivity boost. Despite representing 95.4% of businesses, SMEs contribute just 52% of GDP, and microenterprises only 12.4%.

Regarding the impulses that MSMEs need to survive the pandemic, Molina-Sánchez., García-Pérez-de-Lema., López-Salazar., & Godínez-López (2022) analyze the competitive factors that help make MSMEs successful. To do this in Guanajuato, Mexico. The results of the binary logistic regression analysis show that quality, technology, and innovation are the main variables that determine a company's success. These findings could provide guidelines to help MSMEs improve their competitiveness, and they could help public administrations better support MSME growth, especially in times of crisis. Digitalization represents an opportunity to modernize and boost economic activity.

La digitalization sola no es suficiente para to improve the performance of the development system once the pandemic is over. There are three areas of particular importance for economic recovery: support for the incorporation of digital technologies, incentives for formalizing companies and biosafety protocols. There are also signs of a shift in the way policies are formulated, towards adaptive management models that focus on accountability and the strengthening of public institutions, the deepening of partnerships with the business sector and the consolidation of decentralization dynamics that provide space for participation by local and regional actors according to Dini and Heredia Zurita (2021).

The implementation of this digitalization needs the support of the government since micro and small companies lack funds to obtain the necessary technology and machines. In addition, training for the use of the aforementioned tools. Hence the interest of the study of Sonobe., Takeda, Yoshida, and Truong (2021) say that soon after the outbreak of the COVID-19 pandemic, many governments began extending financial and other forms of support to MSMEs and their workers because smaller firms are more vulnerable to negative shocks to their supply chain, labor supply, and final demand for goods and services than larger firms.

That´s why there is a need for compatibility between industrial and competition policies and for greater coordination among the agencies responsible for data protection and competition policy and among the different government agencies Da Silva and Núñez Reyes (2021).

Since MSMEs are diverse, however, the severity of the pandemic's impact on them varies considerably depending on their characteristics. The research characterizes those firms in South, Southeast, and Northeast Asia that began participating in online commerce and tries to determine how their use of online commerce and their employment are related in this difficult time. And also examines the government support that MSMEs have received and the extent to which it has satisfied their support needs.

As an example of the above analyzed, DAI Global (2022) in a study found that 60 percent of surveyed MSMEs reported that they used digital tools for business purposes in the past year since COVID-19. Also, surveyed online MSMEs looked favorably on digital tool use during the pandemic: 69 percent reported that digital tools were important or essential to keeping their business running during COVID-19. Also, recognized the help that digital tools provided in adapting to the COVID-19 environment. Finally, 72 percent reported that Facebook apps helped them adapt to the COVID-19 environment.

The above shows that without the help of digital tools, many companies will have collapsed during the pandemic. Specifically, about 30% of companies, that is, 3 out of 10 companies, closed during the pandemic. In this regard, Economist Impact (2021b) comments that the covid-19 pandemic had an immediate, negative impact on many of Mexico's MSMEs, forcing them to turn to digital platforms and tools just to survive. The initial financial pain from the pandemic meant those enterprises that could not adapt quickly enough to a digital-first approach to business either had to temporarily suspend operations or shut down for good. Those that survived learned quickly to adapt to e-commerce and use digital tools to thrive.

Other study by Valdez-Juárez, Castillo-Vergara, and Ramos-Escobar (2022) mentions that innovation management has positive and significant effects on the economic indicators and business performance of SMEs. It is also revealed that Open innovation strategies such as electronic commerce have positive and significant effects on innovation management and corporate performance. Similarly, the home office has significant effects on innovation management.

Castillo-Galván and Mendez Palacios (2022) point out that In a world of constant change and accelerated growth, the use of information systems based on digital technology, integrated into manufacturing processes and resource management, has become a necessity for Mexican small and medium-sized companies (SMEs). who intend to grow globally and maintain their competitiveness in the market in which they operate. They see digital technologies as a tool that would allow them to achieve their development and growth plans, based on the concept of exponential growth organizations who, without many physical resources but with intensive use of technology, have managed to grow in short periods of time. However, it is not so simple, they face greater challenges such the lack of expert personnel to advise and guide them in the implementation and management of the technology, this is a barrier that they must overcome in the state of San Luis Potosí.

Finally, SMEs lag in the digital transformation. Emerging technologies, as diverse as they are, offer a range of applications for them to improve performance and overcome the size-related limitations they face in doing business. However, SMEs must be better prepared, and stakes are high. The SME digital gap has increased inequalities among people, places and firms, and there are concerns that the benefits of the digital transformation could accrue to early adopters, further broadening these inequalities. Enabling SME digitalization has become a top policy priority in OECD and Latin America countries (OECD, 2021).

## METHODOLOGY

The study has a qualitative approach; In order to discover and answer the research question, it is based on a data collection method. The latter will be of a documentary nature, relying on secondary sources, that is, on documents of any kind such as bibliographic and hemerographic; the first is based on consulting books and the second on articles or essays in magazines and newspapers. In addition, the present work is based on a non-experimental design, the phenomenon observed within its natural environment is analyzed. In this case, the phenomenon is to analyze some work areas of interest as a result of the COVID-19 pandemic such as Content Marketing and Social Networks, Artificial Intelligence, 3D Printing, Virtual Reality, Big Data, Devices through the Voice, Robotization, automation and digital transformation of companies, Electronic Commerce and Digital Leisure for the development of digital entrepreneurship with the aim of promoting self-employment of young people, mainly from generation Z. Hypotheses are not tested.

## RESULTS OF THE RESEARCH: THE AREAS INDICATED AND THEIR IMPORTANCE IN GENERATING EMPLOYMENT USING TECHNOLOGY

The pandemic crisis paralyzed economic activities and companies looked for alternatives so as not to disappear from the markets. In this scenario, technology has become a great opportunity, as pointed out by Modgil et al. (2022) in a study whose results indicate the emergence of digital entrepreneurship opportunities in technology (EdTech, FinTech, cybersecurity), healthcare (diagnostics, virtual care, fitness), entertainment (over the top, gaming, social media), and e-commerce (contactless delivery, payment methods, augmented reality). This allows the generation of online communities (Meurer et al., 2022). The interest of this section is to show the importance of new forms of work that include technology in times of crisis.

### Content Marketing and Social Networks (CMSN)

The pandemic crisis has been very hard for companies, forcing entrepreneurs to look for alternatives both to continue their activities and to promote their products given the mobility restriction caused by confinement. To find customers, consolidate brands and sell products, content networks are developed. From there, Content Marketing and Social Networks (CMSN) become an opportunity for companies. CMSN is according to Vázquez (2013) is a set of strategies that are aimed at searching, developing and delivering content to users and followers of a brand in order not only to generate traffic, but also to create empathy and discussions around the brand's proposals. In other words, users are given a series of content that will expand the experience and concept of our brand towards social networks.

For the proper functioning of CMSN, it is important to consider the following: a means of concentrating users, understanding the needs and desires of customers, permanent review of the platform, positioning your brand, expanding your market share, improving your customer service, expand your market, develop lasting relationships. Some of the advantages of this activity are advice, feedback and the provision by the company of a full range of possibilities and means of exchange and interactive communication.

In Mexico, the development of technology focused on business is not new as in many countries, but the pandemic crisis accelerated the incorporation process in organizations. According to El-Gohary (2010), due to the existing conditions of internet accessibility in Mexico and that Mexican people are more attracted to use them, it can be said that there are the necessary conditions to display any of the existing communication strategies and social media marketing (SMM). The SMM that can be very useful, due to a great number of advantages at a low cost, this thanks to the massive use of the Internet and mobile devices (cell phones, tablets), that represent many opportunities but also remove many threats.

The foregoing shows that Mexico has the capabilities to develop the area of CMSN and that access is neither restricted nor limited for those entrepreneurs who want to launch into this activity. Then concludes Madrigal Moreno et al. (2016) in a study that it is confirmed that the contemporary society has established the conditions to implement properly social media marketing in Morelia.

## Artificial Intelligence (AI)

A market investigation according to Canals TI (2021) reveals that, in Mexico, 14% of Information Technology (IT) professionals now use artificial intelligence (AI) in their company. Likewise, 40% of them have accelerated their implementation of AI as a result of the COVID-19 pandemic as indicated throughout this investigation. The above shows that artificial intelligence is now more accessible than ever. For Donald (2019), AI is one of the most disruptive technologies of our time.

Another investigation according to Canales TI (September 8, 2021) shows that more than 57% of Mexican companies are exploring the adoption of AI. And half of Mexican professionals say that the pandemic has increased their focus on customer service (47%), followed by marketing and sales (37%) and process automation (26%). AI is already transforming the way businesses operate today, from how they communicate with their customers through virtual assistants, to automating key workflows, and even managing network security. This allows AI to be defined as machines or computers that mimic cognitive functions that humans associate with the human mind, such as learning and problem solving according to Schalkoff (1990).

AI is applied in various areas of the organization as indicated by Yigitcanlar et al. (2020): (a) digital transformation, innovation, and sustainability are the most popular AI application areas in urban planning and development; (b) drones, automation, robotics, and big data are the most popular AI technologies utilized in urban planning and development; and (c) achieving the digital transformation and sustainability of cities through the use of AI technologies—such as big data, automation and robotics—is the central community discussion topic.

Previous studies have shown the importance and adoption of AI in Mexican companies. It has also been shown that the country has the capacity to develop technology. However, entrepreneurs face certain challenges like many other countries in the world. Of these challenges, one can cite a lack of AI skills and a growing complexity in data management.

## 3D Printing

The demand for 3D printing is increasing in the manufacturing industry since it allows faster production and streamlines processes in the automotive industry such as the aerospace industry and the medical sector in the case of Mexico. In fact, according to Tecma (2022) currently, North America, including Mexico and Europe, account for 68% of the revenue generated by 3D printing. The Asia Pacific region accounts for another 27%. Stratasys, the leading manufacturer of 3D printing equipment and supplies estimates that the use of 3D printing in Mexican industry will grow between 30% and 40% in the current year. The company believes that, in the next several years, Mexico will be the Latin American country with the highest adoption rate of this technology.

The above shows that 3D printing in Mexican industry will account for 70% total parts production in the automotive, aerospace, medical devices and household appliances sector, among others.

## Virtual Reality

Knowledge and mastery of spaces are of vital importance for the movements of human beings. Currently, with technological development, this concern finds a solution: Virtual reality. Garcia Reyes et al. (2014) comments that with the help of the internet and the so-called information and communication technologies, a reflection of humanity can be made in virtual spaces. Therefore, artificial intelligence through the creation of virtual reality systems has offered an alternative solution to this need.

Virtual reality can be defined according to Coiffet and Burdea (1996) as a world that, despite not having any physical reality, is capable of giving the user, through adequate stimulation of their sensory system, the perfect impression of being in interaction. with a physical world. This tool is applied in museum tours, archaeological sites, tourism, education, esports, medicine, engineering and other sectors. The foregoing shows that, in Mexico, virtual reality has gained a great boom and has become an essential tool that can refine and extend the skills of professionals, as well as to favor competitiveness in the field of companies.

## Big Data

Like other technological instruments, Big Data is gaining popularity in Mexican companies given its advantages. According to El Universal (April 27, 2022) Investment in Big Data and data analytics around the world reached 215.7 billion dollars in 2021, 10.1% more than in 2020. In Mexico there are almost 978 thousand people trained in IT, of which 72% are men and 28% women. This shows that globally there is a greater demand for data control to analyze and extract knowledge, manage resources and projects, help companies identify trends, get to know their customers and optimize processes.

Also, it is observed that in Mexico there is a greater number of people trained to manage Big Data, however, there is a gender imbalance in the use of this tool, trained men represent more than 2.5 times women. This situation must change if the inclusion of women in the workplace is to be improved. Finally, Big Data generates many benefits for entrepreneurs such as getting to know customers better, optimizing operations, marketing efforts, fostering loyalty and, ultimately, growing the business.

## Devices Through the Voice

The pandemic crisis forced the population to adopt other ways of life and entrepreneurship. The growth of display-based devices has been seen facilitating the growth of smart speakers, due to the evolution of use cases such as video calls, online content viewing, and social media. For Noguez (2021), of the 86.8 million Internet users in Mexico, 1.2% have a virtual assistant, that is, around 1 million 300 thousand people. The foregoing shows that, although the percentage of people who use the tool is not high, its importance cannot be denied, that is, more than one million users.

## Robotization, Automation, and Digital Transformation of Companies

Industry 4.0 implies the digitalization and integration of the processes within the company of the goods and services it offers and, abroad, the development of disruptive business models (Zegarra & Pérez, 2018). The technological revolution is the automation of all industrial processes by means of machines and robots, which coexist with workers within the company, with a strong component in production processes and the interconnection between production units, such that digital production networks are established that lead to an increase in efficiency. It is characterized by four dimensions: automation, digital customer access, connectivity and digital information (Blanco, 2016) and results from the combination of three fundamental components: hardware, software and connectivity (ONUDI, 2019). According to Zegarra and Pérez (2018), automated manufacturing processes will contribute 14% of world GDP in 2030, more than 10 times the Mexican GDP.

## Electronic Commerce

The lack of mobility caused by the health crisis forced them to focus on an intense use of technology, leading companies to define different types of measures, not only to attend to the health emergency, but also to continue their activities during closing and opening gradual. One of these modifications has been online sales or electronic commerce. According to the Mexican Association of Online Sales, in 2020 electronic commerce in Mexico reached 316 billion pesos; that is, a growth of 81% compared to 2019, which represented nine% of total internet retail sales; but also, the adaptation and innovation of retailers to meet this new demand (Boletín UNAM, 2021).

## Digital Leisure

The technological evolution of video games has opened up a new field or business ideas for businessmen and entrepreneurs. There has been a radical change in the way in which the majority of the population enjoys their leisure and free time after the period of confinement. Today electronic sports or eSports are gaining more interest in the population. Its operation is very simple: each eSport has its own rules and has access to different devices and platforms online or offline. For Rodríguez Martínez (2018), eSports are a great opportunity (video game tournaments) because they provide a potential market for entrepreneurs given the increased demand for their video game skills.

# CONCLUSION

The current technological revolution, based on the use of robots, automated processes, the Internet of Things (IoT), Big Data, Content Marketing and Social Networks, Artificial Intelligence, 3D Printing, Virtual Reality, Devices through the Voice, digital transformation of companies, Electronic Commerce and Digital Leisure. It implies a transformation of the productive sectors throughout the value chain, with an impact on competitiveness and productivity in the short and medium terms. Increasingly, Industry 4.0 (I4.0) modifies production processes, industrial links and the way of relating in the market. New technologies contribute in two main areas. On the one hand, they favor the introduction of new products, which generates sources of employment and income opportunities, the emergence of new industries. On the other, it promotes production efficiency, encouraging the use of clean energy, industrial competitiveness and production chains.

This allows us to achieve the objective of this research, which is to analyze some work areas of interest as a result of the COVID-19 pandemic such as Content Marketing and Social Networks, Artificial Intelligence, 3D Printing, Virtual Reality, Big Data, Devices through the Voice, Robotization, automation and digital transformation of companies, Electronic Commerce and Digital Leisure for the development of digital entrepreneurship with the aim of promoting self-employment of young people, mainly from generation Z. The new generation of workers born in the 2000s should take advantage of these areas of opportunity. But for that, a participation of the state is needed to regulate the sector.

However, Mexico faces many barriers to the effective implementation of technology in industries. The first is the institutional barrier characterized by the absence of public policy. The second is ignorance of technology. Many of the executives are from generation X, the one that has not become familiar with technological processes, this situation leads to resistance to change in the decision to implement technology in organizational processes. The third barrier is the high bureaucracy that delays decision-making regarding the incorporation of technology. The fourth barrier is lack of training. Some administrators do not see the need to invest in the training of their employees and the consequence is that the company has low-level workers and this delays the production and evolution of the company. The fifth barrier is the lack of expert personnel to advise and guide them in the implementation and management of the technology.

Continuing with the above, the link in the Mexican economy is the micro, small and medium-sized company and these present a lag in terms of digitalization of processes due to lack of capital among other reasons. Emerging technologies, as diverse as they are, offer a range of applications for them to improve performance and overcome the size-related limitations they face in doing business. However, SMEs must be better prepared, and stakes are high. The SME digital gap has increased inequalities among people, places and firms, and there are concerns that the benefits of the digital transformation could accrue to early adopters, further broadening these inequalities. Enabling SME digitalization has become a top policy priority in Mexico.

Finally, the relevance of establishing a technological policy that considers all technological actors with wide-ranging and long-term promotion measures should be discussed. Thus, it is necessary to strengthen the capacity of the Mexican economy to create, use, produce, sell and distribute technology, and move forward, following collaborative public-private-academy strategies to strengthen institutions, infrastructure and human skills focused on new technologies.

## REFERENCES

Anim-Yeboah, S., Boateng, R., Awuni Kolog, E., Owusu, A., & Bedi, I. (2020). Digital Entrepreneurship in Business Enterprises: A Systematic Review. In Responsible Design, Implementation and Use of Information and Communication Technology. doi:10.1007/978-3-030-44999-5_16

Baltazar Vilchis, C. A., & Velázquez Ramírez, J. M. (2022). La COVID-19 y las microempresas de comercio al por menor de la Región II Atlacomulco, Estado de México. Un acercamiento mediante análisis factorial en el primer trimestre de 2021. *RECAI Revista de Estudios en Contaduría, Administración e Informática, 11*(30), 13-28. DOI: . 2018.v14n34p65 doi:10.19044/esj

Baranauskas, G., & Raišiene, A. G. (2022). Transition to Digital Entrepreneurship with a Quest of Sustainability: Development of a New Conceptual Framework. *Sustainability, 14*(3), 1104. doi:10.3390u14031104

Bejarano, H., Hancevic, P., & Núñez, H. M. (2021). Impacto económico del COVID-19 en negocios pequeños y medianos bajo restricciones voluntarias e impuestas. *EconoQuantum, 18*(2), 23–56. doi:10.18381/eq.v18i2.7229

Blanco, M. (2016). *Beneficios y amenazas de la Industria 4.0.* Retrieved from https://ctxt.es/es/20160831/Firmas/8157/Industria-tecnologia-revolucion-mercado-digital.htm

Boletín UNAM-DGCS-215. (2021). *Acelera la pandemia el comercio electrónico.* https://www.dgcs.unam.mx/boletin/bdboletin/2021_215.html

Canales, T. I. (2021). *México se posiciona para crecimiento en inteligencia artificial.* México se posiciona para crecimiento en inteligencia artificial – Canales TI. itcomunicacion.com.mx

Castillo-Galván, P., & Méndez Palacios, J. J. (2022). Digital technology as a tool for the growth of Mexican SMEs in San Luis Potosi. *13th International Conference on Applied Human Factors and Ergonomics (AHFE 2022).* 10.54941/ahfe1002224

Chaturvedi, R., & Karri, A. (2022). Entrepreneurship in the Times of Pandemic: Barriers and Strategies. *FIIB Business Review, 11*(1), 52–66. doi:10.1177/23197145211043799

Coiffet, P., & Burdea, G. (1996). Tecnologías de la realidad virtual. Academic Press.

Cueva-Rivera, X. E., & Erazo-Álvarez, J. C. (2021). Impacto socioeconómico del COVID-19 en las micro, pequeñas y medianas empresas. *Revista Arbitrada Interdisciplinaria Koinonía, 6*(12). Advance online publication. doi:10.35381/r.k.v6i12.1275

Da Silva, F., & Núñez Reyes, G. (2021). *Free competition in the post-pandemic digital era: The impact on SMEs*. ECLAC.

Dini & Zurita. (2021). *Analysis of policies to support SMEs in confronting the COVID-19 pandemic in Latin America*. ECLAC. LC/TS.2021/29

Donald, M. (2019). *Leading and Managing Change in the Age of Disruption and Artificial Intelligence*. Emerald Group Publishing. doi:10.1108/9781787563674

Durán, P. (2017). *Microempresas, PyMEs y Objetivos de Desarrollo Sostenible*. Nacionales Unidas México. https://bit.ly/3BJF3zZ

Economist Impact. (2021a). *Mexican SMEs: The digital drivers of economic recovery*. Author.

Economist Impact. (2021b). *Developing Digital Mexico: The SME struggle with covid-19*. Author.

El-Gohary, H. (2010). E-Marketing-A literature Review from a Small Businesses perspective. *International Journal of Business and Social Science*, 214–244. http://www.ijbssnet.com/journals/20.pdf

El Universal. (2022). *México crece en Data Science*. eluniversal.com.mx

Fierro Moreno, E., Cuauhtémoc Gaxiola, S., & Linares, R. (2021). Estrategias de respuesta de empresas mexicanas ante los impactos de la crisis por Covid-19. RECAI Revista de Estudios en Contaduría. *Administración e Informática, 10*(29), 65. Advance online publication. doi:10.36677/recai.v10i29.15567

Gálvez Albarracín, E. J., Guauña Aguilar, R. A., & Ravina Ripoll, R. (2020). Actitud e intención emprendedora en estudiantes de administración de empresas y de contaduría pública. *Universidad & Empresa, 22*(38), 79–105. . doi:10.12804/revistas.urosario.edu.co/empresa/a.7230

García Reyes, C., Valdovinos Rosas, R. M., Salgado Gallegos, M., Alejo Eleuterio, R., & Muñoz Jiménez, V. (2014). Realidad virtual y entornos virtuales como apoyo al acercamiento universidad-comunidad: El caso de la Facultad de Ingeniería de la UAEMex. *Apertura (Guadalajara, Jal.), 6*(1), 76–85.

DAI Global. (2022). *Insights from emerging markets. MSMEs and Digital Tool Use Amidst the COVID-19 Pandemic. Mexico Country Brief.* dai.com

Hernández-Ramírez, M., Mora-Esquivel, R., & Leiva, J. C. (2022). Orientación emprendedora y desempeño innovador en mipymes. El rol moderador de la orientación estratégica. *Estudios Gerenciales, 38*(162), 95–108. doi:10.18046/j.estger.2022.162.4519

INEGI. (2022b). *Directorio Estadístico Nacional de Unidades Económicas.* inegi.org.mx

Instituto Nacional de Estadística y Geográfica. (2022a). *Series calculadas por métodos econométricos a partir de la Encuesta Nacional de Ocupación y Empleo.* Author.

Jawad, M., Naz, M., & Maroof, Z. (2020). Era of digital revolution: Digital entrepreneurship and digital transformation in emerging economies. *Business Strategy and Development, 4*(3). doi:10.1002/bsd2.145

Madrigal Moreno, S., Alfaro Calderón, G. G., & Madrigal Moreno, F. (2016). Social Media Marketing Perspectives in the Organization in Morelia, Mexico. *International Journal of Marketing Studies, 8*(2), 128. doi:10.5539/ijms.v8n2p128

Meurer, M. M., Waldkirch, M., Schou, P. K., Bucher, E. L., & Burmeister-Lamp, K. (2022). Digital affordances: How entrepreneurs access support in online communities during the COVID-19 pandemic. *Small Business Economics, 58*(2), 637–663. doi:10.100711187-021-00540-2

Molina-Sánchez, R., García-Pérez-de-Lema, D., López-Salazar, A., & Godínez-López, R. (2022). Determining factors in MSMEs success: An empirical study in Mexico. *Small Business International Review, 6*(1), e384. doi:10.26784bir.v6i1.384

Mora Pabón, R. (2011). Estudio de actitudes emprendedoras con profesionales que crearon empresas. *Rev. Esc. Adm. Neg., 71*, 70-83. scielo.org.co

Naudé, W., & Liebregts, W. (2020). *Digital Entrepreneurship Research: A Concise Introduction. IZA Discussion Papers 13667. Institute of Labor Economics.* IZA.

NobaneeH.NobaneeH.Mehroz NidaD. (August 30, 2020). Digital Entrepreneurship: Concepts, Applications, and Future Research. *Agenda Journal of Critical Reviews,* 7(19). https://ssrn.com/abstract=3688271 doi:10.2139/ssrn.3688271

Noguez, R. (2021). *Alexa y Google Assistant, un negocio que habla cada vez más fuerte en México y el mundo.* forbes.com.mx

OECD. (2021). *The Digital Transformation of SMEs*. OECD Publishing. doi:10.1787/bdb9256a-en

ONUDI. (2019). *La industrialización en la era digital*. Viena: Organización de las Naciones Unidas para el Desarrollo Industrial.

Ortiz García, P. (2016). Actitud emprendedora de los jóvenes españoles en un contexto de crisis. *Revista de Ciencias Sociales*, *22*(1), 139–152. doi:10.31876/rcs.v22i1.24902

Recker, J., & von Briel, F. (2019). The Future of Digital Entrepreneurship Research: Existing and Emerging Opportunities. *Fortieth International Conference on Information Systems, Munich 2019*. core.ac.uk

Rodríguez González, J. A., Tagle Zamora, D., & Granados Márquez, G. (2020). Estrategias empresariales ante la COVID-19: El caso de la industria curtidora de León, Guanajuato. *Entreciencias: Diálogos en la Sociedad del Conocimiento*, *8*(22). Advance online publication. doi:10.22201/enesl.20078064e.2020.22.76844

Rodríguez Martínez, S. A. (2018). *Modelo de negocio a través de los torneos online de eSports en Colombia* [Tesis]. Ciencias Económicas y Administrativas, carrera de administración de empresas. javeriana.edu.co

Sachin Modgil, Y. K., Dwivedi, N. P., Rana, S. G., & Sachin, K. (2022). Has Covid-19 accelerated opportunities for digital entrepreneurship? An Indian perspective. *Technological Forecasting and Social Change*, *175*, 121415. doi:10.1016/j.techfore.2021.121415 PMID:36536802

Santiago Hernández, V. G., Martínez Sandoval, D., Alcaraz Miranda, M., & Córdova Yánez, A. (2021). Efecto del covid-19 en las mipymes de la región serrana del Estado de Sonora. *Revista Mexicana de Agronegocios*, *49*, 19–32.

Sascha Kraus, C. P., Kailer, N., Kallinger, F. L., & Spitzer, J. (2018). Digital entrepreneurship. A research agenda on new business models for the twenty-first century. *International Journal of Entrepreneurial Behaviour & Research*, *25*(2), 353–375. doi:10.1108/IJEBR-06-2018-0425

Schalkoff, R. J. (1990). *Artificial Intelligence: An Engineering Approach*. McGraw-Hill.

Shapero, A. C. (1981). Self-renewing economies. *Economic Development Commentary*, *5*, 19–22.

Sonobe, T., Takeda, A., Yoshida, S., & Truong, H. T. (2021). *The Impacts of the COVID-19 Pandemic on Micro, Small, and Medium Enterprises in Asia and Their Digitalization Responses. ADBI Working Paper 1241.* Asian Development Bank Institute. https://www.adb.org/publications/impacts-covid-19-pandemic-msme-asia-their-digitalizationresponses

Tecma. (2022). *3D printing in Mexican industry, the United States, and Europe account for 68% of revenues generated, while the Asia Pacific region accounts for 27%. The Use of 3D Printing in Mexican Industry is Growing.* tecma.com

Valdez-Juárez, L. E., Castillo-Vergara, M., & Ramos-Escobar, E. A. (2022). Innovative Business Strategies in the Face of COVID-19: An Approach to Open Innovation of SMEs in the Sonora Region of Mexico. *Journal of Open Innovation, 8*(1), 47. doi:10.3390/joitmc8010047

Velázquez, M. M. A., & Rivero, H. M. (2020). Las MiPYMES y el COVID19 en la Región XI del oriente del Estado de México: escenarios de reconfiguración. Instituto de Investigaciones Económicas. In M. Rivero Hernández (Ed.), *Factores críticos y estratégicos en la interacción territorial desafíos actuales y escenarios futuros.* http://ru.iiec.unam.mx/5175/1/1-072-Velazquez-Rivero.pdf

Yigitcanlar, T., Kankanamge, N., Regona, M., Maldonado, A. R., Rowan, B., Ryu, A., Desouza, K. C., Corchado, J. M., Mehmood, R., & Man Li, R. Y. (2020). Artificial Intelligence Technologies and Related Urban Planning and Development Concepts: How Are They Perceived and Utilized in Australia? *Journal of Open Innovation, 6*(4), 187. doi:10.3390/joitmc6040187

Zegarra, C., & Pérez, M. (2018). *Industria 4.0: oportunidades y retos en México.* Retrieved from https://www.forbes.com.mx/industria-4-0-oportunidades-y-retos-en-mexico/

# Chapter 5
# Global Events to Enhance Tourism:
## New Era for Marketing Through Location Analytics

**Lakshmi Shree K.**
https://orcid.org/0000-0002-5940-374X
*Department of Information and Engineering, BMS College of Engineering, India*

**Ashok Kumar R.**
*Department of Information Science and Engineering, BMS College of Engineering, India*

## ABSTRACT

*Targeting tourist behavior at global events could be one of the interesting topics for business houses. Location Based Analytical - Business Intelligent (LBA-BIntelligent) frameworks predict targeted tourist behavior at global events. The organizing countries create new businesses and gain a competitive advantage from tourists. This framework streamlines marketing to the right people at the right time. This study focuses on implementing bagging and boosting ensemble approaches. These classifiers have been evaluated on various parameters such as accuracy, precision, recall, F-score, Kappa score, and ROC-AUC score. The classification results show that the bagging approach gives better results through all the evaluation metrics.*

DOI: 10.4018/978-1-6684-6591-2.ch005

## INTRODUCTION

We explore target tourist behaviour towards business using social analytics. Our proposed framework Business Intelligent System - LBA-BIntelligent is built from social analytics and location intelligence for event-based marketing. LBA-BIntelligent analyses geospatial data associated with the tweets extracted from hashtags related to an event. Rather than using GPS or Trajectories to derive the geo-data we prefer twitter feeds as the data source. Framework implements most well-known ensemble techniques bagging, boosting approaches.

There are studies where Twitter platform is used to understand the spatiotemporal patterns for sentiment analysis (Cao et al., 2018), to increase the marketing (Dhar & Varshney, 2011) and bring new avenue for retailers (Larson, 2005). Our proposal elaborates to transform he/she who tweets into target customers using spatial location for event based marketing. The retail companies near the event venue analyse the target customers behaviour posted as tweets in the social media. Tweets express current state of mind which retail companies can invest for type of services to be suggested in real time. Further, from the operational viewpoint these retail companies make rapid strategic decisions to facilitate customers. Thereby, we build LBA-BIntelligent platform which provides marketers, online retailers an opportunity to expand business.

This paper is organized as follows: Section 2 is the related work to highlight applications of location analytics on twitter social media. Section 3 we propose LBA-BIntelligent framework to investigate various ensemble methods. In section 4, experimental results evaluate spatial location granularity levels, ensemble algorithms and analyse retweet tags at food, product, travel domains. The outcome of our proposed system in the business domain is briefed using sample tweet in Section 5. Finally in section 6 conclusion and future scope of our work is discussed.

## RELATED WORK

Twitter has been a popular platform for people to share their stories. Each day twitter has a new topic trending with hashtags of on-going event, some of the trending hashtags were #GlobalWarming, #WorldCup, #pandemic. Individuals tend to share their reactions during storms (Dunkel et al., 2019), earthquake (Dragovic et al., 2019), geography or weather (André et al., 2015; Denissen, Butalid, Penke, & Van Aken, 2008; Denissen, Butalid, Penke, & Van Aken, 2008; Howarth & Hoffman, 1984; Shah, Martin, Coiera, Mandl, & Dunn, 2019). This popular social media is also used for analysing characteristics of tweets such as spatial and temporal factors

(Baylis, 2015; Klimstra et al., 2011), variation of tweets at different times of the day, day of the week (Egloff et al., 1995; Golder & Macy, 2011).

Business organisations have readily accepted social media to add values to their brand. Business to Business (B2B) advertising can be integrated with social media to enhance business with Hierarchy of Effects (HOE) theory (Juntunen et al., 2019). Other studies investigate twitter as a platform for business organisers to improve marketing (Sen & Dietz, 2019), promote sports teams and influence fans (Lucas et al., 2017), explore favourite sports person based on trending hashtags (Williams et al., 2014). Considering tourism business travel recommendations (Ravi & Vairavasundaram, 2016), personalised content is pushed to travellers by mining their mobility through spatial clustering methods (Dietz et al., 2018). Tourists are recommended travel packages (Dietz & Wörndl, 2019), analyse check-in information (Liu et al., 2011), duration of stay (Dietz et al., 2020) to improve tourism business with location analytics.

In (Dhar & Varshney, 2011) authors bring out potential of mobile advertisements and other location-based services to increase revenue. Food or culinary tourism are chosen as trends for destination marketing linking the destination cuisine image to the destination (Chatterjee & Suklabaidya, 2020). By. Further, project food as a tool to promote any destination which increases the traveller's likelihood of visit. In (Stone et al., n.d.) authors identify elements - food, drink, travel experiences along with location/setting, companions- factors to create a better culinary tourism experience. This kind of linking increases the travel experience and creates positive word of mouth. Researchers suggest travel, vacations (Blank et al., 2018; Chen et al., 2016), price drops divert the minds of people when they are stressed.

## METHODOLOGY

Target customers behaviour can be analysed through posts in twitter social media. Twitter acts as a sound data source for the business industry to gain benefits. We inspect to transform users (who post tweets with spatial-temporal data) into target customers. Inner-city retailers and service providers can acquire Mobile location-based services (LBS) to create new business opportunities (Schwipper et al., 2020). When a user at event tweets "I am craving for some chinese food" the active framework solves *"where to look"* situation of a user.

The LBA-BIntelligent architecture diagram in Figure 1 uses social analytics and location intelligence to analyse business at two global events. Global Events: FIFA Football World Cup 2018 held in Russia and Olympics 2018 held at PyeongChang are taken into consideration.

At FIFA, 32 nations participated, a total of 3.4 billion people were expected to watch the games held at different stadiums across Russia. Similarly, Olympics witness a diverse gathering of people.

The initial stage involves the extraction process of tweets using various hashtags listed in Table 1. Location information attached with tweets is the input to the LBA-BIntelligent. Next, through the filtering process event location tweets (*Event_Loc_Tweets)* are retained. This implies retaining tweets whose location's data matches the countries where events were held. The Event_Loc_Tweets is subjected to data cleansing process to clean the tweet.

LBA-BIntelligent tackles the problem of business requirement at a given location faced by Online retailers and business organisations. Accordingly, guides business houses to follow the famous quote *"delivering the right message to the right customer at the right time*".

*Figure 1. Architecture of LBA-BIntelligent system*

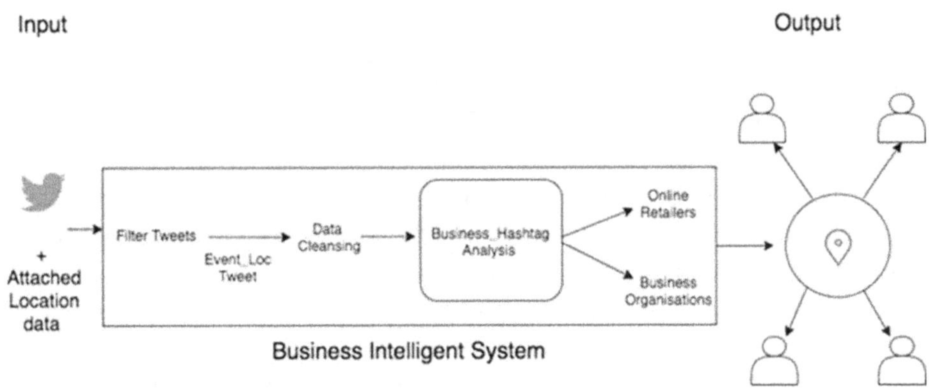


*Table 1. Hashtags used to extract tweets*

| Event Name | Hashtags |
|---|---|
| FIFA | *#worldcup, #worldcupfinal, #FIFAStadium, #Russia2018, #worldcup2018, #FIFA, #WorldCupRussia,* |
| Olympics | *#pyeongchang201, #winterOlympics , #Olympics* |

## Data Cleansing

Twitter Application Programming Interface (API) is used to extract tweets in English as the preferred language. The data cleansing has been applied before modelling the data. Twitter uses hashtags (#), retweets (RT), address (@), stop words ('and', 'the', 'however'), HTML tags and other special characters which do not derive any meaning from the sentence. Tweets are the user's emotions posted as reactions - *'The player made a smarrrrt move!!'* where the substring 'smarrrrt' refers to the smartness of the player.

## Location Data

Twitter API's support tweeters to post tweets with optional geolocation settings - "Tweet with location". Each tweet contains text, emoji's along with timestamp, place attributes (Twitter, n.d.). Place is said to comprise either exact location or latitude and longitude. Location parameters drives towards event based marketing and support other business activities. Such as identify new business opportunities, optimize operations at warehouses and real time marketing suggestions to the tweeters. We confine the tweets extraction process to the event locations (Event_Loc_Tweet). As mentioned in Table 2.

Recently, several studies indicate location factors are associated with sentiment (Shah, Martin, Coiera, Mandl, & Dunn, 2019) and in many other applications. It is believed that location contributes in uplifting business hence the new era of business has started to invest on location-based technologies. They track people to understand their brand value across regions. We work on the same target to analyses and visualizes volumes of location data attached to the tweets shared by people.

Location is defined as a place or a position where an object resides, any activity can be carried out. It can be classified as exact location or approximate location. Each location has hierarchical characteristic described by granularity levels like finer and coarse. For instance, tweet "dining at a restaurant in Kazan" is at the coarse level and another tweet "dining at a Pashmir restaurant in Kazan" is at finer level granularity. At a coarse level, the location level is generic with restaurant names missed in the tweet. Whereas at finer level, we have a more specific location data with restaurant name along with the city name 'Kazan' is specified. One of the observations in extraction process is that tweeters are reluctant to share the exact location.

*Table 2. Locations of FIFA and Olympics events*

| FIFA 2018 | Olympics 2018 |
|---|---|
| Kaliningrad | Pyeongchang-gun |
| Kazan | Korea |
| Moscow | Seoul |
| Nizhny Novgorod | Gangneung-si |
| Rostov-on-Don | Ongjin |
| Saint Petersburg | Wonju |
| Samara | Jeongseo |
| Saransk | Jongno |
| Sochi | Yangyeong |
| Volgograd | Jung-gu |
| Yekaterinburg | - |

We identify few challenges in extracting geolocations of Twitterati communities.

- ***Zombie_LocTweet*:** Individuals maintain privacy about the place of the hangout to be more like a metaphor rather than the exact location. For example, a tweet can be read as *"I am at Hogwarts, near the moon..., somewhere on earth"*.
- ***Error_LocTweet*:** Individuals falsely state where they were or even provide more generic geo-location. For instance, a post "A great Match!! From Russia'' lacks the precise geo-location. Instead the post "A great match!! From Kazan'' builds a specific business intelligence system.
- ***NonRelevant_LocTweet*:** Individuals share irrelevant tweets, which has no contribution in building an intelligent system.

## Domain Specific Dictionary Constructions

LBA-BIntelligent system works on a dictionary built on sports/gaming domain namely Domain-specific Dictionary (DDict). This gaming-based dictionary approach that uses WordNet to acquire the state of mind and classify them into positive or negative reactions. State of mind is briefly analysed by subjecting the tweets to a DDict, represented as a key-value-count triplet. Emotions of the tweets are expressed by words, phrases or tokens which act as keys and sentiment as positive/ negative and a count of the sentiment is placed in the DDict (Tang et al., 2009). Dictionary-based algorithms consider word frequency in documents. Thus, a tweet can have words that are useful to learn opinions related to a given domain. We illustrate few sample tokens based on DDict

Positive = {award, congratulations, enjoy, goal, trophy, success, win}

Negative = {arrogant, down, out, negative, lose, lost, wrong, inferior}

Let's consider a few sample tweets "Congrats to the team, Great to watch!!" and "Player shouted my ball", here the former example is considered a positive opinion, the later example is considered a neutral opinion.

## Analysis and Modelling

Various related work implements ensemble approach for prediction using review datasets (Ghosh & Sanyal, 2018), social media dataset (Lee et al., 2020). In this framework, we have used the ensemble approaches which are highly effective at boosting performance of simple learners (Liu et al., 2017; Sendi et al., 2019). The ensemble methods combine weak learners to create strong learners.

The training set consisted of 18,238 tweets from the location where the events were conducted. Tweets were considered to train the predictive models by dividing the dataset into testing and training datasets with 30% and 70% respectively. The proposed methodology binary classifies the state of mind into positive and negative classes. Cross-validation is used for estimation of the classification models with k parameters to specify the total number of splits. In our case k is 5 is implemented on the training set.

We adopt Bagging (Random Forest) and Boosting approaches (Naïve Bayes, Support Vector Machine, Logistic Regression). The ensemble approaches are used to train the event tweets datasets to assess and compare performance on various metrics. These Algorithms are discussed briefly

- Naïve Bayes approach (McCallum & Nigam, 2004) a supervised learning algorithm based on applying Bayes theorem. It is a simple probabilistic classifier with an assumption of independence between the factors.
- SVM is a supervised learning model (Shmilovici, n.d.) which creates a clear decision boundary using mathematical functions known as hyperplane separated labelled sets of classes. Hyperplanes must be as far from the closest points from each class (Sun et al., 2017; Sundar & Punniyamoorthy, 2019). The closest point is known as support vectors and mathematical functions as kernels. A kernel transforms the input data into required form of the data and makes optimization efficient . SVM kernels map a lower dimensional data into a higher dimensional data, tuned and modelled.
- Logistic Regression (C=1.5) with a Linear model predicts the feature to belong to any of the labelled classes (Kumari et al., 2021). The probability prediction is transformed into binary values for predictions.
- Random forest is a supervised learning algorithm wherein the trees are trained using bagging technique (Shaikhina et al., 2019). Typical feature of Random Forest is that at each stage it selects the best feature from a randomly generated subset of features (Aria et al., 2021). This classification model classifies the object from the set of input vectors. These input vectors shall be put down on each of the trees in the random forest. Each tree provides its decision to generate outcome variables.

## Evaluation

There are several metrics used to evaluate bagging and boosting techniques. Accuracy, precision, F1-score, Cohen's kappa, AUC curve, K-Fold AUC have been taken as the evaluation criteria for testing the robustness of the framework.

The recommended location set can be categorised as relevant or irrelevant. The performance measures (Bao et al., 2015; Isinkaye et al., 2015) to evaluate are as follows a) Precision (P) of a model measures the relevancy provided by the users. Defined as the number of relevant locations over the number of locations recommended. b) Recall (R) of a model measures the probability to select a relevant location to recommend. c) Accuracy measures prediction based on user preferences. Prediction specifies that entire data is classified into the right class. d) F1 Score is the harmonic mean of precision and recall. e) Cohen's kappa coefficient (κ) is defined as a statistic that is used to measure inter-rater reliability (and also intra-rater reliability) for qualitative (categorical) items.

$$P = \frac{N_{rs}}{N_s} \tag{1}$$

$$R = \frac{N_{rs}}{N_r} \tag{2}$$

$$R = \frac{N_{rc}}{N_{rp}} \tag{3}$$

$$F = 2\frac{P.R}{P+R} \tag{4}$$

Where, $N_{rs}$ - Summation of relevant and irrelevant locations which is selected

$N_r$ - Summation of relevant locations which could be either selected or not selected by user

$N_s$ - Total locations selected

$N_{rc}$ - Number of correct recommendations

$N_{rp}$ - Number of possible recommendations

## RESULTS

This section presents the details of i) evaluation of coarse level and fine level tweets ii) evaluation of ensemble algorithms iii) analysing retweet tags

### Evaluation of the Coarse Level and Fine Level Tweets

The framework evaluates tweets granularities as Finer_tweets contribute in predicting precise locations . In the Figure 2, we denote X axis as the percentage of tweets and the Y axis the locations predicted. LBA-BIntelligent predicted higher proportion of finer level tweets (Finer_tweets) compared to coarse level (Coarse_tweets). For instance, we observed higher Finer_tweets locations from the Event_location such Moscow, Samara compared to Russia which belongs to Coarse_tweets. The results clearly show higher tweets to be extracted from nearby vicinities or the from exact stadium locations. These findings suggest the strength of location analytics derived from social analytics to assist retailers in strategizing personalised recommendations.

*Figure 2. Coarse_tweets level vs. Finer_tweets percentage at FIFA*

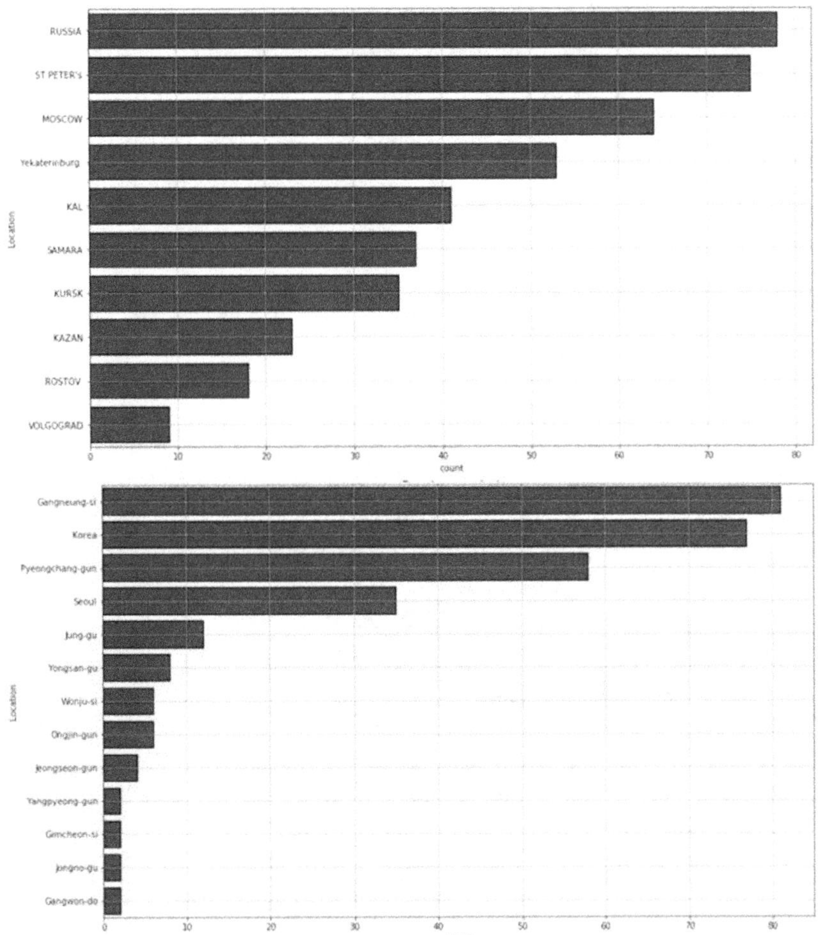


## Evaluation of the Ensemble Techniques

In this section we measure performance of Boosting and Bagging approaches. Ensemble techniques are implemented in the framework to predict the state of mind categorised into positive or negative. The input set consists of tweet, city, timestamp, followers, retweet, hashtags are used to generate output which is either positive or negative. The performances of bagging and boosting classifiers - Logistic Regression (LR), Support Vector Machine (SVM), Naive Bayes (NB) implemented in this study were computed using evaluation metrics and ROC curves. These ensemble techniques are modelled using one versus rest and cross validation approach.

*Figure 3. Coarse_tweets level vs. Finer_tweets percentage at Olympics*

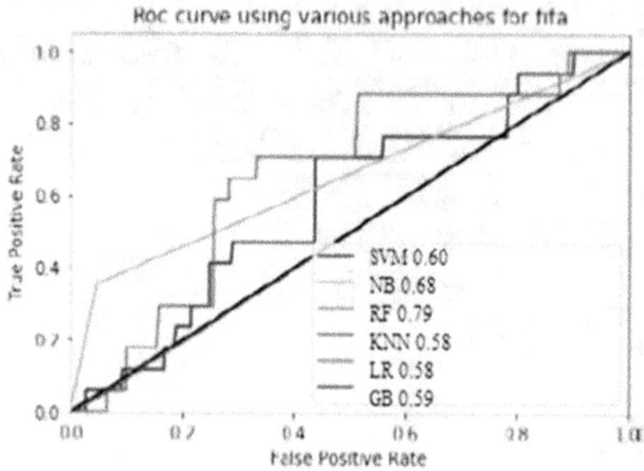


(3a)

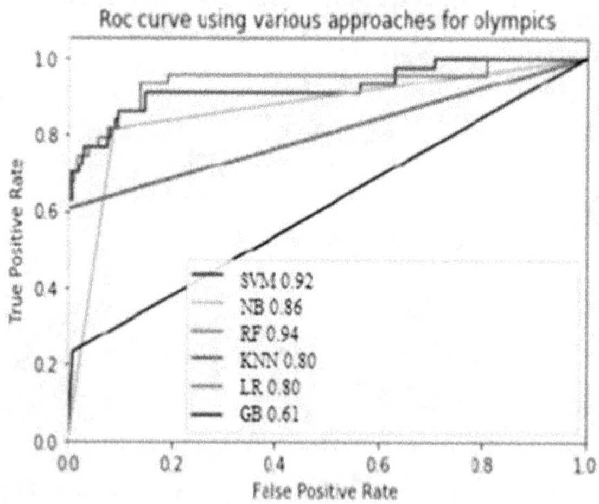


The overall performances of bagging and boosting approaches to classify the state of mind is measured through ROC curves. Figure 3 gives the comparative ROC curves for bagging and boosting classifiers. By exploring these results, it has been observed that RF has more AUC percentage of 79% (Fifa dataset) and 94% (Olympics dataset). Boosting classifiers SVM, NB, KNN, LR, GB have AUC equal to and less than 60% (Fifa dataset) and 92% (Olympics dataset). And the lowest performance of 58% (Fifa dataset) and 80% (Olympics dataset) is present for LR and KNN respectively.

*Figure 4. ROC curve comparision of (a) FIFA dataset and (b) Olympics dataset using bagging and boosting*

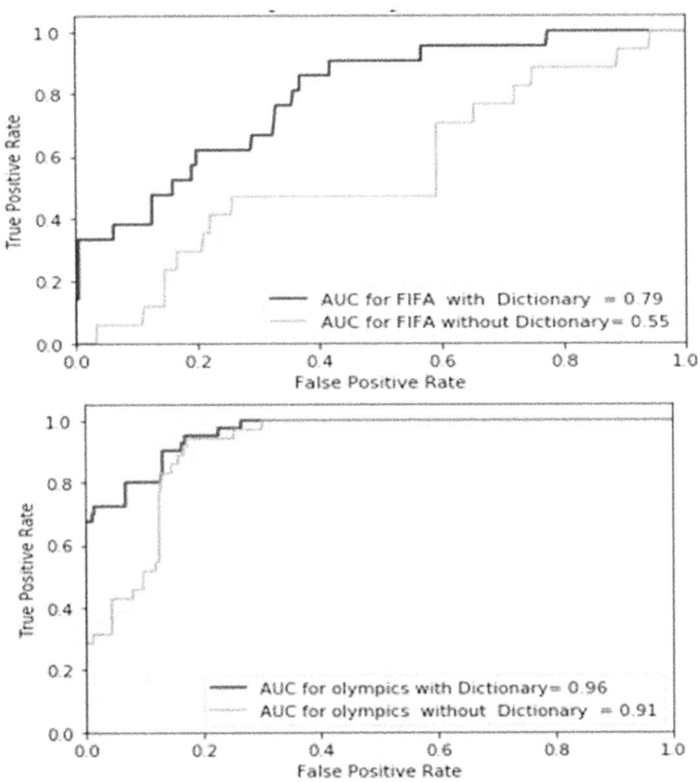


The proposed DDict to explore the reaction emphasizing on sports domain show impressive results compared to EDict. DDict has recorded 76% (Fifa dataset) and 96% (Olympics dataset) in comparison with existing dictionary 59% (Fifa dataset) and 91% (Olympics dataset) as depicted in Figure 4.

Further we assess the ensemble approaches using the metrics mentioned in section 3.5. The metrics such as Accuracy, F1 – score, Cohen's Kappa, AUC and K – Fold AUC has been illustrated in Table 3. The results show that the RF has achieved excellently in comparison to boosting classifiers. The outcomes of ROC curves and metrics prove Random Forest algorithm achieves better scores in contrast to other boosting classifiers - LR, SVM,NB. The results give us a comprehensive comparative study of bagging and boosting ensemble learning methods.

*Figure 5. ROC curve comparision of (a) FIFA dataset and (b) Olympics dataset using RF*

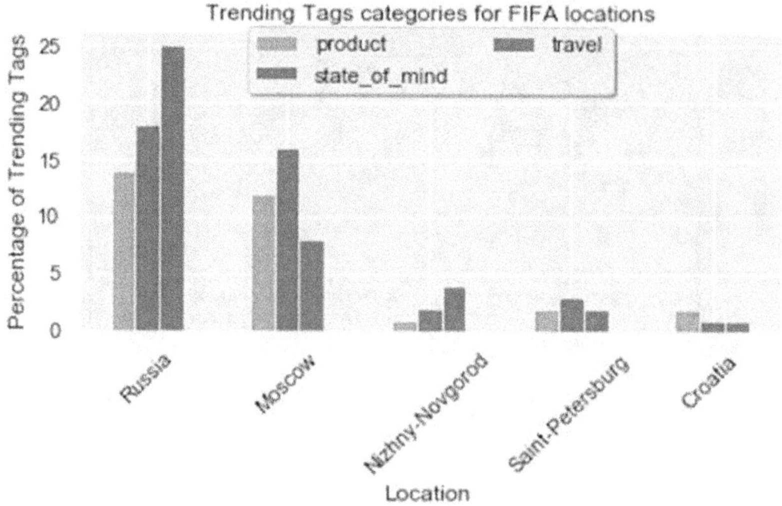


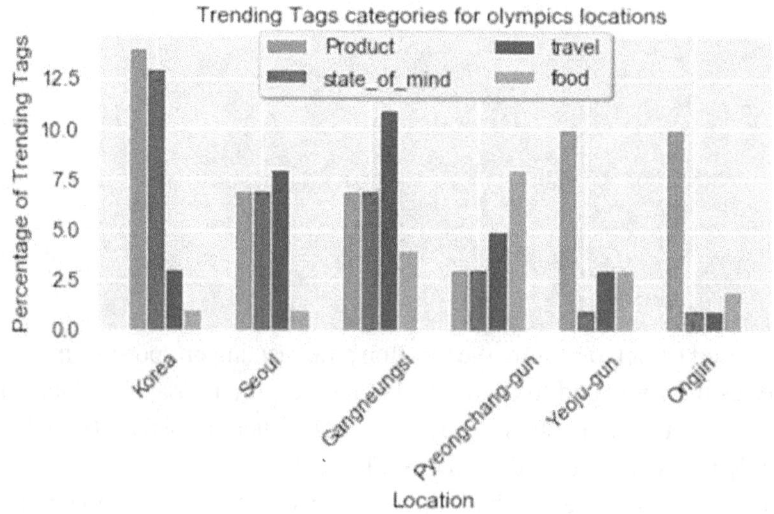


## Analysing Retweet Tags

Another interesting scenario to assist event based marketing is hashtag mining. Retweets have the potential to influence user behaviour, information diffusion (Nadia et al., 2018; Yan et al., n.d.) in social media at the low cost. Retweets are defined as a tweet posted, republished or forwarded to her/his followers aids marketing campaigns and product brand building. This posting of tweet by other followers continues to propagate the information. Based on categorising concepts (Fang & Zhan, 2015) we identify a few categories which shall generate revenue as shown in Table 4.

Business houses, online retailers along with content providers plan to generate revenue to test trending tags popularity. Figure 5, depict insights of trending tags, x axis has the percentage and y axis has geo-tagged data. Locations - Russia (24%) and Korea (13%) witness the highest percentage in the State of Mind category. Other domains Travel at Moscow (15%) and Korea (25%), Product at Russia (13%) and Seoul (9%), and Food categories were null for FIFA and Pyeongchang-gun (4%). This is evident that content providers have extracted Finer_tweets locations with the trending category. The perceived results higher Finer_tweets locations compared to Coarse_tweets. The outcome of this result enriches to understand user interest and provide location based category-aware advertisements.

*Table 3. Performance comparison analysis for Boosting and Bagging approaches at both the events*

| Measures (%) | Ensemble Methods | | | | | | | |
|---|---|---|---|---|---|---|---|---|
| | Boosting | | | | | | Bagging | |
| | LR | | NB | | SVM | | RF | |
| | FIFA | Olympics | FIFA | Olympics | FIFA | Olympics | FIFA | Olympics |
| Accuracy | 58.99 | 82.16 | 68.57 | 86.25 | 60.57 | 92.6 | 79.03 | 94.23 |
| F1 Score | 56.58 | 80.1 | 68.3 | 86.2 | 60 | 92 | 79 | 94.1 |
| Cohen's kappa | 72.30 | 80.2 | 68.31 | 86.33 | 60.62 | 92.1 | 79.11 | 94.26 |
| AUC | 59 | 80 | 68.11 | 86 | 61 | 92 | 82.13 | 94 |
| K-Fold AUC | 58 | 81 | 68.41 | 85 | 61 | 91 | 88.12 | 94.3 |

*Table 4. Trending tags used in categories*

- Food Categories
  food, dinner, lunch, spicy, cook, restaurant, beef, soup,drinks
- Product Categories
  price, trade, sell, sold, service, rate
- State of Mind
  celebration, enjoy, favourite, festival, mood, celebration
- Travel / Place Categories
  journey, show, drama, adventure, parks, museums, historic, guide, transport, venue, event, travel, trip

The category-aware advertisements can either be push based or pull based advertisements. With an goal to evaluate a customer's state of mind, discover and re-examine priorities which could be linked to greater happiness. Let's look more closely at a few sample state of mind tweets and its associated business domain in Table 5. From the samples it is obvious that state of mind has attached trending tags to gain higher business probability and event based marketing.

*Table 5. Domain-based tweet samples*

| Hashtag | Location | State of Mind | Business-Domain |
|---|---|---|---|
| #WinterOlympic<br>#pyeongchang2018<br>#Olympics | South Korea | Host cities hope the #Olympics bring a huge boost in tourism but it often comes at a high price. | Travel |
| #Worldcup | Moscow | Of course I talked about food?? | Food |

## OUTCOME OF THE LBA-BINTELLIGENT

Location granularities offers content providers to gear up precise planning, prediction to execute individual demands. Proposed action planned by the LBA-BIntelligent system based on the tweet reaction is seen in Table 6. There are various types of advertising services such as click to call, Short Message Service (SMS) or Multimedia Messaging Service (MMS), voice calls. Our work recommends to adapt pushed based advertisements which contain discounts, promotional coupons, price elasticities along with the actual purchases. Our work suggest people to be more likely to accept the event based marketing action plans and go ahead for execution.

*Table 6. Action plan proposed by LBA-BIntelligent based on the Tweet Reaction*

| Hashtag | Location | Tweet | Action Planned by the LBA-BIntelligent |
|---|---|---|---|
| #PyeongChang2018 | Yangju-si | Next weekend cannot come fast enough?? | Plan a weekend, Push attractive offers through notifications/pop-up ads to boost the energy level. |
| #WorldCup | Russia | Congratulations to France the st African team to win the cup | Suggest locations to have fun, party, music and movies. |
| #WorldCup | Moscow | Party time in Moscow | |
| #Fifa | Moscow | This guy saves penalties in a match and still does not win that game. Sad story indeed this is just too sad. | Suggest products with discounts, special offers, coupons to eventually change mood. |
| #olympics | Seoul | Disappointed with today's game, sad. | |
| #WorldCup | Samara | A Player shouted, "My Ball". | No Action Planned |

In Figure 5 strongly shows the potential relationship of state of mind in travel, food and product domain. In specific, let us consider one of the tweet reaction captured in Table 5, "Party time in Moscow '' speaks about person's happiness, stress-free mind. The LBA-BIntelligent gives complete statistical report of popular restaurants or pubs, cuisines, prices, reviews and ratings. Consequently, the core functionality - location finder gets activated. Each customer would also be provided with a link to find location information (longitude/latitude, distance from customer location).

*Figure 6. Domain-based notifications generated by LBA-BIntelligent system*

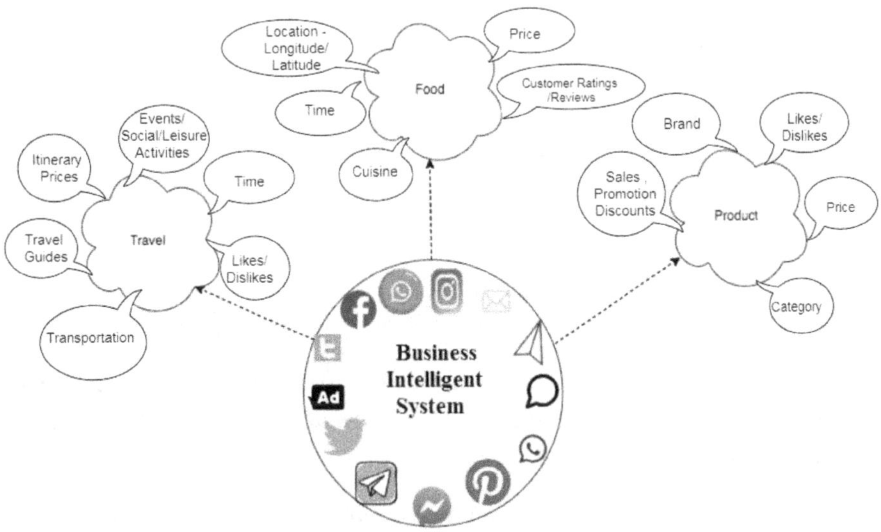


## CONCLUSION AND FUTURE WORK

Location parameters emphasize a larger context to ensure new business openings, optimizing operations at warehouses and immediate marketing to the spectators. Our paper aims at understanding target customers behaviour through tweets shared by spectators after or during the watch. We build LBA-BIntelligent framework provide event marketing, expand marketing strategies and branding in the countries where the event is organised. The geospatial data extracted from spectator's tweets from FIFA and Olympics events. The LBA-BIntelligent system can select players based on popularity who could be considered as brand ambassadors for endorsements. Empirical evaluation of the framework has been conducted with conventional bagging and boosting classifiers. Evaluation scores and ROC curves tested for robustness of the framework prove ensemble to suitable for target customers behaviour prediction.

Also, a comparison of the proposed DDict modelled with Random Forest reveals higher results with the same performance metrics as Edict.

Future research can focus on Twitter data along with other social media like Instagram, Facebook and so on. The results may be varying but guarantees higher income from promotions and endorsements, while locations are extracted from different social media. In this work, we focus only on sports events, other international events such as music concerts, award ceremonies such as MetGala, Cannes Films Festival can be analysed. As these events have huge crowds and witness collaboration of different countries and continents.

## REFERENCES

André, L. F. A., Cláudio de Souza, B., Firmino, A. A., Guimarães de Oliveira, M., & Cardoso de Paiva, A. (2015). A Spatial and Temporal Sentiment Analysis Approach Applied to Twitter Microtexts. –. *Journal of Information and Data Management, 6*, 118–129.

Aria, M., Cuccurullo, C., & Gnasso, A. (2021). A comparison among interpretative proposals for Random Forests. *Machine Learning with Applications, 6*.

Bao, J., Zheng, Y., Wilkie, D., & Mohamed, F. (2015, July 1). Recommendations in location-based social networks: A survey. *GeoInformatica, 19*(3), 525–565. doi:10.100710707-014-0220-8

Baylis, P. (2015). *Temperature and temperament: Evidence from a billion tweets.* Energy Institute at HAAS working paper.

Blank, C., Gatterer, K., & Leichtfried, V. (2018). Short Vacation Improves Stress-Level and Well-Being in German-Speaking Middle-Managers-A Randomized Controlled Trial. *Int J Environ Res Public Health, 15*(1), 130. doi:10.3390/ijerph15010130

Cao, X., MacNaughton, P., Deng, Z., Yin, J., Zhang, X., & Allen, J. (2018). Using Twitter to Better Understand the Spatiotemporal Patterns of Public Sentiment: A Case Study in Massachusetts, USA. *International Journal of Environmental Research and Public Health, 15*(2), 15. doi:10.3390/ijerph15020250 PMID:29393869

Chatterjee & Suklabaidya. (2020). Food image and travel intention: From New Delhi to New York. *Journal of Gastronomy, Hospitality and Travel, 3*(1), 3-19.

Chen, C.-C., Petrick, J. F., & Shahvali, M. (2016, February). Tourism Experiences as a Stress Reliever: Examining the Effects of Tourism Recovery Experiences on Life Satisfaction. *Journal of Travel Research*, *55*(2), 150–160. doi:10.1177/0047287514546223

Denissen, J. J., Butalid, L., Penke, L., & Van Aken, M. A. (2008). The effects of weather on daily mood: A multilevel approach. *Emotion*, *8*(5), 662–667. doi:10.1037/a0013497 PMID:18837616

Dhar, S., & Varshney, U. (2011). Challenges and business models for mobile location-based services and advertising. *Communications of the ACM*, *54*(5), 121–128. doi:10.1145/1941487.1941515

Dietz, L. W., Herzog, D., & Wörndl, W. (2018). Deriving tourist mobility patterns from check-in data. *Proceedings of the WSDM 2018 Workshop on Learning from User Interactions.*

Dietz, L. W., Sen, A., Roy, R., & Wörndl, W. (2020). Mining trips from location-based social networks for clustering travelers and destinations. *Information Technology & Tourism, Vol*, *22*(1), 131–166. doi:10.100740558-020-00170-6

Dietz, L. W., & Wörndl, W. (2019). *How Long to Stay Where?* On the Amount of Item Consumption in Travel Recommendation. –In RecSys.

Dragovic, N., Vasiljevic, D., Stankov, U., & Vujicic, M. (2019). Go social for your own safety! Review of social networks use on natural disasters – Case studies from worldwide. Open Geosciences, 11(1).

Dunkel, Andrienko, Andrienko, Burghardt, Hauthal, & Purves. (2019). A conceptual framework for studying collective reactions to events in location-based social media. *International Journal of Geographical Information Science, 33*(4).

Egloff, B., Tausch, A., Kohlmann, C.-W., & Krohne, H. W. (1995). Relationships between time of day, day of the week, and positive mood: Exploring the role of the mood measure. *Motivation and Emotion*, *19*(2), 99–110. doi:10.1007/BF02250565

Fang & Zhan. (2015). Sentiment analysis using product review data. *Journal of Big Data.*

Ghosh, M., & Sanyal, G. (2018). An ensemble approach to stabilize the features for multi-domain sentiment analysis using supervised machine learning. *Journal of Big Data*, *5*(1), 44. doi:10.118640537-018-0152-5

Golder, S. A., & Macy, M. W. (2011). Diurnal and seasonal mood vary with work, sleep, and day length across diverse cultures. *Science, 333*(6051), 1878–1881. doi:10.1126cience.1202775 PMID:21960633

Howarth & Hoffman. (1984). A multidimensional approach to the relationship between mood and weather. *British Journal of Psychology, 75*(1), 15-23.

Isinkaye, F. O., Folajimi, Y. O., & Ojokoh, B. A. (2015, November). Recommendation systems: Principles, methods and evaluation. *Egyptian Informatics Journal, 16*(3), 261–273. doi:10.1016/j.eij.2015.06.005

Juntunen, M., Ismagilova, E., & Oikarinen, E.-L. (2019). *B2B brands on Twitter: Engaging users with a varying combination of social media content objectives, strategies, and tactics. In Industrial Marketing Management*. Elsevier.

Klimstra, Frijns, Keijsers, Denissen, Raaijmakers, Van Aken, Koot, Van Lier, & Meeu. (2011). Come rain or come shine: Individual differences in how weather affects mood. *Emotion, 11*.

Kumari, S., Kumar, D., & Mittal, M. (2021). An ensemble approach for classification and prediction of diabetes mellitus using soft voting classifier. *International Journal of Cognitive Computing in Engineering, 2*, 40-46.

Larson, J. S. (2005). An Exploratory Look at Supermarket Shopping Paths. *International Journal of Research in Marketing, 22*, 395-414.

Lee, S., Kc, B., & Choeh, J. Y. (2020, June 20). Comparing performance of ensemble methods in predicting movie box office revenue. *Heliyon, 6*(6), e04260. doi:10.1016/j.heliyon.2020.e04260 PMID:32613125

Liu, Q., Ge, Y., Li, Z., Chen, E., & Xiong, H. (2011). Personalized travel package recommendation. In *2011 IEEE 11th International Conference on Data Mining*. IEEE.

Liu, T., Guan, Y., & Lin, Y. (2017). Research on modulation recognition with ensemble learning. *EURASIP Journal on Wireless Communications and Networking, 2017*(1), 179. doi:10.118613638-017-0949-5

Lucas, G. M., Gratch, J., Malandrakis, N., Szablowski, E., Fessler, E., & Nichols, J. (2017). GOAALLL!: Using sentiment in the world cup to explore theories of emotion. *Image and Vision Computing, 65*, 58–65. doi:10.1016/j.imavis.2017.01.006

McCallum & Nigam. (2004). *A Comparison of Event Models for Naive Bayes Text Classification*. cmu.cs.

Nadia, S., Firdaus, C. D., & Sadeghian, A. (2018). Retweet: A popular information diffusion mechanism – A survey paper. *Online Social Networks and Media*, *6*(June), 26–40.

Ravi, L., & Vairavasundaram, S. (2016). A Collaborative Location Based Travel Recommendation System through Enhanced Rating Prediction for the Group of Users. In Computational Intelligence and Neuroscience. Hindawi Publishing Corporation. doi:10.1155/2016/1291358

Schwipper, S., Peche, S., & Schmitz, G. (2020). Mobile Location-Based Services' Value-in-Use in Inner Cities: Do a Customer's Shopping Patterns, Prior User Experience, and Sales Promotions Matter? *Schmalenbach Business Review*, *72*(4), 511–564.

Sen, A., & Dietz, L. W. (2019). Identifying travel regions using location-based social network check-in data. *Frontiers in Big Data*, *2*, 12. doi:10.3389/fdata.2019.00012 PMID:33693335

Sendi, N., Abchiche-Mimouni, N., & Zehraoui, F. (2019). A new Transparent Ensemble Method based on Deep learning. *Procedia Computer Science, 159*, 271-280.

Shah, Z., Martin, P., Coiera, E., Mandl, K. D., & Dunn, A. G. (2019). Modeling Spatiotemporal Factors Associated with Sentiment on Twitter: Synthesis and Suggestions for Improving the Identification of Localized Deviations. *Journal of Medical Internet Research*, *21*(5), e12881. doi:10.2196/12881 PMID:31344669

Shaikhina, T., Lowe, D., Daga, S., Briggs, D., Higgins, R., & Khovanova, N. (2019). Decision tree and random forest models for outcome prediction in antibody incompatible kidney transplantation. *Biomedical Signal Processing and Control, 52*, 456-462.

Shmilovici. (n.d.). *Support Vector Machines, Data Mining and Knowledge Discovery Handbook*. Academic Press.

Stone, Soulard, Migacz, & Wolf. (n.d.). Elements of Memorable Food, Drink, and Culinary Tourism Experiences. *Journal of Travel Research*.

Sun, J., Fujita, H., Chen, P., & Li, H. (2017, March). Dynamic financial distress prediction with concept drift based on time weighting combined with Adaboost support vector machine ensemble. *Knowledge-Based Systems*, *120*(15), 4–14. doi:10.1016/j.knosys.2016.12.019

Sundar, R., & Punniyamoorthy, M. (2019). Performance enhanced Boosted SVM for Imbalanced datasets. *Applied Soft Computing, Elsevier*, *83*(October), 105601.

Tang, H., Tan, S., & Cheng, X. (2009). A survey on sentiment detection of reviews. *Xueqi Cheng Expert Systems with Applications*, *36*(7), 10760–10773. doi:10.1016/j.eswa.2009.02.063

Twitter. (n.d.). https://twitter.com

Williams, J., Chinn, S. J., & Suleiman, J. (2014). The value of Twitter for sports fans. *Journal of Direct, Data and Digital Marketing Practice*, *1*(1), 36–50. doi:10.1057/dddmp.2014.36

Yan, Toriumi, & Sugawara. (n.d.). Understanding how retweets influence the behaviors of social networking service users via agent-based simulation. *Computational Social Networks*.

# Chapter 6
# Trust in Electronic Banking With the Use of Cell Phones for User Satisfaction

**Jose Melchor Medina-Quintero**
*Tamaulipas Autonomous University, Mexico*

**Fernando Ortiz-Rodriguez**
https://orcid.org/0000-0003-2084-3462
*Tamaulipas Autonomous University, Mexico*

**Sanju Tiwari**
*Tamaulipas Autonomous University, Mexico*

**Francisco Isai Morales Saenz**
*Tamaulipas Autonomous University, Mexico*

## ABSTRACT

*Mobile technologies play a transcendental role in the development of organizations. The banking industry has become the world's economic engine, and when combined, they seek to generate a competitive advantage and attract more users. For this reason, this research aims to determine the influence of users' trust in their satisfaction when they use e-banking through mobile phones. A survey was applied to 98 users in Northeastern Mexico who use a commercial banking computer application and inferential analysis with SmartPLS. The main results indicate that trust is essential in using this computer technology to perceive its usefulness and ease of use. However, the most relevant contribution is the use of e-banking by providing greater satisfaction to users.*

DOI: 10.4018/978-1-6684-6591-2.ch006

## INTRODUCTION

Information technologies (IT) since their inception have been advancing by leaps and bounds. Today there is talk of artificial intelligence and Web 4.0 that is nothing other than replacing human labor with computers through artificial intelligence. In the, commercial banking, its users, until ten years ago, mostly interacted directly with employees, and to date, users have greater participation in electronic banking (e-Banking) operations. e-Banking started with automatic teller machines (ATM), then, the ATM set in a network. Today, the Internet revolution has reached them. According to Chmielarz and Zborowski (2018), these technological tools create a competitive advantage for banks and provide services in the most convenient way for users.

The competitive advantages of e-Banking are when users use the app from any place and pay bills, transfer money, manage current accounts (Ataya and Ali, 2019; Medina et al., 2022), reduce operating costs, improve banking services in consumption and expand their participation (Lichtenstein and Williamson, 2006), saving time, banking services 24 hours a day, seven days a week, without unnecessary lines or waiting times (Mansou et al., 2016). E-Banking is defined as all those banking activities and transactions that can be carried out from anywhere and at any time from an electronic device (cell/mobile phone, computer, tablet, SmartTV) connected to the Internet, in which there is no physical contact nor virtual with the banking personnel.

Different factors influence the acceptance of mobile banking, including hedonic motivation (Boonsiritomachai and Pitchayadejanant, 2019), interface and operation guide, consulting service, and humanization (Peng-yu and Xiao-xiao, 2017). Chmielarz and Zborowski (2018), in their literature review, found usability, functionality, interaction, visualization, reliability, and effectiveness as elements for the use of banking technology. To this, it is necessary to add security aspects in the technology that, according to Malinka et al. (2022), require authentication methods, their properties with respect to international standards, and their resistance against cybernetics attacks.

Unfortunately, in terms of research, e-Banking does not have a consolidate theory to support it; it is an area with vast exploration possibilities, a fertile field to test typologies focused on the trust and satisfaction of e-Banking users. Among the theories and models used for their analysis are the Perceived Risk Theory (PRT), the Theory of Planned Behavior (TPB), the Diffusion of Innovation Theory (IDT), the Social Cognitive Theory (SCT), the Theory of Reasoned Action (TRA), the Technology Acceptance Model (TAM) and the Unified Theory of Technology Acceptance and Use (UTAUT). These theories and models have their strengths and weaknesses and the difficulty of taking them as the most appropriate for scientific research.

The relevance that e-Banking has taken is to be appreciated. Considering that many citizens have a cell phone, in such a way, its analysis and research are relevant from a technological, economic, and social point of view. In the literature review, the most used is the TAM; however, some researchers argue that it is too generic and cannot provide a realistic understanding of the adoption of advanced mobile services and technologies (Salimon et al., 2017). However, this research takes it in its essential part; for this, the objective of this study is to determine the influence of trust in e-Banking by mobile phones on user satisfaction. A literature review is carried out, which supports the design of a validated questionnaire to obtain user perceptions about e-Banking. In addition, a second-generation statistical tool based on Structural Equation Modeling (SmartPLS) evaluates a research model to test hypotheses and capture the main contributions to knowledge.

## LITERATURE REVIEW

### Trust

Trust has been classified as one of the most critical factors affecting any economic entity's performance and success. Some empirical results reveal that it is the most significant concern for committing to use e-Banking services (Yu and Asgarkhani, 2015), for which, bank managers must provide the security of their technological systems in order to certify them for their users and make them feel safe and easy in their operation.

Trust has been defined and evaluated very differently, and there is no clear and precise definition; according to Yazir and Majid (2017), it depends on the exchange of information and knowledge. Ataya and Ali (2019) consider that trust and user privacy problems have the most significant influence on the acceptance of e-Banking, which can decrease it and, in return, decrease the number of users. Data from the Federal Reserve Bank of America showed that about 65% of respondents in the United States of America with a mobile phone were concerned about the security of mobile payments or did not see any benefit in its use (Priya et al., 2018), in this way, that is why banks supported by technology is now strengthening their security.

Trust adoption is developed day by day, gaining self-experience and that of the users' acquaintances, since those who have bought online and have a particular skill with computers assume a greater tendency to embrace Internet banking (Serener, 2016). Therefore, finding strategies to generate trust in e-Banking is essential to encourage users to adopt it initially and then continuously use e-Banking services (Wang et al., 2003). Some advances have helped, such as the influence of habit, perceived security, perceived privacy, and trust itself (Moraru and Duhnea, 2018).

Furthermore, it has been found that it is a factor with a high impact on e-Banking (Hammoud et al., 2018) that leads to user satisfaction and service quality (Almurshidee, 2018).

The above are just some crucial elements in the acceptance of e-Banking. Unfortunately, there are also certain downsides, as innovation opens the possibility of fraudulent transactions and scares users away from this fear (Barker, 2018), driven mainly by the underground malware economy (Carminati et al., 2015).

The banking industry should not go trust unnoticed when a user makes use of e-Banking since it is diminished by the fraud committed, which based on the 2021 report of the Internet Crime Report (FBI, 2022), the major crimes are phishing, violation of personal data breach, non-payment/non-delivery, extortion, and technological support.

For this reason, to improve confidence in e-Banking, it is necessary to increase the security and privacy of transactions with digital and personal administrative support for users of these electronic services and get a precise method to create an engaging environment between users and electronic banking, having this the main channel to deploy all digital solutions globally.

## Perceived Utility

The perceived utility is defined as the degree that a person believes using a particular information system improves their performance (Davis, 1989). Acceptance of the technology is the most significant contribution. Some studies argue perceived utility is the most robust component determining the intention of technology adoption (Jieun et al., 2017). For instance, the perceived utility positively affects the adoption in the use of self-service technology in airports, and it also does not require human interaction (Merhi et al., 2019), in fact, in the studies of Luarn and Lin (2005) and Gumussoy et al. (2018) found that the utility of the perceived service is the main reason why users adopted mobile systems to complete banking transactions.

Also, the confirmation of users after the initial use of banking services with cell phones has been determined, and they find a significant impact on the perceived utility (Susanto et al., 2016), which moderates the effect of utility on the perceived value (Jieun et al., 2017). Likewise, in another analysis, the support in TAM to predict the intention of users to adopt Internet banking is confirmed, mainly due to the perceived utility (Wang et al., 2003).

There are e-Banking studies that have found that only three factors are identified as antecedents of attitude towards mobile banking: benefits and ease, service quality and credibility (Mansou et al., 2016), but above all, trust in the Internet (Söllner et al., 2019), with perceived utility being one of the main barriers to the use of e-Banking

(Anouze and Alamro, 2019). In other words, the user must perceive that e-Banking will help them improve their financial life.

That is why banks need to provide training to users to ensure that they have the skills and knowledge necessary to use the mobile banking application (Boonsiritomachai and Pitchayadejanant, 2019), as well as enrich the perceptions of service quality and create awareness among users of its ease of use and utility (George, 2018).

The perceived utility, represent a main role in technology acceptance for users. The banking industry uses IT to grow engagement and to know real needs. The banks are looking to promote a rational and efficient way to use a financial tool, reducing cost, time and efforts providing services.

Therefore, after conducting the literature review, the first working hypothesis to be tested is presented below:

**$H_1$:** User trust in e-Banking through the mobile phone is an essential factor for its perceived usefulness.

## Ease of Use

Ease of use is defined as the degree to which using innovation is effortless (Davis, 1989). In this research, it refers to the user's ability to efficiently operate a mobile phone to make use of e-Banking, because e-Banking will generate profits in the future by providing the user with high-quality services in terms of simplicity (easy to use) and transaction fee (Marku, 2012).

With the use of mobile phones, e-Banking is a tool that can be appreciated by most of the population when organizing banking services through a computer application, easily accessible and operating in an almost intuitive way. Likewise, it is known that the market is receptive to new technologies. If they are easy to use, as it is a crucial element in the behavioral intention of using mobile banking (Gumussoy et al., 2018); however, it is necessary to consider that people are an essential factor to achieve success and the very essence of an organization (Luburić, 2019) and with it its analysis of acceptance of information technologies and more precisely, banking.

The results of Wang et al. (2003), who applied TAM, express their firm support in adopting e-Banking through their perception of ease of use; that is why this concept stands out as a barrier or an opportunity for the intention to use the services of the e-Banking. Thus, the banking industry needs to define and apply strategies for all users to generate quality services, but that does not require a significant effort for their use.

Information technology requires the active participation of all the actors. The ease of use of technology is an essential element that every mobile banking application must have. In other words, skill is the key to operate and use efficiently for the benefit of the users themselves and the banking institutions, significantly that the perceived ease of use will grow as people increase their ability to use this technology, The hypothesis to be tested for this variable:

**$H_2$:** User trust in e-Banking through the mobile phone is critical in perceiving this technology's ease of use.

## Perceived Use

An investment in technology not used is a bad investment and is what every company avoids as much as possible so that it is not an unnecessary expense. However, it requires the collaboration of all those involved in the procedures, in this case, e-Banking. Banks and stakeholders (users, employees, Internet providers, among others) must actively participate so that the end-user can participate in a computer application. Shahabi and Razi (2019) argue that more significant investment in e-Banking can increase online users and, therefore, income, reduce costs (in branches, assets, and personnel) and with-it higher profitability. According to Barker (2018), the aspects concerning the security of transactions are pending matters for bank managers.

Trust in e-Banking is a decisive component influencing the behavioral intention to adopt a technology (Sharma and Sharma, 2019). It is convenient because it has found a positive relationship with banking online (Gerrard and Cunningham, 2003) by increasing user satisfaction when using these services (Asiyanbi and Ishola, 2018). However, bank managers must also improve their use of shared value by collecting data on preferences and user comments (Anouze and Alamro, 2019).

It is necessary to point out a high level of computer operation have a greater tendency to adopt Internet banking (Serener, 2016), and today, young users mostly use cell phones and modern electronic devices, which allows them to generate a positive perception of the use of mobile financial transactions and commerce applications.

TAM has been an efficient precursor of the evaluation to determine the user's intention to use mobile banking. Above all, this technology has become widespread worldwide; its use is a fundamental element in the proper functioning of the technology and an essential indicator to define the efficiency in terms of the services provided in the banking industry, and with the accounting of their accesses, they should evaluate the balance point in the use of e-Banking to make the appropriate decisions.

Perceived use is an important variable in technologies, and the mobile phone has demonstrated the potential to cover needs of users. For this variable, its hypotheses are presented below to analyze and verify in the empirical work:

**$H_3$:** The perceived utility of e-Banking through the mobile phone allows its users greater use of this technology.

**$H_4$:** The ease of use of e-Baking employing the mobile phone allows its users greater use of this technology.

## Satisfaction

Satisfaction can be defined as the psychological state of well-being that the person feels before some life circumstance, this time due to the use of technology. Regarding e-Banking, Hammoud et al. (2018) determine that it is the user's attitude in response to the use of any form of e-Banking services and that many times, according to Asiyanbi and Ishola (2018) it increases when these services are used. Dawood et al. (2019) indicate that users need to be satisfied to obtain a better benefit and reduce risk, considering that e-Banking was about technological innovation in the past. Today, in all business aspects, it is to be focused on the client as a user. Furthermore, Susanto et al. (2016) determined that satisfaction allows generating an environment where the user intends to use this technology continuously.

Banking services have become relevant as they are fundamental in use satisfaction in the e-Banking sector (Kaya and Kahraman, 2011), including reliability, security, and tangibility (Almurshidee, 2018). In this way, banks are obliged to design personalized profiles for efficient segmentation and win their loyalty and satisfaction (Dawood et al., 2019). In addition, if banks understand users' current and future needs, they contribute to the general success since they are the best interpreters and followers of the organization's mission and vision (Siggelkow and Terwiesch, 2019).

Concerning studies on evaluating satisfaction with e-Banking services, the results do not differ according to sex or the residence environment (Merhi et al., 2019). This assessment has been carried out taking into account the variables of TAM (perceived utility, ease of use, credibility) to determine the importance of user satisfaction in accepting this technology with positive results (Priya et al., 2018). It has even been evaluated through word of mouth, the number of complaints and how to deal with them, and loyalty to the service provider (Paul et al., 2016). Therefore, user satisfaction is the goal to be achieved since much of the bank's success and profitability depend on those who use its banking services.

Satisfaction is the main motivator to promote technology. The working hypothesis of this variable reviewed in the literature is defined:

**$H_5$:** The constant use of e-Banking through the mobile phone generates a state of well-being (satisfaction) in users.

## METHOD

E-Banking is a technology that has come to stay. Today it is a competitive advantage in the banking industry, which in the short term will be an urgent need for this type of organization, repeating the life cycle of plastic (cards) to carry out financial operations, electronic funds transfer and ATMs, which right now, without the latter, banks would have no way of surviving the competitive and global market. However, the trend is for them to be replaced for the most part by mobile banking.

In recent years, numerous theories have emerged that offer new ideas to explain the relationship between beliefs, user perceptions, and behavioral intentions to use technology, specifically in e-Banking. As mentioned, PRT, TPB, IDT, SCT, TRA, TAM, and UTAUT are examples of these theories and models, limitations exist in all of them, as the contexts, cultures, and variables analyzed are diverse.

This research takes place in the Mexican state of Tamaulipas, located in the northeast of the country, lays its foundations on the Technology Acceptance Model in conjunction with the most significant variables in previous studies, such as trust and satisfaction of the users. Mexico has an emerging economy that struggles every day to be at the technological forefront and has taken off e-Banking. However, it requires scientific studies that allow it to continue advancing with firmness but safe and constant steps, in which mobile phone penetration per 100 inhabitants is expected to go from 91.83% in 2019 to 94.1% by 2021 (MarketLine, 2019). Of the 62.2 million people who own a mobile phone, 51% have an account in a bank or financial institution, of which 22% operate their bank account through this mobile device (INEGI, 2018), undoubtedly an attractive market for the development of this information technology.

For empirical work, the research users are the population that has used e-Banking for at least six months through mobile phones, people with experience with this technology who can provide information on the use, advantages, and disadvantages that set the guidelines for short-term computing developments. The primary services considered are balance consultation, transfers between own accounts, transfers to other users of the same bank, transfers to other banks, credit card payment, investment funds, payment of services, and cash availability without a bank card.

The dependent and independent variables were analyzed in the literature, which is operationalized as follows:

- **Trust:** Security and privacy.
- **Perceived Utility:** Speed, valuable data, time-saving, facilitation.
- **Ease of Use:** Easy, flexible, interaction, surfing, procedures, services.
- **Use:** Current information, continuous use, best banking option.

- **Satisfaction:** Positive opinion, preference, positive action, satisfaction with the information, adequate attention (when necessary).

With this definition of variables, a questionnaire was developed, reviewed by three academic staff members and two users of this technological tool, and made suitable adjustments with their recommendations. The next step consisted of conducting a pilot study of 35 e-Banking users; the results indicated eliminating five items (Tru3, PerU4, Use1, Use2, and Sat2) that did not reach the minimum reliability and change to 6 that they were not understood in their wording. The seven-point Likert-type scale did not change. It was maintained (1. Strongly Disagree…7. Strongly Agree).

With the final version of the questionnaire, it was applied in the central zone (Victoria City) of the Mexican state of Tamaulipas in a convenience sampling; the process lasted 30 days pressed by the difficulty of the COVID-19 contingency, this situation limited to the obtaining questionnaires for only 98 users that exceed the minimum recommended by the experts. All this information was made known to you that it will be treated confidentially and anonymously; it will only be used for academic and research purposes.

A descriptive analysis is carried out, to later an inferential analysis with a second-generation statistical tool with the help of the SmartPLS software (Ringle et al., 2015) and with a subsampling of 5000 subsamples to obtain crossovers of variables, Average Variance Extracted (AVE), factorial loads, t-statistic, standardized path coefficients (β), explained variance ($R^2$). Furthermore, $f^2$, to validate the values obtained, verify their consistency, homogeneity, and heterogeneity, and accept or reject the five proposed hypotheses.

*Figure 1. E-banking main uses*

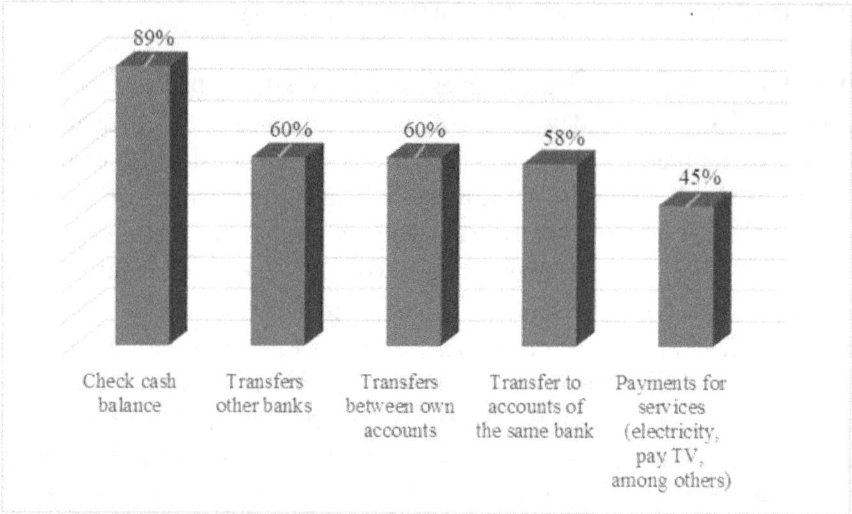


## RESULTS

Within the descriptive aspects, it stands out that 61% are women and 39% men, and their age, for the most part, are young people with a willingness to change and adapt to technological innovations, these data range between 21 and 30 years with 49% followed from 31 to 40 years with 25%. Figure 1 shows the main uses of mobile banking from users.

Regarding inferential analysis, it is carried out using SmartPLS 3.2.8, which is an ideal tool for research in computer technology by allowing evaluation in two stages (Hair et al., 2019): a) Measurement model (properties psychometric of the scale used to mediate a variable), and b) the estimation of the structural model (the strength and direction of the relationships between the variables):

### Measurement Model Validation

- **Item Reliability:** Assessed by examining loads ($\lambda$) or simple correlations. It must have a load equal to or greater than .707 ($\lambda^2$, 50% of the variance is explained) (Chin, 1998). The 17 reflective items present acceptable values (Table 1, Column 2), the loads oscillate between .759 and .907, exceeding the recommended minimums.
- **Composite Reliability (Internal Consistency):** Measured by Cronbach's alpha (.700) and the Fornell and Larcker (1981) statistic of .707. Table 1 (Column 4) shows that this validation is adequate for the investigation.

- **Convergent Validation:** It is carried out through AVE; its values must be greater than .50 (more than 50% of the construct's variance is due to its items) (Fornell and Larcker, 1981). It can only be applied to reflective items, as in this research. The values of the variables presented in Table 1 (Column 7) exceed the accepted minimum of .500, ranging between .652 and .773. Likewise, resampling (5000 subsamples) was carried out to obtain the t-statistic. The results indicate that all were significant (Table 3, Column 3), which gives the guideline for the decision about the hypotheses.

*Table 1. Individual reliability of reflective items and convergent validity*

| | Loading Item | $R^2$ | Cronbach's Alpha | rho_ A | Composite Reliability | AVE |
|---|---|---|---|---|---|---|
| Trust | | Not Apply | .855 | .883 | .911 | .773 |
| Tru1 | .907 | | | | | |
| Tru2 | .837 | | | | | |
| Tru4 | .893 | | | | | |
| Perceived Utility | | .269 | .757 | .789 | .859 | .670 |
| PerU1 | .824 | | | | | |
| PerU2 | .869 | | | | | |
| PerU3 | .759 | | | | | |
| Ease of Use | | .328 | .896 | .900 | .928 | .763 |
| EU1 | .825 | | | | | |
| EU2 | .882 | | | | | |
| EU3 | .918 | | | | | |
| EU4 | .868 | | | | | |
| Use | | .372 | .732 | .731 | .849 | .652 |
| Use3 | .774 | | | | | |
| Use4 | .847 | | | | | |
| Use5 | .800 | | | | | |
| Satisfaction | | .477 | .889 | .894 | .924 | .752 |
| Sat1 | .817 | | | | | |
| Sat3 | .892 | | | | | |
| Sat4 | .863 | | | | | |
| Sat5 | .883 | | | | | |

*Table 2. Correlation of variables*

| | Trust | EU | Sat | Use | PerU |
|---|---|---|---|---|---|
| Trust | .879 | | | | |
| Ease of Use (EU) | .573 | .874 | | | |
| Satisfaction (Sat) | .524 | .585 | .867 | | |
| Use | .381 | .522 | .691 | .807 | |
| Perceived Utility (PerU) | .519 | .662 | .674 | .581 | .819 |

- **Discriminant Validation:** For this assessment, the square root of AVE is used (Fornell and Larcker, 1981), it must be greater than the shared variance between the construct and other constructs in the model. Table 2 (diagonally) shows the discriminant validity for this validation, the variables satisfy this condition. In the same way, the rho_A indicator from Dijkstra and Henseler (2015) is used, which must be greater than .700, Table 1, Column 5, contains values that exceed the recommended minimums.

Note: The diagonal data is the square root of AVE between the variable and its measurements. For discriminant validity, these data must be greater than those in the same row and column (inter-construct).

## Structural Model Validation

Two essential indices are required, the explained variance ($R^2$) and the standardized path coefficients ($\beta$). The $R^2$ indicates the ability to predict the independent variables and the standardized path coefficients identified in the nomogram (PLS graph) employing the arrows that link the constructs in the internal model. For this, Chin (1988) indicates that $\beta$ to be considered significant, should reach at least a value

*Table 3. Summary of results with SmartPLS*

| Hypothesis | β | T-Statistic | $f^2$ | Sig | Remarks |
|---|---|---|---|---|---|
| $H_1$ Trust → Perceived Utility | .519 *** | 6.281 | .368 | .000 | Accepted |
| $H_2$ Trust → Ease Use | .573 *** | 7.688 | .489 | .000 | Accepted |
| $H_3$ Perceived Utility → Use | .419 *** | 3.672 | .157 | .000 | Accepted |
| $H_4$ Ease Use → Use | .262 * | 2.129 | .054 | .046 | Accepted |
| $H_5$ Use → Satisfaction | .691 *** | 10.787 | .914 | .000 | Accepted |

*Figure 2. Evaluated research model*

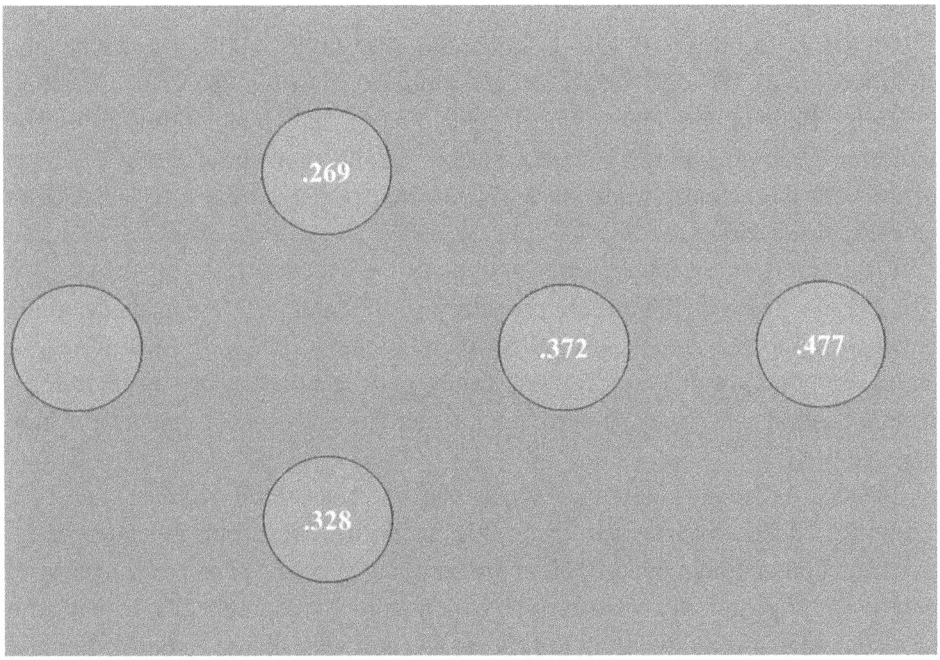


of .2 and ideally be above .3 and remarks that $R^2$ at a level of .67 has a substantial effect, .33 moderate and .19 weak. Also, the significance (p-value) must be less than .05 ($p<.05$). Regarding the effect size ($f^2$), Cohen (1988) indicates that he assesses the degree to which an exogenous variable contributes to explaining an endogenous one in terms of $R^2$, and the minimum accepted value is .02.

Table 3 summarizes the hypotheses raised based on the literature review and the statistical analysis performed. In Figure 2, the evaluated research model is detailed in the PLS nomogram.

When analyzing the results of Table 3, it is possible to verify the approval of the five hypotheses, and Figure 2 also shows that the most significant path is established in the Trust → Perceived_Utility → Use →Satisfaction route. Analyzes are detailed below:

Hypothesis 1 ($H_1$) is accepted (good values in path coefficient=.519, t-statistic=6.281 and significance= $p<.001$), which shows that the user recognizes that his financial information is safe and creates an atmosphere of useful e-Banking (by mobile phone) in terms of speed, time savings, profit, and ease of performing operations. This same confidence allows accepting $H_2$ ($\beta$=.573, t-statistic= 7.688 and significance=$p<.001$) by perceiving that the banking application is easy to use and has some flexibility in its navigation when operations and interactions are easy to understand.

In the same way, the $H_3$ is accepted (β=.419, t-statistic= 3.672 and significance=p<.001, its statistical data supports it, so the speed of operations through e-Banking, the value of the data handled and the saving of time are a clear indicator that users will make constant use of mobile phone instead of going to an office with the inconveniences that it can bring (parking, time invested, lack of empathy from staff).

Likewise, $H_4$ is accepted; however, it is the one with the least statistical weight (β=.262, t-statistic=2.129 and significance =p<.05) and therefore its contribution is not so strong, but it does approve of affirming that e-Banking, which is easy to use to carry out financial operations, is an efficient means of having captive users of mobile banking when they perceive the interactivity and access to the information they require.

Finally, the relationship that shows the greatest solidity, the $H_5$ (β=.691, t-statistic=10.787 and significance=p<.001) and with it, its acceptance. Undoubtedly, the idea of continuing with e-Banking by means of a mobile phone over a physical presence in the bank office and even give it more importance also than with the use of a computer, will allow users to find satisfaction with that technology, because they perceive a positive opinion about online banking, as well as the proper use of their financial information, always meeting their banking needs.

The above, it can be added that security in technology is a relevant aspect for user satisfaction (Raviadaran et al., 2019), therefore, the banking industry must provide a better Internet service and easy-to-use applications.

## CONCLUSION

Technology continues to advance, and the economic growth of a country and organizations often depends on it. Today in the business world, the paradigm shift concentrates on the user as an individual or representative of a public or private company. Therefore, the objective of the research is to analyze the impact of the trust that users have in e-Banking for their satisfaction when they use the mobile phone. The empirical work was carried out in northeastern Mexico on mobile banking users, who adapt to the new role of technologies in the globalized world.

The contributions determine that the user's trust in e-Banking essentially in the security of their transactions when they use it through their mobile phone, influences their satisfaction in the way of reaching that psychological state of well-being in the form of opinion positive that they keep towards this technology that does not require them physically in the bank office and that adequately meets their financial information needs.

This influence in turn, is affected by the constant use that users are giving to e-Banking, especially when they perceive its ease of use and utility. These two variables play a fundamental role within the chain of trust-use-satisfaction management, for which banking institutions need to strengthen these variables for the benefit of their competitive advantage and success as a business. On the part of the user, which must be an immediate requirement by the bank, it provides the highest quality service every day of the year without setbacks so that it generates time savings, increases its efficiency and productivity, and all those advantages that can give digital banking.

The above idealize situations that are currently experienced and that can generate future lines of research: a) users have the knowledge and skills for these innovations, b) users learn quickly with intuitive technologies like other applications, and c) generate appropriate strategies for the short term to integrate more users to banking entities in the mobile format.

Similarly, the results can be used by banking institutions in order to establish and plan relevant strategies and continue to support their strengths and reduce weaknesses to increase the adoption of e-Banking, determine the privileged position in the market and attract more users to the banking business when using their services through the mobile phone always considering the economic, social, technological and cultural environment. Therefore, it is recommended that banks continue to increase security and implementation of emerging technologies (Villazón-Terrazas et al., 2021) in their transactions to strengthen users' trust and satisfaction for their benefit and their users. To do this, banks require technology and databases to be always available (regardless of time or place), confidentiality (that users' data is not shared with anyone) and integrity (without altering the data)

**Limitations:** The research is carried out in the central area of Tamaulipas (Mexico), the results cannot be generalized to the entire country. It requires analysis in other societies and knowledge of its users. The COVID-19 health contingency had an impact on the restriction on obtaining questionnaires. Finally, the research model does not come from a consolidated theory of e-Banking.

## REFERENCES

Almurshidee, K. (2018). SERVPERF-based empirical evidence on e-banking services quality and customer satisfaction from the Saudi banking sector. *International Journal of Advanced and Applied Sciences*, *5*(11), 40–45. doi:10.21833/ijaas.2018.11.005

Anouze, A. L., & Alamro, A. S. (2019). Factors affecting intention to use e-banking in Jordan. *International Journal of Bank Marketing*, *38*(1), 86–112. doi:10.1108/IJBM-10-2018-0271

Asiyanbi, H., & Ishola, A. (2018). E-Banking services impact and customer satisfaction in selected bank branches in Ibadan metropolis, Oyo state, Nigeria. *Accounting*, *4*(4), 153–160. doi:10.5267/j.ac.2018.3.001

Ataya, M. A. M., & Ali, M. A. M. (2019). Acceptance of website security on e-Banking. A-review. *IEEE 10th Control and System Graduate Research Colloquium*. 10.1109/ICSGRC.2019.8837070

Barker, R. (2018). Knowledge management to prevent fraudulent e-banking transactions. *Communitas*, *23*(1), 71–86. doi:10.18820/24150525/Comm.v23.5

Boonsiritomachai, W., & Pitchayadejanant, K. (2019). Determinants affecting mobile banking adoption by generation Y based on the Unified Theory of Acceptance and Use of Technology Model modified by the Technology Acceptance Model concept. *Kasetsart Journal of Social Sciences*, *40*(2), 349–358. doi:10.1016/j.kjss.2017.10.005

Carminati, M., Toberto, C., Maggi, F., Epifani, I., & Zanero, S. (2015). Bank Sealer: A decision support system for online banking fraud analysis and investigation. *Computers & Security*, *3*, 175–186. doi:10.1016/j.cose.2015.04.002

Chin, W. W. (1998). The partial least squares approach to structural equation modelling. In G. A. Marcoulides (Ed.), *Modern methods for business research* (pp. 295–336). Lawrence Erlbaum.

Chmielarz, W., & Zborowski, M. (2018). Analysis of e-Banking Websites' quality with the application of the TOPSIS Method – A Practical Study. *Procedia Computer Science*, *126*, 1964–1976. doi:10.1016/j.procs.2018.07.256

Cohen, J. (1988). *Statistical power analysis for the behavioral science* (2nd ed.). Erlbaum.

Davis, F. D. (1989). Perceived usefulness, perceived ease of use, and user acceptance of information technology. *Management Information Systems Quarterly*, *13*(3), 319–340. doi:10.2307/249008

Dawood, E. A., Elfakhrany, E., & Maghraby, F. A. (2019). Improve Profiling Bank Customer's Behavior Using Machine Learning. *IEEE Access : Practical Innovations, Open Solutions*, *7*, 109320–109327. Advance online publication. doi:10.1109/ACCESS.2019.2934644

Dijkstra, T. K., & Henseler, J. (2015). Consistent Partial Least Squares Path Modeling. *Management Information Systems Quarterly, 39*(2), 297–316. doi:10.25300/MISQ/2015/39.2.02

FBI. (2022). *Internet Crime Report.* Internet Crime Complaint Center. https://www.ic3.gov/Media/PDF/AnnualReport/2022_IC3Report.pd f

Fornell, C., & Larcker, D. F. (1981). Evaluating structural equation models with unobservable variables and measurement error. *JMR, Journal of Marketing Research, 18*(1), 39–5. doi:10.1177/002224378101800104

George, A. (2018). Perceptions of Internet banking users – a structural equation modelling (SEM) approach. *IIMB Management Review, 30*(4), 357–368. doi:10.1016/j.iimb.2018.05.007

Gerrard, P., & Cunningham, J. B. (2003). The diffusion of Internet banking among Singapore consumers. *International Journal of Bank Marketing, 21*(1), 16–28. doi:10.1108/02652320310457776

Gumussoy, C., Kaya, A., & Ozlu, E. (2018). Determinants of mobile banking use: An extended TAM with perceived risk, mobility access, compatibility, perceived self-efficacy and subjective norms. In F. Calisir & H. Camgoz Akdag (Eds.), *Industrial Engineering in the Industry 4.0 Era. Lecture Notes in Management and Industrial Engineering* (pp. 225–228). Springer. doi:10.1007/978-3-319-71225-3_20

Hair, J., Hult, T., Ringle, C., Sarstedt, M., Castillo, J., Cepeda, G., & Roldán, J. L. (2019). *Manual de Partial Least Squares Structural Equation Modeling (PLS-SEM).* SAGE Publishing. doi:10.3926/oss.37

Hammoud, J., Bizri, R. M., & El Baba, I. (2018). The impact of e-banking service quality on customer satisfaction: Evidence from the Lebanese banking sector. *SAGE Open, 8*(Jul-Sep), 1–12. doi:10.1177/2158244018790633

INEGI. (2018). *Encuesta Nacional de Inclusión Financiera (ENIF).* https://www.inegi.org.mx/contenidos/programas/enif/2018/doc/enif_2018_resultados.pdf

Jieun, Y., Lee, H., Ha, I., & Zo, H. (2017). User acceptance of media tablets: An empirical examination of perceived value. *Telematics and Informatics, 34*(4), 206–223. doi:10.1016/j.tele.2015.11.004

Kaya, T., & Kahraman, C. (2011). A fuzzy approach to e-banking website quality assessment based on an integrated ahp-electre method. *Technological and Economic Development of Economy*, *17*(2), 313–334. doi:10.3846/20294913.2011.583727

Lichtenstein, S., & Williamson, K. (2006). Understanding consumer adoption of Internet banking: An interpretive study in the Australian banking context. *Journal of Electronic Commerce Research*, *7*(2), 50–66.

Luarn, P., & Lin, H. (2005). Toward an understanding of the behavioral intention to use mobile Banking. *Computers in Human Behavior*, *21*(6), 873–891. doi:10.1016/j.chb.2004.03.003

Luburić, R. (2019). A Model of Crisis Prevention (based on managing change, quality management and risk management). *Journal of Central Banking Theory and Practice*, *2*(2), 33–49. doi:10.2478/jcbtp-2019-0012

Malinka, K., Hujňák, O., Hanáček, P., & Hellebrandt, L. (2022). E-Banking security study - 10 years later. *IEEE Access : Practical Innovations, Open Solutions*, *10*, 16681–16699. doi:10.1109/ACCESS.2022.3149475

Mansou, I. H. F., Eljelly, A. M. A., & Abdullah, A. M. A. (2016). Consumers' attitude towards e-banking services in Islamic banks: The case of Sudan. *Review of International Business and Strategy*, *26*(2), 244–260. doi:10.1108/RIBS-02-2014-0024

MarketLine. (2019). *Mexico In-depth PESTLE insights. Country Profile Series*. Report Code: ML00002-020. https://www.marketresearch.com/MarketLine-v3883/Mexico-PESTL E-Insights-30069830

Marku, M. (2012). Albanian media and the specifics of the local market. *Studies in Communication Sciences*, *12*(1), 49–52. doi:10.1016/j.scoms.2012.06.010

Medina, J. M., Echeverría, O., & Ortiz, F. (2022). Confianza y calidad de la información para la satisfacción y lealtad del cliente en el e-Banking con el uso del teléfono celular. *Contaduría y Administración*, *67*(1), 283–304. doi:10.22201/fca.24488410e.2022.2965

Merhi, M., Hone, K., & Tarhini, A. (2019). A cross-cultural study of the intention to use mobile banking between Lebanese and British consumers: Extending UTAUT2 with security, privacy, and trust. *Technology in Society*, *59*, 101151. doi:10.1016/j.techsoc.2019.101151

Moraru, A. D., & Duhnea, C. (2018). E-banking and customer satisfaction with banking services. *Strategic Management*, *23*(3), 3–9. doi:10.5937/StraMan1803003M

Paul, J., Mittal, A., & Srivastav, G. (2016). Impact of service quality on customer satisfaction in private and public sector Banks. *International Journal of Bank Marketing*, *34*(5), 606–622. doi:10.1108/IJBM-03-2015-0030

Peng-yu, L., & Xiao-xiao, W. (2017). Service improvement based on E-banking Adoption Model. *International Conference on Management Science & Engineering (24th)*. 10.1109/ICMSE.2017.8574399

Priya, R., Gandhi, A., & Shaikh, A. (2018). Mobile banking adoption in an emerging economy: An empirical analysis of young Indian consumers. *Benchmarking*, *25*(2), 43–762. doi:10.1108/BIJ-01-2016-0009

Raviadaran, H., Dastane, O., Ma'arif, M., & Mohd, N. (2019). Impact of service quality dimensions on internet banking adoption, satisfaction and patronaje. *International Journal of Management. Accounting and Economics*, *6*(10), 709–730.

Ringle, C. M., Wende, S., & Becker, J. M. (2015). *SmartPLS 3.2.8*. Boenningstedt: SmartPLS GmbH. http://www.smartpls.com

Salimon, M., Yusoff, R., & Mokhtar, S. M. (2017). The mediating role of hedonic motivation on the relationship between adoption of e-banking and its determinants. *International Journal of Bank Marketing*, *35*(4), 558–582. doi:10.1108/IJBM-05-2016-0060

Serener, B. (2016). Statistical analysis of Internet banking usage with logistic regression. *Procedia Computer Science*, *102*, 648–653. doi:10.1016/j.procs.2016.09.456

Shahabi, V., & Razi, F. F. (2019). Modeling the effect of electronic banking expansion on profitability using neural networks and system dynamics approach. *Qualitative Research in Financial Markets*, *11*(2), 197–210. doi:10.1108/QRFM-11-2018-0117

Sharma, S. K., & Sharma, M. (2019). Examining the role of trust and quality dimensions in the actual usage of mobile banking services: An empirical investigation. *International Journal of Information Management*, *44*, 65–75. doi:10.1016/j.ijinfomgt.2018.09.013

Siggelkow, N., & Terwiesch, C. (2019). The age of continuous connection. *Harvard Business Review*, (May-June), 64–73.

Söllner, M., Hoffmann, A., & Leimeister, J. M. (2019). Why different trust relationships matter for information systems users. *European Journal of Information Systems, 25*(3), 274–287. doi:10.1057/ejis.2015.17

Susanto, A., Chang, Y., & Ha, Y. (2016). Determinants of continuance intention to use the smartphone banking services: An extension to the expectation-confirmation model. *Industrial Management & Data Systems, 116*(3), 508–525. doi:10.1108/IMDS-05-2015-0195

Villazón-Terrazas, B., Ortiz, F., Tiwari, S., Ayush, G., & Jabbar, M. A. (2021). Knowledge Graphs and Semantic Web. *Communications in Computer and Information Science, 1459*, 1–331. doi:10.1007/978-3-030-91305-2

Wang, Y., Wang, Y., Lin, H., & Tang, T. (2003). Determinants of user acceptance of Internet banking: An empirical study. *International Journal of Service Industry Management, 14*(5), 501–519. doi:10.1108/09564230310500192

Yazir, M., & Majid, A. (2017). Impact of knowledge management enablers on knowledge sharing: Is trust a mission link in SMEs of emerging economies? *World Journal of Entrepreneurship, Management and Sustainable Development, 13*(1), 16–33. doi:10.1108/WJEMSD-02-2016-0010

Yu, C. S., & Asgarkhani, M. (2015). An investigation of trust in e-banking. Evidence from Taiwan and New Zealand empirical studies. *Management Research Review, 38*(2), 1267–1284. doi:10.1108/MRR-09-2014-0210

# Chapter 7
# ICTs for Manufacturing and Trade in the Global Economy

**Oshiel Martinez. Chapa**
*Tamaulipas Autonomous University, Mexico*

**Vicente Villanueva Hernández**
*Tamaulipas Autonomous University, Mexico*

**Daniel Avila-Guzman**
*Tamaulipas Autonomous University, Mexico*

**Ramon Gerardo Tijerina**
*Tamaulipas Autonomous University, Mexico*

## ABSTRACT

*In a globalized world, companies must be effective and efficient with all resources (tangible and intangible and personal). The information and communication technologies (ICTs) were built quickly due to the large and different social problems, in addition to trying to exclude all the barriers of MiPymes that have arisen over time through the implemented information systems. On the other hand, the high demand of companies has marked certain precedents that have determined competitive excellence and increased productivity, which makes technologies such as the internet, social media, connectivity, and the internet of things (IoT) necessary to the daily technological activities that help to make decisions in the different types of MiPymes (homes, offices, workshops, banks, pharmacies, convenience stores, etc.).*

DOI: 10.4018/978-1-6684-6591-2.ch007

## INTRODUCTION

The development of MiPymes in our country is more demanding within all functional areas as well as in the productive area. ICTs have become an essential tool for changes and modifications of the processes that exist within these areas to have the updated information in real-time, be able to solve problems, and make decisions when the updated information of each generated movement within the company arrives.

ICTs are understood as "those tools and methods used to collect, retain, manipulate or distribute information", they are generally associated with computers and related technologies applied to decision making" (Bologna & Walsh, 1997).

In addition, all the tangible and non-tangible parts that are derived from the previous concept and combined with other human elements, communications, investments and are integrated, related to, and interrelated with the entire information technology system on the management of these metadata, with the objective of obtaining a detailed analysis for decision-making and thus serve as support for increasing productivity, competitiveness and reducing costs, time and money, for the development of certain strategic processes in certain MiPymes established in economies from advanced countries.

### Generalities

The increase in productivity is imperative for organizations. In this sense, the use of cutting-edge technologies that are currently available in developed countries are required. Unfortunately, this is not the situation in emerging countries. In recent decades, ICTs have become crucial in order to intensify connectivity that can help markets expand their coverage.

Production and marketing have always been related, now more in the context of the global economy. The old economy has been left behind and today a greater promotion and advertising strategy for goods and services is required in national and international markets. Reliable supply chains and communication infrastructure are equally critical.

According to Meza Rodríguez (2022) the use of ICTs is crucial in modern life. These types of technologies are fundamental and their diffusion is increasingly wide. However, there is a digital gap with respect to what happens in developed countries. In the context of Latin America, the use of these has increased, with which they become allies of productivity and the reinvention of processes. This has contributed to the reduction of labor costs and the intensification of communications in general. However, the biggest challenge is to have people with the necessary qualifications for the operation and expansion of these organizations.

Within the literature that deserves to be cited are authors of the current neoclassical economy. According to Romer (1986), technological progress must be incorporated in the context of the search for innovations with which gains derived from knowledge and research are obtained. Economic incentives are at the core of this type of process. Technological progress originates from the need to raise productivity given the intense competition that is waged in fields such as manufacturing, services, and international trade.

According to Jones (2000), it often happens that organizations do not recognize the effect of capital accumulation because it is small in relation to the size of the economy. Firms do not add capital to improve technology, but rather accumulate capital because it is a useful input for production. However, it turns out that the accumulation of capital provides the rest of the economy with a useful and unexpected benefit: it results in new knowledge.

Knowledge and technology are driving forces of work productivity therefore, the State and productive organizations must be in the same tune. The creation of clear rules and regulations is necessary for the expansion of organizations. At present, fields and activities such as electronics, and air travel, among other inventions, have become relevant. We are witnessing, therefore, the present revolution in the economy, which is related to fields and activities that include medicine, mass education, computing, telecommunications, robotics, and the so-called information economy. The common factor is the use of knowledge, which is reinforced with technology (Martinez Chapa, 2019).

The phenomenon of globalization is characterized, among other aspects, by the dynamics of flows. According to Barayre (2022), the requirements to boost production and get it to consumer markets through digital commerce has to do with actions such as those described below:

According to Laura E. Fischer and Jorge Espejo (2017), it says: "Electronic commerce is all the transactions on the internet that an organization carries out with its markets via the internet."

The following formats can be set:

- **B2B:** Business to business
- **B2C:** Business to consumer
- **B2G:** Business to government
- **C2C:** Consumer to consumer
- **C2B:** Consumer to business
- **C2G:** Consumer to government
- **G2C:** Government to consumer
- **G2B:** Government to business
- **G2G:** Government to government

In all these ways is how electronic commerce can be presented, considering its policies, education, simplicity to make digital commerce.

Likewise, information technologies (IT) represent important benefits such as economic development, access to national and international markets, improving quality of life and the development of the information society in addition to being one of the sustainable development objectives of the 2030 agenda which has been increasing (Méndez, 2021). So, the above demonstrates the need for human capital that facilitates through the design and development of technological solutions for different sectors of society. IT has a broad influence on the activities of different sectors of society. The use of ICT in different areas of companies has led to cost and time savings, helping them in turn with better management of information flows allowing to add value to operational and business management activities, allowing companies to obtain competitive advantages, remain in the market and focus on their business. Companies change their organizational structure, towards structures with greater flexibility and capacity for innovation, as an example of this, there are modular, or knowledge-based ones. The development of ICT in government makes it an open government, as a concept based on the principles of transparency, participation and collaboration, and with technologies as its enabling element. In the education sector, thanks to the familiarization of ICT, there is a new digital and learning culture (Casanovas, et al., 2014).

## Policies to Make Digital Trade More Sustainable and Inclusive

- Affordable and reliable ICTs connectivity for individuals and businesses
- An open and transparent telecommunications market to attract national and foreign investment
- Infrastructure sharing, efficient spectrum management and reduction of taxes and fees on ICT equipment and services

### Education, Skills, and Awareness

- Integrate ICTs at all educational levels and collaborate in the development of study plans
- Reform teaching methods to promote complementary non-cognitive skills
- Support the recycling of workers and teachers and the improvement of their skills
- Carry out awareness campaigns on the opportunities and risks of digital commerce

## Policies to Make Digital Commerce More Sustainable

- Adapt to e-commerce a greater number of small packages
- Modernize and streamline customs processes and single windows
- Simplify export processes for low-weight, low-value shipments
- Promote the use of ICTs in MiPymes to allow integration into global value chains
- Education and training to build skills for e-commerce and digital delivery
- Tailor trade promotion by leveraging online platforms and online marketing channels
- Support companies in complying with various regulations applicable in the target markets.

## Digital Marketing as a Tool for Solutions to Technology Companies

Faced with imminent competition, companies are looking for actions that favor and make the relationship with their customers more effective, always thinking about the administration of their resource, market analysis and the recognition or positioning of this. That is why in this chapter technological tools will be addressed that allow the solution to these problems, in digital marketing we will propose two lines of action which are: personalization and massiveness this will lead us to discover the importance of the 4F of digital marketing (Flow, functionality, feedback, loyalty, as mentioned by Paul Fleming in his book Let's talk about interactive marketing.

Today there are very powerful tools and strategies that allow them to be incorporated into those already established previously (traditional marketing), this will help to have better control, analysis and implementation of Branding.

The use of ICTs at the international level has grown unevenly as shown in Table 1. The most developed countries show greater use and coverage, which facilitates transactions and communications. The ease of accessing this type of technology, the culture and diffusion of these, as well as the need to have the necessary infrastructures, has substantially boosted them.

*Table 1. Percentage of the population that uses ICTs in some countries 2019-2021*

| | Computers | Internet | Cell Phones |
|---|---|---|---|
| Canada | ... | 92.3 | ... |
| China | ... | 73.1 | ... |
| Finland | ... | 92.8 | ... |
| France | ... | 86.1 | ... |
| Japan | 75.5 | 90.2 | 79.1 |
| South Korea | 82.3 | 97.6 | 99.9 |
| Mexico | 38.0 | 72.0 | 75.5 |
| Spain | 74.0 | 93.9 | 98.9 |
| United States | ... | 89.4 | ... |

Source: https://www.itu.int/en/itu-d/statistics/pages/stat/default.aspx

At the Mexican level, Table 2 shows how the number of cell phone and internet users has grown over time. Growth has been significant, as can be seen, and this is explained by a variety of factors, including competition between companies, access to these technologies at low costs, a wide range of access facilities, as well as the growth of infrastructure for its better use and exploitation. Connectivity is presented to us as an essential factor to increase productivity and therefore economic development.

*Table 2. Growth of cell phone and internet users in Mexico*

| | Cell Phone Users (in Millions of Users) | Internet Users (in Percentage) |
|---|---|---|
| 2000 | 14,077,880.00 | 5.08 |
| 2001 | 21,757,559.00 | 7.04 |
| 2002 | 25,928,266.00 | 11.90 |
| 2003 | 30,097,700.00 | 12.90 |
| 2004 | 38,451,135.00 | 14.10 |
| 2005 | 47,128,746.00 | 17.21 |
| 2006 | 55,395,461.00 | 19.52 |
| 2007 | 66,559,462.00 | 20.81 |
| 2008 | 75,303,469.00 | 21.71 |
| 2009 | 83,193,574.00 | 26.34 |
| 2010 | 91,383,493.00 | 31.05 |
| 2011 | 94,583,253.00 | 37.18 |
| 2012 | 100,727,228.00 | 39.75 |
| 2013 | 106,747,373.00 | 43.46 |
| 2014 | 104,948,339.00 | 44.39 |
| 2015 | 107,688,282.00 | 57.43 |
| 2016 | 111,730,635.00 | 59.54 |
| 2017 | 114,329,353.00 | 63.85 |
| 2018 | 120,165,322.00 | 65.77 |
| 2019 | 122,035,192.00 | 70.07 |
| 2020 | 122,898,392.00 | 71.97 |
| 2021 | 123,920,752.00 | 71.97 |
| 2022 | 144,908,958.81 | 74.16 |
| 2023 * | 149,614,122.41 | 77.72 |

*Prediction

Source: https://www.itu.int/en/ITU-D/Statistics/Pages/stat/default.aspx

According to the National Survey of Financing of Companies from INEGI, the financial actions carried out by these show a pattern of growth, especially those related to the use of ICTs. Thus, it is observed that resorting to communication and promotion actions, typical of the traditional economy, has been left behind, especially in the case of large corporations.

*Figure 1. Financial actions carried out by companies to continue or improve their operation in Mexico*
*Source: Encuesta Nacional de financiamiento de las empresas en 2021, INEGI.*

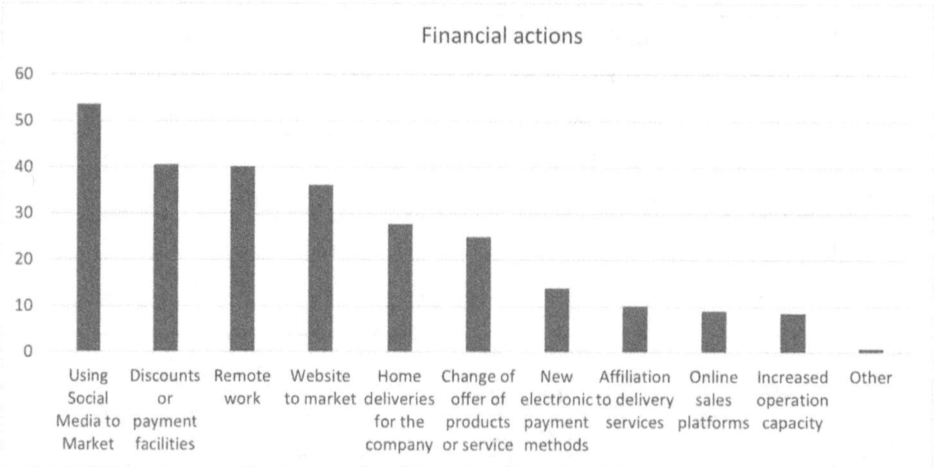


On the other hand, according to the National Survey of Financing of Companies from INEGI, in Mexico financial operations related to strategies tend to position themselves competitively were carried out, highlighting those that have to do with the use of ICTs (internet, mobile applications, among others).

*Figure 2. Means by which companies carried out financial operations in Mexico*
*Source: Encuesta Nacional de financiamiento de las empresas en 2021 INEGI.*

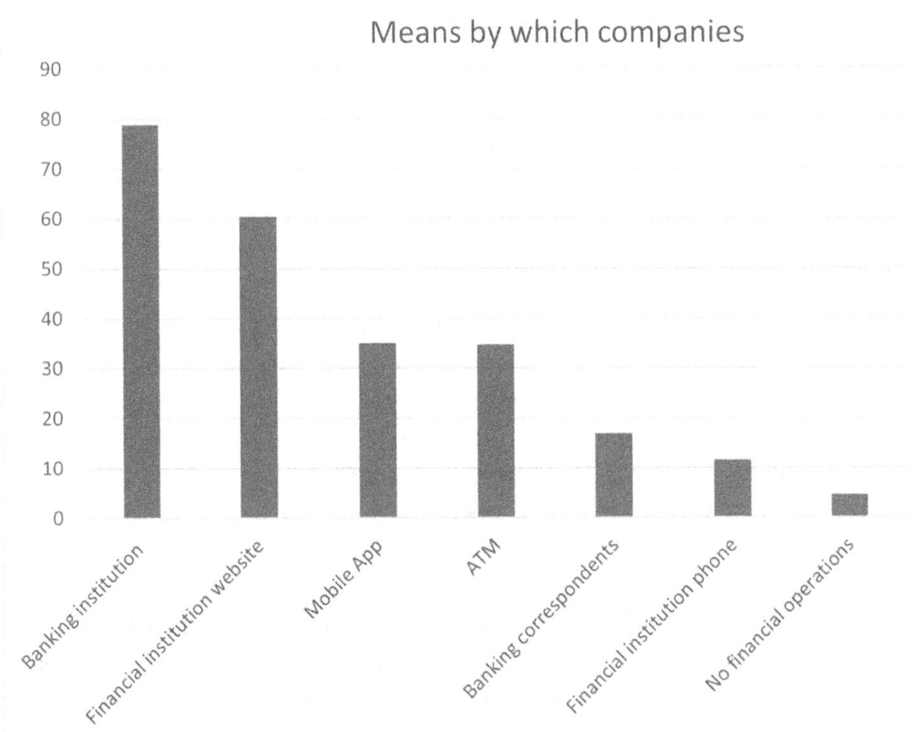


Regarding the use of ICTs in manufacturing in Mexico, Graph 3 reveals growth in 2021 compared to 2019. In fact, it should be noted that COVID-19 implied confinement and a decrease in the activities of the traditional economy. However, the need to increase the production and marketing of goods and services meant the use of applications (free and low cost) and a strong push for ICTs worldwide. However, it should be noted that the citizens of developing countries, to a large extent, have not had access to this technological progress.

The use of ICTs is associated with increased profits, since lower operating costs are implied. As can be seen in graph 4, there is growth in income in Mexican manufacturing companies in the 2019-2021 period. Revenues have increased significantly for technology corporations and less for local companies that previously promoted and advertised in the media (local television, print, and radio stations). Now a larger audience is sought in social networks, applications, web pages, and others. Corporations such as Mercado Libre, Alibaba, eBay, Amazon, Ali Express, etc., as well as large companies from Mexico and abroad, have been big winners in this process.

## CONCLUSION

ICTs have come to consolidate and become necessary in all areas of the world economy. Its impacts are diverse and its scope has reached very diverse activities such as commerce, services, public administration, and of course, manufacturing. In the case of manufacturing processes, as noted, greater integration and coordination are required in real-time. In this sense, the challenge for companies is to reinvent their processes despite the fact that we find ourselves in a global context of political uncertainty, inflation, problems with supply chains, unemployment, and other challenges. In addition to this, it is required to have trained personnel, which, because it is in high demand in this type of job, becomes expensive. However, educational institutions are in charge of training cadres of technicians and professionals for the planning and implementation of these operations.

Technological changes are increasingly positive in the lives of human beings and therefore is reflected in the field of industry, bringing as positive consequences more efficient processes, minimization of errors, automated and remote work (work at home). However, all this is raised through digital transformation, which will have to be incorporated gradually and thus face this changing environment, such as the different areas: artificial intelligence, software development, analyst in big data, etc.

## REFERENCES

Barro, R. J., & Sala-i-Martin, X. (2012). *Crecimiento económico*. Editorial Reverté.

Bologna & Walsh. (1997). The accountant's handbook of information technology. Academic Press.

Brayre, C. (2022). *Transformación digital del comercio: Tendencias, oportunidades y retos*. UNCTAD. https://unctad.org/system/files/non-official-document/decb_ecde_p01_barayre_es.pdf

Fischer & Espejo. (2017). *Mercadotecnia*. McGraw-Hill.

Fleming, P. (2000). *Hablemos del marketing interactivo.* Encuesta Nacional de financiamiento de las empresas (2021) INEGI. https://www.inegi.org.mx/programas/enafin/2021/

Jones, C. (2000). *Introducción al crecimiento económico*. Pearson.

Martínez Chapa, O. (2019). El papel del conocimiento en las organizaciones productivas: Aspectos teóricos y reflexiones. *RIDE Revista Iberoamericana para la Investigación y el Desarrollo Educativo*, *9*(18), 412–422. doi:10.23913/ride.v9i18.430

Meza Rodríguez, E. (2022). *Empresas de LATAM apuestan por tecnologías emergentes para aumentar la productividad y reinventar los procesos*. El Economista. https://www.eleconomista.com.mx/el-empresario/Empresas-de-LATAM-apuestan-por-tecnologias-emergentes-para-aumentar-la-productividad-y-reinventar-los-procesos-20221201-0092.html

Romer, P. (1986). Increasing returns and long-run growth. *Journal of Political Economy*, 4.

# Chapter 8
# Political Marketing App Based on Citizens

**Ruben Mizael Barrera**
*Autonomous University of Tamaulipas, Mexico*

**Jose L. Martinez-Rodriguez**
*Autonomous University of Tamaulipas, Mexico*

**Sanju Tiwari**
*Autonomous University of Tamaulipas, Mexico*

**Viridiana Barrera**
*Autonomous University of Tamaulipas, Mexico*

## ABSTRACT

*The chapter addressed what smartphones, mobile applications, programming languages, and mobile operating systems are. The development, implementation, and results obtained from mobile applications in the following areas are discussed in detail: educational platforms, citizen participation with the government, teaching the pronunciation of the English language, and citizen participation in public security. Android, being the main operating system for smartphones, is the most suitable for the development of mobile applications since it guarantees that it will have the greatest possible visibility and reach, not only for its popularity but for its presence in many devices other than cell phones and its "open system" feature so that everyone who wants it can develop compatible software.*

DOI: 10.4018/978-1-6684-6591-2.ch008

## INTRODUCTION

The smartphone is one of the few devices that have completely changed people's lives. In its beginnings the cell phone or mobile phone fulfilled the function of making and receiving calls from anywhere, in addition to issuing and receiving short text messages known as SMS. Today its basic functions are falling into disuse, however, in its time it was a complete revolution. In situations of risk, immediate communication with authorities or relatives was available. Little by little, more functions such as camera, video games, clock, agenda among others were added.

The second revolution took place when the cell phone became a smartphone. A whole range of possibilities were opened to the public, access to the internet anywhere, consultation of emails, digital agendas, taking high quality pictures and the possibility of sharing them instantly using social networks.

With the popularization of smartphones, costs were lowered, companies were forced to respond in the same way; Improving services, coverage areas, data upload/download speeds and flexible data and internet plans that adapt to the needs of users.

A side effect of the popularization of the smartphone was the reduction of the digital divide. In some countries the following transition took place: desktop computer, laptop computer, smartphone. However, in other countries the transition was different, people who never had access to a desktop or laptop directly acquired a smartphone given the simplicity of handling it, and the growing need for communication.

Along with the smartphone comes a new concept, the mobile application, popularly known as "app". In a simplified way, apps are programs that take advantage of the characteristics of the device, to offer facilities to the user. An example is online banking applications, with which it is already possible to check the balance of an account, among other things, without having to go personally to an ATM. While this is also possible from a computer, having the possibility of doing it from a device that fits in your pocket and anywhere with an internet connection, makes it the favorite option for many thanks to its unparalleled comfort.

The most popular applications are those that give access to social networks; however, it does not mean applications with other purposes cannot proliferate, applications whose purpose is to bring the citizen closer to the government, facilitate the use of university services to students or even applications for personal and educational development.

According to an article published by El Economista "In Mexico… at the end of 2018, a total of 121.8 million mobile lines were counted, of which an impressive number of 106.7 million are smart devices or smartphones." Given these numbers it is logical to think that the various government and school institutions would launch their own applications to take advantage of the potential scope they would have, although some states of the republic and governments have made available to citizens local applications to carry out procedures and consult information, it is not a situation that is universalized in countries. On the other hand, users constantly complain about performance, functionality, and reliability of these apps. That is in cases where cities or entities have official applications, there are cases where there is not this type of application at all (Aja, 2019).

In other words, it can be clearly seen that there is a shortage of applications and mobile content for public and school services that are of quality, reliable, intuitive and, above all, that really represent an improvement for the user.

## BACKGROUND

### Smartphone

A “smartphone” is an electronic device that functions like a mobile phone with characteristics like those of a personal computer. It is an element halfway between a classic mobile phone and a PDA since it allows you to make calls and send text messages like a conventional mobile but also includes features close to those of a personal computer. An important feature of almost all smartphones is that they allow the installation of programs to increase data processing and connectivity. These applications can be developed by the device manufacturer, by the operator or by a third party. Smartphones are distinguished by many features, among which touch screens, an operating system, as well as Internet connectivity and email access stand out. Full email support seems to be an indispensable feature found in all existing models and announced in 2007, 2008 and 2009. Other applications that are usually present are integrated cameras, contact management, multimedia software for music playback and viewing of photos and video clips and some navigation programs, as well as, occasionally, the ability to read business documents in a variety of formats such as PDF and Microsoft Office. A feature common to most smartphones is a contact list capable of storing as many contacts as free memory allows, in contrast to classic phones that have a limit to the maximum number of contacts that can be stored. Almost all smartphones also allow the user to install additional programs. (Alonso, Artime, Rodriguez, & Baniello, 2011)

### Android

Android is an operating system and software platform, based on Linux for mobile phones. Android allows programming in a Java framework, applications on a Dalvik virtual machine (a variation of the Java machine with runtime compilation) (Baez, Borrego, Cordero, & Cruz).

## Mobile Application

A mobile app, more commonly known as an app, is a type of app software designed to run on a mobile device, such as a smartphone or tablet. Mobile applications often serve to provide users with services like those accessed on PCs. Applications are generally small individual software units with limited functions. This use of the app's software was originally popularized by Apple Inc. and its App Store, which offers thousands of apps for iPhone, iPad, and iPod Touch. A mobile app can also be known as an app, web app, online app, iPhone app, or smartphone app (Techopedia, 2020).

## Programming Language

Computer programming languages allow us to give instructions to a computer in a language that the computer understands. The part of language that a computer can understand is called "binary." Translating the programming language into binary is known as "compilation." Each language, from C to Python, has its own distinct characteristics, although there are often commonalities between programming languages. These languages allow computers to process large, complex swaths of information quickly and efficiently (ComputerScience.org, 2020).

# RELATED WORK

## Security Applications

### PF Mobile, Mexico (Government Application)

In 2013 the Federal Police decided to launch an application to be able to issue complaints, in the format of voice message, photographs or videos without people having to share their identity (Villasana, 2013).

## Governance Applications

### App CDMX

App CDMX centralizes access to the existing applications of the different governmental entities of the public administration of the city. Its objective is to facilitate and improve the lives of citizens by making available information that is of interest to them (Google Play, 2020).

## School Applications

### PumaMovil

To improve the mobility of its students within its central campus, the National Autonomous University of Mexico (UNAM) launched the PumaMóvil application, developed by the Center for Complexity Sciences (C3).

This mobile application offers real-time information on the internal transport network that circulates around the city (Pumabús and Bicipuma); in addition to offering its students information about activities, calls, and services; and data on access spaces for people with disabilities (Sanchez, 2019).

## Language Teaching Applications

### Babbel

Babbel is a language learning app that is subscription-based to help people learn 14 languages offered on its platform. The format of the application is based on the curriculum with pre-recorded content and there is no live interaction (Rype, 2020).

### Duolingo

Duolingo is the most popular language learning platform and the most downloaded educational app in the world, with over 300 million users. The company's mission is to make education free, fun and accessible to all. Duolingo is designed to feel like a game. In addition to its core platform, the company created the Duolingo English Test (DET), an affordable and convenient language certification option that is accepted by more than 200 universities (Duolingo, 2018).

## Development

### Methodology Employed

It was decided to use the SCRUM methodology for the development of applications because it was the most appropriate for the purposes pursued. This methodology is ideal when what is sought is the delivery of products in short periods. The short duration of the iterations prevents development from stalling in some section, whatever the problem. By making an iteration of maximum two weeks, it is ensured that at the end of this period a prototype of functional software is delivered, this is thanks to the fact that it only focuses on adding what is necessary to meet the requirements indicated by the client. At the end of the iteration, the software is evaluated to find flaws and areas of opportunity in terms of design, functionality, and usability.

## Applications

### APPVISO

Development was carried out in one-month iterations or sprints over 4 months, each as follows:

**First Week:** The main idea of the application is described. A paper design is made for the graphical interface. The order and shape of the buttons and the location of the elements in general are determined.

**Second Week:** A flowchart is made for each of the buttons and elements, explaining what actions it performs and with which other elements it interacts or affects. A map is made where all the activities are shown (screens, sales, sections) describing what action or event is the one that leads to that place.

**Third Week:** The buttons are elaborated in some graphic design software. The graphical interface of the application is designed, the corresponding elements are added. All the aesthetic elements that are necessary are designed and elaborated, images, buttons or custom elements, proprietary sounds, the application icon, among others.

**Fourth Week:** Routines are created for each of the elements of the application. They are created in the different activities. Elements such as the permissions that the application must access to function properly are configured.

Once the sprint or iteration is finished, the product is presented for evaluation in the following aspects: aesthetics, design, functionality, and reliability.

The group of evaluators consisted of students.

Minimum requirements for using the application.

The following features or higher are required to use the app on Android devices:

- Operating System: Android 4.4.2
- Processor: Qualcomm MSM8916 Snapdragon 410 at 1.2 Ghz single core.
- RAM: 1GB
- Connectivity: WIFI, compatibility with 3g and 4g networks
- Sensors: GPS
- Resolution: 540 x 960

In case of not complying with any of the characteristics, compatibility or correct operation is not ensured (Ortiz-Rodriguez, Barrera, Villanueva, Medina, & Gauna, 2020).

### *Faculty and Students Engagement APP*

The development was carried out in two-week iterations, as follows:

**Week 1:** The main idea of the application is described. A design is made on the paper for the graphical interface that will be had. Determines the order and shape of the buttons, the location of the elements.

**Week 2:** The buttons are made in different programs. The interface of the application is designed, the corresponding elements are added. The different routines and instructions are programmed for each element of the application. A website is created to serve as an intermediary between the app and the university's News Feed.

The first step towards implementation was carried out through interviews with users (students and teachers) and with questionnaires to ensure the main services to be modeled.

The last step was to implement it in a university scenario, the case study population reaches 3000 students and professors (Zuñiga, Ortiz-Rodriguez, & Barrera, 2018).

### *Ubiquitous Information Systems for Government and Public Services*

The development was carried out in one-week iterations:

**Day 1.** The application is described. Fundamental characteristics are listed. A design is made on paper.

**Day 2.** Design of the graphical interface.

**Day 3.** The map of the application is made, functionality and correspondence of each button are detailed.

**Day 4.** Elaboration of buttons and images making use of various drawing and graphic design programs.

**Day 5.** Programming of the different routines and instructions for the correct functioning of the application.

**Day 6.** The product is presented to a group of users outside the development team to evaluate the application. The feedback is expected to include aspects of usability, how well it responds to pulsations, events in which it is cycled, mobile data usage.

**Day 7.** Analysis of data obtained by the evaluation group, as well as analysis of extra functionalities at the request of the group (Medina, Valdez, Guerrero, Ortiz-Rodriguez, & Abrego, 2019).

## Phonemapp

The development was carried out in two-week iterations:

**Week 1.** First, the essential requirements that the application must meet are analyzed. Paper design of menus, graphical interface, and navigation map. Selection of general aesthetics of the application. Obtaining sample graphic elements and multimedia elements. Determination of minimum requirements in which the program will run.

**Week 2.** Elaboration of the elements of the graphical interface. Integration of graphic elements. Programming routines for the correct functioning of the application. Integration of multimedia elements. Performing compatibility tests on various Android devices. Usability testing and bug finding.

## Results

### Appviso

As a result, an intuitive, responsive, and functional application was obtained that meets the expectations of functionality that were foreseen for a first version of the product.

The main function of the application is to grant the user the possibility of reporting a risk event to the public. The application allows users to view a real-time map of the city and specifically the surrounding area where the user is. This map shows reports from other users, warning of possible risk situations. Risk situations are displayed as different icons on the map, each identifying a different danger such as shootings, shootings, armed confrontations, robberies, tire punches among others. This in order that people have knowledge of the events around them and can protect themselves from danger. Also, when a person is a victim of one of these events or witnesses one can alert the public reporting what happened, for this it is enough to select the type of event that is developing, press the "Report" button and what was described above will happen.

The main menu of the application also allows to show historical and statistical data of the city, this in order that users are aware of which are the places where more criminal activities have been developed and what type they have been so that they take precautions.

The various screens or activities that make up the application will be explained below and in the following order: App logo on Android, Home screen, Main Menu, Statistics, Real-time status, and City map.

*Figure 1. Appviso icon*

Here it can be seen the icon of the application on the Android desktop, it is represented by a yellow speaker enclosed in a square, the icon is yellow to give the feeling of a warning. It is based on the amber color of the traffic lights, this is so to give the same type of message, caution.

*Figure 2. Appviso Home screen*

When the app is opened the first thing to be noticed is the home screen. The application welcomes users with the logo. This screen unfolds and takes users to the next menu automatically, the duration is 5 seconds.

Below the logo it can be seen the slogan "Helping one report at a time". This refers to the fact that for this application to be successful in its mission, the joint effort of all users is needed to report the various risk situations.

*Figure 3. Appviso main menu*

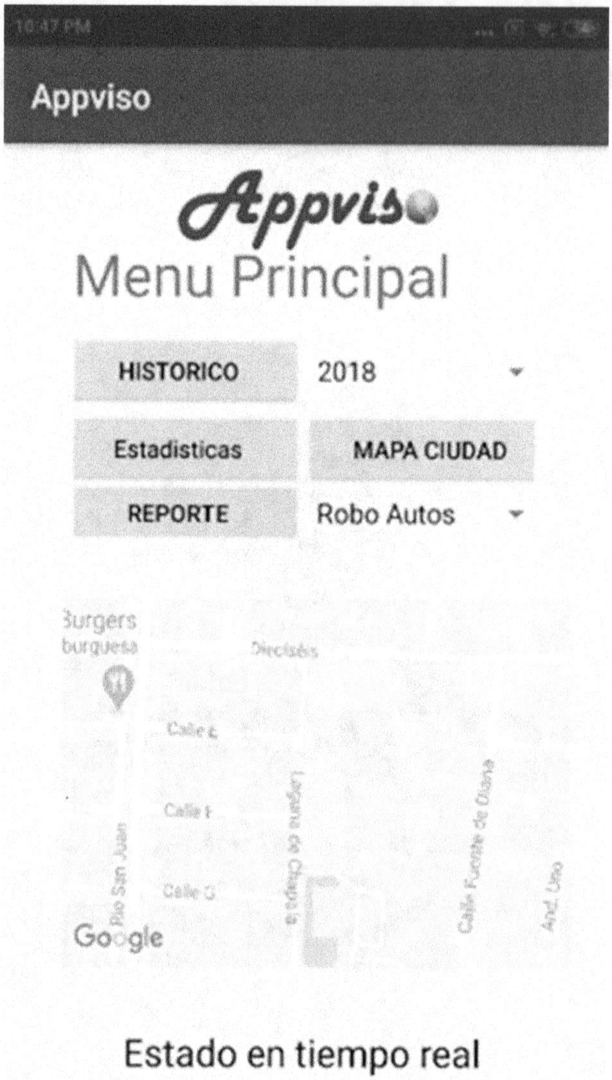


Main menu of the application. At the top is an alternative logo adapted to smaller spaces to match the aesthetics of the menu.

At the bottom of the screen is an element of type "Google Maps" this is an element of Google which is responsible for doing all the programming and processes necessary to display a Google map automatically. The function it fulfills is to display a map of the city oriented to show the surroundings in which the user is currently located. The map is programmed to always have the user's location as the central axis. In addition, this is where the iconography of the events of the city is shown, whether current or historical or those that the same user reports. Below the map is a label that identifies the status of the map, that is, if it is in real time or the last time it was updated.

Starting with the top-down and left-to-right description:

**"Historical" Button:** This element is a button with the text "Historical", it fulfills the function of displaying on the map the icons corresponding to the various eventualities that occurred in the city corresponding to the selected year. The icon is displayed on the map with the corresponding coordinate. The year to display is selected from a drop list item next to the button.

**Drop List "Year":** This element is a drop list (drop-down list) that is used for the user to select the year in which he wants to visualize the events that occurred in the city. The eligible years are as follows: 2018, 2017 and 2016. The icons displayed on the map are three different colors: blue for 2018, orange for 2017, and yellow for 2016.

*Figure 4. Iconography of the most reported events per year*

The previous figure displays all the symbology used in the icons; these are the ones that will appear on the map to identify risk situations. They are the following along with their acronyms:

**"Statistics" Button:** By pressing this button the user is taken to the "Statistical Data" screen, it has no other function.

**"City Map" Button:** This button has the function of taking to the "City Map" screen, it has no more functions.

**"Report" Button:** This button is used to report any eventuality in the city. First, select the event to report from the drop list to the right of the button. Once it is selected, press the button, when doing this the application takes the GPS data of the device, specifically speaking the coordinates of latitude and longitude and then shows on the map an arrow indicating that a situation is developing.

**Drop List "Events":** This drop list element is made to be used in conjunction with the previous button. Pressing the small triangle on the right displays a list with the following options: Carjacking, murder, shooting, blockade, armed people, illegal surveillance, persecution, tire punch and drug sales. These options correspond to the previous figure.

*Figure 5. Statistical data screen year 2016-17*

Datos Estadisticos

Año 2016

| EVENTO | OCTUBRE | NOVIEMBRE | DICIEMBRE |
|---|---|---|---|
| | | | |
| Autos Robados | 1 | 0 | 0 |
| Asesinados | 2 | 2 | 1 |
| Balacera (sdr) | 23 | 32 | 18 |
| Bloqueos | 14 | 2 | 1 |
| Crimen Organizado (co) | 0 | 2 | 1 |
| Daño Colateral | 0 | 1 | 0 |
| Fuerzas Armadas (FA) | 0 | 0 | 1 |
| Gente Armada(GA) | 7 | 6 | 8 |
| Halcon (GH) | 2 | 1 | 1 |
| Persecusion | 3 | 3 | 1 |
| Ponchallantas (PLL) | 7 | 14 | 11 |
| Venta de Droga | 0 | 0 | 0 |

Año 2017

| EVENTO | ENERO | FEBRERO | MARZO |
|---|---|---|---|
| | | | |
| Autos Robados | 0 | 1 | 1 |

*Figure 6. Statistical data year 2018*

| EVENTO | ENERO | FEBRERO | MARZO |
|---|---|---|---|
| | | | |
| Autos Robados | 1 | 2 | 0 |
| Asesinados | 3 | 0 | 6 |
| Balacera (sdr) | 44 | 27 | 39 |
| Bloqueos | 12 | 2 | 0 |
| Crimen Organizado (co) | 11 | 0 | 0 |
| Daño Colateral | 0 | 2 | 3 |
| Fuerzas Armadas (FA) | 1 | 0 | 0 |
| Gente Armada(GA) | 4 | 2 | 8 |
| Halcon (GH) | 0 | 0 | 0 |
| Persecusion | 2 | 1 | 3 |
| Ponchallantas (PLL) | 0 | 1 | 3 |
| Venta de Droga | 2 | 3 | 0 |

| EVENTO | ABRIL | MAYO | JUNIO |
|---|---|---|---|
| | | | |
| Autos Robados | 0 | 0 | 4 |
| Asesinados | 8 | 3 | 6 |
| Balacera (sdr) | 30 | 32 | 43 |
| Bloqueos | 0 | 4 | 1 |
| Crimen Organizado (co) | 0 | 0 | 0 |
| Daño Colateral | 0 | 0 | 2 |
| Fuerzas Armadas (FA) | 0 | 0 | 1 |
| Gente Armada(GA) | 3 | 2 | 7 |
| Halcon (GH) | 0 | 0 | 4 |
| Persecusion | 1 | 2 | 6 |

**"Statistics" Screen.** This screen is accessed after pressing the "Statistics" button. Here graphs are displayed with the statistical data of the different events that have arisen in the city. The categories shown are as follows: Stolen cars, murders, shootings, blockades, organized crime, collateral damage, armed forces, armed people, illegal surveillance, persecution, punches, drug sales. They are spread over years and each year is assigned a color for a simpler differentiation. Year 2016 is the first, with a single graph and no color. Year 2017 is the second year, it is identified by the color purple, there are three graphs in this period: the first from January to March, the next from April to June and the last from October to December. Finallythe graphs belonging to 2018, in this three graphs identified with the blue color, they cover from the month of January to September, each graph comprises three months.

*Figure 7. Using the "report" function*

**Main Menu, "Report" functionality.** This screenshot shows the change that occurs in the city map when a user presses the "Report" button. The application takes GPS data to put an indicator in the coordinates where the user is, it has an approximate accuracy of 20 meters. Other users will be able to visualize on their maps that there is an indicative of an event, if they are at a distance less than one kilometer the application will send an alert in the form of a message warning that they are close to an eventuality. The specific icon of the selected event is displayed on the map after half an hour.

*Figure 8. "City Map" screen*

**"City Map" Screen.** This screen is accessed by pressing the "City Map" button in the main menu of the app. In the figure above is displayed a full-screen map of the city. It is configured so that the central axis is the current location of the user, however, free navigation is avaliable. In this case, the historical data of the previous years is displayed on the map, this to observe how often and in what places a particular event has occurred.

## Faculty and Students Engagement App

At the end of the development, a simple, intuitive, and responsive application was obtained.

This application works as a meeting point that brings together all the online services and web pages that encompass the Autonomous University of Tamaulipas.

The university already has a group of varied services ranging from a newsletter, online campus, re-enrollment system among others. The problem that arises is that all these services are dispersed, they are not easy to find, the specific pages of each campus have links, but these are not easy to identify, in some cases such as the job bank, it is necessary to navigate in various menus to reach the corresponding link. While it is true that a simple search on the search engine of choice should be enough to reach the desired platform this is far from ideal.

*Figure 9. Faculty app main menu*

**Main Menu.** The main screen of the application. For the explanation, the screen will be divided into the following sectors: upper, upper center, lower center, and bottom.

**Upper Sector.** In this sector are the logo of the Autonomous University of Tamaulipas and on its right side, in this case, the logo of the Reynosa-Aztlan Multidisciplinary Academic Unit. In both cases they are image button elements, the function they fulfill is quite simple, when pressed they work as a link to the website of the university and when pressing the logo of the Aztlan unit, they lead to the website of that academic unit.

**Upper Central Sector.** In this area of the screen highlights the element known as web view, it is the rectangle with text that can be seen in the image. A web view allows to view web pages, it is basically a thumbnail window of a common browser. It is used to display the latest news to the user, it is configured to display the news section of the page of the specific academic unit for which the application was made. It allows to interact in a basic way with the page, the user can scroll down or up and press the different links it may contain, doing this will open the mobile browser application and proceed normally.

**Lower Central Sector.** In this sector six button-type elements with a circular appearance are shown, this to fit with the general aesthetics of the product. Here each button serves as a link to the specific page of each service, pressing a button opens the user's preferred browser and displays the corresponding page. By doing this, users save themselves the time of searching for the link on the university's homepage. The buttons belong to the following online services, from left to right and top to bottom: SIIA, UAT Tutorials, Online Campus (Black Board), UAT calendar, and Social Service.

**Lower Sector.** This sector fulfills the same function as the previous one, here the buttons lead to the various pages of the specific academic unit within social networks. This in order that students can access them quickly and conveniently.

## Ubiquitous Information Systems for Government and Public Services

The development resulted in a product that can be classified as functional and efficient according to the objectives that were set at the beginning.

This app serves as a central point for the different online services, links, web pages and in general all the content and contacts that the government of the state of Tamaulipas makes available to citizens. The problem is that many citizen communication portals with the government are not visible enough or are lost among the different menus and options that the pages give. Some are not even publicized.

With this application, all citizens are given easy access to these different services so that there is effective communication and constant participation.

The product obtained is responsive since all the buttons and links work correctly, intuitive since it has an easy-to-understand interface. It is reliable since no screen freezes occur or has loading screens, finally, it protects the privacy and anonymity of users since it does not ask for any type of information or store any user data. All information that is sent to the government is the same as they already ask for to make a report, the application does not collect additional data.

*Figure 10. Main menu ubiquitous information systems for government and public services*

**Main Screen.** When the application is opened, the screen in the previous figure is shown. The application does not have more activities, so a navigation map is not necessary. For the explanation, the screen will be divided into four sectors, which are: upper, upper center, lower center, and bottom.

**Upper Sector.** In this sector there is an element named image button. It is an element that behaves like an image container, when click on it, it behaves like a button. In this case it serves in the first instance as a banner to display the state government logos. When pressed, it opens the user's default navigation and redirects to the main page of the state government.

**Upper Central Sector.** This section introduces a view Web Part, this element is used to display the newsletter that is on the state government page. It allows basic interaction such as clicking links and filling out forms.

**Lower Central Sector.** Six button-type elements are found in this section. They serve to open links to the different services, pages, and portals of the government.

**Lower Sector.** In this sector there are five buttons that serve as a link to the different social networks of the government, YouTube, Twitter, Facebook, Instagram and additionally includes a button to make calls to government offices. The number to which it is dialed is the same as that available on the official government portal.

## Phonemapp

As a result of the development, a responsive, simple, and compatible application was obtained. The main objective was its compatibility with as many mobile devices as possible. This was achieved through using an API that was old enough to be compatible with 100% of devices in use, this could bring complications since the use of this limited the number of tools for development, however, this problem was solved by relying solely on simple programming, direct storage within the application of all sounds and iconography used. The weight of the app is increased by this decision; however, it is not disproportionate, additionally, the need to use the internet once the app was downloaded for the first time is eliminated.

All the icons used to make the graphic representation of the sounds were made considering the corresponding mnemonics and using the appropriate colors for a correct representation.

The menus and backgrounds were also developed to be consistent with a general aesthetic whose purpose is to recall a classroom, specifically, a chalk board.

In this version the phonemes that are available are categorized under the concept of "alphabet". In later versions, specific categories will be incorporated for different careers and levels of knowledge of English.

The application teaches people to correctly pronounce the English language by teaching the pronunciation of phonemes. It has a group of buttons, each button has a drawing for the user to associate the object of the drawing with the sound and in the upper left corner the graphic representation of the phoneme itself, once the icon is pressed, the phoneme is shown in a bar as it is, and while the phoneme is displayed the application plays the corresponding sound. When several icons are pressed in a row, the application can play all the sounds in a chain and thus show in a basic way how a phrase or word is pronounced.

*Figure 11. Phonemapp icon*

In the previous figure can be seen the icon in the Android interface that represents Phonemapp, in this case the text "InglesAPP" appears, which is the name that the application received when it was still in pre-beta phase and its official name had not been defined.

The design of the icon is based on a chalk board, according to the general aesthetics of the application that should remind a class room, this to give seriousness in the subject of teaching and learning. The letters P and H are observed, which are the first two letters of the English word "phonema" which means phoneme in Spanish. On its right side is the icon of a speaker or speaker that symbolizes that the important thing about the application is to teach about sounds.

*Figure 12. Phonemapp home screen*

**Welcome Screen.** When open the welcome screen will be displayed, this screen will be displayed for three seconds. The logo of the Autonomous University of Tamaulipas is appreciated, adapted to the blackboard style. There are no more functions on this screen.

*Figure 13. Phonemapp main menu*

**Main Menu.** After the welcome screen is closed, the main menu is displayed. In large letters the phrase "Main Menu" appears to denote the user where he is. At the bottom there are four elements of image button type, the buttons were stylized to look like something written on a blackboard. Each button corresponds to a category in which the different phonemes are grouped, pressing a button takes users to a different screen where the buttons of that category are displayed. In the alphabet category the phonemes are ordered by their common alphabetical order, so, first, it will be finding what sound represents the letter a, then the letter b and in this way until reaching the z.

The other buttons lead to a screen where phonemes are grouped by words or terms relevant to the specific career or topic, they are no longer individual letters.

The last button that has the text "Level 1" corresponds to a category that includes phrases and terms corresponding to the knowledge in English that a person of level 1, that is, basic, must learn to pronounce correctly.

*Figure 14. Phonemapp screen alphabet*

**Alphabet Screen.** This screen is accessed by pressing the "ALPHABET" button in the main menu of the application. A blank space on the screen is displayed, this is where the different phonemes will appear once one of the buttons that are at the bottom is pressed.

The first two buttons observed are "play" and "clear". The first button fulfills the function of reproducing all the phonemes that are shown at the top, one after the other in the case of being more than one, this to concatenate phonemes and form phrases. The second button present has the function of deleting the phonemes.

*Figure 15. Phonemapp, alphabet screen, simple phoneme*

The matrix of figures that can be seen at the bottom are button-type elements. Each button when pressed reproduces the sound corresponding to the phoneme it represents, also displays at the top the specific phoneme of the image, as shown in the previous figure. In this case the first button was pressed with an image of an apple and shows the phoneme at the top.

*Figure 16. Phonemapp, alphabet screen, phoneme string*

Figure 16 shows how several buttons have already been pressed and their phonemes are displayed at the top of the screen, so the user can press the "play" button to play them all in a chain and thus form a sentence.

*Figure 17. Phonemapp, alphabet screen, lower phonemes*

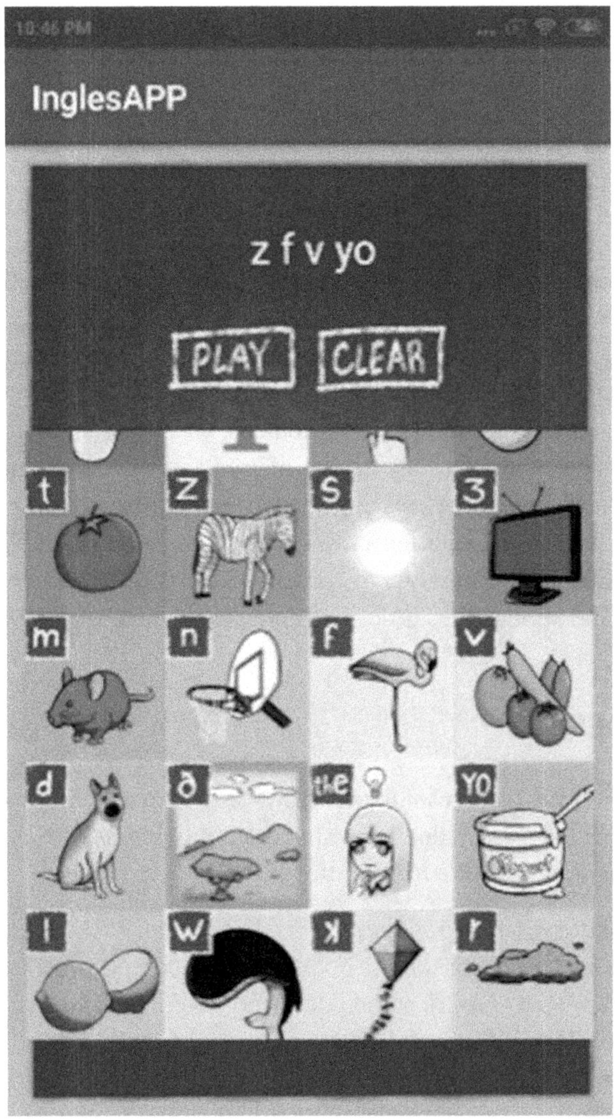

In Figure 17 can be appreciated how there are other buttons on the screen, these are accessed through scrolling down. Other phonemes are also shown at the top, these like the previous ones can also be played in chain with the use of the "PLAY" button.

## CONCLUSION

It can be observed with the results obtained from the applications that people are willing to participate in digital platforms that suppose a personal and community benefit when these are intuitive, functional, and easily accessible.

At present, the preferred device of the population for consultations on the internet is the smartphone, however, it is not usually used for procedures and similar unless the institution or agency has a dedicated application, mainly because the mobile version of the online portals is poorly designed, has restricted functions compared to the desktop version or there is no mobile version at all.

Widespread access to ubiquitous software is of vital importance today when it comes to applications whose objective is citizen participation in matters of security, governance, and access to educational resources.

The conversion of the various digital platforms from an exclusively desktop environment to a hybrid one where importance and optimization is given to mobile applications is a natural evolution of software. The trend is the development of software that allows the generation of content of all kinds on smartphones, not just consuming it. The applications described above contribute to this evolution.

## REFERENCES

Aja, A. (2019). *Un estudio sobre smartphones en México*. From Periodico El Economista S.A. de C.V.: https://www.eleconomista.com.mx/opinion/Un-estudio-sobre-smartphones-en-Mexico-20190320-0134.html

Alonso, A. B., Artime, I. F., Rodriguez, M. A., & Baniello, R. G. (2011). *Dispositivos Moviles*. From https://s3.amazonaws.com/academia.edu.documents/34258261/dispostivos_moviles_y_su_clasificacion.pdf?response-content-disposition=inline%3B%20filename%3DDispositivos_moviles.pdf&X-Amz-Algorithm=AWS4-HMAC-SHA256&X-Amz-Credential=AKIAIWOWYYGZ2Y53UL3A%2F20200

Baez, M., Borrego, A., Cordero, J., & Cruz, L. (n.d.). *Introduccion a Android*. E.M.E. Editorial.

ComputerScience.org. (2020). *Computer Programming Lenguages.* From Computer Science: https://www.computerscience.org/resources/computer-programming-languages/

Duolingo. (2018). *What is Duolingo?* From https://support.duolingo.com/hc/en-us/articles/204829090-What-is-Duolingo-

Google Play. (2020). From Google: https://play.google.com/store/apps/details?id=mx.gob.cdmx.adip.apps&hl=en

Medina, M., Valdez, D., Guerrero, P., Ortiz-Rodriguez, F., & Abrego, D. (2019). Ubicuos Citizens Services: A Mexican innovation study case at public sector. *PUBSIC 2019.*

Ortiz-Rodriguez, F., Barrera, R., Villanueva, V., Medina, M., & Gauna, A. (2020). *APPVISO: citizen digital communication to prevent risk events in real time.* From The 21st Annual International Conference on Digital Government Research (dg.o '20): 10.1145/3396956.3397019

Rype. (2020). *Babbel Review.* From RYPE, INC.: https://www.rypeapp.com/babbel-review/

Sanchez, J. (2019). *PumaMóvil, la app de la UNAM para que no te pierdas en Ciudad Universitaria.* From El Sol de Mexico: https://www.elsoldemexico.com.mx/metropoli/cdmx/pumamovil-la-app-de-la-unam-para-que-no-te-pierdas-en-ciudad-universitaria-4044444.html

Techopedia. (2020). *Mobile Application (Mobile App).* From Techopedia Inc.: https://www.techopedia.com/definition/2953/mobile-application-mobile-app

Villasana, J. (2013). *Presenta Policía Federal de México su aplicación para móviles.* From Xataka Mexico: https://www.xataka.com.mx/aplicaciones/presenta-policia-federal-de-mexico-su-aplicacion-para-moviles

Zuñiga, M., Ortiz-Rodriguez, F., & Barrera, R. (2018). Faculty and students engagement app: A Mexican digital strategy to improve university services. *ICERI*, 2927-2932.

# Chapter 9
# English as a Main Driver for International Business:
## A Northern Mexican Case

**Areli Y. Rodriguez-Elizondo**
*Autonomous University of Tamaulipas, Mexico*

**Ruben Mizael Barrera**
*Tamaulipas Autonomous University, Mexico*

**Viridiana Barrera**
*Tamaulipas Autonomous University, Mexico*

**Gerardo Tijerina**
*Tamaulipas Autonomous University, Mexico*

## ABSTRACT

*The city of Reynosa, Tamaulipas is full of maquiladoras that come from abroad to settle. In turn, these export mostly to the United States, because Reynosa is a border with the aforementioned country. Businesses and agreements have been created that until now have prospered successfully. Speaking English has long ceased to be an added value, and its importance is increasingly evident to professionals and companies, who see this language as the door to better job opportunities, expansion into the world, and new businesses. In Reynosa, there are about 125,945 students pursuing a university degree, among which are, to mention a few: bachelor's degree in economics, international trade, computer systems engineering, architecture, production systems engineering, industrial engineering, and mechatronics engineering, among others. The present research is expected to show the main factor as to why students from 18 to 23 years old in Reynosa, Tamaulipas between 2022 and 2023 are interested in learning English.*

DOI: 10.4018/978-1-6684-6591-2.ch009

## INTRODUCTION

In Reynosa the main source of work are the maquiladoras companies, which we have a variety of them, of different kind of products and services, these are foreign companies that are ubicated here due the low cost of labor, because they are foreign companies the owners are not Mexican, some of them are American (or Chinese), this due that Reynosa is in the border with the USA, because of that the majority of the exportations we do are to the already mentioned country, in this way is that exist the business relation between these two countries that have been doing business very well in the last couple of years.

Speak English is no longer a value added and its importance is more evident to the professionals and the companies, that see in this language the door to new labor opportunities, the expansion to the world and new business. Speak English open doors to you, if the companies see the potential on you, many times they send their employees to work in another country in their own companies.

In Reynosa are around 125,945 students doing a degree, some of them are economy, international trade, computational systems, mechatronic, etc.

This Project is focus on a real problem, the impact that English has in the hiring of students in Reynosa, it is relevant to study the impact that it has and if the students know the importance of it, as well as their interest of learn it. It is possible to solve this by an investigation could get to a conclusion.

With this work we hope to know if the students know English, if they are interested in learning it and if the know the importance that this language have could get to the labor area. This way the investigation is considered f, besides it would be a knowledge generator.

## DELIMITATION

### Spacial Delimitation

The present investigation will be focus in the city of Reynosa, Tamaulipas, this because this area is accessible to could make a study.

### Temporal Delimitation

This investigation will be focus between 2022 and 2023 (time that this investigation will last), this because we are going to be focus in the currently time that is relevant for this work.

## Social Delimitation

This investigation will be focus in students between the age of 18 – 23 that is the age that the students go into college and is when they still have the opportunity of learn English in time.

## Topic Delimitation

This investigation will be focus in if the students are interested in learning English and what are the factors that take them to want to learn it.

# RESEARCH STATEMENT

In Reynosa, Tamaulipas which is the main factor that take the students between the age of 18 – 23 between the years 2022 – 2023 to be interested in learn English?

## Hypothesis

In Reynosa, Tamaulipas the main factor that take the students between the age of 18 – 23 between the years 2022 – 2023 to be interested in learning English is because they know the importance that it has in the labor area.

## Justification

The present investigation is important and necessary due that people think that nowadays a huge part of students that are doing a degree do not know English, however, they do want to learn it, one of the possible factors is because they do know the importance of speak English has in the labor area.

This investigation is important to the young students because in this way people could be more conscious of the fact of the importance of English in the labor area and of the many doors this second language could open, and to make students not only have the intention of learn it but also to start learning it as soon as possible and practice it while they still have time.

## General Objective

The general objective this investigation has is determinate the main factor that takes students between the age of 18 – 23 in Reynosa, Tamaulipas between the years

2022 – 2023, to be interested in learning English is because the importance this language has in the labor area.

## STATE OF THE ART

### Main Factor

The main factor is the element or cause for which something happens, in a certain situation, whether desired or not, at different times of our life we have experienced moments or situations which predominate from a main factor, in this way we know that it is a concept with which we are related however we do not have it present all the time.

### Definition of Main Factor

According to Moreno (2017) the acquisition of a foreign language is affected by emotional variables such as motivation, anxiety and self-esteem. Stephen Krashen called it the affective filter hypothesis. Students assume a negative attitude towards the target language that interferes with their behavior because they feel vulnerable to a language in which they are not competent. After conducting a systematic descriptive study of the existing literature on the influence of the affective filter, emotional factors and affective strategies used in the acquisition of second languages, it was determined that they are natural psychological factors and tend to influence negatively when they are not provided with prepared teachers, methodologies appropriate to the level and reality of the students, In addition to the importance of strategies that focus on the humanistic part. This indicates the need for behavioral and methodological changes in teaching to facilitate the acquisition of a second language.

According to Sanchez (2017) insufficient time dedicated to study (TI) is the main factor of low performance in English according to students. The number 2 position is occupied by the lack of good study strategies (CE). In Position 3 and 4 are laziness or laziness to study (PE) and little or no knowledge of the subject (PC) respectively. These two factors are recognized as those that have the least influence on English failure.

According to Krause (2022) in everyday language, the word factor is generally used to name an element or cause within others that generate a certain effect, whether desired or not.

According to Bembimbre (2022) we understand by factors those elements that can condition a situation, becoming the cause of the evolution or transformation of the facts. One factor is what contributes to certain outcomes by falling on the responsibility for variation or change.

A main factor is the element that contributes to different aspects, for something to happen or not, and as mentioned above is present at different times of our lives.

## Decisions

Previously we saw what it is a factor, as a result of different types of factors we get to make decisions that impact our day to day, then we will see more thoroughly what it is a decision.

According to R. (2021) a decision is a response with will with which a conflict is resolved, or the fate of a thing or situation is determined. Perez Porto (2009) tells us that the decision is a determination or resolution that is made about a thing. Usually, the decision is a beginning to end a situation; that is, it imposes a change of state. For Chiavenato (2009) decision-making is a process that consists of making an analysis and choosing among several actions a course of action.

As it could be deduced a decision is vital in our life, and this must be thought of thoroughly since it can harm or help us, in addition to being taken on time.

As discussed above, all decisions influence our lives, whether positive or negative, from the most insignificant decision to the most important. B. (2018) tells us about the constant making of decisions that we make in our lives from the simplest as what we are going to eat today, what we are going to use, to the most important ones such as what we are going to do in our lives, take that job opportunity, etc., and how these from the smallest to the biggest can change and have a great impact on our lives, could change it for better or worse forever.

According to Rojas (n.d.) when the outcome of a decision depends on the course of action, we change one or more factors of the situational problem in order to cause a desirable change in some other factor of it. We will succeed if we can know the behavior about the interactions between the components of the problem.

Posada (n.d.) tells us that a decision made in time gives us the opportunity, however, if we do not do it in due time the universe will take care of taking it for us.

A decision made in time composes the control and knowledge of several factors on a personal level, such as realizing what you are doing, how and what you are doing it for.

Most young students have the most important decisions of their lives that they have to make at a certain moment, which determines much of their life.

According to Rossana (2021) a student is any subject who, within the academic field, has as his main occupation to study. It is therefore a person who is dedicated to the deep understanding of different topics that may serve you in the future.

According to Perez Porto (2008) student is a word that allows to refer to those who are dedicated to the apprehension, implementation and reading of knowledge about some science, discipline or art. It is usual for a student to be enrolled in a formal study program, although he can also dedicate himself to the search for knowledge autonomously and informally.

Redalyc (2022) tells us that, in short, students include, in turn, a large part of youth defined by living conditions that go beyond the university itself, and they are also students proper, defined by particular study conditions.

Vigotsky (2022) describes the student as an active participant with a lot of potential for the teaching-learning process, but this must be formed through learning experiences that favor social interaction.

A student has the responsibility to fulfill their obligations in school, most of the students are made up of youth, whether they are studying university or private studies. There are several types of students, each of them has its own way of being and its own way of learning, which must be identified in order to better acquire the knowledge that is objective.

According to Martos (2022) there are 13 types of students. According to Staff (2019) there are 4 different types of students that will be thoroughly seen below. Four types of students according to Vazquez (2022):

In this way, by knowing all these types of students and studying each of them in depth, you can get to identify when you are a teacher and in this way be able to help the student to acquire better knowledge, if on the contrary the student is self-taught, he can identify himself and, in this way, create an adequate curriculum.

## Second language

Speaking a second language, whatever you want to learn has its degree of complexity, however, learning any of them enriches us in many ways since you also learn from new cultures and in this way we know more from around the world.

According to Ribeiro Guevara (2021) a second language is the one spoken by a person without it being their native language, more specifically it is the language that a person learned after having developed their native language during their childhood.

According to Martin Martin (n.d.) the denomination of a second language is not very precise, because it includes not only a second language but also a third or fourth, it refers in short to any language that is not the native language, so second language is equivalent to target language.

Nordquist, ThoughtCo (2020) tell us that a second language is any language that a person uses other than a first or native language. Contemporary linguist and educators commonly use the term L1 to refer to a first or native language, and the term L2 to refer to a second language or a foreign language that's being studied.

A second language is one that a person learns after mastering his native language, and he uses it to learn that second language he wants to know.

The benefits obtained from learning a second language are many, from physical, mental, social and even work.

According to Runiewicz (2016) the research shows that there are many benefits of speaking additional languages. Having a second language appears to have a very positive impact on your brain, improves your creativity and increases your awareness and cultural understanding.

In a recent review, Li et al. (2014a) examined neuroanatomical changes in the brain as a function of L2 experience and training, relating these findings to the literature on functional brain activations for L2 tasks. Several studies have specifically focused on the effects of L2 training on brain structure in response to intensive L2 training over the course of several months, including increased cortical thickness (CT) and gray matter volume (GMV) in the inferior frontal gyrus (IFG; Hosoda et al., 2013; Mårtensson et al., 2012; Stein et al., 2012), middle frontal gyrus (MFG; Mårtensson et al., 2012), temporal superior gyrus (STG; Mårtensson et al., 2012), and former temporal lobe (Stein et al., 2012). Notably, these structural brain changes may be dependent on continued practice for long-lasting effects: Hosoda et al. (2013) analyzed participant's gray matter volume one year after L2 training and found that participants who continued practicing in the L2 showed increased gray matter volume in the right IFG, whereas gray matter volume in this structure for those who did not practice their L2 returned to pretraining levels. This is perhaps one of the most convincing findings in support of L2-dependent neuroplasticity.

Learning a second language stimulates our brain, even helps us to better master our creativity and of course the way to communicate even in the native language.

English is one of the many languages that exist in the world, however, this is the universal language, with which all the habitants of the world communicate, when making work meetings, in tourism, on airplanes, etc. (Potter, 2022) The English language is an Indo-European language in the West Germanic language group. Modern English is widely considered to be the lingua franca of the world and is the standard language in a wide variety of fields, including computer coding, international business, and higher education. (Nordquist, 2020) The term "English" is derived from *Anglisc*, the speech of the Angles—one of the three Germanic tribes that invaded England during the fifth century. The English language is the primary language of several countries, including Australia, Canada, New Zealand, the United Kingdom and many of its former colonies, and the United States, and the second language in a number of multilingual countries, including India, Singapore, and the Philippines.

English belongs to everyone. English is everything and nothing. English is not just a language, with a magnificent literature written in it, but an evolving construct which draws the globe together. English is big enough for different people to see it in different ways. All three presenters like to read it, write it, and teach it. Alas we all must test it too (Hands, 2019).

English is a language spoken in different countries and is used as a universal language, with which all those who speak different languages can communicate, it is a magnificent language that enriches us in many different ways.

Speaking English is very important today in order to continue communicating with the world, to be able to expand and leave the comfort zone and thus seek new opportunities and adventures.

Knowledge of English is a required skill in many high performing companies. Individuals who can communicate in this language have vast employability opportunities. Plus, they are not only tied to national market. They can look for their dream job across many different countries (Bravo, 2022).

English have impacted the job market in a huge way. Many businesses these days consist of international teams which work remotely. It accelerates performance of companies and improves overall employability for those with knowledge of this language.

English has had a huge impact on international education (Bravo, 2022). It is currently mandatory subject in most schools across the world and for good reason, as some of the world best universities teach lessons in this language. English can also help students in their personal lives. Learning a new language can help broaden student's minds, while also help them develop emotional skills. As we already mentioned, it provides job opportunities and help people communicate through the internet (Bravo, 2022). English has a huge impact on globalization, as it allows all of us to speak in one common language. This is something unique that has never been possible before in history. We are able to communicate and understand each other's point of view, which supports trade, international dialogue and cooperation. People are now roaming freely across countries, English being global language allows them to look for help on airports or tourist information points.

English is the language of business, in the era of globalization many companies decided to expand to foreign markets (Bravo, 2022). This is not an easy task, and requires a deep search for possible partners and knowledge of local law, etc. English allows swift communication between both parties involved.

Job opportunities are what open doors and help to scale to better areas, through new experiences and better conditions. Baptista (2019) defines job opportunity as that which refers to the convenience of a context and the confluence of a space and an appropriate time period that is desired to obtain a benefit or fulfill an objective. Opportunities, therefore, are the instants or deadlines that are propitious to perform an action.

Nowadays this concept is used specially to refer to professional or work opportunities, referring to the chances that a person must improve their situation at work. Team (2021) says that career opportunities refer to any opportunities that take you closer to your career goals. This can be a job, an internship opportunity or a training programmer that helps you excel in your career. You may have opportunities to advance your career within an organization or you may take a job in a different company for career advancement. Some people build their career in a particular industry, such as construction or IT, while others may work in different sectors throughout their career.

According to Fernandez (2022) career opportunities refer to any opportunity that brings you closer to your career goals. This can be a job, an internship opportunity, or a training program that helps you excel in your career.

Career opportunity, by definition, refers to a particular job that can be a steppingstone to higher ambitions. Jimenez (2022) tells us that career opportunities refer to any opportunity that brings you closer to your career goals. This can be a job, an internship opportunity, or a training program that helps you excel in your career.

Job or career opportunities are those that help an individual climb the career ladder through something that makes him stand out from other employees or candidates.

Career or job opportunities help us grow both professionally and in our lives in different ways.

Indeed Editorial Team (2021) says that It's important to take advantage of career development opportunities for several reasons. Here are some key examples of why career development opportunities are so important, regardless of your profession:

- Introduce you to new areas of professional interest:

By taking part in career development opportunities, you could potentially identify one or more alternative career paths that align you with your interest and professional goals.

- Ensures you stay motivated and inspired:

Partaking in career development opportunities helps remind you of your goals and why you're working in a particular job field. This further helps enhance your current job motivation to preform to the best of your ability and reach new milestones.

- Provides you with a sense of fulfillment:

When you stay at one job for a long period of time or consistently work in the same role job, you might start to long for a new challenge. This is when career development opportunities can help you. You could achieve new qualifications and take the next step in your career to a role that gives you the revised sense of fulfillment in your personal and professional life.

- Helps guide your job search decisions:

Through career development opportunities like networking, you may learn about employers with job openings to apply for. Achieving advanced certifications also allows you to expand your job search to more senior o specialty roles.

Sarokin (2020) tell us the follow benefits of career development:

- **Evaluation:** Understanding one's long-term goals, capabilities and gaps in experience or education, usually through the creation of a personalized medium-range or long-range plan.
- **Mentoring:** Meeting regularly with a senior leader in the organization who can help guide your developmental activities and solve professional problems as they arise.
- **Shadowing:** Spending a fixed period of time, such as a day or a week, following senior personnel throughout their workday to learn how work is carried out at the upper levels of the organization.

Abinaya (n.d.). gives us the follow benefits of a career development:

1. Provides equal opportunity employment

When considering a career development programme, there is the possibility of equal opportunity jobs since these programmes define each person on their merits. Highly efficient individuals and the results shown by the individual are used as a criterion for their growth rather than other criteria, demonstrating equal opportunity.

2. Improves quality of work-life of employees

Career Development assists workers in learning better working practices, work ethics, and other key aspects of the job.

3. Increases the skill of the employees

If an employee participates in a career development program, his or her skills will grow. These programs aim to improve different aspects of a worker's life, allowing them to perform better at work.

4. Reduces attrition of employees

A career development program helps to improve employee satisfaction and, as a result, reduces the number of individuals who plan to leave the organization.

5. Improves the use of the employees

Employees should learn more about their jobs and grow their skills through career growth. It also assists them in effectively managing their time and ensuring that the use of workers increases over time.

6. Improves the organization's overall

Employees have gained a better understanding of the firm's different operations as a result of a career development program. As a result, information sharing and work ethics tend to strengthen the organization.

7. Cost reduction strategies of the organization

Organizational cost-cutting techniques are, once again, extremely risky for those who are not prepared to advance to the next level. If corporations must reduce their operating expenses, the job of those persons who are unemployed or have not performed satisfactorily in the past is jeopardized. Employees must constantly update themselves and demonstrate their talent to stay in organizations for an extended period.

8. Information Technology Innovations

Change is often brought about by continuous improvements and advancements in technology. Some people can keep up with evolving technology and are often eager to learn and implement new IT applications, while others exhibit extreme resistance, which is unacceptable to organizations. Employees must stay up to date and demonstrate a willingness to embrace and mould themselves in response to changes.

9. Economic Downsizing

The most significant factor affecting the careers of millions of people is economic downsizing. Organizations' jobs are slashed, and only the fittest of all workers survive. Employees who consistently learn new and improved skills are less likely to be negatively impacted by economic conditions than most people.

10. Delayering

De-layering means work reclassification. This is an organisational change effort in which a corporation chooses to reclassify jobs in a broader sense. However, old reporting lines remain in place to keep management in control, so certain jobs may be eliminated or reduced during the process. Individuals who are not qualified enough to be transferred to another job of a different nature must once again leave the group.

Taking courses in different ways to improve or develop the career that was studied helps to have an added value in order to excel in your work area and this brings you different benefits both in your career and in your life.

## METHODOLOGY

The scope is the Reynosa City in Tamaulipas, and research is looking to the main factor that influences young people aged 18-23 between the years 2022-2023 if that they are interested in learning English? They believe is that in Reynosa, Tamaulipas the main factor that influences young people from 18 to 23 years old between 2022 – 2023 for them to be interested in learning English is because they know the importance that has this second language to obtain a job opportunity.

To develop the project, it is intended to apply as a Likert Research Method. The value and Likert estimation scales are those that are used to determine the perception of some variable. It has been widely used in social studies where perceptions about a specific topic are collected (Song of Ghent, 2020).

The present research is quantitative, quantitative methods, the main characteristic of quantitative data is that they are composed of information that can be, in one way or another, quantifiable. In other words, we can convert quantitative data into numbers, figures and graphs and process them using statistical procedures. When we do quantitative analysis, what we are usually interested in finding out is how much or how many cases there are of whatever interests us (Rasinger, 2020).

In the present work a descriptive and exploratory research will be carried out, in the Exploratory LCANCE They study problems or factors that have been little analyzed or that still have contradictory data, identify promising fields of research, analyze problems with a new perspective and in descriptive scope specify properties of variables, define and measure variables, quantify and show the dimensions of a phenomenon or context (Alvarez Rico, 2020)..

In turn it will be field research since according to Sanchez (2019), field research is the collection of new data from primary sources for a specific purpose.

## Theoretical Framework

First, an analysis was made to the hypothesis question and the hypothesis in Reynosa, Tamaulipas, what is the main factor that influences young people aged 18 - 23 between 2022 – 2023 so that they are interested in learning English? In Reynosa, Tamaulipas the main factor that influences young people from 18 to 23 years between 2022/2023 for them to be interested in learning English is because they know the importance who has this second language to get a job opportunity. From this a list of nouns was extracted to begin with the realization of the theoretical framework.

After having the list of nouns, information began to be collected through google, using filters such as google scholar where truthful and reliable information could be found.

After finding the definitions of the nouns, they were read, the most important thing was underlined and with that paraphrases were formulated, there are different definitions on paraphrase in a general way, it is understood by it, the interpretation by the writer of an idea presented by another author, that is, it constitutes the personalization of an idea of an author or base text (Castillo Cuevas, 2020) as well as synthesis, according to Quesada (2020) synthesis is the inverse operation, which mentally establishes the union or combination of the previously analyzed parts and makes it possible to discover relationships and general characteristics between the elements of reality. It is based on the generalization of some characteristics defined from the analysis. The analysis is produced by synthesizing the properties and characteristics of each part of the whole, while synthesis is performed on the basis of the results of the analysis. In research, one or the other procedure may predominate at a certain stage.

From this, all the different definitions were compared and thus a general personal conclusion was obtained about everything that could be acquired from the theoretical framework carried out and how it relates and helps the present research.

## Operation of Variables

The research problem for this research is in Reynosa, Tamaulipas, what is the main factor that influences young people from 18 to 23 years old between 2022-2023 so that they are interested in learning English? And the possible result is that in Reynosa, Tamaulipas the main factor that influences young people from 18 to 23 years old between 2022-2023 so that they are interested in learning English is because they know the importance of this second language to be able to obtain a job opportunity. To determine the variables, an analysis of the hypothesis was made, in which dependent variables and independent variables were divided. The dependent variable is the main factor that influences them to be interested in learning English and the dependent variable is because they know the importance of this second language in order to obtain a job opportunity.

From the variables of disaggregated the indicators, for the dependent variable is: young people. For the independent variable is: other reasons why they might be interested in learning English.

With the indicators it was possible to break down items for every indicator. For the youth indicator the items are: age, if they can speak English, level of knowledge of the English language, in case they do not know, do they want to learn it? For the indicator reasons why they are interested in learning English the items are: because they like it, because they need the credits of English to obtain their degree, because their parents instilled them in them, because the job opportunities.

## Design of Instruments to Collect Data From Variables

According to the table of operationalization of the variables of the hypothesis, the most appropriate interrogation research technique was selected as the most appropriate because it is the best way to formulate the data that we want to know for the present research.

From this chosen research technique, it is considered that the appropriate research instruments are survey and interview, considering them more useful because the application of these is easy and the interpretation of the results will also be easier with the instruments already mentioned.

According to the table of operation of the quantitative variables, we proceed to design the appropriate instruments for the items, determining that for all items the appropriate instrument is survey, due to its easy handling and also easy application for both the interviewer and the respondent.

The poll will be as follows: Item: knowledge of the language; Do you know English? Level of knowledge of the English language?; item: forms of learning; Did you learn by yourself?, Did you learn in school?, Item: obstacles; Haven't you learned for economic reasons? Have you not learned because you have not found the right course for you?, Have you not learned because the methodology of the existing courses are not adequate?, motivating items; Do you want to learn or did you learn because you like it?, Do you want to learn or did you learn because you need the credits to obtain your degree?, Do you want to learn or did you learn because your parents instilled it in you?, Do you want to learn or did you learn because of the importance of this language to obtain a job opportunity?

## Universe, Population, and Sample

In the present research, a universe will be taken into account, which is defined as elements (people, objects, programs, systems, events, database...) global, finite and infinite (Condori-Ojeda, 2020), so the universe of this research is determined as the number of students studying a university career.

In turn, the population is defined as accessible elements or unit of analysis that belong to the special field where the study is developed (Condori-Ojeda, 2020). For the present research, it is determined as the population of students between the age of 18-23 years of the current year 2023.

For the present project the type of simple random sampling is applicable, it ensures that each element of the population has the same probability of being chosen. From an available sample frame (census of the population where all the coded units appear) the selection is made using tables or procedures based on random numbers (Immaculate, 2020). It is understood as a representative sample of the population, with the same general characteristics of the population (Condori-Ojeda, 2020). As margin of error is defined as the interval in which I expect reality to be (Inmaculada, 2020). For the present investigation the margin of error to be used will be 5%.

This research is a case study because it is a current case of real life, with the results obtained it will be possible to define the priorities of the students, if the system that is being used is adequate for the correct learning, etc.

## The Analysis and Interpretation Procedure

The surveys will be applied online, to make it more practical both for the respondent and for those who are applying it, also helping the environment by not doing them on paper.

The analytical method that was chosen for the present research is the inferential statistical analysis is one that deals with inferring important conclusions of a population from a representative sample. This inference is not entirely accurate; For this reason, in this type of statistic, probabilities must be taken into account to establish conclusions. Statistical inference also deals with structuring a representative sample of the population under study, to design models, inferences, trends, and predictions about their behavior from the randomness of the observations (Villegas-Zamora, 2019), being the reason why it is the most suitable for present research.

The procedure that will be used to interpret the results of the surveys will be through graphs made in the Excel 2017 program, in turn, the media will be taken and in this way have a more accurate answer.

This research will be approved if most of the answers of university students infer the question with the item that refers to choosing to study and learn English due to its importance to obtain a job opportunity. On the other hand, it will be taken as dis-proven if it is the case that derives from any other item, more specifically that university students learn English because they like it, because they need the points to obtain their degree, or because their parents instilled them in them.

## CONCLUSION

This research aims to discover students thinking about English language and it importance in professional career.

With the above concepts you can better understand this research, and the way in which they relate to each other, can be understood why English is an important language and the great usefulness it has in our lives, even mostly for better job.

## REFERENCES

Abinaya. (n.d.). *OpenEducationPortal*. Obtained from https://www.openeducationportal.com/importance-of-career-dev elopment/

Alvarez Rico, A. (2020). *Classification of investigations*. University of Lima, Faculty of Business and Economic Sciences, International Business Career. Obtained from https://repositorio.ulima.edu.pe/bitstream/handle/20.500.12724/10818/Note%20Acad%c3%a9mic%202%20%2818.04.2021%29%20-%20Clasificaci%c3%b3n%20of%20investigations.pdf?sequence=4&isAll owed=y

B. (2018). *The Universal*. Academic Press.

Baptista, J. (2019). *LinkedIn*. Obtained from https://es.linkedin.com/pulse/opportunity-laboral-jennifer-baptista-cal

Bembimbre, C. (2022). *Definition ABC*. Obtained from https://www.definitionabc.com/general/factores.php

Bravo, J. (2022). *The impact of english language in our society*. Obtained from TraslateDay: https://www.translateday.com/impact-english-language-in-our-society/

Castillo Cuevas, M. (2020). *Paraphrase. Elements for its writing.* Obtained from https://d1wqtxts1xzle7.cloudfront.net/64576591/PARAPHRASIS__ELEMENTS_FOR_ITS_REDACT%C3%93N.-free.pdf?1601589506=&response-content-disposition=inline%3B+filename%3DParaphrasis_Elements_for_its_redaction.pdf&Expires=1675718922&Signature=KF1Lfg~oNdZ7E31QKG

Chiavenato. (2009). *Library.* Obtained from https://1library.co/article/types-factors-factors-influence-take-decisions.q0x2l99q

Condori-Ojeda, P. (2020). *Universe, Population and Sample.* Workshop.

Fernandez, A. (2022). *ILJobsCareer.com.* Obtained from https://iljobscareers.com/what-is-a-definition-of-career -opportunity /

Hands, T. (2019). *Attain.* Obtained from https://attain.guide/features/what-is-english

Immaculate, G. G. (2020). *Research design: Questionnaire and sample.* Academic Press.

Indeed Editorial Team. (2021). *Indeed.* Obtained from https://www.indeed.com/career-advice/career-development/career-development-opportunities#:~:text=Why%20is%20it%20important%20to%20take%20advantage%20of,4%20Helps%20guide%20your%20job%20search%20decisions%20

Jimenez, J. (2022). *JobsCareerQuestions.com.* Obtained from https://jobscareerquestions.com/what-is-the-definition-of-professional-opportunity /

Krause, G. (2022). *Definition.* Obtained from https://definition.com/factor/

Martin Martin, J. (n.d.). *The maternal language in the learning of a second language.* Seville University.

Martos, C. (2022). *Fivenews.* Obtained from https://www.fivenews.com/types-of-students/

MorenoK. (2017). Obtained from https://d1wqtxts1xzle7.cloudfront.net/54189891/MORENO_KARINA_-_FILTER_AFCETIVE-free.pdf?1503257845=&response-content-disposition=inline%3B+filename%3DEMOTIONAL_FACTORS_THAT_INFLUENCE_IN_FIL.pdf&Expires=1675286199&Signature=GVrtWAGzI2npbxhtrOOT66a9u6kMI~

NordquistR. (2020a). *ThoughtCo.* Obtained from https://www.thoughtco.com/second-language-1691930

NordquistR. (2020b). *ThoughtCo.* Obtained from https://www.thoughtco.com/what-is-the-english-language-1690652

Perez Porto, J. G. (2008). *Definition.* Obtained from https://definition.of/student/

Perez Porto, J. G. (2009). *Definition.* Obtained from https://definition.of/factor/

Posada, J. (n.d.). *I think that.* Obtained from https://www.thecolombian .com/blogs/ithinkthat/tag/effects-of-the-decision

Potter, S. (2022). English language. In *Encyclopedia Britannica.* Obtained from de https://www.britannica.com/topic/English-language

Quesada, A. M. A. (2020). *Theoretical research methods: Analysis-synthesis, induction-deduction.* Obtained from https://www.researchgate.net/publication/347987929_METHODS_THEORICS_OF_RESEARCH_ANALYSIS-SYNTHESIS_INDUCTION-DEDUCTION_ABSTRACT_-CONCRETE_AND_HISTORIC-LOGIC

R. (2021). *Concept.* Obtained from https://conceptdefinition.of/decision/

Rasinger, M. S. (2020). *Qualitative research in linguistics.* Akal S.A.

Redalyc. (2022). *Philosophy.* Obtained from https://. co/general/definition-of-pupil-according-to-authors/#:~:text=student%20is%20a%20what%20what%20provie%20of%20pupils%20pupils%2C.is%20a%20pers%20that%20that%20is%A1%20dedicated%20to%20learning.

Ribeiro GuevaraS. (2021). *YuBrain.* Obtained from https://www.yubrain.com/humanities/linguistic/second -language/

Rojas, A. (n.d.). *Press Room*. Obtained from https://www.aiu.edu/Spanish/publications/student/spanish/TAKE%20OF%DECISIONS%20-%20Decisions%20Making.html#:~:text=when%20the%20result%20of%20a%20decisi%C3%B3n%20depends%20of,about%20the%20intetactions%20between%20the%20components%20of%20problem

Rossana, A. (2021). *Concept.* Obtained from https://conceptdefinition.of/student/

RuniewiczM. (2016). *LinkedIn*. Obtained from https://www.linkedin.com/pulse/advantages-speaking-second-language-mark-runiewicz#:~:text=The%20research%20shows%20that%20there%20are%20many%20benefits,creativity%20and%20increases%20your%20awareness%20and%20cultural%20understanding

SanchezA. (2019). *Question pro.* Obtained from https://www.questionpro.com/is/research-of-field.html

SanchezA. B. (2017). Obtained from https://www.researchgate.net/profile/Raquel-Morquecho-Sanchez/publication/351094563_Volume_1_Number_2_-octuber_-dicember_-2017/links/6085f695907dcf667bc457bc/Volume-1-number-2-octuber-dicember-2017.pdf#page=35

SarokinD. (2020). *Chron*. Obtained from https://work.chron.com/advantages-career-development-training-6783.html

Song of Ghent. (2020). Likert scale: An alternative to elaborate and interpret an instrument of social perception. *Magazine of High Technology and Society, 38.*

Staff. (2019). *Got from what are the main types of students?* https://www.iwanttolearnlanguages.com/training-online/main-types-of-students/

TeamI. E. (2021). *Indeed*. Obtained from https://in.indeed.com/career-advice/career-development/what-are-career-opportunities?fbclid=IwAR0mX2FetEtblNo-EJm4P7C6QqMuscrbp1SfmjY3YL-gXTqHJ0S0ahpDfy8

VazquezS. (2022). *Gostudent.* Obtained from https://insights.gostudent.org/is/types-of-students

Vigotsky. (2022). *Filosofia.* Obtained from https:// filosofia.co/general/definition-of-student-according -to-authors/#:~:text=Student%20is%20a%20concept%20thta%20com es%20from%20alumnus%2C,is %20a%20person%20that%20is%C3%A1%20 dedicated%20to%20learnlng.

Villegas-Zamora, D. A. (2019). The importance of applied statistics for decision-making in Marketing. *Magazine Research and Business.*

# Chapter 10
# E-Government Success:
## An End-User Perspective

**Fernando Ortiz**
*Tamaulipas Autonomous University, Mexico*

**Sanju Tiwari**
*Tamaulipas Autonomous University, Mexico*

**Fatima Zahra Amara**
*Khenchela University, Algeria*

**Miguel Sahagun**
*High Point University, USA*

## ABSTRACT

*The objective of this research is to determine the critical success factors of a tax collector website in a country with an emerging economy. In the method, a questionnaire is applied to 488 taxpayers in Northeastern Mexico, and factor analysis is a statistical tool. The results show that the top five success factors are citizen satisfaction, service quality, information quality, ease of use, and confidence. The results show the need to adapt the technologies to the citizens for their better performance and usefulness, so the originality of the research is that there are few empirical studies in the country.*

DOI: 10.4018/978-1-6684-6591-2.ch010

## INTRODUCTION

The access and use of information technologies (IT) are substantial factors in the generation and distribution of data, information and knowledge, as they are key enablers in the organizational transformation, which together with the Internet, led the government to rethink the use of IT for better communication with citizens, businesses and other government entities. However, barriers arose such as lack of financing, technical personnel, resistance to change, poor technological infrastructure and legal issues such as privacy-data security (Wirtz et al., 2017). In other words, IT has forced governments to have tools that allow greater communication with citizens seen as taxpayers, users or customers of their services.

The common definition of electronic government (e-Gov) refers to the use of IT by the government to deliver information and services to citizens, businesses and public agencies (Horsburgh, Goldfinch and Gauld, 2011), in an attempt to facilitate access to government services in an efficient manner. In the same way, it improves transparency and efficiency in government with the use of electronic devices, which will serve both citizens and companies (Šimić, 2019).

The study of the direct acceptance of e-Gov services is in its beginnings, little is known about the attitude of citizens towards the various channels of service provision (Lamberti, Benedetti and Chen, 2014) and under the guideline from cost savings, using services and improving infrastructure by and for citizens, governments are trying to move traditional public service channels to more effective channels such as e-Gov (Ali, Mazen and Hassanein, 2018), but they need to ensure that their procedures are carried out with precision and quality for citizens, for this, they use IT and specifically the Internet.

The application of the e-Gov by itself is an innovation and at the same time a competitive advantage for all types of organizations and people, unfortunately in countries with emerging economies, not everyone has access to it. Gulati, Williams and Yates (2014) argue that the richest and most prosperous countries in the technological development of society are in a stronger position to respond to the demands of citizens, because there are still many of them who have never visited a Government website (Wang, 2014), so it is necessary to consider the technological culture of each country (Nguyen, 2016).

The lack of research on the public value of the e-Gov in industrialized countries and a total absence in countries with emerging economies has been determined (Twizeyimana and Andersson, 2019), often due to a common evil of governments in the world: inadequate infrastructure, non-existent service, low or no IT budget, software licenses and support, and difficulties in migration, integration and management of software and hardware (Ali et al., 2018), where there is little public awareness of the government data and information (Arwati and Verdania, 2019).

Therefore, it is necessary to detect those critical factors for success (CFS), in the e-Gov, these elements have been defined as those key areas of an institution that are essential to work in an adequate and coordinated way with the firm purpose of achieving the success. Public services are not left out of this context, their evaluation by governments is a current issue, which includes issues such as confidence, easiness of use, satisfaction, citizen technology, decision-making, security, privacy, risks, accessibility, utility, awareness, quality, among others. Osei-Kojo (2017) found that technological infrastructure and poor population development in emerging economies are serious weaknesses for their development. In Mexico, where this research takes place, it has been detected that it is the reduction of costs, personalization of the interface, efficiency in the processes, promotion of e-democracy, less corruption and better services quality (Luna-Reyes and Gil -García, 2014). Other elements are the value, effectiveness of the website, user needs and alternative sources of information (Wang, 2014), for this, transactions, transparency and interactivity are important factors that directly affect the e-Gov and indirectly confidence (Welch and Pandey, 2005), unfortunately in Mexico there are no important advances in terms of information transparency (Sandoval-Almazan, 2019).

Despite the lack of equal treatment of taxpayers in Latin America by governments that causes poor tax collection or evasion (Castañeda, 2017), many countries are looking for new ways to collect taxes and streamline bureaucratic processes for citizens, and with the help of information technology it has become a valuable means to eliminate tedious administrative processes and to some extent, corruption. In this sense, government authorities, and specifically tax authorities, should implement easy-to-use e-Gov solutions and motivate taxpayers and businesses to use them, which according to Wirtz et al. (2017), with the e-Gov it is possible to generate quality in the service, in the administration processes and the saving of costs and time for the benefit of the citizen and the companies that can lead to an increase in the receipt of taxes.

Based on the above, the research question consists of answering what are the key elements that citizens take into account to make constant use of the e-Gov? For this, the objective of this research is to determine the critical success factors of a tax collector website. To achieve the goal, the literature review of the most studied elements in the state of the art is carried out. Next, the research method based on the application of a questionnaire to taxpayers who make constant use of this governmental technological platform is described, a multivariate study is carried out through exploratory factor analysis, to end with the main contributions to knowledge.

## REVIEW OF LITERATURE

### Resources of the Citizens as Users

The possibility of accessing government services is now an advantage for citizens, but they require the appropriate telecommunications infrastructure from the government, which on many occasions affects the failure of the e-Gov, in addition, the *computational requirements* (hardware and software) reflect the degree to which users make efforts to acquire the necessary computer equipment to use a service, its absence is a barrier to the use of technology (Venkatesh, Chan and Thong, 2012).

It is precise to describe the relevant characteristics of users for the use of a Website, which include knowledge, skills, experience, education, training, and motor and sensory capacities (ISO, 1998); however, Venkatesh et al. (2012) indicate that few citizens consider *computational requirements*, most focus on other attributes, in addition, some results indicate the importance of an organizational strategy for the community in order to ensure Internet access, coordinate education and training and to support the use of the Internet to initiate participation in the e-Gov among the techno-disadvantaged.

Another important element is *computer skills*, which have been proven to increase online participation and users with a greater positive attitude and trained in technology more feasible to use the e-Gov (Lee and Porumbescu, 2019), and together with the IT experience, work experience and educational level influence satisfaction (Chopra and Rajan, 2016). In this sense, Van Deursen and Vaan Dijk (2009) indicate that citizens with a high level of skills in information and strategies will use it for their own goals, so they require: *i)* operational to handle the new media, *ii)* formal to the management of new media, *iii)* informational to search and select relevant information, and *iv)* strategic to use the information obtained and achieve certain goals. It is also true that if a country does not create the skills and resources required for the use and availability of the e-Gov to all citizens equally, the country cannot expect the same ability from them to adopt the technology (Shareef et al., 2011), consequently, it is understood that citizens with greater education will participate with greater commitment in e-Gov activities.

In addition to the above, *citizen support* refers to providing help from the e-Gov in assisting citizens in their requests for information or during their transactions (Papadomichelaki and Mentzas, 2012), which can be through chat on line, telephone, Facebook, Twitter, e-mail, among others, since if users do not find a service when they require it, they will feel that they are being treated unfairly (Shareef et al., 2011) and with adequate technical support, citizens may be able to carry out their operations in an autonomous way when they carry out activity in the services of the e-Gov.

Three fundamental issues have been proposed that governments must take into consideration if they want to evolve towards the e-Gov (Twizeyimana and Andersson, 2019): improved public services, improved administration and improved social value, including open government, improved ethical behavior and professionalism, confidence in government, better social value and well-being. Undoubtedly, the essential technological requirements of the users are necessary in order to have an efficient development in the use of a Website, which will allow them to make its use a normal activity, accept said technology and make more and better decisions.

On the other hand, the e-Gov is an Internet-based application, so data protection issues can be considered an important policy in the area (Wu, 2014), because the characteristics that distinguish the user for adoption of the e-Gov consists of the perception of *risk, security and privacy* (Kumar et al., 2007) especially when they are mobile payments (Liu et al., 2019). For this, security is defined based on what is proposed by Papadomichelaki and Mentzas (2012) who indicate that it is essentially the protection of citizens/users from the risk of loss of financial information or fraud, especially when it is protected with anonymity and the secure safeguarding of personal data.

Various scientific articles by e-Gov show that security and risk are predominant factors for your satisfaction and confidence (Aggarwal and Rahul, 2018), since government websites can collect large volumes of personal information that is almost always sensitive and may involve potentially, infringements of the privacy of information (Wu, 2014) and that by allowing users to access services from anywhere, many of the times without restrictions, can become an avalanche of both administrative and technical problems.

Likewise, it is well known that quality is a key element in any type of organization in today's globalized world, however, Nishant, Srivastava and Teo (2019) determined with the use of polynomial models that, for government websites electronic, both the agreement and the disagreement between the expected and perceived quality of the service of this technology, are positively associated with the intention of continuous use by the citizen.

Regarding the *information quality*, which in the literature review is considered to acquire this concept when it is accurate, timely, complete, relevant and consistent (Ritchi, Wahyudi and Susanto, 2015; Medina-Quintero et al., 2018) and Kumar et al. (2007) believe that the content, organization and presentation of the information (accurate, current, relevant, satisfactory, its compliance, its linking, complete, thorough, organized, timely) are potential contributors to create a perception of reliability that influences in the acceptance of the e-Gov by the user. In this sense, Li and Shang (2019) found a strong relationship between the quality of the service and the quality of the information, which becomes an important incentive to improve technology (quality) and people (service); in the end, the information quality is a predictor of the adoption of the e-Gov and is undoubtedly a goal to be reached immediately, which will ensure the harmonious development of the processes that are followed on the Website and which will have an impact directly in its efficient use (Wirtz et al., 2016), more precisely in the collection of taxes.

Regarding the *service, quality* it is aimed at the satisfaction that ensures the regular use of the e-Gov through its various clients or stakeholders such as citizens, companies and other public institutions, for this, Janita and Miranda (2018) determined four basic dimensions to measure the quality of electronic services: information quality, technical efficiency, privacy and communication, to which it is added that Belanche and Casaló (2015) found that the perceived quality of public electronic services has a positive effect on trust in public administration and the e-Gov.

The success of the initiatives to put into operation an e-Gov Website are intermittent until the citizens adopt the services; in this sense, Osei-Kojo (2017) argues that service quality is created when efficiency is increased, costs are reduced, the service is always available and citizen satisfaction is achieved. In the same way, three aspects of the quality of the electronic service have been detected for its adoption by citizens: social influence, the expectation of effort and the expectation of performance (Osmanbegović and Lugavić, 2018). Li and Shang (2019) found that the e-Gov service quality concept has eight dimensions: system quality, reliability, security, accessibility, information quality, service capacity, interactivity, and responsiveness.

Without a doubt, the basic resources of the citizen/user, whether technological or non-technological, are necessary so that they can work in harmony and efficiently with the use of the e-Gov and with the least setbacks.

## Benefits to the Citizen as User

In order to have an appropriate evaluation of tangible and intangible *benefits* of the e-Gov, successful projects involve decision-making activities (Sundberg and Larsson, 2017), so governments need to introduce new options in their e-policies and strategies in order to better serve the people. In the same way, you can find additional benefits such as ease of use, comfort, customer service, innovations, new forms of communication and security that have changed the behavior and attitude of citizens towards the use of the services of e-Gov (Kumar, Sachan and Mukherjee, 2017).

The e-Gov offers many benefits to its end users, including financial incentives and improved services (Shareef et al., 2011), and these researchers believe that it has been seen as an important way to break down barriers and bring the government to the citizens, since with the adoption of e-Gov systems, a user can gain many relative and absolute benefits such as effectiveness, efficiency, availability, access from anywhere, comfort in use, time saving, decrease in costs and convenience. Skybe (2016) considers the quality and efficiency of public services as accessible, transparent, cost reduction, less administrative burden and citizen integration. Other researchers such as Lamberti et al. (2014) believe that the benefits perceived by citizens with the e-Gov approach are cost savings, time savings, unrestricted access, multimedia access, security, democracy, transparency, user friendliness, quality, interactivity, system customization and integration.

On the other hand, *ease of use* is defined as the degree to which using a product, process or technology does not require a major effort, because citizens prefer e-Gov services in a few steps (Venkatesh et al., 2012) and linked to this concept is the usability/usefulness of IT. For this, models and theories have emerged, such is the case of the Diffusion of Innovation model and the TAM (Technology Acceptance Model) that indicate that citizens, personally and in their performance in an organization, will use technology until they perceive its usefulness to meet their objectives. Furthermore, it has been widely recognized that the system quality is a direct source of utility and ease of use (Kimathi, Zhang and Longji, 2019), for this, Hamida and Razakb (2016) found that the perceived utility and ease of use perceived were positively related to the intention of continuing the use of the e-Gov.

Regarding *Confidence* in the e-Gov Website, it is defined in terms of timeliness, technical functionality (access and provision), accuracy and promise of service (Papadomichelaki and Mentzas, 2012). That is to say, the confidence of citizens towards the Website has a positive effect on the behavioral intention to use electronic government services (Kurfal et al., 2017) reinforced mainly by the security on the e-Gov Website (Janita and Miranda, 2018). In addition, the studies carried out on the subject essentially focus on trust in the government and the Internet and when talking about citizens, their personality, culture, sex, experience, educational level and beliefs (Alzahrani, Al-Karaghouli and Weerakkody, 2017).

The review of the state of the art has shown that technologies increase trust in the e-Gov, but at the same time there is a rejection of some organizations and citizens in particular. Undoubtedly, confidence is a multidimensional concept that can be studied from the point of view of various social and economic disciplines and becomes a crucial ingredient for any successful e-Gov project, where users who make intensive use of the Internet, have greater confidence in the services provided by the e-Gov (Horsburgh et al., 2011) and privacy is the key element in building citizen trust and their intention to continue using the e-Gov service (Kimathi et al., 2019; Susanto and Aljoza, 2015).

On the other hand, one of the most recognized aspects as a key factor in the success of the use and acceptance of technology is satisfaction, which measures the degree to which users/clients are free from non-conformities and negative attitudes towards the use of a product (ISO, 1998), in addition, higher levels of satisfaction (safe, reliable, smooth, participatory experience) leads to higher levels of adoption (Kumar et al., 2007) and with regard to the Internet, satisfaction in the information of the Website, the system itself and electronic services in general, lead to electronic satisfaction, noting that citizens who are more satisfied with the e-Gov also trust the government more (Welch and Pandey, 2005), which leads to a greater intention of use (Li and Shang, 2019).

Satisfaction is important to provide feedback to e-Gov Websites by knowing the experiences of its users. Unfortunately, despite the large investments by governments in the introduction of their online services to link them to citizens, their penetration is unsatisfactory and they do not provide an adequate return on investment (Lamberti et al., 2014) and some Websites are negatively related to citizen satisfaction and perceptions of public sector reliability, even Kumar, Sachan and Mukherjee (2017) indicate that until today, there is no satisfactory experience due to a limited set of characteristics and a poor service quality in terms of access and design.

However, technology allows applications to be easily accessible to government services, but they do not ensure citizen satisfaction, which is the main and final objective of the e-Gov, considering at the same time what was found by Krairit (2018) who points out that recently a new type of user called self-satisfaction has been defined, which may be a link with the theory of satisfaction in economics.

## Method

Information technologies are key in the development and survival of any institution and in governments they can be used as an important link with citizens. The goal of this study is to determine the technological and non-technological factors that most impact the perception of success of an e-Gov Website, in particular, the tax collector, seen from the point of view of its taxpayers.

The process followed to achieve the objective began in the first stage with the review of the state of the art in order to identify the variables and items of the most relevant factors detected by the e-Gov and analyze the main research centers and national universities, the result is that there are not enough studies of this type in the area under analysis or in Mexico, hence its importance. Based on the above, a questionnaire was designed that was reviewed by experts both academics (two people) and those dedicated to daily practice in tax operations (three people) to provide feedback on the instrument, for which the observations made were incorporated. Immediately, a pilot study was carried out with 31 contributors that resulted in the elimination of 7 items that were not understood or had no statistical significance and the modification of 12 items in order to achieve greater validity and thus establish the final document, made up of two sections, the first one captures demographic data such as sex, age, educational level, the most used procedures on the Website, business line of business and number of employees. And the second section composed of 63 questions evaluated on a 7-point Likert scale (1. Strongly disagree… 7. Strongly agree).

The empirical work was carried out in the Mexican state of Tamaulipas and with the validated questionnaire, it was applied to a convenience sample that lasted approximately one month. It is necessary to point out that the participation by taxpayers and users representing the company is still poor, in the end 488 valid surveys were reached in the main cities of the state of Tamaulipas: Nuevo Laredo (98), Reynosa (95), Matamoros (69), Ciudad Victoria (109) and Tampico (117). The target population was defined as the taxpayers who make constant use of the Tax Administration Service (SAT in Spanish) website in order to carry out any administrative or fiscal procedure. The SAT was selected because it is the most important way and it tends to be the only way to carry out tax obligations for citizens in Mexico. Subsequently, based on the information obtained, the data analysis is derived, carried out in the same way in two stages, in the first, the descriptive statistics basically with frequencies and tables, and the second part, with factorial analysis in SPSS version 21. Finally, the conclusions and contributions to knowledge are developed, taking into account the analysis carried out for this purpose.

## Results

After applying the questionnaire and using factor analysis, the demographic results indicate that 48% are men and 52% are women, so there is a balance in this aspect when making use of information technologies and this Website SAT government. Of the taxpayers surveyed, the majority went to university (undergraduate or graduate) (66%), 22% had a Baccalaureate, 6% only had a High School and the rest (6%) did not answer. Among the main activities carried out in the e-Gov, they highlight that the majority (71%) use it to consult the registration card before the public treasury in Mexico, known as the Federal Taxpayers Registry (RFC in Spanish), that is, an underutilization of the government's technological infrastructure by citizens, lower in percentage (49%) they use it to carry out electronic invoicing and only 42% for the tax return.

The second part corresponds to the inferential analysis. There are things that cannot be measured directly, they are known as latent variables, for this, the most appropriate statistical tool for this type of scientific analysis is the exploratory factor analysis (EFA) for the construction of the scale and the definition of the critical factors success of the use of the e-Gov by taxpayers.

A critical assumption underlying the adequacy of factor analysis is to ensure that the data matrix has the necessary correlation for its application. The first step is to identify those factor loadings greater than .300, since Hair et al. (2018) consider them significant for factor analysis, with a sample greater than 350 cases;

Therefore, and with the firm intention of making the validation more robust, it was based on this guideline, with values equal to or greater than .500 to be considered valid within the study.

Likewise, it is necessary to determine the matrix correlation of Bartlett's Test Sphericity, which provides the probability or statistical test to analyze the presence of significant correlations between the variables. The results obtained were significant at levels of p <0.001, that is, suitable for factor analysis, requiring at least p<0.05. Regarding the Kaiser-Meyer-Olkin (KMO) test, which measures the adequacy of the data in order to quantify the degree of intercorrelations between the variables, this data reached a value of .960, which are reliable for factor analysis.

The principal components factor analysis model was then executed, which according to Hair et al. (2018), consider the total variance and estimate the factors that contain low proportions of the unique variance. From the above, the orthogonal rotation was performed with the Varimax method. The process ended in three iterations, for which seven items were eliminated. In Table 1, it can be seen that the 10 factors obtained cover 74.021% of the total variance, a value considered good, taking into account that it is an exploratory study.

*Table 1. Total variance explained*

| Component | Initial Eigenvalues | | | Extraction Sums of Squared Loadings | | | Rotation Sums of Squared Loadings | | |
|---|---|---|---|---|---|---|---|---|---|
| | Total | % of Variance | Cumulative % | Total | % of Variance | Cumulative % | Total | % of Variance | Cumulative % |
| 1 | 24.287 | 41.874 | 41.874 | 24.287 | 41.874 | 41.874 | 5.958 | 10.272 | 10.272 |
| 2 | 4.035 | 6.957 | 48.831 | 4.035 | 6.957 | 48.831 | 5.450 | 9.397 | 19.669 |
| 3 | 3.033 | 5.230 | 54.061 | 3.033 | 5.230 | 54.061 | 4.955 | 8.543 | 28.211 |
| 4 | 2.201 | 3.796 | 57.857 | 2.201 | 3.796 | 57.857 | 4.795 | 8.266 | 36.478 |
| 5 | 2.008 | 3.463 | 61.320 | 2.008 | 3.463 | 61.320 | 4.493 | 7.746 | 44.224 |
| 6 | 1.888 | 3.255 | 64.574 | 1.888 | 3.255 | 64.574 | 4.302 | 7.417 | 51.640 |
| 7 | 1.546 | 2.666 | 67.240 | 1.546 | 2.666 | 67.240 | 4.267 | 7.357 | 58.998 |
| 8 | 1.355 | 2.337 | 69.577 | 1.355 | 2.337 | 69.577 | 3.915 | 6.751 | 65.749 |
| 9 | 1.301 | 2.243 | 71.820 | 1.301 | 2.243 | 71.820 | 2.719 | 4.689 | 70.437 |
| 10 | 1.277 | 2.202 | 74.021 | 1.277 | 2.202 | 74.021 | 2.079 | 3.584 | 74.021 |
| Extraction Method: Principal Component Analysis. | | | | | | | | | |

Table 2 shows the final rotations and factor loadings for each accepted item. Ten elements have been identified as critical success factors of the e-Gov and named: *i*) User Satisfaction, *ii*) Service Quality, *iii*) Information Quality, *iv*) Ease of Use, *v*)

Confidence, *vi*) System Quality, *vii*) Perceived Benefits, *viii*) Utility, *ix*) Computer Skills, and *x*) Technological Resources.

*Table 2. Rotated factor matrix*

| **User Satisfaction** | | **Service Quality** | |
|---|---|---|---|
| SAT1. I think it is a positive idea to carry out my tax activities on the SAT website | .524 | SUPPORT1. When I have a problem on the SAT website, the SAT contact center shows sincere interest in solving it | .643 |
| SAT2. I have a positive opinion about the SAT website | .609 | SUPPORT2. The SAT contact center is always ready to help me | .739 |
| SAT3. The SAT website meets my needs for procedures and tax services | .662 | SUPPORT3. The SAT contact center has the knowledge to answer my questions | .790 |
| SAT4. The SAT website lives up to my expectations | .700 | SUPPORT 4. The SAT contact center understands my specific needs | .778 |
| SAT5. I am satisfied with the information on the SAT website | .708 | SUPPORT5. The SAT contact center gives adequate answers | .759 |
| SAT6. The SAT website adequately meets my information needs | .685 | SUPPORT6. When I make a request on the SAT website, I get prompt and timely attention | .702 |
| SAT7. I feel satisfied when I use the SAT website | .667 | SUPPORT 7. The support provided by the SAT contact center is useful to me | .670 |
| SAT8. I would recommend the SAT website to someone seeking my advice. | .646 | | |
| SAT9. If I have to do another procedure or service in the tax field, I would choose the SAT website again | .641 | | |
| | | | |
| **Information Quality** | | **Ease of Use** | |
| IQ1. The SAT website provides me with relevant information | .588 | EU1. The SAT website is easy to use | .741 |
| IQ 2. The SAT website provides me with accurate and easy-to-understand information | .662 | EU 2. It is easy to become proficient in using the SAT website | .740 |
| IQ 3. The SAT website provides me with timely information | .708 | EU 3. I require the minimum of fields and screens to carry out my procedure on the SAT website | .703 |
| IQ 4. The information obtained from the SAT website is reliable to me | .760 | EU 4. Carrying out the procedures and operations on the SAT website is easy for me | .757 |
| IQ 5. The information obtained from the SAT website is useful to me | .734 | EU 5. The queries or access to the information required on the SAT website are easy to do | .771 |

*Continued on following page*

*Table 2. Continued*

| User Satisfaction | | | Service Quality | |
|---|---|---|---|---|
| IQ 6. The information obtained from the SAT website is sufficient and of high quality for me. | .668 | | EU 6. The SAT website has a clear design | .708 |
| IQ. The SAT website provides me with updated information | .618 | | | |
| | | | | |
| **Confidence** | | | **System Quality** | |
| CONF1. The SAT website certifies that it will keep my information secure | .801 | | VALUE1. The SAT website reduces the operating costs of my tax procedures and services | .569 |
| CONF2. I trust that my procedures/ services on the SAT website are carried out with an adequate level of security | .897 | | VALUE2. The SAT website saves me time | .621 |
| CONF3. I trust that the SAT website will keep my personal information safe | .895 | | VALUE3. The SAT website facilitates my tax procedures and services | .669 |
| CONF4. The SAT website has the security and privacy required for the management of my information | .887 | | VALUE4. The SAT website helps me make better and faster decisions | .690 |
| CONF5. I trust that the administrators of the SAT website will not misuse my information | .830 | | VALUES5. The SAT website improves the quality of my work | .721 |
| | | | VALUE6. With the use of the SAT website, I improve the service to my clients | .749 |
| | | | | |
| **Perceived Benefits** | | | **Utility** | |
| INTER4. On the SAT website, I wait a short time between my actions and the response of the site | .598 | | UTIL1. The SAT website improves the effectiveness of the activities I carry out | .664 |
| INTER5. The SAT Web page, accessed from any browser (Explorer, Chrome, FireFox, etc.) | .693 | | UTIL2. All my procedures and required services can be completed through the SAT website | .681 |
| INTER6. SAT web pages load quickly | .821 | | UTIL3. I consider that the functions of the SAT website are useful | .608 |
| INTER7. In relation to other similar government sites, the SAT website is fast to load | .805 | | UTIL4. The SAT website is more useful to me to complete my procedures and services instead of calling or sending an email to an executive of the SAT | .657 |
| INTER8. The speed of issuing reports and information on the SAT website is reasonable | .734 | | UTIL5. The SAT website allows me to do my homework quickly | .610 |
| INTER9. The SAT website is always operating or is always online | .571 | | UTIL6. The SAT website increases my productivity | .561 |
| | | | | |
| **Computer Skills** | | | **Technological Resources** | |

*Continued on following page*

*Table 2. Continued*

| User Satisfaction | | | Service Quality | |
|---|---|---|---|---|
| HC1. I have the necessary knowledge to operate a computer. | .921 | | RT1. I have an adequate Information Technology (IT) infrastructure. | .793 |
| HC2. I have the necessary knowledge to make good use of the Internet. | .920 | | RT2. I have Internet connectivity to access the electronic services of the SAT. | .734 |
| HC3. I have the computer skills to efficiently use the SAT website and carry out procedures or services over the Internet. | .781 | | RT3. The SAT in their offices provides me with adequate IT infrastructure to access their electronic services. | .684 |

Extraction method: Principal component analysis.
Rotation method: Varimax with Kaiser normalization

a. Rotation converged in 7 iterations.

After performing the exploratory factor analysis, each of the elements obtained is briefly described below:

Factor 1, called *User Satisfaction* ensures that the taxpayer/user reaches that psychological state of well-being while performing their tax obligations with the Government. Factor 2 is called *Service Quality or Citizen Support*. This variable analyzes the attitude of government employees who are the operators of the Website, in the sense of their willingness to help, the knowledge they possess, empathy, guidance and support for taxpayers.

For Factor 3, *Information Quality*, it aims to identify if the Website provides precise, accurate, timely, reliable, useful, sufficient and quality information. And as for Factor 4, it has been called *Ease of Use*, with this variable it is intended that the Website be perceptible, easy to operate for the taxpayer, that they find it attractive and understandable.

The next factor (5) is *Confidence*, it essentially refers to the fact that the taxpayer is convinced that the operation of the Website is safe and that it will keep the data provided there confidentially (privacy), and Factor 6, *Perceived Benefits*, is referred to better decision-making and an increase in the quality of the activities carried out by the user.

As for Factor 7 called *System Quality*, it is relative to the waiting time to send and receive information on the Website, interoperability with various Internet browsers and permanent availability. For Factor 8, *Utility*, it is essentially the importance of the technological platform to improve activities, perception of increased personal productivity, saving time in physical transfers and speed in handling information, and Factor 9, *Computer Skills*, seeks to determine the technical knowledge of the taxpayer to make efficient use of the computer and the Internet when carrying out their operations on the SAT Website.

Last but not least is Factor 10, it has been named *Technological Resources,* it implies that the taxpayer has the computer equipment and the adequate Internet connection to be able to access and operate the Website.

Finally, in Figure 1, you can see a Research Model for future research. The diagram represents an opportunity to confirm or expand on issues related to electronic government that provide more elements for the benefit of government services. It should be noted that this proposed activity can be carried out with a second generation tool such as Structural Equation Modeling and determine the relationship of the various actors that can influence the harmonious development between citizens and the government.

*Figure 1. Research model for future research*

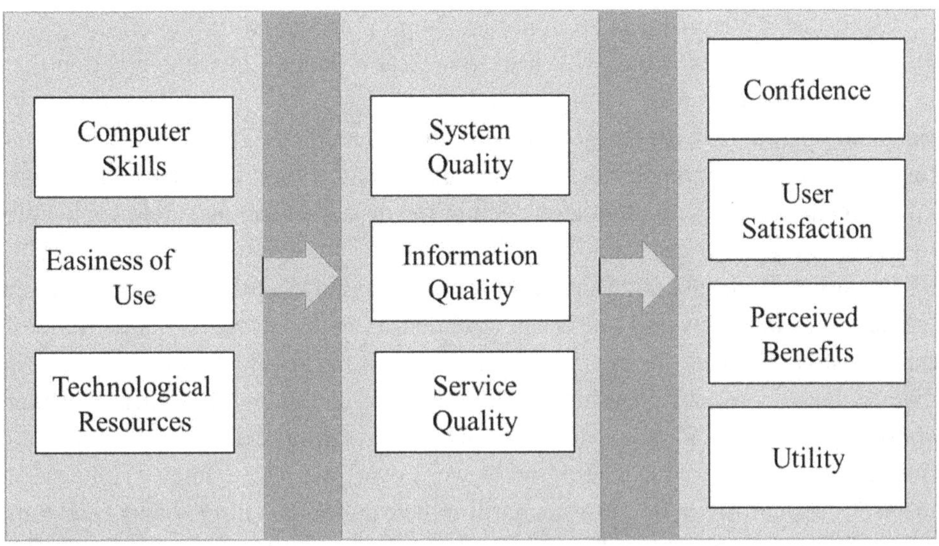


## CONCLUSION

The information technologies continue with their vertiginous advance and in ascent day by day and the organizations follow the step that the computer science tools are providing. For this reason, the invaluable value that the Internet revolution has brought with it cannot be denied; more precisely, in this third millennium, the era of globalization and the generation of knowledge, require an almost immediate adaptation to the new world realities, which includes government activities at all levels.

In order to address the above, the objective of this research is to determine the factors with the greatest influence on the use and operation of the Tax Collection Website in Mexico. The results obtained allow us to point out that the critical success factors of the e-Gov for the northeast region of the country that has an emerging economy are: *i)* Citizen Satisfaction, *ii)* Service Quality, *iii)* Information Quality, *iv)* Ease of Use, *v)* Confidence, *vi)* Perceived Benefits, *vii)* System Quality, *viii)* Utility, *ix)* Computational Skills, and *x)* Technological Resources.

Also note that citizens are more communicated with computers and the Internet, their involvement and participation in government activities has increased; in this way, governments should communicate to citizens the existence of this e-Government platform, its advantages, its benefits, its benevolences, the links with other government offices, among others. In these ideas, the e-Gov has allowed the saving of valuable costs and time that is not recoverable, both for the government and for the citizens/taxpayers, it has increased the quality of the data and the availability of the information, all this, thanks to the benefits it offers in conjunction with information technologies.

Electronic government is an important step in the search for the efficiency of government activities, which will lead to a great reduction in the corruption that so afflicts some countries, to eliminate intermediaries who make large profits in financial operations with the government, the reduction of administrative burden for taxpayers (and companies), increase confidence in the government and other government functions and that at the end of the day, is a virtuous circle applicable to all government offices.

Regarding the implications, governments, it is essential that they jointly support the activities of e-Gov and coexist in communion with citizens or, in the case of this investigation, with the captive taxpayers that it has. Undoubtedly, the scope is diverse, but it is necessary to highlight the need to continue developing computer applications according to the true needs of citizens, taking them into account at all times. In the same way, it is required to work overtime on the interoperability of the Website platform in order to standardize the data for the entire country and thus have relevant information and above all, always listen to the real needs of its users.

Finally, the limitations are in the sense that the questionnaire can vary its validity in a culture other than Mexican, the size of the sample, the ages, the possible bias in the educational level and the excessive number of items in the instrument. Likewise, increase the sample to other Mexican states so that the validity is conclusive.

## ACKNOWLEDGMENT

Our most sincere appreciation for all the support to PRODEP of the Ministry of Public Education (Mexico) and the EP project. IDCA: 23370 and Code: UAT-CA-132.

## REFERENCES


Aggarwal, A., & Rahul, M. (2018). The effect of perceived security on consumer purchase intensions in electronic commerce. *International Journal of Public Sector Performance Management*, *4*(1), 1–20. doi:10.1504/IJPSPM.2018.088691

Ali, K. E., Mazen, Sh. A., & Hassanein, E. E. (2018). A proposed hybrid model for adopting cloud computing in e-Government. *Future Computing and Informatics Journal*, *3*(2), 286–295. doi:10.1016/j.fcij.2018.09.001

Alzahrani, L., Al-Karaghouli, W., & Weerakkody, V. (2017). Analysing the critical factors influencing trust in e-government adoption from citizens' perspective: A systematic review and a conceptual framework. *International Business Review*, *26*(1), 164–175. doi:10.1016/j.ibusrev.2016.06.004

Arwati, D., & Verdania, D. L. (2019). Factors inhibiting public participation in corruption prevention through e-Government application in Indonesia. *Global Business and Management Research*, *11*(1), 81–86.

Belanche, D., & Casaló, L. V. (2015). Rebuilding public trust in government administrations through e-Government actions. *Revista Española de Investigación de Marketing ESIC*, *19*(1), 1–11. doi:10.1016/j.reimke.2014.07.001

Castañeda, V. M. (2017). La equidad del sistema tributario y su relación con la moral tributaria. Un estudio para América Latina. *Investigacion Economica*, *76*(299), 25–152. doi:10.1016/j.inveco.2017.02.002

Chopra, S., & Rajan, P. (2016). Modeling intermediary satisfaction with mandatory adoption of e-Government technologies for food distribution. *Information Technologies and International Development*, *12*(1), 15–34.

Gulati, G. J., Williams, C. B., & Yates, D. J. (2014). Predictors of on-line and e-participation: A cross-national comparison. *Government Information Quarterly*, *31*(4), 526–533. doi:10.1016/j.giq.2014.07.005

Hair, J. F., Babin, B. J., Anderson, R. E., & Black, W. C. (2018). *Multivariate Data Analysis* (8th ed.). CENGAGE.

Hamida, A. A., & Razakb, F. Z. A. (2016). The effects of perceived usefulness and perceived ease of use on continuance intention to use e-Government. *Procedia Economics and Finance*, *35*, 644–649. doi:10.1016/S2212-5671(16)00079-4

Horsburgh, S., Goldfinch, S., & Gauld, R. (2011). Is public trust in government associated with trust in e-Government? *Social Science Computer Review*, *29*(2), 232–241. doi:10.1177/0894439310368130

ISO. (1998). *ISO 9241-11. Ergonomic requirements for office work with visual display terminals (VDTs) - Part 11: Guidance on usability*: Recuperado de: http://www.it.uu.se/edu/course/homepage/acsd/vt09/ISO9241part11.pdf

Janita, M. S., & Miranda, F. J. (2018). Quality in e-Government services: A proposal of dimensions from the perspective of public sector employees. *Telematics and Informatics*, *35*(2), 457–469. doi:10.1016/j.tele.2018.01.004

Kimathi, F. A., Zhang, Y., & Longji, H. (2019). Citizens' acceptance of e-Government service: Examining E-Tax Filing and Payment System (ETFPS) in Tanzania. *African Journal of Library Archives and Information Science*, *29*(1), 45–62.

Krairit, D. (2018). The new face of Internet user typology: The case of Thailand. *Journal of Theoretical and Applied Electronic Commerce Research, 13*(2), 58-79. doi:10.4067/S0718-18762018000200106

Kumar, R., Sachan, A., & Mukherjee, A. (2017). Qualitative approach to determine user experience of e-government services. *Computers in Human Behavior*, *71*, 299–306. doi:10.1016/j.chb.2017.02.023

Kumar, V., Mukerji, B., Butt, I., & Persaud, A. (2007). Factors for successful e-Government adoption: A conceptual framework. *The Electronic Journal of E-Government*, *5*(1), 63–76.

Kurfal, M., Arifoglu, A., Tokdemir, G., & Paçin, Y. (2017). Adoption of e-Government services in Turkey. *Computers in Human Behavior*, *66*, 168–178. doi:10.1016/j.chb.2016.09.041

Lamberti, L., Benedetti, M., & Chen, S. (2014). Benefits sought by citizens and channel attitudes for multichannel payment services: Evidence from Italy. *Government Information Quarterly*, *31*(4), 596–609. doi:10.1016/j.giq.2014.03.002

Lee, J. B., & Porumbescu, G. A. (2019). Engendering inclusive e-government use through citizen IT training programs. *Government Information Quarterly*, *36*(1), 69–76. doi:10.1016/j.giq.2018.11.007

Li, Y., & Shang, H. (2019). Service quality, perceived value, and citizens' continuous-use intention regarding e-government: Empirical evidence from China. *Information & Management*. Advance online publication. doi:10.1016/j.im.2019.103197

Liu, Y., Wang, M., Huang, D., Huang, Q., Yang, H., & Li, Z. (2019). The impact of mobility, risk, and cost on the users' intention to adopt mobile payments. *Information Systems and e-Business Management*, *17*(2-4), 1–24. doi:10.100710257-019-00449-0

Luna-Reyes, L. F., & Gil-García, J. R. (2014). Digital government transformation and Internet portals: The co-evolution of technology, organizations, and institutions. *Government Information Quarterly*, *31*(4), 545–555. doi:10.1016/j.giq.2014.08.001

Medina-Quintero, J. M., Abrego-Almazán, D., & Ortiz-Rodríguez, F. (2018). Use and usefulness of the information systems measurement. A quality approach at the Mexican Northeastern Region. *Cuadernos Americanos*, *31*(56), 7–30. doi:10.11144/Javeriana.cao.31-56.ubwm

Nguyen, A. (2016). A cross-cultural study on e-Government services delivery. *The Electronic Journal Information Systems Evaluation*, *19*(2), 121–134.

Nishant, R., Srivastava, S. C., & Teo, T. (2019). Using polynomial modeling to understand service quality in e-Government websites. *MIS Quarterly*, *43*(3), 807-826. doi:10.25300/MISQ/2019/12349

Osei-Kojo, A. (2017). E-government and public service quality in Ghana. *Journal of Public Affairs*, *17*(3), e1620. doi:10.1002/pa.1620

Osmanbegović, E., & Lugavić, Z. (2018). Influencing factors of e-government services adoption in Bosnia and Herzegovina. *Economic Review: Journal of Economics and Business*, *16*(2), 39–51.

Papadomichelaki, X., & Mentzas, G. (2012). E-GovQual: A multiple-item scale for assessing e-government service quality. *Government Information Quarterly*, *29*(1), 98–109. doi:10.1016/j.giq.2011.08.011

Ritchi, H., Wahyudi, I., & Susanto, A. (2015). Research program on key success factors of e-Government an their impacto on accounting inforarion quality. *Procedia - Social and Behavioral Sciences*, *211*, 673-680. doi:10.1016/j.sbspro.2015.11.102

Sandoval-Almazan, R. (2019). Gobierno abierto y transparencia en México: Estudio longitudinal 2015-2018. *Innovar (Universidad Nacional de Colombia)*, *29*(74), 115–131. doi:10.15446/innovar.v29n74.82097

Shareef, M. A., Kumar, V., Kumar, U., & Dwivedi, Y. K. (2011). e-Government Adoption Model (GAM): Differing service maturity levels. *Government Information Quarterly*, *28*(1), 17–35. doi:10.1016/j.giq.2010.05.006

Šimić, G. P. (2019). Improving e-government services for advanced search. *Military Technical Courier*, *67*(2), 307–325. doi:10.5937/vojtehg67-20356

Skybe, M. V. (2016). Improving e-government as one of the preconditions for economic development. *Economic Processes Management: International Scientific E-Journal, 3*. Recuperado de: http://epm.fem.sumdu.edu.ua/download/2016_3/epm2016_3_6.pdf

Sundberg, L., & Larsson, A. (2017). The impact of formal decision processes on e-Government projects. *Administrative Sciences*, *7*(14), 2–12. doi:10.3390/admsci7020014

Susanto, T. D., & Aljoza, M. (2015). Individual acceptance of e-government services in a developing country: Dimensions of perceived usefulness and perceived ease of use and the importance of trust and social influence. *Procedia Computer Science, 72*, 622-629. http:// doi:10.1016/j.procs.2015.12.171

Twizeyimana, J. D., & Andersson, A. (2019). The public value of E-Government – A literature review. *Government Information Quarterly*, *36*(2), 167–178. doi:10.1016/j.giq.2019.01.001

Van Deursen, A. J., & van Dijk, J. A. (2009). Improving digital skills for the use of online public information and services. *Government Information Quarterly*, *26*(2), 333–340. doi:10.1016/j.giq.2008.11.002

Venkatesh, V., Chan, F., & Thong, J. (2012). Designing e-government services: Key service attributes and citizens' preference. *Journal of Operations Management, 30*(1-2), 116–133. doi:10.1016/j.jom.2011.10.001

Wang, F. (2014). Explaining the low utilization of government websites: Using a grounded theory approach. *Government Information Quarterly*, *31*(4), 610–621. doi:10.1016/j.giq.2014.04.004

Welch, E. W., & Pandey, S. (2005). E-Government and network technologies: Does bureaucratic red tape inhibit, promote or fall victim to intranet technology implementation? *Proceedings of the 38th Hawaii International Conference on System Sciences, 5*, 122.3. 10.1109/HICSS.2005.215

Wirtz, B., Weyerer, J., Thomas, M. C., & Möller, A. (2017). E-Government Implementation: Theoretical Aspects and Empirical Evidence. *Public Organization Review*, *17*(1), 101–120. doi:10.100711115-015-0330-2

Wirtz, B. W., Piehler, R., Rieger, V., & Daiser, P. (2016). E-government portal information performance and the role of local community interest. Empirical support for a model of citizen perceptions. *Public Administration Quarterly*, *40*(1), 48–83.

Wu, Y. (2014). Protecting personal data in E-government: A cross-country study. *Government Information Quarterly*, *31*(1), 150–159. doi:10.1016/j.giq.2013.07.003

# Compilation of References


A., R., O. V., M., & R., J. (2020). Additive Manufacturing of Nickel-Based Super Alloys for Aero Engine Applications . In Balasubramanian, K., & Senthilkumar, V. (Ed.), *Additive Manufacturing Applications for Metals and Composites* (pp. 48-70). IGI Global. https://doi.org/ doi:10.4018/978-1-7998-4054-1.ch003

Abdallah, S. (2020). Social Interactions in Electronic Networks of Practice. [IJeC]. *International Journal of e-Collaboration, 16*(2), 27–44. doi:10.4018/IJeC.2020040103

Abdelkader, A. A., & Ebrahim, R. S. (2021). Decomposing Customer Engagement Effect Between Marketer- and User-Generated Content and Repurchase Intention in the Online Airline Service Community. [IJOM]. *International Journal of Online Marketing, 11*(4), 1–22. doi:10.4018/IJOM.2021100101

Abel, K. M., & Reiter, E. M. (2022). Health and Race in America at the Macro, Meso, and Micro Levels. In T. R. Flockhart, A. Reiter, & M. R. Hassett (Eds.), *The Reproduction and Maintenance of Inequalities in Interpersonal Relationships* (pp. 255–272). IGI Global., doi:10.4018/978-1-6684-4128-2.ch014

Abinaya. (n.d.). *OpenEducationPortal*. Obtained from https://www.openeducationportal.com/importance-of-career-dev
elopment/

Abir, J. I., & Shamim, T. F. (2020). What Compels Journalists to Take a Step Back? In S. Jamil (Ed.), *Handbook of Research on Combating Threats to Media Freedom and Journalist Safety* (pp. 38–53). IGI Global., doi:10.4018/978-1-7998-1298-2.ch003

Abokhoza, R. R., & Sobieh, Y. M. (2021). The Role of Virtual Reality to Enhance Cultural Communication. [IJWP]. *International Journal of Web Portals, 13*(2), 20–35. doi:10.4018/IJWP.2021070102

Abrar, M., Khan, A. S., & Xiang, L. (2022). Impact of Employee-Based Brand Equity on Customer-Based Brand Equity. In M. Bari, M. Abrar, & E. Alaverdov (Eds.), *Antecedents and Outcomes of Employee-Based Brand Equity* (pp. 16–30). IGI Global., doi:10.4018/978-1-6684-3621-9.ch002

Abubaker, F., & El-Badri, H. A. (2022). Using Digital Storytelling as a Tool for Reflection in the Libyan EFL Literature Classroom. In W. M. El-Henawy & M. del Mar Suárez (Eds.), *English as a Foreign Language in a New-Found Post-Pandemic World* (pp. 182–205). IGI Global., doi:10.4018/978-1-6684-4205-0.ch009

Adah, P. (2022). Navigating Marginalization Through a Motivational Weapon and Resilience. In Haas, L.Tussey, J. T. (Eds.), Disciplinary Literacy as a Support for Culturally and Linguistically Responsive Teaching and Learning (pp. 217-246). IGI Global. https://doi.org/ doi:10.4018/978-1-6684-4215-9.ch011

Adams, A. T. (2022). From Courageous to Unapologetic Conversations About School Discipline Disparities. In A. T. Adams (Ed.), *Approaching Disparities in School Discipline* (pp. 271–294). IGI Global., doi:10.4018/978-1-6684-3359-1.ch012

Adegbore, A. M. (2020). Digital Storytelling, Podcasting, and New Format of Messaging in the Libraries. In A. Tella (Ed.), *Handbook of Research on Digital Devices for Inclusivity and Engagement in Libraries* (pp. 185–207). IGI Global., doi:10.4018/978-1-5225-9034-7.ch009

Adeyinka-Skold, S. (2020). Barriers in Women's Romantic Partner Search in the Digital Age. In R. Kalish (Ed.), *Young Adult Sexuality in the Digital Age* (pp. 113–137). IGI Global., doi:10.4018/978-1-7998-3187-7.ch007

Adkins, S. (1999). Cause related marketing: who cares wins. Butterworth-Heinemann.

Adkins-Sharif, J. (2021). A Black Principal's Decolonizing Journey for Racial Justice. In Rodriguez, S.Brown, K. (Eds.), Black and Brown Leadership and the Promotion of Change in an Era of Social Unrest (pp. 271-297). IGI Global. https://doi.org/ doi:10.4018/978-1-7998-7235-1.ch012

Aggarwal, A., & Rahul, M. (2018). The effect of perceived security on consumer purchase intensions in electronic commerce. *International Journal of Public Sector Performance Management*, *4*(1), 1–20. doi:10.1504/IJPSPM.2018.088691

Agrawal, C., & Duggal, T. (2021). A Study of Consumer Switching Behaviour in the Indian Context With Respect to Recycled Products. In B. N. Gopalakrishnan, T. Duggal, & T. Tewary (Eds.), *Examining the Intersection of Circular Economy, Forestry, and International Trade* (pp. 142–153). IGI Global., doi:10.4018/978-1-7998-4990-2.ch012

Ahmad, N. (2020). What Determine Indonesian Commercial News TV Channels' Political News Production and Publication in the Post-Soeharto Regime. In Karlidag, S.Bulut, S. (Eds.), Handbook of Research on the Political Economy of Communications and Media (pp. 134-160). IGI Global. https://doi.org/ doi:10.4018/978-1-7998-3270-6.ch008

Ahmad, B., Göç, K., & Yin, X. (2022). Employee-Based Brand Equity. In M. Bari, M. Abrar, & E. Alaverdov (Eds.), *Antecedents and Outcomes of Employee-Based Brand Equity* (pp. 72–80). IGI Global., doi:10.4018/978-1-6684-3621-9.ch005

Aja, A. (2019). *Un estudio sobre smartphones en México*. From Periodico El Economista S.A. de C.V.: https://www.eleconomista.com.mx/opinion/Un-estudio-sobre-smartphones-en-Mexico-20190320-0134.html

Akansel, I. (2020). The Relationship Between Old Institutional Economics (OIE) and Feminist Economics. In I. Akansel (Ed.), *Examining the Relationship Between Economics and Philosophy* (pp. 1–26). IGI Global., doi:10.4018/978-1-7998-1037-7.ch001

Akbar, M., Suaib, M., Husain, M. S., & Shukla, S. (2020). A Compendium of Cloud Forensics. In M. Husain & M. Khan (Eds.), *Critical Concepts, Standards, and Techniques in Cyber Forensics* (pp. 215–227). IGI Global., doi:10.4018/978-1-7998-1558-7.ch012

Al Janabi, M. A. (2020). Risk Management in Emerging and Islamic Markets in Light of the Subprime Global Financial Crisis. In N. Naifar (Ed.), *Impact of Financial Technology (FinTech) on Islamic Finance and Financial Stability* (pp. 98–127). IGI Global., doi:10.4018/978-1-7998-0039-2.ch006

Al Tamimi, W. S. (2022). Education for Women and Girls in Iraq. In Boivin, J. A.Pacheco-Guffrey, H. (Eds.), Education as the Driving Force of Equity for the Marginalized (pp. 272-289). IGI Global. https://doi.org/ doi:10.4018/978-1-7998-8025-7.ch013

Alan, A., Kabadayi E. & Yilmaz, C. (2015). Cognitive and affective constituents of the consumption experience in retail service settings: effects on store loyalty. *Service Business, 10*(4), 715-735. doi:10.1007/s11628-015-0288-8

Alawdat, M., & Hodges, R. (2021). Quaran-Teens 2020 Blog Series. In E. B. Hancı-Azizoglu & M. Alawdat (Eds.), *Rhetoric and Sociolinguistics in Times of Global Crisis* (pp. 56–78). IGI Global., doi:10.4018/978-1-7998-6732-6.ch004

Alazrak, N. N. (2020). Making Sense of Journalists' Safety and Media Freedom in Egypt Between Different Types of Threats and the Ruling Legislative Context. In S. Jamil (Ed.), *Handbook of Research on Combating Threats to Media Freedom and Journalist Safety* (pp. 172–185). IGI Global., doi:10.4018/978-1-7998-1298-2.ch010

Alboul, L., Beer, M., & Nisiotis, L. (2019). Merging Realities in Space and Time. In M. Dimitrova & H. Wagatsuma (Eds.), *Cyber-Physical Systems for Social Applications* (pp. 156–183). IGI Global., doi:10.4018/978-1-5225-7879-6.ch007

Alexander-Ashley, B. M. (2022). Reducing Mass Incarceration Through Trauma-Informed Pedagogy. In C. Bernadowski (Ed.), *Strategies and Methods for Implementing Trauma-Informed Pedagogy* (pp. 123–143). IGI Global., doi:10.4018/978-1-7998-7473-7.ch007

Ali, M. B. (2021). Internet of Things (IoT) to Foster Communication and Information Sharing. In Ali, M. B.Wood-Harper, T. (Eds.), Fostering Communication and Learning With Underutilized Technologies in Higher Education (pp. 1-20). IGI Global. https://doi.org/ doi:10.4018/978-1-7998-4846-2.ch001

Ali, N. (2021). Racialization of Religion. In Rodriguez, S.Brown, K. (Eds.), Black and Brown Leadership and the Promotion of Change in an Era of Social Unrest (pp. 247-270). IGI Global. https://doi.org/ doi:10.4018/978-1-7998-7235-1.ch011

Ali, K. E., Mazen, Sh. A., & Hassanein, E. E. (2018). A proposed hybrid model for adopting cloud computing in e-Government. *Future Computing and Informatics Journal*, *3*(2), 286–295. doi:10.1016/j.fcij.2018.09.001

Aliprantis, J., & Caridakis, G. (2019). A Survey of Augmented Reality Applications in Cultural Heritage. [IJCMHS]. *International Journal of Computational Methods in Heritage Science*, *3*(2), 118–147. doi:10.4018/IJCMHS.2019070107

Ali, S. A., Yassin, M., & AbuRaya, R. (2020). The Impact of Firm Characteristics on Corporate Financial Performance in Emerging Markets. [IJCRMM]. *International Journal of Customer Relationship Marketing and Management*, *11*(4), 70–89. doi:10.4018/IJCRMM.2020100105

Al-Malkawi, H. N., Pillai, R., & AlShiab, M. S. (2020). Evaluating Microeconomic Factors, Financial Crisis, and Stock Price Dynamics. In L. Farinha, A. B. Cruz, & J. R. Sebastião (Eds.), *Handbook of Research on Accounting and Financial Studies* (pp. 131–153). IGI Global., doi:10.4018/978-1-7998-2136-6.ch007

Almazari, A. A. (2020). Valuation of Banking Sector. In Köseoğlu, S. D. (Eds.), Valuation Challenges and Solutions in Contemporary Businesses (pp. 175-200). IGI Global. https://doi.org/ doi:10.4018/978-1-7998-1086-5.ch010

Almurshidee, K. (2018). SERVPERF-based empirical evidence on e-banking services quality and customer satisfaction from the Saudi banking sector. *International Journal of Advanced and Applied Sciences*, *5*(11), 40–45. doi:10.21833/ijaas.2018.11.005

Alonso, A. B., Artime, I. F., Rodriguez, M. A., & Baniello, R. G. (2011). *Dispositivos Moviles*. From https://s3.amazonaws.com/academia.edu.documents/34258261/dispostivos_moviles_y_su_clasificacion.pdf?response-content-disposition=inline%3B%20filename%3DDispositivos_moviles.pdf&X-Amz-Algorithm=AWS4-HMAC-SHA256&X-Amz-Credential=AKIAIWOWYYGZ2Y53UL3A%2F20200

Alqurashi, E., & Siegelman, A. R. (2019). Designing and Evaluating Technology-Based Formative Assessments. In A. Elçi, L. L. Beith, & A. Elçi (Eds.), *Handbook of Research on Faculty Development for Digital Teaching and Learning* (pp. 222–244). IGI Global., doi:10.4018/978-1-5225-8476-6.ch012

Al-Rashed, A., & Al-Gilani, M. (2020). Gender Equity in Surgical Academia in Kuwait and the Arabian Gulf Region. In M. I. Bellini & V. E. Papalois (Eds.), *Gender Equity in the Medical Profession* (pp. 237–251). IGI Global., doi:10.4018/978-1-5225-9599-1.ch017

Altin, H. (2022). The Effect of the COVID-19 Pandemic on International Stock Exchanges. In Sloboda, B. W.Sissoko, Y. (Eds.), Economic Impact and Recovery Following a Global Health Crisis (pp. 106-143). IGI Global. https://doi.org/ doi:10.4018/978-1-7998-6900-9.ch005

Altınırmak, S., Şahin, C., Karamaşa, Ç., & Okoth, B. O. (2020). Participative Banking in Turkey. In A. Rafay (Ed.), *Growth and Emerging Prospects of International Islamic Banking* (pp. 141–154). IGI Global., doi:10.4018/978-1-7998-1611-9.ch008

Alturki, N. (2022). Nada Alturki. In Goodman Hayward, P., Rehman, S.Yan, Z. (Eds.), Women Community Leaders and Their Impact as Global Changemakers (pp. 280-285). IGI Global. https://doi.org/ doi:10.4018/978-1-6684-2490-2.ch047

Alvarado, L. E., & Rossatto, C. A. (2022). Allies in Solidarity Transcend Guilt and Unlearn Patriarchal Privileges. In J. Keengwe (Ed.), *Handbook of Research on Social Justice and Equity in Education* (pp. 203–222). IGI Global., doi:10.4018/978-1-7998-9567-1.ch010

Alvarez Rico, A. (2020). *Classification of investigations.* University of Lima, Faculty of Business and Economic Sciences, International Business Career. Obtained from https://repositorio.ulima.edu.pe/bitstream/handle/20.500.12724/10818/Note%20Acad%c3%a9mic%202%20%2818.04.2021%29%20-%20Clasificaci%c3%b3n%20of%20investigations.pdf?sequence=4&isAllowed=y

Álvarez, M., Guerrero, C., & Larios, M. (2021). Mercadotecnia con causa en tiempos de Coronavirus. *Revista de Investigaciones Universidad Del Quindío*, *33*(S1), 96–112. doi:10.33975/riuq.vol33nS1.486

Alzahrani, L., Al-Karaghouli, W., & Weerakkody, V. (2017). Analysing the critical factors influencing trust in e-government adoption from citizens' perspective: A systematic review and a conceptual framework. *International Business Review*, *26*(1), 164–175. doi:10.1016/j.ibusrev.2016.06.004

Al-Zaman, M. S., & Puja, P. P. (2021). Storytelling and the Rhetoric of Rumor in Social Media. In L. C. Mihăeş, R. Andreescu, & A. Dimitriu (Eds.), *Handbook of Research on Contemporary Storytelling Methods Across New Media and Disciplines* (pp. 40–62). IGI Global., doi:10.4018/978-1-7998-6605-3.ch003

Amaladas, S. (2021). COVID-19 and the Call for Elder Change Leadership. In Al-Aali, E.Masmoudi, M. (Eds.), Global Perspectives on Change Management and Leadership in the Post-COVID-19 Era (pp. 218-239). IGI Global. https://doi.org/ doi:10.4018/978-1-7998-6948-1.ch014

Ambikar, R., Szrot, L., Greer, C., & Peterson, D. (2021). Curriculum for Compassion. In C. Reneau & M. Villarreal (Eds.), *Handbook of Research on Leading Higher Education Transformation With Social Justice, Equity, and Inclusion* (pp. 198–217). IGI Global., doi:10.4018/978-1-7998-7152-1.ch014

Amhag, L. (2020). *Reflection and Self-Assessment in Smart Education.* IGI Global., doi:10.4018/978-1-7998-4183-8.ch006

Amirsadeghi, L. (2020). Location-Based Entertainment. In Morie, J. F.McCallum, K. (Eds.), Handbook of Research on the Global Impacts and Roles of Immersive Media (pp. 284-313). IGI Global. https://doi.org/ doi:10.4018/978-1-7998-2433-6.ch015

Anand, A., & Muthusamy, A. (2020). Data Security and Privacy-Preserving in Cloud Computing Paradigm. In S. Gochhait, D. T. Shou, & S. Fazalbhoy (Eds.), *Cloud Computing Applications and Techniques for E-Commerce* (pp. 99–133). IGI Global., doi:10.4018/978-1-7998-1294-4.ch006

Andrade, L. J., & Ferreira, M. J. (2022). The Influence of Storytelling Strategies on Attitude and Purchase Intention. In A. Campos & S. Almeida (Eds.), *Global Perspectives on Strategic Storytelling in Destination Marketing* (pp. 94–115). IGI Global., doi:10.4018/978-1-6684-3436-9.ch006

André, L. F. A., Cláudio de Souza, B., Firmino, A. A., Guimarães de Oliveira, M., & Cardoso de Paiva, A. (2015). A Spatial and Temporal Sentiment Analysis Approach Applied to Twitter Microtexts. –. *Journal of Information and Data Management*, *6*, 118–129.

Andrews, S. K., & Crawford, C. M. (2021). Barriers, Issues, and Similarities Among Women in eSports and Similar Mixed Gender Sports. In S. Andrews & C. M. Crawford (Eds.), *Handbook of Research on Pathways and Opportunities Into the Business of Esports* (pp. 25–46). IGI Global., doi:10.4018/978-1-7998-7300-6.ch002

Anim-Yeboah, S., Boateng, R., Awuni Kolog, E., Owusu, A., & Bedi, I. (2020). Digital Entrepreneurship in Business Enterprises: A Systematic Review. In Responsible Design, Implementation and Use of Information and Communication Technology. doi:10.1007/978-3-030-44999-5_16

Anouze, A. L., & Alamro, A. S. (2019). Factors affecting intention to use e-banking in Jordan. *International Journal of Bank Marketing*, *38*(1), 86–112. doi:10.1108/IJBM-10-2018-0271

Anthony, B. Jr. (2020). Green Information Systems Refraction for Corporate Ecological Responsibility Reflection in ICT Based Firms. [JCIT]. *Journal of Cases on Information Technology*, *22*(1), 14–37. doi:10.4018/JCIT.2020010102

Appiah-Adjei, G. (2021). Confronting Freedom to Inform With Freedom of Expression. In Jamil, S., Çoban, B., Ataman, B.Appiah-Adjei, G. (Eds.), Handbook of Research on Discrimination, Gender Disparity, and Safety Risks in Journalism (pp. 269-296). IGI Global. https://doi.org/doi:10.4018/978-1-7998-6686-2.ch015

Appiah-Adjei, G. (2020). The Role of Ghanaian News Media Organisations in Countering Threats to Media Freedom and Journalists' Safety. In S. Jamil (Ed.), *Handbook of Research on Combating Threats to Media Freedom and Journalist Safety* (pp. 186–213). IGI Global., doi:10.4018/978-1-7998-1298-2.ch011

Araujo, J. J., & Araujo, D. L. (2021). What Counts as Literacy for the 21st Century Youth. In L. Haas & J. Tussey (Eds.), *Connecting Disciplinary Literacy and Digital Storytelling in K-12 Education* (pp. 298–315). IGI Global., doi:10.4018/978-1-7998-5770-9.ch015

Arda, Ö., & Akmeşe, Z. (2021). Media Ethics. In M. N. Taskiran & F. Pinarbaşi (Eds.), *Multidisciplinary Approaches to Ethics in the Digital Era* (pp. 96–110). IGI Global., doi:10.4018/978-1-7998-4117-3.ch007

Ardıç Çobaner, A. (2021). Representation of Syrian Children in Turkish Media From a Child-Oriented Rights Journalism Perspective. In F. Özsungur (Ed.), *Handbook of Research on Policies, Protocols, and Practices for Social Work in the Digital World* (pp. 355–375). IGI Global., doi:10.4018/978-1-7998-7772-1.ch020

Argus, S., Vaccaro, A., Coiro, J., Hos, R., & Deeney, T. (2022). Equitable Teaching Practices in Higher Education. In J. Keengwe (Ed.), *Handbook of Research on Social Justice and Equity in Education* (pp. 92–113). IGI Global., doi:10.4018/978-1-7998-9567-1.ch005

Aria, M., Cuccurullo, C., & Gnasso, A. (2021). A comparison among interpretative proposals for Random Forests. *Machine Learning with Applications, 6.*

Armie, M. (2020). Between Tradition and Innovation. In Membrive, V.Armie, M. (Eds.), Using Literature to Teach English as a Second Language (pp. 1-33). IGI Global. https://doi.org/doi:10.4018/978-1-7998-4670-3.ch001

Armistead, K. J., & Woods, V. (2021). Fostering and Developing Culturally-Aware Mentorship Practices. In C. Reneau & M. Villarreal (Eds.), *Handbook of Research on Leading Higher Education Transformation With Social Justice, Equity, and Inclusion* (pp. 126–140). IGI Global., doi:10.4018/978-1-7998-7152-1.ch009

Armstrong, C. L., & Towery, N. A. (2021). How Individuals Hypothetically and Realistically Respond to Media Messages About Severe Weather. [IJDREM]. *International Journal of Disaster Response and Emergency Management, 4*(1), 47–62. doi:10.4018/IJDREM.2021010104

Armstrong, G., & Kotler, P. (2017). *Fundamentos de Marketing* (P. Educación, Ed.).

Arnold, J. M., & Sableski, M. (2020). Building Reflective Practices Through a Digital Literacy Portfolio in an Online Context. In R. Karchmer-Klein & K. E. Pytash (Eds.), *Effective Practices in Online Teacher Preparation for Literacy Educators* (pp. 45–64). IGI Global., doi:10.4018/978-1-7998-0206-8.ch003

Arnould, E., & Thompson, C. (2005). Consumer Culture Theory (CCT): Twenty years of research. *The Journal of Consumer Research, 31*(4), 868–882. doi:10.1086/426626

Arslan, H., & Topal, A. (2021). Evaluation of Women's Perspectives in the East Societies on New Media News. In Tombul, I. & Sarı, G. (Ed.), Handbook of Research on Contemporary Approaches to Orientalism in Media and Beyond (pp. 778-798). IGI Global. https://doi.org/doi:10.4018/978-1-7998-7180-4.ch044

Artan Özoran, B. (2021). Digital Storytelling and Public Relations. In E. Esiyok (Ed.), *Handbook of Research on New Media Applications in Public Relations and Advertising* (pp. 217–233). IGI Global., doi:10.4018/978-1-7998-3201-0.ch013

Arvanitis, P., & Krystalli, P. (2021). Digital Storytelling and Augmented Reality-Based Scenarios for Foreign Language Teaching. In M. Montebello (Ed.), *Digital Pedagogies and the Transformation of Language Education* (pp. 1–22). IGI Global., doi:10.4018/978-1-7998-6745-6.ch001

Arwati, D., & Verdania, D. L. (2019). Factors inhibiting public participation in corruption prevention through e-Government application in Indonesia. *Global Business and Management Research, 11*(1), 81–86.

Asano, G., Cheng, T. P., Rhodes, J., & Lok, P. (2019). The Influence of Online Reviews and Brand Trust and Customer Equity. [JECO]. *Journal of Electronic Commerce in Organizations, 17*(4), 30–43. doi:10.4018/JECO.2019100103

Asha, J. O. (2021). Phenomenology of Religious Experience. In E. D. Essien (Ed.), *Phenomenological Approaches to Religion and Spirituality* (pp. 251–267). IGI Global., doi:10.4018/978-1-7998-4595-9.ch013

Asiyanbi, H., & Ishola, A. (2018). E-Banking services impact and customer satisfaction in selected bank branches in Ibadan metropolis, Oyo state, Nigeria. *Accounting, 4*(4), 153–160. doi:10.5267/j.ac.2018.3.001

Assay, B. E. (2019). Social Media and the Challenges of Curtailing the Spread of Fake News in Nigeria. In Chiluwa, I. E.Samoilenko, S. A. (Eds.), Handbook of Research on Deception, Fake News, and Misinformation Online (pp. 226-263). IGI Global. https://doi.org/ doi:10.4018/978-1-5225-8535-0.ch014

Ataman, B., Çoban, B., & Erkmen, Ö. (2020). A Review on the Safety of Journalists in Turkey. In S. Jamil (Ed.), *Handbook of Research on Combating Threats to Media Freedom and Journalist Safety* (pp. 148–171). IGI Global., doi:10.4018/978-1-7998-1298-2.ch009

Ataya, M. A. M., & Ali, M. A. M. (2019). Acceptance of website security on e-Banking. A-review. *IEEE 10th Control and System Graduate Research Colloquium.* 10.1109/ICSGRC.2019.8837070

Atef, N. (2020). Can Revolutionary Media Be Made Online? In A. M. Solo (Ed.), *Handbook of Research on Politics in the Computer Age* (pp. 203–216). IGI Global., doi:10.4018/978-1-7998-0377-5.ch012

Atienza, V. (2020). Waste Management in the Philippines. In Pariatamby, A., Shahul Hamid, F.Bhatti, M. S. (Eds.), Sustainable Waste Management Challenges in Developing Countries (pp. 270-286). IGI Global. https://doi.org/ doi:10.4018/978-1-7998-0198-6.ch011

Atlı, D., Kose, S. B., & Sezen, A. N. (2019). A Neuromarketing Based Approach on the Usage of Narratives in the Advertising. In R. Yilmaz (Ed.), *Handbook of Research on Narrative Advertising* (pp. 251–268). IGI Global., doi:10.4018/978-1-5225-9790-2.ch022

Attuel-Mendes, L., Assadi, D., & Raymond, S. (2021). Investors' Motivations in Different Types of Crowdfunding. In C. S. Negrão & J. F. Brito (Eds.), *Multidisciplinary Approaches to Crowdfunding Platforms* (pp. 21–54). IGI Global., doi:10.4018/978-1-7998-3226-3.ch002

Aureli, S., & Graziano, H. (2020). When Ethical Values Drive the Creation and Development of Sporting Events. In A. Fotiadis & C. Vassiliadis (Eds.), *Principles and Practices of Small-Scale Sport Event Management* (pp. 217–232). IGI Global., doi:10.4018/978-1-7998-4757-1.ch011

Awad, A. W., Awwad, B. S., & Sharabati, A. A. (2021). Evaluating Mergers as a Tool to Strengthen and Modernize the Palestinian Banking System. In Y. A. Albastaki, A. Razzaque, & A. M. Sarea (Eds.), *Innovative Strategies for Implementing FinTech in Banking* (pp. 201–221). IGI Global., doi:10.4018/978-1-7998-3257-7.ch013

Ayad, S. M., Dunn, R. A., & Marshall, S. W. (2020). Political Advertising Effects on Perceived Bias, Value, and Credibility in Online News. In K. Dalkir & R. Katz (Eds.), *Navigating Fake News, Alternative Facts, and Misinformation in a Post-Truth World* (pp. 184–202). IGI Global., doi:10.4018/978-1-7998-2543-2.ch008

Ayar Senturk, H. (2021). Digital Storytelling and Parasocial Interaction for Brand-Consumer Relationship. In N. Mohd Suki (Ed.), *Handbook of Research on Technology Applications for Effective Customer Engagement* (pp. 197–214). IGI Global., doi:10.4018/978-1-7998-4772-4.ch013

Ayish, M., & Dahdal, S. (2021). Going Mobile in Journalism Education. [IJSEUS]. *International Journal of Smart Education and Urban Society*, *12*(2), 21–31. doi:10.4018/IJSEUS.2021040103

B. (2018). *The Universal.* Academic Press.

Babel, S., Ta, A. T., & Habarakada Liyanage, T. U. (2020). Current Situation and Challenges of Waste Management in Thailand. In Pariatamby, A., Shahul Hamid, F., & Bhatti, M. S. (Ed.), Sustainable Waste Management Challenges in Developing Countries (pp. 409-440). IGI Global. https://doi.org/ doi:10.4018/978-1-7998-0198-6.ch017

Baek, E., Choo, H., & Lee, S. (2018). Using warmth as the visual design of a store: Intimacy, relational needs, and approach intentions. *Journal of Business Research*, *88*, 91–101. doi:10.1016/j.jbusres.2018.03.013

Baez, M., Borrego, A., Cordero, J., & Cruz, L. (n.d.). *Introduccion a Android.* E.M.E. Editorial.

Bain, A. S. (2022). Diversity and Equity in Healthcare. In Reeves, E. K.McIntyre, C. J. (Eds.), Multidisciplinary Perspectives on Diversity and Equity in a Virtual World (pp. 163-183). IGI Global. https://doi.org/ doi:10.4018/978-1-7998-8028-8.ch010

Baker, C. (2022). From Story-Based to Story-Interactive Experiences. In Campos, A.Almeida, S. (Eds.), Global Perspectives on Strategic Storytelling in Destination Marketing (pp. 74-93). IGI Global. https://doi.org/ doi:10.4018/978-1-6684-3436-9.ch005

Baker, P. J. (2020). Afrocentric Thought in Adult Education. In Okojie, M. C.Boulder, T. C. (Eds.), Handbook of Research on Adult Learning in Higher Education (pp. 175-198). IGI Global. https://doi.org/ doi:10.4018/978-1-7998-1306-4.ch007

Bal, S. (2022). Gendering the EU's Western Balkan Enlargement. In B. F. Costa (Ed.), *Challenges and Barriers to the European Union Expansion to the Balkan Region* (pp. 153–170). IGI Global., doi:10.4018/978-1-7998-9055-3.ch008

Baltazar Vilchis, C. A., & Velázquez Ramírez, J. M. (2022). La COVID-19 y las microempresas de comercio al por menor de la Región II Atlacomulco, Estado de México. Un acercamiento mediante análisis factorial en el primer trimestre de 2021. *RECAI Revista de Estudios en Contaduría, Administración e Informática*, *11*(30), 13-28. DOI: . 2018.v14n34p65 doi:10.19044/esj

Bang, H. J., Fabienke, N., & Tyson, C. A. (2022). Creating Diverse, Equitable, and Inclusive Digital Learning Platforms for Young Children. In A. L. Betts & K. Thai (Eds.), *Handbook of Research on Innovative Approaches to Early Childhood Development and School Readiness* (pp. 577–601). IGI Global., doi:10.4018/978-1-7998-8649-5.ch024

Banner, D. (2022). Storytelling in Peace Leadership. In E. P. Schellhammer (Ed.), *Evolution of Peace Leadership and Practical Implications* (pp. 273–292). IGI Global., doi:10.4018/978-1-7998-9736-1.ch015

Bao, J., Zheng, Y., Wilkie, D., & Mohamed, F. (2015, July 1). Recommendations in location-based social networks: A survey. *GeoInformatica*, *19*(3), 525–565. doi:10.100710707-014-0220-8

Baporikar, N. (2021). Effect of Reward on Motivation and Job Satisfaction. [IJAMSE]. *International Journal of Applied Management Sciences and Engineering*, *8*(1), 12–51. doi:10.4018/IJAMSE.2021010102

Baporikar, N. (2021). Health Institution Governance. [IJPAE]. *International Journal of Political Activism and Engagement*, *8*(4), 1–19. doi:10.4018/IJPAE.2021100101

Baporikar, N. (2021). Stakeholder Approach for Land Reform Programme to Enhance Access and Equity. [IJPAE]. *International Journal of Political Activism and Engagement*, *8*(2), 40–63. doi:10.4018/IJPAE.2021040103

Baptista, J. (2019). *LinkedIn.* Obtained from https://es.linkedin.com/pulse/opportunity-laboral-jennifer-baptista-cal

Baquee, A., & Sevukan, R. (2019). Marketing of Information Products and Services through Library Websites: An Analytical Study of Indian Central University Library. *Library Philosophy and Practice.* Available at: https://digitalcommons.unl.edu/libphilprac/2652

Baranauskas, G., & Raišiene, A. G. (2022). Transition to Digital Entrepreneurship with a Quest of Sustainability: Development of a New Conceptual Framework. *Sustainability*, *14*(3), 1104. doi:10.3390u14031104

Bari, M. W., & Shahzadi, I. (2022). Employee-Based Brand Equity and Factors of Employee-Brand Association. In M. Bari, M. Abrar, & E. Alaverdov (Eds.), *Antecedents and Outcomes of Employee-Based Brand Equity* (pp. 1–15). IGI Global., doi:10.4018/978-1-6684-3621-9.ch001

Barker, R. (2018). Knowledge management to prevent fraudulent e-banking transactions. *Communitas*, *23*(1), 71–86. doi:10.18820/24150525/Comm.v23.5

Barrett, S. J. (2021). Exploring Diversity and Inclusion Leadership in Complex Organizations. In R. D. Johnson (Ed.), *Handbook of Research on Multidisciplinary Perspectives on Managerial and Leadership Psychology* (pp. 320–353). IGI Global., doi:10.4018/978-1-7998-3811-1.ch016

Barrios, M. (2012). Marketing de la experiencia: Principales conceptos y características. *Palermo Business Review*, *7*, 67–89.

Barro, R. J., & Sala-i-Martin, X. (2012). *Crecimiento económico*. Editorial Reverté.

Bashir, M., Bhutta, M. K., & Shahi, S. G. (2022). Knowledge-Sharing Culture and Employee-Based Brand Equity. In M. Bari, M. Abrar, & E. Alaverdov (Eds.), *Antecedents and Outcomes of Employee-Based Brand Equity* (pp. 119–137). IGI Global., doi:10.4018/978-1-6684-3621-9.ch009

Basile, V. (2019). Building a Strong Brand Equity in Pharmaceutical Industry. [IJCRMM]. *International Journal of Customer Relationship Marketing and Management*, *10*(3), 1–20. doi:10.4018/IJCRMM.2019070101

Basnal, G. (2022). Assessment of 21st Century Skills. In Chakravarti, S.Boukareva, B. (Eds.), Cases on Global Innovative Practices for Reforming Education (pp. 202-221). IGI Global. https://doi.org/ doi:10.4018/978-1-7998-8310-4.ch010

Baylis, P. (2015). *Temperature and temperament: Evidence from a billion tweets*. Energy Institute at HAAS working paper.

Beasley, M., Tunstall, J., Blackmon, S., & Smith, M. (2022). Make Space, Take Space. In E. Cain-Sanschagrin, R. A. Filback, & J. Crawford (Eds.), *Cases on Academic Program Redesign for Greater Racial and Social Justice* (pp. 1–21). IGI Global., doi:10.4018/978-1-7998-8463-7.ch001

Beevor, M. C., Campos, A. C., & Guerreiro, M. M. (2022). Storytelling and Experience Design in Heritage Tourism. In A. Campos & S. Almeida (Eds.), *Global Perspectives on Strategic Storytelling in Destination Marketing* (pp. 1–21). IGI Global., doi:10.4018/978-1-6684-3436-9.ch001

Bejarano, H., Hancevic, P., & Núñez, H. M. (2021). Impacto económico del COVID-19 en negocios pequeños y medianos bajo restricciones voluntarias e impuestas. *EconoQuantum*, *18*(2), 23–56. doi:10.18381/eq.v18i2.7229

Belanche, D., & Casaló, L. V. (2015). Rebuilding public trust in government administrations through e-Government actions. *Revista Española de Investigación de Marketing ESIC*, *19*(1), 1–11. doi:10.1016/j.reimke.2014.07.001

Bello, L. K., Ojebisi, A. O., & Adebanjo, A. A. (2021). The Impact of Perceived Relevance and Technology Anxiety on Readiness to Use Digital Storytelling. [IJTEPD]. *International Journal of Teacher Education and Professional Development*, *4*(2), 82–96. doi:10.4018/IJTEPD.2021070106

Bembimbre, C. (2022). *Definition ABC*. Obtained from https://www.definitionabc.com/general/factores.php

Ben Mim, S., & Mbarki, Y. (2021). Corporate Governance in Islamic Banks. In A. Alqatan, K. Hussainey, & H. Khlif (Eds.), *Corporate Governance and Its Implications on Accounting and Finance* (pp. 322–337). IGI Global., doi:10.4018/978-1-7998-4852-3.ch015

Benson, O. V., Udo-Anyanwu, A. J., & Onuoha, C. O. (2016). *Strategies Used in Marketing Library and Information Services in Tertiary Institutions in Imo State. Journal of Applied Information Science and Technology, 9(1).*

Berg, G. A. (2020). Equity and Diversity in the 21st Century University. In Berg, G. A.Venis, L. (Eds.), Accessibility and Diversity in the 21st Century University (pp. 1-19). IGI Global. https://doi.org/ doi:10.4018/978-1-7998-2783-2.ch001

Bergman, T. (2020). Critical Political Economy and Content Analysis. In Karlidag, S.Bulut, S. (Eds.), Handbook of Research on the Political Economy of Communications and Media (pp. 242-255). IGI Global. https://doi.org/ doi:10.4018/978-1-7998-3270-6.ch013

Besong, E. N. (2022). Nigerian Media's Poor Representation and Negligence of Minorities as a Breach of Ethical Journalism. In Okocha, D. O., Onobe, M. J.Alike, M. N. (Eds.), Handbook of Research on Connecting Philosophy, Media, and Development in Developing Countries (pp. 352-364). IGI Global. https://doi.org/ doi:10.4018/978-1-6684-4107-7.ch024

Betts, A. L., Fabienke, N., & Farber, M. (2021). The Quest for Learning. In L. Haas & J. Tussey (Eds.), *Disciplinary Literacy Connections to Popular Culture in K-12 Settings* (pp. 203–230). IGI Global., doi:10.4018/978-1-7998-4721-2.ch010

Bhattacharyya, M. (2021). Safety and Security of Journalists in India. In Jamil, S., Çoban, B., Ataman, B.Appiah-Adjei, G. (Eds.), Handbook of Research on Discrimination, Gender Disparity, and Safety Risks in Journalism (pp. 119-142). IGI Global. https://doi.org/ doi:10.4018/978-1-7998-6686-2.ch008

Bhattacharyya, R. (2019). Financial Globalization and Trade Openness in China and India. [IJABIM]. *International Journal of Asian Business and Information Management*, *10*(3), 22–48. doi:10.4018/IJABIM.2019070102

Bienvenido, H. P., Barinaga, B., & Mora-Fernandez, J. (2021). A Historical Review of Immersive Storytelling Technologies. In V. Chkoniya (Ed.), *Handbook of Research on Applied Data Science and Artificial Intelligence in Business and Industry* (pp. 569–597). IGI Global., doi:10.4018/978-1-7998-6985-6.ch027

Billen, M. T., Ward, N. A., DeHart, J. D., Moran, R. R., & Yang, S. (2021). StoryVisualizer by LEGO Education. In L. Haas & J. Tussey (Eds.), *Connecting Disciplinary Literacy and Digital Storytelling in K-12 Education* (pp. 148–168). IGI Global., doi:10.4018/978-1-7998-5770-9.ch008

Bintz, W., Ciecierski, L. M., & Royan, E. (2021). Using Picture Books With Instructional Strategies to Address New Challenges and Teach Literacy Skills in a Digital World. In L. Haas & J. Tussey (Eds.), *Connecting Disciplinary Literacy and Digital Storytelling in K-12 Education* (pp. 38–58). IGI Global., doi:10.4018/978-1-7998-5770-9.ch003

Biswas, D., Lund, K., & Szocs, C. (2018). Sounds like a healthy retail atmospheric strategy: Effects of ambient music and background noise on food sales. *Journal of the Academy of Marketing Science*, *47*(1), 37–55. doi:10.100711747-018-0583-8

Biswas, D., & Szocs, C. (2019). The Smell of Healthy Choices: Cross-Modal Sensory Compensation Effects of Ambient Scent on Food Purchases. *JMR, Journal of Marketing Research*, *56*(1), 123–141. doi:10.1177/0022243718820585

Biswas, D., Szocs, C., & Abell, A. (2019b). Extending the Boundaries of Sensory Marketing and Examining the Sixth Sensory System: Effects of Vestibular Sensations for Sitting versus Standing Postures on Food Taste Perception. *The Journal of Consumer Research*, *46*(5), 1–17. doi:10.1093/jcr/ucz018

Bitrus-Ojiambo, U. A., & King'ori, M. E. (2020). Media and Child Rights in Africa. In O. Oyero (Ed.), *Media and Its Role in Protecting the Rights of Children in Africa* (pp. 125–148). IGI Global., doi:10.4018/978-1-7998-0329-4.ch007

Black, E., & Kirkwood, K. (2022). Twice as Good to Get Half. In Alvarez, W. & De Walt, P. S. (Ed.), Voicing Diverse Teaching Experiences, Approaches, and Perspectives in Higher Education (pp. 17-27). IGI Global. https://doi.org/ doi:10.4018/978-1-7998-9000-3.ch002

Blanco Sánchez, T., & Castillo Díaz, A. (2022). Research in Public Relations in Spain Through the State Research Plans 2013-2020. In M. Carrillo-Durán & M. Pérez Pulido (Eds.), *Cases on Developing Effective Research Plans for Communications and Information Science* (pp. 189–214). IGI Global., doi:10.4018/978-1-6684-4523-5.ch010

Blanco, M. (2016). *Beneficios y amenazas de la Industria 4.0.* Retrieved from https://ctxt.es/es/20160831/Firmas/8157/Industria-tecnologia -revolucion-mercado-digital.htm

Blank, C., Gatterer, K., & Leichtfried, V. (2018). Short Vacation Improves Stress-Level and Well-Being in German-Speaking Middle-Managers-A Randomized Controlled Trial. *Int J Environ Res Public Health*, *15*(1), 130. doi:10.3390/ijerph15010130

Bledsoe, T., & Setterlund, K. (2021). *All About the Classroom!* IGI Global., doi:10.4018/978-1-7998-4069-5.ch008

Bledsoe, T., & Setterlund, K. (2021). *Background Experiences, Developmental Perspectives.* IGI Global., doi:10.4018/978-1-7998-4069-5.ch003

Bledsoe, T., & Setterlund, K. (2021). *The Power of Narratives.* IGI Global., doi:10.4018/978-1-7998-4069-5.ch001

Bloom, L., Noltensmeyer, C. J., Hahn, S. A., Rush, C. B., Heidlebaugh-Buskey, P., & Westbrook, T. M. (2020). Pedagogical Considerations in Teaching Implicit Bias. [IJBIDE]. *International Journal of Bias, Identity and Diversities in Education*, *5*(1), 46–63. doi:10.4018/IJBIDE.2020010103

Bobbert, Y., Chtepen, M., Kumar, T., Vanderbeken, Y., & Verslegers, D. (2021). *Findings and Core Practices in the Domain of CI/CD and DevOps on Security Compliance.* IGI Global., doi:10.4018/978-1-7998-7367-9.ch009

Bobbert, Y., Chtepen, M., Kumar, T., Vanderbeken, Y., & Verslegers, D. (2021). *Research Findings in the Domain of CI/CD and DevOps on Security Compliance*. IGI Global., doi:10.4018/978-1-7998-7367-9.ch008

Bocci, M. C. (2022). Guiding School-Based Service-Learning With Youth Participatory Action Research. In Management Association, I. (Eds.), Research Anthology on Service Learning and Community Engagement Teaching Practices (pp. 186-205). IGI Global. https://doi.org/ doi:10.4018/978-1-6684-3877-0.ch011

Boguszewicz-Kreft, M., Kreft, J., & Żurek, P. (2019). Myth and Storytelling. In J. Kreft, S. Kuczamer-Kłopotowska, & A. Kalinowska-Żeleźnik (Eds.), *Myth in Modern Media Management and Marketing* (pp. 22–49). IGI Global., doi:10.4018/978-1-5225-9100-9.ch002

Bolat, N. (2022). The Narrative of Violence in the Framework of the Post-Truth Concept in Television Series. In Yılmaz, R.Koç, B. (Eds.), Narrative Theory and Therapy in the Post-Truth Era (pp. 43-60). IGI Global. https://doi.org/ doi:10.4018/978-1-7998-9251-9.ch004

Bolat, N. (2021). Cross-Media as a Multi-Platform Narrative Interaction Form. In R. Yilmaz (Ed.), *Handbook of Research on Narrative Interactions* (pp. 274–291). IGI Global., doi:10.4018/978-1-7998-4903-2.ch015

Boletín UNAM-DGCS-215. (2021). *Acelera la pandemia el comercio electrónico*. https://www.dgcs.unam.mx/boletin/bdboletin/2021_215.html

Bologna & Walsh. (1997). The accountant's handbook of information technology. Academic Press.

Bolyard, C. S., Baker, A. M., & Rudnick, D. L. (2022). Dilemmas in Asynchronous Multicultural Teacher Education From a Relational Pedagogy Perspective. In S. P. Huffman, D. D. Cunningham, M. Shavers, & R. Adamson (Eds.), *Handbook of Research on Opening Pathways for Marginalized Individuals in Higher Education* (pp. 123–146). IGI Global., doi:10.4018/978-1-6684-3819-0.ch008

Bondad-Brown, B., & Haras, C. (2022). Alt-Instruction. In P. Sullivan, B. Sullivan, & J. Lantz (Eds.), *Cases on Innovative and Successful Uses of Digital Resources for Online Learning* (pp. 178–203). IGI Global., doi:10.4018/978-1-7998-9004-1.ch008

Boonsiritomachai, W., & Pitchayadejanant, K. (2019). Determinants affecting mobile banking adoption by generation Y based on the Unified Theory of Acceptance and Use of Technology Model modified by the Technology Acceptance Model concept. *Kasetsart Journal of Social Sciences*, *40*(2), 349–358. doi:10.1016/j.kjss.2017.10.005

Boult, J., Whited, J. E., & Easley, T. M. (2021). An Ethics-of-Care Approach to Developing Students' Antiracist Practice in SLP Curricula. In R. Horton (Ed.), *Critical Perspectives on Social Justice in Speech-Language Pathology* (pp. 198–223). IGI Global., doi:10.4018/978-1-7998-7134-7.ch010

Bowen, A. M., Robinson, S., & Lane, J. (2021). Black Female Education Leaders and Intersectionality. In S. Rodriguez & K. Brown (Eds.), *Black and Brown Leadership and the Promotion of Change in an Era of Social Unrest* (pp. 101–123). IGI Global., doi:10.4018/978-1-7998-7235-1.ch005

Bozkurt, Y. (2019). Expectation Horizon in Narrative Advertising. In R. Yilmaz (Ed.), *Handbook of Research on Narrative Advertising* (pp. 22–35). IGI Global., doi:10.4018/978-1-5225-9790-2.ch003

Bradish, C. L., & Burton, N. (2021). Media and Content in an Active Economy. In D. J. Finch & D. Legg (Eds.), *Understanding the Active Economy and Emerging Research on the Value of Sports, Recreation, and Wellness* (pp. 239–246). IGI Global., doi:10.4018/978-1-7998-7939-8.ch011

Brakus, J., Schmitt, B., & Zhang, S. (2009). Experiential product attributes and preferences for new products: The role of processing fluency. *Journal of Business Research*, *67*(11), 2291–2298. doi:10.1016/j.jbusres.2014.06.017

Brandão, A. M., & Machado, S. M. (2020). How Consumers Respond to Editorial Communication Strategies. In S. M. Loureiro & H. R. Kaufmann (Eds.), *Exploring the Power of Electronic Word-of-Mouth in the Services Industry* (pp. 364–389). IGI Global., doi:10.4018/978-1-5225-8575-6.ch020

Brand, S. T., & Tutwiler, M. S. (2022). Beyond Critical Race Theory. In J. Keengwe (Ed.), *Handbook of Research on Social Justice and Equity in Education* (pp. 160–182). IGI Global., doi:10.4018/978-1-7998-9567-1.ch008

Bratitsis, T. (2022). Cultural Heritage Redesigned Through Digital Storytelling. In Papadakis, S.Kapaniaris, A. (Eds.), The Digital Folklore of Cyberculture and Digital Humanities (pp. 296-311). IGI Global. https://doi.org/ doi:10.4018/978-1-6684-4461-0.ch016

Bravo, J. (2022). *The impact of english language in our society.* Obtained from TraslateDay: https://www.translateday.com/impact-english-language-in-our-society/

Bravo, I. R., & Rubio-Hernández, M. D. (2020). An Analysis of Netflix España Campaigns. In V. Hernández-Santaolalla & M. Barrientos-Bueno (Eds.), *Handbook of Research on Transmedia Storytelling, Audience Engagement, and Business Strategies* (pp. 367–381). IGI Global., doi:10.4018/978-1-7998-3119-8.ch024

Brayre, C. (2022). *Transformación digital del comercio: Tendencias, oportunidades y retos.* UNCTAD. https://unctad.org/system/files/non-official-document/decb_ecde_p01_barayre_es.pdf

Bright, A., Acosta, S., & Parker, B. (2020). Humility Matters. In J. Keengwe (Ed.), *Handbook of Research on Diversity and Social Justice in Higher Education* (pp. 19–40). IGI Global., doi:10.4018/978-1-7998-5268-1.ch002

Bright, A., Hendryx-Dobson, J. N., & Johnson, S. (2022). Contending With Word Choices in Cross-Cultural Teacher Preparation. In J. Keengwe (Ed.), *Handbook of Research on Social Justice and Equity in Education* (pp. 22–45). IGI Global., doi:10.4018/978-1-7998-9567-1.ch002

Brooks-Eaves, M. (2022). From the Schoolhouse to the Prison Yard. In A. T. Adams (Ed.), *Approaching Disparities in School Discipline* (pp. 257–270). IGI Global., doi:10.4018/978-1-6684-3359-1.ch011

Broughton, A. (2019). *Green Thumb Educating*. IGI Global., doi:10.4018/978-1-5225-8867-2.ch004

Brown, S. (2020). Literacy in Early Childhood. In Mitchell, J. S.Vaughn, E. N. (Eds.), Participatory Literacy Practices for P-12 Classrooms in the Digital Age (pp. 1-19). IGI Global. https://doi.org/ doi:10.4018/978-1-7998-0000-2.ch001

Brown, T. Y., Cornell, N., Tevlin, J. M., Williams, D., & Mulvaney, T. (2022). Inclusion, Diversity Belonging, Equity, and Accessibility Principles on College Campuses. In A. El-Amin (Ed.), *Implementing Diversity, Equity, Inclusion, and Belonging Management in Organizational Change Initiatives* (pp. 202–215). IGI Global., doi:10.4018/978-1-6684-4023-0.ch011

Brulles, D., & Naglieri, J. A. (2022). A Social Justice Approach to Developing Equity and Diversity in Gifted Programming. In J. L. Nyberg & J. A. Manzone (Eds.), *Creating Equitable Services for the Gifted* (pp. 103–119). IGI Global., doi:10.4018/978-1-7998-8153-7.ch008

Buckley-Marudas, M., & Ellenbogen, C. (2020). Fostering Participatory Literacies in English Language Arts Instruction Using Student-Authored Podcasts. In J. S. Mitchell & E. N. Vaughn (Eds.), *Participatory Literacy Practices for P-12 Classrooms in the Digital Age* (pp. 20–39). IGI Global., doi:10.4018/978-1-7998-0000-2.ch002

Buil, I., Melero, I., & Montaner, T. (2012). La estrategia de marketing con causa: Factores determinantes de su éxito. *Universia Business Review*, *36*, 90–107.

Bulut, S. (2020). The Political Economy of News Production. In Karlidag, S.Bulut, S. (Eds.), Handbook of Research on the Political Economy of Communications and Media (pp. 98-114). IGI Global. https://doi.org/ doi:10.4018/978-1-7998-3270-6.ch006

Burciaga, L. (2022). Trauma-Engaged and Culturally Responsive Schools. In K. Johns (Ed.), *Counseling Strategies for Children and Families Impacted by Incarceration* (pp. 209–238). IGI Global., doi:10.4018/978-1-7998-9209-0.ch012

Burrell, D. N. (2021). Black American Men and Complex Societal Educational Navigation of the Emergency Public Health Pandemic of COVID 19. [IJSEUS]. *International Journal of Smart Education and Urban Society*, *12*(2), 1–9. doi:10.4018/IJSEUS.2021040101

Burrell, D. N. (2021). Creating Diverse and Religiously Inclusive Workplace Cultures in Hyper-Connected, Technical, and Cyber-Driven Organizations. [IJSKD]. *International Journal of Sociotechnology and Knowledge Development*, *13*(3), 17–32. doi:10.4018/IJSKD.2021070102

Burrell, D. N., Barrett, S. J., Lewis, E. J., Dawson, M., Bovell, K., & Crowe, M. (2021). Creating Inclusive Workplaces for Women in Health Organizations Engaging in Digital Economy-Driven Innovations. [IJIDE]. *International Journal of Innovation in the Digital Economy*, *12*(2), 18–31. doi:10.4018/IJIDE.2021040102

Burrell, D. N., Lu, S., Lindsay, P. V., Burton, S. L., French, R., Finch, A., McLester, Q., & Springs, D. (2021). Sexual Harassment Training Focused Solely on Protecting Organizations From Lawsuits Won't Change a Toxic Culture for Women to an Inclusive One. [IJPSS]. *International Journal of Public Sociology and Sociotherapy*, *1*(1), 12–25. doi:10.4018/IJPSS.2021010102

Burrell, D. N., Modeste, R. L., & Finch, A. (2021). Responsible Church Leaders Should Be Educating Their Congregations About Racism and Serving the Community Concerning the Black Lives Matter movement. [IJSEUS]. *International Journal of Smart Education and Urban Society*, *12*(3), 38–49. doi:10.4018/IJSEUS.2021070104

Burrell, D. N., Modeste, R., Aridi, A. S., DiPeri, D., Jones, D., & Clay, L. (2021). Addressing Workplace Sexual Harassment in a Government Contracting Company Through Organizational Consulting. [IJSEUS]. *International Journal of Smart Education and Urban Society*, *12*(1), 18–29. doi:10.4018/IJSEUS.2021010102

Burrell, D. N., Shufutinsky, A., Bland, S., Cole, C. M., Wright, J. B., Crowe, M., Aridi, A. S., & Mairs-Levy, J. (2020). A Case Study of a Hospital Workplace Culture of Injustice for Women Physicians. [IJPCH]. *International Journal of Patient-Centered Healthcare*, *10*(1), 15–36. doi:10.4018/IJPCH.2020010102

Burton, S. L. (2021). Technological Digital Disruption in the Age of Artificial Intelligence. In L. S. Byrd (Ed.), *Cultivating Entrepreneurial Changemakers Through Digital Media Education* (pp. 1–35). IGI Global., doi:10.4018/978-1-7998-5808-9.ch001

Bushur-Harris, L. (2022). Leadership Using Internal Controls for a Decentralized (Remote) Workforce. In Heinzman, J. R., Judge, D. S., Franklin, V. S.McCleskey, J. A. (Eds.), Business Models to Promote Technology, Culture, and Leadership in Post-COVID-19 Organizations (pp. 74-92). IGI Global. https://doi.org/ doi:10.4018/978-1-6684-4358-3.ch004

Butler, M., & Whitehead, M. (2022). Did You Get the Memo? In H. W. Pichon & Y. Mutakabbir (Eds.), *African American Leadership and Mentoring Through Purpose, Preparation, and Preceptors* (pp. 101–125). IGI Global., doi:10.4018/978-1-7998-8206-0.ch006

Byrd, L. S. (2021). At the Intersection of Media Innovation and Solutions Journalism. In L. S. Byrd (Ed.), *Cultivating Entrepreneurial Changemakers Through Digital Media Education* (pp. 208–222). IGI Global., doi:10.4018/978-1-7998-5808-9.ch014

Byrd, L. S. (2021). Future Forward. In L. S. Byrd (Ed.), *Cultivating Entrepreneurial Changemakers Through Digital Media Education* (pp. 223–236). IGI Global., doi:10.4018/978-1-7998-5808-9.ch015

Cabrera-Gala, R. (2022). Research in the Field of Communication in Mexico. In Carrillo-Durán, M.Pérez Pulido, M. (Eds.), Cases on Developing Effective Research Plans for Communications and Information Science (pp. 166-188). IGI Global. https://doi.org/ doi:10.4018/978-1-6684-4523-5.ch009

Çakın, Ö. (2019). The Structural Transformation of Narrative Advertising in Turkic Republics. In R. Yilmaz (Ed.), *Handbook of Research on Narrative Advertising* (pp. 108–120). IGI Global., doi:10.4018/978-1-5225-9790-2.ch010

Çal, B. (2020). Firm-Specific Moderators in Recovery From Brand Scandals. In R. Leon (Ed.), *Strategies for Business Sustainability in a Collaborative Economy* (pp. 122–140). IGI Global., doi:10.4018/978-1-7998-4543-0.ch007

Calder, C., & Walker, Q. (2022). Facilitating Anti-Racism in Counselor Education. In S. N. Brant-Rajahn, E. M. Gibson, & M. Cook Sandifer (Eds.), *Developing, Delivering, and Sustaining School Counseling Practices Through a Culturally Affirming Lens* (pp. 248–270). IGI Global., doi:10.4018/978-1-7998-9514-5.ch013

Camilleri, C., Vella, J. G., & Nezval, V. (2020). ThespisTRX. [IJITWE]. *International Journal of Information Technology and Web Engineering, 15*(1), 1–16. doi:10.4018/IJITWE.2020010101

Camillo, A. (2021). *Finance.* IGI Global., doi:10.4018/978-1-7998-4342-9.ch009

Campbell, S. (2022). An Examination of Racial Trauma and Multicultural Counseling. In Brant-Rajahn, S. N., Gibson, E. M.Cook Sandifer, M. (Eds.), Developing, Delivering, and Sustaining School Counseling Practices Through a Culturally Affirming Lens (pp. 58-75). IGI Global. https://doi.org/ doi:10.4018/978-1-7998-9514-5.ch004

Campbell, D. M. (2019). Depicting Political Dynamics of Migrant "Blackness" in the Era of Trumpism. In F. P. Endong (Ed.), *Popular Representations of America in Non-American Media* (pp. 134–160). IGI Global., doi:10.4018/978-1-5225-9312-6.ch006

Canales, T. I. (2021). *México se posiciona para crecimiento en inteligencia artificial.* México se posiciona para crecimiento en inteligencia artificial – Canales TI. itcomunicacion.com.mx

Canniford, R., Riach, K., & Hill, T. (2018). Nosenography: How smell constitutes meaning, identity and temporal experience in spatial assemblages. *Marketing Theory, 18*(2), 234–248. doi:10.1177/1470593117732462

Cantimur, S., & Bolat, N. (2022). Representation of Violence Against Women in Television News. In R. Yılmaz & B. Koç (Eds.), *Narrative Theory and Therapy in the Post-Truth Era* (pp. 79–99). IGI Global., doi:10.4018/978-1-7998-9251-9.ch006

Cao, X., MacNaughton, P., Deng, Z., Yin, J., Zhang, X., & Allen, J. (2018). Using Twitter to Better Understand the Spatiotemporal Patterns of Public Sentiment: A Case Study in Massachusetts, USA. *International Journal of Environmental Research and Public Health, 15*(2), 15. doi:10.3390/ijerph15020250 PMID:29393869

Çapan, S. A. (2020). Using Digital Storytelling to Handle Second Language Writing Anxiety and Attitudes. In Kruk, M.Peterson, M. (Eds.), New Technological Applications for Foreign and Second Language Learning and Teaching (pp. 157-178). IGI Global. https://doi.org/ doi:10.4018/978-1-7998-2591-3.ch008

Carbajal, D., & Ramirez, Q. A. (2022). Applying Theoretical Perspectives to Social Media Influencers. In M. N. Al-Suqri, J. Alsalmi, & O. Al-Shaqsi (Eds.), *Mass Communications and the Influence of Information During Times of Crises* (pp. 69–98). IGI Global., doi:10.4018/978-1-7998-7503-1.ch004

Cardona-Moltó, M. C., & Miralles-Cardona, C. (2022). Education for Gender Equality in Teacher Preparation. In J. A. Boivin & H. Pacheco-Guffrey (Eds.), *Education as the Driving Force of Equity for the Marginalized* (pp. 65–89). IGI Global., doi:10.4018/978-1-7998-8025-7.ch004

Carminati, M., Toberto, C., Maggi, F., Epifani, I., & Zanero, S. (2015). Bank Sealer: A decision support system for online banking fraud analysis and investigation. *Computers & Security*, *3*, 175–186. doi:10.1016/j.cose.2015.04.002

Carrizo, A., Freitas, P., & Ferreira, V. (2017). Les effets des expériences de marque sur la qualité, la satisfaction et la fidélité: Une étude empirique dans le domaine des services multiples de télécommunications. *Innovar (Universidad Nacional de Colombia)*, *27*(64), 23–38. doi:10.15446/innovar.v27n64.62366

Carr-Winston, M. A. (2019). Consequences of Inequality and Exclusion on the Culture of Higher Education Institutions. In Wisdom, S., Leavitt, L.Bice, C. (Eds.), Handbook of Research on Social Inequality and Education (pp. 91-110). IGI Global. https://doi.org/ doi:10.4018/978-1-5225-9108-5.ch005

Cartagena, S., & Pike, L. (2022). Defying Deficit Thinking. In R. D. Williams (Ed.), *Handbook of Research on Challenging Deficit Thinking for Exceptional Education Improvement* (pp. 101–126). IGI Global., doi:10.4018/978-1-7998-8860-4.ch005

Carvalho, L. M., & Noronha, A. B. (2020). An Outlook About the Application of Digital Storytelling in Higher Education. In L. C. Carvalho, A. B. Noronha, & C. L. Souza (Eds.), *Learning Styles and Strategies for Management Students* (pp. 35–48). IGI Global., doi:10.4018/978-1-7998-2124-3.ch003

Casado-Aranda, L., Sánchez-Fernández, J., & Paço, A. (2021). Exploring the Effectiveness of Storytelling in Advertising Through Eye-Tracking. In L. C. Mihăeş, R. Andreescu, & A. Dimitriu (Eds.), *Handbook of Research on Contemporary Storytelling Methods Across New Media and Disciplines* (pp. 158–179). IGI Global., doi:10.4018/978-1-7998-6605-3.ch009

Casale, R., & Mentor, D. (2022). Digital Film-Making Response to a Hate Crime. In D. Mentor (Ed.), *Handbook of Research on New Media, Training, and Skill Development for the Modern Workforce* (pp. 210–233). IGI Global., doi:10.4018/978-1-6684-3996-8.ch010

Castañeda, V. M. (2017). La equidad del sistema tributario y su relación con la moral tributaria. Un estudio para América Latina. *Investigacion Economica, 76*(299), 25–152. doi:10.1016/j.inveco.2017.02.002

Castillo Cuevas, M. (2020). *Paraphrase. Elements for its writing.* Obtained from https://d1wqtxts1xzle7.cloudfront.net/64576591/PARAPHRASIS__ELEMENTS_FOR_ITS_REDACT%C3%93N.-free.pdf?1601589506=&response-content-disposition=inline%3B+filename%3DParaphrasis_Elements_for_its_redaction.pdf&Expires=1675718922&Signature=KF1Lfg~oNdZ7E31QKG

Castillo-Galván, P., & Méndez Palacios, J. J. (2022). Digital technology as a tool for the growth of Mexican SMEs in San Luis Potosi. *13th International Conference on Applied Human Factors and Ergonomics (AHFE 2022).* 10.54941/ahfe1002224

Cavazos, J. A., & Puente, R. D. (2014). Conceptualización y características de la mercadotecnia relacionada con causas. In Facultad de Contaduría y Administración (Ed.), Mercadotecnia Sustentable y su aplicación en México y Latinoamérica (pp. 1–43). Academic Press.

Cervantes-Guzmán, J. N. (2021). Evolution of Entrepreneur Women From Traditional Companies to E-Business. [IJBSA]. *International Journal of Business Strategy and Automation, 2*(2), 26–40. doi:10.4018/IJBSA.20210401.oa3

Çetinkaya, Ö. A. (2019). Brand Storytelling and Narrative Advertising. In R. Yilmaz (Ed.), *Handbook of Research on Narrative Advertising* (pp. 281–291). IGI Global., doi:10.4018/978-1-5225-9790-2.ch024

Chaiya, C., & Ahmad, M. M. (2022). The Student Loan Fund and the Education for All in Thailand. In J. A. Boivin & H. Pacheco-Guffrey (Eds.), *Education as the Driving Force of Equity for the Marginalized* (pp. 135–157). IGI Global., doi:10.4018/978-1-7998-8025-7.ch007

Cha, J. (2019). Legitimacy of Crowdfunding. [JMME]. *Journal of Media Management and Entrepreneurship, 1*(2), 31–47. doi:10.4018/JMME.2019070103

Chajdas, T. (2019). Misleading Media Portrayals in a Globalized World. In Chiluwa, I. E.Samoilenko, S. A. (Eds.), Handbook of Research on Deception, Fake News, and Misinformation Online (pp. 45-64). IGI Global. https://doi.org/ doi:10.4018/978-1-5225-8535-0.ch004

Chakabwata, W. (2022). An Intersectional Study of the Funding Experiences of South African University Students After Majority Rule. In J. Keengwe (Ed.), *Handbook of Research on Social Justice and Equity in Education* (pp. 242–258). IGI Global., doi:10.4018/978-1-7998-9567-1.ch012

Chalamandaris, G., & Antonopoulos, D. (2020). Algorithmic Trading and Transaction Costs. In C. Zopounidis, D. Kenourgios, & G. Dotsis (Eds.), *Recent Advances and Applications in Alternative Investments* (pp. 189–219). IGI Global., doi:10.4018/978-1-7998-2436-7.ch009

Chaman, S., & Shaheen, S. (2022). Linking Psychological Contract With Employee-Based Brand Equity. In M. Bari, M. Abrar, & E. Alaverdov (Eds.), *Antecedents and Outcomes of Employee-Based Brand Equity* (pp. 186–197). IGI Global., doi:10.4018/978-1-6684-3621-9.ch013

Chamblin, M., Newland, L. Z., Kelly, J., & Silva Thompson, L. M. (2022). Sistas in Action. In J. T. Butcher (Ed.), *Black Female Leaders in Academia* (pp. 97–120). IGI Global., doi:10.4018/978-1-7998-9774-3.ch006

Chandra, A. (2019). Gender Gap in Skill Development. In Bala, S.Singhal, P. (Eds.), Gender Issues in Technical and Vocational Education Programs (pp. 1-22). IGI Global. https://doi.org/ doi:10.4018/978-1-5225-8443-8.ch001

Chatterjee & Suklabaidya. (2020). Food image and travel intention: From New Delhi to New York. *Journal of Gastronomy, Hospitality and Travel, 3*(1), 3-19.

Chaturvedi, R., & Karri, A. (2022). Entrepreneurship in the Times of Pandemic: Barriers and Strategies. *FIIB Business Review, 11*(1), 52–66. doi:10.1177/23197145211043799

Chen, C.-C., Petrick, J. F., & Shahvali, M. (2016, February). Tourism Experiences as a Stress Reliever: Examining the Effects of Tourism Recovery Experiences on Life Satisfaction. *Journal of Travel Research, 55*(2), 150–160. doi:10.1177/0047287514546223

Cheshire, T. C., Martinez-Alire, C. D., Esquivido, V., & Springer, M. (2021). The Transformational Change Agent Equation. In S. Rodriguez & K. Brown (Eds.), *Black and Brown Leadership and the Promotion of Change in an Era of Social Unrest* (pp. 208–229). IGI Global., doi:10.4018/978-1-7998-7235-1.ch009

Chiavenato. (2009). *Library*. Obtained from https://1library.co/article/types-factors-factors-influence-take-decisions.q0x2l99q

Chin, W. W. (1998). *The partial least squares approach for structural equation modeling. Modern Methods for Business Research, 2, 295–336.*

Chin, W. W. (1998). The partial least squares approach to structural equation modelling. In G. A. Marcoulides (Ed.), *Modern methods for business research* (pp. 295–336). Lawrence Erlbaum.

Chiou, S. (2020). Data-Driven Stochastic Optimization for Transportation Road Network Design Under Uncertainty. In F. P. Garcia Marquez (Ed.), *Handbook of Research on Big Data Clustering and Machine Learning* (pp. 231–278). IGI Global., doi:10.4018/978-1-7998-0106-1.ch012

Chisita, C. T., Shoko, M., Rusero, A. M., & Ngoaketse, J. (2020). Media, Libraries, and Archives. In C. T. Chisita (Ed.), *Cooperation and Collaboration Initiatives for Libraries and Related Institutions* (pp. 243–272). IGI Global., doi:10.4018/978-1-7998-0043-9.ch013

Chiu, H., & Wagner, E. (2020). CEO Bonus Pay and Firm Credit Risk. [IJRCM]. *International Journal of Risk and Contingency Management, 9*(1), 1–19. doi:10.4018/IJRCM.2020010101

Chmielarz, W., & Zborowski, M. (2018). Analysis of e-Banking Websites' quality with the application of the TOPSIS Method – A Practical Study. *Procedia Computer Science*, *126*, 1964–1976. doi:10.1016/j.procs.2018.07.256

Choistealbha, J. U., & Colum, M. (2022). You Can't Be What You Can't See. In J. A. Boivin & H. Pacheco-Guffrey (Eds.), *Education as the Driving Force of Equity for the Marginalized* (pp. 113–134). IGI Global., doi:10.4018/978-1-7998-8025-7.ch006

Chopra, S., & Nagaraj, S. (2023). Business Tech in Media and Entertainment. In S. Nagaraj & K. Kumar (Eds.), *AI-Driven Intelligent Models for Business Excellence* (pp. 81–94). IGI Global., doi:10.4018/978-1-6684-4246-3.ch005

Chopra, S., & Rajan, P. (2016). Modeling intermediary satisfaction with mandatory adoption of e-Government technologies for food distribution. *Information Technologies and International Development*, *12*(1), 15–34.

Chung, M. (2021). Digital Storytelling Project for Language Teachers. In Ramírez-Verdugo, M. D.Otcu-Grillman, B. (Eds.), Interdisciplinary Approaches Toward Enhancing Teacher Education (pp. 50-68). IGI Global. https://doi.org/ doi:10.4018/978-1-7998-4697-0.ch004

Chu, S., Tu, S., Wang, N., & Zhang, W. (2020). Information Equity and Cultural Sharing. [IJLIS]. *International Journal of Library and Information Services*, *9*(1), 10–24. doi:10.4018/IJLIS.2020010102

Ciftci, D. (2021). Political Marketing and New Media Election Campaigning. In E. Esiyok (Ed.), *Handbook of Research on New Media Applications in Public Relations and Advertising* (pp. 355–379). IGI Global., doi:10.4018/978-1-7998-3201-0.ch021

Cinar, D. (2021). New Event Trends as a Tool of Digital Marketing Communication. In Birdir, K., Birdir, S., Dalgic, A.Toksoz, D. (Eds.), Impact of ICTs on Event Management and Marketing (pp. 216-241). IGI Global. https://doi.org/ doi:10.4018/978-1-7998-4954-4.ch013

Clara, S., & Barbosa, B. (2021). People Make Places, What Do Stories Do? In L. C. Mihăeş, R. Andreescu, & A. Dimitriu (Eds.), *Handbook of Research on Contemporary Storytelling Methods Across New Media and Disciplines* (pp. 79–99). IGI Global., doi:10.4018/978-1-7998-6605-3.ch005

Cohen, J. (1988). *Statistical power analysis for the behavioral science* (2nd ed.). Erlbaum.

Cohen, J. (1988). *Statistical Power Analysis for the Behavioral Sciences* (2nd ed.). Lawrence Erlbaum Associates, Publishers.

Coiffet, P., & Burdea, G. (1996). Tecnologías de la realidad virtual. Academic Press.

Cole, C. M., Burrell, D. N., & Springs, D. (2020). Exploring Organizational Development Intervention Around Sexual Harassment in Technical Firms. [IJHIoT]. *International Journal of Hyperconnectivity and the Internet of Things*, *4*(1), 29–42. doi:10.4018/IJHIoT.2020010103

ComputerScience.org. (2020). *Computer Programming Lenguages.* From Computer Science: https://www.computerscience.org/resources/computer-programming-languages/

Condie, C. (2022). Using Writing Workshops in Teacher Education to Build Writing Pedagogy and Equity-Oriented Mindsets. In T. S. Hodges (Ed.), *Handbook of Research on Teacher Practices for Diverse Writing Instruction* (pp. 248–269). IGI Global., doi:10.4018/978-1-6684-6213-3.ch013

Condori-Ojeda, P. (2020). *Universe, Population and Sample.* Workshop.

Contreras Aguirre, H. C. (2022). Navigating College as Latina STEM Students at Hispanic-Serving Institutions. In Huffman, S. P., Cunningham, D. D., Shavers, M.Adamson, R. (Eds.), Handbook of Research on Opening Pathways for Marginalized Individuals in Higher Education (pp. 244-265). IGI Global. https://doi.org/ doi:10.4018/978-1-6684-3819-0.ch014

Contreras, E. R. (2013). El concepto de estrategia como fundamento de la planeación estratégica. *Pensamiento y Gestión, 35*(8), 152–181.

Cook, B. L. (2021). The Voice of Social Media, 1997-2018. In Khosrow-Pour D.B.A., M. (Eds.), Encyclopedia of Information Science and Technology, Fifth Edition (pp. 1461-1468). IGI Global. https://doi.org/ doi:10.4018/978-1-7998-3479-3.ch100

Copeland, K., & Tarver, E. N. (2020). Diversity, Equity, and Inclusiveness in Higher Education. In Freeman, J. P., Keller, C. L. & Cambiano, R. L. (Ed.), Higher Education Response to Exponential Societal Shifts (pp. 313-329). IGI Global. https://doi.org/ doi:10.4018/978-1-7998-2410-7.ch015

Corces-Zimmerman, C., & Southern, D. E. (2021). Disrupting Structural Whiteness in Higher Education. In C. Reneau & M. Villarreal (Eds.), *Handbook of Research on Leading Higher Education Transformation With Social Justice, Equity, and Inclusion* (pp. 306–325). IGI Global., doi:10.4018/978-1-7998-7152-1.ch020

Costa, R. P. (2021). "All the World's a Stage" and Sociologists Its Storytellers. In Mihăeş, L. C., Andreescu, R.Dimitriu, A. (Eds.), Handbook of Research on Contemporary Storytelling Methods Across New Media and Disciplines (pp. 1-16). IGI Global. https://doi.org/ doi:10.4018/978-1-7998-6605-3.ch001

Costa, P. T., & Pereira, A. S. (2022). Storytelling by the Sea. In A. Campos & S. Almeida (Eds.), *Global Perspectives on Strategic Storytelling in Destination Marketing* (pp. 164–191). IGI Global., doi:10.4018/978-1-6684-3436-9.ch009

Crawford, C. M., Simons, M. A., & Walters, R. (2021). Social Learning Through a Participative Storytelling Framework. In C. M. Crawford & M. A. Simons (Eds.), *eLearning Engagement in a Transformative Social Learning Environment* (pp. 44–67). IGI Global., doi:10.4018/978-1-7998-6956-6.ch003

Crawford, J., Cain, E. C., & Hamilton, E. (2022). Building Racial Justice Into a Master's Program. In E. Cain-Sanschagrin, R. A. Filback, & J. Crawford (Eds.), *Cases on Academic Program Redesign for Greater Racial and Social Justice* (pp. 98–124). IGI Global., doi:10.4018/978-1-7998-8463-7.ch005

Cronovich, P., & Mitchell, J. (2022). Redesigning GE Language. In E. Cain-Sanschagrin, R. A. Filback, & J. Crawford (Eds.), *Cases on Academic Program Redesign for Greater Racial and Social Justice* (pp. 22–40). IGI Global., doi:10.4018/978-1-7998-8463-7.ch002

Cubbage, J. (2021). So They Might Tell Their Own Stories. In L. S. Byrd (Ed.), *Cultivating Entrepreneurial Changemakers Through Digital Media Education* (pp. 78–94). IGI Global., doi:10.4018/978-1-7998-5808-9.ch005

Cueva-Rivera, X. E., & Erazo-Álvarez, J. C. (2021). Impacto socioeconómico del COVID-19 en las micro, pequeñas y medianas empresas. *Revista Arbitrada Interdisciplinaria Koinonía*, *6*(12). Advance online publication. doi:10.35381/r.k.v6i12.1275

Cupid, S., Marina, B. L., & Canton, M. (2022). When and Where We Enter. In Msengi, C. M., Lartey, G. K., & Sprott, K. R. (Ed.), Contemporary Issues in Multicultural and Global Education (pp. 193-216). IGI Global. https://doi.org/ doi:10.4018/978-1-7998-7404-1.ch011

Cyrulnik, N. (2022). To Identify the Evolution of Tourism Practices in a Sensitive Way Through Documentary. In Andrade, P.Martins, M. D. (Eds.), Handbook of Research on Urban Tourism, Viral Society, and the Impact of the COVID-19 Pandemic (pp. 538-555). IGI Global. https://doi.org/ doi:10.4018/978-1-6684-3369-0.ch026

Da Silva, F., & Núñez Reyes, G. (2021). *Free competition in the post-pandemic digital era: The impact on SMEs*. ECLAC.

DAI Global. (2022). *Insights from emerging markets. MSMEs and Digital Tool Use Amidst the COVID-19 Pandemic. Mexico Country Brief.* dai.com

Dal Canbazoğlu, A. (2021). Gender and Patriarchy in Turkish Advertising. In Mihăeş, L. C., Andreescu, R.Dimitriu, A. (Eds.), Handbook of Research on Contemporary Storytelling Methods Across New Media and Disciplines (pp. 138-157). IGI Global. https://doi.org/ doi:10.4018/978-1-7998-6605-3.ch008

Dalvi, D. S. (2021). Employer Brand Equity and Its Impact on the Application Intent of the Prospective Employees. [IJBIR]. *International Journal of Business Intelligence Research*, *12*(1), 1–25. doi:10.4018/IJBIR.20210101.oa1

Daradkeh, M. K. (2021). An Empirical Examination of the Relationship Between Data Storytelling Competency and Business Performance. [JOEUC]. *Journal of Organizational and End User Computing*, *33*(5), 42–73. doi:10.4018/JOEUC.20210901.oa3

Dar, W. A. (2021). Constructivism, Pluralism, and Pedagogy From Below in India. In N. Mthembu (Ed.), *Ethical Research Approaches to Indigenous Knowledge Education* (pp. 110–126). IGI Global., doi:10.4018/978-1-7998-1249-4.ch005

Darwish, E. (2020). Perceptions of the UAE's Government Communicators Regarding Social Media Roles. [IJCRMM]. *International Journal of Customer Relationship Marketing and Management, 11*(4), 20–35. doi:10.4018/IJCRMM.2020100102

Das, S. (2020). Innovations in Digital Banking Service Brand Equity and Millennial Consumerism. In K. Sandhu (Ed.), *Digital Transformation and Innovative Services for Business and Learning* (pp. 62–79). IGI Global., doi:10.4018/978-1-7998-5175-2.ch004

Davis-Cotton, D. (2021). Marginalized Communities, Curriculum, Children (MC3). In M. C. Grant (Ed.), *Emerging Strategies for Public Education Reform* (pp. 126–160). IGI Global., doi:10.4018/978-1-7998-5695-5.ch005

Davis, F. D. (1989). Perceived usefulness, perceived ease of use, and user acceptance of information technology. *Management Information Systems Quarterly, 13*(3), 319–340. doi:10.2307/249008

Davis, L. (2020). Don't Hide the Hurt. In A. M. Ellsworth (Ed.), *Cases on Emotionally Responsive Teaching and Mentoring* (pp. 13–26). IGI Global., doi:10.4018/978-1-7998-2971-3.ch002

Dawood, E. A., Elfakhrany, E., & Maghraby, F. A. (2019). Improve Profiling Bank Customer's Behavior Using Machine Learning. *IEEE Access : Practical Innovations, Open Solutions, 7*, 109320–109327. Advance online publication. doi:10.1109/ACCESS.2019.2934644

De Blasio, E., Rega, R., & Valente, M. (2022). Polarization and Platformization of News in Italian Journalism. In D. Palau-Sampio, G. López García, & L. Iannelli (Eds.), *Contemporary Politics, Communication, and the Impact on Democracy* (pp. 74–92). IGI Global., doi:10.4018/978-1-7998-8057-8.ch005

Decré, B., & Cloonan, C. (2019). A touch of gloss: Haptic perception of packaging and consumers' reactions. *Journal of Product and Brand Management, 28*(1), 117–132. doi:10.1108/JPBM-05-2017-1472

Deeb, A. M., & Bromer, B. L. (2022). Spotlighting Diversity, Equity, Inclusion, and Belonging in Higher Education During the COVID-19 Pandemic. In B. L. Bromer & C. M. Crawford (Eds.), *Handbook of Research on Learner-Centered Approaches to Teaching in an Age of Transformational Change* (pp. 226–247). IGI Global., doi:10.4018/978-1-6684-4240-1.ch012

Degener, R., Castillo, B., & Beschorner, B. (2022). Evaluating Antiracist Dispositions. In von Hohenberg, S. C. (Ed.), Dispositional Development and Assessment in Teacher Preparation Programs (pp. 273-288). IGI Global. https://doi.org/ doi:10.4018/978-1-6684-4089-6.ch015

DeHart, J. D. (2021). The Emotional Affordances of Visual Literacy Pedagogy. In Tussey, J.Haas, L. (Eds.), Handbook of Research on Supporting Social and Emotional Development Through Literacy Education (pp. 73-87). IGI Global. https://doi.org/ doi:10.4018/978-1-7998-7464-5.ch004

DeHart, J. (2022). *Authorial Work With Film.* IGI Global., doi:10.4018/978-1-7998-9136-9.ch006

DeHart, J. (2022). *Implications for Choosing Film.* IGI Global., doi:10.4018/978-1-7998-9136-9.ch002

DeHart, J. D. (2023). Traveling Across Media. In J. D. DeHart (Ed.), *Exploring Comics and Graphic Novels in the Classroom* (pp. 279–291). IGI Global., doi:10.4018/978-1-6684-4313-2.ch015

Del Priore, A. (2022). Mentoring for Career Advancement. In Pichon, H. W.Mutakabbir, Y. (Eds.), African American Leadership and Mentoring Through Purpose, Preparation, and Preceptors (pp. 222-250). IGI Global. https://doi.org/ doi:10.4018/978-1-7998-8206-0.ch011

DeMartino, L., & Weiser, S. G. (2021). Striving for Equity in Pandemic Times. In L. Kyei-Blankson, J. Blankson, & E. Ntuli (Eds.), *Handbook of Research on Inequities in Online Education During Global Crises* (pp. 199–223). IGI Global., doi:10.4018/978-1-7998-6533-9.ch011

Dempsey, A., M'gadzah, S., & Watson, S. D. (2022). Diversity and Racism in Higher Education. In E. Meletiadou (Ed.), *Handbook of Research on Practices for Advancing Diversity and Inclusion in Higher Education* (pp. 354–376). IGI Global., doi:10.4018/978-1-7998-9628-9.ch018

Denissen, J. J., Butalid, L., Penke, L., & Van Aken, M. A. (2008). The effects of weather on daily mood: A multilevel approach. *Emotion*, *8*(5), 662–667. doi:10.1037/a0013497 PMID:18837616

Dennis, B., Li, P., Ross, K., & Zhao, P. (2021). Pedagogy as a Form of Praxis and Commitment. In T. S. Jenkins (Ed.), *Reshaping Graduate Education Through Innovation and Experiential Learning* (pp. 1–22). IGI Global., doi:10.4018/978-1-7998-4836-3.ch001

Derindere Köseoğlu, S., & Awad Almeany, S. S. (2020). Introduction to Business Valuation. In Köseoğlu, S. D. (Ed.), Valuation Challenges and Solutions in Contemporary Businesses (pp. 1-23). IGI Global. https://doi.org/ doi:10.4018/978-1-7998-1086-5.ch001

Dewsbury, B. (2020). A Worthy Burden. In Brand, S. T.Ciccomascolo, L. E. (Eds.), Social Justice and Putting Theory Into Practice in Schools and Communities (pp. 29-43). IGI Global. https://doi.org/ doi:10.4018/978-1-5225-9434-5.ch003

Dhar, S., & Chowdhury, M. A. (2021). Impact of Environmental Accounting Reporting Practices on Financial Performance. [IJABIM]. *International Journal of Asian Business and Information Management*, *12*(1), 24–42. doi:10.4018/IJABIM.20210101.oa2

Dhar, S., & Varshney, U. (2011). Challenges and business models for mobile location-based services and advertising. *Communications of the ACM*, *54*(5), 121–128. doi:10.1145/1941487.1941515

Díaz, N. C., & Castaño, C. A. (2013). El Valor Compartido como Nueva Estrategia de Desarrollo Empresarial. *International Journal of Good Conscience*, *8*(2), 82–100.

Dickson, T. A. (2022). Advancing Equity, Diversity, and Inclusion Through the Transformation of Nursing Education. In McCune, N. M. (Eds.), Advancing DEI and Creating Inclusive Environments in the Online Space (pp. 94-109). IGI Global. https://doi.org/ doi:10.4018/978-1-6684-5146-5.ch006

Dietz, L. W., Herzog, D., & Wörndl, W. (2018). Deriving tourist mobility patterns from check-in data. *Proceedings of the WSDM 2018 Workshop on Learning from User Interactions*.

Dietz, L. W., Sen, A., Roy, R., & Wörndl, W. (2020). Mining trips from location-based social networks for clustering travelers and destinations. *Information Technology & Tourism, Vol, 22*(1), 131–166. doi:10.100740558-020-00170-6

Dietz, L. W., & Wörndl, W. (2019). *How Long to Stay Where?* On the Amount of Item Consumption in Travel Recommendation. –In RecSys.

Díez-Garrido, M., Calvo, D., & Cano-Orón, L. (2022). The Mirage of Truth. In D. Palau-Sampio, G. López García, & L. Iannelli (Eds.), *Contemporary Politics, Communication, and the Impact on Democracy* (pp. 133–151). IGI Global., doi:10.4018/978-1-7998-8057-8.ch008

Dijkstra, T. K., & Henseler, J. (2015). Consistent Partial Least Squares Path Modeling. *Management Information Systems Quarterly, 39*(2), 297–316. doi:10.25300/MISQ/2015/39.2.02

Dinesh Kumar, J., & Sriram, A. (2021). Information and Communication Technologies Use and Its Influence in Family Functioning. [IJTD]. *International Journal of Technology Diffusion, 12*(1), 28–52. doi:10.4018/IJTD.2021010102

Dini & Zurita. (2021). *Analysis of policies to support SMEs in confronting the COVID-19 pandemic in Latin America.* ECLAC. LC/TS.2021/29

Donald, M. (2019). *Leading and Managing Change in the Age of Disruption and Artificial Intelligence.* Emerald Group Publishing. doi:10.1108/9781787563674

Dönmez, S. C., & Yegen, C. (2021). Eleven Eleven VR. In R. Yilmaz (Ed.), *Handbook of Research on Narrative Interactions* (pp. 292–305). IGI Global., doi:10.4018/978-1-7998-4903-2.ch016

Dos, D. (2021). Unlimiting Perspectives. In Reneau, C. Villarreal, M. (Eds.), Handbook of Research on Leading Higher Education Transformation With Social Justice, Equity, and Inclusion (pp. 89-106). IGI Global. https://doi.org/ doi:10.4018/978-1-7998-7152-1.ch007

Dove, K. G. (2021). Classroom Equity and the Role of a Teacher Leader. In B. S. Zugelder (Ed.), *Empowering Formal and Informal Leadership While Maintaining Teacher Identity* (pp. 109–134). IGI Global., doi:10.4018/978-1-7998-6500-1.ch005

Dragovic, N., Vasiljevic, D., Stankov, U., & Vujicic, M. (2019). Go social for your own safety! Review of social networks use on natural disasters – Case studies from worldwide. Open Geosciences, 11(1).

Dua, S., Dua, S., & Singh, I. (2021). i-Branding as a Tool of Integrated Marketing. In Singh, A. (Ed.), Big Data Analytics for Improved Accuracy, Efficiency, and Decision Making in Digital Marketing (pp. 183-195). IGI Global. https://doi.org/ doi:10.4018/978-1-7998-7231-3.ch013

Dua, S., Singh, I., & Das, S. (2021). Banking Innovative Service With Digital Brand Equity for New Age Consumers. In S. Das & S. R. Mondal (Eds.), *Innovations in Digital Branding and Content Marketing* (pp. 134–159). IGI Global., doi:10.4018/978-1-7998-4420-4.ch007

Dunkel, Andrienko, Andrienko, Burghardt, Hauthal, & Purves. (2019). A conceptual framework for studying collective reactions to events in location-based social media. *International Journal of Geographical Information Science, 33*(4).

Duolingo. (2018). *What is Duolingo?* From https://support.duolingo.com/hc/en-us/articles/204829090-Wha t-is-Duolingo-

Durán, P. (2017). *Microempresas, PyMEs y Objetivos de Desarrollo Sostenible*. Nacionales Unidas México. https://bit.ly/3BJF3zZ

Duval, S., & Foerster Luu, A. M. (2020). Transforming the Education of Immigrant Youth. In L. Cardozo-Gaibisso & M. Vazquez Dominguez (Eds.), *Handbook of Research on Advancing Language Equity Practices With Immigrant Communities* (pp. 87–106). IGI Global., doi:10.4018/978-1-7998-3448-9.ch005

Dwivedi, R., Shukla, B., & Malik, G. (2022). Waste to Wealth Enterprises. In H. Magd, D. Singh, R. T. Syed, & D. Spicer (Eds.), *International Perspectives on Value Creation and Sustainability Through Social Entrepreneurship* (pp. 223–238). IGI Global., doi:10.4018/978-1-6684-4666-9.ch011

Easa, N. F., & Bazzi, A. M. (2020). The Influence of Employer Branding on Employer Attractiveness and Employee Engagement and Retention. [IJCRMM]. *International Journal of Customer Relationship Marketing and Management, 11*(4), 48–69. doi:10.4018/IJCRMM.2020100104

Economist Impact. (2021a). *Mexican SMEs: The digital drivers of economic recovery*. Author.

Economist Impact. (2021b). *Developing Digital Mexico: The SME struggle with covid-19*. Author.

Egloff, B., Tausch, A., Kohlmann, C.-W., & Krohne, H. W. (1995). Relationships between time of day, day of the week, and positive mood: Exploring the role of the mood measure. *Motivation and Emotion, 19*(2), 99–110. doi:10.1007/BF02250565

Ejiogu, A. O., & Adikaibe, P. (2019). Socioeconomic Analysis of the Relationship between the Socioeconomic Characteristics and the Leverage Ratio of Rice Farmers in Anambra State, Nigeria. [IJSEM]. *International Journal of Sustainable Economies Management, 8*(4), 1–12. doi:10.4018/IJSEM.2019100101

El Gody, A. (2020). Social Media Economy and Newsroom Convergence in Egyptian Media. In Karlidag, S.Bulut, S. (Eds.), Handbook of Research on the Political Economy of Communications and Media (pp. 115-133). IGI Global. https://doi.org/ doi:10.4018/978-1-7998-3270-6.ch007

El Gody, A. (2020). Social Networks, Media, and the Egyptian Revolution. In Kumar, V.Malhotra, G. (Eds.), Examining the Roles of IT and Social Media in Democratic Development and Social Change (pp. 133-155). IGI Global. https://doi.org/ doi:10.4018/978-1-7998-1791-8.ch006

El Universal. (2022). *México crece en Data Science*. eluniversal.com.mx

El-Amin, A. (2022). Organizational Climate Change. In A. El-Amin (Ed.), *Implementing Diversity, Equity, Inclusion, and Belonging Management in Organizational Change Initiatives* (pp. 1–23). IGI Global., doi:10.4018/978-1-6684-4023-0.ch001

Elastic, P., Bakhtiar, T., & Jaharuddin. (2020). An Optimal Control Problem of Knowledge Dissemination. In Idemudia, E. C. (Ed.), *Handbook of Research on Social and Organizational Dynamics in the Digital Era* (pp. 461-482). IGI Global. https://doi.org/ doi:10.4018/978-1-5225-8933-4.ch022

*Elavazhagan, K. (n.d.). Marketing of information products and Services. Being a Course Material for Library and Information Science.* Bharathidasan University.

Elder, R., & Krishna, A. (2022). A Review of Sensory Imagery for Consumer Psychology. *Journal of Consumer Psychology, 32*(2), 293–315. doi:10.1002/jcpy.1242

El-Gohary, H. (2010). E-Marketing-A literature Review from a Small Businesses perspective. *International Journal of Business and Social Science*, 214–244. http://www.ijbssnet.com/journals/20.pdf

Eliasson, M. N. (2023). Trayvon Martin. In L. J. Leonard (Ed.), *Cases on Crimes, Investigations, and Media Coverage* (pp. 94–116). IGI Global., doi:10.4018/978-1-7998-9668-5.ch006

Elikci, C. (2021). Integration of Artificial Intelligence Into Austrian Journalism. In Musiolik, T. H.Cheok, A. D. (Eds.), Analyzing Future Applications of AI, Sensors, and Robotics in Society (pp. 182-200). IGI Global. https://doi.org/ doi:10.4018/978-1-7998-3499-1.ch011

Ellao, J. A., Roxas, E. F., & Torres, T. P. (2021). Dealing With Sexual Harassment. In S. Jamil, B. Çoban, B. Ataman, & G. Appiah-Adjei (Eds.), *Handbook of Research on Discrimination, Gender Disparity, and Safety Risks in Journalism* (pp. 24–42). IGI Global., doi:10.4018/978-1-7998-6686-2.ch003

Ellington, L. M. (2022). Anti-Racism Movement on Campus and Educational Leadership. In V. Wang (Ed.), *Handbook of Research on Educational Leadership and Research Methodology* (pp. 256–272). IGI Global., doi:10.4018/978-1-6684-4144-2.ch014

Ellington, L. M. (2022). Character Development. In A. Courtney-Dattola (Ed.), *Handbook of Research on Adapting Remote Learning Practices for Early Childhood and Elementary School Classrooms* (pp. 65–76). IGI Global., doi:10.4018/978-1-7998-8405-7.ch004

Elwood, S. A., Kesterson, M. R., Bippert, K., DeGrande, H., & Boyson, P. (2022). Formative Journeys. In J. Keengwe (Ed.), *Handbook of Research on Digital-Based Assessment and Innovative Practices in Education* (pp. 1–29). IGI Global., doi:10.4018/978-1-6684-2468-1.ch001

Ershov, B., & Ashmarov, I. (2022). *Church as a Social and Spiritual Institution of Society*. IGI Global., doi:10.4018/978-1-6684-4915-8.ch004

Espinoza, K., Machado-Casas, M., & Martinez-Suarez, A. (2021). Disruption Through Concientización. In G. Onchwari & J. Keengwe (Eds.), *Bridging Family-Teacher Relationships for ELL and Immigrant Students* (pp. 65–82). IGI Global., doi:10.4018/978-1-7998-4712-0.ch004

Esqueda, R. W., Mendoza, L., & Quiroga, F. (2021). Marketing, network marketing y marketing digital: antecedentes, tendencias y principales características. Teoría y Estudios Regionales de la toma de decisiones de marketing, 15-66.

Esquivel Martin, T., Pérez Martín, J. M., & Bravo Torija, B. (2021). The Use of Storytelling to Promote Literacy Skills in Biology Education. In M. D. Ramírez-Verdugo & B. Otcu-Grillman (Eds.), *Interdisciplinary Approaches Toward Enhancing Teacher Education* (pp. 155–177). IGI Global., doi:10.4018/978-1-7998-4697-0.ch009

Everett, D. L., & Harris, W. G. (2021). A Model for Institutional Equity. In A. J. Griffen (Ed.), *Challenges to Integrating Diversity, Equity, and Inclusion Programs in Organizations* (pp. 1–11). IGI Global., doi:10.4018/978-1-7998-4093-0.ch001

Ezikwelu, E. (2022). Racialized Social Perceptions. In Msengi, C. M., Lartey, G. K.Sprott, K. R. (Eds.), Contemporary Issues in Multicultural and Global Education (pp. 16-30). IGI Global. https://doi.org/ doi:10.4018/978-1-7998-7404-1.ch002

Falcone, P. (2020). Heritage Storytelling. In A. D. Queirós (Ed.), *Examining a New Paradigm of Heritage With Philosophy, Economy, and Education* (pp. 142–156). IGI Global., doi:10.4018/978-1-7998-3636-0.ch010

Falk, A. F., Carrasco-Velez, R. T., Shannon, M., & Proulx, E. (2022). Advancing College Diversity and Access Through Partnership. In E. Meletiadou (Ed.), *Handbook of Research on Practices for Advancing Diversity and Inclusion in Higher Education* (pp. 149–170). IGI Global., doi:10.4018/978-1-7998-9628-9.ch008

Fallah, S., Reynolds, B., & Murawski, W. (2020). *Results of a Mixed-Methods Study on One CLD Group*. IGI Global., doi:10.4018/978-1-7998-2069-7.ch007

Fang & Zhan. (2015). Sentiment analysis using product review data. *Journal of Big Data*.

Faraon, M., Jaff, A., Nepomuceno, L. P., & Villavicencio, V. (2020). Fake News and Aggregated Credibility. [IJACI]. *International Journal of Ambient Computing and Intelligence*, *11*(4), 93–117. doi:10.4018/IJACI.20201001.oa1

FBI. (2022). *Internet Crime Report*. Internet Crime Complaint Center. https://www.ic3.gov/Media/PDF/AnnualReport/2022_IC3Report.pd
f

Fernández Gómez, J. D. (2020). An Approach to Motivation Research From Advertising Strategy. In Hernández-Santaolalla, V.Barrientos-Bueno, M. (Eds.), Handbook of Research on Transmedia Storytelling, Audience Engagement, and Business Strategies (pp. 239-253). IGI Global. https://doi.org/ doi:10.4018/978-1-7998-3119-8.ch016

Fernandez, A. (2022). *ILJobsCareer.com*. Obtained from https://iljobscareers.com/what-is-a-definition-of-career -op portunity /

Fernández, C., Arribas, F., & Martín, C. (2020). Marketing sensorial en el sector de la moda femenina: El olor de las tiendas en Madrid. *Revista Academia & Negocios*, *7*(1), 31–40. doi:10.29393/RAN6-1SMCF20001

Fernández, R., Ángeles, M., & Bonillo, I. (2009). La estética y la diversión como factores generadores de valor en la experiencia de consumo en servicios. *Innovar (Universidad Nacional de Colombia)*, *19*(34), 7–24. http://www.scielo.org.co/scielo.php?script=sci_arttext&pid=S0121-50512009000200002

Ferraro, A. (2022). Framing Higher Education Through the Social Determinants of Health. In McCune, N. M. (Eds.), Advancing DEI and Creating Inclusive Environments in the Online Space (pp. 210-224). IGI Global. https://doi.org/ doi:10.4018/978-1-6684-5146-5.ch013

Ferraz-Caetano, J., & Dias, D. (2021). Chemistry Edutainment. In L. C. Mihăeş, R. Andreescu, & A. Dimitriu (Eds.), *Handbook of Research on Contemporary Storytelling Methods Across New Media and Disciplines* (pp. 364–391). IGI Global., doi:10.4018/978-1-7998-6605-3.ch019

Fierro Moreno, E., Cuauhtémoc Gaxiola, S., & Linares, R. (2021). Estrategias de respuesta de empresas mexicanas ante los impactos de la crisis por Covid-19. RECAI Revista de Estudios en Contaduría. *Administración e Informática*, *10*(29), 65. Advance online publication. doi:10.36677/recai.v10i29.15567

Figueiredo, C. (2020). Working to Produce Consensus. In Karlidag, S.Bulut, S. (Eds.), Handbook of Research on the Political Economy of Communications and Media (pp. 18-36). IGI Global. https://doi.org/ doi:10.4018/978-1-7998-3270-6.ch002

Figueiredo, G. V., & Neto, J. P. (2022). Digital Marketing as a Driver of Tourism. In N. Gustavo, J. Pronto, L. Carvalho, & M. Belo (Eds.), *Optimizing Digital Solutions for Hyper-Personalization in Tourism and Hospitality* (pp. 214–230). IGI Global., doi:10.4018/978-1-7998-8306-7.ch011

Filbeck, G., & Zhao, X. (2020). Supply Chain Disruptions. [IJISSCM]. *International Journal of Information Systems and Supply Chain Management*, *13*(3), 78–108. doi:10.4018/IJISSCM.2020070105

Fischer & Espejo. (2017). *Mercadotecnia*. McGraw-Hill.

Fleming, J. (2022). Why Are Finland Women Scholars Not Finnish-ing the Race Towards Science, Engineering, and Technology. In Boivin, J. A.Pacheco-Guffrey, H. (Eds.), Education as the Driving Force of Equity for the Marginalized (pp. 247-271). IGI Global. https://doi.org/ doi:10.4018/978-1-7998-8025-7.ch012

Fleming, P. (2000). *Hablemos del marketing interactivo.* Encuesta Nacional de financiamiento de las empresas (2021) INEGI. https://www.inegi.org.mx/programas/enafin/2021/

Flores, M. D. (2022). Intermedia Agenda-Setting Effect of Latino Television in the 2020 U.S. Presidential Election. In Palau-Sampio, D., López García, G.Iannelli, L. (Eds.), Contemporary Politics, Communication, and the Impact on Democracy (pp. 186-208). IGI Global. https://doi.org/ doi:10.4018/978-1-7998-8057-8.ch011

Fogel, J., & Wahba, V. (2021). Physician Rating Websites and Use or Non-Use of a Physician After Reading These Reviews. [JECO]. *Journal of Electronic Commerce in Organizations*, *19*(2), 55–73. doi:10.4018/JECO.2021040104

Forero, Y. M. (2012). *Creación de valor compartido*. Ploutos.

Fornell, C., & Larcker, D. F. (1981). Evaluating structural equation models with unobservable variables and measurement error. *JMR, Journal of Marketing Research*, *18*(1), 39–5. doi:10.1177/002224378101800104

Forrest, J. Y., Liu, J., Martorell, G., Xu, L., & Liu, Y. (2021). Role of Manufacturing Sector in the Forthcoming National Industrial Transformations. [IJSKD]. *International Journal of Sociotechnology and Knowledge Development*, *13*(2), 153–167. doi:10.4018/IJSKD.2021040109

Fourour, S., & Lebbah, Y. (2020). Equitable Optimization for Multicast Communication. [IJDSST]. *International Journal of Decision Support System Technology*, *12*(3), 1–25. doi:10.4018/IJDSST.2020070101

Fovet, F. (2021). Using Universal Design for Learning to Create Inclusive Provisions for Indigenous Students in Higher Education. In L. N. Roberts (Ed.), *Redesigning Teaching, Leadership, and Indigenous Education in the 21st Century* (pp. 253–274). IGI Global., doi:10.4018/978-1-7998-5557-6.ch013

Fox, B. C. (2022). The New Chief Diversity Officer. In A. El-Amin (Ed.), *Implementing Diversity, Equity, Inclusion, and Belonging Management in Organizational Change Initiatives* (pp. 24–44). IGI Global., doi:10.4018/978-1-6684-4023-0.ch002

Frazier, C. J., & Bazner, K. (2022). Who Gets Tapped by Whom? In H. W. Pichon & Y. Mutakabbir (Eds.), *African American Leadership and Mentoring Through Purpose, Preparation, and Preceptors* (pp. 89–100). IGI Global., doi:10.4018/978-1-7998-8206-0.ch005

Frizzell, M. M., Brownlee, Y., & Moffett, N. L. (2021). Graduating From the School of Noranology. In Moffett, N. L. (Ed.), Navigating Post-Doctoral Career Placement, Research, and Professionalism (pp. 301-320). IGI Global. https://doi.org/ doi:10.4018/978-1-7998-5065-6.ch014

Froehlich, T. J. (2020). Ten Lessons for the Age of Disinformation. In Dalkir, K.Katz, R. (Eds.), Navigating Fake News, Alternative Facts, and Misinformation in a Post-Truth World (pp. 36-88). IGI Global. https://doi.org/ doi:10.4018/978-1-7998-2543-2.ch003

Froemming, C. Y., Fahrenbruck, M. L., & Rutledge, D. W. (2022). App Smashing to Bolster Preservice Teachers' Digital Teaching Repertoires. In C. L. Webb & A. L. Lindner (Eds.), *Preparing Pre-Service Teachers to Integrate Technology in K-12 Classrooms* (pp. 167–190). IGI Global., doi:10.4018/978-1-6684-5478-7.ch010

Frolova, N., & Frolov, E. (2021). Estimation of Securities Positioning Efficiency in Commercial Banks. In T. Škrinjarić, M. Čižmešija, & B. Christiansen (Eds.), *Recent Applications of Financial Risk Modelling and Portfolio Management* (pp. 235–256). IGI Global., doi:10.4018/978-1-7998-5083-0.ch012

Fronza, F. C., Ferrari, E. P., Ramos, D. K., Sartori, A. S., & Cardoso, F. L. (2019). Cognitive Content of Commercial Exergames. [IJGBL]. *International Journal of Game-Based Learning, 9*(3), 23–37. doi:10.4018/IJGBL.2019070102

Gabriel, M. L. (2021). ¿Cuándo Podemos Descansar? When Can We Rest? In Rodriguez, S.Brown, K. (Eds.), Black and Brown Leadership and the Promotion of Change in an Era of Social Unrest (pp. 1-25). IGI Global. https://doi.org/ doi:10.4018/978-1-7998-7235-1.ch001

Galan, M. L., Galera, C. C., & Alves, H. M. (2021). Cause-Related Marketing Case Studies from a Global Perspective Classroom Companion: Business. In M. L. Galan, C. C. Galera, & H. Alves (Eds.), Cause-Related Marketing: case studies from a Global Perspective (pp. 1–18). Springer. doi:10.1007/978-3-030-54205-4_333

Galán, M., Clementina, L., Casquet, G., & Amaro, V. (2005). *El marketing con causa como estrategia publicitaria.* Academic Press.

Gallavan, N. P. (2022). Delving Into Expectations, Experiences, Exploitations, and Erosion of Tenure-Track Faculty. In Huffman, S. P., Cunningham, D. D., Shavers, M.Adamson, R. (Eds.); Handbook of Research on Opening Pathways for Marginalized Individuals in Higher Education (pp. 330-352). IGI Global. https://doi.org/ doi:10.4018/978-1-6684-3819-0.ch018

Galus, W., & Starzyk, J. (2021). *Embodiment and Phenomenal Consciousness.* IGI Global., doi:10.4018/978-1-7998-5653-5.ch002

Galvão, R. M. (2021). Financial Analysis and Value Creation. In Costa, T. G., Lisboa, I.Teixeira, N. M. (Eds.), Handbook of Research on Reinventing Economies and Organizations Following a Global Health Crisis (pp. 244-271). IGI Global. https://doi.org/ doi:10.4018/978-1-7998-6926-9.ch014

Galvão, R., & Teixeira, A. B. (2021). Analyzing the Impact of the COVID-19 Pandemic on Value Creation. In Teixeira, N. M. & Lisboa, I. (Ed.), Handbook of Research on Financial Management During Economic Downturn and Recovery (pp. 153-173). IGI Global. https://doi.org/ doi:10.4018/978-1-7998-6643-5.ch009

Gálvez Albarracín, E. J., Guauña Aguilar, R. A., & Ravina Ripoll, R. (2020). Actitud e intención emprendedora en estudiantes de administración de empresas y de contaduría pública. *Universidad & Empresa, 22*(38), 79–105. . doi:10.12804/revistas.urosario.edu.co/empresa/a.7230

Gambarato, R. R., & Medvedev, S. (2020). ICT and Transmedia Storytelling for Democratic Development in the Russian Political Landscape. In V. Kumar & G. Malhotra (Eds.), *Examining the Roles of IT and Social Media in Democratic Development and Social Change* (pp. 55–91). IGI Global., doi:10.4018/978-1-7998-1791-8.ch003

Gambrell, J. A., & Bright, A. (2022). Interrogating White Saviorism, Fragility, and Innocence in K-12 Teacher Education. In J. Keengwe (Ed.), *Handbook of Research on Social Justice and Equity in Education* (pp. 114–137). IGI Global., doi:10.4018/978-1-7998-9567-1.ch006

Gao, G., Wang, T., Zheng, X., Chen, Y., & Xu, X. (2019). A Systems Dynamics Simulation Study of Network Public Opinion Evolution Mechanism. [JGIM]. *Journal of Global Information Management, 27*(4), 189–207. doi:10.4018/JGIM.2019100110

Garaus, M. (2017). Atmospheric harmony in the retail environment: Its influence on store satisfaction and re-patronage intention. *Journal of Consumer Behaviour, 16*(3), 265–278. doi:10.1002/cb.1626

García Reyes, C., Valdovinos Rosas, R. M., Salgado Gallegos, M., Alejo Eleuterio, R., & Muñoz Jiménez, V. (2014). Realidad virtual y entornos virtuales como apoyo al acercamiento universidad-comunidad: El caso de la Facultad de Ingeniería de la UAEMex. *Apertura (Guadalajara, Jal.), 6*(1), 76–85.

Garrido, M. (2020). The Pitfalls and Perils of Being a Digital Journalist in Venezuela. In S. Jamil (Ed.), *Handbook of Research on Combating Threats to Media Freedom and Journalist Safety* (pp. 319–337). IGI Global., doi:10.4018/978-1-7998-1298-2.ch017

Garry, V., & Boyer, P. G. (2021). First-Year Teachers' Preparedness in Using Student Assessment Data. [IJTEPD]. *International Journal of Teacher Education and Professional Development, 4*(1), 102–114. doi:10.4018/IJTEPD.2021010107

Gates, D. (2021). Exploring Superior-Subordinate Communication From the Perspectives of African American and Latino American Subordinates. In R. D. Johnson (Ed.), *Handbook of Research on Multidisciplinary Perspectives on Managerial and Leadership Psychology* (pp. 148–166). IGI Global., doi:10.4018/978-1-7998-3811-1.ch008

Gates, Z. Y. (2022). The People v. Critical Race Theory. In J. Keengwe (Ed.), *Handbook of Research on Social Justice and Equity in Education* (pp. 138–159). IGI Global., doi:10.4018/978-1-7998-9567-1.ch007

Gbadebo, A. O. (2020). Uncommon Sources of Finance and Sustainability, Growth and Development of Small Medium-Scale Enterprises in Nigeria. In I. Oncioiu (Ed.), *Improving Business Performance Through Innovation in the Digital Economy* (pp. 200–214). IGI Global., doi:10.4018/978-1-7998-1005-6.ch014

George, A. (2018). Perceptions of Internet banking users – a structural equation modelling (SEM) approach. *IIMB Management Review, 30*(4), 357–368. doi:10.1016/j.iimb.2018.05.007

Gerrard, P., & Cunningham, J. B. (2003). The diffusion of Internet banking among Singapore consumers. *International Journal of Bank Marketing, 21*(1), 16–28. doi:10.1108/02652320310457776

Gersamia, M., Toradze, M., & Markariani, L. (2021). The Voice of Women and Challenges of Gender Equality in Georgian Media. In S. Jamil, B. Çoban, B. Ataman, & G. Appiah-Adjei (Eds.), *Handbook of Research on Discrimination, Gender Disparity, and Safety Risks in Journalism* (pp. 232–250). IGI Global., doi:10.4018/978-1-7998-6686-2.ch013

Gertrudix, M., Rubio-Tamayo, J. L., Wuebben, D., & Sanchez-Acedo, A. (2022). XR Journalism Lab. In A. Correia & V. Viegas (Eds.), *Methodologies and Use Cases on Extended Reality for Training and Education* (pp. 1–20). IGI Global., doi:10.4018/978-1-6684-3398-0.ch001

Getfield, J. (2022). Family Engagement in a Pandemic. In Fox, K. R.Szech, L. E. (Eds.), Handbook of Research on Family Literacy Practices and Home-School Connections (pp. 176-195). IGI Global. https://doi.org/ doi:10.4018/978-1-6684-4569-3.ch011

Gezmen, B., & Eken, I. (2019). The Periods of Crisis in the Ownership of the Media of Large Enterprises in Turkey. In H. Dinçer & S. Yüksel (Eds.), *Handbook of Research on Global Issues in Financial Communication and Investment Decision Making* (pp. 276–315). IGI Global., doi:10.4018/978-1-5225-9265-5.ch014

Ghosh, S. K. (2020). Waste Management Under the Legal Framework in India. In Pariatamby, A., Shahul Hamid, F.Bhatti, M. S. (Eds.), Sustainable Waste Management Challenges in Developing Countries (pp. 144-165). IGI Global. https://doi.org/ doi:10.4018/978-1-7998-0198-6.ch006

Ghosh, M., & Sanyal, G. (2018). An ensemble approach to stabilize the features for multi-domain sentiment analysis using supervised machine learning. *Journal of Big Data*, *5*(1), 44. doi:10.118640537-018-0152-5

Gibson, A. N. (2021). Becoming an Intersectional Educator. In Wellner, L.Pierce-Friedman, K. (Eds.), Supporting Early Career Teachers With Research-Based Practices (pp. 214-231). IGI Global. https://doi.org/ doi:10.4018/978-1-7998-6803-3.ch011

Gilblom, E. A. (2022). The Shape of Educational Equity. In Neimann, T., Felix, J. J., Shliakhovchuk, E.Hindman, L. L. (Eds.), Policy and Practice Challenges for Equality in Education (pp. 172-187). IGI Global. https://doi.org/ doi:10.4018/978-1-7998-7379-2.ch008

Gilblom, E. A., & Sang, H. I. (2020). Using Geographic Information Systems in Educational Research. In E. Kennedy & Y. Qian (Eds.), *Advancing Educational Research With Emerging Technology* (pp. 173–210). IGI Global., doi:10.4018/978-1-7998-1173-2.ch009

Gkadolou, E. (2019). Spatial Organization and Semantic Modelling of Historical Data. [IJCMHS]. *International Journal of Computational Methods in Heritage Science*, *3*(2), 43–57. doi:10.4018/IJCMHS.2019070103

Goker, O., & Derindere Köseoğlu, S. (2020). Challenges in Valuation by Using Discounted Free Cash Flow Method. In Köseoğlu, S. D. (Ed.), Valuation Challenges and Solutions in Contemporary Businesses (pp. 60-78). IGI Global. https://doi.org/ doi:10.4018/978-1-7998-1086-5.ch004

Golden Julie, E. (2019). Waste Management System for Smart City Using IoT. In Goyal, D., Balamurugan, S., Peng, S.Jat, D. S. (Eds.), The IoT and the Next Revolutions Automating the World (pp. 1-15). IGI Global. https://doi.org/ doi:10.4018/978-1-5225-9246-4.ch001

Golder, S. A., & Macy, M. W. (2011). Diurnal and seasonal mood vary with work, sleep, and day length across diverse cultures. *Science*, *333*(6051), 1878–1881. doi:10.1126cience.1202775 PMID:21960633

Gómez, R., & Mejía, J. E. (2012). La gestión del Marketing que conecta con los sentidos. *Revista Escuela de Administración de Negocios*, *73*(2), 168–183. doi:10.21158/01208160.n73.2012.592

Gómez-Suárez, M., Yagüe, M. J., Schmitz, A., & García-Gumiel, C. (2020). Sensorial and Experiential Marketing in Shopping Centers: Effects on Retailer Performance. In F. Musso & E. Druica (Eds.), *Handbook of Research on Retailing Techniques for Optimal Consumer Engagement and Experiences* (pp. 162–182). IGI Global. doi:10.4018/978-1-7998-1412-2.ch008

González, N. H., Guzmán, J. C., Olguin, J. A., & Gamboa, F. (2019). La mercadotecnia sensorial en la zona comercial del sur de Tamaulipas, México. *Revista Observatorio de la Economía Latinoamericana*. Recuperado de: https://www.eumed.net/rev/oel/2019/10/mercadotecnia-sensorial-mexico.html

Google Play. (2020). From Google: https://play.google.com/store/apps/details?id=mx.gob.cdmx.adip.apps&hl=en

Grant, C. S. (2020). Rediscovering Our Original Selves. In Leggett-Robinson, P. M.Villa, B. C. (Eds.), Overcoming Barriers for Women of Color in STEM Fields (pp. 141-171). IGI Global. https://doi.org/ doi:10.4018/978-1-7998-4858-5.ch007

Grant-Smith, D., & Winter, A. (2022). The Temporal Disciplining of Doctoral Research in the Neoliberal Academy. In T. Neimann, J. J. Felix, E. Shliakhovchuk, & L. L. Hindman (Eds.), *Policy and Practice Challenges for Equality in Education* (pp. 238–258). IGI Global., doi:10.4018/978-1-7998-7379-2.ch011

Gray, J. (2022). Counseling Strategies to Disrupt the School-Prison Nexus. In K. Johns (Ed.), *Counseling Strategies for Children and Families Impacted by Incarceration* (pp. 139–158). IGI Global., doi:10.4018/978-1-7998-9209-0.ch008

Green, A. (2022). Improving Diversity in Military Medicine Through Collaborative Leadership. In A. El-Amin (Ed.), *Implementing Diversity, Equity, Inclusion, and Belonging in Educational Management Practices* (pp. 120–155). IGI Global., doi:10.4018/978-1-6684-4803-8.ch007

Green, C. (2021). *Culture, Race, and Ethnicity*. IGI Global., doi:10.4018/978-1-7998-3874-6.ch003

Groshek, J. (2020). Exploring a Methodological Model for Social Media Gatekeeping on Contentious Topics. In M. Adria (Ed.), *Using New Media for Citizen Engagement and Participation* (pp. 97–111). IGI Global., doi:10.4018/978-1-7998-1828-1.ch006

Grossman, R. C. (2020). The Gender Pay Gap in Medicine. In Bellini, M. I.Papalois, V. E. (Eds.), Gender Equity in the Medical Profession (pp. 110-127). IGI Global. https://doi.org/ doi:10.4018/978-1-5225-9599-1.ch008

Grottis, L. R. (2022). Black Women in Higher Education Leadership. In J. T. Butcher (Ed.), *Black Female Leaders in Academia* (pp. 58–72). IGI Global., doi:10.4018/978-1-7998-9774-3.ch004

Guarinos, V., & Cobo Durán, S. (2020). The Expanded Story From Transmedia as a Business Model. In V. Hernández-Santaolalla & M. Barrientos-Bueno (Eds.), *Handbook of Research on Transmedia Storytelling, Audience Engagement, and Business Strategies* (pp. 382–395). IGI Global., doi:10.4018/978-1-7998-3119-8.ch025

Guedes, M. J., Saraiva, T. M., & Felício, T. (2021). Does the Capital Structure of New Ventures Differ as a Response to a Financial Crisis? In Teixeira, N. M., & Lisboa, I. (Ed.), Handbook of Research on Financial Management During Economic Downturn and Recovery (pp. 77-93). IGI Global. https://doi.org/ doi:10.4018/978-1-7998-6643-5.ch005

Gulati, G. J., Williams, C. B., & Yates, D. J. (2014). Predictors of on-line and e-participation: A cross-national comparison. *Government Information Quarterly*, *31*(4), 526–533. doi:10.1016/j.giq.2014.07.005

Gumussoy, C., Kaya, A., & Ozlu, E. (2018). Determinants of mobile banking use: An extended TAM with perceived risk, mobility access, compatibility, perceived self-efficacy and subjective norms. In F. Calisir & H. Camgoz Akdag (Eds.), *Industrial Engineering in the Industry 4.0 Era. Lecture Notes in Management and Industrial Engineering* (pp. 225–228). Springer. doi:10.1007/978-3-319-71225-3_20

Gunawardana, K. D. (2020). Success Factors of the Implementation of Crowdfunding for Start-Ups. [IJSKD]. *International Journal of Sociotechnology and Knowledge Development*, *12*(4), 89–105. doi:10.4018/IJSKD.2020100106

Gunawardana, K. D. (2021). An Analysis of Financial Distress Prediction of Selected Listed Companies in Colombo Stock Exchange. [IJSKD]. *International Journal of Sociotechnology and Knowledge Development*, *13*(2), 48–70. doi:10.4018/IJSKD.2021040104

Günaydin, A. D. (2021). Predicting Equity Returns in Developed Markets. In Škrinjarić, T., Čižmešija, M.Christiansen, B. (Eds.), Recent Applications of Financial Risk Modelling and Portfolio Management (pp. 68-90). IGI Global. https://doi.org/ doi:10.4018/978-1-7998-5083-0.ch004

Günaydin, R., & Yıldız, E. (2021). Determining the Motives and Behaviors of Brand Hate. In B. Christiansen & T. Škrinjarić (Eds.), *Handbook of Research on Applied AI for International Business and Marketing Applications* (pp. 474–498). IGI Global., doi:10.4018/978-1-7998-5077-9.ch023

Gunther, C. B., Cross-Denny, B., Reyes, M. M., & Provenzano, D. (2022). Framing eHealth Design on Critical Race Theory to Mitigate Barriers in Access to Healthcare. In S. R. Tamim (Ed.), *Instructional Design Exemplars in eHealth and mHealth Education Interventions* (pp. 55–74). IGI Global., doi:10.4018/978-1-7998-9490-2.ch003

Gupta, A., & Verma, M. (2022). Pandemic and Sustainability Practices. In R. K. Kovid & V. Kumar (Eds.), *Cases on Emerging Market Responses to the COVID-19 Pandemic* (pp. 259–283). IGI Global., doi:10.4018/978-1-6684-3504-5.ch013

Gupta, D., Montgomery, M. S., Eddy, C. M., Kalinec-Craig, C. A., Morton, K., Hulme, K., & Mahdi, F. (2021). Developing and Supporting Mathematics Teacher Educators Through Virtual Collaborations. In C. M. Crawford (Ed.), *Shifting to Online Learning Through Faculty Collaborative Support* (pp. 279–293). IGI Global., doi:10.4018/978-1-7998-6944-3.ch015

Gupta, R., Pal, S. K., & Muttoo, S. K. (2020). Data Analytics for Better Branding of E-Governance and E-Business Systems. In N. Vij Mali (Ed.), *Leveraging Digital Innovation for Governance, Public Administration, and Citizen Services* (pp. 51–78). IGI Global., doi:10.4018/978-1-5225-5412-7.ch003

Gürer, M. D. (2020). Pre-Service Language Teachers' Experiences in the Digital Storytelling Process. In Makewa, L. N.Ngussa, B. M. (Eds.), IT Issues in Higher Education (pp. 87-112). IGI Global. https://doi.org/ doi:10.4018/978-1-7998-1029-2.ch005

Gürer, M. D. (2020). Should Pre-Service Language Teachers Develop Digital Stories? In E. Alqurashi (Ed.), *Handbook of Research on Fostering Student Engagement With Instructional Technology in Higher Education* (pp. 429–445). IGI Global., doi:10.4018/978-1-7998-0119-1.ch023

Gürsakal, N., Ozkan, E., Yılmaz, F. M., & Oktay, D. (2020). How Should Data Science Education Be? [IJEOE]. *International Journal of Energy Optimization and Engineering*, *9*(2), 25–36. doi:10.4018/IJEOE.2020040103

Gurses, M. E., & Sahin, S. (2021). Reality Augmented Nightmares or Experiences of Fear. In M. N. Erdem, N. Kocabay-Sener, & T. Demir (Eds.), *Handbook of Research on Aestheticization of Violence, Horror, and Power* (pp. 592–620). IGI Global., doi:10.4018/978-1-7998-4655-0.ch029

Gurses, M. E., & Tugran, F. E. (2021). The Real Westworlds. In R. Yilmaz (Ed.), *Handbook of Research on Narrative Interactions* (pp. 86–105). IGI Global., doi:10.4018/978-1-7998-4903-2.ch006

Haase, J., Wiedmann, J., & Bettels, J. (2020). Sensory imagery in advertising: How the senses affect perceived product design and consumer attitude. *Journal of Marketing Communications*, *26*(5), 475–487. doi:10.1080/13527266.2018.1518257

Haase, J., & Wiedmann, K. (2020). The implicit sensory association test (ISAT): A measurement approach for sensory perception. *Journal of Business Research*, *109*, 236–245. doi:10.1016/j.jbusres.2019.12.005

Hafeez, E., & Zahid, L. (2021). Sexism and Gender Discrimination in Pakistan's Mainstream News Media. In S. Jamil, B. Çoban, B. Ataman, & G. Appiah-Adjei (Eds.), *Handbook of Research on Discrimination, Gender Disparity, and Safety Risks in Journalism* (pp. 60–89). IGI Global., doi:10.4018/978-1-7998-6686-2.ch005

Hagan, D. (2020). The Effect of Blogging on Fashion Consumption. In S. S. Dadwal (Ed.), *Handbook of Research on Innovations in Technology and Marketing for the Connected Consumer* (pp. 315–335). IGI Global., doi:10.4018/978-1-7998-0131-3.ch015

Hai-Jew, S. (2021). *Creating and Advancing Storylines for Learning With Visuals*. IGI Global., doi:10.4018/978-1-7998-3946-0.ch003

Hai-Jew, S. (2022). *"Generous" and "Stingy" Advice Sharing Among Peer Freelancers in Professional and Creative Project Work Considering Competitive Advantage*. IGI Global., doi:10.4018/978-1-7998-6496-7.ch004

Hair, J. F., Babin, B. J., Anderson, R. E., & Black, W. C. (2018). *Multivariate Data Analysis* (8th ed.). CENGAGE.

Hair, J., Hult, T., Ringle, C., Sarstedt, M., Castillo, J., Cepeda, G., & Roldán, J. L. (2019). *Manual de Partial Least Squares Structural Equation Modeling (PLS-SEM)*. SAGE Publishing. doi:10.3926/oss.37

Hair, J., Risher, J., Sarstedt, M., & Ringle, C. (2019). When and how to report the results of PLS-SEM. *European Business Review*, *31*(1), 2–24. doi:10.1108/EBR-11-2018-0203

Hairston, K. R. (2021). The Impact of a Pandemic on Historically Black College/University Educators. In Hairston, K. R., Edmonds, W. M.Clark, S. P. (Eds.), The Black Experience and Navigating Higher Education Through a Virtual World (pp. 1-21). IGI Global. https://doi.org/doi:10.4018/978-1-7998-7537-6.ch001

Hamacher, K., & Buckremer, R. (2022). Measuring Online Sensory Consumer Experience: Introducing the Online Sensory Marketing Index (OSMI) as a Structural Modeling Approach. *Journal of Theoretical and Applied Electronic Commerce Research*, *17*(2), 751–772. doi:10.3390/jtaer17020039

Hamida, A. A., & Razakb, F. Z. A. (2016). The effects of perceived usefulness and perceived ease of use on continuance intention to use e-Government. *Procedia Economics and Finance*, *35*, 644–649. doi:10.1016/S2212-5671(16)00079-4

Hamilton, E., Cain-Sanschagrin, E., & Crawford, J. (2022). Implementing a Critical Community of Practice Within a University-Based Teacher Induction Program. In E. Cain-Sanschagrin, R. A. Filback, & J. Crawford (Eds.), *Cases on Academic Program Redesign for Greater Racial and Social Justice* (pp. 125–149). IGI Global., doi:10.4018/978-1-7998-8463-7.ch006

Hammoud, J., Bizri, R. M., & El Baba, I. (2018). The impact of e-banking service quality on customer satisfaction: Evidence from the Lebanese banking sector. *SAGE Open*, *8*(Jul-Sep), 1–12. doi:10.1177/2158244018790633

Hanaysha, J. R., Saleh, I., Hussain, S., Lee, K. L., & Abu Bakar, Z. (2021). Determinants of Firm Performance in Automotive Industry. [IJSSMET]. *International Journal of Service Science, Management, Engineering, and Technology*, *12*(4), 132–148. doi:10.4018/IJSSMET.2021070108

Hancı-Azizoglu, E. B., & Kavaklı Ulutaş, N. (2021). Creative Digital Writing. In M. Montebello (Ed.), *Digital Pedagogies and the Transformation of Language Education* (pp. 250–266). IGI Global., doi:10.4018/978-1-7998-6745-6.ch013

Hands, T. (2019). *Attain.* Obtained from https://attain.guide/features/what-is-english

Harris, D. C. (2022). Unconscious Bias Towards African American Women in the Education Workforce. In Butcher, J. T.Baker, W. C. (Eds.), Addressing Issues of Systemic Racism During Turbulent Times (pp. 23-43). IGI Global. https://doi.org/ doi:10.4018/978-1-7998-8532-0.ch002

Harris, K. I., Teitelbaum, A. M., & Holets, M. B. (2022). Cultivating Nourishment and Compassion for Young Children's Minds, Hearts, and Souls Using Spiritual Literacy. In Fox, K. R., & Szech, L. E. (Ed.), Handbook of Research on Family Literacy Practices and Home-School Connections (pp. 286-305). IGI Global. https://doi.org/ doi:10.4018/978-1-6684-4569-3.ch017

Harris, H. R. (2021). No More War Stories. In L. S. Byrd (Ed.), *Cultivating Entrepreneurial Changemakers Through Digital Media Education* (pp. 190–207). IGI Global., doi:10.4018/978-1-7998-5808-9.ch013

Harvey, J. (2019). Deconstructing Representations of African Americans in the Media. In Hoffman-Miller, P. H., James, M.Hermond, D. (Eds.), African American Suburbanization and the Consequential Loss of Identity (pp. 20-27). IGI Global. https://doi.org/ doi:10.4018/978-1-5225-7835-2.ch002

Hatton, C. E., & Clemons, K. L. (2022). School Counselors as Social Justice Advocates. In S. N. Brant-Rajahn, E. M. Gibson, & M. Cook Sandifer (Eds.), *Developing, Delivering, and Sustaining School Counseling Practices Through a Culturally Affirming Lens* (pp. 76–96). IGI Global., doi:10.4018/978-1-7998-9514-5.ch005

Heller, C. (2020). Bringing the Human Dimension to Virtual Experience. In Morie, J. F.McCallum, K. (Eds.), Handbook of Research on the Global Impacts and Roles of Immersive Media (pp. 158-175). IGI Global. https://doi.org/ doi:10.4018/978-1-7998-2433-6.ch009

Helmefalk, M. (2019). Browsing behaviour as a mediator: The impact of multi-sensory cues on purchasing. *Journal of Consumer Marketing*, *36*(2), 253–263. doi:10.1108/JCM-10-2017-2392

Hemani, C. K. (2021). Demonstrating Wet Waste Composting as a Greening Society Initiative. In Karmaoui, A., Ben Salem, A.Anees, M. T. (Eds.), Handbook of Research on Environmental Education Strategies for Addressing Climate Change and Sustainability (pp. 84-115). IGI Global. https://doi.org/ doi:10.4018/978-1-7998-7512-3.ch005

Hendy, N. T. (2022). The Role of Intellectual Humility in Leadership and Promoting Workplace Diversity, Equity, Inclusion, and Belongingness. In A. El-Amin (Ed.), *Implementing Diversity, Equity, Inclusion, and Belonging Management in Organizational Change Initiatives* (pp. 81–98). IGI Global., doi:10.4018/978-1-6684-4023-0.ch005

Henning, G., & Lundquist, A. E. (2021). Centering Learners in Assessment. In A. Peck & D. DeSawal (Eds.), *Applying Design Thinking to the Measurement of Experiential Learning* (pp. 1–11). IGI Global., doi:10.4018/978-1-7998-7768-4.ch001

Hepola, J., Karjaluoto, H., & Hintikka, A. (2017). The effect of sensory brand experience and involvement on brand equity directly and indirectly through consumer brand engagement. *Journal of Product and Brand Management*, *26*(3), 282–293. doi:10.1108/JPBM-10-2016-1348

Heredia-Torres, M. (2020). Audience Engagement and Transmedia Adaptation. In Hernández-Santaolalla, V.Barrientos-Bueno, M. (Eds.), Handbook of Research on Transmedia Storytelling, Audience Engagement, and Business Strategies (pp. 56-75). IGI Global. https://doi.org/ doi:10.4018/978-1-7998-3119-8.ch005

Hernandez, J., Thompson, J., & Mark Brookshire, T. (2022). Post-COVID Lesson Learned. In S. Ramlall, T. Cross, & M. Love (Eds.), *Handbook of Research on Future of Work and Education* (pp. 159–174). IGI Global., doi:10.4018/978-1-7998-8275-6.ch010

Hernández-Ramírez, M., Mora-Esquivel, R., & Leiva, J. C. (2022). Orientación emprendedora y desempeño innovador en mipymes. El rol moderador de la orientación estratégica. *Estudios Gerenciales*, *38*(162), 95–108. doi:10.18046/j.estger.2022.162.4519

Heuston, B. (2022). Pursuing Excellence and Equity in Education. In Betts, A. L.Thai, K. (Eds.), Handbook of Research on Innovative Approaches to Early Childhood Development and School Readiness (pp. 637-664). IGI Global. https://doi.org/ doi:10.4018/978-1-7998-8649-5.ch026

He, Y., & Bagwell, D. (2022). Professional Learning in Hybrid Spaces. In B. S. Zugelder & M. L'Esperance (Eds.), *Handbook of Research on the Educator Continuum and Development of Teachers* (pp. 1–23). IGI Global., doi:10.4018/978-1-6684-3848-0.ch007

Hill, J. T. (2022). Reimagining HBCUs in the Future of P-20 Black Education. In Bagasra, A., Mc Letchie, A.Wesley, J. (Eds.), Contributions of Historically Black Colleges and Universities in the 21st Century (pp. 41-67). IGI Global. https://doi.org/ doi:10.4018/978-1-6684-3814-5.ch003

Hisle, N. (2022). Racial Trauma-Informed Pedagogy Strategies for Educational Professionals. In C. Bernadowski (Ed.), *Strategies and Methods for Implementing Trauma-Informed Pedagogy* (pp. 20–38). IGI Global., doi:10.4018/978-1-7998-7473-7.ch002

Hisle, N. (2022). The Intersectionality of Race and Trauma in Children and Teens Who Are Black, Indigenous, and People of Color (BIPOC). In C. Bernadowski (Ed.), *Strategies and Methods for Implementing Trauma-Informed Pedagogy* (pp. 39–64). IGI Global., doi:10.4018/978-1-7998-7473-7.ch003

Hoguane, J. J., Tavares, M. N., & Boto, S. (2020). The Use of Media Convergence in the Preservation and Dissemination of Cultural Assets. [IJCICG]. *International Journal of Creative Interfaces and Computer Graphics*, *11*(2), 16–26. doi:10.4018/IJCICG.2020070102

Holmes, Q. D., Sr. (2022). The Impact of Implicit Bias on Policing Communities of Color. In Butcher, J. T.Baker, W. C. (Eds.), Addressing Issues of Systemic Racism During Turbulent Times (pp. 224-238). IGI Global. https://doi.org/ doi:10.4018/978-1-7998-8532-0.ch014

Homza, A., & Fontno, T. J. (2021). Supporting Teacher Candidates as Social Justice Change-Makers. In D. E. Hartsfield (Ed.), *Handbook of Research on Teaching Diverse Youth Literature to Pre-Service Professionals* (pp. 398–421). IGI Global., doi:10.4018/978-1-7998-7375-4.ch020

Hood, C. (2021). Kindergarten Writing. In Onchwari, G.Keengwe, J. (Eds.), Bridging Family-Teacher Relationships for ELL and Immigrant Students (pp. 302-315). IGI Global. https://doi.org/ doi:10.4018/978-1-7998-4712-0.ch016

Horak, J., Machova, V., & Vrbka, J. (2021). Financial Management for the Successful Company Value. In Teixeira, N. M., & Lisboa, I. (Ed.), Handbook of Research on Financial Management During Economic Downturn and Recovery (pp. 126-152). IGI Global. https://doi.org/ doi:10.4018/978-1-7998-6643-5.ch008

Hornak, A. M. (2021). Designing Learning Environments That Integrate With Students' Academic Learning in a Community College Setting. In Peck, A.DeSawal, D. (Eds.), Applying Design Thinking to the Measurement of Experiential Learning (pp. 134-145). IGI Global. https://doi.org/ doi:10.4018/978-1-7998-7768-4.ch009

Horsburgh, S., Goldfinch, S., & Gauld, R. (2011). Is public trust in government associated with trust in e-Government? *Social Science Computer Review, 29*(2), 232–241. doi:10.1177/0894439310368130

Horsfall, M. N. (2020). Marketing of Library and Information Services in the Digital Age: Challenges, Strategies and Implications. *Journal of Information and Knowledge Management, 11*(2), 13–20. doi:10.4314/iijikm.v11i2.2

Horton, R. (2020). Systems-Based Approaches to Speech-Language Pathology Service Delivery for School Age Children. In D. M. Scott (Ed.), *Cases on Communication Disorders in Culturally Diverse Populations* (pp. 113–136). IGI Global., doi:10.4018/978-1-7998-2261-5.ch006

Hosen, M., Imran, M., & Chowdhury, M. A. (2021). Nexus Between Sectoral Shift and Stock Return. [IJABIM]. *International Journal of Asian Business and Information Management, 12*(1), 75–93. doi:10.4018/IJABIM.20210101.oa5

Hossain, M. I. (2021). Effects of E-Banking Adoption on the Financial Performance of State-Owned Commercial Banks in Bangladesh. [IRMJ]. *Information Resources Management Journal, 34*(4), 93–112. doi:10.4018/IRMJ.20211001.oa1

Howarth & Hoffman. (1984). A multidimensional approach to the relationship between mood and weather. *British Journal of Psychology, 75*(1), 15-23.

Howell, E., & Kelley, A. D. (2021). Bridging New Media Literacies and the Common Core Through Narrative. In L. Haas & J. Tussey (Eds.), *Connecting Disciplinary Literacy and Digital Storytelling in K-12 Education* (pp. 85–103). IGI Global., doi:10.4018/978-1-7998-5770-9.ch005

Huerta, J. O., Prybutok, G. L., & Prybutok, V. R. (2021). Using Data Science Software to Address Health Disparities. [IJBDAH]. *International Journal of Big Data and Analytics in Healthcare, 6*(2), 45–58. doi:10.4018/IJBDAH.20210701.oa4

Humphrey, S., Ngo, T., & Wang, T. (2021). Digital Storytelling and Teachers' Disciplinary Multiliteracies. In L. Haas & J. Tussey (Eds.), *Connecting Disciplinary Literacy and Digital Storytelling in K-12 Education* (pp. 59–84). IGI Global., doi:10.4018/978-1-7998-5770-9.ch004

Humphreys, D., & Hinton, M. D. (2022). Seeking Equity, Quality, and Purpose as Higher Education Transforms. In A. M. Brower & R. J. Specht-Boardman (Eds.), *New Models of Higher Education: Unbundled, Rebundled, Customized, and DIY* (pp. 257–271). IGI Global., doi:10.4018/978-1-6684-3809-1.ch013

Hurst, B. S. (2020). Cinematic Virtual Reality. In Morie, J. F.McCallum, K. (Eds.), Handbook of Research on the Global Impacts and Roles of Immersive Media (pp. 221-236). IGI Global. https://doi.org/ doi:10.4018/978-1-7998-2433-6.ch012

Hutson, K. M. (2021). Missing Faces. In Gaines, C. B.Hutson, K. M. (Eds.), Promoting Positive Learning Experiences in Middle School Education (pp. 200-216). IGI Global. https://doi.org/ doi:10.4018/978-1-7998-7057-9.ch011

Ibrahim, A. M. (2019). Theorizing the Journalism Model of Disinformation and Hate Speech Propagation in a Nigerian Democratic Context. [IJEP]. *International Journal of E-Politics*, *10*(2), 60–73. doi:10.4018/IJEP.2019070105

Ibrahim, A. M., Pate, U. A., & Usman, A. M. (2020). Silencing the Media and Chaining the Watchdog. In S. Jamil (Ed.), *Handbook of Research on Combating Threats to Media Freedom and Journalist Safety* (pp. 214–240). IGI Global., doi:10.4018/978-1-7998-1298-2.ch012

Ibrahim, H. J., & Spikin, B. R. (2021). Female Journalists and Safety Challenges in Selected Media Organizations in Kano State, Nigeria. In S. Jamil, B. Çoban, B. Ataman, & G. Appiah-Adjei (Eds.), *Handbook of Research on Discrimination, Gender Disparity, and Safety Risks in Journalism* (pp. 366–393). IGI Global., doi:10.4018/978-1-7998-6686-2.ch019

Immaculate, G. G. (2020). *Research design: Questionnaire and sample*. Academic Press.

Indeed Editorial Team. (2021). *Indeed*. Obtained from https://www.indeed.com/career-advice/career-development/career-development-opportunities#:~:text=Why%20is%20it%20important%20to%20take%20advantage%20of,4%20Helps%20guide%20your%20job%20search%20decisions%20

Indira Barrón, D. (2021). *Influence of Mexicanas Americanas*. IGI Global., doi:10.4018/978-1-7998-3763-3.ch002

INEGI. (2018). *Encuesta Nacional de Inclusión Financiera (ENIF)*. https://www.inegi.org.mx/contenidos/programas/enif/2018/doc/enif_2018_resultados.pdf

INEGI. (2022b). *Directorio Estadístico Nacional de Unidades Económicas*. inegi.org.mx

Inman, L. D., & Fortner, K. M. (2021). Leading for Liberation. In S. Rodriguez & K. Brown (Eds.), *Black and Brown Leadership and the Promotion of Change in an Era of Social Unrest* (pp. 26–54). IGI Global., doi:10.4018/978-1-7998-7235-1.ch002

Instituto Nacional de Estadística y Geográfica. (2022a). *Series calculadas por métodos econométricos a partir de la Encuesta Nacional de Ocupación y Empleo*. Author.

Isika, N., Mendoza, A., & Bosua, R. (2020). An Affordance Perspective on the Enabling and Disruptive Effects of Social Media Tools on Self-Management of Chronic Illness. In K. Sandhu (Ed.), *Opportunities and Challenges in Digital Healthcare Innovation* (pp. 36–56). IGI Global., doi:10.4018/978-1-7998-3274-4.ch003

Isinkaye, F. O., Folajimi, Y. O., & Ojokoh, B. A. (2015, November). Recommendation systems: Principles, methods and evaluation. *Egyptian Informatics Journal*, *16*(3), 261–273. doi:10.1016/j.eij.2015.06.005

Islam, M. A., Quarmal, S. B., & Das, A. (2021). An investigation Into Risks to Mental Health of Bangladeshi Journalists. In S. Jamil, B. Çoban, B. Ataman, & G. Appiah-Adjei (Eds.), *Handbook of Research on Discrimination, Gender Disparity, and Safety Risks in Journalism* (pp. 167–193). IGI Global., doi:10.4018/978-1-7998-6686-2.ch010

ISO. (1998). *ISO 9241-11. Ergonomic requirements for office work with visual display terminals (VDTs) - Part 11: Guidance on usability*: Recuperado de: http://www.it.uu.se/edu/course/homepage/acsd/vt09/ISO9241part11.pdf

İstanbullu Dinçer, F. F., & Özdemir Akgül, S. (2022). Digital Cultural Heritage. In L. Oliveira (Ed.), *Handbook of Research on Digital Communications, Internet of Things, and the Future of Cultural Tourism* (pp. 183–202). IGI Global., doi:10.4018/978-1-7998-8528-3.ch010

Iyanga-Mambo, E. (2021). Online Personal Narratives. In Mihăeş, L. C., Andreescu, R.Dimitriu, A. (Eds.), Handbook of Research on Contemporary Storytelling Methods Across New Media and Disciplines (pp. 17-39). IGI Global. https://doi.org/ doi:10.4018/978-1-7998-6605-3.ch002

Jackson, T. R. (2020). An Assessment of School Segregation and Its Impact on STEM Education. In Leggett-Robinson, P. M.Villa, B. C. (Eds.), Overcoming Barriers for Women of Color in STEM Fields (pp. 34-53). IGI Global. https://doi.org/ doi:10.4018/978-1-7998-4858-5.ch002

Jackson, T. R. (2022). The Exploration of Diversity and Inclusion Programs Within Institutions of Higher Education. In E. Meletiadou (Ed.), *Handbook of Research on Practices for Advancing Diversity and Inclusion in Higher Education* (pp. 315–332). IGI Global., doi:10.4018/978-1-7998-9628-9.ch016

Jacob, R., & Rani, D. (2020). Do Pregnant Women Using Smartphones Care About Their Privacy? [IJICTHD]. *International Journal of Information Communication Technologies and Human Development*, *12*(4), 19–36. doi:10.4018/IJICTHD.2020100102

Jacobs, M., & Ellis, C. (2021). Research Methodology to Examine Disparities in Communication Disorders in Underrepresented and Vulnerable Populations. In R. Horton (Ed.), *Critical Perspectives on Social Justice in Speech-Language Pathology* (pp. 151–179). IGI Global., doi:10.4018/978-1-7998-7134-7.ch008

Jacobs, M., Jebahi, F., & Ellis, C. (2021). The Determinants of Health. In R. Horton (Ed.), *Critical Perspectives on Social Justice in Speech-Language Pathology* (pp. 39–58). IGI Global., doi:10.4018/978-1-7998-7134-7.ch003

Jamalova, M., & Constantinovits, M. (2021). The Influence of Gender on Smartphone Adoption of Young Adults in Hungary. [IJEIS]. *International Journal of Enterprise Information Systems, 17*(3), 47–65. doi:10.4018/IJEIS.2021070104

Jamil, S., & Appiah-Adjei, G. (2021). Discrimination, Gender Disparity, and Safety Risks in Journalism. In S. Jamil, B. Çoban, B. Ataman, & G. Appiah-Adjei (Eds.), *Handbook of Research on Discrimination, Gender Disparity, and Safety Risks in Journalism* (pp. 1–7). IGI Global., doi:10.4018/978-1-7998-6686-2.ch001

Jan, A., & Marimuthu, M., bin Mohd @ Mat Isa, M. P., & Shad, M. K. (2019). Bankruptcy Forecasting and Economic Sustainability Profile of the Market Leading Islamic Banking Countries. [IJABIM]. *International Journal of Asian Business and Information Management, 10*(2), 73–90. doi:10.4018/IJABIM.2019040104

Jang, H., & Lee, S. (2019). Applying Effective Sensory Marketing to Sustainable Coffee Shop Business Management. *Sustainability, 11*(22), 6430. doi:10.3390u11226430

Janita, M. S., & Miranda, F. J. (2018). Quality in e-Government services: A proposal of dimensions from the perspective of public sector employees. *Telematics and Informatics, 35*(2), 457–469. doi:10.1016/j.tele.2018.01.004

Jawad, M., Naz, M., & Maroof, Z. (2020). Era of digital revolution: Digital entrepreneurship and digital transformation in emerging economies. *Business Strategy and Development, 4*(3). doi:10.1002/bsd2.145

Jeris, S. S. (2021). Factors Influencing Bank Profitability in a Developing Economy. [IJABIM]. *International Journal of Asian Business and Information Management, 12*(3), 333–346. doi:10.4018/IJABIM.20210701.oa20

Jieun, Y., Lee, H., Ha, I., & Zo, H. (2017). User acceptance of media tablets: An empirical examination of perceived value. *Telematics and Informatics, 34*(4), 206–223. doi:10.1016/j.tele.2015.11.004

Jiménez Sánchez, Á., & Frontera Sánchez, M. R. (2020). Audiovisual Storytelling Approaches in the Marketing of Luxury Clothing Brands. In Margalina, V. & Lavín, J. M. (Ed.), Management and Inter/Intra Organizational Relationships in the Textile and Apparel Industry (pp. 263-283). IGI Global. https://doi.org/ doi:10.4018/978-1-7998-1859-5.ch012

Jimenez, J. (2022). *JobsCareerQuestions.com.* Obtained from https://jobscareerquestions.com/what-is-the-definition-of-pr ofessional-opportunity /

Jimenez, C. (2019). America as Ambivalent Superpower in Recent Mexican, Australian, and Chinese Media. In F. P. Endong (Ed.), *Popular Representations of America in Non-American Media* (pp. 29–54). IGI Global., doi:10.4018/978-1-5225-9312-6.ch002

Jobe, R. L., McCune, N. M., & Lynn, L. K. (2022). A Framework to Measure Inclusion. In McCune, N. M. (Ed.), Advancing DEI and Creating Inclusive Environments in the Online Space (pp. 153-165). IGI Global. https://doi.org/ doi:10.4018/978-1-6684-5146-5.ch010

Johnson Austin, S., Walker, B. L., Moore, L. L., Holley, M. B., Wright, S. L. Sr, & Knight, L. M. (2022). "RISE" Up Reduce School Suspensions. In A. El-Amin (Ed.), *Implementing Diversity, Equity, Inclusion, and Belonging in Educational Management Practices* (pp. 156–173). IGI Global., doi:10.4018/978-1-6684-4803-8.ch008

Johnson, L., & Pierre, Y. (2021). Solving Wicked Diversity, Equity, and Inclusive Problems From a Design Thinking Lens. In A. Peck & D. DeSawal (Eds.), *Applying Design Thinking to the Measurement of Experiential Learning* (pp. 60–76). IGI Global., doi:10.4018/978-1-7998-7768-4.ch004

Johnson, N. N. (2022). Central Office Leadership. In A. El-Amin (Ed.), *Implementing Diversity, Equity, Inclusion, and Belonging in Educational Management Practices* (pp. 14–32). IGI Global., doi:10.4018/978-1-6684-4803-8.ch002

Johnson, P., & Punnett, I. (2022). *Extended Reality and the Future of Digital Advertising*. IGI Global., doi:10.4018/978-1-7998-3844-9.ch008

Johnson, P., & Punnett, I. (2022). *Imagined Futures*. IGI Global., doi:10.4018/978-1-7998-3844-9.ch002

Johnson, P., & Punnett, I. (2022). *The Future Around Journalism*. IGI Global., doi:10.4018/978-1-7998-3844-9.ch001

Johnson, P., & Punnett, I. (2022). *The Future Electronic News Media*. IGI Global., doi:10.4018/978-1-7998-3844-9.ch006

Johnson, P., & Punnett, I. (2022). *The Future Is Africa*. IGI Global., doi:10.4018/978-1-7998-3844-9.ch021

Johnson, P., & Punnett, I. (2022). *The Future of Fake News*. IGI Global., doi:10.4018/978-1-7998-3844-9.ch003

Johnson, P., & Punnett, I. (2022). *The Future of Journalism in the Robotic Age*. IGI Global., doi:10.4018/978-1-7998-3844-9.ch007

Johnson, P., & Punnett, I. (2022). *The Future of Photojournalism*. IGI Global., doi:10.4018/978-1-7998-3844-9.ch016

Johnson, P., & Punnett, I. (2022). *The History of Black Journalism Is the Future for All Journalism*. IGI Global., doi:10.4018/978-1-7998-3844-9.ch005

Johnson, P., & Punnett, I. (2022). *The Social and Technological Revolution in Sports Journalism*. IGI Global., doi:10.4018/978-1-7998-3844-9.ch009

Johnson, P., & Punnett, I. (2022). *Visual Journalism and the Future of News Consumption.* IGI Global., doi:10.4018/978-1-7998-3844-9.ch015

Johnson, V. D. (2022). Race Conflicts and Discrimination as a Challenge for Peace Leadership. In E. P. Schellhammer (Ed.), *Evolution of Peace Leadership and Practical Implications* (pp. 181–196). IGI Global., doi:10.4018/978-1-7998-9736-1.ch010

Jones, C. (2000). *Introducción al crecimiento económico.* Pearson.

Jones, J. L., & Jones, L. L. (2022). A Space Is a Terrible Thing to Waste. In A. El-Amin (Ed.), *Implementing Diversity, Equity, Inclusion, and Belonging Management in Organizational Change Initiatives* (pp. 234–247). IGI Global., doi:10.4018/978-1-6684-4023-0.ch013

Jones, J. R., Telinhos, A., Hughes, J. M., & Patel, S. Y. (2020). A Multiple-Choice Test for the Ages. In B. Christiansen (Ed.), *Global Applications of Multigenerational Management and Leadership in the Transcultural Era* (pp. 1–39). IGI Global., doi:10.4018/978-1-5225-9906-7.ch001

Jordan, K., Lapidus, S. M., & Ramaswamy, S. (2022). Analyzing the Role of Implicit Bias From a DisCrit Perspective. In T. Neimann, J. J. Felix, E. Shliakhovchuk, & L. L. Hindman (Eds.), *Policy and Practice Challenges for Equality in Education* (pp. 102–122). IGI Global., doi:10.4018/978-1-7998-7379-2.ch006

Joseph, J., & Parameswari, B. (2002). Marketing of Information Products and Services for Libraries in India. *Library Philosophy and Practice.* Available at: https://digitalcommons.unl.edu/libphilprac/32

Jowallah, R. J. (2020). A Multilayered Approach for Addressing Poverty and Education in African American Communities. In P. W. Jones (Ed.), *Fostering Collaborations Between African American Communities and Educational Institutions* (pp. 155–172). IGI Global., doi:10.4018/978-1-7998-1181-7.ch008

Juntunen, M., Ismagilova, E., & Oikarinen, E.-L. (2019). *B2B brands on Twitter: Engaging users with a varying combination of social media content objectives, strategies, and tactics. In Industrial Marketing Management.* Elsevier.

Kaale, K. B., & Mgeta, M. B. (2020). Photojournalism Ethics. In O. Oyero (Ed.), *Media and Its Role in Protecting the Rights of Children in Africa* (pp. 149–168). IGI Global., doi:10.4018/978-1-7998-0329-4.ch008

Kalogeras, S. (2021). Transmedia Storytelling Edutainment and the New Testament Lesson. In Mihăeş, L. C., Andreescu, R.Dimitriu, A. (Eds.), Handbook of Research on Contemporary Storytelling Methods Across New Media and Disciplines (pp. 392-406). IGI Global. https://doi.org/ doi:10.4018/978-1-7998-6605-3.ch020

Kalogeras, S. (2021). Social Entrepreneurship, Smart Brands, and Epic Social Learning Networks. In P. K. Wamuyu (Ed.), *Analyzing Global Social Media Consumption* (pp. 1–15). IGI Global., doi:10.4018/978-1-7998-4718-2.ch001

Kalpana, A. R., Parveen, N., Singh, D. V., & Azam, Z. (2020). Generation and Management of Biomedical Waste. In Bhat, R. A., Qadri, H., Wani, K. A., Dar, G. H., & Mehmood, M. A. (Ed.), Innovative Waste Management Technologies for Sustainable Development (pp. 98-121). IGI Global. https://doi.org/ doi:10.4018/978-1-7998-0031-6.ch006

Kamine, D., & Stewart, R. (2020). Strategic Partnerships for Pre-K-12 Journalism Education. In R. F. Kronick (Ed.), *Emerging Perspectives on Community Schools and the Engaged University* (pp. 22–39). IGI Global., doi:10.4018/978-1-7998-0280-8.ch002

Kansiime, P., Said, S. J., & Eyaa, S. (2022). What Kind of Blackfella Are You Anyway? In F. Özsungur (Ed.), *Handbook of Research on Cyber Approaches to Public Administration and Social Policy* (pp. 420–443). IGI Global., doi:10.4018/978-1-6684-3380-5.ch017

Kantor, J. (2020). Discovering a Language of Stories in Immersive Storytelling. In Morie, J. F.McCallum, K. (Eds.), Handbook of Research on the Global Impacts and Roles of Immersive Media (pp. 142-157). IGI Global. https://doi.org/ doi:10.4018/978-1-7998-2433-6.ch008

Kapaniaris, A. G. (2022). Folk Culture and Cutting-Edge Technologies. In Papadakis, S.Kapaniaris, A. (Eds.), The Digital Folklore of Cyberculture and Digital Humanities (pp. 1-12). IGI Global. https://doi.org/ doi:10.4018/978-1-6684-4461-0.ch001

Karantalis, N., Koukopoulos, D., & Koutromanos, G. (2022). Digital Narrative as an Educational Tool for Cultural Heritage Teaching. In S. Papadakis & A. Kapaniaris (Eds.), *The Digital Folklore of Cyberculture and Digital Humanities* (pp. 117–141). IGI Global., doi:10.4018/978-1-6684-4461-0.ch007

Karaoglan Yilmaz, F. G., Koseoglu, B., Ayvali, C., & Ozturk, T. (2020). The Effect of Using Digital Stories in Teaching English as a Second Language. In Meri Yilan, S., & Koruyan, K. (Ed.), ICT-Based Assessment, Methods, and Programs in Tertiary Education (pp. 191-208). IGI Global. https://doi.org/ doi:10.4018/978-1-7998-3062-7.ch010

Karcı, H. D. (2021). Transmedia Storytelling in Advertising. In Tombul, I.Sarı, G. (Eds.), Handbook of Research on Contemporary Approaches to Orientalism in Media and Beyond (pp. 818-837). IGI Global. https://doi.org/ doi:10.4018/978-1-7998-7180-4.ch046

Karno, D., & Fish, L. A. (2021). Digital Nature Explorations. In J. Burris, D. Rosen, & D. Karno (Eds.), *Handbook of Research on Empowering Early Childhood Educators With Technology* (pp. 227–246). IGI Global., doi:10.4018/978-1-7998-6888-0.ch012

Kasoma, T. (2021). Ubuntu as a Springboard for Service-Learning. In Mukuni, J.Tlou, J. (Eds.), Understanding Ubuntu for Enhancing Intercultural Communications (pp. 141-155). IGI Global. https://doi.org/ doi:10.4018/978-1-7998-7947-3.ch012

Kaushal, V., Sharma, S., & Ali, N. (2019). Empirical Investigation of Relationship Among Destination Brand Equity Dimensions. [IJABIM]. *International Journal of Asian Business and Information Management, 10*(3), 74–90. doi:10.4018/IJABIM.2019070105

Kaya, T., & Kahraman, C. (2011). A fuzzy approach to e-banking website quality assessment based on an integrated ahp-electre method. *Technological and Economic Development of Economy*, *17*(2), 313–334. doi:10.3846/20294913.2011.583727

Kazlauskiene, V., & Draksaite, A. (2020). Green Investment Financing Instruments. In A. Kuna-Marszałek & A. Kłysik-Uryszek (Eds.), *CSR and Socially Responsible Investing Strategies in Transitioning and Emerging Economies* (pp. 189–213). IGI Global., doi:10.4018/978-1-7998-2193-9.ch010

Keiffer-Lewis, V. A. (2022). Cultural Humility as a Path to Equity in Higher Education. In Cain-Sanschagrin, E., Filback, R. A.Crawford, J. (Eds.), Cases on Academic Program Redesign for Greater Racial and Social Justice (pp. 262-280). IGI Global. https://doi.org/ doi:10.4018/978-1-7998-8463-7.ch013

Keiffer-Lewis, V., & Berman, J. (2022). Preparing Managers to Lead for Diversity, Equity, and Inclusion. In L. C. Carvalho, N. Teixeira, & P. Pardal (Eds.), *Interdisciplinary and Practical Approaches to Managerial Education and Training* (pp. 174–192). IGI Global., doi:10.4018/978-1-7998-8239-8.ch010

Keller Nicol, M., & Best, S. (2022). Disability Life Writing. In R. D. Williams (Ed.), *Handbook of Research on Challenging Deficit Thinking for Exceptional Education Improvement* (pp. 329–346). IGI Global., doi:10.4018/978-1-7998-8860-4.ch015

Keller-Bell, Y. D. (2021). Disproportionate Representation in Special Education and the Intersectionality of Race, Ethnicity, and Socioeconomic Status. In R. Horton (Ed.), *Critical Perspectives on Social Justice in Speech-Language Pathology* (pp. 1–17). IGI Global., doi:10.4018/978-1-7998-7134-7.ch001

Keller, T. M. (2021). Story Shaping Ideology. In A. Bhusal (Ed.), *Teaching Practices and Language Ideologies for Multilingual Classrooms* (pp. 1–26). IGI Global., doi:10.4018/978-1-7998-3339-0.ch001

Kelley, D. R., & Williams, M. A. (2022). A Culture of Care. In C. Ward (Ed.), *Achieving Equity in Higher Education Using Empathy as a Guiding Principle* (pp. 48–74). IGI Global., doi:10.4018/978-1-7998-9746-0.ch003

Kelly, M., & Fields, C. W. (2020). Unlocking the Doors. In C. K. Clausen & S. R. Logan (Eds.), *Integrating Social Justice Education in Teacher Preparation Programs* (pp. 1–28). IGI Global., doi:10.4018/978-1-7998-5098-4.ch001

Kendadamath, G. C. (n.d). Marketing of Library and Information Services. In D. De & B. Jirli (Eds.), *Communication Support for Sustainable Development* (p. 221001). GangaKaveri Publishing House.

Kew, S. N., Tan, S., Liew, T. W., & Tasir, Z. (2022). English Language Learner Pedagogical Performance and Experience Through Digital Video Production. In Zou, B., Thomas, M., Barr, D., & Jia, W. (Ed.), Emerging Concepts in Technology-Enhanced Language Teaching and Learning (pp. 111-127). IGI Global. https://doi.org/ doi:10.4018/978-1-7998-8981-6.ch006

Khan, A. R. (2020). Political Economy of the Relationship Between Crony Capitalism and the Private Television Channel Boom in Bangladesh. In Karlidag, S.Bulut, S. (Eds.), Handbook of Research on the Political Economy of Communications and Media (pp. 161-180). IGI Global. https://doi.org/ doi:10.4018/978-1-7998-3270-6.ch009

Khan, A., & Moseki, M. (2020). Reconceptualising Migration in South Africa. In M. A. Mafukata & K. A. Tshikolomo (Eds.), *African Perspectives on Reshaping Rural Development* (pp. 233–248). IGI Global., doi:10.4018/978-1-7998-2306-3.ch011

Kibet Ngetich, J. (2021). Role of Journalists in Development. In Akwala, A. O., Ngetich, J. K.Theuri, A. W. (Eds.), Dialectical Perspectives on Media, Health, and Culture in Modern Africa (pp. 137-151). IGI Global. https://doi.org/ doi:10.4018/978-1-5225-8091-1.ch008

Kibler, K. W., & de Oliveira, L. C. (2020). Professional Learning Recommendations for Teachers of Late-Entering Newcomers With Interrupted Formal Education. In L. Cardozo-Gaibisso & M. Vazquez Dominguez (Eds.), *Handbook of Research on Advancing Language Equity Practices With Immigrant Communities* (pp. 266–282). IGI Global., doi:10.4018/978-1-7998-3448-9.ch014

Kier, M., & Khalil, D. (2021). An Emerging Methodological Approach to Anti-Racist Design and Implementation. In V. Wang (Ed.), *Promoting Qualitative Research Methods for Critical Reflection and Change* (pp. 153–179). IGI Global., doi:10.4018/978-1-7998-7600-7.ch009

Kimathi, F. A., Zhang, Y., & Longji, H. (2019). Citizens' acceptance of e-Government service: Examining E-Tax Filing and Payment System (ETFPS) in Tanzania. *African Journal of Library Archives and Information Science*, *29*(1), 45–62.

Kincey, S. D., Zemrani, A., & Bailey, T. L. (2022). Demystifying Diversity, Equity, and Inclusion Among Students in Higher Education. In J. T. Butcher & W. C. Baker (Eds.), *Addressing Issues of Systemic Racism During Turbulent Times* (pp. 93–104). IGI Global., doi:10.4018/978-1-7998-8532-0.ch006

Kırık, A. M., & Çetinkaya, A. (2022). The Relationship Between Digital Literacy and Cyberchondria. In H. Aker & M. Aiken (Eds.), *Handbook of Research on Cyberchondria, Health Literacy, and the Role of Media in Society's Perception of Medical Information* (pp. 298–311). IGI Global., doi:10.4018/978-1-7998-8630-3.ch016

Klimstra, Frijns, Keijsers, Denissen, Raaijmakers, Van Aken, Koot, Van Lier, & Meeu. (2011). Come rain or come shine: Individual differences in how weather affects mood. *Emotion, 11*.

Koirala, S. (2020). Practices of Self-Censorship Among Nepali Journalists. In S. Jamil (Ed.), *Handbook of Research on Combating Threats to Media Freedom and Journalist Safety* (pp. 72–82). IGI Global., doi:10.4018/978-1-7998-1298-2.ch005

Koku, P. S. (2022). Critical Perspectives on Diversity, Equity, and Inclusion in Marketing. In A. Gbadamosi (Ed.), *Critical Perspectives on Diversity, Equity, and Inclusion in Marketing* (pp. 142–153). IGI Global., doi:10.4018/978-1-6684-3590-8.ch008

Kolodnicki, P. A. (2019). Integrating Media Literacy Into Mathematics. In Yildiz, M. N., Fazal, M., Ahn, M., Feirsen, R.Ozdemir, S. (Eds.), Handbook of Research on Media Literacy Research and Applications Across Disciplines (pp. 27-49). IGI Global. https://doi.org/ doi:10.4018/978-1-5225-9261-7.ch003

Komla, V. K. (2020). Strategic Responses to Disruptive Digital Innovation and Their Effects in the News Media Industry. In R. Boateng (Ed.), *Handbook of Research on Managing Information Systems in Developing Economies* (pp. 532–539). IGI Global., doi:10.4018/978-1-7998-2610-1.ch027

Kong, P. A., Zhang, X., Sachdev, A., Dzotsenidze, N., & Yu, X. (2021). Racial Socialization and Multicultural Education of Asian Families in the United States. In R. K. Gordon, K. Ahmed, & M. Hosoda (Eds.), *Evolving Multicultural Education for Global Classrooms* (pp. 40–67). IGI Global., doi:10.4018/978-1-7998-7649-6.ch003

Koş, F. C., & Gasseloğlu, M. A. (2021). Responsive Tectonics. In E. Garip & S. Garip (Eds.), *Handbook of Research on Methodologies for Design and Production Practices in Interior Architecture* (pp. 440–465). IGI Global., doi:10.4018/978-1-7998-7254-2.ch021

Koszembar, M. (2019). Sensory Marketing - Sensory Communication and its Social Perception. *Communication Today*, *10*(2), 146–156.

Kotler, P. (1973). Atmospherics as a marketing tool. *Journal of Retailing*, *49*(4), 48–64.

Kotler, P., & Andreasen, R. (1996). Strategic Marketing for Nonprofit Organization. *Journal of Marketing*, (43), 37–44.

Krairit, D. (2018). The new face of Internet user typology: The case of Thailand. *Journal of Theoretical and Applied Electronic Commerce Research, 13*(2), 58-79. doi:10.4067/S0718-18762018000200106

Kramer, B. N. (2020). Teaching Diversity in the Utah Bubble. In Clausen, C. K.Logan, S. R. (Eds.), Integrating Social Justice Education in Teacher Preparation Programs (pp. 165-184). IGI Global. https://doi.org/ doi:10.4018/978-1-7998-5098-4.ch008

Krause, G. (2022). *Definition.* Obtained from https://definition.com/factor/

Krey, N. L. T. E. (2016). *Enough is enough! Understanding environmentally driven multisensory experiences* [Doctoral dissertation]. https://digitalcommons.latech.edu/dissertations/141

Krishna, A. (2012). Sensory marketing: research on the sensuality of products. Routledge, Taylor & Francis Group, USA

Krishna, A., & Schwarz, N. (2014). Sensory marketing, embodiment, and grounded cognition: A review and introduction. *Journal of Consumer Psychology*, *24*(2), 159–168. doi:10.1016/j.jcps.2013.12.006

Krishnamurthy, S., Fudurich, G., & Rao, P. (2019). Circular Economy for India. In Ferreira, A., Marques, R., Azevedo, G., Inácio, H., & Santos, C. (Ed.), Modernization and Accountability in the Social Economy Sector (pp. 272-298). IGI Global. https://doi.org/ doi:10.4018/978-1-5225-8482-7.ch015

Krsmanovic, M. (2022). "Outsiders" Hurting From Within. In Huffman, S. P., Cunningham, D. D., Shavers, M.Adamson, R. (Eds.), Handbook of Research on Opening Pathways for Marginalized Individuals in Higher Education (pp. 210-224). IGI Global. https://doi.org/ doi:10.4018/978-1-6684-3819-0.ch012

Kuchirko, Y., & Nayfeld, I. (2020). Language Gap. In C. Huertas-Abril & M. E. Gómez-Parra (Eds.), *International Approaches to Bridging the Language Gap* (pp. 32–53). IGI Global., doi:10.4018/978-1-7998-1219-7.ch003

Küçükkambak, S. E. (2022). Creating Brand Experience Based on Brand Equity in Tourism Destinations. In G. Akel (Ed.), *Handbook of Research on Interdisciplinary Reflections of Contemporary Experiential Marketing Practices* (pp. 121–141). IGI Global., doi:10.4018/978-1-6684-4380-4.ch007

Kuehn, C. (2020). College-Going and College-Staying Capital. In Berg, G. A.Venis, L. (Eds.), Accessibility and Diversity in the 21st Century University (pp. 68-98). IGI Global. https://doi.org/ doi:10.4018/978-1-7998-2783-2.ch004

Kumar, A. (2014), Marketing of Information Products & Services in Kurukshetra University Library in the Disciplines of Social Science: A study. *IOSR Journal of Humanities and Social Science, 19*(2), 72-85. Available at: www.iosrjournals.org

Kumar, A., & Diksha, J. S. (2014). Marketing of Information Products & Services by the Research Scholars & Scientists in Central Soil Salinity Research Institute, Karnal: A study. *IOSR Journal of Humanities and Social Science, 19*(11), 58-78. Available at: www.iosrjournals.org

Kumari, S., Kumar, D., & Mittal, M. (2021). An ensemble approach for classification and prediction of diabetes mellitus using soft voting classifier. *International Journal of Cognitive Computing in Engineering, 2*, 40-46.

Kumar, J. D., & Sriram, A. (2019). The Role of Information and Communication Technologies in Family Dynamics. [IJICTHD]. *International Journal of Information Communication Technologies and Human Development, 11*(3), 1–20. doi:10.4018/IJICTHD.2019070101

Kumar, P., Paul, A., & Kumar, M. A. (2021). Risk Optimisation Analytics. [IJSESD]. *International Journal of Social Ecology and Sustainable Development, 12*(2), 48–62. doi:10.4018/IJSESD.2021040103

Kumar, R., Sachan, A., & Mukherjee, A. (2017). Qualitative approach to determine user experience of e-government services. *Computers in Human Behavior, 71*, 299–306. doi:10.1016/j.chb.2017.02.023

Kumar, V., Mukerji, B., Butt, I., & Persaud, A. (2007). Factors for successful e-Government adoption: A conceptual framework. *The Electronic Journal of E-Government*, *5*(1), 63–76.

Kundu, P., & Bhuiyan, M. M. (2021). Online Harassment of Female Journalists in Bangladesh. In S. Jamil, B. Çoban, B. Ataman, & G. Appiah-Adjei (Eds.), *Handbook of Research on Discrimination, Gender Disparity, and Safety Risks in Journalism* (pp. 143–166). IGI Global., doi:10.4018/978-1-7998-6686-2.ch009

Kupatadze, K. (2020). Ecological Chemistry Through Popular Scientific Articles. In Duca, G.Vaseashta, A. (Eds.), Handbook of Research on Emerging Developments and Environmental Impacts of Ecological Chemistry (pp. 531-542). IGI Global. https://doi.org/ doi:10.4018/978-1-7998-1241-8.ch025

Kurchenko, L. (2022). Invisible Barriers, Undeclared Wars. In Neimann, T., Felix, J. J., Shliakhovchuk, E.Hindman, L. L. (Eds.), Policy and Practice Challenges for Equality in Education (pp. 1-23). IGI Global. https://doi.org/ doi:10.4018/978-1-7998-7379-2.ch001

Kurfal, M., Arifoglu, A., Tokdemir, G., & Paçin, Y. (2017). Adoption of e-Government services in Turkey. *Computers in Human Behavior*, *66*, 168–178. doi:10.1016/j.chb.2016.09.041

Kwende, M. F., Bourgeois, J. W., Henderson, H., & Scott, J. (2022). Separate and Still Unequal. In A. T. Adams (Ed.), *Approaching Disparities in School Discipline* (pp. 136–165). IGI Global., doi:10.4018/978-1-6684-3359-1.ch006

Kyriakides, L., & Charalambous, E. (2021). Establishing Links Between Teacher Effectiveness Research and Research on Teacher Improvement. In L. W. Grant, J. H. Stronge, & X. Xu (Eds.), *International Beliefs and Practices That Characterize Teacher Effectiveness* (pp. 85–124). IGI Global., doi:10.4018/978-1-7998-7908-4.ch004

L. Guo-BrennanM. Guo-Brennan (2022). *Advancing Equity and Inclusion in Internationalization*. IGI Global. https://doi.org/ doi:10.4018/978-1-6684-4528-0.ch005

Labeeb, H. A. (2022). How Could Egyptian Young Adults Detect False Information About COVID-19 on Social Media Platforms? In Abdrabo, A. A.Galaby, A. A. (Eds.), Societal Resilience and Response to Contagious Diseases and Pandemics (pp. 155-177). IGI Global. https://doi.org/ doi:10.4018/978-1-7998-8973-1.ch008

Lachman, R., & Joffe, M. (2021). Applications of Artificial Intelligence in Media and Entertainment. In T. H. Musiolik & A. D. Cheok (Eds.), *Analyzing Future Applications of AI, Sensors, and Robotics in Society* (pp. 201–220). IGI Global., doi:10.4018/978-1-7998-3499-1.ch012

Lalas, J. W., & Strikwerda, H. L. (2020). Driving Equity in Action Through a Socially and Culturally Situated Pedagogy. In P. D. Keough (Ed.), *Overcoming Current Challenges in the P-12 Teaching Profession* (pp. 291–315). IGI Global., doi:10.4018/978-1-7998-1177-0.ch013

Lamberti, L., Benedetti, M., & Chen, S. (2014). Benefits sought by citizens and channel attitudes for multichannel payment services: Evidence from Italy. *Government Information Quarterly*, *31*(4), 596–609. doi:10.1016/j.giq.2014.03.002

Lambert, R., Greene, Q., & Lai, V. (2022). DeleteDeficitThinking. In R. D. Williams (Ed.), *Handbook of Research on Challenging Deficit Thinking for Exceptional Education Improvement* (pp. 127–143). IGI Global., doi:10.4018/978-1-7998-8860-4.ch006

Lamonaca, S. (2021). Journalism and Communication at School in Order to Form Critical Citizens. In Panconesi, G.Guida, M. (Eds.), Handbook of Research on Teaching With Virtual Environments and AI (pp. 210-235). IGI Global. https://doi.org/ doi:10.4018/978-1-7998-7638-0.ch010

Lamphere, R. D., & Pomykacz, C. R. (2022). Love and Discrimination. In T. R. Flockhart, A. Reiter, & M. R. Hassett (Eds.), *The Reproduction and Maintenance of Inequalities in Interpersonal Relationships* (pp. 23–46). IGI Global., doi:10.4018/978-1-6684-4128-2.ch002

Lampprecht, T., Salb, D., Mauser, M., van de Wetering, H., Burch, M., & Kloos, U. (2020). Visual Classification of Formula One Races by Events, Drivers, and Time Periods. In M. Sarfraz (Ed.), *Advancements in Computer Vision Applications in Intelligent Systems and Multimedia Technologies* (pp. 101–114). IGI Global., doi:10.4018/978-1-7998-4444-0.ch006

Lane, C. (2019). Digitizing Learning. In Sein-Echaluce, M. L., Fidalgo-Blanco, Á.García-Peñalvo, F. (Eds.), Innovative Trends in Flipped Teaching and Adaptive Learning (pp. 138-161). IGI Global. https://doi.org/ doi:10.4018/978-1-5225-8142-0.ch007

Lantz, J. L., Myers, J., & Wilson, R. (2020). Digital Storytelling and Young Children. In P. M. Sullivan, J. L. Lantz, & B. A. Sullivan (Eds.), *Handbook of Research on Integrating Digital Technology With Literacy Pedagogies* (pp. 212–231). IGI Global., doi:10.4018/978-1-7998-0246-4.ch010

Larson, J. S. (2005). An Exploratory Look at Supermarket Shopping Paths. *International Journal of Research in Marketing, 22*, 395-414.

Lasisi, J. O. (2022). Structural Integration Theory as Underpinning for Discourse of Diversity, Equity, and Inclusion. In Raimi, L.Kah, J. M. (Eds.), Mainstreaming Diversity, Equity, and Inclusion as Future Workplace Ethics (pp. 182-199). IGI Global. https://doi.org/ doi:10.4018/978-1-6684-3657-8.ch009

Lattimer, H., & Pizarro, M. (2021). Building a Framework for Transformation in Higher Education. In C. Reneau & M. Villarreal (Eds.), *Handbook of Research on Leading Higher Education Transformation With Social Justice, Equity, and Inclusion* (pp. 71–88). IGI Global., doi:10.4018/978-1-7998-7152-1.ch006

Latunde, C. Y. (2022). Toward the Promise. In Cain-Sanschagrin, E., Filback, R. A.Crawford, J. (Eds.), Cases on Academic Program Redesign for Greater Racial and Social Justice (pp. 176-189). IGI Global. https://doi.org/ doi:10.4018/978-1-7998-8463-7.ch008

Laughlin, T. (2021). A Vision for Deeper Agency and Personalization in Micro-Credentials. In Northrup, P., Rasmussen, K.Colson, R. (Eds.), Career Ready Education Through Experiential Learning (pp. 19-45). IGI Global. https://doi.org/ doi:10.4018/978-1-7998-1928-8.ch002

Lauritzen, J. (2021). Culturally Responsive Instruction as Computer-Based Reading Engagement and Literacy Among Native American Students. In R. Throne (Ed.), *Indigenous Research of Land, Self, and Spirit* (pp. 82–101). IGI Global., doi:10.4018/978-1-7998-3729-9.ch006

Lawa, K. O. (2020). Challenges and Opportunities for News Media and Journalism in an Increasingly Digital Mobile. In Suki, N. M.Suki, N. M. (Eds.), Leveraging Consumer Behavior and Psychology in the Digital Economy (pp. 46-59). IGI Global. https://doi.org/ doi:10.4018/978-1-7998-3042-9.ch003

Lawrence, S. A., Labissiere, T., & Stone, M. C. (2021). The 4Cs of Academic Language and Literacy. In M. L. Niess & H. Gillow-Wiles (Eds.), *Handbook of Research on Transforming Teachers' Online Pedagogical Reasoning for Engaging K-12 Students in Virtual Learning* (pp. 297–316). IGI Global., doi:10.4018/978-1-7998-7222-1.ch015

Lawton, P. H. (2021). Re-Discovering Graphics. In Bobick, B.DiCindio, C. (Eds.), Engaging Communities Through Civic Engagement in Art Museum Education (pp. 97-125). IGI Global. https://doi.org/ doi:10.4018/978-1-7998-7426-3.ch005

Le Rossignol, K. (2022). Digital Storyworlds. In C. Lane (Ed.), *Handbook of Research on Acquiring 21st Century Literacy Skills Through Game-Based Learning* (pp. 302–319). IGI Global., doi:10.4018/978-1-7998-7271-9.ch016

Leandros, N., & Papadopoulou, L. (2020). Strategic Business Models in Times of Transformational Change and Crisis. [JMME]. *Journal of Media Management and Entrepreneurship*, *2*(1), 28–41. doi:10.4018/JMME.2020010102

Lebedeva, N. A. (2022). Media Development Trends as a Counter for Terrorism in Ukraine. In Ismayil, E.Karadogan Ismayil, E. (Eds.), Media and Terrorism in the 21st Century (pp. 124-143). IGI Global. https://doi.org/ doi:10.4018/978-1-7998-9755-2.ch008

Lederer, M., & Riedl, J. (2020). Data Science Techniques in Knowledge-Intensive Business Processes. [IJDA]. *International Journal of Data Analytics*, *1*(1), 52–67. doi:10.4018/IJDA.2020010104

Lee, C. (2022). Using Multicultural Children's Literature to Leverage Student Cultural Competence and Promote Social Justice. In J. Keengwe (Ed.), *Handbook of Research on Social Justice and Equity in Education* (pp. 223–241). IGI Global., doi:10.4018/978-1-7998-9567-1.ch011

Lee, C.-Y., Chang, W.-C., & Lee, H.-C. (2017). An investigation of the effects of corporate social responsibility on corporate reputation and customer loyalty – evidence from the Taiwan non-life insurance industry. *Social Responsibility Journal*, *13*(2), 355–369. doi:10.1108/SRJ-01-2016-0006

Lee, J. B., & Porumbescu, G. A. (2019). Engendering inclusive e-government use through citizen IT training programs. *Government Information Quarterly*, *36*(1), 69–76. doi:10.1016/j.giq.2018.11.007

Lee, S., Kc, B., & Choeh, J. Y. (2020, June 20). Comparing performance of ensemble methods in predicting movie box office revenue. *Heliyon*, *6*(6), e04260. doi:10.1016/j.heliyon.2020.e04260 PMID:32613125

Leeson, S., & Kovid, R. K. (2023). Resurgence of Crowdfunding During the Corona Pandemic. In W. J. Aloulou (Ed.), *Handbook of Research on Entrepreneurship and Organizational Resilience During Unprecedented Times* (pp. 352–368). IGI Global., doi:10.4018/978-1-6684-4605-8.ch016

Leggett-Robinson, P. M. (2020). Celebrating Transformations Through STEM Storytelling. In Leggett-Robinson, P. M.Villa, B. C. (Eds.), Overcoming Barriers for Women of Color in STEM Fields (pp. 54-81). IGI Global. https://doi.org/ doi:10.4018/978-1-7998-4858-5.ch003

Lehner, E., & Ziegler, J. R. (2019). Re-Conceptualizing Race in New York City's High School Social Studies Classrooms. In S. Wisdom, L. Leavitt, & C. Bice (Eds.), *Handbook of Research on Social Inequality and Education* (pp. 24–45). IGI Global., doi:10.4018/978-1-5225-9108-5.ch002

Leija, M. G., & Fránquiz, M. E. (2021). Building Bridges Between School and Home. In G. Onchwari & J. Keengwe (Eds.), *Bridging Family-Teacher Relationships for ELL and Immigrant Students* (pp. 100–121). IGI Global., doi:10.4018/978-1-7998-4712-0.ch006

Lekic-Subasic, Z. (2021). Women and Media. In Jamil, S., Çoban, B., Ataman, B.Appiah-Adjei, G. (Eds.), Handbook of Research on Discrimination, Gender Disparity, and Safety Risks in Journalism (pp. 8-23). IGI Global. https://doi.org/ doi:10.4018/978-1-7998-6686-2.ch002

Leonard, B. (2020). Virtual eXperience as a Mass Market Phenomenon. In Morie, J. F.McCallum, K. (Eds.), Handbook of Research on the Global Impacts and Roles of Immersive Media (pp. 200-220). IGI Global. https://doi.org/ doi:10.4018/978-1-7998-2433-6.ch011

Leonard, L. J. (2023). An Analysis of Biases in US Policing and Subsequent Media Coverage in Response to the Ferguson Shooting of 2014. In L. J. Leonard (Ed.), *Cases on Crimes, Investigations, and Media Coverage* (pp. 169–191). IGI Global., doi:10.4018/978-1-7998-9668-5.ch009

Levay, K., Scheib, C., & Grossman, T. (2022). Effects of Racial and Ethnic Matching of Teacher Candidates of Color With Mentors. In B. S. Zugelder & M. L'Esperance (Eds.), *Handbook of Research on the Educator Continuum and Development of Teachers* (pp. 99–119). IGI Global., doi:10.4018/978-1-6684-3848-0.ch006

Lever, M. W., & Elliot, S. (2022). Show Me a Story. In A. Campos & S. Almeida (Eds.), *Global Perspectives on Strategic Storytelling in Destination Marketing* (pp. 230–245). IGI Global., doi:10.4018/978-1-6684-3436-9.ch012

Lewis, D. R. (2022). Examining the Deficit Narrative. In R. D. Williams (Ed.), *Handbook of Research on Challenging Deficit Thinking for Exceptional Education Improvement* (pp. 347–367). IGI Global., doi:10.4018/978-1-7998-8860-4.ch016

Liao, Y. K., Truong, G. N., & Nguyen, P. M. (2020). Psychological and Relational Moderators for the Relationship Between Brand Equity and Its Consequences. [JECO]. *Journal of Electronic Commerce in Organizations*, *18*(4), 93–116. doi:10.4018/JECO.2020100105

Lichtenstein, S., & Williamson, K. (2006). Understanding consumer adoption of Internet banking: An interpretive study in the Australian banking context. *Journal of Electronic Commerce Research, 7*(2), 50–66.

Li, M., & Akoto, M. (2021). Review of Recent Research on L2 Digital Multimodal Composing. [IJCALLT]. *International Journal of Computer-Assisted Language Learning and Teaching, 11*(3), 1–16. doi:10.4018/IJCALLT.2021070101

Lima, A. M., Teixeira, S. F., & Barbosa, B. (2022). Newspaper Digital Content During and After the Silly Season. In J. Remondes & S. Teixeira (Eds.), *Implementing Automation Initiatives in Companies to Create Better-Connected Experiences* (pp. 215–232). IGI Global., doi:10.4018/978-1-6684-5538-8.ch010

Lim, Y. J., & Lemanski, J. (2021). Individual Journalistic Bias Leads to Public Propaganda. In L. Shedletsky (Ed.), *Rationalist Bias in Communication Theory* (pp. 140–154). IGI Global., doi:10.4018/978-1-7998-7439-3.ch008

Lin, A., Hardee, S. C., & Bowen, J. (2021). Educating Otherwise. In D. E. Hartsfield (Ed.), *Handbook of Research on Teaching Diverse Youth Literature to Pre-Service Professionals* (pp. 593–613). IGI Global., doi:10.4018/978-1-7998-7375-4.ch029

Lindstrom, M. (2015). *Brand Sense: Convierta su marca en una experiencia de cinco sentidos.* Patria.

Little, C., Patterson, D., Skavronskaya, L., Moyle, B., & Bec, A. (2022). Digital Storytelling and 3D Technologies for Visitor Experience and Contested Heritage Preservation. In A. Campos & S. Almeida (Eds.), *Global Perspectives on Strategic Storytelling in Destination Marketing* (pp. 215–229). IGI Global., doi:10.4018/978-1-6684-3436-9.ch011

Liu, Q., Ge, Y., Li, Z., Chen, E., & Xiong, H. (2011). Personalized travel package recommendation. In *2011 IEEE 11th International Conference on Data Mining*. IEEE.

Liu, P. (2021). Information Dissemination Mechanism Based on Cloud Computing Cross-Media Public Opinion Network Environment. [IJITSA]. *International Journal of Information Technologies and Systems Approach, 14*(2), 70–83. doi:10.4018/IJITSA.2021070105

Liu, T., Guan, Y., & Lin, Y. (2017). Research on modulation recognition with ensemble learning. *EURASIP Journal on Wireless Communications and Networking, 2017*(1), 179. doi:10.118613638-017-0949-5

Liu, Y., Wang, M., Huang, D., Huang, Q., Yang, H., & Li, Z. (2019). The impact of mobility, risk, and cost on the users' intention to adopt mobile payments. *Information Systems and e-Business Management, 17*(2-4), 1–24. doi:10.100710257-019-00449-0

Liu, Z., & Chen, Y. (2020). Valuation Method of Equity Incentives of Listed Companies Based on the Black-Scholes Model. [IJISSS]. *International Journal of Information Systems in the Service Sector, 12*(2), 36–49. doi:10.4018/IJISSS.2020040103

Li, Y., & Shang, H. (2019). Service quality, perceived value, and citizens' continuous-use intention regarding e-government: Empirical evidence from China. *Information & Management*. Advance online publication. doi:10.1016/j.im.2019.103197

Logan, S. R. (2022). Teaching While Black, Oh and a Woman. In Logan, S. R.Good, T. L. (Eds.), Black Women Navigating Historically White Higher Education Institutions and the Journey Toward Liberation (pp. 137-160). IGI Global. https://doi.org/ doi:10.4018/978-1-6684-4626-3.ch007

Lohani, S. N. (2021). Increasing Access to and Success in Higher Education and the Role of Ethical Leadership. In A. Bhusal (Ed.), *Teaching Practices and Language Ideologies for Multilingual Classrooms* (pp. 151–169). IGI Global., doi:10.4018/978-1-7998-3339-0.ch009

Lomidze, M., & Janashia, A. (2022). The Social Potential of Media Literacy and Ways to Implement. In Alaverdov, E. & Bari, M. (Ed.), Regulating Human Rights, Social Security, and Socio-Economic Structures in a Global Perspective (pp. 45-62). IGI Global. https://doi.org/ doi:10.4018/978-1-6684-4620-1.ch004

López, A. C. (2022). Aprendizaje Colectivo en Tiempos de la Pandemia. In Shinas, V. H., Ly, C. N.Ozden, S. Y. (Eds.), Cases on Practical Applications for Remote, Hybrid, and Hyflex Teaching (pp. 88-99). IGI Global. https://doi.org/ doi:10.4018/978-1-7998-9168-0.ch005

Lopez-Cantos, F. (2021). Scientific Image Forgery, Journalism, and Public Communication of Science. [IJSKD]. *International Journal of Sociotechnology and Knowledge Development*, *13*(3), 95–105. doi:10.4018/IJSKD.2021070106

Lopez, M. M., Newman, T., & Day, C. M. (2021). Community Cultural Wealth. In T. S. Jenkins (Ed.), *Reshaping Graduate Education Through Innovation and Experiential Learning* (pp. 82–103). IGI Global., doi:10.4018/978-1-7998-4836-3.ch005

Lopez, P. D., & Duran, A. (2021). The Role of Mentoring on the Retention of Women From Diverse Backgrounds in STEM. In C. Hughes (Ed.), *Implementation Strategies for Improving Diversity in Organizations* (pp. 271–310). IGI Global., doi:10.4018/978-1-7998-4745-8.ch010

López-Paredes, M., & Carrillo-Andrade, A. (2022). Legitimation by Digital Discourses. In M. Carrillo-Durán & M. Pérez Pulido (Eds.), *Cases on Developing Effective Research Plans for Communications and Information Science* (pp. 235–250). IGI Global., doi:10.4018/978-1-6684-4523-5.ch012

Loranc-Paszylk, B., & Firla, M. (2019). Engaging Students With Authentic Ways to Learn New Words. In C. A. Lenkaitis & S. M. Hilliker (Eds.), *Engaging Teacher Candidates and Language Learners With Authentic Practice* (pp. 90–102). IGI Global., doi:10.4018/978-1-5225-8543-5.ch006

Luarn, P., & Lin, H. (2005). Toward an understanding of the behavioral intention to use mobile Banking. *Computers in Human Behavior*, *21*(6), 873–891. doi:10.1016/j.chb.2004.03.003

Luburić, R. (2019). A Model of Crisis Prevention (based on managing change, quality management and risk management). *Journal of Central Banking Theory and Practice*, *2*(2), 33–49. doi:10.2478/jcbtp-2019-0012

Lucas, G. M., Gratch, J., Malandrakis, N., Szablowski, E., Fessler, E., & Nichols, J. (2017). GOAALLL!: Using sentiment in the world cup to explore theories of emotion. *Image and Vision Computing*, *65*, 58–65. doi:10.1016/j.imavis.2017.01.006

Lukas, T. (2021). Performance Aspirations and Corporate Tax Avoidance. [IJCFA]. *International Journal of Corporate Finance and Accounting*, *8*(2), 40–58. doi:10.4018/IJCFA.2021070104

Luna-Reyes, L. F., & Gil-García, J. R. (2014). Digital government transformation and Internet portals: The co-evolution of technology, organizations, and institutions. *Government Information Quarterly*, *31*(4), 545–555. doi:10.1016/j.giq.2014.08.001

Lund, C. (2015). Selling through the Senses: Sensory Appeals in the Fashion Retail Environment. Fashion Practice. *Journal of Design Creative Process & The Fashion Industry*, *7*(1), 9–30. doi: 0.2752/175693815X14182200335619

Lundquist, F. (2022). Give and Take, the Love and Hate Relationship. In Logan, S. R.Good, T. L. (Eds.), Black Women Navigating Historically White Higher Education Institutions and the Journey Toward Liberation (pp. 192-228). IGI Global. https://doi.org/ doi:10.4018/978-1-6684-4626-3.ch010

Lundquist, A. E., & Henning, G. (2020). From Avoiding Bias to Social Justice. In A. D. Spicer-Runnels & T. E. Simpson (Eds.), *Developing an Intercultural Responsive Leadership Style for Faculty and Administrators* (pp. 47–61). IGI Global., doi:10.4018/978-1-7998-4108-1.ch004

Ly, C. N., & Soutter, M. (2022). Technological Pedagogical Content Knowledge Framework as a Lens for Transformative Social and Emotional Learning Online. In V. H. Shinas, C. N. Ly, & S. Y. Ozden (Eds.), *Cases on Practical Applications for Remote, Hybrid, and Hyflex Teaching* (pp. 71–87). IGI Global., doi:10.4018/978-1-7998-9168-0.ch004

Lynch, E. (2021). Sex, Scholarship, and Service. In Etim, A. S.Etim, J. (Eds.), Overcoming Challenges and Barriers for Women in Business and Education (pp. 162-185). IGI Global. https:// doi.org/ doi:10.4018/978-1-7998-3814-2.ch009

Lyons, N., & Smith, M. (2021). From Overlay to Interplay. In L. C. Mihăeş, R. Andreescu, & A. Dimitriu (Eds.), *Handbook of Research on Contemporary Storytelling Methods Across New Media and Disciplines* (pp. 200–223). IGI Global., doi:10.4018/978-1-7998-6605-3.ch011

Lypka, A. E., & De Felice, D. (2020). Telecollaborative Storytelling. In G. Neokleous, A. Krulatz, & R. Farrelly (Eds.), *Handbook of Research on Cultivating Literacy in Diverse and Multilingual Classrooms* (pp. 146–165). IGI Global., doi:10.4018/978-1-7998-2722-1.ch008

Madrigal Moreno, S., Alfaro Calderón, G. G., & Madrigal Moreno, F. (2016). Social Media Marketing Perspectives in the Organization in Morelia, Mexico. *International Journal of Marketing Studies*, *8*(2), 128. doi:10.5539/ijms.v8n2p128

Madzharov, A. (2019). Self-Control and Touch: When Does Direct Versus Indirect Touch Increase Hedonic Evaluations and Consumption of Food. *Journal of Retailing*, *95*(4), 170–185. doi:10.1016/j.jretai.2019.10.009

Magyar, C. K. (2022). Addressing "Another" in the Aftermath of School Shootings Using Dance and Rhetoric. In G. A. Crews (Ed.), *Impact of School Shootings on Classroom Culture, Curriculum, and Learning* (pp. 89–112). IGI Global., doi:10.4018/978-1-7998-5200-1.ch006

Maher, D. (2020). Pre-Service Teachers' Digital Competencies to Support School Students' Digital Literacies. In Keengwe, J.Onchwari, G. (Eds.), Handbook of Research on Literacy and Digital Technology Integration in Teacher Education (pp. 29-46). IGI Global. https://doi.org/ doi:10.4018/978-1-7998-1461-0.ch002

Mahmood, F. (2020). Combating Bullets With a Pen. In S. Jamil (Ed.), *Handbook of Research on Combating Threats to Media Freedom and Journalist Safety* (pp. 54–71). IGI Global., doi:10.4018/978-1-7998-1298-2.ch004

Maiti, A., & Jana, S. K. (2022). Diversity and Equity in Higher Education. In E. Meletiadou (Ed.), *Handbook of Research on Practices for Advancing Diversity and Inclusion in Higher Education* (pp. 263–280). IGI Global., doi:10.4018/978-1-7998-9628-9.ch013

Majumdar, S. (2022). Recreating "Home" in Exile. In Pourya Asl, M. (Eds.), Gender, Place, and Identity of South Asian Women (pp. 252-274). IGI Global. https://doi.org/ doi:10.4018/978-1-6684-3626-4.ch013

Makarova, N. S. (2020). Trade-Off Between Intergenerational Equity and Economic Growth. In M. Ziolo (Ed.), *Social, Economic, and Environmental Impacts Between Sustainable Financial Systems and Financial Markets* (pp. 201–230). IGI Global., doi:10.4018/978-1-7998-1033-9.ch010

Makhado, M. P., & Tshisikhawe, T. R. (2021). How Apartheid Education Encouraged and Reinforced Tribalism and Xenophobia in South Africa. In M. A. Mafukata (Ed.), *Impact of Immigration and Xenophobia on Development in Africa* (pp. 131–151). IGI Global., doi:10.4018/978-1-7998-7099-9.ch008

Malegiannaki, I., Daradoumis, T., & Retalis, S. (2021). Using a Story-Driven Board Game to Engage Students and Adults With Cultural Heritage. [IJGBL]. *International Journal of Game-Based Learning, 11*(2), 1–19. doi:10.4018/IJGBL.2021040101

Malerba, R. C., Fernandes, C. I., & Veiga, P. (2020). What Do We Know About Destination Branding? In S. J. Teixeira & J. M. Ferreira (Eds.), *Multilevel Approach to Competitiveness in the Global Tourism Industry* (pp. 211–228). IGI Global., doi:10.4018/978-1-7998-0365-2.ch013

Malinka, K., Hujňák, O., Hanáček, P., & Hellebrandt, L. (2022). E-Banking security study - 10 years later. *IEEE Access : Practical Innovations, Open Solutions, 10*, 16681–16699. doi:10.1109/ACCESS.2022.3149475

Mallawaarachchi, C. (2019). Significant Influences of Digital Literacy to Promote Gender Equity and Equality in Education. In Bala, S.Singhal, P. (Eds.), Gender Issues in Technical and Vocational Education Programs (pp. 218-234). IGI Global. https://doi.org/ doi:10.4018/978-1-5225-8443-8.ch011

Manríquez, S., Gallegos, J., & Valenzuela, I. (2005). Análisis y aplicación de la medición y gestión del valor económico agregado (EVA) a una empresa que cotiza en la bolsa. *Capic Review*, *3*, 4.

Mansou, I. H. F., Eljelly, A. M. A., & Abdullah, A. M. A. (2016). Consumers' attitude towards e-banking services in Islamic banks: The case of Sudan. *Review of International Business and Strategy*, *26*(2), 244–260. doi:10.1108/RIBS-02-2014-0024

Manzone, J. A., & Nyberg, J. L. (2021). Instruction Expanded. In D. AuCoin (Ed.), *Building Integrated Collaborative Relationships for Inclusive Learning Settings* (pp. 240–265). IGI Global., doi:10.4018/978-1-7998-6816-3.ch010

Manzone, J. A., & Nyberg, J. L. (2021). Instruction-Expanded Virtual Education Model. In J. D. Herron & T. Douglas (Eds.), *Strategies for Student Support During a Global Crisis* (pp. 48–70). IGI Global., doi:10.4018/978-1-7998-7000-5.ch004

Manzone, J. A., & Nyberg, J. L. (2022). Constructing Culturally-Authentic Differentiated Access Points Using the Content Imperatives. In J. L. Nyberg & J. A. Manzone (Eds.), *Creating Equitable Services for the Gifted* (pp. 171–188). IGI Global., doi:10.4018/978-1-7998-8153-7.ch012

Manzone, J. A., & Nyberg, J. L. (2022). Creating Culturally Sustainable Literacy Experiences Through Home and Community Connections. In L. Haas & J. T. Tussey (Eds.), *Disciplinary Literacy as a Support for Culturally and Linguistically Responsive Teaching and Learning* (pp. 15–40). IGI Global., doi:10.4018/978-1-6684-4215-9.ch002

Marasco, A., Nicolais, F., Acampa, G., & Balbi, B. (2022). Cinematic Storytelling with Virtual Reality for Cultural Heritage Marketing and Accessibility. In A. Campos & S. Almeida (Eds.), *Global Perspectives on Strategic Storytelling in Destination Marketing* (pp. 193–214). IGI Global., doi:10.4018/978-1-6684-3436-9.ch010

Marin, P., & Gomez, D. (2022). Application of sensory marketing techniques in fashion shops: The case of Zara and Stradivarius. *Vivat Academia*, *155*, 17–32.

MarketLine. (2019). *Mexico In-depth PESTLE insights. Country Profile Series*. Report Code: ML00002-020. https://www.marketresearch.com/MarketLine-v3883/Mexico-PESTLE-Insights-30069830

Marks, R., & Vickland, C. (2021). Expanding Equity and Access in State-Authorized Charter Schools. In A. J. Griffen (Ed.), *Challenges to Integrating Diversity, Equity, and Inclusion Programs in Organizations* (pp. 42–61). IGI Global., doi:10.4018/978-1-7998-4093-0.ch004

Marku, M. (2012). Albanian media and the specifics of the local market. *Studies in Communication Sciences*, *12*(1), 49–52. doi:10.1016/j.scoms.2012.06.010

Marone, F., & Pozzuoli, C. (2022). The Museum of Children. In F. Bifulco & M. Tregua (Eds.), *Handbook of Research on Museum Management in the Digital Era* (pp. 312–330). IGI Global., doi:10.4018/978-1-7998-9656-2.ch017

Marques, M. I., & Heitor, J. C. (2022). Social Media as Storytelling Destination Communication Channels. In A. Campos & S. Almeida (Eds.), *Global Perspectives on Strategic Storytelling in Destination Marketing* (pp. 246–261). IGI Global., doi:10.4018/978-1-6684-3436-9.ch013

Martin Martin, J. (n.d.). *The maternal language in the learning of a second language.* Seville University.

Martin, F. C., II. (2022). Sites of Immanent Social Critique. In Bagasra, A., Mc Letchie, A.Wesley, J. (Eds.), Contributions of Historically Black Colleges and Universities in the 21st Century (pp. 221-238). IGI Global. https://doi.org/ doi:10.4018/978-1-6684-3814-5.ch011

Martin, C. S. (2022). Mathematical Literacy Writing and Equity in the Mathematics Classroom. In T. S. Hodges (Ed.), *Handbook of Research on Writing Instruction Practices for Equitable and Effective Teaching* (pp. 272–290). IGI Global., doi:10.4018/978-1-6684-3745-2.ch014

Martínez Chapa, O. (2019). El papel del conocimiento en las organizaciones productivas: Aspectos teóricos y reflexiones. *RIDE Revista Iberoamericana para la Investigación y el Desarrollo Educativo, 9*(18), 412–422. doi:10.23913/ride.v9i18.430

Martin-Neira, J., Domínguez, M. T., & Olvera-Lobo, M. (2022). Digital Journalism and Transmedia Narratives in the Communication of Science. In R. Pettinger, B. B. Gupta, A. Roja, & D. Cozmiuc (Eds.), *Handbook of Research on Digital Transformation Management and Tools* (pp. 531–555). IGI Global., doi:10.4018/978-1-7998-9764-4.ch024

Martos, C. (2022). *Fivenews.* Obtained from https://www.fivenews.com/types-of-students/

Marzano, G. (2022). *Creativity and Autism Spectrum Disorder.* IGI Global., doi:10.4018/978-1-7998-7840-7.ch009

Masenya, T. M. (2022). Digital Preservation of Indigenous Knowledge in South African Rural Communities. In Tshifhumulo, R.Makhanikhe, T. J. (Eds.), Handbook of Research on Protecting and Managing Global Indigenous Knowledge Systems (pp. 317-340). IGI Global. https://doi.org/ doi:10.4018/978-1-7998-7492-8.ch017

Matey, C. (2021). Heeding the Call of America's Youth. In D. E. Hartsfield (Ed.), *Handbook of Research on Teaching Diverse Youth Literature to Pre-Service Professionals* (pp. 68–85). IGI Global., doi:10.4018/978-1-7998-7375-4.ch004

Matsumoto, K., Hirotani, M., & Fukada, A. (2020). Examining Oral Performance Characteristics of L2 Learners With the CAF Calculator. In A. Andujar (Ed.), *Recent Tools for Computer- and Mobile-Assisted Foreign Language Learning* (pp. 132–148). IGI Global., doi:10.4018/978-1-7998-1097-1.ch006

Mayeaux, A. S., Barber, A., & Adams, M. S. (2022). Supporting the Habits and Practices of Teacher Expertise Development. In B. S. Zugelder & M. L'Esperance (Eds.), *Handbook of Research on the Educator Continuum and Development of Teachers* (pp. 430–452). IGI Global., doi:10.4018/978-1-6684-3848-0.ch021

Mayo-Cubero, M. (2021). Social Media and Digital Information Sources in News Coverage of Crisis, Disaster, and Emergency Situations. In Oliveira, L., Tajariol, F.Gonçalves, L. B. (Eds.), Digital Services in Crisis, Disaster, and Emergency Situations (pp. 268-281). IGI Global. https://doi.org/ doi:10.4018/978-1-7998-6705-0.ch012

Mayowa, A. S. (2020). Development of a 2D Digital Animation for Yorùbá Folktale Narrative. [IJACDT]. *International Journal of Art, Culture, Design, and Technology*, *9*(1), 47–61. doi:10.4018/IJACDT.2020010104

McCallum & Nigam. (2004). *A Comparison of Event Models for Naive Bayes Text Classification*. cmu.cs.

McCallum, K. M. (2020). Immersive Experience. In Morie, J. F.McCallum, K. (Eds.), Handbook of Research on the Global Impacts and Roles of Immersive Media (pp. 453-484). IGI Global. https://doi.org/ doi:10.4018/978-1-7998-2433-6.ch022

McCune, N. M. (2022). Equity in the Online Space? In McCune, N. M. (Eds.), Advancing DEI and Creating Inclusive Environments in the Online Space (pp. 248-266). IGI Global. https://doi.org/ doi:10.4018/978-1-6684-5146-5.ch015

McCune, N. M., & Schulz, W. C., III. (2022). The Social Determinants of Changemakers. In McCune, N. M. (Ed.), Advancing DEI and Creating Inclusive Environments in the Online Space (pp. 268-280). IGI Global. https://doi.org/ doi:10.4018/978-1-6684-5146-5.ch016

McElhone, D., & Yeigh, M. J. (2022). Disrupting the Deficit-Gaze. In von Hohenberg, S. C. (Ed.), Dispositional Development and Assessment in Teacher Preparation Programs (pp. 167-185). IGI Global. https://doi.org/ doi:10.4018/978-1-6684-4089-6.ch009

Md Husin, M., & Haron, R. (2020). Financial Sustainability of SMEs Through Islamic Crowdfunding. In A. Rafay (Ed.), *Handbook of Research on Theory and Practice of Global Islamic Finance* (pp. 321–337). IGI Global., doi:10.4018/978-1-7998-0218-1.ch018

Medina, M., Valdez, D., Guerrero, P., Ortiz-Rodriguez, F., & Abrego, D. (2019). Ubicuos Citizens Services: A Mexican innovation study case at public sector. *PUBSIC 2019.*

Medina, J. M., Echeverría, O., & Ortiz, F. (2022). Confianza y calidad de la información para la satisfacción y lealtad del cliente en el e-Banking con el uso del teléfono celular. *Contaduría y Administración*, *67*(1), 283–304. doi:10.22201/fca.24488410e.2022.2965

Medina-Quintero, J. M., Abrego-Almazán, D., & Ortiz-Rodríguez, F. (2018). Use and usefulness of the information systems measurement. A quality approach at the Mexican Northeastern Region. *Cuadernos Americanos*, *31*(56), 7–30. doi:10.11144/Javeriana.cao.31-56.ubwm

Mehmood, M. (2020). Finance in the Hospitality Industry. In Pius, A., Alharahsheh, H. H.Adesanmi, A. A. (Eds.), Contemporary Management Approaches to the Global Hospitality and Tourism Industry (pp. 185-212). IGI Global. https://doi.org/ doi:10.4018/978-1-7998-2204-2.ch011

Mehrabian, A., & Russell, J. (1974). *An approach to environmental psychology. An approach to environmental psychology*. The MIT Press.

Meletiadou, E. (2022). Profiling the Writing Competency of BAME Undergraduate Students. In E. Meletiadou (Ed.), *Handbook of Research on Practices for Advancing Diversity and Inclusion in Higher Education* (pp. 20–48). IGI Global., doi:10.4018/978-1-7998-9628-9.ch002

Mendoza, P., Cardenas Riaño, F. E., Hoyos Ensuncho, M., & Reina Zambrano, J. (2021). The Case of the International Research Center for the Development of Education (CIIDE). In G. Malfatti (Ed.), *People-Centered Approaches Toward the Internationalization of Higher Education* (pp. 234–253). IGI Global., doi:10.4018/978-1-7998-3796-1.ch012

Mendoza-Reis, N., Louque, A., & Lu, M. (2021). The Resilient Women of Color Leaders. In S. Rodriguez & K. Brown (Eds.), *Black and Brown Leadership and the Promotion of Change in an Era of Social Unrest* (pp. 55–75). IGI Global., doi:10.4018/978-1-7998-7235-1.ch003

Merhi, M., Hone, K., & Tarhini, A. (2019). A cross-cultural study of the intention to use mobile banking between Lebanese and British consumers: Extending UTAUT2 with security, privacy, and trust. *Technology in Society*, *59*, 101151. doi:10.1016/j.techsoc.2019.101151

Merkovity, N. (2019). A Possible Framework for Attention-Based Politics. [IJEP]. *International Journal of E-Politics*, *10*(2), 13–23. doi:10.4018/IJEP.2019070102

Meurer, M. M., Waldkirch, M., Schou, P. K., Bucher, E. L., & Burmeister-Lamp, K. (2022). Digital affordances: How entrepreneurs access support in online communities during the COVID-19 pandemic. *Small Business Economics*, *58*(2), 637–663. doi:10.100711187-021-00540-2

Meza Rodríguez, E. (2022). *Empresas de LATAM apuestan por tecnologías emergentes para aumentar la productividad y reinventar los procesos*. El Economista. https://www.eleconomista.com.mx/el-empresario/Empresas-de-LATAM-apuestan-por-tecnologias-emergentes-para-aumentar-la-productividad-y-reinventar-los-procesos-20221201-0092.html

Miller, O. P., & Banks-Hall, R. L. (2019). Parental Involvement in Education. In P. H. Hoffman-Miller, M. James, & D. Hermond (Eds.), *African American Suburbanization and the Consequential Loss of Identity* (pp. 116–140). IGI Global., doi:10.4018/978-1-5225-7835-2.ch007

Min, E. J. (2022). Equitable Assessment Practices. In Crawford, J.Filback, R. A. (Eds.), TESOL Guide for Critical Praxis in Teaching, Inquiry, and Advocacy (pp. 65-86). IGI Global. https://doi.org/ doi:10.4018/978-1-7998-8093-6.ch004

Mohamad Saleh, M. S., Heinrichs, H., & Nik Hasan, N. N. (2021). Role of Images in Constructing Public Opinion About Environmental Matters in Malaysia. [IJSESD]. *International Journal of Social Ecology and Sustainable Development*, *12*(1), 115–130. doi:10.4018/IJSESD.2021010109

Mohamed, H., & Lamia, M. (2020). Efficacy of the Flipped Classroom to Teach the Digital Storytelling Process. In Soares, F., Lopes, A. P., Brown, K. & Uukkivi, A. (Ed.), Developing Technology Mediation in Learning Environments (pp. 57-77). IGI Global. https://doi.org/ doi:10.4018/978-1-7998-1591-4.ch004

Mokha, A. K. (2021). Brand Equity, Brand Satisfaction, and Brand Loyalty. [IJOM]. *International Journal of Online Marketing, 11*(3), 34–50. doi:10.4018/IJOM.2021070103

Mokuria, V. G., & Chhikara, A. (2022). Narrative Inquiry as a Relational Methodology. In Watson, S. W., Austin, S. & Bell, J. (Ed.), Conceptual Analyses of Curriculum Inquiry Methodologies (pp. 1-27). IGI Global. https://doi.org/ doi:10.4018/978-1-7998-8848-2.ch001

Molina-Sánchez, R., García-Pérez-de-Lema, D., López-Salazar, A., & Godínez-López, R. (2022). Determining factors in MSMEs success: An empirical study in Mexico. *Small Business International Review, 6*(1), e384. doi:10.26784bir.v6i1.384

Monstad, T. H., & Burman, S. (2020). Digital Transformations Carried Out Through Games. In M. Helmefalk & L. Marcusson (Eds.), *Utilizing Gamification in Servicescapes for Improved Consumer Engagement* (pp. 119–147). IGI Global., doi:10.4018/978-1-7998-1970-7.ch005

Montejo, G. A., & Frazier, A. E. (2020). Assessing Quality of Life Across Mexico City Using Socio-Economic and Environmental Factors. [IJAGR]. *International Journal of Applied Geospatial Research, 11*(3), 68–86. doi:10.4018/IJAGR.2020070105

Moore, D. (2014). Is anticipation delicious? Visceral factors as mediators of the effect of olfactory cues on purchase intentions. *Journal of Business Research, 67*(9), 2045–2051. doi:10.1016/j.jbusres.2013.10.005

Mora Pabón, R. (2011). Estudio de actitudes emprendedoras con profesionales que crearon empresas. *Rev. Esc. Adm. Neg., 71*, 70-83. scielo.org.co

Morales, A. R., & Raible, J. (2021). To Teach as We Are Known. In K. Sprott, J. R. O'Connor Jr, & C. Msengi (Eds.), *Designing Culturally Competent Programming for PK-20 Classrooms* (pp. 79–97). IGI Global., doi:10.4018/978-1-7998-3652-0.ch005

Moraru, A. D., & Duhnea, C. (2018). E-banking and customer satisfaction with banking services. *Strategic Management, 23*(3), 3–9. doi:10.5937/StraMan1803003M

Moreira, A., Fortes, N., & Santiago, R. (2017). Influence of sensory stimuli on brand experience, brand equity and purchase intention. *Journal of Business Economics and Management, 18*(1), 68–83. doi:10.3846/16111699.2016.1252793

Moreno-Albarracín, B. (2022). Brand Storytelling in Christmas Commercials of Large Supermarket Chains. In Carrillo-Durán, M.Pérez Pulido, M. (Eds.), Cases on Developing Effective Research Plans for Communications and Information Science (pp. 215-234). IGI Global. https://doi.org/ doi:10.4018/978-1-6684-4523-5.ch011

MorenoK. (2017). Obtained from https://d1wqtxts1xzle7.cloudfront.net/54189891/MORENO_KARINA _-_FILTER_AFCETIVE-free.pdf?1503257845=&response-content-dis position=inline%3B+filename%3DEMOTIONAL_FACTORS_THAT_INFLUEN CE_IN_FIL.pdf&Expires=1675286199&Signature=GVrtWAGzI2npbxhtr OOT66a9u6kMI~

Morgan, R., Fortner, K. M., & Tang, K. (2021). Challenges Experienced by Women of Color in Educational Leadership. In S. Rodriguez & K. Brown (Eds.), *Black and Brown Leadership and the Promotion of Change in an Era of Social Unrest* (pp. 76–100). IGI Global., doi:10.4018/978-1-7998-7235-1.ch004

Morikawa-Zhou, M. (2022). Chimamanda Ngozi Adichie. In Goodman Hayward, P., Rehman, S.Yan, Z. (Eds.), Women Community Leaders and Their Impact as Global Changemakers (pp. 115-119). IGI Global. https://doi.org/ doi:10.4018/978-1-6684-2490-2.ch020

Morim, A. C., Inácio, H., & Vieira, E. (2020). The Implementation of Internal Control in the Financial Services Expenditure in a Hospital Department. In G. Azevedo, J. Oliveira, R. Marques, & A. Ferreira (Eds.), *Tools, Strategies, and Practices for Modern and Accountable Public Sector Management* (pp. 290–323). IGI Global., doi:10.4018/978-1-7998-1385-9.ch011

Morrison, J. A., & Kim, J. (2020). Resisting the "Tyranny of an Expert". In A. S. Zimmerman (Ed.), *Preparing Students for Community-Engaged Scholarship in Higher Education* (pp. 43–60). IGI Global., doi:10.4018/978-1-7998-2208-0.ch003

Mosca, F., Kitchen, P. J., & Chiaudano, V. (2021). Investigating the Impact of Luxury Brands' Traditional and Digital Contents on Customer-Based Brand Equity. In F. Mosca, C. Casalegno, & R. Gallo (Eds.), *Developing Successful Global Strategies for Marketing Luxury Brands* (pp. 81–100). IGI Global., doi:10.4018/978-1-7998-5882-9.ch005

Mossberger, K., & Tolbert, C. J. (2021). Digital Citizenship and Digital Communities. [IJEPR]. *International Journal of E-Planning Research*, *10*(3), 19–34. doi:10.4018/IJEPR.20210701.oa2

Mostafa, R., & Kasamani, T. (2020). Brand experience and brand loyalty: Is it a matter of emotions? *Asia Pacific Journal of Marketing and Logistics*, *33*(4), 1033–1051. doi:10.1108/APJML-11-2019-0669

Moye, S. (2022). Monitor and Adjust. In Logan, S. R.Good, T. L. (Eds.), Black Women Navigating Historically White Higher Education Institutions and the Journey Toward Liberation (pp. 25-50). IGI Global. https://doi.org/ doi:10.4018/978-1-6684-4626-3.ch002

Moyo, O. N. (2020). Examining Oppressions as a Way of Valuing Diversity. In J. Keengwe (Ed.), *Handbook of Research on Diversity and Social Justice in Higher Education* (pp. 55–77). IGI Global., doi:10.4018/978-1-7998-5268-1.ch004

Mudau, T. S. (2021). Community Engagement as a Strategy to Facilitate the Immigrant-Local Cohesion. In M. A. Mafukata (Ed.), *Impact of Immigration and Xenophobia on Development in Africa* (pp. 261–274). IGI Global., doi:10.4018/978-1-7998-7099-9.ch015

Mukba, G. (2022). Therapeutic Storytelling. In Yılmaz, R.Koç, B. (Eds.), Narrative Theory and Therapy in the Post-Truth Era (pp. 191-210). IGI Global. https://doi.org/ doi:10.4018/978-1-7998-9251-9.ch013

Muñoz-Muñoz, E. R., Love, M., McCollum, M. C., Cruz, R. A., Umaña, D., & Nance, C. R. (2022). Mind the Gatekeepers. In Colón, G., & Alsace, T. O. (Ed.), Bilingual Special Education for the 21st Century (pp. 1-24). IGI Global. https://doi.org/ doi:10.4018/978-1-7998-9043-0.ch001

Mupenzi, A. (2022). Navigating the Australian Education System Refugees and New Arrivals. In Smith, C.Zhou, G. (Eds.), Handbook of Research on Teaching Strategies for Culturally and Linguistically Diverse International Students (pp. 265-287). IGI Global. https://doi.org/ doi:10.4018/978-1-7998-8921-2.ch014

Murray-Everett, N. C., & Schroeder, S. (2021). Fostering Inclusive Communities Through Children's Literature. In D. E. Hartsfield (Ed.), *Handbook of Research on Teaching Diverse Youth Literature to Pre-Service Professionals* (pp. 566–592). IGI Global., doi:10.4018/978-1-7998-7375-4.ch028

Musingafi, M., Mafumbate, R., & Khumalo, T. (2021). *Feminist Perspectives on the Self.* IGI Global., doi:10.4018/978-1-7998-4090-9.ch011

Musingafi, M., Mafumbate, R., & Khumalo, T. (2021). *Gender Inequality Theories of Feminism.* IGI Global., doi:10.4018/978-1-7998-4090-9.ch007

Nabb, K. A. (2022). Using the Five Practices to Promote Active and Equitable Learning Environments. In Kartal, O., Popovic, G.Morrissey, S. (Eds.), Global Perspectives and Practices for Reform-Based Mathematics Teaching (pp. 293-322). IGI Global. https://doi.org/ doi:10.4018/978-1-7998-9422-3.ch014

Nadia, S., Firdaus, C. D., & Sadeghian, A. (2018). Retweet: A popular information diffusion mechanism – A survey paper. *Online Social Networks and Media*, *6*(June), 26–40.

Naglieri, J. A., & Lansdowne, K. A. (2022). Equitable Assessment of Gifted Students Using the Naglieri General Ability Tests. In J. L. Nyberg & J. A. Manzone (Eds.), *Creating Equitable Services for the Gifted* (pp. 58–76). IGI Global., doi:10.4018/978-1-7998-8153-7.ch005

Nakae, K. (2021). Incompatible Discrepancy Between Low Proficiency of Arabic Language and Its High Status and Prestige. In A. Wang (Ed.), *Redefining the Role of Language in a Globalized World* (pp. 54–70). IGI Global., doi:10.4018/978-1-7998-2831-0.ch004

Nakamura, J. (2021). Effect of External Activate Factors Serving as Clue. In Ogata, T.Ono, J. (Eds.), Bridging the Gap Between AI, Cognitive Science, and Narratology With Narrative Generation (pp. 338-362). IGI Global. https://doi.org/ doi:10.4018/978-1-7998-4864-6.ch011

Naudé, W., & Liebregts, W. (2020). *Digital Entrepreneurship Research: A Concise Introduction. IZA Discussion Papers 13667. Institute of Labor Economics*. IZA.

Navas, C., Tisi, V., & Close, T. (2021). Grassroots Organization and Justice Through Social Media. In R. Horton (Ed.), *Critical Perspectives on Social Justice in Speech-Language Pathology* (pp. 262–284). IGI Global., doi:10.4018/978-1-7998-7134-7.ch013

Negrão, C. S., & Brito, J. A. (2021). An Empirical Study on the Determinants of Success of Crowdfunding Projects. In C. S. Negrão & J. F. Brito (Eds.), *Multidisciplinary Approaches to Crowdfunding Platforms* (pp. 1–20). IGI Global., doi:10.4018/978-1-7998-3226-3.ch001

Nerren, J. B. (2022). Could There Be an AutCrit? In J. B. Nerren (Ed.), *Rethinking Perception and Centering the Voices of Unique Individuals* (pp. 234–251). IGI Global., doi:10.4018/978-1-6684-5103-8.ch012

Neu, J., & Cox, N. B. (2022). Racism in the United States. In G. D. Luurs (Ed.), *Handbook of Research on Communication Strategies for Taboo Topics* (pp. 86–103). IGI Global., doi:10.4018/978-1-7998-9125-3.ch005

Newman, P. (2021). The Room Is Crooked AF. In Rodriguez, S.Brown, K. (Eds.), Black and Brown Leadership and the Promotion of Change in an Era of Social Unrest (pp. 124-148). IGI Global. https://doi.org/ doi:10.4018/978-1-7998-7235-1.ch006

Ng, G., Cheuk, H., Singh, S., & Sharma, B. (2022). Artificial Intelligence as Virtual Inspector for Construction Waste Dumping. In A. Vaseashta, G. Duca, & S. Travin (Eds.), *Handbook of Research on Water Sciences and Society* (pp. 673–686). IGI Global., doi:10.4018/978-1-7998-7356-3.ch031

Nguyen, A. (2016). A cross-cultural study on e-Government services delivery. *The Electronic Journal Information Systems Evaluation, 19*(2), 121–134.

Nickkar, A., Shin, H., & Farkas, Z. A. (2020). A Spatial Analysis of Commuting Patterns of Electric Vehicle Drivers. [IJSVST]. *International Journal of Smart Vehicles and Smart Transportation, 3*(1), 42–59. doi:10.4018/IJSVST.2020010103

Nicolaou, C. (2021). Development of Business Through the Internet and Social Media. In El-Gohary, H., Edwards, D.Ben Mimoun, M. (Eds.), Handbook of Research on IoT, Digital Transformation, and the Future of Global Marketing (pp. 193-211). IGI Global. https://doi.org/ doi:10.4018/978-1-7998-7192-7.ch012

Nicolaou, C. (2022). Information and Communications Technologies Through Technology-Enhanced Learning in Adult Education. In Krishnan, C., Al-Harthy, F. N.Singh, G. (Eds.), Technology Training for Educators From Past to Present (pp. 73-94). IGI Global. https://doi.org/ doi:10.4018/978-1-6684-4083-4.ch004

Nishant, R., Srivastava, S. C., & Teo, T. (2019). Using polynomial modeling to understand service quality in e-Government websites. *MIS Quarterly, 43*(3), 807-826. doi:10.25300/MISQ/2019/12349

Niyonzima, D., & Bhuju, K. (2021). The Role of Community Radio in Promoting Gender Equality in Rwanda. In S. Jamil, B. Çoban, B. Ataman, & G. Appiah-Adjei (Eds.), *Handbook of Research on Discrimination, Gender Disparity, and Safety Risks in Journalism* (pp. 343–365). IGI Global., doi:10.4018/978-1-7998-6686-2.ch018

Njuguna, J., & Jjuuko, M. (2020). Online Behaviour as Predictive of Professional Online Work Readiness Among Mass Communication Students. [IJICTHD]. *International Journal of Information Communication Technologies and Human Development, 12*(2), 48–61. doi:10.4018/IJICTHD.2020040104

NobaneeH.NobaneeH.Mehroz NidaD. (August 30, 2020). Digital Entrepreneurship: Concepts, Applications, and Future Research. *Agenda Journal of Critical Reviews*, *7*(19). https://ssrn.com/abstract=3688271 doi:10.2139/ssrn.3688271

Nobel, M. M. (2022). Challenging Deficit Thinking in Our Schools. In R. D. Williams (Ed.), *Handbook of Research on Challenging Deficit Thinking for Exceptional Education Improvement* (pp. 27–64). IGI Global., doi:10.4018/978-1-7998-8860-4.ch002

Noguez, R. (2021). *Alexa y Google Assistant, un negocio que habla cada vez más fuerte en México y el mundo.* forbes.com.mx

Nordgren, R. D., & Persson, H. (2020). An Examination of Growth of Publicly-Funded Private Schools in the U.S. and Sweden. In P. D. Keough (Ed.), *Overcoming Current Challenges in the P-12 Teaching Profession* (pp. 247–267). IGI Global., doi:10.4018/978-1-7998-1177-0.ch011

NordquistR. (2020a). *ThoughtCo.* Obtained from https://www.thoughtco.com/second-language-1691930

NordquistR. (2020b). *ThoughtCo.* Obtained from https://www.thoughtco.com/what-is-the-english-language-16906 52

Novak, A. M. (2022). Not White Saviors, but Critical Scholars. In Nyberg, J. L.Manzone, J. A. (Eds.), Creating Equitable Services for the Gifted (pp. 246-262). IGI Global. https://doi.org/ doi:10.4018/978-1-7998-8153-7.ch016

Nunes, C., & Oliveira, N. D. (2022). Developing Communication and Inclusive Literacy Skills Among Children With Profound Intellectual and Multiple Disabilities. In Almeida, A. P. & Esteves, S. (Ed.), Modern Reading Practices and Collaboration Between Schools, Family, and Community (pp. 125-154). IGI Global. https://doi.org/ doi:10.4018/978-1-7998-9750-7.ch006

Nure, G. (2020). Cost Efficiency Analysis in the Banking Industry. [IJCFA]. *International Journal of Corporate Finance and Accounting*, *7*(2), 1–20. doi:10.4018/IJCFA.2020070101

Nurse, S. (2022). Why "Race Neutral" Policy Fails Black Small Business Owners. In Rolle, J. D.Crump, M. (Eds.), Sustainability and the Future of Work and Entrepreneurship for the Underserved (pp. 111-130). IGI Global. https://doi.org/ doi:10.4018/978-1-6684-4322-4.ch006

Oakes, R., Oakeley, A. K., & Goke-Pariola, R. (2021). The Victimization and Disparate Treatment of Racial and Ethnic Minorities. In R. Blasdell, L. Krieger-Sample, & M. Kilburn (Eds.), *Invisible Victims and the Pursuit of Justice* (pp. 353–382). IGI Global., doi:10.4018/978-1-7998-7348-8.ch015

Obialo, F. (2022). Entrepreneurs out of Necessity in the Developing Context. In Raimi, L.Kah, J. M. (Eds.), Mainstreaming Diversity, Equity, and Inclusion as Future Workplace Ethics (pp. 219-242). IGI Global. https://doi.org/ doi:10.4018/978-1-6684-3657-8.ch011

Obuaku-Igwe, C. (2021). Medical Sociology and Storytelling in a Decolonial Context. In Mihăeş, L. C., Andreescu, R.Dimitriu, A. (Eds.), Handbook of Research on Contemporary Storytelling Methods Across New Media and Disciplines (pp. 342-363). IGI Global. https://doi.org/ doi:10.4018/978-1-7998-6605-3.ch018

OECD. (2021). *The Digital Transformation of SMEs*. OECD Publishing. doi:10.1787/bdb9256a-en

Oke, I. A., Salihu, L., Mohammed, I. D., & Afolabi, A. M. (2021). Overview of Solid Waste Management of Healthcare and Related Organisations. In Khosrow-Pour D.B.A., M. (Ed.), Encyclopedia of Information Science and Technology, Fifth Edition (pp. 1336-1352). IGI Global. https://doi.org/ doi:10.4018/978-1-7998-3479-3.ch091

Okocha, D. O., & Ola-Akuma, R. O. (2022). Participatory Communication and Digital Media in Africa. In D. O. Okocha, M. J. Onobe, & M. N. Alike (Eds.), *Handbook of Research on Connecting Philosophy, Media, and Development in Developing Countries* (pp. 149–171). IGI Global., doi:10.4018/978-1-6684-4107-7.ch011

Okon, B. (2022). The Media and Development in an Era of Digitalized Economy. In Okocha, D. O., Onobe, M. J.Alike, M. N. (Eds.), Handbook of Research on Connecting Philosophy, Media, and Development in Developing Countries (pp. 50-68). IGI Global. https://doi.org/ doi:10.4018/978-1-6684-4107-7.ch005

Okwudili, U. M., & Kazaure, J. S. (2020). Digital Activism and Digital Revolution in Objective Journalism. [IJICST]. *International Journal of Interactive Communication Systems and Technologies*, *10*(2), 39–56. doi:10.4018/IJICST.2020070104

Oliveira, N. A., Gabrielli, C., Santos, G. N., & Borges, L. A. (2022). Intersectionality Between Racism and Sexism in the Brazilian Airline Industry. In P. Cembranel, J. R. Soares, & A. R. Perinotto (Eds.), *Promoting Social and Cultural Equity in the Tourism Sector* (pp. 155–176). IGI Global., doi:10.4018/978-1-6684-4194-7.ch009

Omotosho, B. J. (2020). Interrogating Social Negotiations Within Online Discussion Platforms in Nigeria. [IJCBPL]. *International Journal of Cyber Behavior, Psychology and Learning*, *10*(1), 32–40. doi:10.4018/IJCBPL.2020010103

Oni, O., & Mahlangu, P. S. (2021). Promoting Entrepreneurship Education Through Valuation of Cost of Equity. In A. O. Ayandibu (Ed.), *Reshaping Entrepreneurship Education With Strategy and Innovation* (pp. 321–347). IGI Global., doi:10.4018/978-1-7998-3171-6.ch015

ONUDI. (2019). *La industrialización en la era digital.* Viena: Organización de las Naciones Unidas para el Desarrollo Industrial.

Onyebadi, U. T., Bland, D., Howard, H., & Walcott, C. (2020). Issues in Academic Leadership. In U. T. Onyebadi (Ed.), *Multidisciplinary Issues Surrounding African Diasporas* (pp. 220–244). IGI Global., doi:10.4018/978-1-5225-5079-2.ch010

Onyebadi, U. T., Satti, M. A., & Mbunyuza-Memani, L. (2020). Diversity and the Media. In U. T. Onyebadi (Ed.), *Multidisciplinary Issues Surrounding African Diasporas* (pp. 54–79). IGI Global., doi:10.4018/978-1-5225-5079-2.ch003

Oralkan, A. (2021). Narrative Advertising in Destination Branding. In R. Yilmaz (Ed.), *Handbook of Research on Narrative Interactions* (pp. 346–358). IGI Global., doi:10.4018/978-1-7998-4903-2.ch020

Ortiz García, P. (2016). Actitud emprendedora de los jóvenes españoles en un contexto de crisis. *Revista de Ciencias Sociales*, *22*(1), 139–152. doi:10.31876/rcs.v22i1.24902

Ortiz-Rodriguez, F., Barrera, R., Villanueva, V., Medina, M., & Gauna, A. (2020). *APPVISO: citizen digital communication to prevent risk events in real time.* From The 21st Annual International Conference on Digital Government Research (dg.o '20): 10.1145/3396956.3397019

Osei-Kojo, A. (2017). E-government and public service quality in Ghana. *Journal of Public Affairs*, *17*(3), e1620. doi:10.1002/pa.1620

Osmanbegović, E., & Lugavić, Z. (2018). Influencing factors of e-government services adoption in Bosnia and Herzegovina. *Economic Review: Journal of Economics and Business*, *16*(2), 39–51.

Otobrise, H. C., & Omagbon, A. B. (2019). Digital marketing of library, information and knowledge products and services among librarians in selected university libraries in South-South, Nigeria. Journal of ICT Development. *Applications and Research*, *1*, 47–60.

Owa, O. A. (2022). Mainstreaming Diversity, Equity, and Inclusion as Future Workplace Ethics. In Raimi, L.Kah, J. M. (Eds.), Mainstreaming Diversity, Equity, and Inclusion as Future Workplace Ethics (pp. 28-48). IGI Global. https://doi.org/ doi:10.4018/978-1-6684-3657-8.ch002

Ozgen, O., & Turkoglu, E. (2019). Popular Culture and Communication Ethics. In O. Ozgen (Ed.), *Handbook of Research on Consumption, Media, and Popular Culture in the Global Age* (pp. 36–56). IGI Global., doi:10.4018/978-1-5225-8491-9.ch003

Ozturk, E. (2020). The Political Economy of Urban Transformation. In Karlidag, S.Bulut, S. (Eds.), Handbook of Research on the Political Economy of Communications and Media (pp. 322-338). IGI Global. https://doi.org/ doi:10.4018/978-1-7998-3270-6.ch018

Padilla, R., Milton, S., Johnson, L., & Nyadzayo, M. (2017). Impact of service value on satisfaction and repurchase intentions in business-to-business cloud computing. *Service Science*, *9*(1), 5–13. doi:10.1287erv.2016.0163

Page, L. (2022). Implicit Perceptions and Explicit Messages. In Tussey, J.Haas, L. (Eds.), Poverty Impacts on Literacy Education (pp. 130-148). IGI Global. https://doi.org/ doi:10.4018/978-1-7998-8730-0.ch007

Palmer, J. E., Morgan, J. W., Hinojosa, S., Olomi, J. M., Ayala, L., & Rosay, A. B. (2022). Anti-Racist and Intersectional Approaches in Social Science and Community-Based Research. In R. Throne (Ed.), *Social Justice Research Methods for Doctoral Research* (pp. 222–243). IGI Global., doi:10.4018/978-1-7998-8479-8.ch011

Panagiotidis, K., Maniou, T. A., & Veglis, A. (2020). Selfie Journalism and Politics. In Y. Ibrahim (Ed.), *Handbook of Research on Recent Developments in Internet Activism and Political Participation* (pp. 16–32). IGI Global., doi:10.4018/978-1-7998-4796-0.ch002

Paneva-Marinova, D., Goynov, M., Luchev, D., Pavlova, L., Márkus, Z. L., Veres, M., Weisz, Z., Szántó, G., & Szkaliczki, T. (2022). Studying Thracian Civilization Through Serious Games and Storytelling. In O. Bernardes, V. Amorim, & A. C. Moreira (Eds.), *Handbook of Research on Cross-Disciplinary Uses of Gamification in Organizations* (pp. 445–466). IGI Global., doi:10.4018/978-1-7998-9223-6.ch021

Pant, L. D. (2021). Gender Mainstreaming in the Media. In Jamil, S., Çoban, B., Ataman, B. Appiah-Adjei, G. (Eds.), Handbook of Research on Discrimination, Gender Disparity, and Safety Risks in Journalism (pp. 194-210). IGI Global. https://doi.org/ doi:10.4018/978-1-7998-6686-2.ch011

Papadomichelaki, X., & Mentzas, G. (2012). E-GovQual: A multiple-item scale for assessing e-government service quality. *Government Information Quarterly*, *29*(1), 98–109. doi:10.1016/j.giq.2011.08.011

Papadopoulou, L., & Maniou, T. A. (2021). Digital Media and New Forms of Journalism. In Khosrow-Pour D.B.A., M. (Ed.), Encyclopedia of Information Science and Technology, Fifth Edition (pp. 1130-1139). IGI Global. https://doi.org/ doi:10.4018/978-1-7998-3479-3.ch078

Papathanasiou, S., Koutsokostas, D., Balios, D., & Eriotis, N. (2019). Winemaking Sector in Greece. [IJCFA]. *International Journal of Corporate Finance and Accounting*, *6*(2), 1–17. doi:10.4018/IJCFA.2019070101

Parahakaran, S. (2022). Digital Ethnography Within Indigenous Contexts. In Chowdhury, J. S., Wahab, H. A., Saad, R. M., Roy, P. K.Wronka, J. (Eds.), Practices, Challenges, and Prospects of Digital Ethnography as a Multidisciplinary Method (pp. 138-147). IGI Global. https://doi.org/ doi:10.4018/978-1-6684-4190-9.ch010

Parahita, G. D., & Ahmad, N. (2020). What Dampen the Indonesian Journalists' Freedom and Safety in the Post-Soeharto New Order? In S. Jamil (Ed.), *Handbook of Research on Combating Threats to Media Freedom and Journalist Safety* (pp. 83–105). IGI Global., doi:10.4018/978-1-7998-1298-2.ch006

Parente, F., & Pessoa, L. F. (2021). Special Education in Brazil. In A. Singh, C. J. Yeh, S. Blanchard, & L. Anunciação (Eds.), *Handbook of Research on Critical Issues in Special Education for School Rehabilitation Practices* (pp. 126–142). IGI Global., doi:10.4018/978-1-7998-7630-4.ch007

Parham, C. R., Wake, D. G., West, S., & Maxwell, C. D. (2022). Influence Faculty Members' Thinking to Promote Social Justice and Equity. In S. P. Huffman, D. D. Cunningham, M. Shavers, & R. Adamson (Eds.), *Handbook of Research on Opening Pathways for Marginalized Individuals in Higher Education* (pp. 288–309). IGI Global., doi:10.4018/978-1-6684-3819-0.ch016

Park, G., & Xu, Z. (2020). Spatial and Temporal Dynamics of Social Vulnerability in the United States from 1970 to 2010. [IJAGR]. *International Journal of Applied Geospatial Research*, *11*(1), 36–54. doi:10.4018/IJAGR.2020010103

Parveen, N., Singh, D. V., & Azam, R. (2020). Innovations in Recycling for Sustainable Management of Solid Wastes. In R. A. Bhat, H. Qadri, K. A. Wani, G. H. Dar, & M. A. Mehmood (Eds.), *Innovative Waste Management Technologies for Sustainable Development* (pp. 177–210). IGI Global., doi:10.4018/978-1-7998-0031-6.ch010

Patange, J. T. (2013). Marketing of Library and Information Products and Services. *Global Journal of Human, Social Science, Linguistics, and Education, 13*(1).

Pate, U. A., & Dauda, S. (2020). Threats to Media Freedom and the Safety of Journalists in Nigeria. In S. Jamil (Ed.), *Handbook of Research on Combating Threats to Media Freedom and Journalist Safety* (pp. 241–256). IGI Global., doi:10.4018/978-1-7998-1298-2.ch013

Pătrăşcanu, K. (2021). The Viewer-Participant Performing Morality in Interactive Storytelling in Bandersnatch. In Mihăeş, L. C., Andreescu, R.Dimitriu, A. (Eds.), Handbook of Research on Contemporary Storytelling Methods Across New Media and Disciplines (pp. 241-257). IGI Global. https://doi.org/ doi:10.4018/978-1-7998-6605-3.ch013

Paul, J., Mittal, A., & Srivastav, G. (2016). Impact of service quality on customer satisfaction in private and public sector Banks. *International Journal of Bank Marketing, 34*(5), 606–622. doi:10.1108/IJBM-03-2015-0030

Pavlič, J., & Tomažič, T. (2020). 360° Video as an Opportunity for the Inclusion of Product Placement. In V. Hernández-Santaolalla & M. Barrientos-Bueno (Eds.), *Handbook of Research on Transmedia Storytelling, Audience Engagement, and Business Strategies* (pp. 188–214). IGI Global., doi:10.4018/978-1-7998-3119-8.ch014

Payne, A. F., Storbacka, K., & Frow, P. (2008). Managing the co-creation of value. *Journal of the Academy of Marketing Science, 36*(1), 83–96. doi:10.100711747-007-0070-0

Payne, A., Holt, S., & Frow, P. (2001). Relationship Value Management: Exploring the Integration of Employee, Customer and Shareholder Value and Enterprise Performance Models. *Journal of Marketing Management, 17*(7–8), 785–817. doi:10.1362/026725701323366827

Pellicelli, A. C., & Franzé, C. (2021). The Impact of Customer Education on the Perception of Made in Italy Products in the Agri-Food Sector. [IJABE]. *International Journal of Applied Behavioral Economics, 10*(2), 35–52. doi:10.4018/IJABE.2021040103

Pembecioğlu, N., & Gündüz, U. (2021). The Difference Between the Western Reflections of Disaster News and Orientalist Perspectives. In Tombul, I. & Sarı, G. (Ed.), Handbook of Research on Contemporary Approaches to Orientalism in Media and Beyond (pp. 145-164). IGI Global. https://doi.org/ doi:10.4018/978-1-7998-7180-4.ch009

Peneda de Oliveira, C., & Sousa, B. M. (2020). Green Consumer Behavior and Its Implications on Brand Marketing Strategy. In V. Naidoo & R. Verma (Eds.), *Green Marketing as a Positive Driver Toward Business Sustainability* (pp. 69–95). IGI Global., doi:10.4018/978-1-5225-9558-8.ch004

Penelas, A. L., Cuesta, P. V., & Sarro, M. del M. A., & Guriérrez, P. R. (2004). El Marketing y las organizaciones no lucrativas: El marketing con causa (MCC). *Revista Internacional de Marketing Público y No Lucrativo*, *1*(1), 125–137.

Peng-yu, L., & Xiao-xiao, W. (2017). Service improvement based on E-banking Adoption Model. *International Conference on Management Science & Engineering (24th).* 10.1109/ICMSE.2017.8574399

Pereira, E. T., & Salaris, S. (2019). The Evolution of the Role of Women in Labor Markets in Developed Economies. In E. T. Pereira & P. Paoloni (Eds.), *Handbook of Research on Women in Management and the Global Labor Market* (pp. 1–20). IGI Global., doi:10.4018/978-1-5225-9171-9.ch001

Pereira, S. M., & Ferreira, R. N. (2022). Beyond the Corporate Digital Newsroom 2.0. In J. G. Andrade & T. Ruão (Eds.), *Navigating Digital Communication and Challenges for Organizations* (pp. 131–152). IGI Global., doi:10.4018/978-1-7998-9790-3.ch008

Perez Porto, J. G. (2008). *Definition.* Obtained from https://definition.of/student/

Perez Porto, J. G. (2009). *Definition.* Obtained from https://definition.of/factor/

Perreault, G. P., & Perreault, M. F. (2021). eSports as a News Specialty Gold Rush. In Andrews, S. & Crawford, C. M. (Ed.), Handbook of Research on Pathways and Opportunities Into the Business of Esports (pp. 303-320). IGI Global. https://doi.org/ doi:10.4018/978-1-7998-7300-6.ch014

Perumal, S., Ali, J., & Shaarih, H. (2021). Exploring nexus among sensory marketing and repurchase intention: Application of S-O-R Model. *Management Science Letters*, *11*, 1527–1536. doi:10.5267/j.msl.2020.12.020

Perumandla, S., & Kurisetti, P. (2020). An Empirical Investigation on Equity Market Integration of ASEAN-India. In P. Ordoñez de Pablos, X. Zhang, & K. Chui (Eds.), *Innovative Management and Business Practices in Asia* (pp. 29–57). IGI Global., doi:10.4018/978-1-7998-1566-2.ch002

Perumandla, S., & Kurisetti, P. (2021). Commodity Transaction Tax (CTT). [IJABIM]. *International Journal of Asian Business and Information Management*, *12*(2), 16–36. doi:10.4018/ijabim.20210401.oa2

Phillips, B., Hale, M., & Michael, T. (2022). Promoting Campus Wellness Through the Lens of Mental Health Counselors. In C. J. Alexander & A. Tureen (Eds.), *Leadership Wellness and Mental Health Concerns in Higher Education* (pp. 61–88). IGI Global., doi:10.4018/978-1-7998-7693-9.ch004

Pilipenko, A. I., Pilipenko, Z. A., & Pilipenko, O. I. (2022). Patterns of Self-Sufficient Companies' Network Interaction Reorganization Due to COVID-19. In A. Pego (Ed.), *Handbook of Research on Digital Innovation and Networking in Post-COVID-19 Organizations* (pp. 36–67). IGI Global., doi:10.4018/978-1-6684-6762-6.ch003

Pimentel, L. M., & Jorge, S. M. (2019). Earnings Quality and Firm Valuation. In J. D. Oliveira, G. M. Azevedo, & A. D. Ferreira (Eds.), *International Financial Reporting Standards and New Directions in Earnings Management* (pp. 1–31). IGI Global., doi:10.4018/978-1-5225-7817-8.ch001

Pınar, M., & Girard, T. (2020). Comparing Private Label Brand Equity Dimensions of the Same Store. In Y. Arslan (Ed.), *Improving Marketing Strategies for Private Label Products* (pp. 61–82). IGI Global., doi:10.4018/978-1-7998-0257-0.ch004

Pine, J., & Gilmore, J. (2011). *The Experience Economy*. Harvard Business Review Press.

Placide, V., & Vance, M. M. (2022). Supporting Diversity and Inclusiveness Amid a Changing Academic Landscape. In C. R. Ford & K. B. Garza (Eds.), *Handbook of Research on Updating and Innovating Health Professions Education* (pp. 1–23). IGI Global., doi:10.4018/978-1-7998-7623-6.ch001

Polly, D. (2021). Advancing Equity-Based Mathematics Teaching in the Primary Grades. [IJTEPD]. *International Journal of Teacher Education and Professional Development*, *4*(1), 68–88. doi:10.4018/IJTEPD.2021010105

Polly, D., Colonnese, M., Bacak, J., Holshouser, K. O., & Lewis, W. (2022). Promoting Equity in Elementary School Mathematics. In E. K. Reeves & C. J. McIntyre (Eds.), *Multidisciplinary Perspectives on Diversity and Equity in a Virtual World* (pp. 213–232). IGI Global., doi:10.4018/978-1-7998-8028-8.ch012

Porter, E., & Kramer, M. R. (2006). Estrategia y sociedad: El vínculo entre ventaja competitiva y responsabilidad social corporativa. *Harvard Business Review América Latina*, *12*(84), 42–56.

Porter, M. E., & Kramer, M. R. (2011). La creación de valor compartido. *Harvard Business Review*, •••, 32–49.

Porter, T. (2022). Mismatched Students, Missed Opportunities. In R. D. Williams (Ed.), *Handbook of Research on Challenging Deficit Thinking for Exceptional Education Improvement* (pp. 299–328). IGI Global., doi:10.4018/978-1-7998-8860-4.ch014

Posada, J. (n.d.). *I think that*. Obtained from https://www.thecolombian .com/blogs/ithinkthat/tag/effects-of-the-decision

Potter, S. (2022). English language. In *Encyclopedia Britannica*. Obtained from de https://www.britannica.com/topic/English-language

Powell Baker, D., & Cassar, L. (2022). Mentorship of Pre-Health Professional Students. In R. Ganjoo & L. S. Schwartz (Eds.), *Handbook of Research on Developing Competencies for Pre-Health Professional Students, Advisors, and Programs* (pp. 152–173). IGI Global., doi:10.4018/978-1-6684-5969-0.ch008

Powell, A. M. (2022). The Negative Impact of Racial Microaggressions on College Students of Color. In Butcher, J. T.Baker, W. C. (Eds.), Addressing Issues of Systemic Racism During Turbulent Times (pp. 157-169). IGI Global. https://doi.org/ doi:10.4018/978-1-7998-8532-0.ch010

Prahalad, C. K., & Ramaswamy, V. (2004). Co-creation experiences: The next practice in value creation. *Journal of Interactive Marketing*, *18*(3), 5–14. doi:10.1002/dir.20015

Premat, C. E. (2020). Hacktivism and Alternative Journalism. In Khosrow-Pour D.B.A., M. (Eds.), Encyclopedia of Criminal Activities and the Deep Web (pp. 347-361). IGI Global. https://doi.org/ doi:10.4018/978-1-5225-9715-5.ch023

Privette, C. (2021). Critical Race Theory for Speech-Language Pathology. In R. Horton (Ed.), *Critical Perspectives on Social Justice in Speech-Language Pathology* (pp. 84–104). IGI Global., doi:10.4018/978-1-7998-7134-7.ch005

Priyanka, E. B., Thangavel, S., & Prabu, D. V. (2020). Fundamentals of Wireless Sensor Networks Using Machine Learning Approaches. In Sagayam, K., Bhushan, B., Andrushia, A., & Albuquerque, V. C. (Ed.), Deep Learning Strategies for Security Enhancement in Wireless Sensor Networks (pp. 233-254). IGI Global. https://doi.org/ doi:10.4018/978-1-7998-5068-7.ch012

Priya, R., Gandhi, A., & Shaikh, A. (2018). Mobile banking adoption in an emerging economy: An empirical analysis of young Indian consumers. *Benchmarking*, *25*(2), 43–762. doi:10.1108/BIJ-01-2016-0009

Pruitt, E., & Pinchbeck, K. (2022). Empathy-MInded Practice in Higher Education. In C. Ward (Ed.), *Achieving Equity in Higher Education Using Empathy as a Guiding Principle* (pp. 215–238). IGI Global., doi:10.4018/978-1-7998-9746-0.ch010

Quesada, A. M. A. (2020). *Theoretical research methods: Analysis-synthesis, induction-deduction.* Obtained from https://www.researchgate.net/publication/347987929_METHODS_THEORICS_OF_RESEARCH_ANALYSIS-SYNTHESIS_INDUCTION-DEDUCTION_ABSTRACT_-CONCRETE_AND_HISTORIC-LOGIC

R. (2021). *Concept.* Obtained from https://conceptdefinition.of/decision/

R'boul, H. (2021). Interculturally-Critical Digital Storytelling. In Haas, L.Tussey, J. (Eds.), Connecting Disciplinary Literacy and Digital Storytelling in K-12 Education (pp. 278-297). IGI Global. https://doi.org/ doi:10.4018/978-1-7998-5770-9.ch014

R'boul, H., & Bueno-Alastuey, M. C. (2021). Reimagining Multicultural Education. In R. K. Gordon, K. Ahmed, & M. Hosoda (Eds.), *Evolving Multicultural Education for Global Classrooms* (pp. 195–213). IGI Global., doi:10.4018/978-1-7998-7649-6.ch010

Raimi, L., Tariq, M. U., & Kah, J. M. (2022). Diversity, Equity, and Inclusion as the Future Workplace Ethics. In L. Raimi & J. M. Kah (Eds.), *Mainstreaming Diversity, Equity, and Inclusion as Future Workplace Ethics* (pp. 1–27). IGI Global., doi:10.4018/978-1-6684-3657-8.ch001

Raković, R. M. (2020). Application of Cloud Computing in Electric Power Utility Systems. In Stojanović, M. D.Boštjančič Rakas, S. V. (Eds.), Cyber Security of Industrial Control Systems in the Future Internet Environment (pp. 229-247). IGI Global. https://doi.org/ doi:10.4018/978-1-7998-2910-2.ch011

Ramírez-Verdugo, M. D. (2021). International Teacher Education Network. In Ramírez-Verdugo, M. D.Otcu-Grillman, B. (Eds.), Interdisciplinary Approaches Toward Enhancing Teacher Education (pp. 1-19). IGI Global. https://doi.org/ doi:10.4018/978-1-7998-4697-0.ch001

Ramos, J. A., & Cañadillas, I. P. (2003). Delimitación del Marketing con Causa o Marketing Social Corporativo mediante el análisis de empresas que realizan acciones de responsabilidad social. *Cuadernos de Gestión*, *3*(1–2), 65–82.

Ramsey, T. L. (2022). Looking Towards the Sun. In J. T. Butcher (Ed.), *Black Female Leaders in Academia* (pp. 164–183). IGI Global., doi:10.4018/978-1-7998-9774-3.ch008

Randhir, R., Latasha, K., Tooraiven, P., & Monishan, B. (2016). Analyzing the impact of sensory marketing on consumers: A case study of KFC. *Journal of US-China Public Administration*, *13*(4), 278–292. doi:10.17265/1548-6591/2016.04.007

Raposo, D. (2022). *Design, visual communication and branding*. Cambridge Scholars Publishing.

Rascão, J. P. (2021). Freedom of Speech, Privacy, and Ethical and Social Responsibility in Democracy in the Digital Age. [IJRCM]. *International Journal of Risk and Contingency Management*, *10*(3), 34–83. doi:10.4018/IJRCM.2021070104

Rasinger, M. S. (2020). *Qualitative research in linguistics*. Akal S.A.

Ravi, L., & Vairavasundaram, S. (2016). A Collaborative Location Based Travel Recommendation System through Enhanced Rating Prediction for the Group of Users. In Computational Intelligence and Neuroscience. Hindawi Publishing Corporation. doi:10.1155/2016/1291358

Raviadaran, H., Dastane, O., Ma'arif, M., & Mohd, N. (2019). Impact of service quality dimensions on internet banking adoption, satisfaction and patronaje. *International Journal of Management. Accounting and Economics*, *6*(10), 709–730.

Recker, J., & von Briel, F. (2019). The Future of Digital Entrepreneurship Research: Existing and Emerging Opportunities. *Fortieth International Conference on Information Systems, Munich 2019*. core.ac.uk

Redalyc. (2022). *Philosophy*. Obtained from https://. co/general/definition-of-pupil-according-to-authors/#:~:text=student%20is%20a%20what%20what%20provie%20of%20pupils%20pupils%2C.is%20a%20pers%20that%20that%20is%A1%20dedicated%20to%20learning.

Reed, D., Fontenot, C., Peltier-Glaze, B., Hines, M. T., Parker, C. H., & Washington, K. (2022). Nobody Knows the Troubles That I See. In J. T. Butcher (Ed.), *Black Female Leaders in Academia* (pp. 121–163). IGI Global., doi:10.4018/978-1-7998-9774-3.ch007

Reichheld, F. F. (1996). Learning from customer defections. *Harvard Business Review*, *74*(2), 56–67.

Reid, E. K., Matute-Chavarria, M., & Gray, P. (2022). Wading Through Water. In S. R. Logan & T. L. Good (Eds.), *Black Women Navigating Historically White Higher Education Institutions and the Journey Toward Liberation* (pp. 114–135). IGI Global., doi:10.4018/978-1-6684-4626-3.ch006

Reina, M., & Jimenez, D. (2020). Consumer Experience and Omnichannel Behavior in Various Sales Atmospheres. *Frontiers in Psychology*, *11*, 1972. doi:10.3389/fpsyg.2020.01972 PMID:32849155

Reiter, A. (2022). "What Are You?". In Flockhart, T. R., Reiter, A.Hassett, M. R. (Eds.), The Reproduction and Maintenance of Inequalities in Interpersonal Relationships (pp. 134-152). IGI Global. https://doi.org/ doi:10.4018/978-1-6684-4128-2.ch008

Rejón-Guardia, F., Marković, N., & García-Sastre, M. A. (2020). The Development of a Scale to Measure Tourism-Phobia. In Ribeiro de Almeida, C., Quintano, A., Simancas, M., Huete, R., & Breda, Z. (Ed.), Handbook of Research on the Impacts, Challenges, and Policy Responses to Overtourism (pp. 217-236). IGI Global. https://doi.org/ doi:10.4018/978-1-7998-2224-0.ch012

Reneau, C., & Boutakidis, I. (2021). A Modest Proposition. In C. Reneau & M. Villarreal (Eds.), *Handbook of Research on Leading Higher Education Transformation With Social Justice, Equity, and Inclusion* (pp. 339–360). IGI Global., doi:10.4018/978-1-7998-7152-1.ch022

Ressler, M. B., Ressler, J. D., & Gordon, B. (2021). Preparing New Zealand's Teachers to Use Culturally Responsive Relationship-Based Pedagogies. [IJTEPD]. *International Journal of Teacher Education and Professional Development*, *4*(2), 19–33. doi:10.4018/IJTEPD.2021070102

Resuloğlu, F. (2022). No Dress Rehearsal. In A. E. Arimoro (Ed.), *Global Perspectives on the LGBT Community and Non-Discrimination* (pp. 122–140). IGI Global., doi:10.4018/978-1-6684-2428-5.ch006

Reynolds-Mcllnay, R., & Morin, M. (2019). Increasing Shopper Trust in Retailer Technological Interfaces via Auditory Confirmation. *Journal of Retailing*, *95*(4), 128–142. doi:10.1016/j.jretai.2019.10.006

Reynoso, N. M., Foxx, K., Tadesse, A., & Mack, C. (2022). Patching the Pipeline. In H. W. Pichon & Y. Mutakabbir (Eds.), *African American Leadership and Mentoring Through Purpose, Preparation, and Preceptors* (pp. 266–289). IGI Global., doi:10.4018/978-1-7998-8206-0.ch013

Reza, F. (2021). De Facto Segregation and the Digital Divide. In H. K. Dhir (Ed.), *Handbook of Research on Barriers for Teaching 21st-Century Competencies and the Impact of Digitalization* (pp. 145–160). IGI Global., doi:10.4018/978-1-7998-6967-2.ch008

Ribeiro GuevaraS. (2021). *YuBrain*. Obtained from https://www.yubrain.com/humanities/linguistic/second -language/

Ringle, C. M., Wende, S., & Becker, J. M. (2015). *SmartPLS 3.2.8*. Boenningstedt: SmartPLS GmbH. http://www.smartpls.com

Ringler, C., Sirianni, N., Gustafsson, A., & Peck, J. (2019). Look but Don't Touch! The Impact of Active Interpersonal Haptic Blocking on Compensatory Touch and Purchase Behavior. *Journal of Retailing*, *95*(4), 186–203. doi:10.1016/j.jretai.2019.10.007

Ritchi, H., Wahyudi, I., & Susanto, A. (2015). Research program on key success factors of e-Government an their impacto on accounting inforarion quality. *Procedia - Social and Behavioral Sciences, 211*, 673-680. doi:10.1016/j.sbspro.2015.11.102

Rivas-de-Roca, R., & García-Gordillo, M. (2022). Achieving a Representative Democracy in Europe. In D. Palau-Sampio, G. López García, & L. Iannelli (Eds.), *Contemporary Politics, Communication, and the Impact on Democracy* (pp. 19–36). IGI Global., doi:10.4018/978-1-7998-8057-8.ch002

Rivera, S., Hoffman, C., Manierre, M., & Boolani, A. (2022). Beyond the Statement. In E. Cain-Sanschagrin, R. A. Filback, & J. Crawford (Eds.), *Cases on Academic Program Redesign for Greater Racial and Social Justice* (pp. 243–261). IGI Global., doi:10.4018/978-1-7998-8463-7.ch012

Rivera, S., & Ibourk, A. (2020). Incorporating Social Justice Into Science Teacher Education Courses. In C. K. Clausen & S. R. Logan (Eds.), *Integrating Social Justice Education in Teacher Preparation Programs* (pp. 208–224). IGI Global., doi:10.4018/978-1-7998-5098-4.ch010

Robinson, P. A., & Aldana, J. J. (2020). Making Lemonade From the Lemon of Cultural Taxation. In J. Keengwe (Ed.), *Handbook of Research on Diversity and Social Justice in Higher Education* (pp. 1–18). IGI Global., doi:10.4018/978-1-7998-5268-1.ch001

Robinson, P. A., & Stojanović, M. (2022). Critical Considerations for Advancing Gender and Racial Literacies. In J. Keengwe (Ed.), *Handbook of Research on Social Justice and Equity in Education* (pp. 1–21). IGI Global., doi:10.4018/978-1-7998-9567-1.ch001

Rocha, C. J. (2021). Inspiring Inquiry With the i2Flex Model in the World Language Classroom. In Avgerinou, M. D.Pelonis, P. (Eds.), Handbook of Research on K-12 Blended and Virtual Learning Through the i2Flex Classroom Model (pp. 174-187). IGI Global. https://doi.org/ doi:10.4018/978-1-7998-7760-8.ch010

Rodríguez González, J. A., Tagle Zamora, D., & Granados Márquez, G. (2020). Estrategias empresariales ante la COVID-19: El caso de la industria curtidora de León, Guanajuato. *Entreciencias: Diálogos en la Sociedad del Conocimiento*, *8*(22). Advance online publication. doi:10.22201/enesl.20078064e.2020.22.76844

Rodríguez Martínez, S. A. (2018). *Modelo de negocio a través de los torneos online de eSports en Colombia* [Tesis]. Ciencias Económicas y Administrativas, carrera de administración de empresas. javeriana.edu.co

Rodriguez, J. (2022). Practicing Storytelling to Find Meaning and Convey Competencies in the Medical School Application. In Schwartz, L. S.Ganjoo, R. (Eds.), Handbook of Research on Advising and Developing the Pre-Health Professional Student (pp. 269-285). IGI Global. https:// doi.org/ doi:10.4018/978-1-7998-9617-3.ch014

Rodríguez, N. N., Updegraff, A., & Winters, L. A. (2021). Skippyjon, Spanglish, and Stereotypes. In D. E. Hartsfield (Ed.), *Handbook of Research on Teaching Diverse Youth Literature to Pre-Service Professionals* (pp. 103–123). IGI Global., doi:10.4018/978-1-7998-7375-4.ch006

Rodriguez, S. K., & Ricchezza, L. C. (2020). Equity and Social Justice. In S. L. Johnson (Ed.), *Examining Social Change and Social Responsibility in Higher Education* (pp. 1–16). IGI Global., doi:10.4018/978-1-7998-2177-9.ch001

Roggeveen, A., Grewal, D., & Schweiger, E. (2020). The DAST Framework for Retail Atmospherics: The Impact of In- and Out-of-Store Retail Journey Touchpoints on the Customer Experience. *Journal of Retailing*, *96*(1), 128–137. doi:10.1016/j.jretai.2019.11.002

Rojas, A. (n.d.). *Press Room*. Obtained from https://www.aiu.edu/Spanish/publications/student/spanish/TAKE%20OF%DECISIONS%20-%20Decisions%20Making.html#:~:text=when%20the%20result%20of%20a%20decisi%C3%B3n%20depends%20of,about%20the%20intetactions%20between%20the%20components%20of%20problem

Romer, P. (1986). Increasing returns and long-run growth. *Journal of Political Economy*, 4.

Roque, M. I. (2022). Storytelling in Cultural Heritage. In Campos, A.Almeida, S. (Eds.), Global Perspectives on Strategic Storytelling in Destination Marketing (pp. 22-37). IGI Global. https://doi.org/ doi:10.4018/978-1-6684-3436-9.ch002

Rossana, A. (2021). *Concept*. Obtained from https://conceptdefinition.of/student/

Ross, D. B., & Peyton, G. L. (2021). The Never Ending Intellectual Theft of Truth. In R. J. Blankenship (Ed.), *Deep Fakes, Fake News, and Misinformation in Online Teaching and Learning Technologies* (pp. 39–68). IGI Global., doi:10.4018/978-1-7998-6474-5.ch003

Roubides, P. (2021). Learning Design in the 21st Century. In D. Chatham (Ed.), *Advancing Online Course Design and Pedagogy for the 21st Century Learning Environment* (pp. 1–27). IGI Global., doi:10.4018/978-1-7998-5598-9.ch001

Rozman, T., & Rozman, M. F. (2020). Education for Sustainability. [IJSEUS]. *International Journal of Smart Education and Urban Society*, *11*(1), 41–63. doi:10.4018/IJSEUS.2020010104

Ruhe, S. (2020). Fostering (Digital) Media Literacy Skills and Global Citizenship in the EFL Classroom. In Neokleous, G., Krulatz, A.Farrelly, R. (Eds.), Handbook of Research on Cultivating Literacy in Diverse and Multilingual Classrooms (pp. 125-145). IGI Global. https://doi.org/ doi:10.4018/978-1-7998-2722-1.ch007

Ruiz-Molina, M., Gil-Saura, I., & Berenguer-Contrí, G. (2020). Are Retailers' Perceptions of Their Innovativeness and Technology Similar to Those of Consumers? In F. Musso & E. Druica (Eds.), *Handbook of Research on Retailing Techniques for Optimal Consumer Engagement and Experiences* (pp. 310–337). IGI Global., doi:10.4018/978-1-7998-1412-2.ch014

RuniewiczM. (2016). *LinkedIn.* Obtained from https://www.linkedin.com/pulse/advantages-speaking-second-language-mark-runiewicz#:~:text=The%20research%20shows%20that%20there%20are%20many%20benefits,creativity%20and%20increases%20your%20awareness%20and%20cultural%20understanding

Rype. (2020). *Babbel Review.* From RYPE, INC.: https://www.rypeapp.com/babbel-review/

Saad, H., & Hamza, M. (2021). Patterns and Motivations Predicting Mobile Hard News and Soft News Consumption. [IJCRMM]. *International Journal of Customer Relationship Marketing and Management, 12*(3), 49–66. doi:10.4018/IJCRMM.2021070104

Sabela, P. T. (2022). Embedding Afrocentricity in Inclusive Education and Equality. In Maguvhe, M. O.Masuku, M. M. (Eds.), Handbook of Research on Creating Spaces for African Epistemologies in the Inclusive Education Discourse (pp. 25-36). IGI Global. https://doi.org/ doi:10.4018/978-1-6684-4436-8.ch003

Sabu, J. (2022). Testing Models of Data-Driven Reporting in Newspapers for Health Communication. In Al-Suqri, M. N., Alsalmi, J.Al-Shaqsi, O. (Eds.), Mass Communications and the Influence of Information During Times of Crises (pp. 204-235). IGI Global. https://doi.org/ doi:10.4018/978-1-7998-7503-1.ch010

Sachdeva, I., & Goel, S. (2015). Retail store environment and customer experience: A paradigm. *Journal of Fashion Marketing and Management, 19*(3), 290–298. doi:10.1108/JFMM-03-2015-0021

Sachin Modgil, Y. K., Dwivedi, N. P., Rana, S. G., & Sachin, K. (2022). Has Covid-19 accelerated opportunities for digital entrepreneurship? An Indian perspective. *Technological Forecasting and Social Change, 175*, 121415. doi:10.1016/j.techfore.2021.121415 PMID:36536802

Sackey, R., Asiamah, A. A., & Aboagye, L. A. (2021). Newsroom Representation and Discrimination Against Female Journalists in Ghana. In S. Jamil, B. Çoban, B. Ataman, & G. Appiah-Adjei (Eds.), *Handbook of Research on Discrimination, Gender Disparity, and Safety Risks in Journalism* (pp. 297–318). IGI Global., doi:10.4018/978-1-7998-6686-2.ch016

Safeer, A. A., & Khuhro, S. (2022). Employee-Based Brand Equity and Competitive Advantage. In M. Bari, M. Abrar, & E. Alaverdov (Eds.), *Antecedents and Outcomes of Employee-Based Brand Equity* (pp. 54–71). IGI Global., doi:10.4018/978-1-6684-3621-9.ch004

Safeer, A., He, Y., & Abrar, M. (2020). The influence of brand experience on brand authenticity and brand love: An empirical study from Asian consumers' perspective. *Asia Pacific Journal of Marketing and Logistics, 33*(5), 1123–1138. doi:10.1108/APJML-02-2020-0123

Safieddine, F., & Hammad, R. (2020). Fake News. In Y. Ibrahim (Ed.), *Handbook of Research on Recent Developments in Internet Activism and Political Participation* (pp. 103–121). IGI Global., doi:10.4018/978-1-7998-4796-0.ch007

Salato, S. J., & Fifield Brandt, B. (2022). Reflecting on Race and Health Outcomes. In R. Ganjoo & L. S. Schwartz (Eds.), *Handbook of Research on Developing Competencies for Pre-Health Professional Students, Advisors, and Programs* (pp. 305–327). IGI Global., doi:10.4018/978-1-6684-5969-0.ch015

Salazar, L. R., Garcia, N., Diego-Medrano, E., & Castillo, Y. (2021). Workplace Cyberbullying and Cross-Cultural Differences. In L. Ramos Salazar (Ed.), *Handbook of Research on Cyberbullying and Online Harassment in the Workplace* (pp. 284–309). IGI Global., doi:10.4018/978-1-7998-4912-4.ch014

Salimon, M., Yusoff, R., & Mokhtar, S. M. (2017). The mediating role of hedonic motivation on the relationship between adoption of e-banking and its determinants. *International Journal of Bank Marketing, 35*(4), 558–582. doi:10.1108/IJBM-05-2016-0060

Salim, Z. (2020). Mapping Gated Communities. [IJAGR]. *International Journal of Applied Geospatial Research, 11*(3), 48–67. doi:10.4018/IJAGR.2020070104

Salmon, A. K., & Melliou, K. (2021). Understanding and Facing Migration Through Stories for Influence. In I. G. Barreto (Ed.), *Handbook of Research on Promoting Social Justice for Immigrants and Refugees Through Active Citizenship and Intercultural Education* (pp. 205–231). IGI Global., doi:10.4018/978-1-7998-7283-2.ch011

Samoilenko, S. A., & Miroshnichenko, A. (2019). Profiting From the "Trump Bump". In I. E. Chiluwa & S. A. Samoilenko (Eds.), *Handbook of Research on Deception, Fake News, and Misinformation Online* (pp. 375–391). IGI Global., doi:10.4018/978-1-5225-8535-0.ch020

San Martín, H., García-de-los-Salmones, M. M., & Herrero-Crespo, Á. (2020). Citizen Perceptions and Support for Smart City Projects. In J. M. Palma-Ruiz, J. Saiz-Álvarez, & Á. Herrero-Crespo (Eds.), *Handbook of Research on Smart Territories and Entrepreneurial Ecosystems for Social Innovation and Sustainable Growth* (pp. 107–123). IGI Global., doi:10.4018/978-1-7998-2097-0.ch007

Sanchez, J. (2019). *PumaMóvil, la app de la UNAM para que no te pierdas en Ciudad Universitaria.* From El Sol de Mexico: https://www.elsoldemexico.com.mx/metropoli/cdmx/pumamovil-la-app-de-la-unam-para-que-no-te-pierdas-en-ciudad-universitaria-4044444.html

SanchezA. (2019). *Question pro.* Obtained from https://www.questionpro.com/is/research-of-field.html

SanchezA. B. (2017). Obtained from https://www.researchgate.net/profile/Raquel-Morquecho-Sanchez/publication/351094563_Volume_1_Number_2_-octuber_-dicember_-2017/links/6085f695907dcf667bc457bc/Volume-1-number-2-octuber-dicember-2017.pdf#page=35

Sánchez-Connally, P., & Cabello, C. (2022). Resistencia. In Alvarez, W. & De Walt, P. S. (Ed.), Voicing Diverse Teaching Experiences, Approaches, and Perspectives in Higher Education (pp. 191-201). IGI Global. https://doi.org/ doi:10.4018/978-1-7998-9000-3.ch014

Sánchez-Figuera, R., Casado Gutiérrez, F., Luque González, A., & García-Guerrero, J. (2021). Sensationalism vs. Information During COVID-19 in Ecuador. In M. Bari & E. Alaverdov (Eds.), *Impact of Infodemic on Organizational Performance* (pp. 195–216). IGI Global., doi:10.4018/978-1-7998-7164-4.ch012

Sandell, K. (2019). Olfactory cues and purchase behavior: Consumer characteristics as moderators. *European Journal of Marketing*, *53*(7), 1378–1399. doi:10.1108/EJM-12-2017-0918

Sandoval-Almazan, R. (2019). Gobierno abierto y transparencia en México: Estudio longitudinal 2015-2018. *Innovar (Universidad Nacional de Colombia)*, *29*(74), 115–131. doi:10.15446/innovar.v29n74.82097

Sangar, S. (2022). Addressing Low Female Participation in STEM for an Inclusive Industry 4.0. In Bala, S.Singhal, P. (Eds.), Gender Perspectives on Industry 4.0 and the Impact of Technology on Mainstreaming Female Employment (pp. 91-106). IGI Global. https://doi.org/ doi:10.4018/978-1-7998-8594-8.ch005

Santiago Hernández, V. G., Martínez Sandoval, D., Alcaraz Miranda, M., & Córdova Yánez, A. (2021). Efecto del covid-19 en las mipymes de la región serrana del Estado de Sonora. *Revista Mexicana de Agronegocios*, *49*, 19–32.

Santos, I. M., & Wu, W. (2022). Equity Pedagogies for Inclusive Online Classrooms in Higher Education. In S. Ramlall, T. Cross, & M. Love (Eds.), *Handbook of Research on Future of Work and Education* (pp. 379–399). IGI Global., doi:10.4018/978-1-7998-8275-6.ch023

Santos, S., & Santo, P. E. (2021). Brands and Stories in Ads. In L. C. Mihăeş, R. Andreescu, & A. Dimitriu (Eds.), *Handbook of Research on Contemporary Storytelling Methods Across New Media and Disciplines* (pp. 116–137). IGI Global., doi:10.4018/978-1-7998-6605-3.ch007

Saqib, S., Rubab, A., & Pitsaphol, C. (2022). Knowledge-Hiding Behaviors and Employee-Based Brand Equity. In M. Bari, M. Abrar, & E. Alaverdov (Eds.), *Antecedents and Outcomes of Employee-Based Brand Equity* (pp. 81–89). IGI Global., doi:10.4018/978-1-6684-3621-9.ch006

Saridou, T. A., & Veglis, A. (2021). Exploring the Integration of User-Generated Content in Media Organizations Through Participatory Journalism. In Khosrow-Pour D.B.A., M. (Ed.), Encyclopedia of Information Science and Technology, Fifth Edition (pp. 1152-1163). IGI Global. https://doi.org/ doi:10.4018/978-1-7998-3479-3.ch080

Sarkar, A., Jha, A., & Mukherjee, D. (2019). Trucks and Brand. [IJABIM]. *International Journal of Asian Business and Information Management*, *10*(2), 1–30. doi:10.4018/IJABIM.2019040101

SarokinD. (2020). *Chron*. Obtained from https://work.chron.com/advantages-career-development-trainin g-6783.html

Sascha Kraus, C. P., Kailer, N., Kallinger, F. L., & Spitzer, J. (2018). Digital entrepreneurship. A research agenda on new business models for the twenty-first century. *International Journal of Entrepreneurial Behaviour & Research*, *25*(2), 353–375. doi:10.1108/IJEBR-06-2018-0425

Satti, Z., Babar, S., & Ahmad, H. (2019). Exploring mediating role of service quality in the association between sensory marketing and customer satisfaction. *Total Quality Management & Business Excellence*, *32*(7-8), 719–736. doi:10.1080/14783363.2019.1632185

Savino, A. A., & de Titto, E. (2020). Sustainable Waste Management Challenges in Argentina. In Pariatamby, A., Shahul Hamid, F. & Bhatti, M. S. (Ed.), Sustainable Waste Management Challenges in Developing Countries (pp. 1-34). IGI Global. https://doi.org/ doi:10.4018/978-1-7998-0198-6.ch001

Scarpena, K. (2020). Online Doctoral Programs. In Setzekorn, K., Patnayakuni, N.Burton, T. (Eds.), Socioeconomics, Diversity, and the Politics of Online Education (pp. 90-110). IGI Global. https://doi.org/ doi:10.4018/978-1-7998-3583-7.ch006

Schalkoff, R. J. (1990). *Artificial Intelligence: An Engineering Approach.* McGraw-Hill.

Schwartzman, R. (2021). Risky Jews. In L. Shedletsky (Ed.), *Rationalist Bias in Communication Theory* (pp. 1–17). IGI Global., doi:10.4018/978-1-7998-7439-3.ch009

Schwipper, S., Peche, S., & Schmitz, G. (2020). Mobile Location-Based Services' Value-in-Use in Inner Cities: Do a Customer's Shopping Patterns, Prior User Experience, and Sales Promotions Matter? *Schmalenbach Business Review*, *72*(4), 511–564.

Scott, B. (2019). Afro-Caribbean Immigrants in STEM Careers. In Thomas, U.Drake, J. (Eds.), Women's Influence on Inclusion, Equity, and Diversity in STEM Fields (pp. 143-168). IGI Global. https://doi.org/ doi:10.4018/978-1-5225-8870-2.ch006

Scott-Johnson, P. E., & Leggett-Robinson, P. M. (2020). A Journey Worth Traveling. In P. M. Leggett-Robinson & B. C. Villa (Eds.), *Overcoming Barriers for Women of Color in STEM Fields* (pp. 116–140). IGI Global., doi:10.4018/978-1-7998-4858-5.ch006

Scullin, B. L. (2021). Promoting Race Talk With Elementary Preservice Teachers Through Diverse Picture Book Read Alouds. In D. E. Hartsfield (Ed.), *Handbook of Research on Teaching Diverse Youth Literature to Pre-Service Professionals* (pp. 210–234). IGI Global., doi:10.4018/978-1-7998-7375-4.ch011

Seegars, W. (2022). Cultural Bias and Its Implications for Discipline Disparity. In A. T. Adams (Ed.), *Approaching Disparities in School Discipline* (pp. 1–22). IGI Global., doi:10.4018/978-1-6684-3359-1.ch001

Seliskar, H. V., Robinson, C., Early, K. W., Williams, T. N., & Johnson, C. S. (2021). Building Capacity Through Multiculturalism and Diversity in the Online Classroom. In T. P. Fudge & S. S. Ferebee (Eds.), *Curriculum Development and Online Instruction for the 21st Century* (pp. 114–131). IGI Global., doi:10.4018/978-1-7998-7653-3.ch007

Selnes, F. N., & Walulya, G. (2020). Types and Sources of Threats to Media Freedom in Uganda. In S. Jamil (Ed.), *Handbook of Research on Combating Threats to Media Freedom and Journalist Safety* (pp. 257–276). IGI Global., doi:10.4018/978-1-7998-1298-2.ch014

Şen, O. (2022). Informatics Truth. In Yılmaz, R.Koç, B. (Eds.), Narrative Theory and Therapy in the Post-Truth Era (pp. 61-78). IGI Global. https://doi.org/ doi:10.4018/978-1-7998-9251-9.ch005

Sen, A., & Dietz, L. W. (2019). Identifying travel regions using location-based social network check-in data. *Frontiers in Big Data, 2*, 12. doi:10.3389/fdata.2019.00012 PMID:33693335

Sendi, N., Abchiche-Mimouni, N., & Zehraoui, F. (2019). A new Transparent Ensemble Method based on Deep learning. *Procedia Computer Science, 159*, 271-280.

Sera, H., & Wall, A. F. (2021). Ichigo-Ichie. In C. Reneau & M. Villarreal (Eds.), *Handbook of Research on Leading Higher Education Transformation With Social Justice, Equity, and Inclusion* (pp. 1–17). IGI Global., doi:10.4018/978-1-7998-7152-1.ch001

Serener, B. (2016). Statistical analysis of Internet banking usage with logistic regression. *Procedia Computer Science, 102*, 648–653. doi:10.1016/j.procs.2016.09.456

Seward, K., & Gentry, M. (2022). Protocols for Identification. In J. L. Nyberg & J. A. Manzone (Eds.), *Creating Equitable Services for the Gifted* (pp. 1–10). IGI Global., doi:10.4018/978-1-7998-8153-7.ch001

Sezgin, M., & Bayoğlu, F. (2020). Comparison of Public Relations Education at Undergraduate and Graduate Levels in Turkey and EU Member States. In Y. Bayar (Ed.), *Handbook of Research on Social and Economic Development in the European Union* (pp. 510–541). IGI Global., doi:10.4018/978-1-7998-1188-6.ch030

Shabbir, M. S. (2020). Attributes Ensuring Positive Consumer Evaluation in Brand Extension of Pakistan. [IJABIM]. *International Journal of Asian Business and Information Management, 11*(4), 71–84. doi:10.4018/IJABIM.2020100106

Shahabi, V., & Razi, F. F. (2019). Modeling the effect of electronic banking expansion on profitability using neural networks and system dynamics approach. *Qualitative Research in Financial Markets, 11*(2), 197–210. doi:10.1108/QRFM-11-2018-0117

Shaheen, S., Chaman, S., & Zulfiqar, S. (2022). An Exploration of the Factors Affecting Brand Association. In M. Bari, M. Abrar, & E. Alaverdov (Eds.), *Antecedents and Outcomes of Employee-Based Brand Equity* (pp. 106–118). IGI Global., doi:10.4018/978-1-6684-3621-9.ch008

Shah, S. F., Jan, F., & Ittefaq, M. (2021). Health and Safety Risks to Journalists During Pandemics. In S. Jamil, B. Çoban, B. Ataman, & G. Appiah-Adjei (Eds.), *Handbook of Research on Discrimination, Gender Disparity, and Safety Risks in Journalism* (pp. 90–103). IGI Global., doi:10.4018/978-1-7998-6686-2.ch006

Shah, Z., Martin, P., Coiera, E., Mandl, K. D., & Dunn, A. G. (2019). Modeling Spatiotemporal Factors Associated with Sentiment on Twitter: Synthesis and Suggestions for Improving the Identification of Localized Deviations. *Journal of Medical Internet Research, 21*(5), e12881. doi:10.2196/12881 PMID:31344669

Shaikhina, T., Lowe, D., Daga, S., Briggs, D., Higgins, R., & Khovanova, N. (2019). Decision tree and random forest models for outcome prediction in antibody incompatible kidney transplantation. *Biomedical Signal Processing and Control, 52*, 456-462.

Shapero, A. C. (1981). Self-renewing economies. *Economic Development Commentary, 5*, 19–22.

Shareef, M. A., Kumar, V., Kumar, U., & Dwivedi, Y. K. (2011). e-Government Adoption Model (GAM): Differing service maturity levels. *Government Information Quarterly, 28*(1), 17–35. doi:10.1016/j.giq.2010.05.006

Sharma, A. (2022). Understanding the Digitised Labour Market Through a Gendered Lens. In Bala, S.Singhal, P. (Eds.), Gender Perspectives on Industry 4.0 and the Impact of Technology on Mainstreaming Female Employment (pp. 108-131). IGI Global. https://doi.org/ doi:10.4018/978-1-7998-8594-8.ch006

Sharma, S. K., & Sharma, M. (2019). Examining the role of trust and quality dimensions in the actual usage of mobile banking services: An empirical investigation. *International Journal of Information Management, 44*, 65–75. doi:10.1016/j.ijinfomgt.2018.09.013

Sheikh, S. (2021). *AI in Industry*. IGI Global., doi:10.4018/978-1-7998-4607-9.ch005

Shelton, H., He-Weatherford, Z., Peterson, S. R., & Alharthi, A. A. (2021). Framing Crisis in Seattle During COVID-19 and Black Lives Matter. In E. B. Hancı-Azizoglu & M. Alawdat (Eds.), *Rhetoric and Sociolinguistics in Times of Global Crisis* (pp. 342–364). IGI Global., doi:10.4018/978-1-7998-6732-6.ch018

Shinas, V. H., Wen, H., & Guo, D. (2022). Developing Teachers as Writers. In T. S. Hodges (Ed.), *Handbook of Research on Teacher Practices for Diverse Writing Instruction* (pp. 88–107). IGI Global., doi:10.4018/978-1-6684-6213-3.ch006

Shin, D. (2021). A Cross-National Study on the Perception of Algorithm News in the East and the West. [JGIM]. *Journal of Global Information Management, 29*(2), 77–101. doi:10.4018/JGIM.2021030105

Shittu, A. K., Mbada, K. A., & Odeyemi, T. I. (2021). Evaluating the Impact and Effectiveness of Community-Based Health Insurance Policy Among Informal Sector in Lagos State Using Donabedian Model. [IJPPPHCE]. *International Journal of Public and Private Perspectives on Healthcare, Culture, and the Environment, 5*(2), 65–80. doi:10.4018/IJPPPHCE.2021070105

Shmilovici. (n.d.). *Support Vector Machines, Data Mining and Knowledge Discovery Handbook*. Academic Press.

Siggelkow, N., & Terwiesch, C. (2019). The age of continuous connection. *Harvard Business Review*, (May-June), 64–73.

Šimić, G. P. (2019). Improving e-government services for advanced search. *Military Technical Courier*, *67*(2), 307–325. doi:10.5937/vojtehg67-20356

Simon, K. N., Hodgkins, L., & Argent, J. (2022). Small Chunks, Deep Learning. In Y. Huang (Ed.), *Handbook of Research on Credential Innovations for Inclusive Pathways to Professions* (pp. 276–299). IGI Global., doi:10.4018/978-1-7998-3820-3.ch014

Sims, C. (2021). The Impact of Gendered Lookism During Employment Stages. In C. Hughes (Ed.), *Implementation Strategies for Improving Diversity in Organizations* (pp. 75–109). IGI Global., doi:10.4018/978-1-7998-4745-8.ch003

Sina, A., & Kim, H. (2019). Enhancing consumer satisfaction and retail patronage through brand experience, cognitive pleasure, and shopping enjoyment: A comparison between lifestyle and product-centric displays. *Journal of Global Fashion Marketing*, *10*(2), 129–144. doi:10.1080/20932685.2019.1573698

Sindhu, S. (2020). Cause-related marketing— An interpretive structural model approach. *Journal of Nonprofit & Public Sector Marketing*, *00*(00), 1–27. doi:10.1080/10495142.2020.1798851

Sine Nazlı, R., Akbulak, B., & Çat, A. K. (2020). Journalism and Communication Design in New Media. In S. Kır (Ed.), *New Media and Visual Communication in Social Networks* (pp. 70–92). IGI Global., doi:10.4018/978-1-7998-1041-4.ch005

Sithole, P. M., & Bondai, B. M. (2020). Taboos and Storytelling for Teaching and Learning in Zimbabwe. [IJCDLM]. *International Journal of Curriculum Development and Learning Measurement*, *1*(2), 53–65. doi:10.4018/IJCDLM.2020070104

Skybe, M. V. (2016). Improving e-government as one of the preconditions for economic development. *Economic Processes Management: International Scientific E-Journal*, *3*. Recuperado de: http://epm.fem.sumdu.edu.ua/download/2016_3/epm2016_3_6.pdf

Smith-Adams, C. (2022). Path to College Presidency. In J. T. Butcher (Ed.), *Black Female Leaders in Academia* (pp. 213–232). IGI Global., doi:10.4018/978-1-7998-9774-3.ch011

Smith, E. C., & Conrad, M. (2020). Cultivating Magic and Nostalgia. In D. Batabyal (Ed.), *Global Entrepreneurial Trends in the Tourism and Hospitality Industry* (pp. 131–158). IGI Global., doi:10.4018/978-1-7998-2603-3.ch007

Smith, H. L., & Iyengar, K. (2021). "Respectful" Home-School Relationships. In G. Onchwari & J. Keengwe (Eds.), *Bridging Family-Teacher Relationships for ELL and Immigrant Students* (pp. 265–284). IGI Global., doi:10.4018/978-1-7998-4712-0.ch014

Smith, H. L., & Iyengar, K. M. (2019). My Friends and Family. In J. Keengwe & G. Onchwari (Eds.), *Handbook of Research on Assessment Practices and Pedagogical Models for Immigrant Students* (pp. 316–329). IGI Global., doi:10.4018/978-1-5225-9348-5.ch017

Smith-Woofter, M. B., Rumley, M. A., & Barbour, N. N. (2022). School Leaders Serving to Develop Teachers as Equity-Focused Change Agents. In B. S. Zugelder & M. L'Esperance (Eds.), *Handbook of Research on the Educator Continuum and Development of Teachers* (pp. 510–526). IGI Global., doi:10.4018/978-1-6684-3848-0.ch025

Sohal, P. (2020). Shooting the Messenger, Slowly, but Surely. In S. Jamil (Ed.), *Handbook of Research on Combating Threats to Media Freedom and Journalist Safety* (pp. 23–37). IGI Global., doi:10.4018/978-1-7998-1298-2.ch002

Soles, B., Flores, P. III, Domingues, J., & Solis, F. (2020). The Role of Formal and Nonformal Leaders in Creating Culturally Proficient Educational Practices. In P. D. Keough (Ed.), *Overcoming Current Challenges in the P-12 Teaching Profession* (pp. 144–172). IGI Global., doi:10.4018/978-1-7998-1177-0.ch007

Söllner, M., Hoffmann, A., & Leimeister, J. M. (2019). Why different trust relationships matter for information systems users. *European Journal of Information Systems, 25*(3), 274–287. doi:10.1057/ejis.2015.17

Solomon, E. N., Adu-Debrah, L. K., & Braimah, S. M. (2022). Promoting Tourism Destinations Through Storytelling. In A. Campos & S. Almeida (Eds.), *Global Perspectives on Strategic Storytelling in Destination Marketing* (pp. 117–135). IGI Global., doi:10.4018/978-1-6684-3436-9.ch007

Soltani, S. (2020). "Designing Optimal Valuation Model of Bank Stocks". In Köseoğlu, S. D. (Eds.), Valuation Challenges and Solutions in Contemporary Businesses (pp. 212-233). IGI Global. https://doi.org/ doi:10.4018/978-1-7998-1086-5.ch012

Song of Ghent. (2020). Likert scale: An alternative to elaborate and interpret an instrument of social perception. *Magazine of High Technology and Society, 38.*

Sonobe, T., Takeda, A., Yoshida, S., & Truong, H. T. (2021). *The Impacts of the COVID-19 Pandemic on Micro, Small, and Medium Enterprises in Asia and Their Digitalization Responses. ADBI Working Paper 1241.* Asian Development Bank Institute. https://www.adb.org/publications/impacts-covid-19-pandemic-msme-asia-their-digitalizationresponses

Sowad, A. S. (2019). Is Gender a More Important Axis of Representation Than Race, Ethnicity or Class in Politics? [IJSESD]. *International Journal of Social Ecology and Sustainable Development, 10*(2), 29–36. doi:10.4018/IJSESD.2019040103

Sözler, S. (2021). Design Thinking for Online Learning. In Kurubacak-Meric, G.Sisman-Ugur, S. (Eds.), Improving Scientific Communication for Lifelong Learners (pp. 14-37). IGI Global. https://doi.org/ doi:10.4018/978-1-7998-4534-8.ch002

Spears, J. C., Jr., & Coleman, S. T. (2021). The Social Impact of Sport. In Hairston, K. R., Edmonds, W. M. & Clark, S. P. (Ed.), The Black Experience and Navigating Higher Education Through a Virtual World (pp. 97-121). IGI Global. https://doi.org/ doi:10.4018/978-1-7998-7537-6.ch006

Spence, C. (2012). Managing sensory expectations concerning products and brands: Capitalizing on the potential of sound and shape symbolism. *Journal of Consumer Psychology*, *22*(1), 37–54. doi:10.1016/j.jcps.2011.09.004

Spencer, A. D., & Lance, T. A. (2021). Leading Boldly. In A. J. Griffen (Ed.), *Challenges to Integrating Diversity, Equity, and Inclusion Programs in Organizations* (pp. 200–214). IGI Global., doi:10.4018/978-1-7998-4093-0.ch013

Spranger, A. N. (2022). The Inclusive Leader's Toolkit. In Neimann, T., Felix, J. J., Shliakhovchuk, E.Hindman, L. L. (Eds.), Policy and Practice Challenges for Equality in Education (pp. 279-294). IGI Global. https://doi.org/ doi:10.4018/978-1-7998-7379-2.ch013

Staff. (2019). *Got from what are the main types of students?* https://www.iwanttolearnlanguages.com/training-online/main-t ypes-of-students/

Statti, A. L. (2021). Learner-Active Technology-Infused Classroom. [IJSEUS]. *International Journal of Smart Education and Urban Society*, *12*(1), 30–44. doi:10.4018/IJSEUS.2021010103

Stepniak, M., Shaffer, S., & Shaffer, S. (2021). Using Social-Emotional Learning and Literacy Tools to Bridge the Gap During and Beyond COVID-19. In J. Tussey & L. Haas (Eds.), *Handbook of Research on Supporting Social and Emotional Development Through Literacy Education* (pp. 172–194). IGI Global., doi:10.4018/978-1-7998-7464-5.ch009

Stiegler, C. (2020). No Line on the Horizon. In Y. Ibrahim (Ed.), *Handbook of Research on Recent Developments in Internet Activism and Political Participation* (pp. 53–68). IGI Global., doi:10.4018/978-1-7998-4796-0.ch004

Stillman, P., Lee, H., Deng, X., Unnava, H., & Fujita, K. (2020). Examining consumers' sensory experiences with color: A consumer neuroscience approach. *Psychology and Marketing*, *37*(7), 995–1007. doi:10.1002/mar.21360

Stojanović, M., & Robinson, P. A. (2022). A Deep Dive Into How Critical Literacy Experts Advance Equity and Social Justice. In J. Keengwe (Ed.), *Handbook of Research on Social Justice and Equity in Education* (pp. 72–91). IGI Global., doi:10.4018/978-1-7998-9567-1.ch004

Stone, Soulard, Migacz, & Wolf. (n.d.). Elements of Memorable Food, Drink, and Culinary Tourism Experiences. *Journal of Travel Research.*

Strehovec, J. (2020). *Remediating the Social: Impacts of Historical Fascism on Academic Fascism*. IGI Global., doi:10.4018/978-1-7998-3835-7.ch008

Strehovec, J. (2020). *The Word-Image-Virtual Body*. IGI Global., doi:10.4018/978-1-7998-3835-7.ch004

Stufft, C. (2021). Cultivating Social Justice Through Explorations of Multimodal Pop Culture Texts. In Haas, L.Tussey, J. (Eds.), Disciplinary Literacy Connections to Popular Culture in K-12 Settings (pp. 273-291). IGI Global. https://doi.org/ doi:10.4018/978-1-7998-4721-2.ch013

Sundar, R., & Punniyamoorthy, M. (2019). Performance enhanced Boosted SVM for Imbalanced datasets. *Applied Soft Computing, Elsevier*, *83*(October), 105601.

Sundberg, L., & Larsson, A. (2017). The impact of formal decision processes on e-Government projects. *Administrative Sciences*, *7*(14), 2–12. doi:10.3390/admsci7020014

Sun, J., Fujita, H., Chen, P., & Li, H. (2017, March). Dynamic financial distress prediction with concept drift based on time weighting combined with Adaboost support vector machine ensemble. *Knowledge-Based Systems*, *120*(15), 4–14. doi:10.1016/j.knosys.2016.12.019

Surugiu, R. (2022). Bridging Journalists and PR Practitioners in a Digital Context. In Andrade, J. G.Ruão, T. (Eds.), Navigating Digital Communication and Challenges for Organizations (pp. 153-166). IGI Global. https://doi.org/ doi:10.4018/978-1-7998-9790-3.ch009

Susanto, T. D., & Aljoza, M. (2015). Individual acceptance of e-government services in a developing country: Dimensions of perceived usefulness and perceived ease of use and the importance of trust and social influence. *Procedia Computer Science, 72*, 622-629. http:// doi:10.1016/j.procs.2015.12.171

Susanto, A., Chang, Y., & Ha, Y. (2016). Determinants of continuance intention to use the smartphone banking services: An extension to the expectation-confirmation model. *Industrial Management & Data Systems*, *116*(3), 508–525. doi:10.1108/IMDS-05-2015-0195

Švigelj, M. M. (2022). Re-Mediating Narratives. In R. D. Williams (Ed.), *Handbook of Research on Challenging Deficit Thinking for Exceptional Education Improvement* (pp. 380–404). IGI Global., doi:10.4018/978-1-7998-8860-4.ch018

Swanson, J. R., & Johannigman, T. (2022). Autoethnography of Cultural Heritage Tourism Documentary Production. In A. Campos & S. Almeida (Eds.), *Global Perspectives on Strategic Storytelling in Destination Marketing* (pp. 38–51). IGI Global., doi:10.4018/978-1-6684-3436-9.ch003

Taha, N., & Al-Maskeri, A. (2022). The Application of Social Network Theory During a Pandemic. In M. N. Al-Suqri, J. Alsalmi, & O. Al-Shaqsi (Eds.), *Mass Communications and the Influence of Information During Times of Crises* (pp. 188–203). IGI Global., doi:10.4018/978-1-7998-7503-1.ch009

Tajuddin, S. N., & Ali, R. (2020). The Risks and Challenges for Professional Journalism in the Digital Age. In S. Jamil (Ed.), *Handbook of Research on Combating Threats to Media Freedom and Journalist Safety* (pp. 106–123). IGI Global., doi:10.4018/978-1-7998-1298-2.ch007

Talavera, I. (2022). Some Problems in Advancing Academic Inclusion. In V. Wang (Ed.), *Handbook of Research on Educational Leadership and Research Methodology* (pp. 290–310). IGI Global., doi:10.4018/978-1-6684-4144-2.ch016

Tambascia, T. P. (2021). Letters to My 25-Year-Old Self. In Reneau, C.Villarreal, M. (Eds.), Handbook of Research on Leading Higher Education Transformation With Social Justice, Equity, and Inclusion (pp. 18-25). IGI Global. https://doi.org/ doi:10.4018/978-1-7998-7152-1.ch002

Tănase, A. E., Calotă, T. O., & Oncioiu, G. C. (2021). Convergence and Divergence Regarding Business Combinations. In I. Oncioiu, S. Căpuşneanu, D. I. Topor, & D. M. Constantin (Eds.), *Sustainability Reporting, Ethics, and Strategic Management Strategies for Modern Organizations* (pp. 78–91). IGI Global., doi:10.4018/978-1-7998-4637-6.ch005

Tănase, A. E., Stoica, D. A., Trăistaru, N. I., & Sürgün, M. B. (2020). Important Managerial Controversies in Conversion of Financial Statements. In I. Oncioiu, G. Cokins, S. Căpuşneanu, & D. I. Topor (Eds.), *Management Accounting Standards for Sustainable Business Practices* (pp. 227–238). IGI Global., doi:10.4018/978-1-7998-0178-8.ch012

Tandon, U., Kiran, R., & Sah, A. (2017). Customer Satisfaction as mediator between website service quality and repurchase intention: An emerging economy case. *Service Science*, *9*(2), 106–120. doi:10.1287erv.2016.0159

Tang, H., Tan, S., & Cheng, X. (2009). A survey on sentiment detection of reviews. *Xueqi Cheng Expert Systems with Applications*, *36*(7), 10760–10773. doi:10.1016/j.eswa.2009.02.063

Taraktaş, B. (2022). Incorporating Computational Social Science in Political Science. In E. Abanoz (Ed.), *Opportunities and Challenges for Computational Social Science Methods* (pp. 23–44). IGI Global., doi:10.4018/978-1-7998-8553-5.ch002

Targowski, A. (2022). *Digital Humanities Strategy*. IGI Global., doi:10.4018/978-1-7998-8036-3.ch017

Tas Alicenap, C. (2021). The Use of Animation and Storytelling in Science Communication. In Kurubacak-Meric, G.Sisman-Ugur, S. (Eds.), Improving Scientific Communication for Lifelong Learners (pp. 240-250). IGI Global. https://doi.org/ doi:10.4018/978-1-7998-4534-8.ch013

TeamI. E. (2021). *Indeed*. Obtained from https://in.indeed.com/career-advice/career-development/what-are-career-opportunities?fbclid=IwAR0mX2FetEtblNo-EJm4P7C6Qq Muscrbp1SfmjY3YL-gXTqHJ0S0ahpDfy8

Techopedia. (2020). *Mobile Application (Mobile App)*. From Techopedia Inc.: https://www.techopedia.com/definition/2953/mobile-application-mobile-app

Tecma. (2022). *3D printing in Mexican industry, the United States, and Europe account for 68% of revenues generated, while the Asia Pacific region accounts for 27%. The Use of 3D Printing in Mexican Industry is Growing*. tecma.com

Tengler, K. (2022). Developing Storytelling Activities Supporting Computational Thinking Using Educational Robots. In Eteokleous, N.Nisiforou, E. (Eds.), Designing, Constructing, and Programming Robots for Learning (pp. 116-135). IGI Global. https://doi.org/ doi:10.4018/978-1-7998-7443-0.ch006

Thi, K. T. (2020). Internet Technology Application in Production of Internet Radio Programs in Vietnam. In Jamil, G. L., Ribeiro, F., Malheiro da Silva, A.Maravilhas Lopes, S. (Eds.), Handbook of Research on Emerging Technologies for Effective Project Management (pp. 300-322). IGI Global. https://doi.org/ doi:10.4018/978-1-5225-9993-7.ch018

Thomas, M., & Stang, B. (2022). A Serious Game for Cultural Heritage? In O. Bernardes & V. Amorim (Eds.), *Handbook of Research on Promoting Economic and Social Development Through Serious Games* (pp. 334–374). IGI Global., doi:10.4018/978-1-7998-9732-3.ch016

Thompson, J. M. (2022). Sustaining Culturally Affirming and Antiracist Practices. In Brant-Rajahn, S. N., Gibson, E. M.Cook Sandifer, M. (Eds.), Developing, Delivering, and Sustaining School Counseling Practices Through a Culturally Affirming Lens (pp. 174-191). IGI Global. https://doi.org/ doi:10.4018/978-1-7998-9514-5.ch009

Toma, M. J. (2022). Mass Media's Negative Narratives. In G. A. Crews (Ed.), *Impact of School Shootings on Classroom Culture, Curriculum, and Learning* (pp. 190–217). IGI Global., doi:10.4018/978-1-7998-5200-1.ch010

Tomar, R. S., & Kulkarni, M. (2020). Global Racial, Ethnic, and Religious Subculture and Its Impact on Healthcare Organizations. In M. Merviö (Ed.), *Global Issues and Innovative Solutions in Healthcare, Culture, and the Environment* (pp. 253–270). IGI Global., doi:10.4018/978-1-7998-3576-9.ch013

Tombul, I. (2020). Gender Construction in Transmedial Narration. In G. Sarı (Ed.), *Gender and Diversity Representation in Mass Media* (pp. 197–217). IGI Global., doi:10.4018/978-1-7998-0128-3.ch011

Tomin, B., & Jenson, J. (2021). Exploring Science Fictional Futures With Secondary Students. In L. Haas & J. Tussey (Eds.), *Disciplinary Literacy Connections to Popular Culture in K-12 Settings* (pp. 94–114). IGI Global., doi:10.4018/978-1-7998-4721-2.ch005

Tribusean, I. (2020). The Use of VR in Journalism. In S. M. Loureiro (Ed.), *Managerial Challenges and Social Impacts of Virtual and Augmented Reality* (pp. 125–141). IGI Global., doi:10.4018/978-1-7998-2874-7.ch008

Trillo Domínguez, M. (2021). The Digital Realm Blurs the Lines Between Journalistic and Corporate Communication. In Olvera-Lobo, M. D., Gutiérrez-Artacho, J., Rivera-Trigueros, I.Díaz-Millón, M. (Eds.), Innovative Perspectives on Corporate Communication in the Global World (pp. 78-96). IGI Global. https://doi.org/ doi:10.4018/978-1-7998-6799-9.ch005

Tsang, S. J. (2020). Understanding Perceived Fakeness of Online Health News in Hong Kong. [IJDLDC]. *International Journal of Digital Literacy and Digital Competence*, *11*(2), 1–11. doi:10.4018/IJDLDC.2020040101

Tshifhumulo, R., Musvipwa, F. F., Makhanikhe, T. J., & Tshikukuvhe, L. D. (2021). Towards an African-Centered Model of Learning. In N. Mthembu (Ed.), *Ethical Research Approaches to Indigenous Knowledge Education* (pp. 155–177). IGI Global., doi:10.4018/978-1-7998-1249-4.ch007

Tuazon, R. R., & Torres, T. P. (2020). Digital Threats and Attacks on the Philippine Alternative Press. In S. Jamil (Ed.), *Handbook of Research on Combating Threats to Media Freedom and Journalist Safety* (pp. 1–22). IGI Global., doi:10.4018/978-1-7998-1298-2.ch001

Tuazon, R. R., & Torres, T. P. (2021). Threats and Attacks on Women Journalists in the Philippines. In S. Jamil, B. Çoban, B. Ataman, & G. Appiah-Adjei (Eds.), *Handbook of Research on Discrimination, Gender Disparity, and Safety Risks in Journalism* (pp. 43–59). IGI Global., doi:10.4018/978-1-7998-6686-2.ch004

Tu, J., & Yang, C. (2019). Consumer Needs for Hand-Touch Product Designs Based on the Experience Economy. *Sustainability, 11*(7), 2064. doi:10.3390u11072064

Tuncel, I. (2022). Health Journalism and Representation of Campaign News of Spinal Muscular Atrophy (SMA) Patients. In Aker, H.Aiken, M. (Eds.), Handbook of Research on Cyberchondria, Health Literacy, and the Role of Media in Society's Perception of Medical Information (pp. 313-329). IGI Global. https://doi.org/ doi:10.4018/978-1-7998-8630-3.ch017

Tussey, J. T., & Haas, L. (2022). Supporting Students Impacted by Poverty Through Literacy Methods, Resources, and Strategies. In J. Tussey & L. Haas (Eds.), *Poverty Impacts on Literacy Education* (pp. 235–251). IGI Global., doi:10.4018/978-1-7998-8730-0.ch012

Twitter. (n.d.). https://twitter.com

Twizeyimana, J. D., & Andersson, A. (2019). The public value of E-Government – A literature review. *Government Information Quarterly, 36*(2), 167–178. doi:10.1016/j.giq.2019.01.001

Ulaş, S. (2021). The Role of Social Media on Dissemination of Information During the COVID-19 Pandemic. In G. Sarı (Ed.), *Handbook of Research on Representing Health and Medicine in Modern Media* (pp. 216–227). IGI Global., doi:10.4018/978-1-7998-6825-5.ch015

Ulker-Demirel, E. (2019). Development of Digital Communication Technologies and the New Media. In R. Yilmaz (Ed.), *Handbook of Research on Narrative Advertising* (pp. 164–175). IGI Global., doi:10.4018/978-1-5225-9790-2.ch015

Ülkü, A., & Erol, G. (2022). Destination Storytelling as a Destination Branding Tool. In A. Campos & S. Almeida (Eds.), *Global Perspectives on Strategic Storytelling in Destination Marketing* (pp. 136–163). IGI Global., doi:10.4018/978-1-6684-3436-9.ch008

Uniamikogbo, E., Okoye, E. I., & Chinazu, A. (2020). Non-Interest Income and Financial Performance of Selected Deposit Money Banks in Nigeria. [IJBSA]. *International Journal of Business Strategy and Automation, 1*(3), 52–66. doi:10.4018/IJBSA.2020070105

Ursyn, A. (2020). *Active Learning Aimed at Visual Development.* IGI Global., doi:10.4018/978-1-7998-1651-5.ch006

Valandra & Leslie. T. (2022). The History of Incarceration of African Americans/Blacks in the United States. In Johns, K. (Ed.), Counseling Strategies for Children and Families Impacted by Incarceration (pp. 24-46). IGI Global. https://doi.org/ doi:10.4018/978-1-7998-9209-0.ch002

Valderrama, Y. Z. (2020). Journalists' Safety and Multifaceted Censorship in Colombia. In S. Jamil (Ed.), *Handbook of Research on Combating Threats to Media Freedom and Journalist Safety* (pp. 298–318). IGI Global., doi:10.4018/978-1-7998-1298-2.ch016

Valdez-Juárez, L. E., Castillo-Vergara, M., & Ramos-Escobar, E. A. (2022). Innovative Business Strategies in the Face of COVID-19: An Approach to Open Innovation of SMEs in the Sonora Region of Mexico. *Journal of Open Innovation*, *8*(1), 47. doi:10.3390/joitmc8010047

Valdiviezo, J., & Graybill, L. (2020). The Great Race. In J. Bazler & M. L. Van Sickle (Eds.), *Cases on Models and Methods for STEAM Education* (pp. 170–204). IGI Global., doi:10.4018/978-1-5225-9631-8.ch008

Van Deursen, A. J., & van Dijk, J. A. (2009). Improving digital skills for the use of online public information and services. *Government Information Quarterly*, *26*(2), 333–340. doi:10.1016/j.giq.2008.11.002

Vargas-Hernández, J. G. (2020). Rural Migration and Shrinkage Transformation Processes in Mexican Countryside. In D. Ushakov (Ed.), *Migration and Urbanization* (pp. 303–328). IGI Global., doi:10.4018/978-1-7998-0111-5.ch016

Vargas-Hernández, J. G. (2020). Strategic Transformational Transition of Green Economy, Green Growth and Sustainable Development. [IJESGT]. *International Journal of Environmental Sustainability and Green Technologies*, *11*(1), 34–56. doi:10.4018/IJESGT.2020010103

Vargas-Hernández, J. G., & Warner, I. (2020). Necessary Prerequisites for Successful Green Economic Transition and Subsequent Green Development. [IJPPPHCE]. *International Journal of Public and Private Perspectives on Healthcare, Culture, and the Environment*, *4*(2), 25–49. doi:10.4018/IJPPPHCE.2020070103

Vargas-Hernández, J. G., & Zdunek-Wielgołaska, J. A. (2019). Recent trends in Sustainable Urban Planning. [IJSEM]. *International Journal of Sustainable Economies Management*, *8*(3), 29–47. doi:10.4018/IJSEM.2019070103

Varghese, B., Joseph, E. K., & Kallarakal, T. K. (2022). Gender Perspectives. In P. Cembranel, J. R. Soares, & A. R. Perinotto (Eds.), *Promoting Social and Cultural Equity in the Tourism Sector* (pp. 70–84). IGI Global., doi:10.4018/978-1-6684-4194-7.ch005

Varsha, P. S., Akter, S., Kumar, A., Gochhait, S., & Patagundi, B. (2021). The Impact of Artificial Intelligence on Branding. [JGIM]. *Journal of Global Information Management*, *29*(4), 221–246. doi:10.4018/JGIM.20210701.oa10

Varshney, D., Heblikar, S., & K, S. B. (2021). A Study on the Performance of Indian Mutual Funds in Recent Years. In Teixeira, N. M., & Lisboa, I. (Ed.), *Handbook of Research on Financial Management During Economic Downturn and Recovery* (pp. 428-444). IGI Global. https://doi.org/ doi:10.4018/978-1-7998-6643-5.ch024

Vasconcelos, S. V., & Balula, A. (2021). Pitch This. In L. C. Mihăeş, R. Andreescu, & A. Dimitriu (Eds.), *Handbook of Research on Contemporary Storytelling Methods Across New Media and Disciplines* (pp. 100–115). IGI Global., doi:10.4018/978-1-7998-6605-3.ch006

Vasile, A. A. (2020). Lifelong Education. In V. Trif (Ed.), *Analyzing Paradigms Used in Education and Educational Psychology* (pp. 144–168). IGI Global., doi:10.4018/978-1-7998-1427-6.ch007

Vassis, G., Margounakis, D. G., & Tambouris, E. (2021). Review and Evaluation of Systems Supporting Data Journalism. In Khosrow-Pour D.B.A., M. (Ed.), Encyclopedia of Organizational Knowledge, Administration, and Technology (pp. 679-694). IGI Global. https://doi.org/ doi:10.4018/978-1-7998-3473-1.ch050

VazquezS. (2022). *Gostudent*. Obtained from https://insights.gostudent.org/is/types-of-students

Velázquez, M. M. A., & Rivero, H. M. (2020). Las MiPYMES y el COVID19 en la Región XI del oriente del Estado de México: escenarios de reconfiguración. Instituto de Investigaciones Económicas. In M. Rivero Hernández (Ed.), *Factores críticos y estratégicos en la interacción territorial desafíos actuales y escenarios futuros*. http://ru.iiec.unam.mx/5175/1/1-072-Velazquez-Rivero.pdf

Venkatesh, V., Chan, F., & Thong, J. (2012). Designing e-government services: Key service attributes and citizens' preference. *Journal of Operations Management*, *30*(1-2), 116–133. doi:10.1016/j.jom.2011.10.001

Veratti, D. (2020). Victimology of Predatory Crimes and Prevention Techniques. In Balloni, A.Sette, R. (Eds.), Handbook of Research on Trends and Issues in Crime Prevention, Rehabilitation, and Victim Support (pp. 431-446). IGI Global. https://doi.org/ doi:10.4018/978-1-7998-1286-9.ch025

Verma, R., & Kumar, M. (2022). Brand Extension in FMCG Sector Through Social Media Enabled CRM and Investigating Its Impact on Brand Equity. In A. Naim & S. K. Kautish (Eds.), *Building a Brand Image Through Electronic Customer Relationship Management* (pp. 201–236). IGI Global., doi:10.4018/978-1-6684-5386-5.ch009

View, J., DeMulder, E., Stribling, S., & Dallman, L. (2020). *Critical Reflective Practice, Critical Pedagogy, and Culturally Relevant Pedagogy*. IGI Global., doi:10.4018/978-1-7998-5649-8.ch003

View, J., DeMulder, E., Stribling, S., & Dallman, L. (2020). *Teacher Leadership and Collegial Relationships*. IGI Global., doi:10.4018/978-1-7998-5649-8.ch005

View, J., DeMulder, E., Stribling, S., & Dallman, L. (2020). *When Asked, Teachers Said...*. IGI Global., doi:10.4018/978-1-7998-5649-8.ch001

Vigotsky. (2022). *Filosofia*. Obtained from https:// filosofia.co/general/definition-of-student-according -to-authors/#:~:text=Student%20is%20a%20concept%20thta%20com es%20from%20alumnus%2C,is %20a%20person%20that%20is%C3%A1%20dedicated%20to%20 learnlng.

Villasana, J. (2013). *Presenta Policía Federal de México su aplicación para móviles*. From Xataka Mexico: https://www.xataka.com.mx/aplicaciones/presenta-policia-federal-de-mexico-su-aplicacion-para-moviles

Villazón-Terrazas, B., Ortiz, F., Tiwari, S., Ayush, G., & Jabbar, M. A. (2021). Knowledge Graphs and Semantic Web. *Communications in Computer and Information Science*, *1459*, 1–331. doi:10.1007/978-3-030-91305-2

Villegas-Zamora, D. A. (2019). The importance of applied statistics for decision-making in Marketing. *Magazine Research and Business*.

Virvilaitė, R., & Dovalienė, A. (2021). The Concept of Shared Value in the Contexto of Newest Marketing Theories. In *Gamification and Consumer Engagement* (pp. 7–32). https://www.springer.com/series/10440

von Gillern, S., Stufft, C., Marlatt, R., & Nadolny, L. (2022). Minecraft and Elementary Literacy Learning. In C. Lane (Ed.), *Handbook of Research on Acquiring 21st Century Literacy Skills Through Game-Based Learning* (pp. 320–343). IGI Global., doi:10.4018/978-1-7998-7271-9.ch017

Wabwire, J. (2021). Digital Remediation of African Folklore. In Maake, A. O., Maake, B. M.Awuor, F. M. (Eds.), Digital Solutions and the Case for Africa's Sustainable Development (pp. 97-115). IGI Global. https://doi.org/ doi:10.4018/978-1-7998-2967-6.ch007

Waity, J. F., Vanderminden, J., & Robeson, K. (2020). The Fact That the Author Was Male Instead of Female Provided for an Objective Opinion [IJITLHE]. *International Journal of Innovative Teaching and Learning in Higher Education*, *1*(3), 44–60. doi:10.4018/IJITLHE.2020070103

Wang, F. (2014). Explaining the low utilization of government websites: Using a grounded theory approach. *Government Information Quarterly*, *31*(4), 610–621. doi:10.1016/j.giq.2014.04.004

Wang, Q. (2020). The Role of Classroom-Situated Game-Based Language Learning in Promoting Students' Communicative Competence. [IJCALLT]. *International Journal of Computer-Assisted Language Learning and Teaching*, *10*(2), 59–82. doi:10.4018/IJCALLT.2020040104

Wang, Y., Chen, Y., Xu, Q., & Wu, W. (2020). An Empirical Study of ISO 14001 Certification and Firm Environmental Performance. In S. Tsai, Z. Yuan, J. Yu, & X. Liu (Eds.), *Waste Management Techniques for Improved Environmental and Public Health* (pp. 1–28). IGI Global., doi:10.4018/978-1-7998-1966-0.ch001

Wang, Y., Wang, Y., Lin, H., & Tang, T. (2003). Determinants of user acceptance of Internet banking: An empirical study. *International Journal of Service Industry Management*, *14*(5), 501–519. doi:10.1108/09564230310500192

Ward, C. (2022). The Connection Between Empathy and Equity in Higher Education. In C. Ward (Ed.), *Achieving Equity in Higher Education Using Empathy as a Guiding Principle* (pp. 1–27). IGI Global., doi:10.4018/978-1-7998-9746-0.ch001

Ward, M. C., Corr, P. G., Fernes, V. A., & Wang, T. (2022). How an Anti-Racist Organizational Change Model Can Build Capacity to Support Historically Excluded Students. In R. Ganjoo & L. S. Schwartz (Eds.), *Handbook of Research on Developing Competencies for Pre-Health Professional Students, Advisors, and Programs* (pp. 389–414). IGI Global., doi:10.4018/978-1-6684-5969-0.ch019

Warren, A. N., & Ward, N. A. (2020). Using Case Methods in Online Teacher Education to Develop Culturally Sustaining Educators. In R. Karchmer-Klein & K. E. Pytash (Eds.), *Effective Practices in Online Teacher Preparation for Literacy Educators* (pp. 128–149). IGI Global., doi:10.4018/978-1-7998-0206-8.ch007

Welch, E. W., & Pandey, S. (2005). E-Government and network technologies: Does bureaucratic red tape inhibit, promote or fall victim to intranet technology implementation? *Proceedings of the 38th Hawaii International Conference on System Sciences, 5*, 122.3. 10.1109/HICSS.2005.215

Wessels, S., & Trainin, G. (2021). Digital Storytelling With English Language Learning Families. In G. Onchwari & J. Keengwe (Eds.), *Bridging Family-Teacher Relationships for ELL and Immigrant Students* (pp. 27–45). IGI Global., doi:10.4018/978-1-7998-4712-0.ch002

Weston, E. (2020). Case Study of The BizNest. In Morie, J. F.McCallum, K. (Eds.), Handbook of Research on the Global Impacts and Roles of Immersive Media (pp. 176-199). IGI Global. https://doi.org/ doi:10.4018/978-1-7998-2433-6.ch010

Whitaker, M. C. (2020). Utilizing Feminist Pedagogy to Foster Preservice Teachers' Critical Consciousness. In Clausen, C. K.Logan, S. R. (Eds.), Integrating Social Justice Education in Teacher Preparation Programs (pp. 76-100). IGI Global. https://doi.org/ doi:10.4018/978-1-7998-5098-4.ch004

White, P. A. (2022). Reconstructing Reading for Students of Color. In Butcher, J. T.Baker, W. C. (Eds.), Addressing Issues of Systemic Racism During Turbulent Times (pp. 63-72). IGI Global. https://doi.org/ doi:10.4018/978-1-7998-8532-0.ch004

Wibisono, N., & Syah, E. (2019). The rol of experiential marketing towards satisfaction and re-intention to visit a tourist destination. *Journal of Tourism & Sports Management*, *1*(1), 1–14.

Williams, J., Chinn, S. J., & Suleiman, J. (2014). The value of Twitter for sports fans. *Journal of Direct, Data and Digital Marketing Practice*, *1*(1), 36–50. doi:10.1057/dddmp.2014.36

Willis, M., Jagasia, J., & Robinson-Perez, A. (2021). Black and Brown Women Fostering Authentic Activism in Counseling Programs Amid Social Unrest. In S. Rodriguez & K. Brown (Eds.), *Black and Brown Leadership and the Promotion of Change in an Era of Social Unrest* (pp. 149–183). IGI Global., doi:10.4018/978-1-7998-7235-1.ch007

Wilson, A. V. (2022). The Equity of Remote Teaching During COVID-19. In Reeves, E. K.McIntyre, C. J. (Eds.), Multidisciplinary Perspectives on Diversity and Equity in a Virtual World (pp. 138-154). IGI Global. https://doi.org/ doi:10.4018/978-1-7998-8028-8.ch008

Wirtz, B. W., Piehler, R., Rieger, V., & Daiser, P. (2016). E-government portal information performance and the role of local community interest. Empirical support for a model of citizen perceptions. *Public Administration Quarterly*, *40*(1), 48–83.

Wirtz, B., Weyerer, J., Thomas, M. C., & Möller, A. (2017). E-Government Implementation: Theoretical Aspects and Empirical Evidence. *Public Organization Review*, *17*(1), 101–120. doi:10.100711115-015-0330-2

Wiyonoputri, W. T., Eppang, B. M., & Scott, N. (2022). The Development of Stories of Bajo Mola in Wakatobi National Park. In A. Campos & S. Almeida (Eds.), *Global Perspectives on Strategic Storytelling in Destination Marketing* (pp. 52–73). IGI Global., doi:10.4018/978-1-6684-3436-9.ch004

Woiwod, U. (2021). Adaptations of Print Narratives Into Literary Apps. In Haas, L.Tussey, J. (Eds.), Connecting Disciplinary Literacy and Digital Storytelling in K-12 Education (pp. 127-147). IGI Global. https://doi.org/ doi:10.4018/978-1-7998-5770-9.ch007

Wolf, J., Feitosa, F., & Marques, J. L. (2021). Efficiency and Equity in the Spatial Planning of Primary Schools. [IJEPR]. *International Journal of E-Planning Research*, *10*(1), 21–38. doi:10.4018/IJEPR.2021010102

Woodcock, C. A. (2022). Social Action Literacy for Elementary Teachers. In Bromer, B. L.Crawford, C. M. (Eds.), Handbook of Research on Learner-Centered Approaches to Teaching in an Age of Transformational Change (pp. 308-327). IGI Global. https://doi.org/ doi:10.4018/978-1-6684-4240-1.ch016

Woodroof, P. J., Deitz, G. D., Howie, K. M., & Evans, R. D. Jr. (2019). The effect of cause-related marketing on firm value: A look at Fortune's most admired all-stars. *Journal of the Academy of Marketing Science*, *47*(5), 899–918. doi:10.100711747-019-00660-y

Wooten, C. B. (2021). Junior Faculty Scholarly Personal Narrative. In Moffett, N. L. (Eds.), Navigating Post-Doctoral Career Placement, Research, and Professionalism (pp. 104-128). IGI Global. https://doi.org/ doi:10.4018/978-1-7998-5065-6.ch006

Wörfel, P., Frentz, F., & Tautu, C. (2022). Marketing comes to its senses: A bibliometric review and integrated framework of sensory experience in marketing. *European Journal of Marketing*, *56*(3), 704–737. doi:10.1108/EJM-07-2020-0510

Worley, C. (2022). The Red Bandanna. In Haas, L.Tussey, J. T. (Eds.), Disciplinary Literacy as a Support for Culturally and Linguistically Responsive Teaching and Learning (pp. 285-305). IGI Global. https://doi.org/ doi:10.4018/978-1-6684-4215-9.ch014

Wright, M. M., & Edney, N. (2022). Students at the Table. In E. Cain-Sanschagrin, R. A. Filback, & J. Crawford (Eds.), *Cases on Academic Program Redesign for Greater Racial and Social Justice* (pp. 212–225). IGI Global., doi:10.4018/978-1-7998-8463-7.ch010

Wright, W. F., & Wright, M. M. (2021). Characteristics of Successful Securities Crowdfunding Campaigns in the United States. In C. S. Negrão & J. F. Brito (Eds.), *Multidisciplinary Approaches to Crowdfunding Platforms* (pp. 163–197). IGI Global., doi:10.4018/978-1-7998-3226-3.ch007

Wu, Y. (2014). Protecting personal data in E-government: A cross-country study. *Government Information Quarterly*, *31*(1), 150–159. doi:10.1016/j.giq.2013.07.003

Xiao, J. (2021). From Equality to Equity to Justice. In A. Bozkurt (Ed.), *Handbook of Research on Emerging Pedagogies for the Future of Education* (pp. 1–15). IGI Global., doi:10.4018/978-1-7998-7275-7.ch001

Xiao, L. (2021). Is There Racial Discrimination Within the NBA? [IJOCI]. *International Journal of Organizational and Collective Intelligence*, *11*(2), 1–28. doi:10.4018/IJOCI.2021040101

Yagasa, R., Uch, R., & Sam, P. (2020). Solid Waste Management in Cambodia. In Pariatamby, A., Shahul Hamid, F., & Bhatti, M. S. (Ed.), Sustainable Waste Management Challenges in Developing Countries (pp. 56-85). IGI Global. https://doi.org/ doi:10.4018/978-1-7998-0198-6.ch003

Yakhlef, A. (2015). Customer experience within retail environments. *Marketing Theory*, *15*(4), 545–564. doi:10.1177/1470593115569016

Yan, Toriumi, & Sugawara. (n.d.). Understanding how retweets influence the behaviors of social networking service users via agent-based simulation. *Computational Social Networks.*

Yanginlar, G. (2020). The Effect of Reverse Logistics Activities on Brand Equity and Customer Satisfaction. In G. Ç. Ceyhun (Ed.), *Handbook of Research on the Applications of International Transportation and Logistics for World Trade* (pp. 395–414). IGI Global., doi:10.4018/978-1-7998-1397-2.ch021

Yang, K. C., & Kang, Y. (2019). Narrative Adverting and Multi-Platform Storytelling. In R. Yilmaz (Ed.), *Handbook of Research on Narrative Advertising* (pp. 177–195). IGI Global., doi:10.4018/978-1-5225-9790-2.ch016

Yastibaş, A. E., Baturay, M. H., & Çinar, C. A. (2022). Augmented Reality-Based Digital Storytelling in Language Teaching and Learning. In Zou, B., Thomas, M., Barr, D., & Jia, W. (Ed.), Emerging Concepts in Technology-Enhanced Language Teaching and Learning (pp. 42-65). IGI Global. https://doi.org/ doi:10.4018/978-1-7998-8981-6.ch003

Yazir, M., & Majid, A. (2017). Impact of knowledge management enablers on knowledge sharing: Is trust a mission link in SMEs of emerging economies? *World Journal of Entrepreneurship, Management and Sustainable Development*, *13*(1), 16–33. doi:10.1108/WJEMSD-02-2016-0010

Yearta, L., & Kelly, K. (2021). Digital Storytelling to Enhance Social Studies Content Knowledge, Explore Multiple Perspectives, and Advocate for Social Justice. In L. Haas & J. Tussey (Eds.), *Connecting Disciplinary Literacy and Digital Storytelling in K-12 Education* (pp. 235–256). IGI Global., doi:10.4018/978-1-7998-5770-9.ch012

Ye, F. (2022). *Grand Synthetic Model.* IGI Global., doi:10.4018/978-1-6684-4935-6.ch004

Ye, F. (2022). *Social Equity and Fiscal Policy*. IGI Global., doi:10.4018/978-1-6684-4935-6.ch011

Yeung, R. P. (2022). Understanding the Relationship Between White Teacher Implicit Bias and Black Student Academic Disparities and High Discipline Rates. In A. T. Adams (Ed.), *Approaching Disparities in School Discipline* (pp. 23–51). IGI Global., doi:10.4018/978-1-6684-3359-1.ch002

Yigitcanlar, T., Kankanamge, N., Regona, M., Maldonado, A. R., Rowan, B., Ryu, A., Desouza, K. C., Corchado, J. M., Mehmood, R., & Man Li, R. Y. (2020). Artificial Intelligence Technologies and Related Urban Planning and Development Concepts: How Are They Perceived and Utilized in Australia? *Journal of Open Innovation*, *6*(4), 187. doi:10.3390/joitmc6040187

Yıldızgörür, M. R. (2021). New Media and New Journalism. In E. Esiyok (Ed.), *Handbook of Research on New Media Applications in Public Relations and Advertising* (pp. 451–471). IGI Global., doi:10.4018/978-1-7998-3201-0.ch026

Yılmaz Altuntaş, E., & Akgün Çomak, N. (2021). Analysing Digital Media Contents Representing COVID-19 Pandemics With "21-K Method". In G. Sarı (Ed.), *Handbook of Research on Representing Health and Medicine in Modern Media* (pp. 461–478). IGI Global., doi:10.4018/978-1-7998-6825-5.ch028

Yilmaz, B. K., & Dalkilic, O. S. (2022). Token Image in Male-Dominated Professions and Occupational Segregation Based on Gender. In E. B. Uçel (Ed.), *Eastern Perspectives on Women's Roles and Advancement in Business* (pp. 61–87). IGI Global., doi:10.4018/978-1-7998-8742-3.ch004

Yoon, O. (2022). Importance and Educational Possibilities of the Place-Based Education Through Virtual Fieldtrips. In A. García de la Vega (Ed.), *Didactic Strategies and Resources for Innovative Geography Teaching* (pp. 79–101). IGI Global., doi:10.4018/978-1-7998-9598-5.ch004

Yousaf, M., Raza, S. H., & Kamboh, S. A. (2022). Human Development and Advocacy Journalism in the Spotlight. In D. O. Okocha, M. J. Onobe, & M. N. Alike (Eds.), *Handbook of Research on Connecting Philosophy, Media, and Development in Developing Countries* (pp. 97–111). IGI Global., doi:10.4018/978-1-6684-4107-7.ch008

Yu, P., Xu, A., Hanes, E., & Lu, S. (2022). Would Crowdfunding Really Help Startups in China? In Felseghi, R. A., Cobîrzan, N., & Raboaca, M. S. (Ed.), Clean Technologies and Sustainable Development in Civil Engineering (pp. 217-247). IGI Global. https://doi.org/ doi:10.4018/978-1-7998-9810-8.ch009

Yu, B., Epstein, L., & Tisi, V. (2021). A DisCrit-Informed Critique of the Difference vs. Disorder Approach in Speech-Language Pathology. In R. Horton (Ed.), *Critical Perspectives on Social Justice in Speech-Language Pathology* (pp. 105–128). IGI Global., doi:10.4018/978-1-7998-7134-7.ch006

Yu, C. S., & Asgarkhani, M. (2015). An investigation of trust in e-banking. Evidence from Taiwan and New Zealand empirical studies. *Management Research Review*, *38*(2), 1267–1284. doi:10.1108/MRR-09-2014-0210

Yu, P., Tang, S., Ahuja, A., & Chang, X. (2022). Active Equity Investing. In R. Sharma & K. Mehta (Eds.), *Handbook of Research on Stock Market Investment Practices and Portfolio Management* (pp. 301–328). IGI Global., doi:10.4018/978-1-6684-5528-9.ch016

Yusuf, I. U., Ibrahim, A. M., & Liman, M. A. (2022). Emergence of Counternarrative Peace Media in the Northeast of Nigeria. In E. Ismayil & E. Karadogan Ismayil (Eds.), *Media and Terrorism in the 21st Century* (pp. 183–203). IGI Global., doi:10.4018/978-1-7998-9755-2.ch011

Zaluczkowska, A. M. (2019). The Potential of Interactive Negotiated Narratives in Rebuilding and Reimagining Northern Irish Society. [IJEP]. *International Journal of E-Politics*, *10*(2), 44–59. doi:10.4018/IJEP.2019070104

Zameer, H., Wang, Y., Yasmeen, H., & Ahmed, W. (2019). Modeling the Role of Service Quality, Customer Satisfaction and Customer Loyalty in Building Service Brand Equity. [IJABIM]. *International Journal of Asian Business and Information Management*, *10*(2), 55–72. doi:10.4018/IJABIM.2019040103

Zegarra, C., & Pérez, M. (2018). *Industria 4.0: oportunidades y retos en México.* Retrieved from https://www.forbes.com.mx/industria-4-0-oportunidades-y-retos-en-mexico/

Zengaro, S., & Warley, R. (2022). The Fallacy of Higher Education as the Great Social Equalizer. In J. Keengwe (Ed.), *Handbook of Research on Social Justice and Equity in Education* (pp. 46–71). IGI Global., doi:10.4018/978-1-7998-9567-1.ch003

Zengin, F., & Kapır, B. (2021). Aestheticizing Violence Within Transmedia Storytelling Context. In M. N. Erdem, N. Kocabay-Sener, & T. Demir (Eds.), *Handbook of Research on Aestheticization of Violence, Horror, and Power* (pp. 484–500). IGI Global., doi:10.4018/978-1-7998-4655-0.ch024

Zenkov, K., Lague, M., Haddad, K., Gervacio, A., Sabah, M., & Kolapalli, A. (2022). "Storying" Injustice. In T. S. Hodges (Ed.), *Handbook of Research on Teacher Practices for Diverse Writing Instruction* (pp. 224–247). IGI Global., doi:10.4018/978-1-6684-6213-3.ch012

Zha, D., Foroudi, P., Jin, Z., & Melewar, T. (2021). Making sense of sensory brand experience: Constructing an integrative framework for future research. *International Journal of Management Reviews*, 1–38, 130–167.

Zhang, J., Pearlman, A. M., & Kegler, J. L. (2022). Leveraging Interdisciplinary Collaboration to Improve Technology Dependency and Intercultural Competencies. In P. Bawa (Ed.), *Preparing Faculty for Technology Dependency in the Post-COVID-19 Era* (pp. 73–92). IGI Global., doi:10.4018/978-1-7998-9235-9.ch005

Zhang, S. I. (2019). Mobile Experience in War and Conflict Reporting. In X. Xu (Ed.), *Impacts of Mobile Use and Experience on Contemporary Society* (pp. 226–241). IGI Global., doi:10.4018/978-1-5225-7885-7.ch014

Zhao, R., Li, J., & Zheng, J. (2022). Knowledge Services Development in Unprecedented Circumstances. In M. Lamba (Ed.), *Technological Advancements in Library Service Innovation* (pp. 23–42). IGI Global., doi:10.4018/978-1-7998-8942-7.ch002

Zheng, L., & Si, M. (2020). Narrative Strategies in VR Movies, Traditional Movies, and Digital Games. In J. F. Morie & K. McCallum (Eds.), *Handbook of Research on the Global Impacts and Roles of Immersive Media* (pp. 59–78). IGI Global., doi:10.4018/978-1-7998-2433-6.ch004

Zhou, L. J., Qiu, H., & Zhang, X. (2021). How Does the Market React to Corporate Philanthropic Behavior? Evidence from the COVID-19 Pandemic Shock. *Emerging Markets Finance & Trade*, *57*(6), 1613–1627. doi:10.1080/1540496X.2021.1898367

Zuñiga, M., Ortiz-Rodriguez, F., & Barrera, R. (2018). Faculty and students engagement app: A Mexican digital strategy to improve university services. *ICERI*, 2927-2932.

# Related Readings

To continue IGI Global's long-standing tradition of advancing innovation through emerging research, please find below a compiled list of recommended IGI Global book chapters and journal articles in the areas of Academic Library Environments, COVID-19 Pandemic, Digital Age, and Digital Entrepreneurship. These related readings will provide additional information and guidance to further enrich your knowledge and assist you with your own research.

A., R., O. V., M., & R., J. (2020). Additive Manufacturing of Nickel-Based Super Alloys for Aero Engine Applications . In Balasubramanian, K., & Senthilkumar, V. (Ed.), *Additive Manufacturing Applications for Metals and Composites* (pp. 48-70). IGI Global. https://doi.org/ doi:10.4018/978-1-7998-4054-1.ch003

Abdallah, S. (2020). Social Interactions in Electronic Networks of Practice. [IJeC]. *International Journal of e-Collaboration, 16*(2), 27–44. doi:10.4018/IJeC.2020040103

Abdelkader, A. A., & Ebrahim, R. S. (2021). Decomposing Customer Engagement Effect Between Marketer- and User-Generated Content and Repurchase Intention in the Online Airline Service Community. [IJOM]. *International Journal of Online Marketing, 11*(4), 1–22. doi:10.4018/IJOM.2021100101

Abel, K. M., & Reiter, E. M. (2022). Health and Race in America at the Macro, Meso, and Micro Levels. In T. R. Flockhart, A. Reiter, & M. R. Hassett (Eds.), *The Reproduction and Maintenance of Inequalities in Interpersonal Relationships* (pp. 255–272). IGI Global., doi:10.4018/978-1-6684-4128-2.ch014

Abir, J. I., & Shamim, T. F. (2020). What Compels Journalists to Take a Step Back? In S. Jamil (Ed.), *Handbook of Research on Combating Threats to Media Freedom and Journalist Safety* (pp. 38–53). IGI Global., doi:10.4018/978-1-7998-1298-2.ch003

Abokhoza, R. R., & Sobieh, Y. M. (2021). The Role of Virtual Reality to Enhance Cultural Communication. [IJWP]. *International Journal of Web Portals, 13*(2), 20–35. doi:10.4018/IJWP.2021070102

Abrar, M., Khan, A. S., & Xiang, L. (2022). Impact of Employee-Based Brand Equity on Customer-Based Brand Equity. In M. Bari, M. Abrar, & E. Alaverdov (Eds.), *Antecedents and Outcomes of Employee-Based Brand Equity* (pp. 16–30). IGI Global., doi:10.4018/978-1-6684-3621-9.ch002

Abubaker, F., & El-Badri, H. A. (2022). Using Digital Storytelling as a Tool for Reflection in the Libyan EFL Literature Classroom. In W. M. El-Henawy & M. del Mar Suárez (Eds.), *English as a Foreign Language in a New-Found Post-Pandemic World* (pp. 182–205). IGI Global., doi:10.4018/978-1-6684-4205-0.ch009

Adah, P. (2022). Navigating Marginalization Through a Motivational Weapon and Resilience. In Haas, L.Tussey, J. T. (Eds.), Disciplinary Literacy as a Support for Culturally and Linguistically Responsive Teaching and Learning (pp. 217-246). IGI Global. https://doi.org/ doi:10.4018/978-1-6684-4215-9.ch011

Adams, A. T. (2022). From Courageous to Unapologetic Conversations About School Discipline Disparities. In A. T. Adams (Ed.), *Approaching Disparities in School Discipline* (pp. 271–294). IGI Global., doi:10.4018/978-1-6684-3359-1.ch012

Adegbore, A. M. (2020). Digital Storytelling, Podcasting, and New Format of Messaging in the Libraries. In A. Tella (Ed.), *Handbook of Research on Digital Devices for Inclusivity and Engagement in Libraries* (pp. 185–207). IGI Global., doi:10.4018/978-1-5225-9034-7.ch009

Adeyinka-Skold, S. (2020). Barriers in Women's Romantic Partner Search in the Digital Age. In R. Kalish (Ed.), *Young Adult Sexuality in the Digital Age* (pp. 113–137). IGI Global., doi:10.4018/978-1-7998-3187-7.ch007

Adkins-Sharif, J. (2021). A Black Principal's Decolonizing Journey for Racial Justice. In Rodriguez, S.Brown, K. (Eds.), Black and Brown Leadership and the Promotion of Change in an Era of Social Unrest (pp. 271-297). IGI Global. https://doi.org/ doi:10.4018/978-1-7998-7235-1.ch012

Agrawal, C., & Duggal, T. (2021). A Study of Consumer Switching Behaviour in the Indian Context With Respect to Recycled Products. In B. N. Gopalakrishnan, T. Duggal, & T. Tewary (Eds.), *Examining the Intersection of Circular Economy, Forestry, and International Trade* (pp. 142–153). IGI Global., doi:10.4018/978-1-7998-4990-2.ch012

Ahmad, B., Göç, K., & Yin, X. (2022). Employee-Based Brand Equity. In M. Bari, M. Abrar, & E. Alaverdov (Eds.), *Antecedents and Outcomes of Employee-Based Brand Equity* (pp. 72–80). IGI Global., doi:10.4018/978-1-6684-3621-9.ch005

Ahmad, N. (2020). What Determine Indonesian Commercial News TV Channels' Political News Production and Publication in the Post-Soeharto Regime. In Karlidag, S.Bulut, S. (Eds.), Handbook of Research on the Political Economy of Communications and Media (pp. 134-160). IGI Global. https://doi.org/ doi:10.4018/978-1-7998-3270-6.ch008

Akansel, I. (2020). The Relationship Between Old Institutional Economics (OIE) and Feminist Economics. In I. Akansel (Ed.), *Examining the Relationship Between Economics and Philosophy* (pp. 1–26). IGI Global., doi:10.4018/978-1-7998-1037-7.ch001

Akbar, M., Suaib, M., Husain, M. S., & Shukla, S. (2020). A Compendium of Cloud Forensics. In M. Husain & M. Khan (Eds.), *Critical Concepts, Standards, and Techniques in Cyber Forensics* (pp. 215–227). IGI Global., doi:10.4018/978-1-7998-1558-7.ch012

Al Janabi, M. A. (2020). Risk Management in Emerging and Islamic Markets in Light of the Subprime Global Financial Crisis. In N. Naifar (Ed.), *Impact of Financial Technology (FinTech) on Islamic Finance and Financial Stability* (pp. 98–127). IGI Global., doi:10.4018/978-1-7998-0039-2.ch006

Al-Malkawi, H. N., Pillai, R., & AlShiab, M. S. (2020). Evaluating Microeconomic Factors, Financial Crisis, and Stock Price Dynamics. In L. Farinha, A. B. Cruz, & J. R. Sebastião (Eds.), *Handbook of Research on Accounting and Financial Studies* (pp. 131–153). IGI Global., doi:10.4018/978-1-7998-2136-6.ch007

Al-Rashed, A., & Al-Gilani, M. (2020). Gender Equity in Surgical Academia in Kuwait and the Arabian Gulf Region. In M. I. Bellini & V. E. Papalois (Eds.), *Gender Equity in the Medical Profession* (pp. 237–251). IGI Global., doi:10.4018/978-1-5225-9599-1.ch017

Al Tamimi, W. S. (2022). Education for Women and Girls in Iraq. In Boivin, J. A.Pacheco-Guffrey, H. (Eds.), Education as the Driving Force of Equity for the Marginalized (pp. 272-289). IGI Global. https://doi.org/ doi:10.4018/978-1-7998-8025-7.ch013

Al-Zaman, M. S., & Puja, P. P. (2021). Storytelling and the Rhetoric of Rumor in Social Media. In L. C. Mihăeş, R. Andreescu, & A. Dimitriu (Eds.), *Handbook of Research on Contemporary Storytelling Methods Across New Media and Disciplines* (pp. 40–62). IGI Global., doi:10.4018/978-1-7998-6605-3.ch003

Alawdat, M., & Hodges, R. (2021). Quaran-Teens 2020 Blog Series. In E. B. Hancı-Azizoglu & M. Alawdat (Eds.), *Rhetoric and Sociolinguistics in Times of Global Crisis* (pp. 56–78). IGI Global., doi:10.4018/978-1-7998-6732-6.ch004

Alazrak, N. N. (2020). Making Sense of Journalists' Safety and Media Freedom in Egypt Between Different Types of Threats and the Ruling Legislative Context. In S. Jamil (Ed.), *Handbook of Research on Combating Threats to Media Freedom and Journalist Safety* (pp. 172–185). IGI Global., doi:10.4018/978-1-7998-1298-2.ch010

Alboul, L., Beer, M., & Nisiotis, L. (2019). Merging Realities in Space and Time. In M. Dimitrova & H. Wagatsuma (Eds.), *Cyber-Physical Systems for Social Applications* (pp. 156–183). IGI Global., doi:10.4018/978-1-5225-7879-6.ch007

Alexander-Ashley, B. M. (2022). Reducing Mass Incarceration Through Trauma-Informed Pedagogy. In C. Bernadowski (Ed.), *Strategies and Methods for Implementing Trauma-Informed Pedagogy* (pp. 123–143). IGI Global., doi:10.4018/978-1-7998-7473-7.ch007

Ali, M. B. (2021). Internet of Things (IoT) to Foster Communication and Information Sharing. In Ali, M. B.Wood-Harper, T. (Eds.), Fostering Communication and Learning With Underutilized Technologies in Higher Education (pp. 1-20). IGI Global. https://doi.org/ doi:10.4018/978-1-7998-4846-2.ch001

Ali, N. (2021). Racialization of Religion. In Rodriguez, S.Brown, K. (Eds.), Black and Brown Leadership and the Promotion of Change in an Era of Social Unrest (pp. 247-270). IGI Global. https://doi.org/ doi:10.4018/978-1-7998-7235-1.ch011

Ali, S. A., Yassin, M., & AbuRaya, R. (2020). The Impact of Firm Characteristics on Corporate Financial Performance in Emerging Markets. [IJCRMM]. *International Journal of Customer Relationship Marketing and Management, 11*(4), 70–89. doi:10.4018/IJCRMM.2020100105

Aliprantis, J., & Caridakis, G. (2019). A Survey of Augmented Reality Applications in Cultural Heritage. [IJCMHS]. *International Journal of Computational Methods in Heritage Science, 3*(2), 118–147. doi:10.4018/IJCMHS.2019070107

Almazari, A. A. (2020). Valuation of Banking Sector. In Köseoğlu, S. D. (Eds.), Valuation Challenges and Solutions in Contemporary Businesses (pp. 175-200). IGI Global. https://doi.org/ doi:10.4018/978-1-7998-1086-5.ch010

Alqurashi, E., & Siegelman, A. R. (2019). Designing and Evaluating Technology-Based Formative Assessments. In A. Elçi, L. L. Beith, & A. Elçi (Eds.), *Handbook of Research on Faculty Development for Digital Teaching and Learning* (pp. 222–244). IGI Global., doi:10.4018/978-1-5225-8476-6.ch012

Altin, H. (2022). The Effect of the COVID-19 Pandemic on International Stock Exchanges. In Sloboda, B. W.Sissoko, Y. (Eds.), Economic Impact and Recovery Following a Global Health Crisis (pp. 106-143). IGI Global. https://doi.org/ doi:10.4018/978-1-7998-6900-9.ch005

Altınırmak, S., Şahin, C., Karamaşa, Ç., & Okoth, B. O. (2020). Participative Banking in Turkey. In A. Rafay (Ed.), *Growth and Emerging Prospects of International Islamic Banking* (pp. 141–154). IGI Global., doi:10.4018/978-1-7998-1611-9.ch008

Alturki, N. (2022). Nada Alturki. In Goodman Hayward, P., Rehman, S.Yan, Z. (Eds.), Women Community Leaders and Their Impact as Global Changemakers (pp. 280-285). IGI Global. https://doi.org/ doi:10.4018/978-1-6684-2490-2.ch047

Alvarado, L. E., & Rossatto, C. A. (2022). Allies in Solidarity Transcend Guilt and Unlearn Patriarchal Privileges. In J. Keengwe (Ed.), *Handbook of Research on Social Justice and Equity in Education* (pp. 203–222). IGI Global., doi:10.4018/978-1-7998-9567-1.ch010

Amaladas, S. (2021). COVID-19 and the Call for Elder Change Leadership. In Al-Aali, E.Masmoudi, M. (Eds.), Global Perspectives on Change Management and Leadership in the Post-COVID-19 Era (pp. 218-239). IGI Global. https://doi.org/ doi:10.4018/978-1-7998-6948-1.ch014

Ambikar, R., Szrot, L., Greer, C., & Peterson, D. (2021). Curriculum for Compassion. In C. Reneau & M. Villarreal (Eds.), *Handbook of Research on Leading Higher Education Transformation With Social Justice, Equity, and Inclusion* (pp. 198–217). IGI Global., doi:10.4018/978-1-7998-7152-1.ch014

Amhag, L. (2020). *Reflection and Self-Assessment in Smart Education*. IGI Global., doi:10.4018/978-1-7998-4183-8.ch006

Amirsadeghi, L. (2020). Location-Based Entertainment. In Morie, J. F.McCallum, K. (Eds.), Handbook of Research on the Global Impacts and Roles of Immersive Media (pp. 284-313). IGI Global. https://doi.org/ doi:10.4018/978-1-7998-2433-6.ch015

Anand, A., & Muthusamy, A. (2020). Data Security and Privacy-Preserving in Cloud Computing Paradigm. In S. Gochhait, D. T. Shou, & S. Fazalbhoy (Eds.), *Cloud Computing Applications and Techniques for E-Commerce* (pp. 99–133). IGI Global., doi:10.4018/978-1-7998-1294-4.ch006

Andrade, L. J., & Ferreira, M. J. (2022). The Influence of Storytelling Strategies on Attitude and Purchase Intention. In A. Campos & S. Almeida (Eds.), *Global Perspectives on Strategic Storytelling in Destination Marketing* (pp. 94–115). IGI Global., doi:10.4018/978-1-6684-3436-9.ch006

Andrews, S. K., & Crawford, C. M. (2021). Barriers, Issues, and Similarities Among Women in eSports and Similar Mixed Gender Sports. In S. Andrews & C. M. Crawford (Eds.), *Handbook of Research on Pathways and Opportunities Into the Business of Esports* (pp. 25–46). IGI Global., doi:10.4018/978-1-7998-7300-6.ch002

Anthony, B. Jr. (2020). Green Information Systems Refraction for Corporate Ecological Responsibility Reflection in ICT Based Firms. [JCIT]. *Journal of Cases on Information Technology*, *22*(1), 14–37. doi:10.4018/JCIT.2020010102

Appiah-Adjei, G. (2020). The Role of Ghanaian News Media Organisations in Countering Threats to Media Freedom and Journalists' Safety. In S. Jamil (Ed.), *Handbook of Research on Combating Threats to Media Freedom and Journalist Safety* (pp. 186–213). IGI Global., doi:10.4018/978-1-7998-1298-2.ch011

Appiah-Adjei, G. (2021). Confronting Freedom to Inform With Freedom of Expression. In Jamil, S., Çoban, B., Ataman, B.Appiah-Adjei, G. (Eds.), Handbook of Research on Discrimination, Gender Disparity, and Safety Risks in Journalism (pp. 269-296). IGI Global. https://doi.org/ doi:10.4018/978-1-7998-6686-2.ch015

Araujo, J. J., & Araujo, D. L. (2021). What Counts as Literacy for the 21st Century Youth. In L. Haas & J. Tussey (Eds.), *Connecting Disciplinary Literacy and Digital Storytelling in K-12 Education* (pp. 298–315). IGI Global., doi:10.4018/978-1-7998-5770-9.ch015

Arda, Ö., & Akmeşe, Z. (2021). Media Ethics. In M. N. Taskiran & F. Pinarbaşi (Eds.), *Multidisciplinary Approaches to Ethics in the Digital Era* (pp. 96–110). IGI Global., doi:10.4018/978-1-7998-4117-3.ch007

Ardıç Çobaner, A. (2021). Representation of Syrian Children in Turkish Media From a Child-Oriented Rights Journalism Perspective. In F. Özsungur (Ed.), *Handbook of Research on Policies, Protocols, and Practices for Social Work in the Digital World* (pp. 355–375). IGI Global., doi:10.4018/978-1-7998-7772-1.ch020

Argus, S., Vaccaro, A., Coiro, J., Hos, R., & Deeney, T. (2022). Equitable Teaching Practices in Higher Education. In J. Keengwe (Ed.), *Handbook of Research on Social Justice and Equity in Education* (pp. 92–113). IGI Global., doi:10.4018/978-1-7998-9567-1.ch005

Armie, M. (2020). Between Tradition and Innovation. In Membrive, V.Armie, M. (Eds.), Using Literature to Teach English as a Second Language (pp. 1-33). IGI Global. https://doi.org/ doi:10.4018/978-1-7998-4670-3.ch001

Armistead, K. J., & Woods, V. (2021). Fostering and Developing Culturally-Aware Mentorship Practices. In C. Reneau & M. Villarreal (Eds.), *Handbook of Research on Leading Higher Education Transformation With Social Justice, Equity, and Inclusion* (pp. 126–140). IGI Global., doi:10.4018/978-1-7998-7152-1.ch009

Armstrong, C. L., & Towery, N. A. (2021). How Individuals Hypothetically and Realistically Respond to Media Messages About Severe Weather. [IJDREM]. *International Journal of Disaster Response and Emergency Management, 4*(1), 47–62. doi:10.4018/IJDREM.2021010104

Arnold, J. M., & Sableski, M. (2020). Building Reflective Practices Through a Digital Literacy Portfolio in an Online Context. In R. Karchmer-Klein & K. E. Pytash (Eds.), *Effective Practices in Online Teacher Preparation for Literacy Educators* (pp. 45–64). IGI Global., doi:10.4018/978-1-7998-0206-8.ch003

Arslan, H., & Topal, A. (2021). Evaluation of Women's Perspectives in the East Societies on New Media News. In Tombul, I. & Sarı, G. (Ed.), Handbook of Research on Contemporary Approaches to Orientalism in Media and Beyond (pp. 778-798). IGI Global. https://doi.org/ doi:10.4018/978-1-7998-7180-4.ch044

Artan Özoran, B. (2021). Digital Storytelling and Public Relations. In E. Esiyok (Ed.), *Handbook of Research on New Media Applications in Public Relations and Advertising* (pp. 217–233). IGI Global., doi:10.4018/978-1-7998-3201-0.ch013

Arvanitis, P., & Krystalli, P. (2021). Digital Storytelling and Augmented Reality-Based Scenarios for Foreign Language Teaching. In M. Montebello (Ed.), *Digital Pedagogies and the Transformation of Language Education* (pp. 1–22). IGI Global., doi:10.4018/978-1-7998-6745-6.ch001

Asano, G., Cheng, T. P., Rhodes, J., & Lok, P. (2019). The Influence of Online Reviews and Brand Trust and Customer Equity. [JECO]. *Journal of Electronic Commerce in Organizations, 17*(4), 30–43. doi:10.4018/JECO.2019100103

Asha, J. O. (2021). Phenomenology of Religious Experience. In E. D. Essien (Ed.), *Phenomenological Approaches to Religion and Spirituality* (pp. 251–267). IGI Global., doi:10.4018/978-1-7998-4595-9.ch013

Assay, B. E. (2019). Social Media and the Challenges of Curtailing the Spread of Fake News in Nigeria. In Chiluwa, I. E.Samoilenko, S. A. (Eds.), Handbook of Research on Deception, Fake News, and Misinformation Online (pp. 226-263). IGI Global. https://doi.org/ doi:10.4018/978-1-5225-8535-0.ch014

Ataman, B., Çoban, B., & Erkmen, Ö. (2020). A Review on the Safety of Journalists in Turkey. In S. Jamil (Ed.), *Handbook of Research on Combating Threats to Media Freedom and Journalist Safety* (pp. 148–171). IGI Global., doi:10.4018/978-1-7998-1298-2.ch009

Atef, N. (2020). Can Revolutionary Media Be Made Online? In A. M. Solo (Ed.), *Handbook of Research on Politics in the Computer Age* (pp. 203–216). IGI Global., doi:10.4018/978-1-7998-0377-5.ch012

Atienza, V. (2020). Waste Management in the Philippines. In Pariatamby, A., Shahul Hamid, F.Bhatti, M. S. (Eds.), Sustainable Waste Management Challenges in Developing Countries (pp. 270-286). IGI Global. https://doi.org/ doi:10.4018/978-1-7998-0198-6.ch011

Atlı, D., Kose, S. B., & Sezen, A. N. (2019). A Neuromarketing Based Approach on the Usage of Narratives in the Advertising. In R. Yilmaz (Ed.), *Handbook of Research on Narrative Advertising* (pp. 251–268). IGI Global., doi:10.4018/978-1-5225-9790-2.ch022

Attuel-Mendes, L., Assadi, D., & Raymond, S. (2021). Investors' Motivations in Different Types of Crowdfunding. In C. S. Negrão & J. F. Brito (Eds.), *Multidisciplinary Approaches to Crowdfunding Platforms* (pp. 21–54). IGI Global., doi:10.4018/978-1-7998-3226-3.ch002

Aureli, S., & Graziano, H. (2020). When Ethical Values Drive the Creation and Development of Sporting Events. In A. Fotiadis & C. Vassiliadis (Eds.), *Principles and Practices of Small-Scale Sport Event Management* (pp. 217–232). IGI Global., doi:10.4018/978-1-7998-4757-1.ch011

Awad, A. W., Awwad, B. S., & Sharabati, A. A. (2021). Evaluating Mergers as a Tool to Strengthen and Modernize the Palestinian Banking System. In Y. A. Albastaki, A. Razzaque, & A. M. Sarea (Eds.), *Innovative Strategies for Implementing FinTech in Banking* (pp. 201–221). IGI Global., doi:10.4018/978-1-7998-3257-7.ch013

Ayad, S. M., Dunn, R. A., & Marshall, S. W. (2020). Political Advertising Effects on Perceived Bias, Value, and Credibility in Online News. In K. Dalkir & R. Katz (Eds.), *Navigating Fake News, Alternative Facts, and Misinformation in a Post-Truth World* (pp. 184–202). IGI Global., doi:10.4018/978-1-7998-2543-2.ch008

Ayar Senturk, H. (2021). Digital Storytelling and Parasocial Interaction for Brand-Consumer Relationship. In N. Mohd Suki (Ed.), *Handbook of Research on Technology Applications for Effective Customer Engagement* (pp. 197–214). IGI Global., doi:10.4018/978-1-7998-4772-4.ch013

Ayish, M., & Dahdal, S. (2021). Going Mobile in Journalism Education. [IJSEUS]. *International Journal of Smart Education and Urban Society, 12*(2), 21–31. doi:10.4018/IJSEUS.2021040103

Babel, S., Ta, A. T., & Habarakada Liyanage, T. U. (2020). Current Situation and Challenges of Waste Management in Thailand. In Pariatamby, A., Shahul Hamid, F., & Bhatti, M. S. (Ed.), Sustainable Waste Management Challenges in Developing Countries (pp. 409-440). IGI Global. https://doi.org/ doi:10.4018/978-1-7998-0198-6.ch017

Bain, A. S. (2022). Diversity and Equity in Healthcare. In Reeves, E. K.McIntyre, C. J. (Eds.), Multidisciplinary Perspectives on Diversity and Equity in a Virtual World (pp. 163-183). IGI Global. https://doi.org/ doi:10.4018/978-1-7998-8028-8.ch010

Baker, C. (2022). From Story-Based to Story-Interactive Experiences. In Campos, A.Almeida, S. (Eds.), Global Perspectives on Strategic Storytelling in Destination Marketing (pp. 74-93). IGI Global. https://doi.org/ doi:10.4018/978-1-6684-3436-9.ch005

Baker, P. J. (2020). Afrocentric Thought in Adult Education. In Okojie, M. C.Boulder, T. C. (Eds.), Handbook of Research on Adult Learning in Higher Education (pp. 175-198). IGI Global. https://doi.org/ doi:10.4018/978-1-7998-1306-4.ch007

Bal, S. (2022). Gendering the EU's Western Balkan Enlargement. In B. F. Costa (Ed.), *Challenges and Barriers to the European Union Expansion to the Balkan Region* (pp. 153–170). IGI Global., doi:10.4018/978-1-7998-9055-3.ch008

Bang, H. J., Fabienke, N., & Tyson, C. A. (2022). Creating Diverse, Equitable, and Inclusive Digital Learning Platforms for Young Children. In A. L. Betts & K. Thai (Eds.), *Handbook of Research on Innovative Approaches to Early Childhood Development and School Readiness* (pp. 577–601). IGI Global., doi:10.4018/978-1-7998-8649-5.ch024

Banner, D. (2022). Storytelling in Peace Leadership. In E. P. Schellhammer (Ed.), *Evolution of Peace Leadership and Practical Implications* (pp. 273–292). IGI Global., doi:10.4018/978-1-7998-9736-1.ch015

Baporikar, N. (2021). Effect of Reward on Motivation and Job Satisfaction. [IJAMSE]. *International Journal of Applied Management Sciences and Engineering, 8*(1), 12–51. doi:10.4018/IJAMSE.2021010102

Baporikar, N. (2021). Health Institution Governance. [IJPAE]. *International Journal of Political Activism and Engagement, 8*(4), 1–19. doi:10.4018/IJPAE.2021100101

Baporikar, N. (2021). Stakeholder Approach for Land Reform Programme to Enhance Access and Equity. [IJPAE]. *International Journal of Political Activism and Engagement, 8*(2), 40–63. doi:10.4018/IJPAE.2021040103

Bari, M. W., & Shahzadi, I. (2022). Employee-Based Brand Equity and Factors of Employee-Brand Association. In M. Bari, M. Abrar, & E. Alaverdov (Eds.), *Antecedents and Outcomes of Employee-Based Brand Equity* (pp. 1–15). IGI Global., doi:10.4018/978-1-6684-3621-9.ch001

Barrett, S. J. (2021). Exploring Diversity and Inclusion Leadership in Complex Organizations. In R. D. Johnson (Ed.), *Handbook of Research on Multidisciplinary Perspectives on Managerial and Leadership Psychology* (pp. 320–353). IGI Global., doi:10.4018/978-1-7998-3811-1.ch016

Bashir, M., Bhutta, M. K., & Shahi, S. G. (2022). Knowledge-Sharing Culture and Employee-Based Brand Equity. In M. Bari, M. Abrar, & E. Alaverdov (Eds.), *Antecedents and Outcomes of Employee-Based Brand Equity* (pp. 119–137). IGI Global., doi:10.4018/978-1-6684-3621-9.ch009

Basile, V. (2019). Building a Strong Brand Equity in Pharmaceutical Industry. [IJCRMM]. *International Journal of Customer Relationship Marketing and Management, 10*(3), 1–20. doi:10.4018/IJCRMM.2019070101

Basnal, G. (2022). Assessment of 21st Century Skills. In Chakravarti, S.Boukareva, B. (Eds.), Cases on Global Innovative Practices for Reforming Education (pp. 202-221). IGI Global. https://doi.org/ doi:10.4018/978-1-7998-8310-4.ch010

Beasley, M., Tunstall, J., Blackmon, S., & Smith, M. (2022). Make Space, Take Space. In E. Cain-Sanschagrin, R. A. Filback, & J. Crawford (Eds.), *Cases on Academic Program Redesign for Greater Racial and Social Justice* (pp. 1–21). IGI Global., doi:10.4018/978-1-7998-8463-7.ch001

Beevor, M. C., Campos, A. C., & Guerreiro, M. M. (2022). Storytelling and Experience Design in Heritage Tourism. In A. Campos & S. Almeida (Eds.), *Global Perspectives on Strategic Storytelling in Destination Marketing* (pp. 1–21). IGI Global., doi:10.4018/978-1-6684-3436-9.ch001

Bello, L. K., Ojebisi, A. O., & Adebanjo, A. A. (2021). The Impact of Perceived Relevance and Technology Anxiety on Readiness to Use Digital Storytelling. [IJTEPD]. *International Journal of Teacher Education and Professional Development, 4*(2), 82–96. doi:10.4018/IJTEPD.2021070106

Ben Mim, S., & Mbarki, Y. (2021). Corporate Governance in Islamic Banks. In A. Alqatan, K. Hussainey, & H. Khlif (Eds.), *Corporate Governance and Its Implications on Accounting and Finance* (pp. 322–337). IGI Global., doi:10.4018/978-1-7998-4852-3.ch015

Berg, G. A. (2020). Equity and Diversity in the 21st Century University. In Berg, G. A.Venis, L. (Eds.), Accessibility and Diversity in the 21st Century University (pp. 1-19). IGI Global. https://doi.org/ doi:10.4018/978-1-7998-2783-2.ch001

Bergman, T. (2020). Critical Political Economy and Content Analysis. In Karlidag, S.Bulut, S. (Eds.), Handbook of Research on the Political Economy of Communications and Media (pp. 242-255). IGI Global. https://doi.org/ doi:10.4018/978-1-7998-3270-6.ch013

Besong, E. N. (2022). Nigerian Media's Poor Representation and Negligence of Minorities as a Breach of Ethical Journalism. In Okocha, D. O., Onobe, M. J.Alike, M. N. (Eds.), Handbook of Research on Connecting Philosophy, Media, and Development in Developing Countries (pp. 352-364). IGI Global. https://doi.org/ doi:10.4018/978-1-6684-4107-7.ch024

Betts, A. L., Fabienke, N., & Farber, M. (2021). The Quest for Learning. In L. Haas & J. Tussey (Eds.), *Disciplinary Literacy Connections to Popular Culture in K-12 Settings* (pp. 203–230). IGI Global., doi:10.4018/978-1-7998-4721-2.ch010

Bhattacharyya, M. (2021). Safety and Security of Journalists in India. In Jamil, S., Çoban, B., Ataman, B.Appiah-Adjei, G. (Eds.), Handbook of Research on Discrimination, Gender Disparity, and Safety Risks in Journalism (pp. 119-142). IGI Global. https://doi.org/ doi:10.4018/978-1-7998-6686-2.ch008

Bhattacharyya, R. (2019). Financial Globalization and Trade Openness in China and India. [IJABIM]. *International Journal of Asian Business and Information Management, 10*(3), 22–48. doi:10.4018/IJABIM.2019070102

Bienvenido, H. P., Barinaga, B., & Mora-Fernandez, J. (2021). A Historical Review of Immersive Storytelling Technologies. In V. Chkoniya (Ed.), *Handbook of Research on Applied Data Science and Artificial Intelligence in Business and Industry* (pp. 569–597). IGI Global., doi:10.4018/978-1-7998-6985-6.ch027

Billen, M. T., Ward, N. A., DeHart, J. D., Moran, R. R., & Yang, S. (2021). StoryVisualizer by LEGO Education. In L. Haas & J. Tussey (Eds.), *Connecting Disciplinary Literacy and Digital Storytelling in K-12 Education* (pp. 148–168). IGI Global., doi:10.4018/978-1-7998-5770-9.ch008

Bintz, W., Ciecierski, L. M., & Royan, E. (2021). Using Picture Books With Instructional Strategies to Address New Challenges and Teach Literacy Skills in a Digital World. In L. Haas & J. Tussey (Eds.), *Connecting Disciplinary Literacy and Digital Storytelling in K-12 Education* (pp. 38–58). IGI Global., doi:10.4018/978-1-7998-5770-9.ch003

Bitrus-Ojiambo, U. A., & King'ori, M. E. (2020). Media and Child Rights in Africa. In O. Oyero (Ed.), *Media and Its Role in Protecting the Rights of Children in Africa* (pp. 125–148). IGI Global., doi:10.4018/978-1-7998-0329-4.ch007

Black, E., & Kirkwood, K. (2022). Twice as Good to Get Half. In Alvarez, W. & De Walt, P. S. (Ed.), Voicing Diverse Teaching Experiences, Approaches, and Perspectives in Higher Education (pp. 17-27). IGI Global. https://doi.org/ doi:10.4018/978-1-7998-9000-3.ch002

Blanco Sánchez, T., & Castillo Díaz, A. (2022). Research in Public Relations in Spain Through the State Research Plans 2013-2020. In M. Carrillo-Durán & M. Pérez Pulido (Eds.), *Cases on Developing Effective Research Plans for Communications and Information Science* (pp. 189–214). IGI Global., doi:10.4018/978-1-6684-4523-5.ch010

Bledsoe, T., & Setterlund, K. (2021). *All About the Classroom!* IGI Global., doi:10.4018/978-1-7998-4069-5.ch008

Bledsoe, T., & Setterlund, K. (2021). *Background Experiences, Developmental Perspectives*. IGI Global., doi:10.4018/978-1-7998-4069-5.ch003

Bledsoe, T., & Setterlund, K. (2021). *The Power of Narratives*. IGI Global., doi:10.4018/978-1-7998-4069-5.ch001

Bloom, L., Noltensmeyer, C. J., Hahn, S. A., Rush, C. B., Heidlebaugh-Buskey, P., & Westbrook, T. M. (2020). Pedagogical Considerations in Teaching Implicit Bias. [IJBIDE]. *International Journal of Bias, Identity and Diversities in Education*, *5*(1), 46–63. doi:10.4018/IJBIDE.2020010103

Bobbert, Y., Chtepen, M., Kumar, T., Vanderbeken, Y., & Verslegers, D. (2021). *Research Findings in the Domain of CI/CD and DevOps on Security Compliance*. IGI Global., doi:10.4018/978-1-7998-7367-9.ch008

Bobbert, Y., Chtepen, M., Kumar, T., Vanderbeken, Y., & Verslegers, D. (2021). *Findings and Core Practices in the Domain of CI/CD and DevOps on Security Compliance*. IGI Global., doi:10.4018/978-1-7998-7367-9.ch009

Bocci, M. C. (2022). Guiding School-Based Service-Learning With Youth Participatory Action Research. In Management Association, I. (Eds.), Research Anthology on Service Learning and Community Engagement Teaching Practices (pp. 186-205). IGI Global. https://doi.org/ doi:10.4018/978-1-6684-3877-0.ch011

Boguszewicz-Kreft, M., Kreft, J., & Żurek, P. (2019). Myth and Storytelling. In J. Kreft, S. Kuczamer-Kłopotowska, & A. Kalinowska-Żeleźnik (Eds.), *Myth in Modern Media Management and Marketing* (pp. 22–49). IGI Global., doi:10.4018/978-1-5225-9100-9.ch002

Bolat, N. (2021). Cross-Media as a Multi-Platform Narrative Interaction Form. In R. Yilmaz (Ed.), *Handbook of Research on Narrative Interactions* (pp. 274–291). IGI Global., doi:10.4018/978-1-7998-4903-2.ch015

Bolat, N. (2022). The Narrative of Violence in the Framework of the Post-Truth Concept in Television Series. In Yılmaz, R.Koç, B. (Eds.), Narrative Theory and Therapy in the Post-Truth Era (pp. 43-60). IGI Global. https://doi.org/ doi:10.4018/978-1-7998-9251-9.ch004

Bolyard, C. S., Baker, A. M., & Rudnick, D. L. (2022). Dilemmas in Asynchronous Multicultural Teacher Education From a Relational Pedagogy Perspective. In S. P. Huffman, D. D. Cunningham, M. Shavers, & R. Adamson (Eds.), *Handbook of Research on Opening Pathways for Marginalized Individuals in Higher Education* (pp. 123–146). IGI Global., doi:10.4018/978-1-6684-3819-0.ch008

Bondad-Brown, B., & Haras, C. (2022). Alt-Instruction. In P. Sullivan, B. Sullivan, & J. Lantz (Eds.), *Cases on Innovative and Successful Uses of Digital Resources for Online Learning* (pp. 178–203). IGI Global., doi:10.4018/978-1-7998-9004-1.ch008

Boult, J., Whited, J. E., & Easley, T. M. (2021). An Ethics-of-Care Approach to Developing Students' Antiracist Practice in SLP Curricula. In R. Horton (Ed.), *Critical Perspectives on Social Justice in Speech-Language Pathology* (pp. 198–223). IGI Global., doi:10.4018/978-1-7998-7134-7.ch010

Bowen, A. M., Robinson, S., & Lane, J. (2021). Black Female Education Leaders and Intersectionality. In S. Rodriguez & K. Brown (Eds.), *Black and Brown Leadership and the Promotion of Change in an Era of Social Unrest* (pp. 101–123). IGI Global., doi:10.4018/978-1-7998-7235-1.ch005

Bozkurt, Y. (2019). Expectation Horizon in Narrative Advertising. In R. Yilmaz (Ed.), *Handbook of Research on Narrative Advertising* (pp. 22–35). IGI Global., doi:10.4018/978-1-5225-9790-2.ch003

Bradish, C. L., & Burton, N. (2021). Media and Content in an Active Economy. In D. J. Finch & D. Legg (Eds.), *Understanding the Active Economy and Emerging Research on the Value of Sports, Recreation, and Wellness* (pp. 239–246). IGI Global., doi:10.4018/978-1-7998-7939-8.ch011

Brand, S. T., & Tutwiler, M. S. (2022). Beyond Critical Race Theory. In J. Keengwe (Ed.), *Handbook of Research on Social Justice and Equity in Education* (pp. 160–182). IGI Global., doi:10.4018/978-1-7998-9567-1.ch008

Brandão, A. M., & Machado, S. M. (2020). How Consumers Respond to Editorial Communication Strategies. In S. M. Loureiro & H. R. Kaufmann (Eds.), *Exploring the Power of Electronic Word-of-Mouth in the Services Industry* (pp. 364–389). IGI Global., doi:10.4018/978-1-5225-8575-6.ch020

Bratitsis, T. (2022). Cultural Heritage Redesigned Through Digital Storytelling. In Papadakis, S.Kapaniaris, A. (Eds.), The Digital Folklore of Cyberculture and Digital Humanities (pp. 296-311). IGI Global. https://doi.org/ doi:10.4018/978-1-6684-4461-0.ch016

Bravo, I. R., & Rubio-Hernández, M. D. (2020). An Analysis of Netflix España Campaigns. In V. Hernández-Santaolalla & M. Barrientos-Bueno (Eds.), *Handbook of Research on Transmedia Storytelling, Audience Engagement, and Business Strategies* (pp. 367–381). IGI Global., doi:10.4018/978-1-7998-3119-8.ch024

Bright, A., Acosta, S., & Parker, B. (2020). Humility Matters. In J. Keengwe (Ed.), *Handbook of Research on Diversity and Social Justice in Higher Education* (pp. 19–40). IGI Global., doi:10.4018/978-1-7998-5268-1.ch002

Bright, A., Hendryx-Dobson, J. N., & Johnson, S. (2022). Contending With Word Choices in Cross-Cultural Teacher Preparation. In J. Keengwe (Ed.), *Handbook of Research on Social Justice and Equity in Education* (pp. 22–45). IGI Global., doi:10.4018/978-1-7998-9567-1.ch002

Brooks-Eaves, M. (2022). From the Schoolhouse to the Prison Yard. In A. T. Adams (Ed.), *Approaching Disparities in School Discipline* (pp. 257–270). IGI Global., doi:10.4018/978-1-6684-3359-1.ch011

Broughton, A. (2019). *Green Thumb Educating*. IGI Global., doi:10.4018/978-1-5225-8867-2.ch004

Brown, S. (2020). Literacy in Early Childhood. In Mitchell, J. S.Vaughn, E. N. (Eds.), Participatory Literacy Practices for P-12 Classrooms in the Digital Age (pp. 1-19). IGI Global. https://doi.org/ doi:10.4018/978-1-7998-0000-2.ch001

Brown, T. Y., Cornell, N., Tevlin, J. M., Williams, D., & Mulvaney, T. (2022). Inclusion, Diversity Belonging, Equity, and Accessibility Principles on College Campuses. In A. El-Amin (Ed.), *Implementing Diversity, Equity, Inclusion, and Belonging Management in Organizational Change Initiatives* (pp. 202–215). IGI Global., doi:10.4018/978-1-6684-4023-0.ch011

Brulles, D., & Naglieri, J. A. (2022). A Social Justice Approach to Developing Equity and Diversity in Gifted Programming. In J. L. Nyberg & J. A. Manzone (Eds.), *Creating Equitable Services for the Gifted* (pp. 103–119). IGI Global., doi:10.4018/978-1-7998-8153-7.ch008

Buckley-Marudas, M., & Ellenbogen, C. (2020). Fostering Participatory Literacies in English Language Arts Instruction Using Student-Authored Podcasts. In J. S. Mitchell & E. N. Vaughn (Eds.), *Participatory Literacy Practices for P-12 Classrooms in the Digital Age* (pp. 20–39). IGI Global., doi:10.4018/978-1-7998-0000-2.ch002

Bulut, S. (2020). The Political Economy of News Production. In Karlidag, S.Bulut, S. (Eds.), Handbook of Research on the Political Economy of Communications and Media (pp. 98-114). IGI Global. https://doi.org/ doi:10.4018/978-1-7998-3270-6.ch006

Burciaga, L. (2022). Trauma-Engaged and Culturally Responsive Schools. In K. Johns (Ed.), *Counseling Strategies for Children and Families Impacted by Incarceration* (pp. 209–238). IGI Global., doi:10.4018/978-1-7998-9209-0.ch012

Burrell, D. N. (2021). Black American Men and Complex Societal Educational Navigation of the Emergency Public Health Pandemic of COVID 19. [IJSEUS]. *International Journal of Smart Education and Urban Society, 12*(2), 1–9. doi:10.4018/IJSEUS.2021040101

Burrell, D. N. (2021). Creating Diverse and Religiously Inclusive Workplace Cultures in Hyper-Connected, Technical, and Cyber-Driven Organizations. [IJSKD]. *International Journal of Sociotechnology and Knowledge Development, 13*(3), 17–32. doi:10.4018/IJSKD.2021070102

Burrell, D. N., Barrett, S. J., Lewis, E. J., Dawson, M., Bovell, K., & Crowe, M. (2021). Creating Inclusive Workplaces for Women in Health Organizations Engaging in Digital Economy-Driven Innovations. [IJIDE]. *International Journal of Innovation in the Digital Economy, 12*(2), 18–31. doi:10.4018/IJIDE.2021040102

Burrell, D. N., Lu, S., Lindsay, P. V., Burton, S. L., French, R., Finch, A., McLester, Q., & Springs, D. (2021). Sexual Harassment Training Focused Solely on Protecting Organizations From Lawsuits Won't Change a Toxic Culture for Women to an Inclusive One. [IJPSS]. *International Journal of Public Sociology and Sociotherapy*, *1*(1), 12–25. doi:10.4018/IJPSS.2021010102

Burrell, D. N., Modeste, R., Aridi, A. S., DiPeri, D., Jones, D., & Clay, L. (2021). Addressing Workplace Sexual Harassment in a Government Contracting Company Through Organizational Consulting. [IJSEUS]. *International Journal of Smart Education and Urban Society*, *12*(1), 18–29. doi:10.4018/IJSEUS.2021010102

Burrell, D. N., Modeste, R. L., & Finch, A. (2021). Responsible Church Leaders Should Be Educating Their Congregations About Racism and Serving the Community Concerning the Black Lives Matter movement. [IJSEUS]. *International Journal of Smart Education and Urban Society*, *12*(3), 38–49. doi:10.4018/IJSEUS.2021070104

Burrell, D. N., Shufutinsky, A., Bland, S., Cole, C. M., Wright, J. B., Crowe, M., Aridi, A. S., & Mairs-Levy, J. (2020). A Case Study of a Hospital Workplace Culture of Injustice for Women Physicians. [IJPCH]. *International Journal of Patient-Centered Healthcare*, *10*(1), 15–36. doi:10.4018/IJPCH.2020010102

Burton, S. L. (2021). Technological Digital Disruption in the Age of Artificial Intelligence. In L. S. Byrd (Ed.), *Cultivating Entrepreneurial Changemakers Through Digital Media Education* (pp. 1–35). IGI Global., doi:10.4018/978-1-7998-5808-9.ch001

Bushur-Harris, L. (2022). Leadership Using Internal Controls for a Decentralized (Remote) Workforce. In Heinzman, J. R., Judge, D. S., Franklin, V. S.McCleskey, J. A. (Eds.), Business Models to Promote Technology, Culture, and Leadership in Post-COVID-19 Organizations (pp. 74-92). IGI Global. https://doi.org/ doi:10.4018/978-1-6684-4358-3.ch004

Butler, M., & Whitehead, M. (2022). Did You Get the Memo? In H. W. Pichon & Y. Mutakabbir (Eds.), *African American Leadership and Mentoring Through Purpose, Preparation, and Preceptors* (pp. 101–125). IGI Global., doi:10.4018/978-1-7998-8206-0.ch006

Byrd, L. S. (2021). At the Intersection of Media Innovation and Solutions Journalism. In L. S. Byrd (Ed.), *Cultivating Entrepreneurial Changemakers Through Digital Media Education* (pp. 208–222). IGI Global., doi:10.4018/978-1-7998-5808-9.ch014

Byrd, L. S. (2021). Future Forward. In L. S. Byrd (Ed.), *Cultivating Entrepreneurial Changemakers Through Digital Media Education* (pp. 223–236). IGI Global., doi:10.4018/978-1-7998-5808-9.ch015

Cabrera-Gala, R. (2022). Research in the Field of Communication in Mexico. In Carrillo-Durán, M.Pérez Pulido, M. (Eds.), Cases on Developing Effective Research Plans for Communications and Information Science (pp. 166-188). IGI Global. https://doi.org/ doi:10.4018/978-1-6684-4523-5.ch009

Çakın, Ö. (2019). The Structural Transformation of Narrative Advertising in Turkic Republics. In R. Yilmaz (Ed.), *Handbook of Research on Narrative Advertising* (pp. 108–120). IGI Global., doi:10.4018/978-1-5225-9790-2.ch010

Çal, B. (2020). Firm-Specific Moderators in Recovery From Brand Scandals. In R. Leon (Ed.), *Strategies for Business Sustainability in a Collaborative Economy* (pp. 122–140). IGI Global., doi:10.4018/978-1-7998-4543-0.ch007

Calder, C., & Walker, Q. (2022). Facilitating Anti-Racism in Counselor Education. In S. N. Brant-Rajahn, E. M. Gibson, & M. Cook Sandifer (Eds.), *Developing, Delivering, and Sustaining School Counseling Practices Through a Culturally Affirming Lens* (pp. 248–270). IGI Global., doi:10.4018/978-1-7998-9514-5.ch013

Camilleri, C., Vella, J. G., & Nezval, V. (2020). ThespisTRX. [IJITWE]. *International Journal of Information Technology and Web Engineering*, *15*(1), 1–16. doi:10.4018/IJITWE.2020010101

Camillo, A. (2021). *Finance*. IGI Global., doi:10.4018/978-1-7998-4342-9.ch009

Campbell, D. M. (2019). Depicting Political Dynamics of Migrant "Blackness" in the Era of Trumpism. In F. P. Endong (Ed.), *Popular Representations of America in Non-American Media* (pp. 134–160). IGI Global., doi:10.4018/978-1-5225-9312-6.ch006

Campbell, S. (2022). An Examination of Racial Trauma and Multicultural Counseling. In Brant-Rajahn, S. N., Gibson, E. M.Cook Sandifer, M. (Eds.), Developing, Delivering, and Sustaining School Counseling Practices Through a Culturally Affirming Lens (pp. 58-75). IGI Global. https://doi.org/ doi:10.4018/978-1-7998-9514-5.ch004

Cantimur, S., & Bolat, N. (2022). Representation of Violence Against Women in Television News. In R. Yılmaz & B. Koç (Eds.), *Narrative Theory and Therapy in the Post-Truth Era* (pp. 79–99). IGI Global., doi:10.4018/978-1-7998-9251-9.ch006

Çapan, S. A. (2020). Using Digital Storytelling to Handle Second Language Writing Anxiety and Attitudes. In Kruk, M.Peterson, M. (Eds.), New Technological Applications for Foreign and Second Language Learning and Teaching (pp. 157-178). IGI Global. https://doi.org/ doi:10.4018/978-1-7998-2591-3.ch008

Carbajal, D., & Ramirez, Q. A. (2022). Applying Theoretical Perspectives to Social Media Influencers. In M. N. Al-Suqri, J. Alsalmi, & O. Al-Shaqsi (Eds.), *Mass Communications and the Influence of Information During Times of Crises* (pp. 69–98). IGI Global., doi:10.4018/978-1-7998-7503-1.ch004

Cardona-Moltó, M. C., & Miralles-Cardona, C. (2022). Education for Gender Equality in Teacher Preparation. In J. A. Boivin & H. Pacheco-Guffrey (Eds.), *Education as the Driving Force of Equity for the Marginalized* (pp. 65–89). IGI Global., doi:10.4018/978-1-7998-8025-7.ch004

Carr-Winston, M. A. (2019). Consequences of Inequality and Exclusion on the Culture of Higher Education Institutions. In Wisdom, S., Leavitt, L.Bice, C. (Eds.), Handbook of Research on Social Inequality and Education (pp. 91-110). IGI Global. https://doi.org/ doi:10.4018/978-1-5225-9108-5.ch005

Cartagena, S., & Pike, L. (2022). Defying Deficit Thinking. In R. D. Williams (Ed.), *Handbook of Research on Challenging Deficit Thinking for Exceptional Education Improvement* (pp. 101–126). IGI Global., doi:10.4018/978-1-7998-8860-4.ch005

Carvalho, L. M., & Noronha, A. B. (2020). An Outlook About the Application of Digital Storytelling in Higher Education. In L. C. Carvalho, A. B. Noronha, & C. L. Souza (Eds.), *Learning Styles and Strategies for Management Students* (pp. 35–48). IGI Global., doi:10.4018/978-1-7998-2124-3.ch003

Casado-Aranda, L., Sánchez-Fernández, J., & Paço, A. (2021). Exploring the Effectiveness of Storytelling in Advertising Through Eye-Tracking. In L. C. Mihăeş, R. Andreescu, & A. Dimitriu (Eds.), *Handbook of Research on Contemporary Storytelling Methods Across New Media and Disciplines* (pp. 158–179). IGI Global., doi:10.4018/978-1-7998-6605-3.ch009

Casale, R., & Mentor, D. (2022). Digital Film-Making Response to a Hate Crime. In D. Mentor (Ed.), *Handbook of Research on New Media, Training, and Skill Development for the Modern Workforce* (pp. 210–233). IGI Global., doi:10.4018/978-1-6684-3996-8.ch010

Cervantes-Guzmán, J. N. (2021). Evolution of Entrepreneur Women From Traditional Companies to E-Business. [IJBSA]. *International Journal of Business Strategy and Automation*, *2*(2), 26–40. doi:10.4018/IJBSA.20210401.oa3

Çetinkaya, Ö. A. (2019). Brand Storytelling and Narrative Advertising. In R. Yilmaz (Ed.), *Handbook of Research on Narrative Advertising* (pp. 281–291). IGI Global., doi:10.4018/978-1-5225-9790-2.ch024

Cha, J. (2019). Legitimacy of Crowdfunding. [JMME]. *Journal of Media Management and Entrepreneurship, 1*(2), 31–47. doi:10.4018/JMME.2019070103

Chaiya, C., & Ahmad, M. M. (2022). The Student Loan Fund and the Education for All in Thailand. In J. A. Boivin & H. Pacheco-Guffrey (Eds.), *Education as the Driving Force of Equity for the Marginalized* (pp. 135–157). IGI Global., doi:10.4018/978-1-7998-8025-7.ch007

Chajdas, T. (2019). Misleading Media Portrayals in a Globalized World. In Chiluwa, I. E.Samoilenko, S. A. (Eds.), Handbook of Research on Deception, Fake News, and Misinformation Online (pp. 45-64). IGI Global. https://doi.org/ doi:10.4018/978-1-5225-8535-0.ch004

Chakabwata, W. (2022). An Intersectional Study of the Funding Experiences of South African University Students After Majority Rule. In J. Keengwe (Ed.), *Handbook of Research on Social Justice and Equity in Education* (pp. 242–258). IGI Global., doi:10.4018/978-1-7998-9567-1.ch012

Chalamandaris, G., & Antonopoulos, D. (2020). Algorithmic Trading and Transaction Costs. In C. Zopounidis, D. Kenourgios, & G. Dotsis (Eds.), *Recent Advances and Applications in Alternative Investments* (pp. 189–219). IGI Global., doi:10.4018/978-1-7998-2436-7.ch009

Chaman, S., & Shaheen, S. (2022). Linking Psychological Contract With Employee-Based Brand Equity. In M. Bari, M. Abrar, & E. Alaverdov (Eds.), *Antecedents and Outcomes of Employee-Based Brand Equity* (pp. 186–197). IGI Global., doi:10.4018/978-1-6684-3621-9.ch013

Chamblin, M., Newland, L. Z., Kelly, J., & Silva Thompson, L. M. (2022). Sistas in Action. In J. T. Butcher (Ed.), *Black Female Leaders in Academia* (pp. 97–120). IGI Global., doi:10.4018/978-1-7998-9774-3.ch006

Chandra, A. (2019). Gender Gap in Skill Development. In Bala, S.Singhal, P. (Eds.), Gender Issues in Technical and Vocational Education Programs (pp. 1-22). IGI Global. https://doi.org/ doi:10.4018/978-1-5225-8443-8.ch001

Cheshire, T. C., Martinez-Alire, C. D., Esquivido, V., & Springer, M. (2021). The Transformational Change Agent Equation. In S. Rodriguez & K. Brown (Eds.), *Black and Brown Leadership and the Promotion of Change in an Era of Social Unrest* (pp. 208–229). IGI Global., doi:10.4018/978-1-7998-7235-1.ch009

Chiou, S. (2020). Data-Driven Stochastic Optimization for Transportation Road Network Design Under Uncertainty. In F. P. Garcia Marquez (Ed.), *Handbook of Research on Big Data Clustering and Machine Learning* (pp. 231–278). IGI Global., doi:10.4018/978-1-7998-0106-1.ch012

Chisita, C. T., Shoko, M., Rusero, A. M., & Ngoaketse, J. (2020). Media, Libraries, and Archives. In C. T. Chisita (Ed.), *Cooperation and Collaboration Initiatives for Libraries and Related Institutions* (pp. 243–272). IGI Global., doi:10.4018/978-1-7998-0043-9.ch013

Chiu, H., & Wagner, E. (2020). CEO Bonus Pay and Firm Credit Risk. [IJRCM]. *International Journal of Risk and Contingency Management*, *9*(1), 1–19. doi:10.4018/IJRCM.2020010101

Choistealbha, J. U., & Colum, M. (2022). You Can't Be What You Can't See. In J. A. Boivin & H. Pacheco-Guffrey (Eds.), *Education as the Driving Force of Equity for the Marginalized* (pp. 113–134). IGI Global., doi:10.4018/978-1-7998-8025-7.ch006

Chopra, S., & Nagaraj, S. (2023). Business Tech in Media and Entertainment. In S. Nagaraj & K. Kumar (Eds.), *AI-Driven Intelligent Models for Business Excellence* (pp. 81–94). IGI Global., doi:10.4018/978-1-6684-4246-3.ch005

Chu, S., Tu, S., Wang, N., & Zhang, W. (2020). Information Equity and Cultural Sharing. [IJLIS]. *International Journal of Library and Information Services*, *9*(1), 10–24. doi:10.4018/IJLIS.2020010102

Chung, M. (2021). Digital Storytelling Project for Language Teachers. In Ramírez-Verdugo, M. D.Otcu-Grillman, B. (Eds.), Interdisciplinary Approaches Toward Enhancing Teacher Education (pp. 50-68). IGI Global. https://doi.org/doi:10.4018/978-1-7998-4697-0.ch004

Ciftci, D. (2021). Political Marketing and New Media Election Campaigning. In E. Esiyok (Ed.), *Handbook of Research on New Media Applications in Public Relations and Advertising* (pp. 355–379). IGI Global., doi:10.4018/978-1-7998-3201-0.ch021

Cinar, D. (2021). New Event Trends as a Tool of Digital Marketing Communication. In Birdir, K., Birdir, S., Dalgic, A.Toksoz, D. (Eds.), Impact of ICTs on Event Management and Marketing (pp. 216-241). IGI Global. https://doi.org/doi:10.4018/978-1-7998-4954-4.ch013

Clara, S., & Barbosa, B. (2021). People Make Places, What Do Stories Do? In L. C. Mihăeş, R. Andreescu, & A. Dimitriu (Eds.), *Handbook of Research on Contemporary Storytelling Methods Across New Media and Disciplines* (pp. 79–99). IGI Global., doi:10.4018/978-1-7998-6605-3.ch005

Cole, C. M., Burrell, D. N., & Springs, D. (2020). Exploring Organizational Development Intervention Around Sexual Harassment in Technical Firms. [IJHIoT]. *International Journal of Hyperconnectivity and the Internet of Things*, *4*(1), 29–42. doi:10.4018/IJHIoT.2020010103

Condie, C. (2022). Using Writing Workshops in Teacher Education to Build Writing Pedagogy and Equity-Oriented Mindsets. In T. S. Hodges (Ed.), *Handbook of Research on Teacher Practices for Diverse Writing Instruction* (pp. 248–269). IGI Global., doi:10.4018/978-1-6684-6213-3.ch013

Contreras Aguirre, H. C. (2022). Navigating College as Latina STEM Students at Hispanic-Serving Institutions. In Huffman, S. P., Cunningham, D. D., Shavers, M.Adamson, R. (Eds.), Handbook of Research on Opening Pathways for Marginalized Individuals in Higher Education (pp. 244-265). IGI Global. https://doi.org/ doi:10.4018/978-1-6684-3819-0.ch014

Cook, B. L. (2021). The Voice of Social Media, 1997-2018. In Khosrow-Pour D.B.A., M. (Eds.), Encyclopedia of Information Science and Technology, Fifth Edition (pp. 1461-1468). IGI Global. https://doi.org/ doi:10.4018/978-1-7998-3479-3.ch100

Copeland, K., & Tarver, E. N. (2020). Diversity, Equity, and Inclusiveness in Higher Education. In Freeman, J. P., Keller, C. L. & Cambiano, R. L. (Ed.), Higher Education Response to Exponential Societal Shifts (pp. 313-329). IGI Global. https://doi.org/ doi:10.4018/978-1-7998-2410-7.ch015

Corces-Zimmerman, C., & Southern, D. E. (2021). Disrupting Structural Whiteness in Higher Education. In C. Reneau & M. Villarreal (Eds.), *Handbook of Research on Leading Higher Education Transformation With Social Justice, Equity, and Inclusion* (pp. 306–325). IGI Global., doi:10.4018/978-1-7998-7152-1.ch020

Costa, P. T., & Pereira, A. S. (2022). Storytelling by the Sea. In A. Campos & S. Almeida (Eds.), *Global Perspectives on Strategic Storytelling in Destination Marketing* (pp. 164–191). IGI Global., doi:10.4018/978-1-6684-3436-9.ch009

Costa, R. P. (2021). "All the World's a Stage" and Sociologists Its Storytellers. In Mihăeş, L. C., Andreescu, R.Dimitriu, A. (Eds.), Handbook of Research on Contemporary Storytelling Methods Across New Media and Disciplines (pp. 1-16). IGI Global. https://doi.org/ doi:10.4018/978-1-7998-6605-3.ch001

Crawford, C. M., Simons, M. A., & Walters, R. (2021). Social Learning Through a Participative Storytelling Framework. In C. M. Crawford & M. A. Simons (Eds.), *eLearning Engagement in a Transformative Social Learning Environment* (pp. 44–67). IGI Global., doi:10.4018/978-1-7998-6956-6.ch003

Crawford, J., Cain, E. C., & Hamilton, E. (2022). Building Racial Justice Into a Master's Program. In E. Cain-Sanschagrin, R. A. Filback, & J. Crawford (Eds.), *Cases on Academic Program Redesign for Greater Racial and Social Justice* (pp. 98–124). IGI Global., doi:10.4018/978-1-7998-8463-7.ch005

Cronovich, P., & Mitchell, J. (2022). Redesigning GE Language. In E. Cain-Sanschagrin, R. A. Filback, & J. Crawford (Eds.), *Cases on Academic Program Redesign for Greater Racial and Social Justice* (pp. 22–40). IGI Global., doi:10.4018/978-1-7998-8463-7.ch002

Cubbage, J. (2021). So They Might Tell Their Own Stories. In L. S. Byrd (Ed.), *Cultivating Entrepreneurial Changemakers Through Digital Media Education* (pp. 78–94). IGI Global., doi:10.4018/978-1-7998-5808-9.ch005

Cupid, S., Marina, B. L., & Canton, M. (2022). When and Where We Enter. In Msengi, C. M., Lartey, G. K., & Sprott, K. R. (Ed.), Contemporary Issues in Multicultural and Global Education (pp. 193-216). IGI Global. https://doi.org/ doi:10.4018/978-1-7998-7404-1.ch011

Cyrulnik, N. (2022). To Identify the Evolution of Tourism Practices in a Sensitive Way Through Documentary. In Andrade, P.Martins, M. D. (Eds.), Handbook of Research on Urban Tourism, Viral Society, and the Impact of the COVID-19 Pandemic (pp. 538-555). IGI Global. https://doi.org/ doi:10.4018/978-1-6684-3369-0.ch026

Dal Canbazoğlu, A. (2021). Gender and Patriarchy in Turkish Advertising. In Mihăeş, L. C., Andreescu, R.Dimitriu, A. (Eds.), Handbook of Research on Contemporary Storytelling Methods Across New Media and Disciplines (pp. 138-157). IGI Global. https://doi.org/ doi:10.4018/978-1-7998-6605-3.ch008

Dalvi, D. S. (2021). Employer Brand Equity and Its Impact on the Application Intent of the Prospective Employees. [IJBIR]. *International Journal of Business Intelligence Research*, *12*(1), 1–25. doi:10.4018/IJBIR.20210101.oa1

Dar, W. A. (2021). Constructivism, Pluralism, and Pedagogy From Below in India. In N. Mthembu (Ed.), *Ethical Research Approaches to Indigenous Knowledge Education* (pp. 110–126). IGI Global., doi:10.4018/978-1-7998-1249-4.ch005

Daradkeh, M. K. (2021). An Empirical Examination of the Relationship Between Data Storytelling Competency and Business Performance. [JOEUC]. *Journal of Organizational and End User Computing*, *33*(5), 42–73. doi:10.4018/JOEUC.20210901.oa3

Darwish, E. (2020). Perceptions of the UAE's Government Communicators Regarding Social Media Roles. [IJCRMM]. *International Journal of Customer Relationship Marketing and Management, 11*(4), 20–35. doi:10.4018/IJCRMM.2020100102

Das, S. (2020). Innovations in Digital Banking Service Brand Equity and Millennial Consumerism. In K. Sandhu (Ed.), *Digital Transformation and Innovative Services for Business and Learning* (pp. 62–79). IGI Global., doi:10.4018/978-1-7998-5175-2.ch004

Davis, L. (2020). Don't Hide the Hurt. In A. M. Ellsworth (Ed.), *Cases on Emotionally Responsive Teaching and Mentoring* (pp. 13–26). IGI Global., doi:10.4018/978-1-7998-2971-3.ch002

Davis-Cotton, D. (2021). Marginalized Communities, Curriculum, Children (MC3). In M. C. Grant (Ed.), *Emerging Strategies for Public Education Reform* (pp. 126–160). IGI Global., doi:10.4018/978-1-7998-5695-5.ch005

De Blasio, E., Rega, R., & Valente, M. (2022). Polarization and Platformization of News in Italian Journalism. In D. Palau-Sampio, G. López García, & L. Iannelli (Eds.), *Contemporary Politics, Communication, and the Impact on Democracy* (pp. 74–92). IGI Global., doi:10.4018/978-1-7998-8057-8.ch005

Deeb, A. M., & Bromer, B. L. (2022). Spotlighting Diversity, Equity, Inclusion, and Belonging in Higher Education During the COVID-19 Pandemic. In B. L. Bromer & C. M. Crawford (Eds.), *Handbook of Research on Learner-Centered Approaches to Teaching in an Age of Transformational Change* (pp. 226–247). IGI Global., doi:10.4018/978-1-6684-4240-1.ch012

Degener, R., Castillo, B., & Beschorner, B. (2022). Evaluating Antiracist Dispositions. In von Hohenberg, S. C. (Ed.), Dispositional Development and Assessment in Teacher Preparation Programs (pp. 273-288). IGI Global. https://doi.org/ doi:10.4018/978-1-6684-4089-6.ch015

DeHart, J. (2022). *Authorial Work With Film*. IGI Global., doi:10.4018/978-1-7998-9136-9.ch006

DeHart, J. (2022). *Implications for Choosing Film*. IGI Global., doi:10.4018/978-1-7998-9136-9.ch002

DeHart, J. D. (2021). The Emotional Affordances of Visual Literacy Pedagogy. In Tussey, J.Haas, L. (Eds.), Handbook of Research on Supporting Social and Emotional Development Through Literacy Education (pp. 73-87). IGI Global. https://doi.org/ doi:10.4018/978-1-7998-7464-5.ch004

DeHart, J. D. (2023). Traveling Across Media. In J. D. DeHart (Ed.), *Exploring Comics and Graphic Novels in the Classroom* (pp. 279–291). IGI Global., doi:10.4018/978-1-6684-4313-2.ch015

Del Priore, A. (2022). Mentoring for Career Advancement. In Pichon, H. W.Mutakabbir, Y. (Eds.), African American Leadership and Mentoring Through Purpose, Preparation, and Preceptors (pp. 222-250). IGI Global. https://doi.org/ doi:10.4018/978-1-7998-8206-0.ch011

DeMartino, L., & Weiser, S. G. (2021). Striving for Equity in Pandemic Times. In L. Kyei-Blankson, J. Blankson, & E. Ntuli (Eds.), *Handbook of Research on Inequities in Online Education During Global Crises* (pp. 199–223). IGI Global., doi:10.4018/978-1-7998-6533-9.ch011

Dempsey, A., M'gadzah, S., & Watson, S. D. (2022). Diversity and Racism in Higher Education. In E. Meletiadou (Ed.), *Handbook of Research on Practices for Advancing Diversity and Inclusion in Higher Education* (pp. 354–376). IGI Global., doi:10.4018/978-1-7998-9628-9.ch018

Dennis, B., Li, P., Ross, K., & Zhao, P. (2021). Pedagogy as a Form of Praxis and Commitment. In T. S. Jenkins (Ed.), *Reshaping Graduate Education Through Innovation and Experiential Learning* (pp. 1–22). IGI Global., doi:10.4018/978-1-7998-4836-3.ch001

Derindere Köseoğlu, S., & Awad Almeany, S. S. (2020). Introduction to Business Valuation. In Köseoğlu, S. D. (Ed.), Valuation Challenges and Solutions in Contemporary Businesses (pp. 1-23). IGI Global. https://doi.org/ doi:10.4018/978-1-7998-1086-5.ch001

Dewsbury, B. (2020). A Worthy Burden. In Brand, S. T.Ciccomascolo, L. E. (Eds.), Social Justice and Putting Theory Into Practice in Schools and Communities (pp. 29-43). IGI Global. https://doi.org/ doi:10.4018/978-1-5225-9434-5.ch003

Dhar, S., & Chowdhury, M. A. (2021). Impact of Environmental Accounting Reporting Practices on Financial Performance. [IJABIM]. *International Journal of Asian Business and Information Management, 12*(1), 24–42. doi:10.4018/IJABIM.20210101.oa2

Dickson, T. A. (2022). Advancing Equity, Diversity, and Inclusion Through the Transformation of Nursing Education. In McCune, N. M. (Eds.), Advancing DEI and Creating Inclusive Environments in the Online Space (pp. 94-109). IGI Global. https://doi.org/ doi:10.4018/978-1-6684-5146-5.ch006

Díez-Garrido, M., Calvo, D., & Cano-Orón, L. (2022). The Mirage of Truth. In D. Palau-Sampio, G. López García, & L. Iannelli (Eds.), *Contemporary Politics, Communication, and the Impact on Democracy* (pp. 133–151). IGI Global., doi:10.4018/978-1-7998-8057-8.ch008

Dinesh Kumar, J., & Sriram, A. (2021). Information and Communication Technologies Use and Its Influence in Family Functioning. [IJTD]. *International Journal of Technology Diffusion, 12*(1), 28–52. doi:10.4018/IJTD.2021010102

Dönmez, S. C., & Yegen, C. (2021). Eleven Eleven VR. In R. Yilmaz (Ed.), *Handbook of Research on Narrative Interactions* (pp. 292–305). IGI Global., doi:10.4018/978-1-7998-4903-2.ch016

Dos, D. (2021). Unlimiting Perspectives. In Reneau, C.Villarreal, M. (Eds.), Handbook of Research on Leading Higher Education Transformation With Social Justice, Equity, and Inclusion (pp. 89-106). IGI Global. https://doi.org/ doi:10.4018/978-1-7998-7152-1.ch007

Dove, K. G. (2021). Classroom Equity and the Role of a Teacher Leader. In B. S. Zugelder (Ed.), *Empowering Formal and Informal Leadership While Maintaining Teacher Identity* (pp. 109–134). IGI Global., doi:10.4018/978-1-7998-6500-1.ch005

Dua, S., Dua, S., & Singh, I. (2021). i-Branding as a Tool of Integrated Marketing. In Singh, A. (Ed.), Big Data Analytics for Improved Accuracy, Efficiency, and Decision Making in Digital Marketing (pp. 183-195). IGI Global. https://doi.org/ doi:10.4018/978-1-7998-7231-3.ch013

Dua, S., Singh, I., & Das, S. (2021). Banking Innovative Service With Digital Brand Equity for New Age Consumers. In S. Das & S. R. Mondal (Eds.), *Innovations in Digital Branding and Content Marketing* (pp. 134–159). IGI Global., doi:10.4018/978-1-7998-4420-4.ch007

Duval, S., & Foerster Luu, A. M. (2020). Transforming the Education of Immigrant Youth. In L. Cardozo-Gaibisso & M. Vazquez Dominguez (Eds.), *Handbook of Research on Advancing Language Equity Practices With Immigrant Communities* (pp. 87–106). IGI Global., doi:10.4018/978-1-7998-3448-9.ch005

Dwivedi, R., Shukla, B., & Malik, G. (2022). Waste to Wealth Enterprises. In H. Magd, D. Singh, R. T. Syed, & D. Spicer (Eds.), *International Perspectives on Value Creation and Sustainability Through Social Entrepreneurship* (pp. 223–238). IGI Global., doi:10.4018/978-1-6684-4666-9.ch011

Easa, N. F., & Bazzi, A. M. (2020). The Influence of Employer Branding on Employer Attractiveness and Employee Engagement and Retention. [IJCRMM]. *International Journal of Customer Relationship Marketing and Management, 11*(4), 48–69. doi:10.4018/IJCRMM.2020100104

Ejiogu, A. O., & Adikaibe, P. (2019). Socioeconomic Analysis of the Relationship between the Socioeconomic Characteristics and the Leverage Ratio of Rice Farmers in Anambra State, Nigeria. [IJSEM]. *International Journal of Sustainable Economies Management, 8*(4), 1–12. doi:10.4018/IJSEM.2019100101

El-Amin, A. (2022). Organizational Climate Change. In A. El-Amin (Ed.), *Implementing Diversity, Equity, Inclusion, and Belonging Management in Organizational Change Initiatives* (pp. 1–23). IGI Global., doi:10.4018/978-1-6684-4023-0.ch001

El Gody, A. (2020). Social Media Economy and Newsroom Convergence in Egyptian Media. In Karlidag, S.Bulut, S. (Eds.), Handbook of Research on the Political Economy of Communications and Media (pp. 115-133). IGI Global. https://doi.org/ doi:10.4018/978-1-7998-3270-6.ch007

El Gody, A. (2020). Social Networks, Media, and the Egyptian Revolution. In Kumar, V.Malhotra, G. (Eds.), Examining the Roles of IT and Social Media in Democratic Development and Social Change (pp. 133-155). IGI Global. https://doi.org/ doi:10.4018/978-1-7998-1791-8.ch006

Elastic, P., Bakhtiar, T., & Jaharuddin. (2020). An Optimal Control Problem of Knowledge Dissemination. In Idemudia, E. C. (Ed.), *Handbook of Research on Social and Organizational Dynamics in the Digital Era* (pp. 461-482). IGI Global. https://doi.org/ doi:10.4018/978-1-5225-8933-4.ch022

Eliasson, M. N. (2023). Trayvon Martin. In L. J. Leonard (Ed.), *Cases on Crimes, Investigations, and Media Coverage* (pp. 94–116). IGI Global., doi:10.4018/978-1-7998-9668-5.ch006

Elikci, C. (2021). Integration of Artificial Intelligence Into Austrian Journalism. In Musiolik, T. H.Cheok, A. D. (Eds.), Analyzing Future Applications of AI, Sensors, and Robotics in Society (pp. 182-200). IGI Global. https://doi.org/ doi:10.4018/978-1-7998-3499-1.ch011

Ellao, J. A., Roxas, E. F., & Torres, T. P. (2021). Dealing With Sexual Harassment. In S. Jamil, B. Çoban, B. Ataman, & G. Appiah-Adjei (Eds.), *Handbook of Research on Discrimination, Gender Disparity, and Safety Risks in Journalism* (pp. 24–42). IGI Global., doi:10.4018/978-1-7998-6686-2.ch003

Ellington, L. M. (2022). Anti-Racism Movement on Campus and Educational Leadership. In V. Wang (Ed.), *Handbook of Research on Educational Leadership and Research Methodology* (pp. 256–272). IGI Global., doi:10.4018/978-1-6684-4144-2.ch014

Ellington, L. M. (2022). Character Development. In A. Courtney-Dattola (Ed.), *Handbook of Research on Adapting Remote Learning Practices for Early Childhood and Elementary School Classrooms* (pp. 65–76). IGI Global., doi:10.4018/978-1-7998-8405-7.ch004

Elwood, S. A., Kesterson, M. R., Bippert, K., DeGrande, H., & Boyson, P. (2022). Formative Journeys. In J. Keengwe (Ed.), *Handbook of Research on Digital-Based Assessment and Innovative Practices in Education* (pp. 1–29). IGI Global., doi:10.4018/978-1-6684-2468-1.ch001

Ershov, B., & Ashmarov, I. (2022). *Church as a Social and Spiritual Institution of Society*. IGI Global., doi:10.4018/978-1-6684-4915-8.ch004

Espinoza, K., Machado-Casas, M., & Martinez-Suarez, A. (2021). Disruption Through Concientización. In G. Onchwari & J. Keengwe (Eds.), *Bridging Family-Teacher Relationships for ELL and Immigrant Students* (pp. 65–82). IGI Global., doi:10.4018/978-1-7998-4712-0.ch004

Esquivel Martin, T., Pérez Martín, J. M., & Bravo Torija, B. (2021). The Use of Storytelling to Promote Literacy Skills in Biology Education. In M. D. Ramírez-Verdugo & B. Otcu-Grillman (Eds.), *Interdisciplinary Approaches Toward Enhancing Teacher Education* (pp. 155–177). IGI Global., doi:10.4018/978-1-7998-4697-0.ch009

Everett, D. L., & Harris, W. G. (2021). A Model for Institutional Equity. In A. J. Griffen (Ed.), *Challenges to Integrating Diversity, Equity, and Inclusion Programs in Organizations* (pp. 1–11). IGI Global., doi:10.4018/978-1-7998-4093-0.ch001

Ezikwelu, E. (2022). Racialized Social Perceptions. In Msengi, C. M., Lartey, G. K.Sprott, K. R. (Eds.), Contemporary Issues in Multicultural and Global Education (pp. 16-30). IGI Global. https://doi.org/ doi:10.4018/978-1-7998-7404-1.ch002

Falcone, P. (2020). Heritage Storytelling. In A. D. Queirós (Ed.), *Examining a New Paradigm of Heritage With Philosophy, Economy, and Education* (pp. 142–156). IGI Global., doi:10.4018/978-1-7998-3636-0.ch010

Falk, A. F., Carrasco-Velez, R. T., Shannon, M., & Proulx, E. (2022). Advancing College Diversity and Access Through Partnership. In E. Meletiadou (Ed.), *Handbook of Research on Practices for Advancing Diversity and Inclusion in Higher Education* (pp. 149–170). IGI Global., doi:10.4018/978-1-7998-9628-9.ch008

Fallah, S., Reynolds, B., & Murawski, W. (2020). *Results of a Mixed-Methods Study on One CLD Group*. IGI Global., doi:10.4018/978-1-7998-2069-7.ch007

Faraon, M., Jaff, A., Nepomuceno, L. P., & Villavicencio, V. (2020). Fake News and Aggregated Credibility. [IJACI]. *International Journal of Ambient Computing and Intelligence, 11*(4), 93–117. doi:10.4018/IJACI.20201001.oa1

Fernández Gómez, J. D. (2020). An Approach to Motivation Research From Advertising Strategy. In Hernández-Santaolalla, V.Barrientos-Bueno, M. (Eds.), Handbook of Research on Transmedia Storytelling, Audience Engagement, and Business Strategies (pp. 239-253). IGI Global. https://doi.org/ doi:10.4018/978-1-7998-3119-8.ch016

Ferraro, A. (2022). Framing Higher Education Through the Social Determinants of Health. In McCune, N. M. (Eds.), Advancing DEI and Creating Inclusive Environments in the Online Space (pp. 210-224). IGI Global. https://doi.org/ doi:10.4018/978-1-6684-5146-5.ch013

Ferraz-Caetano, J., & Dias, D. (2021). Chemistry Edutainment. In L. C. Mihăeş, R. Andreescu, & A. Dimitriu (Eds.), *Handbook of Research on Contemporary Storytelling Methods Across New Media and Disciplines* (pp. 364–391). IGI Global., doi:10.4018/978-1-7998-6605-3.ch019

Figueiredo, C. (2020). Working to Produce Consensus. In Karlidag, S.Bulut, S. (Eds.), Handbook of Research on the Political Economy of Communications and Media (pp. 18-36). IGI Global. https://doi.org/ doi:10.4018/978-1-7998-3270-6.ch002

Figueiredo, G. V., & Neto, J. P. (2022). Digital Marketing as a Driver of Tourism. In N. Gustavo, J. Pronto, L. Carvalho, & M. Belo (Eds.), *Optimizing Digital Solutions for Hyper-Personalization in Tourism and Hospitality* (pp. 214–230). IGI Global., doi:10.4018/978-1-7998-8306-7.ch011

Filbeck, G., & Zhao, X. (2020). Supply Chain Disruptions. [IJISSCM]. *International Journal of Information Systems and Supply Chain Management, 13*(3), 78–108. doi:10.4018/IJISSCM.2020070105

Fleming, J. (2022). Why Are Finland Women Scholars Not Finnish-ing the Race Towards Science, Engineering, and Technology. In Boivin, J. A.Pacheco-Guffrey, H. (Eds.), Education as the Driving Force of Equity for the Marginalized (pp. 247-271). IGI Global. https://doi.org/ doi:10.4018/978-1-7998-8025-7.ch012

Flores, M. D. (2022). Intermedia Agenda-Setting Effect of Latino Television in the 2020 U.S. Presidential Election. In Palau-Sampio, D., López García, G.Iannelli, L. (Eds.), Contemporary Politics, Communication, and the Impact on Democracy (pp. 186-208). IGI Global. https://doi.org/ doi:10.4018/978-1-7998-8057-8.ch011

Fogel, J., & Wahba, V. (2021). Physician Rating Websites and Use or Non-Use of a Physician After Reading These Reviews. [JECO]. *Journal of Electronic Commerce in Organizations*, *19*(2), 55–73. doi:10.4018/JECO.2021040104

Forrest, J. Y., Liu, J., Martorell, G., Xu, L., & Liu, Y. (2021). Role of Manufacturing Sector in the Forthcoming National Industrial Transformations. [IJSKD]. *International Journal of Sociotechnology and Knowledge Development*, *13*(2), 153–167. doi:10.4018/IJSKD.2021040109

Fourour, S., & Lebbah, Y. (2020). Equitable Optimization for Multicast Communication. [IJDSST]. *International Journal of Decision Support System Technology*, *12*(3), 1–25. doi:10.4018/IJDSST.2020070101

Fovet, F. (2021). Using Universal Design for Learning to Create Inclusive Provisions for Indigenous Students in Higher Education. In L. N. Roberts (Ed.), *Redesigning Teaching, Leadership, and Indigenous Education in the 21st Century* (pp. 253–274). IGI Global., doi:10.4018/978-1-7998-5557-6.ch013

Fox, B. C. (2022). The New Chief Diversity Officer. In A. El-Amin (Ed.), *Implementing Diversity, Equity, Inclusion, and Belonging Management in Organizational Change Initiatives* (pp. 24–44). IGI Global., doi:10.4018/978-1-6684-4023-0.ch002

Frazier, C. J., & Bazner, K. (2022). Who Gets Tapped by Whom? In H. W. Pichon & Y. Mutakabbir (Eds.), *African American Leadership and Mentoring Through Purpose, Preparation, and Preceptors* (pp. 89–100). IGI Global., doi:10.4018/978-1-7998-8206-0.ch005

Frizzell, M. M., Brownlee, Y., & Moffett, N. L. (2021). Graduating From the School of Noranology. In Moffett, N. L. (Ed.), Navigating Post-Doctoral Career Placement, Research, and Professionalism (pp. 301-320). IGI Global. https://doi.org/ doi:10.4018/978-1-7998-5065-6.ch014

Froehlich, T. J. (2020). Ten Lessons for the Age of Disinformation. In Dalkir, K.Katz, R. (Eds.), Navigating Fake News, Alternative Facts, and Misinformation in a Post-Truth World (pp. 36-88). IGI Global. https://doi.org/ doi:10.4018/978-1-7998-2543-2.ch003

Froemming, C. Y., Fahrenbruck, M. L., & Rutledge, D. W. (2022). App Smashing to Bolster Preservice Teachers' Digital Teaching Repertoires. In C. L. Webb & A. L. Lindner (Eds.), *Preparing Pre-Service Teachers to Integrate Technology in K-12 Classrooms* (pp. 167–190). IGI Global., doi:10.4018/978-1-6684-5478-7.ch010

Frolova, N., & Frolov, E. (2021). Estimation of Securities Positioning Efficiency in Commercial Banks. In T. Škrinjarić, M. Čižmešija, & B. Christiansen (Eds.), *Recent Applications of Financial Risk Modelling and Portfolio Management* (pp. 235–256). IGI Global., doi:10.4018/978-1-7998-5083-0.ch012

Fronza, F. C., Ferrari, E. P., Ramos, D. K., Sartori, A. S., & Cardoso, F. L. (2019). Cognitive Content of Commercial Exergames. [IJGBL]. *International Journal of Game-Based Learning*, *9*(3), 23–37. doi:10.4018/IJGBL.2019070102

Gabriel, M. L. (2021). ¿Cuándo Podemos Descansar? When Can We Rest? In Rodriguez, S.Brown, K. (Eds.), Black and Brown Leadership and the Promotion of Change in an Era of Social Unrest (pp. 1-25). IGI Global. https://doi.org/ doi:10.4018/978-1-7998-7235-1.ch001

Gallavan, N. P. (2022). Delving Into Expectations, Experiences, Exploitations, and Erosion of Tenure-Track Faculty. In Huffman, S. P., Cunningham, D. D., Shavers, M.Adamson, R. (Eds.), Handbook of Research on Opening Pathways for Marginalized Individuals in Higher Education (pp. 330-352). IGI Global. https:// doi.org/ doi:10.4018/978-1-6684-3819-0.ch018

Galus, W., & Starzyk, J. (2021). *Embodiment and Phenomenal Consciousness*. IGI Global., doi:10.4018/978-1-7998-5653-5.ch002

Galvão, R., & Teixeira, A. B. (2021). Analyzing the Impact of the COVID-19 Pandemic on Value Creation. In Teixeira, N. M. & Lisboa, I. (Ed.), Handbook of Research on Financial Management During Economic Downturn and Recovery (pp. 153-173). IGI Global. https://doi.org/ doi:10.4018/978-1-7998-6643-5.ch009

Galvão, R. M. (2021). Financial Analysis and Value Creation. In Costa, T. G., Lisboa, I.Teixeira, N. M. (Eds.), Handbook of Research on Reinventing Economies and Organizations Following a Global Health Crisis (pp. 244-271). IGI Global. https:// doi.org/ doi:10.4018/978-1-7998-6926-9.ch014

Gambarato, R. R., & Medvedev, S. (2020). ICT and Transmedia Storytelling for Democratic Development in the Russian Political Landscape. In V. Kumar & G. Malhotra (Eds.), *Examining the Roles of IT and Social Media in Democratic Development and Social Change* (pp. 55–91). IGI Global., doi:10.4018/978-1-7998-1791-8.ch003

Gambrell, J. A., & Bright, A. (2022). Interrogating White Saviorism, Fragility, and Innocence in K-12 Teacher Education. In J. Keengwe (Ed.), *Handbook of Research on Social Justice and Equity in Education* (pp. 114–137). IGI Global., doi:10.4018/978-1-7998-9567-1.ch006

Gao, G., Wang, T., Zheng, X., Chen, Y., & Xu, X. (2019). A Systems Dynamics Simulation Study of Network Public Opinion Evolution Mechanism. [JGIM]. *Journal of Global Information Management, 27*(4), 189–207. doi:10.4018/JGIM.2019100110

Garrido, M. (2020). The Pitfalls and Perils of Being a Digital Journalist in Venezuela. In S. Jamil (Ed.), *Handbook of Research on Combating Threats to Media Freedom and Journalist Safety* (pp. 319–337). IGI Global., doi:10.4018/978-1-7998-1298-2.ch017

Garry, V., & Boyer, P. G. (2021). First-Year Teachers' Preparedness in Using Student Assessment Data. [IJTEPD]. *International Journal of Teacher Education and Professional Development, 4*(1), 102–114. doi:10.4018/IJTEPD.2021010107

Gates, D. (2021). Exploring Superior-Subordinate Communication From the Perspectives of African American and Latino American Subordinates. In R. D. Johnson (Ed.), *Handbook of Research on Multidisciplinary Perspectives on Managerial and Leadership Psychology* (pp. 148–166). IGI Global., doi:10.4018/978-1-7998-3811-1.ch008

Gates, Z. Y. (2022). The People v. Critical Race Theory. In J. Keengwe (Ed.), *Handbook of Research on Social Justice and Equity in Education* (pp. 138–159). IGI Global., doi:10.4018/978-1-7998-9567-1.ch007

Gbadebo, A. O. (2020). Uncommon Sources of Finance and Sustainability, Growth and Development of Small Medium-Scale Enterprises in Nigeria. In I. Oncioiu (Ed.), *Improving Business Performance Through Innovation in the Digital Economy* (pp. 200–214). IGI Global., doi:10.4018/978-1-7998-1005-6.ch014

Gersamia, M., Toradze, M., & Markariani, L. (2021). The Voice of Women and Challenges of Gender Equality in Georgian Media. In S. Jamil, B. Çoban, B. Ataman, & G. Appiah-Adjei (Eds.), *Handbook of Research on Discrimination, Gender Disparity, and Safety Risks in Journalism* (pp. 232–250). IGI Global., doi:10.4018/978-1-7998-6686-2.ch013

Gertrudix, M., Rubio-Tamayo, J. L., Wuebben, D., & Sanchez-Acedo, A. (2022). XR Journalism Lab. In A. Correia & V. Viegas (Eds.), *Methodologies and Use Cases on Extended Reality for Training and Education* (pp. 1–20). IGI Global., doi:10.4018/978-1-6684-3398-0.ch001

Getfield, J. (2022). Family Engagement in a Pandemic. In Fox, K. R.Szech, L. E. (Eds.), Handbook of Research on Family Literacy Practices and Home-School Connections (pp. 176-195). IGI Global. https://doi.org/ doi:10.4018/978-1-6684-4569-3.ch011

Gezmen, B., & Eken, I. (2019). The Periods of Crisis in the Ownership of the Media of Large Enterprises in Turkey. In H. Dinçer & S. Yüksel (Eds.), *Handbook of Research on Global Issues in Financial Communication and Investment Decision Making* (pp. 276–315). IGI Global., doi:10.4018/978-1-5225-9265-5.ch014

Ghosh, S. K. (2020). Waste Management Under the Legal Framework in India. In Pariatamby, A., Shahul Hamid, F.Bhatti, M. S. (Eds.), Sustainable Waste Management Challenges in Developing Countries (pp. 144-165). IGI Global. https://doi.org/ doi:10.4018/978-1-7998-0198-6.ch006

Gibson, A. N. (2021). Becoming an Intersectional Educator. In Wellner, L.Pierce-Friedman, K. (Eds.), Supporting Early Career Teachers With Research-Based Practices (pp. 214-231). IGI Global. https://doi.org/ doi:10.4018/978-1-7998-6803-3.ch011

Gilblom, E. A. (2022). The Shape of Educational Equity. In Neimann, T., Felix, J. J., Shliakhovchuk, E.Hindman, L. L. (Eds.), Policy and Practice Challenges for Equality in Education (pp. 172-187). IGI Global. https://doi.org/ doi:10.4018/978-1-7998-7379-2.ch008

Gilblom, E. A., & Sang, H. I. (2020). Using Geographic Information Systems in Educational Research. In E. Kennedy & Y. Qian (Eds.), *Advancing Educational Research With Emerging Technology* (pp. 173–210). IGI Global., doi:10.4018/978-1-7998-1173-2.ch009

Gkadolou, E. (2019). Spatial Organization and Semantic Modelling of Historical Data. [IJCMHS]. *International Journal of Computational Methods in Heritage Science, 3*(2), 43–57. doi:10.4018/IJCMHS.2019070103

Goker, O., & Derindere Köseoğlu, S. (2020). Challenges in Valuation by Using Discounted Free Cash Flow Method. In Köseoğlu, S. D. (Ed.), Valuation Challenges and Solutions in Contemporary Businesses (pp. 60-78). IGI Global. https://doi.org/ doi:10.4018/978-1-7998-1086-5.ch004

Golden Julie, E. (2019). Waste Management System for Smart City Using IoT. In Goyal, D., Balamurugan, S., Peng, S.Jat, D. S. (Eds.), The IoT and the Next Revolutions Automating the World (pp. 1-15). IGI Global. https://doi.org/ doi:10.4018/978-1-5225-9246-4.ch001

Grant, C. S. (2020). Rediscovering Our Original Selves. In Leggett-Robinson, P. M.Villa, B. C. (Eds.), Overcoming Barriers for Women of Color in STEM Fields (pp. 141-171). IGI Global. https://doi.org/ doi:10.4018/978-1-7998-4858-5.ch007

Grant-Smith, D., & Winter, A. (2022). The Temporal Disciplining of Doctoral Research in the Neoliberal Academy. In T. Neimann, J. J. Felix, E. Shliakhovchuk, & L. L. Hindman (Eds.), *Policy and Practice Challenges for Equality in Education* (pp. 238–258). IGI Global., doi:10.4018/978-1-7998-7379-2.ch011

Gray, J. (2022). Counseling Strategies to Disrupt the School-Prison Nexus. In K. Johns (Ed.), *Counseling Strategies for Children and Families Impacted by Incarceration* (pp. 139–158). IGI Global., doi:10.4018/978-1-7998-9209-0.ch008

Green, A. (2022). Improving Diversity in Military Medicine Through Collaborative Leadership. In A. El-Amin (Ed.), *Implementing Diversity, Equity, Inclusion, and Belonging in Educational Management Practices* (pp. 120–155). IGI Global., doi:10.4018/978-1-6684-4803-8.ch007

Green, C. (2021). *Culture, Race, and Ethnicity*. IGI Global., doi:10.4018/978-1-7998-3874-6.ch003

Groshek, J. (2020). Exploring a Methodological Model for Social Media Gatekeeping on Contentious Topics. In M. Adria (Ed.), *Using New Media for Citizen Engagement and Participation* (pp. 97–111). IGI Global., doi:10.4018/978-1-7998-1828-1.ch006

Grossman, R. C. (2020). The Gender Pay Gap in Medicine. In Bellini, M. I.Papalois, V. E. (Eds.), Gender Equity in the Medical Profession (pp. 110-127). IGI Global. https://doi.org/ doi:10.4018/978-1-5225-9599-1.ch008

Grottis, L. R. (2022). Black Women in Higher Education Leadership. In J. T. Butcher (Ed.), *Black Female Leaders in Academia* (pp. 58–72). IGI Global., doi:10.4018/978-1-7998-9774-3.ch004

Guarinos, V., & Cobo Durán, S. (2020). The Expanded Story From Transmedia as a Business Model. In V. Hernández-Santaolalla & M. Barrientos-Bueno (Eds.), *Handbook of Research on Transmedia Storytelling, Audience Engagement, and Business Strategies* (pp. 382–395). IGI Global., doi:10.4018/978-1-7998-3119-8.ch025

Guedes, M. J., Saraiva, T. M., & Felício, T. (2021). Does the Capital Structure of New Ventures Differ as a Response to a Financial Crisis? In Teixeira, N. M., & Lisboa, I. (Ed.), Handbook of Research on Financial Management During Economic Downturn and Recovery (pp. 77-93). IGI Global. https://doi.org/ doi:10.4018/978-1-7998-6643-5.ch005

Gunawardana, K. D. (2020). Success Factors of the Implementation of Crowdfunding for Start-Ups. [IJSKD]. *International Journal of Sociotechnology and Knowledge Development, 12*(4), 89–105. doi:10.4018/IJSKD.2020100106

Gunawardana, K. D. (2021). An Analysis of Financial Distress Prediction of Selected Listed Companies in Colombo Stock Exchange. [IJSKD]. *International Journal of Sociotechnology and Knowledge Development, 13*(2), 48–70. doi:10.4018/IJSKD.2021040104

Günaydin, A. D. (2021). Predicting Equity Returns in Developed Markets. In Škrinjarić, T., Čižmešija, M.Christiansen, B. (Eds.), Recent Applications of Financial Risk Modelling and Portfolio Management (pp. 68-90). IGI Global. https://doi.org/ doi:10.4018/978-1-7998-5083-0.ch004

Günaydin, R., & Yıldız, E. (2021). Determining the Motives and Behaviors of Brand Hate. In B. Christiansen & T. Škrinjarić (Eds.), *Handbook of Research on Applied AI for International Business and Marketing Applications* (pp. 474–498). IGI Global., doi:10.4018/978-1-7998-5077-9.ch023

Gunther, C. B., Cross-Denny, B., Reyes, M. M., & Provenzano, D. (2022). Framing eHealth Design on Critical Race Theory to Mitigate Barriers in Access to Healthcare. In S. R. Tamim (Ed.), *Instructional Design Exemplars in eHealth and mHealth Education Interventions* (pp. 55–74). IGI Global., doi:10.4018/978-1-7998-9490-2.ch003

Gupta, A., & Verma, M. (2022). Pandemic and Sustainability Practices. In R. K. Kovid & V. Kumar (Eds.), *Cases on Emerging Market Responses to the COVID-19 Pandemic* (pp. 259–283). IGI Global., doi:10.4018/978-1-6684-3504-5.ch013

Gupta, D., Montgomery, M. S., Eddy, C. M., Kalinec-Craig, C. A., Morton, K., Hulme, K., & Mahdi, F. (2021). Developing and Supporting Mathematics Teacher Educators Through Virtual Collaborations. In C. M. Crawford (Ed.), *Shifting to Online Learning Through Faculty Collaborative Support* (pp. 279–293). IGI Global., doi:10.4018/978-1-7998-6944-3.ch015

Gupta, R., Pal, S. K., & Muttoo, S. K. (2020). Data Analytics for Better Branding of E-Governance and E-Business Systems. In N. Vij Mali (Ed.), *Leveraging Digital Innovation for Governance, Public Administration, and Citizen Services* (pp. 51–78). IGI Global., doi:10.4018/978-1-5225-5412-7.ch003

Gürer, M. D. (2020). Pre-Service Language Teachers' Experiences in the Digital Storytelling Process. In Makewa, L. N.Ngussa, B. M. (Eds.), IT Issues in Higher Education (pp. 87-112). IGI Global. https://doi.org/ doi:10.4018/978-1-7998-1029-2.ch005

Gürer, M. D. (2020). Should Pre-Service Language Teachers Develop Digital Stories? In E. Alqurashi (Ed.), *Handbook of Research on Fostering Student Engagement With Instructional Technology in Higher Education* (pp. 429–445). IGI Global., doi:10.4018/978-1-7998-0119-1.ch023

Gürsakal, N., Ozkan, E., Yılmaz, F. M., & Oktay, D. (2020). How Should Data Science Education Be? [IJEOE]. *International Journal of Energy Optimization and Engineering*, *9*(2), 25–36. doi:10.4018/IJEOE.2020040103

Gurses, M. E., & Sahin, S. (2021). Reality Augmented Nightmares or Experiences of Fear. In M. N. Erdem, N. Kocabay-Sener, & T. Demir (Eds.), *Handbook of Research on Aestheticization of Violence, Horror, and Power* (pp. 592–620). IGI Global., doi:10.4018/978-1-7998-4655-0.ch029

Gurses, M. E., & Tugran, F. E. (2021). The Real Westworlds. In R. Yilmaz (Ed.), *Handbook of Research on Narrative Interactions* (pp. 86–105). IGI Global., doi:10.4018/978-1-7998-4903-2.ch006

Hafeez, E., & Zahid, L. (2021). Sexism and Gender Discrimination in Pakistan's Mainstream News Media. In S. Jamil, B. Çoban, B. Ataman, & G. Appiah-Adjei (Eds.), *Handbook of Research on Discrimination, Gender Disparity, and Safety Risks in Journalism* (pp. 60–89). IGI Global., doi:10.4018/978-1-7998-6686-2.ch005

Hagan, D. (2020). The Effect of Blogging on Fashion Consumption. In S. S. Dadwal (Ed.), *Handbook of Research on Innovations in Technology and Marketing for the Connected Consumer* (pp. 315–335). IGI Global., doi:10.4018/978-1-7998-0131-3.ch015

Hai-Jew, S. (2021). *Creating and Advancing Storylines for Learning With Visuals*. IGI Global., doi:10.4018/978-1-7998-3946-0.ch003

Hai-Jew, S. (2022). *"Generous" and "Stingy" Advice Sharing Among Peer Freelancers in Professional and Creative Project Work Considering Competitive Advantage*. IGI Global., doi:10.4018/978-1-7998-6496-7.ch004

Hairston, K. R. (2021). The Impact of a Pandemic on Historically Black College/ University Educators. In Hairston, K. R., Edmonds, W. M.Clark, S. P. (Eds.), The Black Experience and Navigating Higher Education Through a Virtual World (pp. 1-21). IGI Global. https://doi.org/ doi:10.4018/978-1-7998-7537-6.ch001

Hamilton, E., Cain-Sanschagrin, E., & Crawford, J. (2022). Implementing a Critical Community of Practice Within a University-Based Teacher Induction Program. In E. Cain-Sanschagrin, R. A. Filback, & J. Crawford (Eds.), *Cases on Academic Program Redesign for Greater Racial and Social Justice* (pp. 125–149). IGI Global., doi:10.4018/978-1-7998-8463-7.ch006

Hanaysha, J. R., Saleh, I., Hussain, S., Lee, K. L., & Abu Bakar, Z. (2021). Determinants of Firm Performance in Automotive Industry. [IJSSMET]. *International Journal of Service Science, Management, Engineering, and Technology, 12*(4), 132–148. doi:10.4018/IJSSMET.2021070108

Hancı-Azizoglu, E. B., & Kavaklı Ulutaş, N. (2021). Creative Digital Writing. In M. Montebello (Ed.), *Digital Pedagogies and the Transformation of Language Education* (pp. 250–266). IGI Global., doi:10.4018/978-1-7998-6745-6.ch013

Harris, D. C. (2022). Unconscious Bias Towards African American Women in the Education Workforce. In Butcher, J. T.Baker, W. C. (Eds.), Addressing Issues of Systemic Racism During Turbulent Times (pp. 23-43). IGI Global. https://doi.org/ doi:10.4018/978-1-7998-8532-0.ch002

Harris, H. R. (2021). No More War Stories. In L. S. Byrd (Ed.), *Cultivating Entrepreneurial Changemakers Through Digital Media Education* (pp. 190–207). IGI Global., doi:10.4018/978-1-7998-5808-9.ch013

Harris, K. I., Teitelbaum, A. M., & Holets, M. B. (2022). Cultivating Nourishment and Compassion for Young Children's Minds, Hearts, and Souls Using Spiritual Literacy. In Fox, K. R., & Szech, L. E. (Ed.), Handbook of Research on Family Literacy Practices and Home-School Connections (pp. 286-305). IGI Global. https:// doi.org/ doi:10.4018/978-1-6684-4569-3.ch017

Harvey, J. (2019). Deconstructing Representations of African Americans in the Media. In Hoffman-Miller, P. H., James, M.Hermond, D. (Eds.), African American Suburbanization and the Consequential Loss of Identity (pp. 20-27). IGI Global. https://doi.org/ doi:10.4018/978-1-5225-7835-2.ch002

Hatton, C. E., & Clemons, K. L. (2022). School Counselors as Social Justice Advocates. In S. N. Brant-Rajahn, E. M. Gibson, & M. Cook Sandifer (Eds.), *Developing, Delivering, and Sustaining School Counseling Practices Through a Culturally Affirming Lens* (pp. 76–96). IGI Global., doi:10.4018/978-1-7998-9514-5.ch005

He, Y., & Bagwell, D. (2022). Professional Learning in Hybrid Spaces. In B. S. Zugelder & M. L'Esperance (Eds.), *Handbook of Research on the Educator Continuum and Development of Teachers* (pp. 1–23). IGI Global., doi:10.4018/978-1-6684-3848-0.ch007

Heller, C. (2020). Bringing the Human Dimension to Virtual Experience. In Morie, J. F.McCallum, K. (Eds.), Handbook of Research on the Global Impacts and Roles of Immersive Media (pp. 158-175). IGI Global. https://doi.org/ doi:10.4018/978-1-7998-2433-6.ch009

Hemani, C. K. (2021). Demonstrating Wet Waste Composting as a Greening Society Initiative. In Karmaoui, A., Ben Salem, A.Anees, M. T. (Eds.), Handbook of Research on Environmental Education Strategies for Addressing Climate Change and Sustainability (pp. 84-115). IGI Global. https://doi.org/ doi:10.4018/978-1-7998-7512-3.ch005

Hendy, N. T. (2022). The Role of Intellectual Humility in Leadership and Promoting Workplace Diversity, Equity, Inclusion, and Belongingness. In A. El-Amin (Ed.), *Implementing Diversity, Equity, Inclusion, and Belonging Management in Organizational Change Initiatives* (pp. 81–98). IGI Global., doi:10.4018/978-1-6684-4023-0.ch005

Henning, G., & Lundquist, A. E. (2021). Centering Learners in Assessment. In A. Peck & D. DeSawal (Eds.), *Applying Design Thinking to the Measurement of Experiential Learning* (pp. 1–11). IGI Global., doi:10.4018/978-1-7998-7768-4.ch001

Heredia-Torres, M. (2020). Audience Engagement and Transmedia Adaptation. In Hernández-Santaolalla, V.Barrientos-Bueno, M. (Eds.), Handbook of Research on Transmedia Storytelling, Audience Engagement, and Business Strategies (pp. 56-75). IGI Global. https://doi.org/ doi:10.4018/978-1-7998-3119-8.ch005

Hernandez, J., Thompson, J., & Mark Brookshire, T. (2022). Post-COVID Lesson Learned. In S. Ramlall, T. Cross, & M. Love (Eds.), *Handbook of Research on Future of Work and Education* (pp. 159–174). IGI Global., doi:10.4018/978-1-7998-8275-6.ch010

Heuston, B. (2022). Pursuing Excellence and Equity in Education. In Betts, A. L.Thai, K. (Eds.), Handbook of Research on Innovative Approaches to Early Childhood Development and School Readiness (pp. 637-664). IGI Global. https://doi.org/ doi:10.4018/978-1-7998-8649-5.ch026

Hill, J. T. (2022). Reimagining HBCUs in the Future of P-20 Black Education. In Bagasra, A., Mc Letchie, A.Wesley, J. (Eds.), Contributions of Historically Black Colleges and Universities in the 21st Century (pp. 41-67). IGI Global. https://doi.org/ doi:10.4018/978-1-6684-3814-5.ch003

Hisle, N. (2022). Racial Trauma-Informed Pedagogy Strategies for Educational Professionals. In C. Bernadowski (Ed.), *Strategies and Methods for Implementing Trauma-Informed Pedagogy* (pp. 20–38). IGI Global., doi:10.4018/978-1-7998-7473-7.ch002

Hisle, N. (2022). The Intersectionality of Race and Trauma in Children and Teens Who Are Black, Indigenous, and People of Color (BIPOC). In C. Bernadowski (Ed.), *Strategies and Methods for Implementing Trauma-Informed Pedagogy* (pp. 39–64). IGI Global., doi:10.4018/978-1-7998-7473-7.ch003

Hoguane, J. J., Tavares, M. N., & Boto, S. (2020). The Use of Media Convergence in the Preservation and Dissemination of Cultural Assets. [IJCICG]. *International Journal of Creative Interfaces and Computer Graphics*, *11*(2), 16–26. doi:10.4018/IJCICG.2020070102

Holmes, Q. D., Sr. (2022). The Impact of Implicit Bias on Policing Communities of Color. In Butcher, J. T.Baker, W. C. (Eds.), Addressing Issues of Systemic Racism During Turbulent Times (pp. 224-238). IGI Global. https://doi.org/ doi:10.4018/978-1-7998-8532-0.ch014

Homza, A., & Fontno, T. J. (2021). Supporting Teacher Candidates as Social Justice Change-Makers. In D. E. Hartsfield (Ed.), *Handbook of Research on Teaching Diverse Youth Literature to Pre-Service Professionals* (pp. 398–421). IGI Global., doi:10.4018/978-1-7998-7375-4.ch020

Hood, C. (2021). Kindergarten Writing. In Onchwari, G.Keengwe, J. (Eds.), Bridging Family-Teacher Relationships for ELL and Immigrant Students (pp. 302-315). IGI Global. https://doi.org/ doi:10.4018/978-1-7998-4712-0.ch016

Horak, J., Machova, V., & Vrbka, J. (2021). Financial Management for the Successful Company Value. In Teixeira, N. M., & Lisboa, I. (Ed.), Handbook of Research on Financial Management During Economic Downturn and Recovery (pp. 126-152). IGI Global. https://doi.org/ doi:10.4018/978-1-7998-6643-5.ch008

Hornak, A. M. (2021). Designing Learning Environments That Integrate With Students' Academic Learning in a Community College Setting. In Peck, A.DeSawal, D. (Eds.), Applying Design Thinking to the Measurement of Experiential Learning (pp. 134-145). IGI Global. https://doi.org/ doi:10.4018/978-1-7998-7768-4.ch009

Horton, R. (2020). Systems-Based Approaches to Speech-Language Pathology Service Delivery for School Age Children. In D. M. Scott (Ed.), *Cases on Communication Disorders in Culturally Diverse Populations* (pp. 113–136). IGI Global., doi:10.4018/978-1-7998-2261-5.ch006

Hosen, M., Imran, M., & Chowdhury, M. A. (2021). Nexus Between Sectoral Shift and Stock Return. [IJABIM]. *International Journal of Asian Business and Information Management*, *12*(1), 75–93. doi:10.4018/IJABIM.20210101.oa5

Hossain, M. I. (2021). Effects of E-Banking Adoption on the Financial Performance of State-Owned Commercial Banks in Bangladesh. [IRMJ]. *Information Resources Management Journal*, *34*(4), 93–112. doi:10.4018/IRMJ.20211001.oa1

Howell, E., & Kelley, A. D. (2021). Bridging New Media Literacies and the Common Core Through Narrative. In L. Haas & J. Tussey (Eds.), *Connecting Disciplinary Literacy and Digital Storytelling in K-12 Education* (pp. 85–103). IGI Global., doi:10.4018/978-1-7998-5770-9.ch005

Huerta, J. O., Prybutok, G. L., & Prybutok, V. R. (2021). Using Data Science Software to Address Health Disparities. [IJBDAH]. *International Journal of Big Data and Analytics in Healthcare*, *6*(2), 45–58. doi:10.4018/IJBDAH.20210701.oa4

Humphrey, S., Ngo, T., & Wang, T. (2021). Digital Storytelling and Teachers' Disciplinary Multiliteracies. In L. Haas & J. Tussey (Eds.), *Connecting Disciplinary Literacy and Digital Storytelling in K-12 Education* (pp. 59–84). IGI Global., doi:10.4018/978-1-7998-5770-9.ch004

Humphreys, D., & Hinton, M. D. (2022). Seeking Equity, Quality, and Purpose as Higher Education Transforms. In A. M. Brower & R. J. Specht-Boardman (Eds.), *New Models of Higher Education: Unbundled, Rebundled, Customized, and DIY* (pp. 257–271). IGI Global., doi:10.4018/978-1-6684-3809-1.ch013

Hurst, B. S. (2020). Cinematic Virtual Reality. In Morie, J. F.McCallum, K. (Eds.), Handbook of Research on the Global Impacts and Roles of Immersive Media (pp. 221-236). IGI Global. https://doi.org/ doi:10.4018/978-1-7998-2433-6.ch012

Hutson, K. M. (2021). Missing Faces. In Gaines, C. B.Hutson, K. M. (Eds.), Promoting Positive Learning Experiences in Middle School Education (pp. 200-216). IGI Global. https://doi.org/ doi:10.4018/978-1-7998-7057-9.ch011

Ibrahim, A. M. (2019). Theorizing the Journalism Model of Disinformation and Hate Speech Propagation in a Nigerian Democratic Context. [IJEP]. *International Journal of E-Politics*, *10*(2), 60–73. doi:10.4018/IJEP.2019070105

Ibrahim, A. M., Pate, U. A., & Usman, A. M. (2020). Silencing the Media and Chaining the Watchdog. In S. Jamil (Ed.), *Handbook of Research on Combating Threats to Media Freedom and Journalist Safety* (pp. 214–240). IGI Global., doi:10.4018/978-1-7998-1298-2.ch012

Ibrahim, H. J., & Spikin, B. R. (2021). Female Journalists and Safety Challenges in Selected Media Organizations in Kano State, Nigeria. In S. Jamil, B. Çoban, B. Ataman, & G. Appiah-Adjei (Eds.), *Handbook of Research on Discrimination, Gender Disparity, and Safety Risks in Journalism* (pp. 366–393). IGI Global., doi:10.4018/978-1-7998-6686-2.ch019

Indira Barrón, D. (2021). *Influence of Mexicanas Americanas*. IGI Global., doi:10.4018/978-1-7998-3763-3.ch002

Inman, L. D., & Fortner, K. M. (2021). Leading for Liberation. In S. Rodriguez & K. Brown (Eds.), *Black and Brown Leadership and the Promotion of Change in an Era of Social Unrest* (pp. 26–54). IGI Global., doi:10.4018/978-1-7998-7235-1.ch002

Isika, N., Mendoza, A., & Bosua, R. (2020). An Affordance Perspective on the Enabling and Disruptive Effects of Social Media Tools on Self-Management of Chronic Illness. In K. Sandhu (Ed.), *Opportunities and Challenges in Digital Healthcare Innovation* (pp. 36–56). IGI Global., doi:10.4018/978-1-7998-3274-4.ch003

Islam, M. A., Quarmal, S. B., & Das, A. (2021). An investigation Into Risks to Mental Health of Bangladeshi Journalists. In S. Jamil, B. Çoban, B. Ataman, & G. Appiah-Adjei (Eds.), *Handbook of Research on Discrimination, Gender Disparity, and Safety Risks in Journalism* (pp. 167–193). IGI Global., doi:10.4018/978-1-7998-6686-2.ch010

İstanbullu Dinçer, F. F., & Özdemir Akgül, S. (2022). Digital Cultural Heritage. In L. Oliveira (Ed.), *Handbook of Research on Digital Communications, Internet of Things, and the Future of Cultural Tourism* (pp. 183–202). IGI Global., doi:10.4018/978-1-7998-8528-3.ch010

Iyanga-Mambo, E. (2021). Online Personal Narratives. In Mihăeş, L. C., Andreescu, R.Dimitriu, A. (Eds.), Handbook of Research on Contemporary Storytelling Methods Across New Media and Disciplines (pp. 17-39). IGI Global. https://doi.org/ doi:10.4018/978-1-7998-6605-3.ch002

Jackson, T. R. (2020). An Assessment of School Segregation and Its Impact on STEM Education. In Leggett-Robinson, P. M.Villa, B. C. (Eds.), Overcoming Barriers for Women of Color in STEM Fields (pp. 34-53). IGI Global. https://doi.org/ doi:10.4018/978-1-7998-4858-5.ch002

Jackson, T. R. (2022). The Exploration of Diversity and Inclusion Programs Within Institutions of Higher Education. In E. Meletiadou (Ed.), *Handbook of Research on Practices for Advancing Diversity and Inclusion in Higher Education* (pp. 315–332). IGI Global., doi:10.4018/978-1-7998-9628-9.ch016

Jacob, R., & Rani, D. (2020). Do Pregnant Women Using Smartphones Care About Their Privacy? [IJICTHD]. *International Journal of Information Communication Technologies and Human Development, 12*(4), 19–36. doi:10.4018/IJICTHD.2020100102

Jacobs, M., & Ellis, C. (2021). Research Methodology to Examine Disparities in Communication Disorders in Underrepresented and Vulnerable Populations. In R. Horton (Ed.), *Critical Perspectives on Social Justice in Speech-Language Pathology* (pp. 151–179). IGI Global., doi:10.4018/978-1-7998-7134-7.ch008

Jacobs, M., Jebahi, F., & Ellis, C. (2021). The Determinants of Health. In R. Horton (Ed.), *Critical Perspectives on Social Justice in Speech-Language Pathology* (pp. 39–58). IGI Global., doi:10.4018/978-1-7998-7134-7.ch003

Jamalova, M., & Constantinovits, M. (2021). The Influence of Gender on Smartphone Adoption of Young Adults in Hungary. [IJEIS]. *International Journal of Enterprise Information Systems, 17*(3), 47–65. doi:10.4018/IJEIS.2021070104

Jamil, S., & Appiah-Adjei, G. (2021). Discrimination, Gender Disparity, and Safety Risks in Journalism. In S. Jamil, B. Çoban, B. Ataman, & G. Appiah-Adjei (Eds.), *Handbook of Research on Discrimination, Gender Disparity, and Safety Risks in Journalism* (pp. 1–7). IGI Global., doi:10.4018/978-1-7998-6686-2.ch001

Jan, A., & Marimuthu, M., bin Mohd @ Mat Isa, M. P., & Shad, M. K. (2019). Bankruptcy Forecasting and Economic Sustainability Profile of the Market Leading Islamic Banking Countries. [IJABIM]. *International Journal of Asian Business and Information Management, 10*(2), 73–90. doi:10.4018/IJABIM.2019040104

Jeris, S. S. (2021). Factors Influencing Bank Profitability in a Developing Economy. [IJABIM]. *International Journal of Asian Business and Information Management, 12*(3), 333–346. doi:10.4018/IJABIM.20210701.oa20

Jimenez, C. (2019). America as Ambivalent Superpower in Recent Mexican, Australian, and Chinese Media. In F. P. Endong (Ed.), *Popular Representations of America in Non-American Media* (pp. 29–54). IGI Global., doi:10.4018/978-1-5225-9312-6.ch002

Jiménez Sánchez, Á., & Frontera Sánchez, M. R. (2020). Audiovisual Storytelling Approaches in the Marketing of Luxury Clothing Brands. In Margalina, V. & Lavín, J. M. (Ed.), Management and Inter/Intra Organizational Relationships in the Textile and Apparel Industry (pp. 263-283). IGI Global. https://doi.org/ doi:10.4018/978-1-7998-1859-5.ch012

Jobe, R. L., McCune, N. M., & Lynn, L. K. (2022). A Framework to Measure Inclusion. In McCune, N. M. (Ed.), Advancing DEI and Creating Inclusive Environments in the Online Space (pp. 153-165). IGI Global. https://doi.org/ doi:10.4018/978-1-6684-5146-5.ch010

Johnson, L., & Pierre, Y. (2021). Solving Wicked Diversity, Equity, and Inclusive Problems From a Design Thinking Lens. In A. Peck & D. DeSawal (Eds.), *Applying Design Thinking to the Measurement of Experiential Learning* (pp. 60–76). IGI Global., doi:10.4018/978-1-7998-7768-4.ch004

Johnson, N. N. (2022). Central Office Leadership. In A. El-Amin (Ed.), *Implementing Diversity, Equity, Inclusion, and Belonging in Educational Management Practices* (pp. 14–32). IGI Global., doi:10.4018/978-1-6684-4803-8.ch002

Johnson, P., & Punnett, I. (2022). *Extended Reality and the Future of Digital Advertising*. IGI Global., doi:10.4018/978-1-7998-3844-9.ch008

Johnson, P., & Punnett, I. (2022). *The History of Black Journalism Is the Future for All Journalism*. IGI Global., doi:10.4018/978-1-7998-3844-9.ch005

Johnson, P., & Punnett, I. (2022). *Imagined Futures*. IGI Global., doi:10.4018/978-1-7998-3844-9.ch002

Johnson, P., & Punnett, I. (2022). *The Future Around Journalism*. IGI Global., doi:10.4018/978-1-7998-3844-9.ch001

Johnson, P., & Punnett, I. (2022). *The Future Electronic News Media*. IGI Global., doi:10.4018/978-1-7998-3844-9.ch006

Johnson, P., & Punnett, I. (2022). *The Future Is Africa*. IGI Global., doi:10.4018/978-1-7998-3844-9.ch021

Johnson, P., & Punnett, I. (2022). *The Future of Fake News*. IGI Global., doi:10.4018/978-1-7998-3844-9.ch003

Johnson, P., & Punnett, I. (2022). *The Future of Journalism in the Robotic Age*. IGI Global., doi:10.4018/978-1-7998-3844-9.ch007

Johnson, P., & Punnett, I. (2022). *The Future of Photojournalism*. IGI Global., doi:10.4018/978-1-7998-3844-9.ch016

Johnson, P., & Punnett, I. (2022). *The Social and Technological Revolution in Sports Journalism*. IGI Global., doi:10.4018/978-1-7998-3844-9.ch009

Johnson, P., & Punnett, I. (2022). *Visual Journalism and the Future of News Consumption*. IGI Global., doi:10.4018/978-1-7998-3844-9.ch015

Johnson, V. D. (2022). Race Conflicts and Discrimination as a Challenge for Peace Leadership. In E. P. Schellhammer (Ed.), *Evolution of Peace Leadership and Practical Implications* (pp. 181–196). IGI Global., doi:10.4018/978-1-7998-9736-1.ch010

Johnson Austin, S., Walker, B. L., Moore, L. L., Holley, M. B., Wright, S. L. Sr, & Knight, L. M. (2022). "RISE" Up Reduce School Suspensions. In A. El-Amin (Ed.), *Implementing Diversity, Equity, Inclusion, and Belonging in Educational Management Practices* (pp. 156–173). IGI Global., doi:10.4018/978-1-6684-4803-8.ch008

Jones, J. L., & Jones, L. L. (2022). A Space Is a Terrible Thing to Waste. In A. El-Amin (Ed.), *Implementing Diversity, Equity, Inclusion, and Belonging Management in Organizational Change Initiatives* (pp. 234–247). IGI Global., doi:10.4018/978-1-6684-4023-0.ch013

Jones, J. R., Telinhos, A., Hughes, J. M., & Patel, S. Y. (2020). A Multiple-Choice Test for the Ages. In B. Christiansen (Ed.), *Global Applications of Multigenerational Management and Leadership in the Transcultural Era* (pp. 1–39). IGI Global., doi:10.4018/978-1-5225-9906-7.ch001

Jordan, K., Lapidus, S. M., & Ramaswamy, S. (2022). Analyzing the Role of Implicit Bias From a DisCrit Perspective. In T. Neimann, J. J. Felix, E. Shliakhovchuk, & L. L. Hindman (Eds.), *Policy and Practice Challenges for Equality in Education* (pp. 102–122). IGI Global., doi:10.4018/978-1-7998-7379-2.ch006

Jowallah, R. J. (2020). A Multilayered Approach for Addressing Poverty and Education in African American Communities. In P. W. Jones (Ed.), *Fostering Collaborations Between African American Communities and Educational Institutions* (pp. 155–172). IGI Global., doi:10.4018/978-1-7998-1181-7.ch008

Kaale, K. B., & Mgeta, M. B. (2020). Photojournalism Ethics. In O. Oyero (Ed.), *Media and Its Role in Protecting the Rights of Children in Africa* (pp. 149–168). IGI Global., doi:10.4018/978-1-7998-0329-4.ch008

Kalogeras, S. (2021). Social Entrepreneurship, Smart Brands, and Epic Social Learning Networks. In P. K. Wamuyu (Ed.), *Analyzing Global Social Media Consumption* (pp. 1–15). IGI Global., doi:10.4018/978-1-7998-4718-2.ch001

Kalogeras, S. (2021). Transmedia Storytelling Edutainment and the New Testament Lesson. In Mihăeş, L. C., Andreescu, R.Dimitriu, A. (Eds.), Handbook of Research on Contemporary Storytelling Methods Across New Media and Disciplines (pp. 392-406). IGI Global. https://doi.org/ doi:10.4018/978-1-7998-6605-3.ch020

Kalpana, A. R., Parveen, N., Singh, D. V., & Azam, Z. (2020). Generation and Management of Biomedical Waste. In Bhat, R. A., Qadri, H., Wani, K. A., Dar, G. H., & Mehmood, M. A. (Ed.), Innovative Waste Management Technologies for Sustainable Development (pp. 98-121). IGI Global. https://doi.org/ doi:10.4018/978-1-7998-0031-6.ch006

Kamine, D., & Stewart, R. (2020). Strategic Partnerships for Pre-K-12 Journalism Education. In R. F. Kronick (Ed.), *Emerging Perspectives on Community Schools and the Engaged University* (pp. 22–39). IGI Global., doi:10.4018/978-1-7998-0280-8.ch002

Kansiime, P., Said, S. J., & Eyaa, S. (2022). What Kind of Blackfella Are You Anyway? In F. Özsungur (Ed.), *Handbook of Research on Cyber Approaches to Public Administration and Social Policy* (pp. 420–443). IGI Global., doi:10.4018/978-1-6684-3380-5.ch017

Kantor, J. (2020). Discovering a Language of Stories in Immersive Storytelling. In Morie, J. F.McCallum, K. (Eds.), Handbook of Research on the Global Impacts and Roles of Immersive Media (pp. 142-157). IGI Global. https://doi.org/ doi:10.4018/978-1-7998-2433-6.ch008

Kapaniaris, A. G. (2022). Folk Culture and Cutting-Edge Technologies. In Papadakis, S.Kapaniaris, A. (Eds.), The Digital Folklore of Cyberculture and Digital Humanities (pp. 1-12). IGI Global. https://doi.org/ doi:10.4018/978-1-6684-4461-0.ch001

Karantalis, N., Koukopoulos, D., & Koutromanos, G. (2022). Digital Narrative as an Educational Tool for Cultural Heritage Teaching. In S. Papadakis & A. Kapaniaris (Eds.), *The Digital Folklore of Cyberculture and Digital Humanities* (pp. 117–141). IGI Global., doi:10.4018/978-1-6684-4461-0.ch007

Karaoglan Yilmaz, F. G., Koseoglu, B., Ayvali, C., & Ozturk, T. (2020). The Effect of Using Digital Stories in Teaching English as a Second Language. In Meri Yilan, S., & Koruyan, K. (Ed.), ICT-Based Assessment, Methods, and Programs in Tertiary Education (pp. 191-208). IGI Global. https://doi.org/ doi:10.4018/978-1-7998-3062-7.ch010

Karcı, H. D. (2021). Transmedia Storytelling in Advertising. In Tombul, I.Sarı, G. (Eds.), Handbook of Research on Contemporary Approaches to Orientalism in Media and Beyond (pp. 818-837). IGI Global. https://doi.org/ doi:10.4018/978-1-7998-7180-4.ch046

Karno, D., & Fish, L. A. (2021). Digital Nature Explorations. In J. Burris, D. Rosen, & D. Karno (Eds.), *Handbook of Research on Empowering Early Childhood Educators With Technology* (pp. 227–246). IGI Global., doi:10.4018/978-1-7998-6888-0.ch012

Kasoma, T. (2021). Ubuntu as a Springboard for Service-Learning. In Mukuni, J.Tlou, J. (Eds.), Understanding Ubuntu for Enhancing Intercultural Communications (pp. 141-155). IGI Global. https://doi.org/ doi:10.4018/978-1-7998-7947-3.ch012

Kaushal, V., Sharma, S., & Ali, N. (2019). Empirical Investigation of Relationship Among Destination Brand Equity Dimensions. [IJABIM]. *International Journal of Asian Business and Information Management, 10*(3), 74–90. doi:10.4018/IJABIM.2019070105

Kazlauskiene, V., & Draksaite, A. (2020). Green Investment Financing Instruments. In A. Kuna-Marszałek & A. Kłysik-Uryszek (Eds.), *CSR and Socially Responsible Investing Strategies in Transitioning and Emerging Economies* (pp. 189–213). IGI Global., doi:10.4018/978-1-7998-2193-9.ch010

Keiffer-Lewis, V., & Berman, J. (2022). Preparing Managers to Lead for Diversity, Equity, and Inclusion. In L. C. Carvalho, N. Teixeira, & P. Pardal (Eds.), *Interdisciplinary and Practical Approaches to Managerial Education and Training* (pp. 174–192). IGI Global., doi:10.4018/978-1-7998-8239-8.ch010

Keiffer-Lewis, V. A. (2022). Cultural Humility as a Path to Equity in Higher Education. In Cain-Sanschagrin, E., Filback, R. A.Crawford, J. (Eds.), Cases on Academic Program Redesign for Greater Racial and Social Justice (pp. 262-280). IGI Global. https://doi.org/ doi:10.4018/978-1-7998-8463-7.ch013

Keller, T. M. (2021). Story Shaping Ideology. In A. Bhusal (Ed.), *Teaching Practices and Language Ideologies for Multilingual Classrooms* (pp. 1–26). IGI Global., doi:10.4018/978-1-7998-3339-0.ch001

Keller-Bell, Y. D. (2021). Disproportionate Representation in Special Education and the Intersectionality of Race, Ethnicity, and Socioeconomic Status. In R. Horton (Ed.), *Critical Perspectives on Social Justice in Speech-Language Pathology* (pp. 1–17). IGI Global., doi:10.4018/978-1-7998-7134-7.ch001

Keller Nicol, M., & Best, S. (2022). Disability Life Writing. In R. D. Williams (Ed.), *Handbook of Research on Challenging Deficit Thinking for Exceptional Education Improvement* (pp. 329–346). IGI Global., doi:10.4018/978-1-7998-8860-4.ch015

Kelley, D. R., & Williams, M. A. (2022). A Culture of Care. In C. Ward (Ed.), *Achieving Equity in Higher Education Using Empathy as a Guiding Principle* (pp. 48–74). IGI Global., doi:10.4018/978-1-7998-9746-0.ch003

Kelly, M., & Fields, C. W. (2020). Unlocking the Doors. In C. K. Clausen & S. R. Logan (Eds.), *Integrating Social Justice Education in Teacher Preparation Programs* (pp. 1–28). IGI Global., doi:10.4018/978-1-7998-5098-4.ch001

Kew, S. N., Tan, S., Liew, T. W., & Tasir, Z. (2022). English Language Learner Pedagogical Performance and Experience Through Digital Video Production. In Zou, B., Thomas, M., Barr, D., & Jia, W. (Ed.), Emerging Concepts in Technology-Enhanced Language Teaching and Learning (pp. 111-127). IGI Global. https://doi.org/ doi:10.4018/978-1-7998-8981-6.ch006

Khan, A., & Moseki, M. (2020). Reconceptualising Migration in South Africa. In M. A. Mafukata & K. A. Tshikolomo (Eds.), *African Perspectives on Reshaping Rural Development* (pp. 233–248). IGI Global., doi:10.4018/978-1-7998-2306-3.ch011

Khan, A. R. (2020). Political Economy of the Relationship Between Crony Capitalism and the Private Television Channel Boom in Bangladesh. In Karlidag, S.Bulut, S. (Eds.), Handbook of Research on the Political Economy of Communications and Media (pp. 161-180). IGI Global. https://doi.org/ doi:10.4018/978-1-7998-3270-6.ch009

Kibet Ngetich, J. (2021). Role of Journalists in Development. In Akwala, A. O., Ngetich, J. K.Theuri, A. W. (Eds.), Dialectical Perspectives on Media, Health, and Culture in Modern Africa (pp. 137-151). IGI Global. https://doi.org/ doi:10.4018/978-1-5225-8091-1.ch008

Kibler, K. W., & de Oliveira, L. C. (2020). Professional Learning Recommendations for Teachers of Late-Entering Newcomers With Interrupted Formal Education. In L. Cardozo-Gaibisso & M. Vazquez Dominguez (Eds.), *Handbook of Research on Advancing Language Equity Practices With Immigrant Communities* (pp. 266–282). IGI Global., doi:10.4018/978-1-7998-3448-9.ch014

Kier, M., & Khalil, D. (2021). An Emerging Methodological Approach to Anti-Racist Design and Implementation. In V. Wang (Ed.), *Promoting Qualitative Research Methods for Critical Reflection and Change* (pp. 153–179). IGI Global., doi:10.4018/978-1-7998-7600-7.ch009

Kincey, S. D., Zemrani, A., & Bailey, T. L. (2022). Demystifying Diversity, Equity, and Inclusion Among Students in Higher Education. In J. T. Butcher & W. C. Baker (Eds.), *Addressing Issues of Systemic Racism During Turbulent Times* (pp. 93–104). IGI Global., doi:10.4018/978-1-7998-8532-0.ch006

Kırık, A. M., & Çetinkaya, A. (2022). The Relationship Between Digital Literacy and Cyberchondria. In H. Aker & M. Aiken (Eds.), *Handbook of Research on Cyberchondria, Health Literacy, and the Role of Media in Society's Perception of Medical Information* (pp. 298–311). IGI Global., doi:10.4018/978-1-7998-8630-3.ch016

Koirala, S. (2020). Practices of Self-Censorship Among Nepali Journalists. In S. Jamil (Ed.), *Handbook of Research on Combating Threats to Media Freedom and Journalist Safety* (pp. 72–82). IGI Global., doi:10.4018/978-1-7998-1298-2.ch005

Koku, P. S. (2022). Critical Perspectives on Diversity, Equity, and Inclusion in Marketing. In A. Gbadamosi (Ed.), *Critical Perspectives on Diversity, Equity, and Inclusion in Marketing* (pp. 142–153). IGI Global., doi:10.4018/978-1-6684-3590-8.ch008

Kolodnicki, P. A. (2019). Integrating Media Literacy Into Mathematics. In Yildiz, M. N., Fazal, M., Ahn, M., Feirsen, R.Ozdemir, S. (Eds.), Handbook of Research on Media Literacy Research and Applications Across Disciplines (pp. 27-49). IGI Global. https://doi.org/ doi:10.4018/978-1-5225-9261-7.ch003

Komla, V. K. (2020). Strategic Responses to Disruptive Digital Innovation and Their Effects in the News Media Industry. In R. Boateng (Ed.), *Handbook of Research on Managing Information Systems in Developing Economies* (pp. 532–539). IGI Global., doi:10.4018/978-1-7998-2610-1.ch027

Kong, P. A., Zhang, X., Sachdev, A., Dzotsenidze, N., & Yu, X. (2021). Racial Socialization and Multicultural Education of Asian Families in the United States. In R. K. Gordon, K. Ahmed, & M. Hosoda (Eds.), *Evolving Multicultural Education for Global Classrooms* (pp. 40–67). IGI Global., doi:10.4018/978-1-7998-7649-6.ch003

Koş, F. C., & Gasseloğlu, M. A. (2021). Responsive Tectonics. In E. Garip & S. Garip (Eds.), *Handbook of Research on Methodologies for Design and Production Practices in Interior Architecture* (pp. 440–465). IGI Global., doi:10.4018/978-1-7998-7254-2.ch021

Kramer, B. N. (2020). Teaching Diversity in the Utah Bubble. In Clausen, C. K.Logan, S. R. (Eds.), Integrating Social Justice Education in Teacher Preparation Programs (pp. 165-184). IGI Global. https://doi.org/ doi:10.4018/978-1-7998-5098-4.ch008

Krishnamurthy, S., Fudurich, G., & Rao, P. (2019). Circular Economy for India. In Ferreira, A., Marques, R., Azevedo, G., Inácio, H., & Santos, C. (Ed.), Modernization and Accountability in the Social Economy Sector (pp. 272-298). IGI Global. https:// doi.org/ doi:10.4018/978-1-5225-8482-7.ch015

Krsmanovic, M. (2022). "Outsiders" Hurting From Within. In Huffman, S. P., Cunningham, D. D., Shavers, M.Adamson, R. (Eds.), Handbook of Research on Opening Pathways for Marginalized Individuals in Higher Education (pp. 210-224). IGI Global. https://doi.org/ doi:10.4018/978-1-6684-3819-0.ch012

Kuchirko, Y., & Nayfeld, I. (2020). Language Gap. In C. Huertas-Abril & M. E. Gómez-Parra (Eds.), *International Approaches to Bridging the Language Gap* (pp. 32–53). IGI Global., doi:10.4018/978-1-7998-1219-7.ch003

Küçükkambak, S. E. (2022). Creating Brand Experience Based on Brand Equity in Tourism Destinations. In G. Akel (Ed.), *Handbook of Research on Interdisciplinary Reflections of Contemporary Experiential Marketing Practices* (pp. 121–141). IGI Global., doi:10.4018/978-1-6684-4380-4.ch007

Kuehn, C. (2020). College-Going and College-Staying Capital. In Berg, G. A.Venis, L. (Eds.), Accessibility and Diversity in the 21st Century University (pp. 68-98). IGI Global. https://doi.org/ doi:10.4018/978-1-7998-2783-2.ch004

Kumar, J. D., & Sriram, A. (2019). The Role of Information and Communication Technologies in Family Dynamics. [IJICTHD]. *International Journal of Information Communication Technologies and Human Development*, *11*(3), 1–20. doi:10.4018/ IJICTHD.2019070101

Kumar, P., Paul, A., & Kumar, M. A. (2021). Risk Optimisation Analytics. [IJSESD]. *International Journal of Social Ecology and Sustainable Development*, *12*(2), 48–62. doi:10.4018/IJSESD.2021040103

Kundu, P., & Bhuiyan, M. M. (2021). Online Harassment of Female Journalists in Bangladesh. In S. Jamil, B. Çoban, B. Ataman, & G. Appiah-Adjei (Eds.), *Handbook of Research on Discrimination, Gender Disparity, and Safety Risks in Journalism* (pp. 143–166). IGI Global., doi:10.4018/978-1-7998-6686-2.ch009

Kupatadze, K. (2020). Ecological Chemistry Through Popular Scientific Articles. In Duca, G.Vaseashta, A. (Eds.), Handbook of Research on Emerging Developments and Environmental Impacts of Ecological Chemistry (pp. 531-542). IGI Global. https://doi.org/ doi:10.4018/978-1-7998-1241-8.ch025

Kurchenko, L. (2022). Invisible Barriers, Undeclared Wars. In Neimann, T., Felix, J. J., Shliakhovchuk, E.Hindman, L. L. (Eds.), Policy and Practice Challenges for Equality in Education (pp. 1-23). IGI Global. https://doi.org/ doi:10.4018/978-1-7998-7379-2.ch001

Kwende, M. F., Bourgeois, J. W., Henderson, H., & Scott, J. (2022). Separate and Still Unequal. In A. T. Adams (Ed.), *Approaching Disparities in School Discipline* (pp. 136–165). IGI Global., doi:10.4018/978-1-6684-3359-1.ch006

Kyriakides, L., & Charalambous, E. (2021). Establishing Links Between Teacher Effectiveness Research and Research on Teacher Improvement. In L. W. Grant, J. H. Stronge, & X. Xu (Eds.), *International Beliefs and Practices That Characterize Teacher Effectiveness* (pp. 85–124). IGI Global., doi:10.4018/978-1-7998-7908-4.ch004

L. Guo-BrennanM. Guo-Brennan (2022). *Advancing Equity and Inclusion in Internationalization*. IGI Global. https://doi.org/ doi:10.4018/978-1-6684-4528-0.ch005

Labeeb, H. A. (2022). How Could Egyptian Young Adults Detect False Information About COVID-19 on Social Media Platforms? In Abdrabo, A. A.Galaby, A. A. (Eds.), Societal Resilience and Response to Contagious Diseases and Pandemics (pp. 155-177). IGI Global. https://doi.org/ doi:10.4018/978-1-7998-8973-1.ch008

Lachman, R., & Joffe, M. (2021). Applications of Artificial Intelligence in Media and Entertainment. In T. H. Musiolik & A. D. Cheok (Eds.), *Analyzing Future Applications of AI, Sensors, and Robotics in Society* (pp. 201–220). IGI Global., doi:10.4018/978-1-7998-3499-1.ch012

Lalas, J. W., & Strikwerda, H. L. (2020). Driving Equity in Action Through a Socially and Culturally Situated Pedagogy. In P. D. Keough (Ed.), *Overcoming Current Challenges in the P-12 Teaching Profession* (pp. 291–315). IGI Global., doi:10.4018/978-1-7998-1177-0.ch013

Lambert, R., Greene, Q., & Lai, V. (2022). DeleteDeficitThinking. In R. D. Williams (Ed.), *Handbook of Research on Challenging Deficit Thinking for Exceptional Education Improvement* (pp. 127–143). IGI Global., doi:10.4018/978-1-7998-8860-4.ch006

Lamonaca, S. (2021). Journalism and Communication at School in Order to Form Critical Citizens. In Panconesi, G.Guida, M. (Eds.), Handbook of Research on Teaching With Virtual Environments and AI (pp. 210-235). IGI Global. https://doi.org/ doi:10.4018/978-1-7998-7638-0.ch010

Lamphere, R. D., & Pomykacz, C. R. (2022). Love and Discrimination. In T. R. Flockhart, A. Reiter, & M. R. Hassett (Eds.), *The Reproduction and Maintenance of Inequalities in Interpersonal Relationships* (pp. 23–46). IGI Global., doi:10.4018/978-1-6684-4128-2.ch002

Lampprecht, T., Salb, D., Mauser, M., van de Wetering, H., Burch, M., & Kloos, U. (2020). Visual Classification of Formula One Races by Events, Drivers, and Time Periods. In M. Sarfraz (Ed.), *Advancements in Computer Vision Applications in Intelligent Systems and Multimedia Technologies* (pp. 101–114). IGI Global., doi:10.4018/978-1-7998-4444-0.ch006

Lane, C. (2019). Digitizing Learning. In Sein-Echaluce, M. L., Fidalgo-Blanco, Á.García-Peñalvo, F. (Eds.), Innovative Trends in Flipped Teaching and Adaptive Learning (pp. 138-161). IGI Global. https://doi.org/ doi:10.4018/978-1-5225-8142-0.ch007

Lantz, J. L., Myers, J., & Wilson, R. (2020). Digital Storytelling and Young Children. In P. M. Sullivan, J. L. Lantz, & B. A. Sullivan (Eds.), *Handbook of Research on Integrating Digital Technology With Literacy Pedagogies* (pp. 212–231). IGI Global., doi:10.4018/978-1-7998-0246-4.ch010

Lasisi, J. O. (2022). Structural Integration Theory as Underpinning for Discourse of Diversity, Equity, and Inclusion. In Raimi, L.Kah, J. M. (Eds.), Mainstreaming Diversity, Equity, and Inclusion as Future Workplace Ethics (pp. 182-199). IGI Global. https://doi.org/ doi:10.4018/978-1-6684-3657-8.ch009

Lattimer, H., & Pizarro, M. (2021). Building a Framework for Transformation in Higher Education. In C. Reneau & M. Villarreal (Eds.), *Handbook of Research on Leading Higher Education Transformation With Social Justice, Equity, and Inclusion* (pp. 71–88). IGI Global., doi:10.4018/978-1-7998-7152-1.ch006

Latunde, C. Y. (2022). Toward the Promise. In Cain-Sanschagrin, E., Filback, R. A.Crawford, J. (Eds.), Cases on Academic Program Redesign for Greater Racial and Social Justice (pp. 176-189). IGI Global. https://doi.org/ doi:10.4018/978-1-7998-8463-7.ch008

Laughlin, T. (2021). A Vision for Deeper Agency and Personalization in Micro-Credentials. In Northrup, P., Rasmussen, K.Colson, R. (Eds.), Career Ready Education Through Experiential Learning (pp. 19-45). IGI Global. https://doi.org/ doi:10.4018/978-1-7998-1928-8.ch002

Lauritzen, J. (2021). Culturally Responsive Instruction as Computer-Based Reading Engagement and Literacy Among Native American Students. In R. Throne (Ed.), *Indigenous Research of Land, Self, and Spirit* (pp. 82–101). IGI Global., doi:10.4018/978-1-7998-3729-9.ch006

Lawa, K. O. (2020). Challenges and Opportunities for News Media and Journalism in an Increasingly Digital Mobile. In Suki, N. M.Suki, N. M. (Eds.), Leveraging Consumer Behavior and Psychology in the Digital Economy (pp. 46-59). IGI Global. https://doi.org/ doi:10.4018/978-1-7998-3042-9.ch003

Lawrence, S. A., Labissiere, T., & Stone, M. C. (2021). The 4Cs of Academic Language and Literacy. In M. L. Niess & H. Gillow-Wiles (Eds.), *Handbook of Research on Transforming Teachers' Online Pedagogical Reasoning for Engaging K-12 Students in Virtual Learning* (pp. 297–316). IGI Global., doi:10.4018/978-1-7998-7222-1.ch015

Lawton, P. H. (2021). Re-Discovering Graphics. In Bobick, B.DiCindio, C. (Eds.), Engaging Communities Through Civic Engagement in Art Museum Education (pp. 97-125). IGI Global. https://doi.org/ doi:10.4018/978-1-7998-7426-3.ch005

Le Rossignol, K. (2022). Digital Storyworlds. In C. Lane (Ed.), *Handbook of Research on Acquiring 21st Century Literacy Skills Through Game-Based Learning* (pp. 302–319). IGI Global., doi:10.4018/978-1-7998-7271-9.ch016

Leandros, N., & Papadopoulou, L. (2020). Strategic Business Models in Times of Transformational Change and Crisis. [JMME]. *Journal of Media Management and Entrepreneurship*, *2*(1), 28–41. doi:10.4018/JMME.2020010102

Lebedeva, N. A. (2022). Media Development Trends as a Counter for Terrorism in Ukraine. In Ismayil, E.Karadogan Ismayil, E. (Eds.), Media and Terrorism in the 21st Century (pp. 124-143). IGI Global. https://doi.org/ doi:10.4018/978-1-7998-9755-2.ch008

Lederer, M., & Riedl, J. (2020). Data Science Techniques in Knowledge-Intensive Business Processes. [IJDA]. *International Journal of Data Analytics*, *1*(1), 52–67. doi:10.4018/IJDA.2020010104

Lee, C. (2022). Using Multicultural Children's Literature to Leverage Student Cultural Competence and Promote Social Justice. In J. Keengwe (Ed.), *Handbook of Research on Social Justice and Equity in Education* (pp. 223–241). IGI Global., doi:10.4018/978-1-7998-9567-1.ch011

Leeson, S., & Kovid, R. K. (2023). Resurgence of Crowdfunding During the Corona Pandemic. In W. J. Aloulou (Ed.), *Handbook of Research on Entrepreneurship and Organizational Resilience During Unprecedented Times* (pp. 352–368). IGI Global., doi:10.4018/978-1-6684-4605-8.ch016

Leggett-Robinson, P. M. (2020). Celebrating Transformations Through STEM Storytelling. In Leggett-Robinson, P. M.Villa, B. C. (Eds.), Overcoming Barriers for Women of Color in STEM Fields (pp. 54-81). IGI Global. https://doi.org/ doi:10.4018/978-1-7998-4858-5.ch003

Lehner, E., & Ziegler, J. R. (2019). Re-Conceptualizing Race in New York City's High School Social Studies Classrooms. In S. Wisdom, L. Leavitt, & C. Bice (Eds.), *Handbook of Research on Social Inequality and Education* (pp. 24–45). IGI Global., doi:10.4018/978-1-5225-9108-5.ch002

Leija, M. G., & Fránquiz, M. E. (2021). Building Bridges Between School and Home. In G. Onchwari & J. Keengwe (Eds.), *Bridging Family-Teacher Relationships for ELL and Immigrant Students* (pp. 100–121). IGI Global., doi:10.4018/978-1-7998-4712-0.ch006

Lekic-Subasic, Z. (2021). Women and Media. In Jamil, S., Çoban, B., Ataman, B.Appiah-Adjei, G. (Eds.), Handbook of Research on Discrimination, Gender Disparity, and Safety Risks in Journalism (pp. 8-23). IGI Global. https://doi.org/ doi:10.4018/978-1-7998-6686-2.ch002

Leonard, B. (2020). Virtual eXperience as a Mass Market Phenomenon. In Morie, J. F.McCallum, K. (Eds.), Handbook of Research on the Global Impacts and Roles of Immersive Media (pp. 200-220). IGI Global. https://doi.org/ doi:10.4018/978-1-7998-2433-6.ch011

Leonard, L. J. (2023). An Analysis of Biases in US Policing and Subsequent Media Coverage in Response to the Ferguson Shooting of 2014. In L. J. Leonard (Ed.), *Cases on Crimes, Investigations, and Media Coverage* (pp. 169–191). IGI Global., doi:10.4018/978-1-7998-9668-5.ch009

Levay, K., Scheib, C., & Grossman, T. (2022). Effects of Racial and Ethnic Matching of Teacher Candidates of Color With Mentors. In B. S. Zugelder & M. L'Esperance (Eds.), *Handbook of Research on the Educator Continuum and Development of Teachers* (pp. 99–119). IGI Global., doi:10.4018/978-1-6684-3848-0.ch006

Lever, M. W., & Elliot, S. (2022). Show Me a Story. In A. Campos & S. Almeida (Eds.), *Global Perspectives on Strategic Storytelling in Destination Marketing* (pp. 230–245). IGI Global., doi:10.4018/978-1-6684-3436-9.ch012

Lewis, D. R. (2022). Examining the Deficit Narrative. In R. D. Williams (Ed.), *Handbook of Research on Challenging Deficit Thinking for Exceptional Education Improvement* (pp. 347–367). IGI Global., doi:10.4018/978-1-7998-8860-4.ch016

Li, M., & Akoto, M. (2021). Review of Recent Research on L2 Digital Multimodal Composing. [IJCALLT]. *International Journal of Computer-Assisted Language Learning and Teaching, 11*(3), 1–16. doi:10.4018/IJCALLT.2021070101

Liao, Y. K., Truong, G. N., & Nguyen, P. M. (2020). Psychological and Relational Moderators for the Relationship Between Brand Equity and Its Consequences. [JECO]. *Journal of Electronic Commerce in Organizations, 18*(4), 93–116. doi:10.4018/JECO.2020100105

Lim, Y. J., & Lemanski, J. (2021). Individual Journalistic Bias Leads to Public Propaganda. In L. Shedletsky (Ed.), *Rationalist Bias in Communication Theory* (pp. 140–154). IGI Global., doi:10.4018/978-1-7998-7439-3.ch008

Lima, A. M., Teixeira, S. F., & Barbosa, B. (2022). Newspaper Digital Content During and After the Silly Season. In J. Remondes & S. Teixeira (Eds.), *Implementing Automation Initiatives in Companies to Create Better-Connected Experiences* (pp. 215–232). IGI Global., doi:10.4018/978-1-6684-5538-8.ch010

Lin, A., Hardee, S. C., & Bowen, J. (2021). Educating Otherwise. In D. E. Hartsfield (Ed.), *Handbook of Research on Teaching Diverse Youth Literature to Pre-Service Professionals* (pp. 593–613). IGI Global., doi:10.4018/978-1-7998-7375-4.ch029

Little, C., Patterson, D., Skavronskaya, L., Moyle, B., & Bec, A. (2022). Digital Storytelling and 3D Technologies for Visitor Experience and Contested Heritage Preservation. In A. Campos & S. Almeida (Eds.), *Global Perspectives on Strategic Storytelling in Destination Marketing* (pp. 215–229). IGI Global., doi:10.4018/978-1-6684-3436-9.ch011

Liu, P. (2021). Information Dissemination Mechanism Based on Cloud Computing Cross-Media Public Opinion Network Environment. [IJITSA]. *International Journal of Information Technologies and Systems Approach, 14*(2), 70–83. doi:10.4018/IJITSA.2021070105

Liu, Z., & Chen, Y. (2020). Valuation Method of Equity Incentives of Listed Companies Based on the Black-Scholes Model. [IJISSS]. *International Journal of Information Systems in the Service Sector, 12*(2), 36–49. doi:10.4018/IJISSS.2020040103

Logan, S. R. (2022). Teaching While Black, Oh and a Woman. In Logan, S. R.Good, T. L. (Eds.), Black Women Navigating Historically White Higher Education Institutions and the Journey Toward Liberation (pp. 137-160). IGI Global. https://doi.org/ doi:10.4018/978-1-6684-4626-3.ch007

Lohani, S. N. (2021). Increasing Access to and Success in Higher Education and the Role of Ethical Leadership. In A. Bhusal (Ed.), *Teaching Practices and Language Ideologies for Multilingual Classrooms* (pp. 151–169). IGI Global., doi:10.4018/978-1-7998-3339-0.ch009

Lomidze, M., & Janashia, A. (2022). The Social Potential of Media Literacy and Ways to Implement. In Alaverdov, E. & Bari, M. (Ed.), Regulating Human Rights, Social Security, and Socio-Economic Structures in a Global Perspective (pp. 45-62). IGI Global. https://doi.org/ doi:10.4018/978-1-6684-4620-1.ch004

López, A. C. (2022). Aprendizaje Colectivo en Tiempos de la Pandemia. In Shinas, V. H., Ly, C. N.Ozden, S. Y. (Eds.), Cases on Practical Applications for Remote, Hybrid, and Hyflex Teaching (pp. 88-99). IGI Global. https://doi.org/ doi:10.4018/978-1-7998-9168-0.ch005

Lopez, M. M., Newman, T., & Day, C. M. (2021). Community Cultural Wealth. In T. S. Jenkins (Ed.), *Reshaping Graduate Education Through Innovation and Experiential Learning* (pp. 82–103). IGI Global., doi:10.4018/978-1-7998-4836-3.ch005

Lopez, P. D., & Duran, A. (2021). The Role of Mentoring on the Retention of Women From Diverse Backgrounds in STEM. In C. Hughes (Ed.), *Implementation Strategies for Improving Diversity in Organizations* (pp. 271–310). IGI Global., doi:10.4018/978-1-7998-4745-8.ch010

Lopez-Cantos, F. (2021). Scientific Image Forgery, Journalism, and Public Communication of Science. [IJSKD]. *International Journal of Sociotechnology and Knowledge Development*, *13*(3), 95–105. doi:10.4018/IJSKD.2021070106

López-Paredes, M., & Carrillo-Andrade, A. (2022). Legitimation by Digital Discourses. In M. Carrillo-Durán & M. Pérez Pulido (Eds.), *Cases on Developing Effective Research Plans for Communications and Information Science* (pp. 235–250). IGI Global., doi:10.4018/978-1-6684-4523-5.ch012

Loranc-Paszylk, B., & Firla, M. (2019). Engaging Students With Authentic Ways to Learn New Words. In C. A. Lenkaitis & S. M. Hilliker (Eds.), *Engaging Teacher Candidates and Language Learners With Authentic Practice* (pp. 90–102). IGI Global., doi:10.4018/978-1-5225-8543-5.ch006

Lukas, T. (2021). Performance Aspirations and Corporate Tax Avoidance. [IJCFA]. *International Journal of Corporate Finance and Accounting*, *8*(2), 40–58. doi:10.4018/IJCFA.2021070104

Lundquist, A. E., & Henning, G. (2020). From Avoiding Bias to Social Justice. In A. D. Spicer-Runnels & T. E. Simpson (Eds.), *Developing an Intercultural Responsive Leadership Style for Faculty and Administrators* (pp. 47–61). IGI Global., doi:10.4018/978-1-7998-4108-1.ch004

Lundquist, F. (2022). Give and Take, the Love and Hate Relationship. In Logan, S. R.Good, T. L. (Eds.), Black Women Navigating Historically White Higher Education Institutions and the Journey Toward Liberation (pp. 192-228). IGI Global. https://doi.org/ doi:10.4018/978-1-6684-4626-3.ch010

Ly, C. N., & Soutter, M. (2022). Technological Pedagogical Content Knowledge Framework as a Lens for Transformative Social and Emotional Learning Online. In V. H. Shinas, C. N. Ly, & S. Y. Ozden (Eds.), *Cases on Practical Applications for Remote, Hybrid, and Hyflex Teaching* (pp. 71–87). IGI Global., doi:10.4018/978-1-7998-9168-0.ch004

Lynch, E. (2021). Sex, Scholarship, and Service. In Etim, A. S.Etim, J. (Eds.), Overcoming Challenges and Barriers for Women in Business and Education (pp. 162-185). IGI Global. https://doi.org/ doi:10.4018/978-1-7998-3814-2.ch009

Lyons, N., & Smith, M. (2021). From Overlay to Interplay. In L. C. Mihăeş, R. Andreescu, & A. Dimitriu (Eds.), *Handbook of Research on Contemporary Storytelling Methods Across New Media and Disciplines* (pp. 200–223). IGI Global., doi:10.4018/978-1-7998-6605-3.ch011

Lypka, A. E., & De Felice, D. (2020). Telecollaborative Storytelling. In G. Neokleous, A. Krulatz, & R. Farrelly (Eds.), *Handbook of Research on Cultivating Literacy in Diverse and Multilingual Classrooms* (pp. 146–165). IGI Global., doi:10.4018/978-1-7998-2722-1.ch008

Magyar, C. K. (2022). Addressing "Another" in the Aftermath of School Shootings Using Dance and Rhetoric. In G. A. Crews (Ed.), *Impact of School Shootings on Classroom Culture, Curriculum, and Learning* (pp. 89–112). IGI Global., doi:10.4018/978-1-7998-5200-1.ch006

Maher, D. (2020). Pre-Service Teachers' Digital Competencies to Support School Students' Digital Literacies. In Keengwe, J.Onchwari, G. (Eds.), Handbook of Research on Literacy and Digital Technology Integration in Teacher Education (pp. 29-46). IGI Global. https://doi.org/ doi:10.4018/978-1-7998-1461-0.ch002

Mahmood, F. (2020). Combating Bullets With a Pen. In S. Jamil (Ed.), *Handbook of Research on Combating Threats to Media Freedom and Journalist Safety* (pp. 54–71). IGI Global., doi:10.4018/978-1-7998-1298-2.ch004

Maiti, A., & Jana, S. K. (2022). Diversity and Equity in Higher Education. In E. Meletiadou (Ed.), *Handbook of Research on Practices for Advancing Diversity and Inclusion in Higher Education* (pp. 263–280). IGI Global., doi:10.4018/978-1-7998-9628-9.ch013

Majumdar, S. (2022). Recreating "Home" in Exile. In Pourya Asl, M. (Eds.), Gender, Place, and Identity of South Asian Women (pp. 252-274). IGI Global. https://doi.org/ doi:10.4018/978-1-6684-3626-4.ch013

Makarova, N. S. (2020). Trade-Off Between Intergenerational Equity and Economic Growth. In M. Ziolo (Ed.), *Social, Economic, and Environmental Impacts Between Sustainable Financial Systems and Financial Markets* (pp. 201–230). IGI Global., doi:10.4018/978-1-7998-1033-9.ch010

Makhado, M. P., & Tshisikhawe, T. R. (2021). How Apartheid Education Encouraged and Reinforced Tribalism and Xenophobia in South Africa. In M. A. Mafukata (Ed.), *Impact of Immigration and Xenophobia on Development in Africa* (pp. 131–151). IGI Global., doi:10.4018/978-1-7998-7099-9.ch008

Malegiannaki, I., Daradoumis, T., & Retalis, S. (2021). Using a Story-Driven Board Game to Engage Students and Adults With Cultural Heritage. [IJGBL]. *International Journal of Game-Based Learning*, *11*(2), 1–19. doi:10.4018/IJGBL.2021040101

Malerba, R. C., Fernandes, C. I., & Veiga, P. (2020). What Do We Know About Destination Branding? In S. J. Teixeira & J. M. Ferreira (Eds.), *Multilevel Approach to Competitiveness in the Global Tourism Industry* (pp. 211–228). IGI Global., doi:10.4018/978-1-7998-0365-2.ch013

Mallawaarachchi, C. (2019). Significant Influences of Digital Literacy to Promote Gender Equity and Equality in Education. In Bala, S.Singhal, P. (Eds.), Gender Issues in Technical and Vocational Education Programs (pp. 218-234). IGI Global. https://doi.org/ doi:10.4018/978-1-5225-8443-8.ch011

Manzone, J. A., & Nyberg, J. L. (2021). Instruction Expanded. In D. AuCoin (Ed.), *Building Integrated Collaborative Relationships for Inclusive Learning Settings* (pp. 240–265). IGI Global., doi:10.4018/978-1-7998-6816-3.ch010

Manzone, J. A., & Nyberg, J. L. (2021). Instruction-Expanded Virtual Education Model. In J. D. Herron & T. Douglas (Eds.), *Strategies for Student Support During a Global Crisis* (pp. 48–70). IGI Global., doi:10.4018/978-1-7998-7000-5.ch004

Manzone, J. A., & Nyberg, J. L. (2022). Constructing Culturally-Authentic Differentiated Access Points Using the Content Imperatives. In J. L. Nyberg & J. A. Manzone (Eds.), *Creating Equitable Services for the Gifted* (pp. 171–188). IGI Global., doi:10.4018/978-1-7998-8153-7.ch012

Manzone, J. A., & Nyberg, J. L. (2022). Creating Culturally Sustainable Literacy Experiences Through Home and Community Connections. In L. Haas & J. T. Tussey (Eds.), *Disciplinary Literacy as a Support for Culturally and Linguistically Responsive Teaching and Learning* (pp. 15–40). IGI Global., doi:10.4018/978-1-6684-4215-9.ch002

Marasco, A., Nicolais, F., Acampa, G., & Balbi, B. (2022). Cinematic Storytelling with Virtual Reality for Cultural Heritage Marketing and Accessibility. In A. Campos & S. Almeida (Eds.), *Global Perspectives on Strategic Storytelling in Destination Marketing* (pp. 193–214). IGI Global., doi:10.4018/978-1-6684-3436-9.ch010

Marks, R., & Vickland, C. (2021). Expanding Equity and Access in State-Authorized Charter Schools. In A. J. Griffen (Ed.), *Challenges to Integrating Diversity, Equity, and Inclusion Programs in Organizations* (pp. 42–61). IGI Global., doi:10.4018/978-1-7998-4093-0.ch004

Marone, F., & Pozzuoli, C. (2022). The Museum of Children. In F. Bifulco & M. Tregua (Eds.), *Handbook of Research on Museum Management in the Digital Era* (pp. 312–330). IGI Global., doi:10.4018/978-1-7998-9656-2.ch017

Marques, M. I., & Heitor, J. C. (2022). Social Media as Storytelling Destination Communication Channels. In A. Campos & S. Almeida (Eds.), *Global Perspectives on Strategic Storytelling in Destination Marketing* (pp. 246–261). IGI Global., doi:10.4018/978-1-6684-3436-9.ch013

Martin, C. S. (2022). Mathematical Literacy Writing and Equity in the Mathematics Classroom. In T. S. Hodges (Ed.), *Handbook of Research on Writing Instruction Practices for Equitable and Effective Teaching* (pp. 272–290). IGI Global., doi:10.4018/978-1-6684-3745-2.ch014

Martin, F. C., II. (2022). Sites of Immanent Social Critique. In Bagasra, A., Mc Letchie, A.Wesley, J. (Eds.), Contributions of Historically Black Colleges and Universities in the 21st Century (pp. 221-238). IGI Global. https://doi.org/ doi:10.4018/978-1-6684-3814-5.ch011

Martin-Neira, J., Domínguez, M. T., & Olvera-Lobo, M. (2022). Digital Journalism and Transmedia Narratives in the Communication of Science. In R. Pettinger, B. B. Gupta, A. Roja, & D. Cozmiuc (Eds.), *Handbook of Research on Digital Transformation Management and Tools* (pp. 531–555). IGI Global., doi:10.4018/978-1-7998-9764-4.ch024

Marzano, G. (2022). *Creativity and Autism Spectrum Disorder.* IGI Global., doi:10.4018/978-1-7998-7840-7.ch009

Masenya, T. M. (2022). Digital Preservation of Indigenous Knowledge in South African Rural Communities. In Tshifhumulo, R.Makhanikhe, T. J. (Eds.), Handbook of Research on Protecting and Managing Global Indigenous Knowledge Systems (pp. 317-340). IGI Global. https://doi.org/ doi:10.4018/978-1-7998-7492-8.ch017

Matey, C. (2021). Heeding the Call of America's Youth. In D. E. Hartsfield (Ed.), *Handbook of Research on Teaching Diverse Youth Literature to Pre-Service Professionals* (pp. 68–85). IGI Global., doi:10.4018/978-1-7998-7375-4.ch004

Matsumoto, K., Hirotani, M., & Fukada, A. (2020). Examining Oral Performance Characteristics of L2 Learners With the CAF Calculator. In A. Andujar (Ed.), *Recent Tools for Computer- and Mobile-Assisted Foreign Language Learning* (pp. 132–148). IGI Global., doi:10.4018/978-1-7998-1097-1.ch006

Mayeaux, A. S., Barber, A., & Adams, M. S. (2022). Supporting the Habits and Practices of Teacher Expertise Development. In B. S. Zugelder & M. L'Esperance (Eds.), *Handbook of Research on the Educator Continuum and Development of Teachers* (pp. 430–452). IGI Global., doi:10.4018/978-1-6684-3848-0.ch021

Mayo-Cubero, M. (2021). Social Media and Digital Information Sources in News Coverage of Crisis, Disaster, and Emergency Situations. In Oliveira, L., Tajariol, F.Gonçalves, L. B. (Eds.), Digital Services in Crisis, Disaster, and Emergency Situations (pp. 268-281). IGI Global. https://doi.org/ doi:10.4018/978-1-7998-6705-0.ch012

Mayowa, A. S. (2020). Development of a 2D Digital Animation for Yorùbá Folktale Narrative. [IJACDT]. *International Journal of Art, Culture, Design, and Technology, 9*(1), 47–61. doi:10.4018/IJACDT.2020010104

McCallum, K. M. (2020). Immersive Experience. In Morie, J. F.McCallum, K. (Eds.), Handbook of Research on the Global Impacts and Roles of Immersive Media (pp. 453-484). IGI Global. https://doi.org/ doi:10.4018/978-1-7998-2433-6.ch022

McCune, N. M. (2022). Equity in the Online Space? In McCune, N. M. (Eds.), Advancing DEI and Creating Inclusive Environments in the Online Space (pp. 248-266). IGI Global. https://doi.org/ doi:10.4018/978-1-6684-5146-5.ch015

McCune, N. M., & Schulz, W. C., III. (2022). The Social Determinants of Changemakers. In McCune, N. M. (Ed.), Advancing DEI and Creating Inclusive Environments in the Online Space (pp. 268-280). IGI Global. https://doi.org/ doi:10.4018/978-1-6684-5146-5.ch016

McElhone, D., & Yeigh, M. J. (2022). Disrupting the Deficit-Gaze. In von Hohenberg, S. C. (Ed.), Dispositional Development and Assessment in Teacher Preparation Programs (pp. 167-185). IGI Global. https://doi.org/ doi:10.4018/978-1-6684-4089-6.ch009

Md Husin, M., & Haron, R. (2020). Financial Sustainability of SMEs Through Islamic Crowdfunding. In A. Rafay (Ed.), *Handbook of Research on Theory and Practice of Global Islamic Finance* (pp. 321–337). IGI Global., doi:10.4018/978-1-7998-0218-1.ch018

Mehmood, M. (2020). Finance in the Hospitality Industry. In Pius, A., Alharahsheh, H. H.Adesanmi, A. A. (Eds.), Contemporary Management Approaches to the Global Hospitality and Tourism Industry (pp. 185-212). IGI Global. https://doi.org/ doi:10.4018/978-1-7998-2204-2.ch011

Meletiadou, E. (2022). Profiling the Writing Competency of BAME Undergraduate Students. In E. Meletiadou (Ed.), *Handbook of Research on Practices for Advancing Diversity and Inclusion in Higher Education* (pp. 20–48). IGI Global., doi:10.4018/978-1-7998-9628-9.ch002

Mendoza, P., Cardenas Riaño, F. E., Hoyos Ensuncho, M., & Reina Zambrano, J. (2021). The Case of the International Research Center for the Development of Education (CIIDE). In G. Malfatti (Ed.), *People-Centered Approaches Toward the Internationalization of Higher Education* (pp. 234–253). IGI Global., doi:10.4018/978-1-7998-3796-1.ch012

Mendoza-Reis, N., Louque, A., & Lu, M. (2021). The Resilient Women of Color Leaders. In S. Rodriguez & K. Brown (Eds.), *Black and Brown Leadership and the Promotion of Change in an Era of Social Unrest* (pp. 55–75). IGI Global., doi:10.4018/978-1-7998-7235-1.ch003

Merkovity, N. (2019). A Possible Framework for Attention-Based Politics. [IJEP]. *International Journal of E-Politics, 10*(2), 13–23. doi:10.4018/IJEP.2019070102

Miller, O. P., & Banks-Hall, R. L. (2019). Parental Involvement in Education. In P. H. Hoffman-Miller, M. James, & D. Hermond (Eds.), *African American Suburbanization and the Consequential Loss of Identity* (pp. 116–140). IGI Global., doi:10.4018/978-1-5225-7835-2.ch007

Min, E. J. (2022). Equitable Assessment Practices. In Crawford, J.Filback, R. A. (Eds.), TESOL Guide for Critical Praxis in Teaching, Inquiry, and Advocacy (pp. 65-86). IGI Global. https://doi.org/ doi:10.4018/978-1-7998-8093-6.ch004

Mohamad Saleh, M. S., Heinrichs, H., & Nik Hasan, N. N. (2021). Role of Images in Constructing Public Opinion About Environmental Matters in Malaysia. [IJSESD]. *International Journal of Social Ecology and Sustainable Development, 12*(1), 115–130. doi:10.4018/IJSESD.2021010109

Mohamed, H., & Lamia, M. (2020). Efficacy of the Flipped Classroom to Teach the Digital Storytelling Process. In Soares, F., Lopes, A. P., Brown, K. & Uukkivi, A. (Ed.), Developing Technology Mediation in Learning Environments (pp. 57-77). IGI Global. https://doi.org/ doi:10.4018/978-1-7998-1591-4.ch004

Mokha, A. K. (2021). Brand Equity, Brand Satisfaction, and Brand Loyalty. [IJOM]. *International Journal of Online Marketing, 11*(3), 34–50. doi:10.4018/IJOM.2021070103

Mokuria, V. G., & Chhikara, A. (2022). Narrative Inquiry as a Relational Methodology. In Watson, S. W., Austin, S. & Bell, J. (Ed.), Conceptual Analyses of Curriculum Inquiry Methodologies (pp. 1-27). IGI Global. https://doi.org/ doi:10.4018/978-1-7998-8848-2.ch001

Monstad, T. H., & Burman, S. (2020). Digital Transformations Carried Out Through Games. In M. Helmefalk & L. Marcusson (Eds.), *Utilizing Gamification in Servicescapes for Improved Consumer Engagement* (pp. 119–147). IGI Global., doi:10.4018/978-1-7998-1970-7.ch005

Montejo, G. A., & Frazier, A. E. (2020). Assessing Quality of Life Across Mexico City Using Socio-Economic and Environmental Factors. [IJAGR]. *International Journal of Applied Geospatial Research, 11*(3), 68–86. doi:10.4018/IJAGR.2020070105

Morales, A. R., & Raible, J. (2021). To Teach as We Are Known. In K. Sprott, J. R. O'Connor Jr, & C. Msengi (Eds.), *Designing Culturally Competent Programming for PK-20 Classrooms* (pp. 79–97). IGI Global., doi:10.4018/978-1-7998-3652-0.ch005

Moreno-Albarracín, B. (2022). Brand Storytelling in Christmas Commercials of Large Supermarket Chains. In Carrillo-Durán, M.Pérez Pulido, M. (Eds.), Cases on Developing Effective Research Plans for Communications and Information Science (pp. 215-234). IGI Global. https://doi.org/ doi:10.4018/978-1-6684-4523-5.ch011

Morgan, R., Fortner, K. M., & Tang, K. (2021). Challenges Experienced by Women of Color in Educational Leadership. In S. Rodriguez & K. Brown (Eds.), *Black and Brown Leadership and the Promotion of Change in an Era of Social Unrest* (pp. 76–100). IGI Global., doi:10.4018/978-1-7998-7235-1.ch004

Morikawa-Zhou, M. (2022). Chimamanda Ngozi Adichie. In Goodman Hayward, P., Rehman, S.Yan, Z. (Eds.), Women Community Leaders and Their Impact as Global Changemakers (pp. 115-119). IGI Global. https://doi.org/ doi:10.4018/978-1-6684-2490-2.ch020

Morim, A. C., Inácio, H., & Vieira, E. (2020). The Implementation of Internal Control in the Financial Services Expenditure in a Hospital Department. In G. Azevedo, J. Oliveira, R. Marques, & A. Ferreira (Eds.), *Tools, Strategies, and Practices for Modern and Accountable Public Sector Management* (pp. 290–323). IGI Global., doi:10.4018/978-1-7998-1385-9.ch011

Morrison, J. A., & Kim, J. (2020). Resisting the "Tyranny of an Expert". In A. S. Zimmerman (Ed.), *Preparing Students for Community-Engaged Scholarship in Higher Education* (pp. 43–60). IGI Global., doi:10.4018/978-1-7998-2208-0.ch003

Mosca, F., Kitchen, P. J., & Chiaudano, V. (2021). Investigating the Impact of Luxury Brands' Traditional and Digital Contents on Customer-Based Brand Equity. In F. Mosca, C. Casalegno, & R. Gallo (Eds.), *Developing Successful Global Strategies for Marketing Luxury Brands* (pp. 81–100). IGI Global., doi:10.4018/978-1-7998-5882-9.ch005

Mossberger, K., & Tolbert, C. J. (2021). Digital Citizenship and Digital Communities. [IJEPR]. *International Journal of E-Planning Research, 10*(3), 19–34. doi:10.4018/IJEPR.20210701.oa2

Moye, S. (2022). Monitor and Adjust. In Logan, S. R.Good, T. L. (Eds.), Black Women Navigating Historically White Higher Education Institutions and the Journey Toward Liberation (pp. 25-50). IGI Global. https://doi.org/ doi:10.4018/978-1-6684-4626-3.ch002

Moyo, O. N. (2020). Examining Oppressions as a Way of Valuing Diversity. In J. Keengwe (Ed.), *Handbook of Research on Diversity and Social Justice in Higher Education* (pp. 55–77). IGI Global., doi:10.4018/978-1-7998-5268-1.ch004

Mudau, T. S. (2021). Community Engagement as a Strategy to Facilitate the Immigrant-Local Cohesion. In M. A. Mafukata (Ed.), *Impact of Immigration and Xenophobia on Development in Africa* (pp. 261–274). IGI Global., doi:10.4018/978-1-7998-7099-9.ch015

Mukba, G. (2022). Therapeutic Storytelling. In Yılmaz, R.Koç, B. (Eds.), Narrative Theory and Therapy in the Post-Truth Era (pp. 191-210). IGI Global. https://doi.org/ doi:10.4018/978-1-7998-9251-9.ch013

Muñoz-Muñoz, E. R., Love, M., McCollum, M. C., Cruz, R. A., Umaña, D., & Nance, C. R. (2022). Mind the Gatekeepers. In Colón, G., & Alsace, T. O. (Ed.), Bilingual Special Education for the 21st Century (pp. 1-24). IGI Global. https://doi.org/ doi:10.4018/978-1-7998-9043-0.ch001

Mupenzi, A. (2022). Navigating the Australian Education System Refugees and New Arrivals. In Smith, C.Zhou, G. (Eds.), Handbook of Research on Teaching Strategies for Culturally and Linguistically Diverse International Students (pp. 265-287). IGI Global. https://doi.org/ doi:10.4018/978-1-7998-8921-2.ch014

Murray-Everett, N. C., & Schroeder, S. (2021). Fostering Inclusive Communities Through Children's Literature. In D. E. Hartsfield (Ed.), *Handbook of Research on Teaching Diverse Youth Literature to Pre-Service Professionals* (pp. 566–592). IGI Global., doi:10.4018/978-1-7998-7375-4.ch028

Musingafi, M., Mafumbate, R., & Khumalo, T. (2021). *Feminist Perspectives on the Self.* IGI Global., doi:10.4018/978-1-7998-4090-9.ch011

Musingafi, M., Mafumbate, R., & Khumalo, T. (2021). *Gender Inequality Theories of Feminism.* IGI Global., doi:10.4018/978-1-7998-4090-9.ch007

Nabb, K. A. (2022). Using the Five Practices to Promote Active and Equitable Learning Environments. In Kartal, O., Popovic, G.Morrissey, S. (Eds.), Global Perspectives and Practices for Reform-Based Mathematics Teaching (pp. 293-322). IGI Global. https://doi.org/ doi:10.4018/978-1-7998-9422-3.ch014

Naglieri, J. A., & Lansdowne, K. A. (2022). Equitable Assessment of Gifted Students Using the Naglieri General Ability Tests. In J. L. Nyberg & J. A. Manzone (Eds.), *Creating Equitable Services for the Gifted* (pp. 58–76). IGI Global., doi:10.4018/978-1-7998-8153-7.ch005

Nakae, K. (2021). Incompatible Discrepancy Between Low Proficiency of Arabic Language and Its High Status and Prestige. In A. Wang (Ed.), *Redefining the Role of Language in a Globalized World* (pp. 54–70). IGI Global., doi:10.4018/978-1-7998-2831-0.ch004

Nakamura, J. (2021). Effect of External Activate Factors Serving as Clue. In Ogata, T.Ono, J. (Eds.), Bridging the Gap Between AI, Cognitive Science, and Narratology With Narrative Generation (pp. 338-362). IGI Global. https://doi.org/ doi:10.4018/978-1-7998-4864-6.ch011

Navas, C., Tisi, V., & Close, T. (2021). Grassroots Organization and Justice Through Social Media. In R. Horton (Ed.), *Critical Perspectives on Social Justice in Speech-Language Pathology* (pp. 262–284). IGI Global., doi:10.4018/978-1-7998-7134-7.ch013

Negrão, C. S., & Brito, J. A. (2021). An Empirical Study on the Determinants of Success of Crowdfunding Projects. In C. S. Negrão & J. F. Brito (Eds.), *Multidisciplinary Approaches to Crowdfunding Platforms* (pp. 1–20). IGI Global., doi:10.4018/978-1-7998-3226-3.ch001

Nerren, J. B. (2022). Could There Be an AutCrit? In J. B. Nerren (Ed.), *Rethinking Perception and Centering the Voices of Unique Individuals* (pp. 234–251). IGI Global., doi:10.4018/978-1-6684-5103-8.ch012

Neu, J., & Cox, N. B. (2022). Racism in the United States. In G. D. Luurs (Ed.), *Handbook of Research on Communication Strategies for Taboo Topics* (pp. 86–103). IGI Global., doi:10.4018/978-1-7998-9125-3.ch005

Newman, P. (2021). The Room Is Crooked AF. In Rodriguez, S.Brown, K. (Eds.), Black and Brown Leadership and the Promotion of Change in an Era of Social Unrest (pp. 124-148). IGI Global. https://doi.org/ doi:10.4018/978-1-7998-7235-1.ch006

Ng, G., Cheuk, H., Singh, S., & Sharma, B. (2022). Artificial Intelligence as Virtual Inspector for Construction Waste Dumping. In A. Vaseashta, G. Duca, & S. Travin (Eds.), *Handbook of Research on Water Sciences and Society* (pp. 673–686). IGI Global., doi:10.4018/978-1-7998-7356-3.ch031

Nickkar, A., Shin, H., & Farkas, Z. A. (2020). A Spatial Analysis of Commuting Patterns of Electric Vehicle Drivers. [IJSVST]. *International Journal of Smart Vehicles and Smart Transportation*, *3*(1), 42–59. doi:10.4018/IJSVST.2020010103

Nicolaou, C. (2021). Development of Business Through the Internet and Social Media. In El-Gohary, H., Edwards, D.Ben Mimoun, M. (Eds.), Handbook of Research on IoT, Digital Transformation, and the Future of Global Marketing (pp. 193-211). IGI Global. https://doi.org/ doi:10.4018/978-1-7998-7192-7.ch012

Nicolaou, C. (2022). Information and Communications Technologies Through Technology-Enhanced Learning in Adult Education. In Krishnan, C., Al-Harthy, F. N.Singh, G. (Eds.), Technology Training for Educators From Past to Present (pp. 73-94). IGI Global. https://doi.org/ doi:10.4018/978-1-6684-4083-4.ch004

Niyonzima, D., & Bhuju, K. (2021). The Role of Community Radio in Promoting Gender Equality in Rwanda. In S. Jamil, B. Çoban, B. Ataman, & G. Appiah-Adjei (Eds.), *Handbook of Research on Discrimination, Gender Disparity, and Safety Risks in Journalism* (pp. 343–365). IGI Global., doi:10.4018/978-1-7998-6686-2.ch018

Njuguna, J., & Jjuuko, M. (2020). Online Behaviour as Predictive of Professional Online Work Readiness Among Mass Communication Students. [IJICTHD]. *International Journal of Information Communication Technologies and Human Development*, *12*(2), 48–61. doi:10.4018/IJICTHD.2020040104

Nobel, M. M. (2022). Challenging Deficit Thinking in Our Schools. In R. D. Williams (Ed.), *Handbook of Research on Challenging Deficit Thinking for Exceptional Education Improvement* (pp. 27–64). IGI Global., doi:10.4018/978-1-7998-8860-4.ch002

Nordgren, R. D., & Persson, H. (2020). An Examination of Growth of Publicly-Funded Private Schools in the U.S. and Sweden. In P. D. Keough (Ed.), *Overcoming Current Challenges in the P-12 Teaching Profession* (pp. 247–267). IGI Global., doi:10.4018/978-1-7998-1177-0.ch011

Novak, A. M. (2022). Not White Saviors, but Critical Scholars. In Nyberg, J. L.Manzone, J. A. (Eds.), Creating Equitable Services for the Gifted (pp. 246-262). IGI Global. https://doi.org/ doi:10.4018/978-1-7998-8153-7.ch016

Nunes, C., & Oliveira, N. D. (2022). Developing Communication and Inclusive Literacy Skills Among Children With Profound Intellectual and Multiple Disabilities. In Almeida, A. P. & Esteves, S. (Ed.), Modern Reading Practices and Collaboration Between Schools, Family, and Community (pp. 125-154). IGI Global. https://doi.org/ doi:10.4018/978-1-7998-9750-7.ch006

Nure, G. (2020). Cost Efficiency Analysis in the Banking Industry. [IJCFA]. *International Journal of Corporate Finance and Accounting*, *7*(2), 1–20. doi:10.4018/IJCFA.2020070101

Nurse, S. (2022). Why "Race Neutral" Policy Fails Black Small Business Owners. In Rolle, J. D.Crump, M. (Eds.), Sustainability and the Future of Work and Entrepreneurship for the Underserved (pp. 111-130). IGI Global. https://doi.org/ doi:10.4018/978-1-6684-4322-4.ch006

Oakes, R., Oakeley, A. K., & Goke-Pariola, R. (2021). The Victimization and Disparate Treatment of Racial and Ethnic Minorities. In R. Blasdell, L. Krieger-Sample, & M. Kilburn (Eds.), *Invisible Victims and the Pursuit of Justice* (pp. 353–382). IGI Global., doi:10.4018/978-1-7998-7348-8.ch015

Obialo, F. (2022). Entrepreneurs out of Necessity in the Developing Context. In Raimi, L.Kah, J. M. (Eds.), Mainstreaming Diversity, Equity, and Inclusion as Future Workplace Ethics (pp. 219-242). IGI Global. https://doi.org/ doi:10.4018/978-1-6684-3657-8.ch011

Obuaku-Igwe, C. (2021). Medical Sociology and Storytelling in a Decolonial Context. In Mihăeş, L. C., Andreescu, R.Dimitriu, A. (Eds.), Handbook of Research on Contemporary Storytelling Methods Across New Media and Disciplines (pp. 342-363). IGI Global. https://doi.org/ doi:10.4018/978-1-7998-6605-3.ch018

Oke, I. A., Salihu, L., Mohammed, I. D., & Afolabi, A. M. (2021). Overview of Solid Waste Management of Healthcare and Related Organisations. In Khosrow-Pour D.B.A., M. (Ed.), Encyclopedia of Information Science and Technology, Fifth Edition (pp. 1336-1352). IGI Global. https://doi.org/ doi:10.4018/978-1-7998-3479-3.ch091

Okocha, D. O., & Ola-Akuma, R. O. (2022). Participatory Communication and Digital Media in Africa. In D. O. Okocha, M. J. Onobe, & M. N. Alike (Eds.), *Handbook of Research on Connecting Philosophy, Media, and Development in Developing Countries* (pp. 149–171). IGI Global., doi:10.4018/978-1-6684-4107-7.ch011

Okon, B. (2022). The Media and Development in an Era of Digitalized Economy. In Okocha, D. O., Onobe, M. J.Alike, M. N. (Eds.), Handbook of Research on Connecting Philosophy, Media, and Development in Developing Countries (pp. 50-68). IGI Global. https://doi.org/ doi:10.4018/978-1-6684-4107-7.ch005

Okwudili, U. M., & Kazaure, J. S. (2020). Digital Activism and Digital Revolution in Objective Journalism. [IJICST]. *International Journal of Interactive Communication Systems and Technologies, 10*(2), 39–56. doi:10.4018/IJICST.2020070104

Oliveira, N. A., Gabrielli, C., Santos, G. N., & Borges, L. A. (2022). Intersectionality Between Racism and Sexism in the Brazilian Airline Industry. In P. Cembranel, J. R. Soares, & A. R. Perinotto (Eds.), *Promoting Social and Cultural Equity in the Tourism Sector* (pp. 155–176). IGI Global., doi:10.4018/978-1-6684-4194-7.ch009

Omotosho, B. J. (2020). Interrogating Social Negotiations Within Online Discussion Platforms in Nigeria. [IJCBPL]. *International Journal of Cyber Behavior, Psychology and Learning, 10*(1), 32–40. doi:10.4018/IJCBPL.2020010103

Oni, O., & Mahlangu, P. S. (2021). Promoting Entrepreneurship Education Through Valuation of Cost of Equity. In A. O. Ayandibu (Ed.), *Reshaping Entrepreneurship Education With Strategy and Innovation* (pp. 321–347). IGI Global., doi:10.4018/978-1-7998-3171-6.ch015

Onyebadi, U. T., Bland, D., Howard, H., & Walcott, C. (2020). Issues in Academic Leadership. In U. T. Onyebadi (Ed.), *Multidisciplinary Issues Surrounding African Diasporas* (pp. 220–244). IGI Global., doi:10.4018/978-1-5225-5079-2.ch010

Onyebadi, U. T., Satti, M. A., & Mbunyuza-Memani, L. (2020). Diversity and the Media. In U. T. Onyebadi (Ed.), *Multidisciplinary Issues Surrounding African Diasporas* (pp. 54–79). IGI Global., doi:10.4018/978-1-5225-5079-2.ch003

Oralkan, A. (2021). Narrative Advertising in Destination Branding. In R. Yilmaz (Ed.), *Handbook of Research on Narrative Interactions* (pp. 346–358). IGI Global., doi:10.4018/978-1-7998-4903-2.ch020

Owa, O. A. (2022). Mainstreaming Diversity, Equity, and Inclusion as Future Workplace Ethics. In Raimi, L.Kah, J. M. (Eds.), Mainstreaming Diversity, Equity, and Inclusion as Future Workplace Ethics (pp. 28-48). IGI Global. https://doi.org/ doi:10.4018/978-1-6684-3657-8.ch002

Ozgen, O., & Turkoglu, E. (2019). Popular Culture and Communication Ethics. In O. Ozgen (Ed.), *Handbook of Research on Consumption, Media, and Popular Culture in the Global Age* (pp. 36–56). IGI Global., doi:10.4018/978-1-5225-8491-9.ch003

Ozturk, E. (2020). The Political Economy of Urban Transformation. In Karlidag, S.Bulut, S. (Eds.), Handbook of Research on the Political Economy of Communications and Media (pp. 322-338). IGI Global. https://doi.org/ doi:10.4018/978-1-7998-3270-6.ch018

Page, L. (2022). Implicit Perceptions and Explicit Messages. In Tussey, J.Haas, L. (Eds.), Poverty Impacts on Literacy Education (pp. 130-148). IGI Global. https://doi.org/ doi:10.4018/978-1-7998-8730-0.ch007

Palmer, J. E., Morgan, J. W., Hinojosa, S., Olomi, J. M., Ayala, L., & Rosay, A. B. (2022). Anti-Racist and Intersectional Approaches in Social Science and Community-Based Research. In R. Throne (Ed.), *Social Justice Research Methods for Doctoral Research* (pp. 222–243). IGI Global., doi:10.4018/978-1-7998-8479-8.ch011

Panagiotidis, K., Maniou, T. A., & Veglis, A. (2020). Selfie Journalism and Politics. In Y. Ibrahim (Ed.), *Handbook of Research on Recent Developments in Internet Activism and Political Participation* (pp. 16–32). IGI Global., doi:10.4018/978-1-7998-4796-0.ch002

Paneva-Marinova, D., Goynov, M., Luchev, D., Pavlova, L., Márkus, Z. L., Veres, M., Weisz, Z., Szántó, G., & Szkaliczki, T. (2022). Studying Thracian Civilization Through Serious Games and Storytelling. In O. Bernardes, V. Amorim, & A. C. Moreira (Eds.), *Handbook of Research on Cross-Disciplinary Uses of Gamification in Organizations* (pp. 445–466). IGI Global., doi:10.4018/978-1-7998-9223-6.ch021

Pant, L. D. (2021). Gender Mainstreaming in the Media. In Jamil, S., Çoban, B., Ataman, B.Appiah-Adjei, G. (Eds.), Handbook of Research on Discrimination, Gender Disparity, and Safety Risks in Journalism (pp. 194-210). IGI Global. https://doi.org/ doi:10.4018/978-1-7998-6686-2.ch011

Papadopoulou, L., & Maniou, T. A. (2021). Digital Media and New Forms of Journalism. In Khosrow-Pour D.B.A., M. (Ed.), Encyclopedia of Information Science and Technology, Fifth Edition (pp. 1130-1139). IGI Global. https://doi.org/ doi:10.4018/978-1-7998-3479-3.ch078

Papathanasiou, S., Koutsokostas, D., Balios, D., & Eriotis, N. (2019). Winemaking Sector in Greece. [IJCFA]. *International Journal of Corporate Finance and Accounting*, *6*(2), 1–17. doi:10.4018/IJCFA.2019070101

Parahakaran, S. (2022). Digital Ethnography Within Indigenous Contexts. In Chowdhury, J. S., Wahab, H. A., Saad, R. M., Roy, P. K.Wronka, J. (Eds.), Practices, Challenges, and Prospects of Digital Ethnography as a Multidisciplinary Method (pp. 138-147). IGI Global. https://doi.org/ doi:10.4018/978-1-6684-4190-9.ch010

Parahita, G. D., & Ahmad, N. (2020). What Dampen the Indonesian Journalists' Freedom and Safety in the Post-Soeharto New Order? In S. Jamil (Ed.), *Handbook of Research on Combating Threats to Media Freedom and Journalist Safety* (pp. 83–105). IGI Global., doi:10.4018/978-1-7998-1298-2.ch006

Parente, F., & Pessoa, L. F. (2021). Special Education in Brazil. In A. Singh, C. J. Yeh, S. Blanchard, & L. Anunciação (Eds.), *Handbook of Research on Critical Issues in Special Education for School Rehabilitation Practices* (pp. 126–142). IGI Global., doi:10.4018/978-1-7998-7630-4.ch007

Parham, C. R., Wake, D. G., West, S., & Maxwell, C. D. (2022). Influence Faculty Members' Thinking to Promote Social Justice and Equity. In S. P. Huffman, D. D. Cunningham, M. Shavers, & R. Adamson (Eds.), *Handbook of Research on Opening Pathways for Marginalized Individuals in Higher Education* (pp. 288–309). IGI Global., doi:10.4018/978-1-6684-3819-0.ch016

Park, G., & Xu, Z. (2020). Spatial and Temporal Dynamics of Social Vulnerability in the United States from 1970 to 2010. [IJAGR]. *International Journal of Applied Geospatial Research*, *11*(1), 36–54. doi:10.4018/IJAGR.2020010103

Parveen, N., Singh, D. V., & Azam, R. (2020). Innovations in Recycling for Sustainable Management of Solid Wastes. In R. A. Bhat, H. Qadri, K. A. Wani, G. H. Dar, & M. A. Mehmood (Eds.), *Innovative Waste Management Technologies for Sustainable Development* (pp. 177–210). IGI Global., doi:10.4018/978-1-7998-0031-6.ch010

Pate, U. A., & Dauda, S. (2020). Threats to Media Freedom and the Safety of Journalists in Nigeria. In S. Jamil (Ed.), *Handbook of Research on Combating Threats to Media Freedom and Journalist Safety* (pp. 241–256). IGI Global., doi:10.4018/978-1-7998-1298-2.ch013

Pătrăşcanu, K. (2021). The Viewer-Participant Performing Morality in Interactive Storytelling in Bandersnatch. In Mihăeş, L. C., Andreescu, R.Dimitriu, A. (Eds.), Handbook of Research on Contemporary Storytelling Methods Across New Media and Disciplines (pp. 241-257). IGI Global. https://doi.org/ doi:10.4018/978-1-7998-6605-3.ch013

Pavlič, J., & Tomažič, T. (2020). 360° Video as an Opportunity for the Inclusion of Product Placement. In V. Hernández-Santaolalla & M. Barrientos-Bueno (Eds.), *Handbook of Research on Transmedia Storytelling, Audience Engagement, and Business Strategies* (pp. 188–214). IGI Global., doi:10.4018/978-1-7998-3119-8.ch014

Pellicelli, A. C., & Franzé, C. (2021). The Impact of Customer Education on the Perception of Made in Italy Products in the Agri-Food Sector. [IJABE]. *International Journal of Applied Behavioral Economics, 10*(2), 35–52. doi:10.4018/IJABE.2021040103

Pembecioğlu, N., & Gündüz, U. (2021). The Difference Between the Western Reflections of Disaster News and Orientalist Perspectives. In Tombul, I. & Sarı, G. (Ed.), Handbook of Research on Contemporary Approaches to Orientalism in Media and Beyond (pp. 145-164). IGI Global. https://doi.org/ doi:10.4018/978-1-7998-7180-4.ch009

Peneda de Oliveira, C., & Sousa, B. M. (2020). Green Consumer Behavior and Its Implications on Brand Marketing Strategy. In V. Naidoo & R. Verma (Eds.), *Green Marketing as a Positive Driver Toward Business Sustainability* (pp. 69–95). IGI Global., doi:10.4018/978-1-5225-9558-8.ch004

Pereira, E. T., & Salaris, S. (2019). The Evolution of the Role of Women in Labor Markets in Developed Economies. In E. T. Pereira & P. Paoloni (Eds.), *Handbook of Research on Women in Management and the Global Labor Market* (pp. 1–20). IGI Global., doi:10.4018/978-1-5225-9171-9.ch001

Pereira, S. M., & Ferreira, R. N. (2022). Beyond the Corporate Digital Newsroom 2.0. In J. G. Andrade & T. Ruão (Eds.), *Navigating Digital Communication and Challenges for Organizations* (pp. 131–152). IGI Global., doi:10.4018/978-1-7998-9790-3.ch008

Perreault, G. P., & Perreault, M. F. (2021). eSports as a News Specialty Gold Rush. In Andrews, S. & Crawford, C. M. (Ed.), Handbook of Research on Pathways and Opportunities Into the Business of Esports (pp. 303-320). IGI Global. https://doi.org/ doi:10.4018/978-1-7998-7300-6.ch014

Perumandla, S., & Kurisetti, P. (2020). An Empirical Investigation on Equity Market Integration of ASEAN-India. In P. Ordoñez de Pablos, X. Zhang, & K. Chui (Eds.), *Innovative Management and Business Practices in Asia* (pp. 29–57). IGI Global., doi:10.4018/978-1-7998-1566-2.ch002

Perumandla, S., & Kurisetti, P. (2021). Commodity Transaction Tax (CTT). [IJABIM]. *International Journal of Asian Business and Information Management, 12*(2), 16–36. doi:10.4018/ijabim.20210401.oa2

Phillips, B., Hale, M., & Michael, T. (2022). Promoting Campus Wellness Through the Lens of Mental Health Counselors. In C. J. Alexander & A. Tureen (Eds.), *Leadership Wellness and Mental Health Concerns in Higher Education* (pp. 61–88). IGI Global., doi:10.4018/978-1-7998-7693-9.ch004

Pilipenko, A. I., Pilipenko, Z. A., & Pilipenko, O. I. (2022). Patterns of Self-Sufficient Companies' Network Interaction Reorganization Due to COVID-19. In A. Pego (Ed.), *Handbook of Research on Digital Innovation and Networking in Post-COVID-19 Organizations* (pp. 36–67). IGI Global., doi:10.4018/978-1-6684-6762-6.ch003

Pimentel, L. M., & Jorge, S. M. (2019). Earnings Quality and Firm Valuation. In J. D. Oliveira, G. M. Azevedo, & A. D. Ferreira (Eds.), *International Financial Reporting Standards and New Directions in Earnings Management* (pp. 1–31). IGI Global., doi:10.4018/978-1-5225-7817-8.ch001

Pınar, M., & Girard, T. (2020). Comparing Private Label Brand Equity Dimensions of the Same Store. In Y. Arslan (Ed.), *Improving Marketing Strategies for Private Label Products* (pp. 61–82). IGI Global., doi:10.4018/978-1-7998-0257-0.ch004

Placide, V., & Vance, M. M. (2022). Supporting Diversity and Inclusiveness Amid a Changing Academic Landscape. In C. R. Ford & K. B. Garza (Eds.), *Handbook of Research on Updating and Innovating Health Professions Education* (pp. 1–23). IGI Global., doi:10.4018/978-1-7998-7623-6.ch001

Polly, D. (2021). Advancing Equity-Based Mathematics Teaching in the Primary Grades. [IJTEPD]. *International Journal of Teacher Education and Professional Development, 4*(1), 68–88. doi:10.4018/IJTEPD.2021010105

Polly, D., Colonnese, M., Bacak, J., Holshouser, K. O., & Lewis, W. (2022). Promoting Equity in Elementary School Mathematics. In E. K. Reeves & C. J. McIntyre (Eds.), *Multidisciplinary Perspectives on Diversity and Equity in a Virtual World* (pp. 213–232). IGI Global., doi:10.4018/978-1-7998-8028-8.ch012

Porter, T. (2022). Mismatched Students, Missed Opportunities. In R. D. Williams (Ed.), *Handbook of Research on Challenging Deficit Thinking for Exceptional Education Improvement* (pp. 299–328). IGI Global., doi:10.4018/978-1-7998-8860-4.ch014

Powell, A. M. (2022). The Negative Impact of Racial Microaggressions on College Students of Color. In Butcher, J. T.Baker, W. C. (Eds.), Addressing Issues of Systemic Racism During Turbulent Times (pp. 157-169). IGI Global. https://doi.org/ doi:10.4018/978-1-7998-8532-0.ch010

Powell Baker, D., & Cassar, L. (2022). Mentorship of Pre-Health Professional Students. In R. Ganjoo & L. S. Schwartz (Eds.), *Handbook of Research on Developing Competencies for Pre-Health Professional Students, Advisors, and Programs* (pp. 152–173). IGI Global., doi:10.4018/978-1-6684-5969-0.ch008

Premat, C. E. (2020). Hacktivism and Alternative Journalism. In Khosrow-Pour D.B.A., M. (Eds.), Encyclopedia of Criminal Activities and the Deep Web (pp. 347-361). IGI Global. https://doi.org/ doi:10.4018/978-1-5225-9715-5.ch023

Privette, C. (2021). Critical Race Theory for Speech-Language Pathology. In R. Horton (Ed.), *Critical Perspectives on Social Justice in Speech-Language Pathology* (pp. 84–104). IGI Global., doi:10.4018/978-1-7998-7134-7.ch005

Priyanka, E. B., Thangavel, S., & Prabu, D. V. (2020). Fundamentals of Wireless Sensor Networks Using Machine Learning Approaches. In Sagayam, K., Bhushan, B., Andrushia, A., & Albuquerque, V. C. (Ed.), Deep Learning Strategies for Security Enhancement in Wireless Sensor Networks (pp. 233-254). IGI Global. https://doi.org/ doi:10.4018/978-1-7998-5068-7.ch012

Pruitt, E., & Pinchbeck, K. (2022). Empathy-MInded Practice in Higher Education. In C. Ward (Ed.), *Achieving Equity in Higher Education Using Empathy as a Guiding Principle* (pp. 215–238). IGI Global., doi:10.4018/978-1-7998-9746-0.ch010

R'boul, H. (2021). Interculturally-Critical Digital Storytelling. In Haas, L.Tussey, J. (Eds.), Connecting Disciplinary Literacy and Digital Storytelling in K-12 Education (pp. 278-297). IGI Global. https://doi.org/ doi:10.4018/978-1-7998-5770-9.ch014

R'boul, H., & Bueno-Alastuey, M. C. (2021). Reimagining Multicultural Education. In R. K. Gordon, K. Ahmed, & M. Hosoda (Eds.), *Evolving Multicultural Education for Global Classrooms* (pp. 195–213). IGI Global., doi:10.4018/978-1-7998-7649-6.ch010

Raimi, L., Tariq, M. U., & Kah, J. M. (2022). Diversity, Equity, and Inclusion as the Future Workplace Ethics. In L. Raimi & J. M. Kah (Eds.), *Mainstreaming Diversity, Equity, and Inclusion as Future Workplace Ethics* (pp. 1–27). IGI Global., doi:10.4018/978-1-6684-3657-8.ch001

Raković, R. M. (2020). Application of Cloud Computing in Electric Power Utility Systems. In Stojanović, M. D.Boštjančič Rakas, S. V. (Eds.), Cyber Security of Industrial Control Systems in the Future Internet Environment (pp. 229-247). IGI Global. https://doi.org/ doi:10.4018/978-1-7998-2910-2.ch011

Ramírez-Verdugo, M. D. (2021). International Teacher Education Network. In Ramírez-Verdugo, M. D.Otcu-Grillman, B. (Eds.), Interdisciplinary Approaches Toward Enhancing Teacher Education (pp. 1-19). IGI Global. https://doi.org/ doi:10.4018/978-1-7998-4697-0.ch001

Ramsey, T. L. (2022). Looking Towards the Sun. In J. T. Butcher (Ed.), *Black Female Leaders in Academia* (pp. 164–183). IGI Global., doi:10.4018/978-1-7998-9774-3.ch008

Rascão, J. P. (2021). Freedom of Speech, Privacy, and Ethical and Social Responsibility in Democracy in the Digital Age. [IJRCM]. *International Journal of Risk and Contingency Management*, *10*(3), 34–83. doi:10.4018/IJRCM.2021070104

Reed, D., Fontenot, C., Peltier-Glaze, B., Hines, M. T., Parker, C. H., & Washington, K. (2022). Nobody Knows the Troubles That I See. In J. T. Butcher (Ed.), *Black Female Leaders in Academia* (pp. 121–163). IGI Global., doi:10.4018/978-1-7998-9774-3.ch007

Reid, E. K., Matute-Chavarria, M., & Gray, P. (2022). Wading Through Water. In S. R. Logan & T. L. Good (Eds.), *Black Women Navigating Historically White Higher Education Institutions and the Journey Toward Liberation* (pp. 114–135). IGI Global., doi:10.4018/978-1-6684-4626-3.ch006

Reiter, A. (2022). "What Are You?". In Flockhart, T. R., Reiter, A.Hassett, M. R. (Eds.), The Reproduction and Maintenance of Inequalities in Interpersonal Relationships (pp. 134-152). IGI Global. https://doi.org/ doi:10.4018/978-1-6684-4128-2.ch008

Rejón-Guardia, F., Marković, N., & García-Sastre, M. A. (2020). The Development of a Scale to Measure Tourism-Phobia. In Ribeiro de Almeida, C., Quintano, A., Simancas, M., Huete, R., & Breda, Z. (Ed.), Handbook of Research on the Impacts, Challenges, and Policy Responses to Overtourism (pp. 217-236). IGI Global. https://doi.org/ doi:10.4018/978-1-7998-2224-0.ch012

Reneau, C., & Boutakidis, I. (2021). A Modest Proposition. In C. Reneau & M. Villarreal (Eds.), *Handbook of Research on Leading Higher Education Transformation With Social Justice, Equity, and Inclusion* (pp. 339–360). IGI Global., doi:10.4018/978-1-7998-7152-1.ch022

Ressler, M. B., Ressler, J. D., & Gordon, B. (2021). Preparing New Zealand's Teachers to Use Culturally Responsive Relationship-Based Pedagogies. [IJTEPD]. *International Journal of Teacher Education and Professional Development*, *4*(2), 19–33. doi:10.4018/IJTEPD.2021070102

Resuloğlu, F. (2022). No Dress Rehearsal. In A. E. Arimoro (Ed.), *Global Perspectives on the LGBT Community and Non-Discrimination* (pp. 122–140). IGI Global., doi:10.4018/978-1-6684-2428-5.ch006

Reynoso, N. M., Foxx, K., Tadesse, A., & Mack, C. (2022). Patching the Pipeline. In H. W. Pichon & Y. Mutakabbir (Eds.), *African American Leadership and Mentoring Through Purpose, Preparation, and Preceptors* (pp. 266–289). IGI Global., doi:10.4018/978-1-7998-8206-0.ch013

Reza, F. (2021). De Facto Segregation and the Digital Divide. In H. K. Dhir (Ed.), *Handbook of Research on Barriers for Teaching 21st-Century Competencies and the Impact of Digitalization* (pp. 145–160). IGI Global., doi:10.4018/978-1-7998-6967-2.ch008

Rivas-de-Roca, R., & García-Gordillo, M. (2022). Achieving a Representative Democracy in Europe. In D. Palau-Sampio, G. López García, & L. Iannelli (Eds.), *Contemporary Politics, Communication, and the Impact on Democracy* (pp. 19–36). IGI Global., doi:10.4018/978-1-7998-8057-8.ch002

Rivera, S., Hoffman, C., Manierre, M., & Boolani, A. (2022). Beyond the Statement. In E. Cain-Sanschagrin, R. A. Filback, & J. Crawford (Eds.), *Cases on Academic Program Redesign for Greater Racial and Social Justice* (pp. 243–261). IGI Global., doi:10.4018/978-1-7998-8463-7.ch012

Rivera, S., & Ibourk, A. (2020). Incorporating Social Justice Into Science Teacher Education Courses. In C. K. Clausen & S. R. Logan (Eds.), *Integrating Social Justice Education in Teacher Preparation Programs* (pp. 208–224). IGI Global., doi:10.4018/978-1-7998-5098-4.ch010

Robinson, P. A., & Aldana, J. J. (2020). Making Lemonade From the Lemon of Cultural Taxation. In J. Keengwe (Ed.), *Handbook of Research on Diversity and Social Justice in Higher Education* (pp. 1–18). IGI Global., doi:10.4018/978-1-7998-5268-1.ch001

Robinson, P. A., & Stojanović, M. (2022). Critical Considerations for Advancing Gender and Racial Literacies. In J. Keengwe (Ed.), *Handbook of Research on Social Justice and Equity in Education* (pp. 1–21). IGI Global., doi:10.4018/978-1-7998-9567-1.ch001

Rocha, C. J. (2021). Inspiring Inquiry With the i2Flex Model in the World Language Classroom. In Avgerinou, M. D.Pelonis, P. (Eds.), Handbook of Research on K-12 Blended and Virtual Learning Through the i2Flex Classroom Model (pp. 174-187). IGI Global. https://doi.org/ doi:10.4018/978-1-7998-7760-8.ch010

Rodriguez, J. (2022). Practicing Storytelling to Find Meaning and Convey Competencies in the Medical School Application. In Schwartz, L. S.Ganjoo, R. (Eds.), Handbook of Research on Advising and Developing the Pre-Health Professional Student (pp. 269-285). IGI Global. https://doi.org/ doi:10.4018/978-1-7998-9617-3.ch014

Rodríguez, N. N., Updegraff, A., & Winters, L. A. (2021). Skippyjon, Spanglish, and Stereotypes. In D. E. Hartsfield (Ed.), *Handbook of Research on Teaching Diverse Youth Literature to Pre-Service Professionals* (pp. 103–123). IGI Global., doi:10.4018/978-1-7998-7375-4.ch006

Rodriguez, S. K., & Ricchezza, L. C. (2020). Equity and Social Justice. In S. L. Johnson (Ed.), *Examining Social Change and Social Responsibility in Higher Education* (pp. 1–16). IGI Global., doi:10.4018/978-1-7998-2177-9.ch001

Roque, M. I. (2022). Storytelling in Cultural Heritage. In Campos, A.Almeida, S. (Eds.), Global Perspectives on Strategic Storytelling in Destination Marketing (pp. 22-37). IGI Global. https://doi.org/ doi:10.4018/978-1-6684-3436-9.ch002

Ross, D. B., & Peyton, G. L. (2021). The Never Ending Intellectual Theft of Truth. In R. J. Blankenship (Ed.), *Deep Fakes, Fake News, and Misinformation in Online Teaching and Learning Technologies* (pp. 39–68). IGI Global., doi:10.4018/978-1-7998-6474-5.ch003

Roubides, P. (2021). Learning Design in the 21st Century. In D. Chatham (Ed.), *Advancing Online Course Design and Pedagogy for the 21st Century Learning Environment* (pp. 1–27). IGI Global., doi:10.4018/978-1-7998-5598-9.ch001

Rozman, T., & Rozman, M. F. (2020). Education for Sustainability. [IJSEUS]. *International Journal of Smart Education and Urban Society, 11*(1), 41–63. doi:10.4018/IJSEUS.2020010104

Ruhe, S. (2020). Fostering (Digital) Media Literacy Skills and Global Citizenship in the EFL Classroom. In Neokleous, G., Krulatz, A.Farrelly, R. (Eds.), Handbook of Research on Cultivating Literacy in Diverse and Multilingual Classrooms (pp. 125-145). IGI Global. https://doi.org/ doi:10.4018/978-1-7998-2722-1.ch007

Ruiz-Molina, M., Gil-Saura, I., & Berenguer-Contrí, G. (2020). Are Retailers' Perceptions of Their Innovativeness and Technology Similar to Those of Consumers? In F. Musso & E. Druica (Eds.), *Handbook of Research on Retailing Techniques for Optimal Consumer Engagement and Experiences* (pp. 310–337). IGI Global., doi:10.4018/978-1-7998-1412-2.ch014

Saad, H., & Hamza, M. (2021). Patterns and Motivations Predicting Mobile Hard News and Soft News Consumption. [IJCRMM]. *International Journal of Customer Relationship Marketing and Management, 12*(3), 49–66. doi:10.4018/IJCRMM.2021070104

Sabela, P. T. (2022). Embedding Afrocentricity in Inclusive Education and Equality. In Maguvhe, M. O.Masuku, M. M. (Eds.), Handbook of Research on Creating Spaces for African Epistemologies in the Inclusive Education Discourse (pp. 25-36). IGI Global. https://doi.org/ doi:10.4018/978-1-6684-4436-8.ch003

Sabu, J. (2022). Testing Models of Data-Driven Reporting in Newspapers for Health Communication. In Al-Suqri, M. N., Alsalmi, J.Al-Shaqsi, O. (Eds.), Mass Communications and the Influence of Information During Times of Crises (pp. 204-235). IGI Global. https://doi.org/ doi:10.4018/978-1-7998-7503-1.ch010

Sackey, R., Asiamah, A. A., & Aboagye, L. A. (2021). Newsroom Representation and Discrimination Against Female Journalists in Ghana. In S. Jamil, B. Çoban, B. Ataman, & G. Appiah-Adjei (Eds.), *Handbook of Research on Discrimination, Gender Disparity, and Safety Risks in Journalism* (pp. 297–318). IGI Global., doi:10.4018/978-1-7998-6686-2.ch016

Safeer, A. A., & Khuhro, S. (2022). Employee-Based Brand Equity and Competitive Advantage. In M. Bari, M. Abrar, & E. Alaverdov (Eds.), *Antecedents and Outcomes of Employee-Based Brand Equity* (pp. 54–71). IGI Global., doi:10.4018/978-1-6684-3621-9.ch004

Safieddine, F., & Hammad, R. (2020). Fake News. In Y. Ibrahim (Ed.), *Handbook of Research on Recent Developments in Internet Activism and Political Participation* (pp. 103–121). IGI Global., doi:10.4018/978-1-7998-4796-0.ch007

Salato, S. J., & Fifield Brandt, B. (2022). Reflecting on Race and Health Outcomes. In R. Ganjoo & L. S. Schwartz (Eds.), *Handbook of Research on Developing Competencies for Pre-Health Professional Students, Advisors, and Programs* (pp. 305–327). IGI Global., doi:10.4018/978-1-6684-5969-0.ch015

Salazar, L. R., Garcia, N., Diego-Medrano, E., & Castillo, Y. (2021). Workplace Cyberbullying and Cross-Cultural Differences. In L. Ramos Salazar (Ed.), *Handbook of Research on Cyberbullying and Online Harassment in the Workplace* (pp. 284–309). IGI Global., doi:10.4018/978-1-7998-4912-4.ch014

Salim, Z. (2020). Mapping Gated Communities. [IJAGR]. *International Journal of Applied Geospatial Research, 11*(3), 48–67. doi:10.4018/IJAGR.2020070104

Salmon, A. K., & Melliou, K. (2021). Understanding and Facing Migration Through Stories for Influence. In I. G. Barreto (Ed.), *Handbook of Research on Promoting Social Justice for Immigrants and Refugees Through Active Citizenship and Intercultural Education* (pp. 205–231). IGI Global., doi:10.4018/978-1-7998-7283-2.ch011

Samoilenko, S. A., & Miroshnichenko, A. (2019). Profiting From the "Trump Bump". In I. E. Chiluwa & S. A. Samoilenko (Eds.), *Handbook of Research on Deception, Fake News, and Misinformation Online* (pp. 375–391). IGI Global., doi:10.4018/978-1-5225-8535-0.ch020

San Martín, H., García-de-los-Salmones, M. M., & Herrero-Crespo, Á. (2020). Citizen Perceptions and Support for Smart City Projects. In J. M. Palma-Ruiz, J. Saiz-Álvarez, & Á. Herrero-Crespo (Eds.), *Handbook of Research on Smart Territories and Entrepreneurial Ecosystems for Social Innovation and Sustainable Growth* (pp. 107–123). IGI Global., doi:10.4018/978-1-7998-2097-0.ch007

Sánchez-Connally, P., & Cabello, C. (2022). Resistencia. In Alvarez, W. & De Walt, P. S. (Ed.), Voicing Diverse Teaching Experiences, Approaches, and Perspectives in Higher Education (pp. 191-201). IGI Global. https://doi.org/ doi:10.4018/978-1-7998-9000-3.ch014

Sánchez-Figuera, R., Casado Gutiérrez, F., Luque González, A., & García-Guerrero, J. (2021). Sensationalism vs. Information During COVID-19 in Ecuador. In M. Bari & E. Alaverdov (Eds.), *Impact of Infodemic on Organizational Performance* (pp. 195–216). IGI Global., doi:10.4018/978-1-7998-7164-4.ch012

Sangar, S. (2022). Addressing Low Female Participation in STEM for an Inclusive Industry 4.0. In Bala, S.Singhal, P. (Eds.), Gender Perspectives on Industry 4.0 and the Impact of Technology on Mainstreaming Female Employment (pp. 91-106). IGI Global. https://doi.org/ doi:10.4018/978-1-7998-8594-8.ch005

Santos, I. M., & Wu, W. (2022). Equity Pedagogies for Inclusive Online Classrooms in Higher Education. In S. Ramlall, T. Cross, & M. Love (Eds.), *Handbook of Research on Future of Work and Education* (pp. 379–399). IGI Global., doi:10.4018/978-1-7998-8275-6.ch023

Santos, S., & Santo, P. E. (2021). Brands and Stories in Ads. In L. C. Mihăeş, R. Andreescu, & A. Dimitriu (Eds.), *Handbook of Research on Contemporary Storytelling Methods Across New Media and Disciplines* (pp. 116–137). IGI Global., doi:10.4018/978-1-7998-6605-3.ch007

Saqib, S., Rubab, A., & Pitsaphol, C. (2022). Knowledge-Hiding Behaviors and Employee-Based Brand Equity. In M. Bari, M. Abrar, & E. Alaverdov (Eds.), *Antecedents and Outcomes of Employee-Based Brand Equity* (pp. 81–89). IGI Global., doi:10.4018/978-1-6684-3621-9.ch006

Saridou, T. A., & Veglis, A. (2021). Exploring the Integration of User-Generated Content in Media Organizations Through Participatory Journalism. In Khosrow-Pour D.B.A., M. (Ed.), Encyclopedia of Information Science and Technology, Fifth Edition (pp. 1152-1163). IGI Global. https://doi.org/ doi:10.4018/978-1-7998-3479-3.ch080

Sarkar, A., Jha, A., & Mukherjee, D. (2019). Trucks and Brand. [IJABIM]. *International Journal of Asian Business and Information Management, 10*(2), 1–30. doi:10.4018/IJABIM.2019040101

Savino, A. A., & de Titto, E. (2020). Sustainable Waste Management Challenges in Argentina. In Pariatamby, A., Shahul Hamid, F. & Bhatti, M. S. (Ed.), Sustainable Waste Management Challenges in Developing Countries (pp. 1-34). IGI Global. https://doi.org/ doi:10.4018/978-1-7998-0198-6.ch001

Scarpena, K. (2020). Online Doctoral Programs. In Setzekorn, K., Patnayakuni, N.Burton, T. (Eds.), Socioeconomics, Diversity, and the Politics of Online Education (pp. 90-110). IGI Global. https://doi.org/ doi:10.4018/978-1-7998-3583-7.ch006

Schwartzman, R. (2021). Risky Jews. In L. Shedletsky (Ed.), *Rationalist Bias in Communication Theory* (pp. 1–17). IGI Global., doi:10.4018/978-1-7998-7439-3.ch009

Scott, B. (2019). Afro-Caribbean Immigrants in STEM Careers. In Thomas, U.Drake, J. (Eds.), Women's Influence on Inclusion, Equity, and Diversity in STEM Fields (pp. 143-168). IGI Global. https://doi.org/ doi:10.4018/978-1-5225-8870-2.ch006

Scott-Johnson, P. E., & Leggett-Robinson, P. M. (2020). A Journey Worth Traveling. In P. M. Leggett-Robinson & B. C. Villa (Eds.), *Overcoming Barriers for Women of Color in STEM Fields* (pp. 116–140). IGI Global., doi:10.4018/978-1-7998-4858-5.ch006

Scullin, B. L. (2021). Promoting Race Talk With Elementary Preservice Teachers Through Diverse Picture Book Read Alouds. In D. E. Hartsfield (Ed.), *Handbook of Research on Teaching Diverse Youth Literature to Pre-Service Professionals* (pp. 210–234). IGI Global., doi:10.4018/978-1-7998-7375-4.ch011

Seegars, W. (2022). Cultural Bias and Its Implications for Discipline Disparity. In A. T. Adams (Ed.), *Approaching Disparities in School Discipline* (pp. 1–22). IGI Global., doi:10.4018/978-1-6684-3359-1.ch001

Seliskar, H. V., Robinson, C., Early, K. W., Williams, T. N., & Johnson, C. S. (2021). Building Capacity Through Multiculturalism and Diversity in the Online Classroom. In T. P. Fudge & S. S. Ferebee (Eds.), *Curriculum Development and Online Instruction for the 21st Century* (pp. 114–131). IGI Global., doi:10.4018/978-1-7998-7653-3.ch007

Selnes, F. N., & Walulya, G. (2020). Types and Sources of Threats to Media Freedom in Uganda. In S. Jamil (Ed.), *Handbook of Research on Combating Threats to Media Freedom and Journalist Safety* (pp. 257–276). IGI Global., doi:10.4018/978-1-7998-1298-2.ch014

Şen, O. (2022). Informatics Truth. In Yılmaz, R.Koç, B. (Eds.), Narrative Theory and Therapy in the Post-Truth Era (pp. 61-78). IGI Global. https://doi.org/doi:10.4018/978-1-7998-9251-9.ch005

Sera, H., & Wall, A. F. (2021). Ichigo-Ichie. In C. Reneau & M. Villarreal (Eds.), *Handbook of Research on Leading Higher Education Transformation With Social Justice, Equity, and Inclusion* (pp. 1–17). IGI Global., doi:10.4018/978-1-7998-7152-1.ch001

Seward, K., & Gentry, M. (2022). Protocols for Identification. In J. L. Nyberg & J. A. Manzone (Eds.), *Creating Equitable Services for the Gifted* (pp. 1–10). IGI Global., doi:10.4018/978-1-7998-8153-7.ch001

Sezgin, M., & Bayoğlu, F. (2020). Comparison of Public Relations Education at Undergraduate and Graduate Levels in Turkey and EU Member States. In Y. Bayar (Ed.), *Handbook of Research on Social and Economic Development in the European Union* (pp. 510–541). IGI Global., doi:10.4018/978-1-7998-1188-6.ch030

Shabbir, M. S. (2020). Attributes Ensuring Positive Consumer Evaluation in Brand Extension of Pakistan. [IJABIM]. *International Journal of Asian Business and Information Management, 11*(4), 71–84. doi:10.4018/IJABIM.2020100106

Shah, S. F., Jan, F., & Ittefaq, M. (2021). Health and Safety Risks to Journalists During Pandemics. In S. Jamil, B. Çoban, B. Ataman, & G. Appiah-Adjei (Eds.), *Handbook of Research on Discrimination, Gender Disparity, and Safety Risks in Journalism* (pp. 90–103). IGI Global., doi:10.4018/978-1-7998-6686-2.ch006

Shaheen, S., Chaman, S., & Zulfiqar, S. (2022). An Exploration of the Factors Affecting Brand Association. In M. Bari, M. Abrar, & E. Alaverdov (Eds.), *Antecedents and Outcomes of Employee-Based Brand Equity* (pp. 106–118). IGI Global., doi:10.4018/978-1-6684-3621-9.ch008

Sharma, A. (2022). Understanding the Digitised Labour Market Through a Gendered Lens. In Bala, S.Singhal, P. (Eds.), Gender Perspectives on Industry 4.0 and the Impact of Technology on Mainstreaming Female Employment (pp. 108-131). IGI Global. https://doi.org/ doi:10.4018/978-1-7998-8594-8.ch006

Sheikh, S. (2021). *AI in Industry*. IGI Global., doi:10.4018/978-1-7998-4607-9.ch005

Shelton, H., He-Weatherford, Z., Peterson, S. R., & Alharthi, A. A. (2021). Framing Crisis in Seattle During COVID-19 and Black Lives Matter. In E. B. Hancı-Azizoglu & M. Alawdat (Eds.), *Rhetoric and Sociolinguistics in Times of Global Crisis* (pp. 342–364). IGI Global., doi:10.4018/978-1-7998-6732-6.ch018

Shin, D. (2021). A Cross-National Study on the Perception of Algorithm News in the East and the West. [JGIM]. *Journal of Global Information Management, 29*(2), 77–101. doi:10.4018/JGIM.2021030105

Shinas, V. H., Wen, H., & Guo, D. (2022). Developing Teachers as Writers. In T. S. Hodges (Ed.), *Handbook of Research on Teacher Practices for Diverse Writing Instruction* (pp. 88–107). IGI Global., doi:10.4018/978-1-6684-6213-3.ch006

Shittu, A. K., Mbada, K. A., & Odeyemi, T. I. (2021). Evaluating the Impact and Effectiveness of Community-Based Health Insurance Policy Among Informal Sector in Lagos State Using Donabedian Model. [IJPPPHCE]. *International Journal of Public and Private Perspectives on Healthcare, Culture, and the Environment, 5*(2), 65–80. doi:10.4018/IJPPPHCE.2021070105

Simon, K. N., Hodgkins, L., & Argent, J. (2022). Small Chunks, Deep Learning. In Y. Huang (Ed.), *Handbook of Research on Credential Innovations for Inclusive Pathways to Professions* (pp. 276–299). IGI Global., doi:10.4018/978-1-7998-3820-3.ch014

Sims, C. (2021). The Impact of Gendered Lookism During Employment Stages. In C. Hughes (Ed.), *Implementation Strategies for Improving Diversity in Organizations* (pp. 75–109). IGI Global., doi:10.4018/978-1-7998-4745-8.ch003

Sine Nazlı, R., Akbulak, B., & Çat, A. K. (2020). Journalism and Communication Design in New Media. In S. Kır (Ed.), *New Media and Visual Communication in Social Networks* (pp. 70–92). IGI Global., doi:10.4018/978-1-7998-1041-4.ch005

Sithole, P. M., & Bondai, B. M. (2020). Taboos and Storytelling for Teaching and Learning in Zimbabwe. [IJCDLM]. *International Journal of Curriculum Development and Learning Measurement, 1*(2), 53–65. doi:10.4018/IJCDLM.2020070104

Smith, E. C., & Conrad, M. (2020). Cultivating Magic and Nostalgia. In D. Batabyal (Ed.), *Global Entrepreneurial Trends in the Tourism and Hospitality Industry* (pp. 131–158). IGI Global., doi:10.4018/978-1-7998-2603-3.ch007

Smith, H. L., & Iyengar, K. (2021). "Respectful" Home-School Relationships. In G. Onchwari & J. Keengwe (Eds.), *Bridging Family-Teacher Relationships for ELL and Immigrant Students* (pp. 265–284). IGI Global., doi:10.4018/978-1-7998-4712-0.ch014

Smith, H. L., & Iyengar, K. M. (2019). My Friends and Family. In J. Keengwe & G. Onchwari (Eds.), *Handbook of Research on Assessment Practices and Pedagogical Models for Immigrant Students* (pp. 316–329). IGI Global., doi:10.4018/978-1-5225-9348-5.ch017

Smith-Adams, C. (2022). Path to College Presidency. In J. T. Butcher (Ed.), *Black Female Leaders in Academia* (pp. 213–232). IGI Global., doi:10.4018/978-1-7998-9774-3.ch011

Smith-Woofter, M. B., Rumley, M. A., & Barbour, N. N. (2022). School Leaders Serving to Develop Teachers as Equity-Focused Change Agents. In B. S. Zugelder & M. L'Esperance (Eds.), *Handbook of Research on the Educator Continuum and Development of Teachers* (pp. 510–526). IGI Global., doi:10.4018/978-1-6684-3848-0.ch025

Sohal, P. (2020). Shooting the Messenger, Slowly, but Surely. In S. Jamil (Ed.), *Handbook of Research on Combating Threats to Media Freedom and Journalist Safety* (pp. 23–37). IGI Global., doi:10.4018/978-1-7998-1298-2.ch002

Soles, B., Flores, P. III, Domingues, J., & Solis, F. (2020). The Role of Formal and Nonformal Leaders in Creating Culturally Proficient Educational Practices. In P. D. Keough (Ed.), *Overcoming Current Challenges in the P-12 Teaching Profession* (pp. 144–172). IGI Global., doi:10.4018/978-1-7998-1177-0.ch007

Solomon, E. N., Adu-Debrah, L. K., & Braimah, S. M. (2022). Promoting Tourism Destinations Through Storytelling. In A. Campos & S. Almeida (Eds.), *Global Perspectives on Strategic Storytelling in Destination Marketing* (pp. 117–135). IGI Global., doi:10.4018/978-1-6684-3436-9.ch007

Soltani, S. (2020). "Designing Optimal Valuation Model of Bank Stocks". In Köseoğlu, S. D. (Eds.), Valuation Challenges and Solutions in Contemporary Businesses (pp. 212-233). IGI Global. https://doi.org/ doi:10.4018/978-1-7998-1086-5.ch012

Sowad, A. S. (2019). Is Gender a More Important Axis of Representation Than Race, Ethnicity or Class in Politics? [IJSESD]. *International Journal of Social Ecology and Sustainable Development, 10*(2), 29–36. doi:10.4018/IJSESD.2019040103

Sözler, S. (2021). Design Thinking for Online Learning. In Kurubacak-Meric, G.Sisman-Ugur, S. (Eds.), Improving Scientific Communication for Lifelong Learners (pp. 14-37). IGI Global. https://doi.org/ doi:10.4018/978-1-7998-4534-8.ch002

Spears, J. C., Jr., & Coleman, S. T. (2021). The Social Impact of Sport. In Hairston, K. R., Edmonds, W. M. & Clark, S. P. (Ed.), The Black Experience and Navigating Higher Education Through a Virtual World (pp. 97-121). IGI Global. https://doi.org/ doi:10.4018/978-1-7998-7537-6.ch006

Spencer, A. D., & Lance, T. A. (2021). Leading Boldly. In A. J. Griffen (Ed.), *Challenges to Integrating Diversity, Equity, and Inclusion Programs in Organizations* (pp. 200–214). IGI Global., doi:10.4018/978-1-7998-4093-0.ch013

Spranger, A. N. (2022). The Inclusive Leader's Toolkit. In Neimann, T., Felix, J. J., Shliakhovchuk, E.Hindman, L. L. (Eds.), Policy and Practice Challenges for Equality in Education (pp. 279-294). IGI Global. https://doi.org/ doi:10.4018/978-1-7998-7379-2.ch013

Statti, A. L. (2021). Learner-Active Technology-Infused Classroom. [IJSEUS]. *International Journal of Smart Education and Urban Society, 12*(1), 30–44. doi:10.4018/IJSEUS.2021010103

Stepniak, M., Shaffer, S., & Shaffer, S. (2021). Using Social-Emotional Learning and Literacy Tools to Bridge the Gap During and Beyond COVID-19. In J. Tussey & L. Haas (Eds.), *Handbook of Research on Supporting Social and Emotional Development Through Literacy Education* (pp. 172–194). IGI Global., doi:10.4018/978-1-7998-7464-5.ch009

Stiegler, C. (2020). No Line on the Horizon. In Y. Ibrahim (Ed.), *Handbook of Research on Recent Developments in Internet Activism and Political Participation* (pp. 53–68). IGI Global., doi:10.4018/978-1-7998-4796-0.ch004

Stojanović, M., & Robinson, P. A. (2022). A Deep Dive Into How Critical Literacy Experts Advance Equity and Social Justice. In J. Keengwe (Ed.), *Handbook of Research on Social Justice and Equity in Education* (pp. 72–91). IGI Global., doi:10.4018/978-1-7998-9567-1.ch004

Strehovec, J. (2020). *Remediating the Social: Impacts of Historical Fascism on Academic Fascism*. IGI Global., doi:10.4018/978-1-7998-3835-7.ch008

Strehovec, J. (2020). *The Word-Image-Virtual Body*. IGI Global., doi:10.4018/978-1-7998-3835-7.ch004

Stufft, C. (2021). Cultivating Social Justice Through Explorations of Multimodal Pop Culture Texts. In Haas, L.Tussey, J. (Eds.), Disciplinary Literacy Connections to Popular Culture in K-12 Settings (pp. 273-291). IGI Global. https://doi.org/ doi:10.4018/978-1-7998-4721-2.ch013

Surugiu, R. (2022). Bridging Journalists and PR Practitioners in a Digital Context. In Andrade, J. G.Ruão, T. (Eds.), Navigating Digital Communication and Challenges for Organizations (pp. 153-166). IGI Global. https://doi.org/ doi:10.4018/978-1-7998-9790-3.ch009

Švigelj, M. M. (2022). Re-Mediating Narratives. In R. D. Williams (Ed.), *Handbook of Research on Challenging Deficit Thinking for Exceptional Education Improvement* (pp. 380–404). IGI Global., doi:10.4018/978-1-7998-8860-4.ch018

Swanson, J. R., & Johannigman, T. (2022). Autoethnography of Cultural Heritage Tourism Documentary Production. In A. Campos & S. Almeida (Eds.), *Global Perspectives on Strategic Storytelling in Destination Marketing* (pp. 38–51). IGI Global., doi:10.4018/978-1-6684-3436-9.ch003

Taha, N., & Al-Maskeri, A. (2022). The Application of Social Network Theory During a Pandemic. In M. N. Al-Suqri, J. Alsalmi, & O. Al-Shaqsi (Eds.), *Mass Communications and the Influence of Information During Times of Crises* (pp. 188–203). IGI Global., doi:10.4018/978-1-7998-7503-1.ch009

Tajuddin, S. N., & Ali, R. (2020). The Risks and Challenges for Professional Journalism in the Digital Age. In S. Jamil (Ed.), *Handbook of Research on Combating Threats to Media Freedom and Journalist Safety* (pp. 106–123). IGI Global., doi:10.4018/978-1-7998-1298-2.ch007

Talavera, I. (2022). Some Problems in Advancing Academic Inclusion. In V. Wang (Ed.), *Handbook of Research on Educational Leadership and Research Methodology* (pp. 290–310). IGI Global., doi:10.4018/978-1-6684-4144-2.ch016

Tambascia, T. P. (2021). Letters to My 25-Year-Old Self. In Reneau, C.Villarreal, M. (Eds.), Handbook of Research on Leading Higher Education Transformation With Social Justice, Equity, and Inclusion (pp. 18-25). IGI Global. https://doi.org/ doi:10.4018/978-1-7998-7152-1.ch002

Tănase, A. E., Calotă, T. O., & Oncioiu, G. C. (2021). Convergence and Divergence Regarding Business Combinations. In I. Oncioiu, S. Căpuşneanu, D. I. Topor, & D. M. Constantin (Eds.), *Sustainability Reporting, Ethics, and Strategic Management Strategies for Modern Organizations* (pp. 78–91). IGI Global., doi:10.4018/978-1-7998-4637-6.ch005

Tănase, A. E., Stoica, D. A., Trăistaru, N. I., & Sürgün, M. B. (2020). Important Managerial Controversies in Conversion of Financial Statements. In I. Oncioiu, G. Cokins, S. Căpuşneanu, & D. I. Topor (Eds.), *Management Accounting Standards for Sustainable Business Practices* (pp. 227–238). IGI Global., doi:10.4018/978-1-7998-0178-8.ch012

Taraktaş, B. (2022). Incorporating Computational Social Science in Political Science. In E. Abanoz (Ed.), *Opportunities and Challenges for Computational Social Science Methods* (pp. 23–44). IGI Global., doi:10.4018/978-1-7998-8553-5.ch002

Targowski, A. (2022). *Digital Humanities Strategy*. IGI Global., doi:10.4018/978-1-7998-8036-3.ch017

Tas Alicenap, C. (2021). The Use of Animation and Storytelling in Science Communication. In Kurubacak-Meric, G.Sisman-Ugur, S. (Eds.), Improving Scientific Communication for Lifelong Learners (pp. 240-250). IGI Global. https:// doi.org/ doi:10.4018/978-1-7998-4534-8.ch013

Tengler, K. (2022). Developing Storytelling Activities Supporting Computational Thinking Using Educational Robots. In Eteokleous, N.Nisiforou, E. (Eds.), Designing, Constructing, and Programming Robots for Learning (pp. 116-135). IGI Global. https://doi.org/ doi:10.4018/978-1-7998-7443-0.ch006

Thi, K. T. (2020). Internet Technology Application in Production of Internet Radio Programs in Vietnam. In Jamil, G. L., Ribeiro, F., Malheiro da Silva, A.Maravilhas Lopes, S. (Eds.), Handbook of Research on Emerging Technologies for Effective Project Management (pp. 300-322). IGI Global. https://doi.org/ doi:10.4018/978-1-5225-9993-7.ch018

Thomas, M., & Stang, B. (2022). A Serious Game for Cultural Heritage? In O. Bernardes & V. Amorim (Eds.), *Handbook of Research on Promoting Economic and Social Development Through Serious Games* (pp. 334–374). IGI Global., doi:10.4018/978-1-7998-9732-3.ch016

Thompson, J. M. (2022). Sustaining Culturally Affirming and Antiracist Practices. In Brant-Rajahn, S. N., Gibson, E. M.Cook Sandifer, M. (Eds.), Developing, Delivering, and Sustaining School Counseling Practices Through a Culturally Affirming Lens (pp. 174-191). IGI Global. https://doi.org/ doi:10.4018/978-1-7998-9514-5.ch009

Toma, M. J. (2022). Mass Media's Negative Narratives. In G. A. Crews (Ed.), *Impact of School Shootings on Classroom Culture, Curriculum, and Learning* (pp. 190–217). IGI Global., doi:10.4018/978-1-7998-5200-1.ch010

Tomar, R. S., & Kulkarni, M. (2020). Global Racial, Ethnic, and Religious Subculture and Its Impact on Healthcare Organizations. In M. Merviö (Ed.), *Global Issues and Innovative Solutions in Healthcare, Culture, and the Environment* (pp. 253–270). IGI Global., doi:10.4018/978-1-7998-3576-9.ch013

Tombul, I. (2020). Gender Construction in Transmedial Narration. In G. Sarı (Ed.), *Gender and Diversity Representation in Mass Media* (pp. 197–217). IGI Global., doi:10.4018/978-1-7998-0128-3.ch011

Tomin, B., & Jenson, J. (2021). Exploring Science Fictional Futures With Secondary Students. In L. Haas & J. Tussey (Eds.), *Disciplinary Literacy Connections to Popular Culture in K-12 Settings* (pp. 94–114). IGI Global., doi:10.4018/978-1-7998-4721-2.ch005

Tribusean, I. (2020). The Use of VR in Journalism. In S. M. Loureiro (Ed.), *Managerial Challenges and Social Impacts of Virtual and Augmented Reality* (pp. 125–141). IGI Global., doi:10.4018/978-1-7998-2874-7.ch008

Trillo Domínguez, M. (2021). The Digital Realm Blurs the Lines Between Journalistic and Corporate Communication. In Olvera-Lobo, M. D., Gutiérrez-Artacho, J., Rivera-Trigueros, I.Díaz-Millón, M. (Eds.), Innovative Perspectives on Corporate Communication in the Global World (pp. 78-96). IGI Global. https://doi.org/ doi:10.4018/978-1-7998-6799-9.ch005

Tsang, S. J. (2020). Understanding Perceived Fakeness of Online Health News in Hong Kong. [IJDLDC]. *International Journal of Digital Literacy and Digital Competence, 11*(2), 1–11. doi:10.4018/IJDLDC.2020040101

Tshifhumulo, R., Musvipwa, F. F., Makhanikhe, T. J., & Tshikukuvhe, L. D. (2021). Towards an African-Centered Model of Learning. In N. Mthembu (Ed.), *Ethical Research Approaches to Indigenous Knowledge Education* (pp. 155–177). IGI Global., doi:10.4018/978-1-7998-1249-4.ch007

Tuazon, R. R., & Torres, T. P. (2020). Digital Threats and Attacks on the Philippine Alternative Press. In S. Jamil (Ed.), *Handbook of Research on Combating Threats to Media Freedom and Journalist Safety* (pp. 1–22). IGI Global., doi:10.4018/978-1-7998-1298-2.ch001

Tuazon, R. R., & Torres, T. P. (2021). Threats and Attacks on Women Journalists in the Philippines. In S. Jamil, B. Çoban, B. Ataman, & G. Appiah-Adjei (Eds.), *Handbook of Research on Discrimination, Gender Disparity, and Safety Risks in Journalism* (pp. 43–59). IGI Global., doi:10.4018/978-1-7998-6686-2.ch004

Tuncel, I. (2022). Health Journalism and Representation of Campaign News of Spinal Muscular Atrophy (SMA) Patients. In Aker, H.Aiken, M. (Eds.), Handbook of Research on Cyberchondria, Health Literacy, and the Role of Media in Society's Perception of Medical Information (pp. 313-329). IGI Global. https://doi.org/doi:10.4018/978-1-7998-8630-3.ch017

Tussey, J. T., & Haas, L. (2022). Supporting Students Impacted by Poverty Through Literacy Methods, Resources, and Strategies. In J. Tussey & L. Haas (Eds.), *Poverty Impacts on Literacy Education* (pp. 235–251). IGI Global., doi:10.4018/978-1-7998-8730-0.ch012

Ulaş, S. (2021). The Role of Social Media on Dissemination of Information During the COVID-19 Pandemic. In G. Sarı (Ed.), *Handbook of Research on Representing Health and Medicine in Modern Media* (pp. 216–227). IGI Global., doi:10.4018/978-1-7998-6825-5.ch015

Ulker-Demirel, E. (2019). Development of Digital Communication Technologies and the New Media. In R. Yilmaz (Ed.), *Handbook of Research on Narrative Advertising* (pp. 164–175). IGI Global., doi:10.4018/978-1-5225-9790-2.ch015

Ülkü, A., & Erol, G. (2022). Destination Storytelling as a Destination Branding Tool. In A. Campos & S. Almeida (Eds.), *Global Perspectives on Strategic Storytelling in Destination Marketing* (pp. 136–163). IGI Global., doi:10.4018/978-1-6684-3436-9.ch008

Uniamikogbo, E., Okoye, E. I., & Chinazu, A. (2020). Non-Interest Income and Financial Performance of Selected Deposit Money Banks in Nigeria. [IJBSA]. *International Journal of Business Strategy and Automation*, *1*(3), 52–66. doi:10.4018/IJBSA.2020070105

Ursyn, A. (2020). *Active Learning Aimed at Visual Development*. IGI Global., doi:10.4018/978-1-7998-1651-5.ch006

Valandra & Leslie. T. (2022). The History of Incarceration of African Americans/Blacks in the United States. In Johns, K. (Ed.), Counseling Strategies for Children and Families Impacted by Incarceration (pp. 24-46). IGI Global. https://doi.org/doi:10.4018/978-1-7998-9209-0.ch002

Valderrama, Y. Z. (2020). Journalists' Safety and Multifaceted Censorship in Colombia. In S. Jamil (Ed.), *Handbook of Research on Combating Threats to Media Freedom and Journalist Safety* (pp. 298–318). IGI Global., doi:10.4018/978-1-7998-1298-2.ch016

Valdiviezo, J., & Graybill, L. (2020). The Great Race. In J. Bazler & M. L. Van Sickle (Eds.), *Cases on Models and Methods for STEAM Education* (pp. 170–204). IGI Global., doi:10.4018/978-1-5225-9631-8.ch008

Vargas-Hernández, J. G. (2020). Rural Migration and Shrinkage Transformation Processes in Mexican Countryside. In D. Ushakov (Ed.), *Migration and Urbanization* (pp. 303–328). IGI Global., doi:10.4018/978-1-7998-0111-5.ch016

Vargas-Hernández, J. G. (2020). Strategic Transformational Transition of Green Economy, Green Growth and Sustainable Development. [IJESGT]. *International Journal of Environmental Sustainability and Green Technologies, 11*(1), 34–56. doi:10.4018/IJESGT.2020010103

Vargas-Hernández, J. G., & Warner, I. (2020). Necessary Prerequisites for Successful Green Economic Transition and Subsequent Green Development. [IJPPPHCE]. *International Journal of Public and Private Perspectives on Healthcare, Culture, and the Environment, 4*(2), 25–49. doi:10.4018/IJPPPHCE.2020070103

Vargas-Hernández, J. G., & Zdunek-Wielgołaska, J. A. (2019). Recent trends in Sustainable Urban Planning. [IJSEM]. *International Journal of Sustainable Economies Management, 8*(3), 29–47. doi:10.4018/IJSEM.2019070103

Varghese, B., Joseph, E. K., & Kallarakal, T. K. (2022). Gender Perspectives. In P. Cembranel, J. R. Soares, & A. R. Perinotto (Eds.), *Promoting Social and Cultural Equity in the Tourism Sector* (pp. 70–84). IGI Global., doi:10.4018/978-1-6684-4194-7.ch005

Varsha, P. S., Akter, S., Kumar, A., Gochhait, S., & Patagundi, B. (2021). The Impact of Artificial Intelligence on Branding. [JGIM]. *Journal of Global Information Management, 29*(4), 221–246. doi:10.4018/JGIM.20210701.oa10

Varshney, D., Heblikar, S., & K, S. B. (2021). A Study on the Performance of Indian Mutual Funds in Recent Years. In Teixeira, N. M., & Lisboa, I. (Ed.), *Handbook of Research on Financial Management During Economic Downturn and Recovery* (pp. 428-444). IGI Global. https://doi.org/ doi:10.4018/978-1-7998-6643-5.ch024

Vasconcelos, S. V., & Balula, A. (2021). Pitch This. In L. C. Mihăeş, R. Andreescu, & A. Dimitriu (Eds.), *Handbook of Research on Contemporary Storytelling Methods Across New Media and Disciplines* (pp. 100–115). IGI Global., doi:10.4018/978-1-7998-6605-3.ch006

Vasile, A. A. (2020). Lifelong Education. In V. Trif (Ed.), *Analyzing Paradigms Used in Education and Educational Psychology* (pp. 144–168). IGI Global., doi:10.4018/978-1-7998-1427-6.ch007

Vassis, G., Margounakis, D. G., & Tambouris, E. (2021). Review and Evaluation of Systems Supporting Data Journalism. In Khosrow-Pour D.B.A., M. (Ed.), Encyclopedia of Organizational Knowledge, Administration, and Technology (pp. 679-694). IGI Global. https://doi.org/ doi:10.4018/978-1-7998-3473-1.ch050

Veratti, D. (2020). Victimology of Predatory Crimes and Prevention Techniques. In Balloni, A.Sette, R. (Eds.), Handbook of Research on Trends and Issues in Crime Prevention, Rehabilitation, and Victim Support (pp. 431-446). IGI Global. https://doi.org/ doi:10.4018/978-1-7998-1286-9.ch025

Verma, R., & Kumar, M. (2022). Brand Extension in FMCG Sector Through Social Media Enabled CRM and Investigating Its Impact on Brand Equity. In A. Naim & S. K. Kautish (Eds.), *Building a Brand Image Through Electronic Customer Relationship Management* (pp. 201–236). IGI Global., doi:10.4018/978-1-6684-5386-5.ch009

View, J., DeMulder, E., Stribling, S., & Dallman, L. (2020). *Critical Reflective Practice, Critical Pedagogy, and Culturally Relevant Pedagogy*. IGI Global., doi:10.4018/978-1-7998-5649-8.ch003

View, J., DeMulder, E., Stribling, S., & Dallman, L. (2020). *Teacher Leadership and Collegial Relationships*. IGI Global., doi:10.4018/978-1-7998-5649-8.ch005

View, J., DeMulder, E., Stribling, S., & Dallman, L. (2020). *When Asked, Teachers Said…*. IGI Global., doi:10.4018/978-1-7998-5649-8.ch001

von Gillern, S., Stufft, C., Marlatt, R., & Nadolny, L. (2022). Minecraft and Elementary Literacy Learning. In C. Lane (Ed.), *Handbook of Research on Acquiring 21st Century Literacy Skills Through Game-Based Learning* (pp. 320–343). IGI Global., doi:10.4018/978-1-7998-7271-9.ch017

Wabwire, J. (2021). Digital Remediation of African Folklore. In Maake, A. O., Maake, B. M.Awuor, F. M. (Eds.), Digital Solutions and the Case for Africa's Sustainable Development (pp. 97-115). IGI Global. https://doi.org/ doi:10.4018/978-1-7998-2967-6.ch007

Waity, J. F., Vanderminden, J., & Robeson, K. (2020). The Fact That the Author Was Male Instead of Female Provided for an Objective Opinion [IJITLHE]. *International Journal of Innovative Teaching and Learning in Higher Education, 1*(3), 44–60. doi:10.4018/IJITLHE.2020070103

Wang, Q. (2020). The Role of Classroom-Situated Game-Based Language Learning in Promoting Students' Communicative Competence. [IJCALLT]. *International Journal of Computer-Assisted Language Learning and Teaching, 10*(2), 59–82. doi:10.4018/IJCALLT.2020040104

Wang, Y., Chen, Y., Xu, Q., & Wu, W. (2020). An Empirical Study of ISO 14001 Certification and Firm Environmental Performance. In S. Tsai, Z. Yuan, J. Yu, & X. Liu (Eds.), *Waste Management Techniques for Improved Environmental and Public Health* (pp. 1–28). IGI Global., doi:10.4018/978-1-7998-1966-0.ch001

Ward, C. (2022). The Connection Between Empathy and Equity in Higher Education. In C. Ward (Ed.), *Achieving Equity in Higher Education Using Empathy as a Guiding Principle* (pp. 1–27). IGI Global., doi:10.4018/978-1-7998-9746-0.ch001

Ward, M. C., Corr, P. G., Fernes, V. A., & Wang, T. (2022). How an Anti-Racist Organizational Change Model Can Build Capacity to Support Historically Excluded Students. In R. Ganjoo & L. S. Schwartz (Eds.), *Handbook of Research on Developing Competencies for Pre-Health Professional Students, Advisors, and Programs* (pp. 389–414). IGI Global., doi:10.4018/978-1-6684-5969-0.ch019

Warren, A. N., & Ward, N. A. (2020). Using Case Methods in Online Teacher Education to Develop Culturally Sustaining Educators. In R. Karchmer-Klein & K. E. Pytash (Eds.), *Effective Practices in Online Teacher Preparation for Literacy Educators* (pp. 128–149). IGI Global., doi:10.4018/978-1-7998-0206-8.ch007

Wessels, S., & Trainin, G. (2021). Digital Storytelling With English Language Learning Families. In G. Onchwari & J. Keengwe (Eds.), *Bridging Family-Teacher Relationships for ELL and Immigrant Students* (pp. 27–45). IGI Global., doi:10.4018/978-1-7998-4712-0.ch002

Weston, E. (2020). Case Study of The BizNest. In Morie, J. F.McCallum, K. (Eds.), Handbook of Research on the Global Impacts and Roles of Immersive Media (pp. 176-199). IGI Global. https://doi.org/ doi:10.4018/978-1-7998-2433-6.ch010

Whitaker, M. C. (2020). Utilizing Feminist Pedagogy to Foster Preservice Teachers' Critical Consciousness. In Clausen, C. K.Logan, S. R. (Eds.), Integrating Social Justice Education in Teacher Preparation Programs (pp. 76-100). IGI Global. https://doi.org/ doi:10.4018/978-1-7998-5098-4.ch004

White, P. A. (2022). Reconstructing Reading for Students of Color. In Butcher, J. T.Baker, W. C. (Eds.), Addressing Issues of Systemic Racism During Turbulent Times (pp. 63-72). IGI Global. https://doi.org/ doi:10.4018/978-1-7998-8532-0.ch004

Willis, M., Jagasia, J., & Robinson-Perez, A. (2021). Black and Brown Women Fostering Authentic Activism in Counseling Programs Amid Social Unrest. In S. Rodriguez & K. Brown (Eds.), *Black and Brown Leadership and the Promotion of Change in an Era of Social Unrest* (pp. 149–183). IGI Global., doi:10.4018/978-1-7998-7235-1.ch007

Wilson, A. V. (2022). The Equity of Remote Teaching During COVID-19. In Reeves, E. K.McIntyre, C. J. (Eds.), Multidisciplinary Perspectives on Diversity and Equity in a Virtual World (pp. 138-154). IGI Global. https://doi.org/ doi:10.4018/978-1-7998-8028-8.ch008

Wiyonoputri, W. T., Eppang, B. M., & Scott, N. (2022). The Development of Stories of Bajo Mola in Wakatobi National Park. In A. Campos & S. Almeida (Eds.), *Global Perspectives on Strategic Storytelling in Destination Marketing* (pp. 52–73). IGI Global., doi:10.4018/978-1-6684-3436-9.ch004

Woiwod, U. (2021). Adaptations of Print Narratives Into Literary Apps. In Haas, L.Tussey, J. (Eds.), Connecting Disciplinary Literacy and Digital Storytelling in K-12 Education (pp. 127-147). IGI Global. https://doi.org/ doi:10.4018/978-1-7998-5770-9.ch007

Wolf, J., Feitosa, F., & Marques, J. L. (2021). Efficiency and Equity in the Spatial Planning of Primary Schools. [IJEPR]. *International Journal of E-Planning Research, 10*(1), 21–38. doi:10.4018/IJEPR.2021010102

Woodcock, C. A. (2022). Social Action Literacy for Elementary Teachers. In Bromer, B. L.Crawford, C. M. (Eds.), Handbook of Research on Learner-Centered Approaches to Teaching in an Age of Transformational Change (pp. 308-327). IGI Global. https://doi.org/ doi:10.4018/978-1-6684-4240-1.ch016

Wooten, C. B. (2021). Junior Faculty Scholarly Personal Narrative. In Moffett, N. L. (Eds.), Navigating Post-Doctoral Career Placement, Research, and Professionalism (pp. 104-128). IGI Global. https://doi.org/ doi:10.4018/978-1-7998-5065-6.ch006

Worley, C. (2022). The Red Bandanna. In Haas, L.Tussey, J. T. (Eds.), Disciplinary Literacy as a Support for Culturally and Linguistically Responsive Teaching and Learning (pp. 285-305). IGI Global. https://doi.org/ doi:10.4018/978-1-6684-4215-9.ch014

Wright, M. M., & Edney, N. (2022). Students at the Table. In E. Cain-Sanschagrin, R. A. Filback, & J. Crawford (Eds.), *Cases on Academic Program Redesign for Greater Racial and Social Justice* (pp. 212–225). IGI Global., doi:10.4018/978-1-7998-8463-7.ch010

Wright, W. F., & Wright, M. M. (2021). Characteristics of Successful Securities Crowdfunding Campaigns in the United States. In C. S. Negrão & J. F. Brito (Eds.), *Multidisciplinary Approaches to Crowdfunding Platforms* (pp. 163–197). IGI Global., doi:10.4018/978-1-7998-3226-3.ch007

Xiao, J. (2021). From Equality to Equity to Justice. In A. Bozkurt (Ed.), *Handbook of Research on Emerging Pedagogies for the Future of Education* (pp. 1–15). IGI Global., doi:10.4018/978-1-7998-7275-7.ch001

Xiao, L. (2021). Is There Racial Discrimination Within the NBA? [IJOCI]. *International Journal of Organizational and Collective Intelligence*, *11*(2), 1–28. doi:10.4018/IJOCI.2021040101

Yagasa, R., Uch, R., & Sam, P. (2020). Solid Waste Management in Cambodia. In Pariatamby, A., Shahul Hamid, F., & Bhatti, M. S. (Ed.), Sustainable Waste Management Challenges in Developing Countries (pp. 56-85). IGI Global. https:// doi.org/ doi:10.4018/978-1-7998-0198-6.ch003

Yang, K. C., & Kang, Y. (2019). Narrative Adverting and Multi-Platform Storytelling. In R. Yilmaz (Ed.), *Handbook of Research on Narrative Advertising* (pp. 177–195). IGI Global., doi:10.4018/978-1-5225-9790-2.ch016

Yanginlar, G. (2020). The Effect of Reverse Logistics Activities on Brand Equity and Customer Satisfaction. In G. Ç. Ceyhun (Ed.), *Handbook of Research on the Applications of International Transportation and Logistics for World Trade* (pp. 395–414). IGI Global., doi:10.4018/978-1-7998-1397-2.ch021

Yastibaş, A. E., Baturay, M. H., & Çinar, C. A. (2022). Augmented Reality-Based Digital Storytelling in Language Teaching and Learning. In Zou, B., Thomas, M., Barr, D., & Jia, W. (Ed.), Emerging Concepts in Technology-Enhanced Language Teaching and Learning (pp. 42-65). IGI Global. https://doi.org/ doi:10.4018/978-1-7998-8981-6.ch003

Ye, F. (2022). *Grand Synthetic Model.* IGI Global., doi:10.4018/978-1-6684-4935-6.ch004

Ye, F. (2022). *Social Equity and Fiscal Policy*. IGI Global., doi:10.4018/978-1-6684-4935-6.ch011

Yearta, L., & Kelly, K. (2021). Digital Storytelling to Enhance Social Studies Content Knowledge, Explore Multiple Perspectives, and Advocate for Social Justice. In L. Haas & J. Tussey (Eds.), *Connecting Disciplinary Literacy and Digital Storytelling in K-12 Education* (pp. 235–256). IGI Global., doi:10.4018/978-1-7998-5770-9.ch012

Yeung, R. P. (2022). Understanding the Relationship Between White Teacher Implicit Bias and Black Student Academic Disparities and High Discipline Rates. In A. T. Adams (Ed.), *Approaching Disparities in School Discipline* (pp. 23–51). IGI Global., doi:10.4018/978-1-6684-3359-1.ch002

Yıldızgörür, M. R. (2021). New Media and New Journalism. In E. Esiyok (Ed.), *Handbook of Research on New Media Applications in Public Relations and Advertising* (pp. 451–471). IGI Global., doi:10.4018/978-1-7998-3201-0.ch026

Yilmaz, B. K., & Dalkilic, O. S. (2022). Token Image in Male-Dominated Professions and Occupational Segregation Based on Gender. In E. B. Uçel (Ed.), *Eastern Perspectives on Women's Roles and Advancement in Business* (pp. 61–87). IGI Global., doi:10.4018/978-1-7998-8742-3.ch004

Yılmaz Altuntaş, E., & Akgün Çomak, N. (2021). Analysing Digital Media Contents Representing COVID-19 Pandemics With "21-K Method". In G. Sarı (Ed.), *Handbook of Research on Representing Health and Medicine in Modern Media* (pp. 461–478). IGI Global., doi:10.4018/978-1-7998-6825-5.ch028

Yoon, O. (2022). Importance and Educational Possibilities of the Place-Based Education Through Virtual Fieldtrips. In A. García de la Vega (Ed.), *Didactic Strategies and Resources for Innovative Geography Teaching* (pp. 79–101). IGI Global., doi:10.4018/978-1-7998-9598-5.ch004

Yousaf, M., Raza, S. H., & Kamboh, S. A. (2022). Human Development and Advocacy Journalism in the Spotlight. In D. O. Okocha, M. J. Onobe, & M. N. Alike (Eds.), *Handbook of Research on Connecting Philosophy, Media, and Development in Developing Countries* (pp. 97–111). IGI Global., doi:10.4018/978-1-6684-4107-7.ch008

Yu, B., Epstein, L., & Tisi, V. (2021). A DisCrit-Informed Critique of the Difference vs. Disorder Approach in Speech-Language Pathology. In R. Horton (Ed.), *Critical Perspectives on Social Justice in Speech-Language Pathology* (pp. 105–128). IGI Global., doi:10.4018/978-1-7998-7134-7.ch006

Yu, P., Tang, S., Ahuja, A., & Chang, X. (2022). Active Equity Investing. In R. Sharma & K. Mehta (Eds.), *Handbook of Research on Stock Market Investment Practices and Portfolio Management* (pp. 301–328). IGI Global., doi:10.4018/978-1-6684-5528-9.ch016

Yu, P., Xu, A., Hanes, E., & Lu, S. (2022). Would Crowdfunding Really Help Startups in China? In Felseghi, R. A., Cobîrzan, N., & Raboaca, M. S. (Ed.), Clean Technologies and Sustainable Development in Civil Engineering (pp. 217-247). IGI Global. https://doi.org/ doi:10.4018/978-1-7998-9810-8.ch009

Yusuf, I. U., Ibrahim, A. M., & Liman, M. A. (2022). Emergence of Counternarrative Peace Media in the Northeast of Nigeria. In E. Ismayil & E. Karadogan Ismayil (Eds.), *Media and Terrorism in the 21st Century* (pp. 183–203). IGI Global., doi:10.4018/978-1-7998-9755-2.ch011

Zaluczkowska, A. M. (2019). The Potential of Interactive Negotiated Narratives in Rebuilding and Reimagining Northern Irish Society. [IJEP]. *International Journal of E-Politics*, *10*(2), 44–59. doi:10.4018/IJEP.2019070104

Zameer, H., Wang, Y., Yasmeen, H., & Ahmed, W. (2019). Modeling the Role of Service Quality, Customer Satisfaction and Customer Loyalty in Building Service Brand Equity. [IJABIM]. *International Journal of Asian Business and Information Management*, *10*(2), 55–72. doi:10.4018/IJABIM.2019040103

Zengaro, S., & Warley, R. (2022). The Fallacy of Higher Education as the Great Social Equalizer. In J. Keengwe (Ed.), *Handbook of Research on Social Justice and Equity in Education* (pp. 46–71). IGI Global., doi:10.4018/978-1-7998-9567-1.ch003

Zengin, F., & Kapır, B. (2021). Aestheticizing Violence Within Transmedia Storytelling Context. In M. N. Erdem, N. Kocabay-Sener, & T. Demir (Eds.), *Handbook of Research on Aestheticization of Violence, Horror, and Power* (pp. 484–500). IGI Global., doi:10.4018/978-1-7998-4655-0.ch024

Zenkov, K., Lague, M., Haddad, K., Gervacio, A., Sabah, M., & Kolapalli, A. (2022). "Storying" Injustice. In T. S. Hodges (Ed.), *Handbook of Research on Teacher Practices for Diverse Writing Instruction* (pp. 224–247). IGI Global., doi:10.4018/978-1-6684-6213-3.ch012

Zhang, J., Pearlman, A. M., & Kegler, J. L. (2022). Leveraging Interdisciplinary Collaboration to Improve Technology Dependency and Intercultural Competencies. In P. Bawa (Ed.), *Preparing Faculty for Technology Dependency in the Post-COVID-19 Era* (pp. 73–92). IGI Global., doi:10.4018/978-1-7998-9235-9.ch005

Zhang, S. I. (2019). Mobile Experience in War and Conflict Reporting. In X. Xu (Ed.), *Impacts of Mobile Use and Experience on Contemporary Society* (pp. 226–241). IGI Global., doi:10.4018/978-1-5225-7885-7.ch014

Zhao, R., Li, J., & Zheng, J. (2022). Knowledge Services Development in Unprecedented Circumstances. In M. Lamba (Ed.), *Technological Advancements in Library Service Innovation* (pp. 23–42). IGI Global., doi:10.4018/978-1-7998-8942-7.ch002

Zheng, L., & Si, M. (2020). Narrative Strategies in VR Movies, Traditional Movies, and Digital Games. In J. F. Morie & K. McCallum (Eds.), *Handbook of Research on the Global Impacts and Roles of Immersive Media* (pp. 59–78). IGI Global., doi:10.4018/978-1-7998-2433-6.ch004

# About the Contributors

**Jose Melchor Medina** is a Doctor in Business Information Systems from the Polytechnic University of Madrid (Spain) and expert in Information Technologies and Systems. Leader of the research group Information Technologies and Strategy (UAT-CA-132), for which he has published 22 papers in high-impact journals (Scopus and JCR) both in Mexico and internationally: Journal of Computer Information Systems, Journal of Information Systems and Technology Management, Innovar Journal, Cuadernos de Administración, Management Studies, Nova Scientia, Accounting and Administration, among others. He is the co-author of 20 book chapters on information technologies and systems. He wrote the book Information Systems Project Planning and co-authored a leading-edge statistical book such as Multivariate Analysis Techniques. Applied to the social sciences, co-author in 6 books with a business administration approach, and coordinator of 5 books. He has supervised 73 theses between graduate, master, and doctorate. Some of the research projects in which Dr. Medina has participated: i) Study of the administrative profile of the SMEs in the state of Tamaulipas, ii) Consolidation of the scientific and technological infrastructure for the exploration and sustainable exploitation of unconventional hydrocarbons, oil/gas shale in Mexico, iii) Institutional Repository of the Autonomous University of Tamaulipas, iv) Information technologies and systems in public and private organizations in the state of Tamaulipas, v) e-Government: Tax collector, vi) e-Banking for customer loyalty and satisfaction, among others. Since 2010, he is a member of the National System of Researchers in Mexico.

**Miguel Sahagun** is an Associate Professor of Marketing at High Point University (HPU), Dr. Sahagun obtained his Ph.D. from The University of Texas-Pan American (UTPA), his Master of Business Administration from the University of Texas-Brownsville (UTB), and his Bachelor's degree in Industrial Engineering from the Instituto Tecnologico y de Estudios Superiores de Occidente (ITESO). Dr. Sahagun has 28 years of corporate and academic experience. He is an active member of AMA, SMA, and ISoF. Dr. Sahagun has published and presented his research at various scientific journals, book chapters, and international conferences in Peru, Mexico,

Romania, Ecuador, Cuba, Canada, China, Chile, Portugal, Morocco, Greece, and the United States of America.

**Jorge Alfaro** is currently the Director of the School of Engineering at Universidad Católica del Norte, Chile. He also leads the MSc. in Technology and Information Management. Dr. Alfaro develops teaching, research, and business consulting responsibilities in IT business management, digital organization, and university coaching. He received his doctorate in 2006 from the Universidad Politécnica de Madrid, Spain.

**Fernando Ortiz-Rodriguez** is a full professor at Tamaulipas Autonomous University, a Member of National Research Council level C, and director of the Social Research Centre at UAT, Mexico. He is a member of the Information Technology research group and part of the Knowledge Graph and Semantic Web Community. He had published, Journal Articles, Book Chapters, and as a book editor from reputed editorials as Springer and Elsevier. Also, he had presented many conference articles in Europe, the United States, and Mexico. Main chair and organizer of KGSWC multi-series conference.

* * *

**Demian Ábrego Almazán** has a PhD in Administrative Sciences from the Autonomous University of Tamaulipas (UAT), Mexico. He is a full-time professor at the same institution and teaches at the bachelor's/undergraduate level, as well as at the master's and doctoral levels. In his scientific dissemination work, he has published various articles in high-impact national and international journals: He is also the co-author of papers, books, and book chapters focused on technologies, information systems, and strategic management, as well as multivariate statistics. . Since 2017, he is a member of the CONACYT National System of Researchers (level 1). Google Scholar League. liga de Scopus , ORCID ).

**Madelyn Avila Vera** is a PhD candidate in Strategic Business Management at the Faculty of Commerce and Administration of the Autonomous University of Tamaulipas, Tampico, she has a Masters degree in Social Sciences with orientation in Sustainable Development at the Institute of Social Research of the Autonomous University of Nuevo Leon (IINSO-UANL), she also has a Bachelor's Degree in Economics from the Faculty of Law and Social Sciences of the Autonomous University of Tamaulipas (FADYCS-UAT). She is currently a Professor of Economics and Finance in the economics and finance degree of the faculty of law and social sciences of the UAT. Her research interests are Regional Development, Sustainability and Public Policies

**Daniel Avila-Guzman** is a professor and coordinator of the career: Bachelor of Information Technology at Tamaulipas Autonomous University, previously he was coordinator of the Reynosa School and deputy director at the Reforma School, in the same way he collaborated in the administrative area at the Tamaulipas Project Center.

**Ruben Barrera** is a graduate student at the Autonomous University of Tamaulipas, originally from the city of Reynosa, Tamaulipas Mexico. Bachelor's degree in information technology from the aforementioned university. Since the middle of his university career, he has been dedicated to scientific research in different areas, mainly focused on issues of education and citizen participation and involvement with government. He has participated in various scientific congresses such as: CSCE 2018, WIR 2019, PUBSIC 2019 and ICERI 2018 - 2019.

**Viridiana Barrera** is a graduate student at the North Tamaulipas University of Technology, originally from the city of Reynosa, Tamaulipas, Mexico. Bachelor's degree in information technology from the aforementioned university. Studying a master's degree in computer science and technology at the Autonomous University of Tamaulipas, dedicated to scientific research on machine learning mainly focused on public health.

**Cesaire Chiatchoua** is a researcher at the Higher School of Economics, Micro and Small Business issues. He proposed a methodology to measure the technological innovation capacities of MYPES. He also works on Foreign Direct Investment and International Trade issues, as well as Economic Development. He has been an evaluator of National Postgraduate Quality Programs. Finally, he teaches at the undergraduate and postgraduate level.

**Ramiro Esqueda-Walle** is a professor-researcher at the Universidad Autónoma de Tamaulipas (UAT), PhD in Regional Economics from the Socioeconomic Research Center of the UADEC (PNPC-CONACYT). He holds a Master's degree in International Business from the Universidad de Alcalá (Spain) and a Bachelor's degree in Economics from the UAT. He is a member of the National System of Researchers, certified with desirable profile by PRODEP. He has experience as a consultant in the private and public sectors. His publications, conferences and teaching deal with a wide range of economic and social topics. As research techniques he has implemented both quantitative and qualitative methods. He has moderated and participated in scientific and professional panels with Mexico's leading economic speakers and analysts. He is editor of a journal and contributor to the editorial staff and referee of a dozen national and foreign journals.

**Lakshmi Shree K.** has pursued her Master's degree in computer science domain from Visveshraya Technological University. Currently a research scholar interested in location analytics and also working as faculty. Also keen on working on the next generation business models using location and social media. She has 10 years of research experience in wireless networking, data mining. Published conference papers and journals in wireless medium and location analytics.

**Jose L. Martinez-Rodriguez** received his Ph.D. in Computer Science from Cinvestav Tamaulipas, Mexico (2018). He is a full-time professor in the Multidisciplinary Academic Unit Reynosa Rodhe at the Autonomous University of Tamaulipas. His research interests include Semantic Web representation, Data Mining, Information Extraction, and Cloud Computing.

**Francisco Isaí Morales-Sáenz** is a professor-researcher at the Faculty of Commerce and Administration Victoria. His research line is information technology and strategy. Currently is a PHD student in administrative economic sciences at the Autonomous University of Tamaulipas.

**Peter Olubiyo** is the Head of Cataloguing and Classification Section in Adeyemi Federal University of Education Library, Ondo.

**Ashok Kumar R.** is a Professor in the Department of Information Science and Engineering at BMSCE, Bangalore, India. He received his BE degree in Information Science & Engineering from Bangalore University, and MTech in Computer Science & Engineering from Visvesvaraya Technological University, Belgaum, India. PhD in the School of Information Technology and Engineering at VIT University, Vellore, India. His area of interest is Information and Cyber Security, Brain Computer Interface, Social Network Analysis. Current research scholar working on social network analysis.

**Lidia Rangel Blanco** is a Professor-Researcher at the Universidad Autónoma de Tamaulipas (UAT). She is a member of the National System of Researchers (Level I). She has a PhD in Environment, a Masters degree in Regional Development and a Bachelor degree in Economics by the UAT. She is a full time professor in the Bachelor's Degree in Economics and Finance at the Faculty of Law and Social Sciences (FADYCS).

**Ramon Tijerina** graduated from Tamaulipas Technical Institute, Victoria, Tamaulipas. Mexico. Postgraduate in Quality of Education by Tamaulipas Autonomous University. Professor since 2022 at UATMRR, Reynosa, Tamaulipas, Mexico.

**Sanju Mishra Tiwari** has worked as a Research Associate for a sponsored research project "Intelligent Real time Situation Awareness and Decision Support System for Indian Defence" funded by DRDO in Department of Computer Applications, National Institute of Technology, Kurukshetra. Her current research interests include Knowledge Based Systems, Ontologism, Intelligent Decision Support, Semantic/ Intelligent Query Search Engines, Intrusion Detection, Swarm Intelligence. She has to-date published 19 research papers one 1 book chapter with international and national publishers. She has 10 years experience in teaching field and 2 years for research field for developing ontologies. She is the member of IEEE. She is working as an organizing committee member of MIR Labs, USA.

**Sofía Villegas Garza** is currently a professor and a researcher at Universidad Autónoma de Tamaulipas, México. She is a PhD Administrative Sciences student. Anabel Sofía develops teaching, research, business consulting, visual merchandiser, and graphic movie designer.

**Fatima Zahra**, Ph.D. student in Computer Science at the University of Khenchela, Algeria, obtained her bachelor's and master's degrees in computer science from the same university in 2016 and 2018, respectively. Her research interests include semantic interoperability, Internet of Things, knowledge representation, ontology engineering, and semantic reasoning.

# Index

## R



## S



## T



## U

www.ingramcontent.com/pod-product-compliance
Lightning Source LLC
LaVergne TN
LVHW080341011026
849161LV00009B/2150